De Renne

Dara,

   It was a pleasure to meet you and your crew. Thank you for your thoughtful attention to Wormsloe while you were here.

                                        Sarah Ross

WORMSLOE FOUNDATION PUBLICATIONS

NUMBER TWENTY-ONE

Dave,

We hope you and your family will return to Wormsloe often and always feel welcome.

Craig & Diana

7/29/09

WILLIAM HARRIS BRAGG

Three Generations of a

DE RENNE

Georgia Family

The University of Georgia Press
Athens and London

© 1999 by the University of Georgia Press
Athens, Georgia 30602

Printed in the United States of America
03 02 01 00 99   C   5 4 3 2 1

Library of Congress Cataloging in Publication Data
Bragg, William Harris.
De Renne : three generations of a Georgia family / William Harris Bragg.
    p.   cm. — (Wormsloe Foundation publications ; no. 21)
Includes bibliographical references and index.
ISBN 0-8203-2089-7 (alk. paper)
1. Georgia—Historiography.   2. Georgia—History—1775–1865.
3. Georgia—History—1865–   4. De Renne family.   5. Georgia—
Biography.   I. Title.   II. Series: Publications (Wormsloe Foundation) ;
no. 21.
F285.2.B73   1999
975.8'03—dc21   98-51167

British Library Cataloging in Publication Data available

On the title page and part titles:
The Library at Wormsloe, c. 1928. Etching by Christopher Murphy Jr.
(1902–1973), from a reverse image photograph. Courtesy of Eudora
De Renne Roebling.

To the Memory of

GEORGE WYMBERLEY JONES DE RENNE

1827–1880

Family connexions are part of the poetry of history. They call to mind the generations of men and women who were born, married and died, and perhaps bequeathed to their descendants some trait of their personality, some tradition of behaviour, which did not perish with the passing of the years but persisted in their grand-children and their grandchildren's children, and so made the past immortal.

—N. G. ANNAN

DE RENNE

Contents

Preface

It is very seldom that the preface of a work is read. . . . I deem it, however, advisable to write a preface, and to this I humbly call the attention of the courteous reader, as its perusal will not a little tend to the proper understanding and appreciation of this volume.

— GEORGE BORROW

This book, the twenty-first of the Wormsloe Foundation Publications, is a direct descendant of the first of the series, Professor E. Merton Coulter's *Wormsloe: Two Centuries of a Georgia Family*, which appeared in 1955. As such, it is a biographical narrative, based primarily on original sources. It focuses on the lives of several members of the De Renne family during the years 1827 to 1970, with particular emphasis on their activities in collecting, printing, and preserving historical materials, principally Georgiana.

Hampered by lack of primary sources, Professor Coulter found it impossible to tell the story of the De Rennes with the detail that he could accord their ancestors, the three generations of the Jones family that preceded them. Consequently, *Wormsloe* devoted only some forty-odd pages to the subjects of *De Renne: Three Generations of a Georgia Family*. The present book, which expands and elaborates Professor Coulter's work through the use of considerable masses of manuscript material only recently accessible, represents in part the completion of unfinished business.

More than four decades have passed since *Wormsloe* was published. In that time historiography has undergone significant expansion and elaboration, producing lively skirmishing between proponents of the Old History and the New, between supporters of the traditional narrative and partisans of the analytic approach. Understandably, some scholars will expect *De Renne* to conform to the history of the family and the history of the book, as those disciplines have been defined in the fairly recent past. Instead, they will encounter a book that seeks mainly to answer what have been described as Old History's questions: "What happened?" and "How did it happen?" But although this book concentrates on lives, there remains—as Michael O'Brien remarked in similar circumstances—the opportunity for these lives, "once documented," to be "of service to other historians with wider concerns."

The Honor of the Past

He does not feel himself a mere individual link in creation, responsible only for his own brief term of being. He carries back his existence in proud recollection, and he extends it forward in honorable anticipation. He lives with his ancestry, and he lives with his posterity. . . . As he has received much from those that have gone before, so he feels bound to transmit much to those that are to come after him.
——WASHINGTON IRVING

Shortly before sunrise on May 18, 1880, an unusual procession left Savannah, Georgia, and made its way southeast down the Thunderbolt road. Although deserted at night, this route was well-traveled by day; at its end lay a spot of extraordinary beauty that for many years had drawn local citizens and visitors alike. No account of the attractions of Georgia's coastal metropolis was complete without mention of the somber enchantments of Evergreen Cemetery, popularly known as Bonaventure. Bound there on this warm, clear morning were several generations of Georgia's oldest family, borne in a line of wagons accompanied by a carriage. Within this last conveyance rode the only living member of this particular family group, the bibliophile and philanthropist George Wymberley Jones De Renne. The wagons carried nine new coffin cases freighted with the remains of his Jones ancestors, newly taken from Savannah's Old Cemetery. Some hours earlier, the eighteenth-century family vault had been opened under De Renne's supervision, by the light of lanterns and a quarter moon. Its breached wall rebricked, the barrel-roofed crypt now stood empty.[1]

As thin dawn light began to penetrate Bonaventure's famous canopy of live oaks, the procession approached its destination. The wagons rolled past pallid sepulchral monuments—slabs, sarcophagi, shafts, and statuary—turning to the right near the tomb of the Kollocks (a gabled stone house, it seemed, sunk to its eaves) and the obelisk-marked plot of the Tattnall family. From colonial times the Tattnalls had held the surrounding acreage as Bonaventure Plantation. Now, however, they owned only the few square yards that held their dead. As signs of their occupancy, there remained only the oak and palmetto avenues and the tabby buttresses of their terraced gardens.[2]

The wagons followed a short, sandy lane called Druades Walk and stopped near an impressive marble monument, its face deeply incised to the memory of "George Jones of Wormsloe." Here lay the father of De Renne, whose distinctive name was the product of a legal change years earlier. This transformation indicated neither lack of pride in his family nor a want of respect for its traditions, however, for both had brought De Renne on this solemn errand.[3]

Upon reaching the family plot, De Renne stepped from his carriage—a neatly dressed, middle-aged gentleman, bearded, thin, and frail. He had ordered an underground vault constructed behind his father's monument and crypt to receive the family remains that had for decades lain in the Savannah burying ground. Long years of neglect and vandalism, as well as its attractions as a playground for Savannah's children, had made the overcrowded Old Cemetery an unsuitable place for the Jones dead; new burials there were forbidden, and there were rumors that the cemetery would soon be "broken up."[4]

Until the cemetery's dissolution, however, De Renne intended to leave two family monuments in place. One he himself had erected to the memory of his great-grandfather Noble Jones, founder of his line in the New World, whose remains occupied one of the nine coffin cases. On the sides of his progenitor's Savannah monument—a cenotaph shaped like a gable-lidded sarcophagus—De Renne had placed that information about his great-grandfather that he thought most important:

NOBLE JONES of WORMSLOE Esquire,
Senior Judge of the General Court
and acting Chief Justice of the Province of Georgia:
For twenty one years Member and sometime
President of His Majesty's Council.
Colonel of the First Georgia Regiment   Died Nov. 2d 1775 aged 73.

Though the monument had been placed in the cemetery only ten years before, its design and appearance suggested that it could have been there since the time of Noble Jones's death. Intricate designs (one of them armorial) decorated the monument's head and foot, and the inscription employed the archaic "long s," for the great-grandson of Noble Jones had an antiquarian's sense of what was appropriate.[5]

In 1733, almost a full century before De Renne's birth, Noble Jones had arrived at the site of Savannah aboard the ship *Anne*. A member of the first group of English settlers to arrive in Georgia, he was accompanied by his wife, two children, and two servants. Climbing the steep river bluff, he first viewed the forested plateau that he would help cut into lots and squares. Soon, however, he turned his eyes to the countryside, for he had a great hunger for land. As rapidly as possible, he made claim to parcels near the coast, and when the trust colony became a royal province—and the limits on landholding were relaxed—he began to acquire more acreage for himself and his children.[6]

Five miles due south of Bonaventure, over land and marsh and river, lay the acreage most firmly associated with Noble Jones: a plantation called Wormsloe. It was still marked by the tabby ruins of the fortified residence Jones had constructed there in the 1740s, near an island redoubt he had also built—protection for Savannah against raiding Yamasee Indians or marauding Spaniards. Wormsloe Plantation occupied the southern third of the Isle of Hope, or Hope's Isle, though "isle" was a misnomer for a roughly anchor-shaped peninsula. The anchor's head joined the mainland, and its short shaft supported a causeway with a bridge at its center. It connected with the narrow, lengthy flange—a mile across at its widest—that ran four miles north to south. A saltwater river and a true islet, Long Island, separated the Isle of Hope from the great bulk of Skidaway Island. Beyond it lay Romerly Marsh, Wassaw Island, and the sea.[7]

Wormsloe gave the descendants of Noble Jones their *nom de terre*, for they were *of* Wormsloe, which had received the body of Noble Jones at his death in 1775. De Renne approved of Jones's reliance on land as the basis of his fortune in the New World, for De Renne—always conscious of the importance of land—had become convinced of its great value when his properties had helped save him from utter ruin following the Civil War.[8]

Before being granted his largest parcels of land, Noble Jones had made himself useful to the Trustees who governed the Georgia colony. They employed him as surveyor, ranger, and Indian agent, among other official jobs, while he also turned his hand at other pursuits—too many to suit his critics. At best they saw him as too overburdened to attend effectively to all his responsibilities; at worst, they called him negligent. At any rate, it could not be gainsaid that he accepted "more offices than he had time to fill." There was no questioning his energy, however. And it was coupled with a strong constitution that saw him through the "seasoning," that grim onslaught of sickness that had left scores of his fellow colonists in early graves. He also had a persistence that kept him in the Georgia colony when other survivors of the seasoning abandoned the young province for the Carolinas and elsewhere.[9]

Noble Jones's accomplishments were many. A self-taught doctor, he had a knowledge of "physick" that served him well in peace and war, and he would train his son Noble Wimberly Jones in the arts of medicine. In turn, this second-generation physician would train his own son, so that the family's commitment to the medical profession was well established. De Renne himself, though he never practiced, had become the first university-educated doctor in the family, and now, with his son Everard soon to graduate from medical school, the line of physicians stretched unbroken into the fifth generation.[10]

But closest to the heart of Noble Jones were his skills as surveyor, draftsman, and builder. Though the *Anne*'s passenger list labeled him merely a "carpenter," the term then encompassed a variety of skills in the construction trade. Surveying was among them—and Jones's work as surveyor at Savannah, Augusta, and Ebenezer was invaluable, despite the criticisms that accompanied it—and drafting and drawing were among his talents as well. His admiration for the massive edifice at Bethesda, for which he cleared an avenue to provide a vista from Wormsloe, was translated into a handsome sketch that was engraved in England and used to illustrate one of the books of the Reverend George Whitefield, Bethesda's founder. As a builder, Jones had in England participated in the seemingly unending work at Westminster Abbey. In the New World he had to his credit his own fortified tabby residence at Wormsloe and the machicolated redoubt he had constructed on an island nearby. And as attested even by William Stephens (normally not among his admirers), Jones made significant contributions to the construction of Savannah's first house of worship, Christ Church.[11]

As a draftsman and builder, Jones was proud to share the surname of the great Inigo, the "English Palladio," of whom, tradition said, Noble Jones was a collateral relation. In any case, Noble Jones had arranged for the marriage that had begun his family to be solemnized in the exquisite chapel at Lincoln's Inn attributed to Inigo Jones.[12]

The Trustees intended that their male colonists be militiamen, ever ready to defend the colony, and Noble Jones, large-framed and resilient, added martial distinctions to his other qualities. During the war with Spain, he oversaw the strategic timber fort that guarded the inland passage joining Spanish Florida and English Georgia. And he also commanded, as captain of marines, a scout boat that plied the coastal waters. He was said to have taken part in both the ill-fated siege of St. Augustine by General James Oglethorpe and his subsequent defense of Fort Frederica. After the Spanish threat passed, Captain Jones continued to serve in various military capacities and often led the troops in parade on Rejoicing Days in Savannah. At a more critical time, he was instrumental in pacifying "Queen of the Creeks" Mary Musgrove and her followers, when they threatened the peace of Georgia's principal town.[13]

Proud to be an Englishman, friend and "companion of Oglethorpe," Noble Jones was the king's good servant, and he filled several high appointive offices capably; he lived and died faithful to the Crown. Fortunately for him, his death occurred in 1775, just when the feeling in Georgia against the king broke into open rebellion; among the rebel leaders was his own son Noble Wimberly Jones. Being on opposite sides in such a momentous struggle was painful for both father and son and must have strained their relations. But the two had such mutual respect and love for each other that there was no real danger of conflict or estrangement.[14]

Born in the shadow of St. Paul's Cathedral, within that square mile that had been London since Roman times, Noble Jones died beneath Wormsloe's oaks and was buried there, near his old bastioned house. Subsequently moved to the Savannah cemetery, the much-traveled dust of Noble Jones had now come to its final resting place at Bonaventure.[15]

Accompanying the coffin of Noble Jones into the vault was that of his son. Despite political differences with his loyalist father, Noble Wimberly Jones had resembled him closely in other respects, particularly in having embarked on a medical career, though he also served in the military organizations of both province and state. He was a crack shot with a pistol and went armed when summoned by patients into the countryside. During the Revolution, however, he made his mark not as a warrior but as a politician who became revered as the "Morning Star of Liberty." Indeed, De Renne had received from the historian George Bancroft a transcript of a letter from Samuel Adams to Noble Wimberly Jones. Therein, Adams—whose good opinion Bancroft admitted he would have coveted most among the patriot fathers—addressed Jones flatteringly as "a warm and able friend of the Liberties of America." And Benjamin Franklin conducted a friendly correspondence with Jones as well.[16]

In the late 1760s and early 1770s, Jones proved to be the bane of Sir James Wright, Georgia's royal governor; Wright several times dissolved the Commons House of Assembly in retaliation for the members' electing as speaker such an unacceptable Whig firebrand as Jones. Elected three times to the Continental Congress, he twice was unable to attend—once because of the fatal illness of his father—but in Georgia he was continuously active in attacking the king's authority, most spectacularly in leading a raid on Savannah's royal magazine, some of whose powder was said to have been sent to Boston in time to be used at Bunker Hill. Though they ultimately deposed Governor Wright, Jones and his fellow Whigs soon found that their own days in power would be brief. Following Savannah's fall to British forces and Governor Wright's reinstatement in 1778, Jones and his family fled to Charleston. He was captured there when that city fell to the enemy two years later and was sent to St. Augustine as a prisoner of war.[17]

Ironically, this involuntary trip to Florida led Noble Wimberly Jones to Pennsylvania, where a prisoner exchange freed him in Philadelphia in 1782. This fortuitous circumstance would forge a link between the Jones family and the Quaker City that lasted for many generations to come. Before returning to Savannah, Dr. Jones practiced medicine for a time in Philadelphia and there became a friend and protégé of the famed physician

Benjamin Rush. For the rest of his life, medicine rather than politics would be Jones's most absorbing interest, and he was recognized as an innovative, progressive physician, widely considered an authority on obstetrics. One of his last acts was to help organize the Georgia Medical Society, whose first president he became. His death in 1805 occasioned great mourning; his funeral "was attended . . . [by a] great a concourse of citizens," with a tolling of the bells of "the Exchange and places of public worship . . . as a particular mark of respect to the deceased." [18]

The Bonaventure vault that now received these and other Jones remains lay adjacent to the crypt of De Renne's father (and Noble Wimberly Jones's son), Dr. George Jones. Like both his sire and grandsire, he had become a physician. Like his father, he had entered the political arena: in the 1790s he had attacked the Yazooists with the same passionate determination his father had deployed against the Crown, and he later helped lead the convention that drafted the last of Georgia's eighteenth-century constitutions. In writing George Jones's epitaph, however, De Renne listed only what he considered the two most salient honors of his father's long career: his superior court judgeship—bestowed on him even though he had no training in law—and his brief tenure in the U.S. Senate, which raised the grandson of one of Georgia's first colonists to the highest office the state could bestow. [19]

By the end of his long life George Jones had reached a state of prosperity unrivaled by his predecessors and left a considerable estate in stocks, land, and slaves to be divided among numerous heirs. But to De Renne, his sole surviving son, he had left—among many handsome bequests—the legacy and responsibility of Wormsloe, to be maintained and preserved for posterity. Bonaventure itself served as a powerful admonition to De Renne; it ominously symbolized what could happen when a family lost possession of its ancestral estate. [20]

By nine o'clock all the boxes had been "safely deposited," and a small corner of Bonaventure had become much richer in historical associations. De Renne had done what he could to protect the remains and preserve the memories of his forefathers. Now the present called him to travel to Philadelphia to attend to pressing business matters. For the future, he looked confidently to three bright, robust sons, at that moment scattered from Texas to Germany. For them (and from them) he had few fears, for he had fashioned a remarkable will that would maintain them comfortably (and their invalid sister as well, should she long survive) while protecting the family wealth. His cautious planning forestalled any danger that his children might fall victim to fortune hunters or that they themselves might develop into a backsliding generation and deplete his estate.[21]

De Renne had written to his kinsman George Noble Jones, on the birth of that gentleman's third son: "In Heraldry the nobler descent is ever by the male—and so a son is a more honourable birth—as an increased security against the lapse of the inheritance to a female—always esteemed a reproach to a race. . . . With three securities you must be perfectly safe." Now he himself had three such securities. But on that morning in 1880 George Noble Jones lay in a vault nearby; his only married son lay with him, and his family's survival in direct line rested tenuously with one young grandson.[22]

As De Renne departed from Bonaventure, it was merciful that he could not see beyond the present. It was best that he not know how soon he would permanently return and kindness that he not foresee that his family was soon to be subjected to something very like a famous poetic curse: "frequent hearses shall besiege your gates." A century after G. W. J. De Renne's death, there would remain only two descendants who had been born with the distinctive surname that he had devised, and, though Wormsloe would survive, it would be transformed in ways he could not have imagined. But had he been able to look into the future, De Renne would have found some comfort there as well because of three facts that he had particular reason to understand: ideas are often more tenacious of life than their formulators, traditions can prove to be much less mutable than flesh, and monuments "more enduring than bronze" can be as lasting as earth and as seemingly fragile as paper.[23]

PART ONE

Exemplars, 1827–1887

CHAPTER 1

The Pierian Spring

The desire of knowledge increases ever with the acquisition of it.
—LAURENCE STERNE

When Dr. George Jones married Eliza Smith at Philadelphia on October 24, 1822, he had reached the age of fifty-six and had buried two other wives and seven of his eight children. The greatest public honors of his life had already been won: his judgeships, his sessions in the state legislature, his terms as mayor of Savannah, his brief elevation to the United States Senate—all were years in the past. Nonetheless, the remaining days of his life would be full, his energies channeled into numerous business pursuits, philanthropic endeavors, and family responsibilities. The last mentioned would have totally occupied a lesser man, for by this time in his life Jones very closely resembled "the head of a tribe or clan," composed not only of his own children and grandchildren (along with a large assortment of nieces and nephews) but also of stepchildren and step-grandchildren from his second marriage.[1]

His third wife's father, Thomas Smith, born in Scotland in 1745, had ended his life as a justice of the Pennsylvania Supreme Court. As a young man he had traveled to America with his older half-brother, the Episcopal clergyman and educator Dr. William Smith, then already famous as a protégé of Benjamin Franklin and first provost of the institution that became the University of Pennsylvania. Like Noble Jones, Thomas Smith first worked as a surveyor in the New World, but subsequently he followed the legal profession. During the Revolution he also served as a militia officer, helped to frame Pennsylvania's constitution of 1776, and—like Dr. George Jones's father, Noble Wimberly Jones—became a member of the Second Continental Congress. Among his other distinctions, Smith acted as George Washington's attorney from 1784 to 1791, handling several cases that arose from Washington's land acquisitions near Fort Pitt.[2]

Nearer Philadelphia was Dr. William Smith's country place, just west of town. John Van Deren's mill was nearby, set amid surroundings of great natural beauty at the falls of Wissahickon Creek, a site captured on canvas by the painter Charles Willson Peale. Long favored as a destination of courting couples, the mill and falls formed the backdrop of Thomas Smith's courtship of the miller's daughter Letitia during the last years of the Revolution. In November 1781, with Dr. Smith officiating, Thomas wed Miss Van Deren, whose German grandfather—a turbulent Lutheran minister—had established his family in New York sixty years earlier.[3]

In August 1782 Letitia Smith was safely delivered of her first child, Eliza, who would marry George Jones four decades later. As siblings joined her, Eliza became an indispensable helper to her mother and, like her, was considered "as remarkable for her industry, as for her economy." Her father also prided himself on Eliza's success in her studies (particularly her aptitude for French), for the main reason he had moved from the countryside into Philadelphia during the late 1790s was to facilitate his children's education. He made a home for them on High Street, "a favorite with national and state government officers"; President John Adams lived nearby in the executive mansion, before his removal in 1800 to the new national capital in Washington City.[4]

Concerned with his daughter's soul as much as her mind, Thomas Smith gave his wife the responsibility of Eliza's spiritual training in the Episcopal faith. He noted that the mother's example made religion "amiable" to Eliza and her sisters; they regularly walked before their parents to Christ Church, where the family after 1800 occupied the "President's Pew." Mrs. Smith would bear nine other children, though of her three sons, only one—her last child, born in 1800—would survive infancy.[5]

Justice Smith died in 1809, his wife two years later. As eldest child, Eliza became de facto head of the family, though the Smith children were under the guardianship of Chief Justice William Tilghman of the Pennsylvania Supreme Court, a longtime associate and close friend of Justice Smith. Eliza would devote many more years of her life to caring for her brother and sisters; she thus admirably fulfilled her father's expectation that she would have the ability to "keep house & manage the affairs of the family" in such difficult circumstances. The Smith siblings formed an extremely close-knit family, and Dr. George Jones would spend much time with his wife among his Smith in-laws in Philadelphia, the city that also was home to his beloved daughter-in-law Sarah Jones—widow of Noble Wimberly Jones II.[6]

Eliza's marriage to Dr. Jones followed closely that of her sister Maria, the only other child of Thomas and Letitia Smith ever to wed. Maria's husband, Frederick Campbell Stewart (sometimes styled Campbell-Stewart), was widower of one of her Van Deren cousins, who had given him a daughter; another daughter came of his union with Maria Smith. Though born in Virginia, where he was master of a Westmoreland County plantation called Pomona, Stewart was—as Frederick Campbell Stewart of Ascog—heir to various Scottish estates and thus had to become a naturalized British citizen. Already a hemorrhaging consumptive at the time of his second marriage, Stewart spent his seven years of married life with Maria trying unsuccessfully to recover his health at various European spas and resorts. Though inveterate travelers, the Stewarts were drawn most strongly to France and to Nice (then in the Kingdom of Sardinia); there Frederick Campbell Stewart died in 1827, soon followed by his two daughters. Maria chose to reside in France for her four decades of widowhood.[7]

Though Dr. George Jones's third marriage surprised his relations, his eleven-year-old grandson could not have been among the least astonished. Known then as George Jones, Jr., (and later known as George Noble Jones), he had long been the sole hope for the continuation of the Jones family in the direct line. The child of Noble Wimberly Jones II—Dr. Jones's only son to reach maturity—he must have viewed with wonder and a mixture of other feelings the two births that followed in the years after his grandfather's wedding. A daughter, Letitia Georgina Telfair, was born in 1823. Four years later, during the year that Dr. Jones turned sixty-one, came the portentous arrival of a tiny uncle for George Noble Jones. Though the birth of this male heir signified a dramatic turn in his fortunes, Jones would always maintain amicable relations with this late addition to the family.[8]

Born in 1827, the son of George and Eliza Jones was christened, like his sister, with a ponderous load of names: George Frederick Tilghman. The first name honored both his father and his mother's brother, George Washington Smith, while his second and third names memorialized his uncle Frederick Campbell Stewart and his mother's former guardian Chief Justice Tilghman, both of whom had died shortly before the child's birth.[9]

From his earliest days, the young Jones heir would be a nomad, splitting each year between the North and the South. As he accompanied his parents on their travels, he became intimately familiar with all manner of coaches, inns, and ships' cabins, for the elder Joneses traveled often, their strong constitutions long resistant to bone-jarring road journeys and the tossing of heavy seas. To young George, fall and winter meant the South: Savannah— with its sandy streets, wooded squares, and bustling waterfront—and, increasingly, his father's Wormsloe Plantation. Spring and summer in the North offered a variety of destinations.[10]

For long years, his father's principal country seat had been Newton Plantation, seven miles west of Savannah, near the headwaters of the Little Ogeechee River. Though a center for rice culture, Newton had a closer claim to the heart of Dr. Jones, for it was there that he bred fine horses for racing. Tragically, in 1825 a faulty chimney had started a disastrous fire that destroyed the dwelling house at Newton and spread to the stables, killing many of the Jones thoroughbreds. Instead of rebuilding in that now unhappy spot, Dr. Jones decided to have a new residence constructed at the oldest of the Jones family's several plantations, Wormsloe.[11]

Entirely unpretentious, the new house at Wormsloe was a "two story Timber and shingled building," apparently based on one of the carpenter-architect Asher Benjamin's plans for "a house intended for the country." Its foundation, which enclosed basement rooms, was of tabby like the colonial ruins that crumbled half a mile southward. The house's forty-foot front faced the river, little more than a hundred yards distant, and the marshes and islands beyond. Its two-story section was twenty feet deep, with brick chimneys venting fireplaces on all floors, including the basement, where a kitchen was located.[12]

Significantly, this house was built during the infancy of George Frederick Tilghman Jones and would be the only Georgia home that he would associate with his father. It could not help conjuring ancestral memories, particularly since the oak-sheltered old Wormsloe burial ground lay so near, just adjacent to the ruins of Noble Jones's bastioned house. Wormsloe's secluded location made it a perfect sanctuary, though one seeming more tropical than otherwise, with its stands of palmettos and pines and clumps of Spanish bayonet—an otherworldly place, "adorned with eternal verdure" like an equatorial forest. This refuge would have a strong appeal to the intensely private person that young Jones would become, and his family's portion of the Isle of Hope would always be precious to him.[15]

When he became old enough to understand such documents as wills, the young heir would learn that Wormsloe had been treasured by his forefathers as well. Above all his other holdings, Noble Jones had endeavored to keep this particular Crown grant sacred to his family by charging his descendants to keep it "for ever" and preserve it "in good and sufficient repair," seeing that it "remain in the Name and family." His son Noble Wimberly Jones, despite a less personal attachment, had exercised a similar caution toward retaining Wormsloe, which his own son, George Jones, would match. G. F. T. Jones would prove a careful custodian as well, though in his own fashion, for he would be responsible for modifying the traditional spelling, "Wormslow," and would ultimately change his surname to De Renne, partially in compliment to his mother's family.[14]

Though Wormsloe was foremost in the affections of young Jones, next in his heart was his mother's Philadelphia—as flat as Savannah, with its own (though fewer) squares and teeming riverfront, but with almost nine times the Georgia port's population of eleven thousand souls, in a county whose inhabitants exceeded a quarter million. More particularly, Philadelphia meant the Smith family's home, now in Dugan's Row, on Spruce Street near Twelfth, with its clutch of doting aunts and the benign and rumpled presence of his bookish uncle. Unquestionably, living for part of each year in the most historic city of the young American republic nurtured a lifelong interest in the past. And the boy's father encouraged his reading of history as a worthwhile study, no matter what profession the young man might ultimately choose. In any case, reading was practically inescapable because books were abundant in the Quaker City, with its scores of publishers, its numerous, well-stocked bookshops, and its eight public libraries.[15]

For travels in the Northeast beyond Philadelphia, there was New York City, invitingly near, and other attractions as well such as Niagara Falls.

There were also frequent stops at various fashionable resorts and healthful watering places, from Newport, Rhode Island, to Saratoga Springs, New York.[16]

As the young heir came of age for formal schooling, another northern town figured in his itinerary, for Dr. Jones was certain that the South's sultry climate was "inimical to the studious." Thirty miles upstream from Philadelphia was Bordentown, New Jersey; its picturesque setting on a breeze-swept hill made it a popular resort for wealthy Philadelphians who found the city too warm in summer. Dr. Jones, who found a temperature of ninety degrees excessively hot (a good reason for his status as one of Savannah's summer refugees), placed his son in school at Bordentown during the summer of 1837 and stayed there with him. No doubt he enjoyed Bordentown's "gracious social life" along with its climate, and it was conveniently near Burlington, where his daughter Letitia pursued her own studies. Many years earlier, during his son Noble's school years at nearby Princeton and elsewhere, Dr. Jones had wanted to be close at hand but had felt compelled by business to deny himself the pleasure. This time he was determined to follow his wishes where his children's education was concerned.[17]

Always responsive to natural beauty, young G. F. T. Jones found Bordentown very agreeable; its hilltop location afforded vistas of the Delaware River and the surrounding sweep of "fertile and well cultivated" countryside. The town itself, population just over one thousand, was considered "remarkable for its healthiness and cleanliness, and the neatness of its dwellings," which were fronted by tree-shaded brick sidewalks.[18]

Bordentown also offered much to feed the young boy's growing appetite for history. During the Revolution, the patriot forces in the town had launched their celebrated "mechanical keg plot," sending explosives floating downriver toward the British fleet at Philadelphia. The act did little damage to the ships but provoked a destructive reprisal on the town.[19]

Bordentown as well was home to a very vivid reminder of a more recent, more massive conflict. The town's most exotic inhabitant—drawn like many others by the area's natural beauty—was Joseph Bonaparte, Count of Survilliers, quondam king of both Naples and Spain and eldest brother of the great Napoleon. This "heavy-set, genial exile" was owner of a seventeen-hundred-acre estate, where he lived in great comfort in a mansion whose grounds—decorated with marble statuary and beautified by a variety of gardens—he generously opened to the public.[20]

As interesting as was Joseph Bonaparte, it was his younger brother who would increasingly fascinate young Jones. Partially he may have been drawn to Napoleon because of the romantic view of him that was commonplace in the middle decades of the 1800s. Certainly he would come to share the younger Bonaparte's taste for objets d'art with an Egyptian motif. But he may have also been aware that he shared physical similarities with the emperor of the French; both had gray eyes, dark brown hair, and short stature: at maturity neither exceeded five and a half feet in height.[21]

After the Bordentown summer of 1837, young Jones would share little over a year more with his father, who died in Savannah in November 1838 at the age of seventy-two. Dr. Jones's health had steadily declined for several years, and in 1834 he had been all but broken by grief when Sarah Jones Cuthbert, the last surviving child of his first marriage, had died at age forty-five. Nonetheless, his death came as a shock to his family and friends. For whatever consolation it offered, the son could not doubt the esteem his father had enjoyed in Savannah as he heard the doleful tolling of the city's bells and saw the mute throng of mourners that followed the hearse on foot as it made its way to the Old Cemetery.[22]

Although Jones was only eleven when his father died, Dr. Jones nonetheless had a profound influence in shaping his life. George Jones had often had to communicate advice and counsel to his first son by letter, because the two were frequently separated, particularly during the years of Noble's early manhood. The force of the father's moral precepts was even more impressive to the second son, since young George had more often received them in person. From his father's life and words, young Jones learned of a philosophy that taught that wealth and social status carried responsibilities to society and that a paramount goal in life was to be found in a seemingly prosaic phrase: to be useful. The son (though not lacking a sense of humor) also inherited a fundamental seriousness from his father, probably reinforced by being from youth thrown so much into the company of older people, most of whom placed great emphasis on piety and rectitude. [23]

Dr. Jones had tried to lead an exemplary life (and had succeeded in doing so); his judgeships, for example, had been bestowed because of his moral authority—he was never a lawyer, and his legal knowledge was absorbed on the bench and in the study. His benevolence often expressed itself through his memberships in various philanthropic organizations, including the Union Society (the oldest such organization in the state), the Savannah

Library Society, and the Savannah Anti-Duelling Association, along with trusteeships such as the one that he held for Bethesda College. He was an active Episcopal churchman as well, a member of Savannah's Christ Church, as had been his forefathers. In his own father's life, Dr. Jones had seen a pattern worthy of emulation: "Imitate, my son," George Jones had once written to his son Noble, "his temperance, chastity & every virtue & like him you may sleep away life, with the composure of a Christian, after long usefulness, greatly beloved & generally regretted." These words could as fittingly describe the life and death of Dr. George Jones.[24]

Dr. Jones's beneficence outlived him. His will—of which his grandson George Noble Jones was executor—made it plain that he had done his best to distribute his vast estate equitably among his constellation of relatives. Though his widow and surviving son and daughter received handsome bequests, including Wormsloe (left to his son following his widow's "decease or marriage"), other Joneses—as well as members of the Bulloch, Kollock, Cumming, Hunter, Habersham, and Glen families—were remembered generously. George Noble Jones received the thousand-acre Chatham County plantation of Dean Forest, and his mother and sisters were left separate, adjoining plantations in Jefferson County, near Georgia's old capital Louisville. Other relatives received over two hundred acres of Wimberly, a previously partitioned Jones plantation on the Isle of Hope that bordered Wormsloe to the north. There was much to distribute: property in Savannah, acreage in Chatham and other counties, stocks and bonds, and numerous slaves, the majority of whom were left to Dr. Jones's son and daughter.[25]

Several years and a mountain of paperwork would be required to settle the estate, a monumental task that George Noble Jones acquitted well. Meanwhile, Dr. Jones's widow and children were required to keep records of expenses ("extremely irksome," young Jones thought) and to apply to the executor for funds. As their father would have been pleased to see, the children often listed among their expenditures charitable contributions, along with purchases of books.[26]

After the death of his father, young Jones's subsequent education was planned by his mother and his uncle Washington Smith. They had, however, been left a pattern by Dr. Jones, who had sent his other namesakes, grandson George Noble Jones and step-grandson George Jones Kollock, to Round Hill School at Northampton, Massachusetts. It was run by Joseph Green Cogswell and George Bancroft, who was then a poet and professor, his days as historian and diplomat in the future. Dr. Jones approved of the rigorous curriculum devised by the two, as well as the "rough measure of democracy" they gave their charges, sons of gentlemen wealthy enough to pay the annual $300 tuition—almost double that paid by Harvard students at the time. The young mens' studies at Round Hill, 1825–28, had enabled them to enter the senior class at Yale College; graduating in 1829, they entered Yale Law School and received their degrees in 1832.[27]

But by the time Dr. Jones's surviving son was of age to enter Round Hill as preparation for his own time at Yale, the school had closed, so an equally demanding institution was selected: St. Paul's College and School, located at College Point, three miles north of Flushing, New York, and nine country miles from New York City. When young Jones arrived in 1839, St. Paul's, though in existence for only a few years, was already a "flourishing institution" with over one hundred students, a faculty of ten professors and seven instructors, and a library containing seven thousand volumes. The campus of almost two hundred acres had a mile-long frontage along the East River. Its most curious feature was a knoll occupied by the ten-foot-high stone foundation of what was originally to have been the central college building. The promised funds for this structure had evaporated during the Panic of 1837, and William Augustus Muhlenberg, the school's founder and rector, was able neither to achieve his aim nor fully abandon it: the roofless basement was to be a feature of St. Paul's for the college's entire existence. To accommodate the students, substantial but less expensive wooden buildings were built; they stretched along the base of the knoll toward the riverfront.[28]

Coincidentally, Muhlenberg, a native Philadelphian and Episcopal clergyman, was descended from Heinrich Melchior Muhlenberg, who had played an important role in the religious history of the province of Georgia. As Lutheran patriarch of Philadelphia, the earlier Muhlenberg had in 1774 visited Ebenezer, the Salzburger settlement near Savannah, and closed a schism dividing the Georgia Lutherans.[29]

The education Muhlenberg offered at College Point was decidedly sectarian, no doubt an important factor to the devout Mrs. Jones. The "fundamental principles" of St. Paul's College (named for "the most educated of the apostles") intended to ensure that "human wisdom . . . be consecrated with the spirit and made subservient to the interests of the Gospel." At St. Paul's it was believed that "the study of the ancient languages and of the exact sciences forms the true groundwork of a liberal education; that in the discipline of the intellect there can be no substitute for the old process of patient application; that moral and religious training must go hand in hand with the cultivation of the intellect; that the religious instruction must be in accordance with the creed of some particular church"—in this case, that of the Protestant Episcopal Church.[50]

Training in the Latin classics, a lifelong passion of Jones's (as well as a requisite for further studies), was rigorous, with examinations of astonishing thoroughness. "Passages taken at random . . . ," wrote one impressed observer, "were translated accurately, neatly, and often beautifully; then analyzed and parsed. Portions were also recited memoriter in the original. Suddenly the professor would call for the remainder of the passage in English, then go back to the original, and the students would, without hesitation, fulfill the required task."[51]

Other subjects demanded similar diligence, but the boys' souls were targeted as much as their minds. Attendance at morning and evening prayer was mandatory, and there was an optional noon service as well. During services, the rector would read from the Bible, after which the boys would chant part of the Nineteenth Psalm: "The law of the Lord is an undefiled law." After silent prayer and the reading of collects, a benediction would conclude the ten-minute service.[52]

Muhlenberg appealed to his charges through a dramatic use of symbols that was less the ritualism of the burgeoning Oxford Movement than a manifestation of the rector's own imagination and aesthetic sense. "Lent . . . was sombre; . . . Holy Week was quiet, and Good Friday like a day of mourning," with a picture of the Crucifixion, draped in black, stationed above the chapel altar. But Easter began at sunrise, and the chapel was filled with candles, calla lilies, and hyacinths. At Christmas, also from a point behind the altar, the Virgin Mary and the Christ Child looked out from a holly-wreathed painting. All of the chapel services were complemented by choral music; many pieces were the rector's own compositions, and he often played accompaniment on the organ, leading the singing in a "fine baritone."[53]

Despite the emphasis on the intellectual and spiritual spheres, there was room for physical pursuits as well, whether of the gymnasium or the playing field, and the nearby river not only provided for swimming but was often "astir with boys and boats, colors streaming, oars flashing." Personal gardens were also allowed to the boys "who fancied horticulture," among them young Jones. And he fancied music enough to take lessons in the flute.[54]

Discipline at the school included "a provision for parental *interest and affection*, as well as for parental power." The latter was seen as "unavailing" unless there was "a good degree of the former." Self-discipline, however, was best, whether applied to behavior or studies. There were no prizes for excellence as at many other schools; the rector's plan was to substitute "Christian endeavor for emulation" and to stimulate learning only through "motives of duty"—for he feared competition was "damaging to character." Competence at studies was the scholars' sole reward, lack of mastery the only punishment.[55]

Its conspicuous excellence had won St. Paul's an enviable nationwide reputation. Among those who looked to it as a model was a visitor from Savannah, well known to young Jones: Stephen Elliott, the recently consecrated first bishop of the Episcopal Diocese of Georgia. Making an inspection tour in 1841—the same year he opened his own school, Montpelier Institute in central Georgia—Bishop Elliott saw much that was impressive. But no doubt he also made one observation that had not escaped young Jones: Muhlenberg was a thorough abolitionist who considered slavery "an immense national evil." He once corrected with an impromptu verse a student who had spoken "grandiloquently" of the national flag:

The stars are the scars,
And the stripes are the wipes,
Of the lash on the negro's back.[56]

Nonetheless, Muhlenberg accepted the $300 annual tuition from slave-holding and abolitionist families alike, and, as events would prove, Jones himself seems not to have been led to entertain any serious questions about his section's most defining institution. Bishop Elliott, moreover, for all his interest in the educational methods and philosophy of St. Paul's, intended to follow at least partially the plan of another institution of learning—George Whitefield's Bethesda College—in deriving part of the support of his school from its own corps of slaves. Despite their fundamental difference on the issue of slavery, Elliott and Muhlenberg were alike in being the source of their institutions' vitality; neither school would long outlast its founder's departure. Montpelier and St. Paul's, like Round Hill before them, depended for their survival on the charismatic personalities that had created them.[37]

Young Jones left College Point in 1843 to pursue an undergraduate degree at Yale. He had received a first-rate education at St. Paul's, particularly in the classics; his firm grounding in Latin would help him pursue both his medical studies and his interest in Roman literature and history. Soon after his arrival at New Haven, however, Jones was summoned to Philadelphia because of the terminal illness of his sister.[38]

Letitia Jones—"Leta" as she was known in the family—had become ill in the fall of 1839. At that time Eliza Jones had recently moved to New Rochelle so that she could be near her children while they were educated in the environs of New York. Leta's illness, however, persuaded her mother of the necessity of returning to Philadelphia, where she was familiar with the doctors and her family could assist her; and there mother and daughter stayed until Leta's death on October 19, 1843, three days after her twentieth birthday. Having lost both her husband and daughter within the past five years, Mrs. Jones wanted her remaining child to come and live with her. Consequently, young George returned to the city where his mother had passed most of her days and where she was anchored by her siblings and friends.[39]

Leta's casket was sent to Savannah, where it was bricked into the vault with that of her father. Other than memories, little remained: a few sketches of her as a child, a silhouette of her as a young woman, and her prayer book, with the poignant notation of a comforting passage from 2 Kings: "Thus saith the Lord . . . I have heard thy prayer, I have seen thy tears: behold, I will heal thee." There was also a poem, written by one who knew her well, printed austerely on single sheets for distribution as a memorial to family and friends. It said in part:

> Parental love watched o'er her infancy
> And childhood's bloom with ceaseless care,
> Nor, with the snares of youthful life, relaxed—
> But still, with wise monition, toiled. . . .
> She formed the centre of the social ring;
> All hearts were turned to her, as to a star
> Whose brightness shed a halo all around;
> She moved in grace and sweetness, beaming joy,
> And youthful gaiety, and sparkling wit.

All who approached her owned her influence,
And all who knew her, loved.
A Brother's warm affection glowed for her,
And fortune laid her favours at her feet,
But could not with the boon corrupt her heart.[40]

If young Jones was fated to return to Pennsylvania to resume his education, it seemed fitting that he attend the University of Pennsylvania, whose earliest history was intimately connected with his grandfather's half-brother Dr. William Smith. And so the young man returned to Philadelphia to join the university's junior class.[41]

While a student he lived with his mother in the recently purchased family home in Portico Square, a block of sixteen "elaborately designed" row houses on Spruce Street between Ninth and Tenth. Portico Square offered residences that were spacious, well-appointed, and equipped with all the amenities for comfortable city living. Like its neighbors, the Jones residence, Number 12, was red brick with marble trim, three and a half stories over a raised, paved basement, with a piazza to the rear. Since the houses were in pairs, the Jones's front entrance shared a three-columned Ionic portico with an adjoining residence. The house's high-ceilinged, well-lit rooms boasted walnut and mahogany trim and marble mantels, and its more private chambers were also handsomely outfitted. The large bathroom was floored with marble, and the water closets were paneled with walnut; these rooms, as well as the kitchen, were furnished with "Fairmount water," pumped through iron pipes from reservoirs at the falls of the Schuylkill River.[42]

Just a few streets north of Portico Square, G. F. T. Jones pursued his studies within a single city block on Ninth Street, between Market and Chestnut. There, occupying "a pleasant enclosure," were the two massive neoclassical university buildings, one for the Department of Arts, the other for the Department of Medicine; both would become very familiar to Jones. Following the regular course, he studied subjects grouped under such general categories as classics, moral and natural philosophy, rhetoric and English literature, and mathematics. In July 1845 he received his bachelor of arts degree.[43]

A powerful influence on him was Henry Hope Reed, professor of rhetoric and belles lettres, whose popularity spread past the campus into Philadelphia at large. His well-attended lectures, open to the public, communicated his love of English literature, particularly poetry (he was an early champion and interpreter of his friend William Wordsworth), as well as his enthusiasm for British and American history.[14]

But Jones's thirst for knowledge could not be slaked by lectures and course-related studies alone, particularly in the field that fascinated him most: history. Then normally considered a branch of literature, history was seldom offered as a separate course of study in colleges and universities. American history, in particular, was neglected, though the University of Pennsylvania finally allowed a short-lived, unsalaried professorship in the subject two years after Jones's graduation. The teacher was Professor Reed's brother, the lawyer and diplomat William Bradford Reed. In an address to Jones and other university alumni, Reed lamented that "Ignorance of History, deep, dark ignorance of our own history is the crying intellectual defect of our country." Jones agreed with Reed.[15]

He also took seriously Alexander Pope's famous admonition: "Drink deep, or taste not the Pierian spring"; he could never be content with "shallow draughts." What he taught himself through wide reading rivaled what he absorbed from his professors. And the voracious love of books and reading that would be a lifelong trait was soon translated into a passion for book collecting.[16]

As a child born into a family of wealth, cultivation, and refinement, Jones had been aware of books from his early days, though not in the quantities he would come to prefer. His uncle Washington Smith had a decent collection, but, sadly, most of the books owned by the first two generations of Joneses in America had been lost to fires, and almost all of the books owned by Dr. George Jones were sold when his estate was settled. In any case, no member of either branch of his family had created a library that rivaled those of such members of Georgia's planter elite as Thomas Spalding of Sapelo and James Hamilton Couper or of any number of Philadelphia bibliophiles. If young Jones were to have a library, he would have to build it himself.[17]

Whether or not grief over the death of his sister in 1843 played any part in Jones's becoming a book collector, it is certain that he did not collect in any significant way during her lifetime; only after she was forever gone from the house in Portico Square did its study begin to fill with books. Shortly after he began collecting seriously, Jones saw his keen love of books evolve into something that went past bibliophily, and he was not ashamed to call it bibliomania—book-madness—the overpowering desire to collect the choicest of books.[48]

Among his major expenses for 1844 were dollars spent for books and cases to contain them. He was fortunate to be in one of the best cities in North America for book buying and collecting. Philadelphia not only boasted numerous publishing houses and bookshops but had been home to many notable bookmen, including both James Logan (1674–1751), assembler of "the finest private library of colonial times," and William Mackenzie (1758–1828), America's first collector of rare books.[49]

Several blocks from Portico Square, on Fourth Street near Market, was the popular bookshop of John Penington, who looked upon bookselling as "not so much a trade as an art." His establishment had the reputation of being a splendid source not only for books but for conversation about books as well, for many of the city's antiquarians and bibliophiles frequented Penington's shop.[50]

Jones's purchases from Penington formed the nucleus of a splendid library of over thirteen hundred volumes that he would gather with care and taste over a period of seventeen years; most of his collecting was done during the first decade of that time. He would add to his library through judicious purchases from other Philadelphia booksellers, including George S. Appleton, Smith & English, and J. W. Moore; from stores in Baltimore, Maryland (just six hours away by train); from the Savannah establishment of Philadelphia-born William Thorne Williams; and from numerous shops visited in several countries during his European travels in 1850 and 1852–53.[51]

Though his books relating to Georgia were closest to his heart, in numbers his library was strongest in British literature; it included a wide array of novels, essays, and poetry. American literature had only a token representation (mainly Washington Irving, James Fenimore Cooper, Ralph Waldo Emerson, Nathaniel Hawthorne, and Herman Melville), while the novels of southern authors were all but ignored and, in the case of William Gilmore Simms, entirely disregarded.[52]

Larger subsections of the library included Latin classics, religious works (with multiple copies of Bibles and Books of Common Prayer), and histories—almost twice as many books on English than American history. In Jones's library, studies of England's past encompassed such volumes as the

Latin histories of Gildas and Nennius, the Elizabethan antiquary William Camden's *Remains Concerning Britain*, and the lengthy chronicles of such luminaries as the earl of Clarendon, Bishop Gilbert Burnet, and G. B. Macaulay. There were also excursions into ancient history, together with a contemporary report of excavations into the storied past: Sir Austen Layard's electrifying account of his discovery of the ruins of Nineveh. There were also works relating to the histories of France (including books from the pens of François Guizot and L.-A. F. de Bourrienne) and Italy (from J. C. L. S. de Sismondi and others).[53]

As an indication of Jones's ravenous intellect and sharpening critical faculty there were the sixteen volumes of Pierre Bayle's *Dictionnaire historique et critique* (1697), one of the collector's costliest acquisitions. "What treasures are to be found in Bayle," one authority declared (while observing that his work was best studied by "young scholars burning with intellectual curiosity"). Bayle, a French philosopher-historian whose "forbidding erudition" was leavened by a somewhat Horatian sense of humor, subjected the "whole scheme of ideas, assumptions, and dogmas to an equal and unceremonious examination." And, most satisfying to the young iconoclast Jones was becoming, Bayle's *Dictionnaire* presents a "thin rivulet of certain facts . . . [flowing] over great depths of footnotes, where skeptical analysis demolishes . . . legend, conjecture, rumor, hearsay, falsehood, myth."[54]

But even youthful skeptics have their articles of faith. One small but choice group of Jones's books had books (and love of books) as its subject; three of the more famous were the *Philobiblon* of Richard de Bury, the fourteenth-century bishop of Durham, reputedly the first book collector (and bibliomaniac); Thomas Frognall Dibdin's famous treatise on bibliomania itself; and James Beresford's *Bibliosophia* (1810), which described the love for book collecting as "a high and dignified passion."[55]

In Philadelphia book lovers' most demanding and catholic tastes could be satisfied by John Penington, who provided books for collecting as well as reading. From him Jones bought one of his most valued volumes, an Ovid published in 1502 by the renowned Venetian scholar-printer Aldus Manutius. The device of Aldus, a sinuous dolphin entwining an anchor, also appeared in scores of other purchases, mainly relating to British literature; these were published by Aldus's self-styled nineteenth-century English disciple, William Pickering, who popularized cloth binding and produced books that were handsome, well-edited, and moderately priced. Some of the volumes in Pickering's Aldine Edition of the British Poets were among Jones's first purchases. Penington could also satisfy Jones's desires for French novels and works of nonfiction, for he imported large supplies of books from the Continent and was well acquainted with the Parisian bibliographer Jacques-Charles Brunet. Jones fit perfectly Penington's idea of the preferred customer: one "who knew what he wanted and why he wanted it." [56]

A lover of beautifully designed books, Jones purchased not only masterpieces of the printer's art but some of the binder's craft as well; he prized two lustrous books bound by James Hayday, the premier English binder of the early nineteenth century. Many of Jones's books were covered in morocco leather, in several colors; some in calfskin—either tanned or polished into vellum; and others in spicily scented Russia leather. His more sumptuous volumes had silk linings and leather joints, and all of them had on their pastedowns his elaborate armorial bookplate, based on an eighteenth-century specimen that had been engraved for Noble Jones. [57]

Young Jones was guided in some of his purchases not only by Penington, whom he knew well, but also by a man he never met, the eccentric British clergyman and bibliographer Thomas Frognall Dibdin, bibliomaniac extraordinaire. Though the Reverend Dibdin wrote about books with more enthusiasm than accuracy, his enthusiasm was his chief charm; his *Introduction to the Knowledge of Rare and Valuable Editions of the Greek and Latin Classics*, with its loving descriptions of the various editions available, had its place in Jones's collection. He also owned *Aedes Althorpiana*, Dibdin's description of the country house and library of his patron, the Earl Spencer, "one of the few noblemen of the time with an eccentric taste for books rather than bloodstock and gambling." [58]

Dibdin's heyday had followed the landmark year of 1812, when—at the sale by auction of the Duke of Roxburghe's library—a rare book had for the first time brought a four-figure sum. In various publications, Dibdin chronicled the collecting ventures of those Englishmen who had subsequently been stricken by bibliomania, a term he himself popularized. He tirelessly promoted the idea that the collecting of rare books was among the most tasteful and intellectually rewarding of pursuits, and his tantalizing descriptions publicized the titles of numerous books, many of which found their way into the libraries of such collectors as Jones. [59]

Led by both Dibdin's advice and his own tastes, Jones added to his choice selection of Greek and Latin classics such volumes as an eighteenth-century

Anacreon, the "chef-d'oeuvre" of the Italian printer Giambattista Bodoni; a "very beautiful" Catullus, published by John Baskerville, as well as one of that master's "most finished specimens of typography": a quarto edition of Virgil; "one of the most beautiful and correct" editions of the *Satyricon* of Petronius, published in seventeenth-century Amsterdam; and a diminutive four-volume set of the works of Seneca, issued by the Elzevirs in Leiden in 1640.[60]

His appreciation for rarities did not prevent Jones from enjoying the simpler and less expensive pleasures of buying new books—those that were, according to William Hazlitt's description, "teeming hot from the press," so that the buyer could be the one to "cut open the leaves, to inhale the fragrance of the scarcely dry paper, to examine the type . . . to launch out into regions of thought and invention never trod till now."[61]

To make a record of all the books he collected, new and old, Jones mastered the terminology of the bibliographer and prepared an alphabetical guide to his collection. It offered all the particulars of his acquisitions, including the prices he paid for almost all of them. His love of books never led him to spend vast amounts of money in an attempt to emulate Philadelphia's most committed bibliophiles. Neither did he try to match the achievements of such Savannah collectors as Alexander A. Smets and Israel K. Tefft or the country's premier collector of Americana, Peter Force of Washington City, famed for reprinting many of his rare holdings.[62]

The French-born Smets, whose nationally known library was the largest private collection in Savannah, published a catalog raisonne that suggested a major interest in books as objects, but it listed scarcely a tenth of his more than two thousand titles. A fortune made in the lumber trade and other businesses enabled Smets to retire in 1849 and devote much of his leisure to securing copies of "the classics of every country and time." Among his treasures were an Egyptian papyrus containing a fragment of the "Ritual of the Dead," incunabula from such printing pioneers as Johannes Gutenberg and William Caxton, and choice volumes from the presses of Aldus and others. He had representative contemporary books as well, including sixteen of Thomas Frognall Dibdin's titles.[63]

Between the wonders of Smets and the collections in other private Savannah libraries—which mainly held readily available books in standard editions—Jones took a middle road. He apparently bought few books that he did not intend to read and indulged himself only occasionally in purchasing a rare item. He did not, for instance, join, as Smets did, in the mania for collecting books in black letter but instead gathered a variety of books whose typographical excellence was paired with subjects that interested him, such as *Poetry of the Anti-Jacobin*, from the press of William Bulmer.[64]

Israel Tefft, Smet's closest friend, had his own national reputation, based on an extensive collection of over twenty-five thousand autographs—normally signed letters or documents rather than mere scraps of paper—dating principally from colonial and revolutionary times. But he also loved and collected books. Though his salary as an employee of the Bank of the State of Georgia did not allow him great scope, Tefft formed a library "large and valuable for one of his limited means." On occasion, Jones would ask permission to bring a "bibliomaniacal friend" to see some of Tefft's treasures. The young man found, moreover, that the cognoscenti of autograph seekers and bibliophiles such as the famed Philadelphia collector Edward Ingraham or his own close friend Winthrop Sargent knew Tefft independently of him. Such was Tefft's renown that no celebrated writer came to Savannah without a letter of introduction to him. Eventually, Jones would also pursue Tefft's interest in manuscripts and autographs, though in a smaller way, for his own library would contain more transcripts of manuscripts than original materials. Jones soon had more Georgia materials of all types than either Smets or Tefft, however, and he once showed Tefft the extraordinary generosity of giving him such a rarity as an autograph of Button Gwinnett.[65]

Though Peter Force's book collection could not rival those of Smets and Tefft in dignity and orderliness, it was, to such a rapt visitor as young Jones, a "noble library." Pleasantly overcrowded, chaotic, and decidedly spartan, it contained around sixty thousand volumes. As one observer noted, "No luxurious library appointments, no glazed bookcases of walnut or mahogany, no easy chairs inviting to soft repose or slumber were there; but only plain, rough pine shelves and pine tables, heaped and piled with books, pamphlets, and journals, which overflowed seven spacious rooms and littered the floors. Among them moved familiarly two or more cats and a favorite old dog, for the lonely scholar was fond of pets." Though Force's collection was heterogeneous, its abundance of American historical works was remarkable. Practically the entire listing of Obadiah Rich's comprehensive *Bibliotheca Americana Nova* was there, with each volume holding a slip of paper giving the book's date and the catalog number that Rich had assigned it.[66]

Jones's library differed conspicuously from those of Smets, Tefft, and Force in his concentration on religious works. The young man's spiritual interests were manifest in the numerous volumes he selected, though his aesthetic concerns remained obvious as well. Of his several editions of the Bible, the most sumptuous was a gilt-edged imperial quarto in two volumes, bound in blue morocco by James Hayday. His prayer books, printed in five languages, included one in Latin produced by William Bagster, the English paragon of ecclesiastical publishing. Bagster's *Hexapla* was among Jones's books as well: a compendium of "the six most important versions in [English] of the New Testament," from John Wycliffe to King James. Related works abounded: histories, commentaries, and discourses by authors from Hugo Grotius to J. D. Michaelis.[67]

Other books (including Bayle's *Dictionnaire*) show that, even in the religious sphere, Jones did not confine himself to authors who confirmed ideas he had already accepted. He found space, for example, for a copy of D. F. Strauss's controversial study of Christ—which had helped shatter the faith of George Eliot, one of its translators—though part of its attraction to Jones may have been that Strauss held the life of Christ up to rigorous historical scrutiny.[68]

More conventionally, Jones's membership in the Episcopal Church led him to gather numerous works bearing on his denomination. They ranged from Bishop Samuel Wilberforce's history of the church in America to accounts of such current controversies as the proceedings against B. T. Onderdonk, the bishop of New York.[69]

The library's pronounced emphasis on works relating to religion did not signify that its owner was a dour prude, for further along the shelves were François Rabelais and George Sand, together with such works as *L'Amour* and *La Femme*. And the numerous Greek and Latin classics, of course, contained passages not for the puritanical, as did later Latin works that Jones owned, such as the mildly erotic *Basia* of Secundus. As a collector, Jones displayed a multiplicity of interests.[70]

Numerous other books also show that he was not without a sense of humor; *Don Quixote* was prominent among his favorites, and he owned a large bronze statuette of the title character consulting a folio of that "best of all books of its kind," *Amadis of Gaul*. Even among his art books, which contained reproductions of paintings, as well as many volumes of etchings and engravings, there were the often satiric works of William Hogarth and the whimsical grotesqueries of Grandville.[71]

Of all the authors whose works Jones owned, highest in his affections were two Horaces, separated by seventeen centuries: Quintus Horatius Flaccus and Horace Walpole, both famed in part for vivid evocations of their respective Augustan ages. The Roman Horace was, to be sure, the colossus of the two, and his graceful lines on diverse topics, his essential humanity, and his lightness of touch made him unfailingly attractive to Jones. He owned multiple copies of Horace's works, including an exquisitely small edition produced by William Pickering, a stately octavo printed by D. A. Talboys at Oxford, and an eighteenth-century gilt-edged quarto, "very beautiful and extremely scarce . . . the rarest of all Baskerville's editions."[72]

With the later Horace, the poet of Augustus and Maecenas shared a habit of amused mockery, though Walpole's had a sharper edge. The "modern" Horace had the advantage of having written —through his deftly entertaining, absorbingly detailed letters— the perfect companion and guide to the era that enchanted Jones: the eighteenth century. In addition to his ten volumes of Walpole's letters, Jones also owned a copy of *The Castle of Otranto*, printed at Parma by Bodoni during Walpole's lifetime; the five-volume *Anecdotes of Painting in England; Historic Doubts on the Life and Reign of King Richard the Third;* and "the most perfect specimen" of the Strawberry Hill Press: Lucan's *Pharsalia*, the only classical work ever printed by Walpole.[73]

Two personal relationships of Jones's university years also formed his developing mind and tastes in ways that rivaled his studies, his reading, and his collecting activities. His bonds with his uncle Washington Smith were strengthened during the period, as Smith increasingly served as the young man's mentor and, in some ways, as his father in all but name, mirroring the role that Chief Justice Tilghman had played in Smith's youth. Jones would come to resemble his uncle in many respects. They shared a philanthropic tendency, along with a passion for privacy and reluctance to bring attention to themselves, which would lead them to "do good by stealth," in Pope's phrase. Both—deeply interested in history, literature, and religion—were constant readers, as well as ardent supporters of their churches, of libraries, and of historical organizations such as the Historical Society of Pennsylvania (of which Smith was a founder) and the Georgia Historical Society (whose presidency Jones would later hold). In business both had an abiding appreciation for investments in stocks, bonds, and real estate, and, insofar as either of them could have been said to have had an occupation, it was managing their investments and properties.[74]

Both would be the first generation of their families to follow no profession; although both were formally schooled in their fathers' professions—Smith in law and Jones in medicine—neither would actively practice. Though both had an interest in science, the younger, befitting his southern agrarian heritage, would be most strongly drawn to scientific agriculture, while the elder's more mechanical interests drew him toward railroads and locomotives, on which he was considered an authority. (His early belief in the future of railways had seemingly been a factor in the wise railroad investments of his brother-in-law Dr. George Jones.) Smith was also interested in penology and wrote several essays on the subject, including one approving the Eastern Penitentiary of Pennsylvania, with its system of solitary confinement at labor for all inmates—the prison that so horrified a visiting Charles Dickens.[75]

Jones's other formative relationship of his university years was with a like-minded young man named Winthrop Sargent. Jones joined the junior class with Sargent at the University of Pennsylvania in early 1844, and the two graduated the following summer. Sargent, two years Jones's senior, shared most of his interests, including the Roman classics and French literature, and he was, not surprisingly, a bibliomaniac.[76]

In its treasures, Sargent's library was closer to Smets's collection than that of his friend Jones. An ardent aficionado of fine binding and its related arts, Sargent collected such gems as a Vulgate *Novum Testamentum*, bound in dark blue morocco, "with gold edges and bands," by the eighteenth-century French binder Bozerian; and he had a "diminutive Johannes Secundus," covered with "scarlet morocco, with plain gold lines and bands." His favorite specimen from the bindery of James Hayday was a prayer book whose fore-edges displayed a painting of the Transfiguration.[77]

One of Jones's and Sargent's strongest shared enthusiasms, however, may have struck some friends and acquaintances as perverse or at least ironic. Though they resided in Philadelphia—a major center of the Whig cause during the Revolution, meeting place of the Continental Congresses, and sometime headquarters of General George Washington—the two were happily enchained by the history of the Loyalists. Their passion for the story of the proponents of the Tory cause existed despite the fact that both young men's grandfathers had been rebels of note: Noble Wimberly Jones as one of the leaders of Georgia's fight for independence, Sargent's namesake as one of the officers of Washington's army, and, after the war, a founder of the Society of the Cincinnati.[78]

Their ancestries held unexpected correspondences. Despite their grandsires' disparate backgrounds in Georgia and New England, both men had been slave owners and had left human property as part of their legacies. Soon after Colonel Sargent had moved to Natchez in the late 1790s as governor of the Mississippi Territory (recently Georgia's westernmost lands), he accumulated—by purchase and through marriage—extensive acres and hundreds of slaves to cultivate them. His bondsmen had also constructed his brick mansion house, called Gloster Place in honor of his Massachusetts birthplace. After the colonel's death, the plantation passed from the family's hands, but by the time Jones and Sargent knew each other, Sargent's father, George Washington Sargent, had bought back most of the old Sargent lands, along with Gloster Place, now embowered among mossy oaks as was Wormsloe House. The Sargents would divide their time between Natchez and Philadelphia, where until 1844 the colonel's widow, known as "Madam Sargent," lived in a large house on Chestnut Street "in much state and dignity."[79]

Jones greatly admired Sargent. He recorded in one of his commonplace books a good number of Sargent's more memorable comments (in both English and Latin), including jests, witticisms, and harmless ribaldries. And once Jones's bibliomania progressed into printing books in limited editions, he would dedicate two of them to his friend. Together they enjoyed good food and drink, along with lengthy visits to John Penington's store for books and conversation. Both young men held strong opinions—particularly on art, history, and literature—and expressed them readily; they also shared an iconoclastic streak that made them eager to expose the errors of supposed experts in their fields of interest. The two loved to "shake the yoke of authority and opinion" and showed a marked unwillingness to accept any views untested and unconfirmed by themselves. Both proved implacable where "sham and pretense" were concerned.[80]

Though they were closest during their years as upperclassmen at the university, the two continued their friendship after Sargent's return to Massachusetts, where he obtained his law degree at his grandfather's alma mater, Harvard, while Jones was pursuing his medical studies. Sargent assisted Jones in his historical pursuits by searching in Harvard's mammoth library for material relating to the early days of Georgia and welcomed him to Cambridge when he came to conduct research on his own.[81]

Though Jones was the first of the two to begin fulfilling his literary aspirations, Sargent would become much more widely known, appearing during his lifetime in Austin Allibone's compendium (faintly praised as "an intelligent antiquary"). Some of Sargent's productions would be similar to those of Jones, limited editions of rare works which he edited. He also wrote and edited a few books that created a stir, particularly his collection of Loyalist verse and a sympathetic biography of Benedict Arnold's co-conspirator, John André. Sargent's documentary account of Major General Edward Braddock's doomed expedition against Fort Duquesne was praised by Washington Irving as "ably edited, with an admirable introductory memoir." Sargent also wrote for periodicals, principally for his friend Jared Sparks's *North American Review*, which published his historical and review essays, as well as loving surveys of bibliomania and bibliopegia, the art of bookbinding. Surveying his friend's literary endeavors, Jones was moved to bestow the supreme compliment: Sargent was, he wrote, "cut out for an American Walpole."[82]

Winthrop Sargent had the distinction of being one of Jones's few close friends near his own age. As a serious and precocious child raised by elderly parents, Jones apparently developed a preference for the companionship of men older than he, who would include William Neyle Habersham, George Noble Jones, Israel Tefft, and, most particularly, William Brown Hodgson.[83]

While Sargent was away at law school, Jones began his medical studies in 1845; he proceeded slowly and methodically, taking both university classes and private courses. As the fourth generation of his family to be drawn to medicine, Jones was well placed to be the first to be professionally trained as a physician. Long unchallenged as the premier medical school in the United States, the University of Pennsylvania School of Medicine attracted the majority of medical scholars who came to Philadelphia during Jones's student days.[84]

Patterned after the medical school of the University of Edinburgh and still basking in the reflected glory of its eminent past professor Benjamin

Rush, the school had the benefit of an excellent seven-man faculty. The professors (who themselves received the students' fees, rather than the university) taught mainly through lectures. During the two-year course of study, in sessions running from October through March, they offered the Theory and Practice of Physic, Chemistry, Surgery, Anatomy, Materia Medica, Physiology (then known as the Institutes of Medicine), and Obstetrics/ Diseases of Women and Children. For practical experience and application, the university's medical students worked at the university dispensary and also trained with local physicians (sometimes their professors), known as preceptors.[85]

Jones's preceptor was Dr. Samuel Jackson, his physiology professor. A venerable figure—one of the links between Jones's time and the age of Rush—Jackson had a vitality and vivacity that continued to enliven his classroom for years after Jones's graduation. One student recalled Jackson's effect during his lectures: "With his bright eyes beaming, his face full of enthusiasm, and his white hair streaming over his shoulders, he was truly picturesque. Leaning forward, he narrated with great animation the happenings of the day . . . as they appeared to the eyes of the great French physiologists."[86]

Among the requirements of candidates for the M.D. degree was an inaugural dissertation. Many of these papers were simply regurgitations of lecture notes, though they were nonetheless held to exacting standards: poor spelling and faulty grammar could "preclude a candidate from examination for a degree." Jones's composition was no rehash of faculty lectures, and its literary qualities were impeccable. Characteristically, it showed both a lively curiosity and an unwillingness to accept received wisdom unless tested. There was a conspicuous tinge of iconoclasm as well, for the paper attacked—successfully—some recent findings regarding cathartics made by the eminent French physiologist Jean-Louis-Marie Poiseuille. The thesis, "Experimental Inquiry into the Correctness of M. Poiseuille's Explanation of the Purgative Action of Certain Substances," attacked the Frenchman's theory with humor and irony. On a practical level, it demonstrated its points with endosmometers fitted with animal and human membranes. In 1848—the same year that Jones received his medical and master's degrees—the *American Journal of the Medical Sciences* printed a précis of his dissertation.[87]

During the same year, nonetheless, the newly minted doctor made it plain that his passion was not for medicine but for literature and history—for the study, not the examining room or the hospital ward. So, instead of choosing a profession, he came to be categorized under what was known in the social nomenclature of the time as a "quality," that of gentleman—the closest thing in America to a title of rank—and, supported by his inheritance, he would lead the life of a gentleman of leisure. Though he would busy himself with investments, in property and otherwise, and also eventually attend to the cultivation of his lands, much of his time would remain free for literary and historical pursuits.[88]

Those who knew the history of Jones's family might have expected him to make political commitments and to accept civic responsibilities, since there had been a century of public service, in peace and war, by the first three generations of his family. In the previous century, Horace Walpole had found himself in a similar situation (though, as the son of Sir Robert Walpole, expectations of him had been much higher). Nonetheless, the younger Walpole had essentially followed his own road, busying himself in many of the same ways that Jones would, at the risk of their being thought inconsequential. In meditating on the circumstances of his decision, Walpole had been drawn to some peculiarly apt lines from Jacques-Auguste de Thou's seventeenth-century classic *Historia sui temporis*. Decades later, these words seemed to fit Jones: "All gave grounds to hope that he would excel the example of his ancestors which he strove to imitate; yet, despite all this, he preferred to seek the obscure easeful retreats of the Muses . . . he chose the ivy and the laurel that grow wild rather than the spoils of battle or triumphs that batten on a hungry peace."[89]

CHAPTER 2

Agricola

A wise skepticism is the first attribute of a good critic.
—JAMES RUSSELL LOWELL

G eorge F. T. Jones came to an early understanding of his
family's heritage and of the significant role his forefathers
had played in the history of Georgia. The simple fact of ancestry
put him in the interesting position of being able to study the story
of colonial, revolutionary, and federal Georgia from a historical
and a genealogical perspective at a time when American historiography and genealogy were enjoying new heights of popularity.[1]

Historical works held a prominent place in the library Jones
created. The American section was heavy with volumes relating
to the colonial and revolutionary periods such as John Huddlestone Wynne's *General History of the British Empire in America*
(1770) and Alexander Garden's *Anecdotes of the Revolutionary
War in America* (1822). As would be expected, there were several
titles relating to the Loyalists (including one fictional work, John
Pendleton Kennedy's *Horse-Shoe Robinson: A Tale of the Tory As-
cendancy*, the only novel by a southern author in Jones's library).
From the general chronicles of the United States, he selected,
among others, the multivolume accounts of the Scotsman James
Grahame and of the immensely popular George Bancroft. But the

young man's historical imagination, like that of many others of his generation, was honed on no American source but on one that was distinctively Scottish.[2]

By the time the boy was old enough to read, the entirety of Sir Walter Scott's Waverley novels awaited him, along with Scott's "Tales of My Landlord" series, and Jones found these romances very appealing. In particular, there was that magical talent of the "Wizard of the North" for making history come alive, for endowing the past with vividness and immediacy. And there was substantial material relating to subjects that held a special fascination for Jones, such as heraldry, which received extensive coverage in the early pages of *Waverley*. Bibliophily figured prominently as well, in such books as Sir Walter's own favorite, *The Antiquary*; it contained many passages on the allure of books, including one in which the first bibliomaniac was identified as Don Quixote de la Mancha, one of Jones's preferred literary characters. *The Antiquary* also meditated on the nature of history and mused on its multiple attractions. Several other novels presented the Scottish rebellions of the early 1700s; these appealed irresistibly to a young man whose maternal grandfather had been born in Jacobite Aberdeen during the "Forty-five," while the Young Pretender was occupying Edinburgh. Finally, brooding over much of Scott's work—and speaking very clearly to Jones—was a preoccupation with continuity: "the unbroken line from past to present—the sense of oneness with earlier generations."[3]

It was neither historical novels nor histories that drew Jones most strongly, however, but the raw materials of history, particularly early publications and manuscripts that related to the colonization of Georgia. Happily, the expatriate American book dealer Obadiah Rich had published in 1835 the first volume of his *Bibliotheca Americana Nova;* it showed the young student much of what had been published on Georgia during the eighteenth century. In his copy of Rich, Jones found not only pamphlets from the 1700s relating to his state's origins but materials in manuscript as well, along with their locations—and he ordered transcriptions of those distant sources that he coveted most.[4]

Jones soon assembled a Georgia historical collection, mainly primary sources, that would impress one authority as the finest he had seen in private hands. Among the titles were *A New and Accurate Account of the Provinces of South Carolina and Georgia*, published in London in 1732, the year

Georgia was chartered, and a folio volume printed nine years later: *An Account Shewing the Progress of the Colony of Georgia in America, from Its First Establishment*. There were accounts of General James Oglethorpe's siege of St. Augustine and of redcoat Colonel Banastre Tarleton's operations in the "Southern Provinces." Journals of sojourners in Georgia, including those of Baron von Reck (1734) and William Bartram (1794), had a place on Jones's shelves, as did works ranging from Patrick Tailfer's 1741 salvo against the Georgia colony's Trustees to relatively staid productions by the Reverend George Whitefield, dealing with the Orphan House at Bethesda. In transcript from the British Museum there was a Latin work on the Salzburger settlement in Georgia, copied from the original published at Augsburg in 1747. And there were such oddities as the fabulously rare *Account of the Remarkable Conversion of Jachiel Heishel from the Jewish to the Christian Religion*, published at Savannah in 1770—the earliest of his Georgia publications. Nonetheless, Jones's volumes relating strictly to Georgia numbered fewer than fifty titles. Though seemingly a small number, it far exceeded that found in some institutions. The library of the University of Georgia, for example, during the 1850s held only about a half dozen books on Georgia history.[5]

Jones found a marked scarcity of book-length productions on Georgia's early history. Alexander Hewat's *Historical Account of the Rise and Progress of the Colonies of South Carolina and Georgia*, published anonymously in London in 1779, placed its greatest emphasis on South Carolina; nonetheless, it also contained interesting matter on Georgia, including an account of the confrontation between Captain Noble Jones and Mary Musgrove's Creek insurgents. Also, since it was written from a Loyalist perspective, Hewat's chronicle appealed strongly to Jones's sympathies.[6]

The only other book available, Captain Hugh McCall's *History of Georgia*, published in Savannah in two volumes (1811 and 1816), added only five years to the time span covered by Hewat and commandeered vast portions of Hewat's text, incorporating them without attribution. These borrowings incensed Jones even more than did the numerous mistakes for which McCall was usually castigated.[7]

Except for two biographies of Oglethorpe, neither of which impressed Jones, no other lengthy studies bearing on colonial Georgia had been produced in the early nineteenth century. Was it time for the production of a new history of Georgia? Jones thought not. It was time, he felt, not for writing but for a concerted effort at gathering, analyzing, and comparing the wide array of primary material available on the history of Georgia, found in both America and England. In the meantime, students of Georgia history could cast light on their subject and help pave the way for future historians by producing essays and monographs drawing on original materials. But by the time Jones published this opinion in 1846, events had followed a somewhat erratic course, and he found that those who had taken charge of Georgia's history were not in full agreement with him.[8]

During the 1820s, the decade of Jones's birth, the gathering of Georgia's historical records had proceeded by fits and starts. Amassing a true state archive depended on the unreliable support of the state's General Assembly— and particularly the legislators' willingness to spend public money to locate and organize materials held by the various departments of state government itself and (for the colonial period) to purchase copies of documents in various British depositories. Encouragingly, the General Assembly had voted in December 1824 to pay the state's first official historian, Joseph Vallence Bevan, the sum of $400 "for the purpose of collating, arranging and publishing all papers pertaining to the original settlement or political history of [Georgia], now in the Executive or Secretary of State's office." Working with an energy and enthusiasm that far surpassed his meager funding, Bevan had soon gathered an impressive collection, not only of papers in the statehouse in Milledgeville but of others elsewhere, most notably papers of Captain Hugh McCall, former governor James Jackson, and Dr. George Jones.[9]

Perhaps Bevan's greatest coup, however, came in 1826, when the British government, in response to his request, opened its archives for research in Georgia documents dated before 1776. Unfortunately, the General Assembly's support ebbed at this crucial moment. It was impossible to have the material from the British archives located and copied, and in 1830 Bevan went to an early grave.[10]

Eight years after Bevan's death, the tide turned. The General Assembly, prodded by the Senatus Academicus, paid $4,000 to the Reverend Charles Wallace Howard to travel to England to obtain copies of many of the coveted records, the housing and organization of which the British government was perfecting. Later the legislators even agreed to send an additional $2,500 to allow its agent to complete his job. Consequently, Howard returned to Georgia in late 1839 with twenty-two folio volumes of "closely-written" transcripts.[11]

Earlier the same year, three Savannahians had banded together to create the Georgia Historical Society. Jones would claim two of them—Israel Tefft and Dr. Richard Arnold—as lifelong friends and would have a notable encounter with the third, Dr. William Bacon Stevens. It was probably said then—and was certainly said later—that Stevens and Tefft, at least, had selfish motives in organizing the society.[12] Stevens wanted an entity to help him realize his dream of writing a history of Georgia. And the inveterate autograph collector Tefft saw the society, of which he would long be corresponding secretary, as a means of acquiring additional letters and documents for his collection. Fittingly, the final decision to form the society was made in the library of Tefft's home on St. Julian Street, where the three founders were surrounded by his remarkable trove of manuscripts and books. Though charged with selfishness, the founders actually had mixed motives, most of them unrelated to self-aggrandizement, and the organization they created—initially composed of 240 regular and honorary members—would prove useful and beneficial in numerous ways unrelated to any personal aims. Dr. Arnold always considered Tefft the "source and origin" of the society and revered him for it.[13]

Among the society's stated aims, collecting and preserving the materials of Georgia history were foremost, and it actively solicited a wide range of donations. Stevens was particularly interested in manuscripts that were "dispersed in many of the old families" of Savannah. In the second-floor room at Whitaker Street and Bay Lane that the society shared with the Savannah Library Society, the shelves and cases soon began to fill with "books and manuscripts and letters of great value."[14]

In 1840, in accordance with the society's other stated aim of "diffusion," Stevens edited and saw through the press the society's first contribution to Georgia historiography, Volume 1 of the *Collections of the Georgia Historical Society;* it featured an oration by William Law touching on earlier efforts to provide a history of the state and reprinted several rare pamphlets of the colonial era, much in the manner of the historical publications of Peter Force. A second, similar volume of the *Collections,* also edited by Stevens, appeared in 1842. By that time Stevens had entered the literary orbit of Tefft's close friend William Gilmore Simms of South Carolina and had begun to publish historical articles in such periodicals as the *Magnolia* and the *Orion*. And he had also begun delivering a series of lectures on Georgia history, presented on behalf of the society to audiences in Savannah and elsewhere.[15]

Stevens pursued his historical activities with an uncommon energy, particularly for someone who had arrived in Georgia as a semi-invalid seeking to stave off "incipient consumption." Born in Maine but a Bostonian since infancy, Stevens had visited several ports of call, including the Sandwich Islands and China, before landing in Savannah and finding that its climate agreed with him. He married the daughter of a local doctor, soon becoming a physician himself, and grew affluent practicing privately and filling several appointive medical positions. Because he was considered sound on the slavery issue, he was enthusiastically welcomed into his adopted community and was admitted to all aspects of life in Savannah open to the gentry (including membership in the celebrated Georgia Hussars, an elite volunteer militia unit) and soon converted from the Congregational to the Episcopal faith.[16]

In recognition of his tireless promotion of the activities of the Georgia Historical Society, Stevens was selected in 1841 to deliver the 12 February oration, scheduled annually by the society to celebrate the founding of the Georgia colony by General James Oglethorpe. With some pomp, the society members, together with such organizations as the Hibernian Society and the German Friendly Society, gathered with other interested townspeople before the City Exchange and marched up Bull Street with Dr. Stevens to the Unitarian church, accompanied by elaborately uniformed escorts from various military units. In the sanctuary the assemblage heard Stevens deliver "a discourse replete with historical information, studiously collected and happily introduced"; the subtext of his oration was a broad hint that he was now prepared to produce a suitable history of Georgia. Ultimately, both the society and the General Assembly decided to give Stevens their support, and he was soon in possession of all the bound transcripts from London, as well as all other historical materials at the command of the society and its membership.[17]

Stevens seemed preeminently qualified for his task. Though William Gilmore Simms had tentatively begun writing Georgia's history himself (an act many patriotic Georgians would not have welcomed from any South Carolinian), he gladly deferred to Stevens. He took the adopted Georgian at his own high valuation, asserting that Stevens had "the whole body of American History at his finger ends." [18]

Another admirer of Dr. Stevens was Bishop Stephen Elliott, the recently elected first Episcopal bishop of Georgia, but his plans would divert Steven's career from medicine and historiography into a new direction, leading to unexpected consequences. While listening to the 1841 oration that had helped win Stevens the role of Georgia's historian, the bishop had found himself moved by more than the historical theme. He commented, "I wish I had that man in the pulpit." Thus Stevens fell under the irresistible sway of the bishop of Georgia and changed his career from medicine to the ministry. [19]

Bishop Elliott was conscious of his church's image as a bastion of high social rank—a characterization lent credence by its limited membership (less than 2 percent of Georgia's churchgoers, attending only half a dozen mainly urban churches) and of such exclusionary practices as the renting of pews. He knew likewise that some of Georgia's Episcopal ministers had the reputation of being house clergy to the wealthy, similar to Jane Austen's Mr. Collins or Henry Fielding's Parson Supple. The bishop resolved to correct these impressions. He determined to make the church more accessible to all Georgians (including slaves) and to send eloquent men such as Stevens into the state's hinterlands as Episcopal missionaries. [20]

Another of Stevens's well-wishers made the bishop's plan possible, for Stevens could not have completed his ministerial studies (even the abbreviated one-year course of study proposed by Elliott) without a source of income to support his family. His patron was William Hunter Bulloch, a cousin of young Jones and proprietor of the *Savannah Daily Georgian.* The newspaper, which in the past had been owned by both Israel Tefft and Dr. Richard Arnold, had always been in the forefront of matters historical. Under Bulloch, a charter member of the Georgia Historical Society, the paper had been a promoter and defender of the society in general and of Stevens in particular. To ease Stevens's financial concerns during his studies, Bulloch paid him $1,500 to write occasional historical columns for the *Georgian.* These articles, Stevens noted with a characteristic lack of modesty, "elevated the tone and literary value" of the newspaper. Bulloch could hardly have agreed more; he seldom mentioned Stevens by name in the newspaper, most often identifying him simply as "the Historiographer," suggesting a very exalted status. [21]

Following his ordination as deacon in 1843, Stevens was posted to the town of Athens. There he entered the priesthood the following year, and Bishop Elliott's influence as one of the University of Georgia's trustees presumably helped him secure a faculty position to supplement his salary as rector of Emmanuel Church, along with housing, also compliments of the university. Stevens's original title was "Professor of Oratory and Belles-Lettres," but he was soon made "Professor of Evidences of Christianity and History" as well. How his activities as missionary and professor squared with his responsibilities as historiographer apparently troubled some society members. Having been persuaded that this local doctor was best qualified to be the state's historian, they had now seen him abandon his medical practice for preaching, then leave Savannah for double duties in Athens. Would his history ever be completed? In 1845 society members, impatient at the delays, appointed a committee to try to find the answer.[22]

How much George F. T. Jones knew of Stevens and his activities is uncertain; following his father's death in 1838, Jones seems to have spent only one winter in Savannah until the mid-1840s. But the two were destined to cross paths. By early 1846, the young man—now in possession of his bachelor's degree and beginning his medical studies—had been reading deeply in Georgia history, among his own books and in various Philadelphia libraries. Though not yet twenty-one and, consequently, not old enough to be a member of the Georgia Historical Society, he possessed a large fund of historical knowledge and had strong opinions on the subject of Georgia historiography. Eager to share both, he chose to do so in a common forum of the day—the daily newspaper—through a widely used medium—the pseudonymous letter. Whether he intended to do so or not, he was bearding the Georgia Historical Society in its den, for it was to his kinsman William Hunter Bulloch that he sent his first composition. Consequently, the readers of the *Georgian* of January 7, 1846, encountered a double column entitled "Essays on the History of Georgia, No. 1" printed above the pen name "Agricola."[23]

Why did he choose this particular nom de plume? The simplest answer may be the best: it was a close Latin translation of his Greek-based Christian name. And since both "George" and "Agricola" essentially mean "farmer," Jones may also have been making a reference to that status he would soon assume, however reluctantly, which he would later describe as "gentleman farmer." There may also have been a subtle allusion to one of the most famous scenes in Scott's *The Antiquary*. Therein the title character, Jonathan Oldbuck, displays the specious expertise and ludicrous credulity that won some antiquarians the scorn of serious historical scholars like Jones. Oldbuck shows a guest an earthen ruin that he identifies as the Praetorium of one of the Roman governor Agricola's Scottish fortifications. A rustic, however, embarrasses the antiquary by revealing the eathwork's true identity as a shelter, built only twenty years before.[24]

The essays of Agricola would run to six numbers over several months, ending on April 3, 1846, and would be followed by two unnumbered pieces. They were remarkable productions for a young man who had not yet reached his majority. Agricola proved himself a lucid stylist, a learned historian, and a classicist who ornamented all his pieces with Latin quotations. He obviously relished the aggressive "cut and rip" that characterized some of the reviewing columns of the British literary periodicals of the early 1800s, and, like John Wilson Croker and others, he soon showed that he would not abstain from personal attacks. But Agricola's essays were marked above all else by a combination of passion and conviction regarding historical matters. Beneath the easy expression and humorous asides was an intelligence both uncompromising and exacting; it promised little tolerance for dissent.[25]

The introductory essay surveyed the few existing secondary works on colonial Georgia. Agricola took offense at those misconceptions regarding Georgia's origin that were particularly cherished in New England, where the Trustees' utopia was regarded as a penal colony. While he quickly admitted Georgia's own negligence in not providing accurate accounts, the essayist argued that state pride was now correcting this slackness—pride fostered by the accomplishments of such nationally celebrated Georgians as John Forsyth and William H. Crawford, famed for their accomplishments as U.S. senators, diplomats, and cabinet officers. This growing state patriotism, he asserted, had inspired such advances as the establishment of the Georgia Historical Society.[26]

Concluding his general observations, the writer took the genesis of Georgia as the main topic of his first essay. With masterful precision he traced the causes that produced the colony; his summary's only weakness—a minor one—was a dramatic overemphasis of the role of the South Sea Bubble in the Georgia story. Before the first essay concluded, however, Agricola allowed a brief appearance by a figure he much admired, General James

Edward Oglethorpe, whose "disinterested benevolence" had been responsible for Georgia's creation.[27]

Agricola returned to Oglethorpe in the second essay, which dealt mainly with the activities of the Trustees who founded Georgia and with the *Anne*'s voyage to the New World with the first group of settlers. Returning to the subject of Oglethorpe, the essayist wrote, "Pure philanthropy was his only motive; the approbation of the good, his only reward." But despite editor Bulloch's printed misgivings, the critic gave a much less glowing assessment of the late Thaddeus Mason Harris. A Massachusetts divine forced South by poor health, he had in 1841 prepared a biography of Oglethorpe with the enthusiastic assistance of Stevens and the Georgia Historical Society. Consequently, the author had dedicated his work to the "President, the Vice Presidents, the Officers and Members" of the society—producing a book "almost sinking under the weight of its dedications," thought Agricola. He liked nothing about the work, beginning with its title: *Biographical Memorials of James Oglethorpe;* he found the omission of Oglethorpe's military rank "a mawkish affectation of republican simplicity." The book itself manifested "far more curiosity than research" and contained numerous errors, one of which Argicola corrected, identifying it as a perpetuation of one of the many mistakes of McCall's *History of Georgia.*[28]

But the second essay's major concern was to list the four most important sources of Georgia history. These, he noted, had to be gathered and refined before there could be "even a tolerably correct, or anything approaching to a complete history of Georgia":

1. Books and pamphlets . . . published in London, Charleston, Philadelphia, &c., from the year 1731 inclusive.
2. Contemporaneous periodical publications, [such] as the Gentleman's Magazine, the London Magazine, the Political State of Great Britain, &c.
3. Contemporaneous *ephemeral* publications; i.e., the daily and weekly papers; among the best of which for the purposes are the London Journal, the London Gazette, the South Carolina and Georgia Gazettes, the American Weekly Mercury, &c.; although all the London papers of the period may be examined with advantage.
4. Manuscript letters and journals, and the official or other documents of the Trustees, preserved in England and Georgia.[29]

In the third essay, Agricola corrected more historians' mistakes—including one by George Bancroft—but Harris emerged as whipping boy and suffered more abuse, this time because of his confusion over an early pamphlet titled *A New Voyage to Georgia*. The essayist supplied complete bibliographic information on the book, using eighteenth-century British periodicals and Rich's *Bibliotheca Americana Nova*. Interestingly, some of Harris's statements had been echoed by William Bacon Stevens in his introduction to the version of *A New Voyage to Georgia* printed in the second volume of the society's *Collections* in 1842. Was Agricola attacking Stevens through his friend Harris?[50]

Answering some of his own Savannah critics, who thought the corrections he supplied were unimportant, Agricola responded that if a fact was "worth stating at all, it was worth stating correctly." This principle, he declared, was the basis of his essays.[51]

Included in the essayist's third piece was a digression on the three classes of minds, a subject akin to the meditations on madness that Jones would soon publish. In his view, it was not the men of genius or the men of talent whose minds changed the world but the minds of men of "indomitable perseverance, invincible resolution, and unconquerable will"; he included Oglethorpe in this last class and paid tribute to the general with a long passage from a Horatian ode.[52]

This and the other essays mentioning Oglethorpe reveal Jones as an ardent admirer of Oglethorpe though, unlike Harris and others, he stopped short of hagiography. He did not ignore Oglethorpe's crotchets and shortcomings or attempt to transform the general's occasional foolish statements into something more palatable. Agricola did not condemn out of hand or belittle Oglethorpe's contemporaries (like Walpole) and recent critics who had made negative remarks about the general; instead, he analyzed the criticism and agreed or disagreed with it according to its merits. Perhaps most surprisingly, he held that "Oglethorpe's military talents [had] been rated much too highly and lauded on inadequate grounds." Though excellent as a "subordinate under the supervision of his superior," Oglethorpe lacked "that imperturbable coolness and self-possession . . . , that deliberative, clear (yet not transparent) mind, so necessary to a commander-in-chief." Oglethorpe's strengths and virtues lay elsewhere, Agricola asserted, particularly in his humanitarian efforts in England and his role in establishing the Georgia colony: "A philanthropist, he deserves the applause of mankind; the founder of their State, he merits from Georgians all the respect and reverence which is due so exalted a character."[53]

Noble Jones, not Oglethorpe, was the unidentified focus of several passages in Essays IV and V; they made plain (to those who knew Agricola's identity) Jones's interest in his family's beginnings in the New World. The author described the gradations of social class that later arose among the settlers sent to Georgia by the Trustees. Correcting those who considered the Georgia colony another Botany Bay, he noted that the Trustees' policy for screening the colonists was rigorous and that they set high standards for admittance into the colony. In a passage that suggested his theory of what brought Noble Jones to Georgia, he noted that among the colonists were "gentlemen of education and respectability," though "it would be folly to suppose that men of rank *and fortune* in England would emigrate to an uncultivated wilderness."[54]

Through Agricola, Jones also explored the process that led to the creation in the new land of a kind of aristocracy, a caste to which Noble Jones presumably belonged: "personal qualities, talents, or acquirements" would raise their possessors "above their fellow men. . . . The different members of society [would then] assume their proper stations, and distinction of ranks . . . [would] again [be] established—but on a widely dissimilar basis." High station could be gotten and kept only by "individual ability," however. "The honor that great men acquire, they transmit to their descendants, and posterity thus inherits the rank it could obtain in no other way." He attacked as fatuous John Locke's suggestion that hereditary noblemen be sent to become colonists; for building a colony, the need was instead for the "great middle class, which is the true source of a nation's strength."[55]

Though by this time some readers had undoubtably been irritated by some of Agricola's pronouncements, only the sixth essay provoked a full-scale controversy. While the previous pieces had contained some plaudits for the Georgia Historical Society, there had been barbs as well, notably in the passages devoted to the shortcomings of the society's protégé Harris. The sixth essay returned to this target, though its ostensible purpose was to review another Oglethorpe biography, published by William Bourn Oliver Peabody in 1844. This critique—actually more the author's survey of Oglethorpe's life than a review of someone else's account of it—was preceded by an attack. Agricola assailed both of the Oglethorpe biographies, as well as both volumes of the Georgia Historical Society's *Collections,* for their New England origins. It seemed most regrettable to Agricola that all books on Georgia—even those prepared in Georgia—apparently had to "proceed from the press of Massachusetts." In a comment that could be seen as directed toward the Boston printers—or even toward former Bostonian William Bacon Stevens himself—the essayist asserted that it was not "very honorable to the literary character of the Georgians, that their history should be illustrated by strangers." This he regarded as a disparagement of Georgians' "patriotism or their abilities."[56]

In a brief preface to the essay, editor Bulloch made it clear that he was not comfortable with its "sectional allusions," even though the author had denied in a private note to the editor that any of his "strictures" were directed toward "Northern friends who have adopted Georgia as their home" or any other Northerners, except those who "have laid themselves open to censure." Bulloch no doubt recalled Agricola's epithets in the first essay for northerners he considered "open to censure": those who considered themselves superior to southerners, particularly the "calculating descendants of the canting murderers of their King—a people as remarkable for their own spirit and pride, as for their love of humbling it in others" and the "riotous sons of Dutch boors and Quaker tradesmen." Agricola closed his communication to Bulloch by noting that "the friends of the Yankee literati" could refute his charges if he was in error.[57]

Jones seemed to be making a obvious distinction between northerners (people who lived in the North) and Yankees (northerners unfriendly to the South). But his unabashed sectionalism indicated that despite his long residence in the North and his numerous personal and family ties there, he was an unapologetic southern partisan. His identity as a southerner and a Georgian came from his father's people; no family had deeper roots in Georgia. But as a slave-holding family, the Joneses, like the slave South itself, had become increasingly beleaguered, beginning with ominous events that had formed part of the backdrop of Jones's early childhood. The Southampton slave insurrection of 1831 and the Nullification Crisis of 1832, compounded by an increasingly aggressive antislavery crusade (and other factors), had helped form a South unlike the one known by his forebears—a South whose fundamental economic and social underpinnings seemed threatened as never before.[58]

As a self-proclaimed southerner in Philadelphia, Jones was relatively unthreatened. He was living and writing in "the most southern of northern cities," a city with a long history of hospitality toward visitors or emigrants from the slave states—particularly if they were from the upper classes—a city that enjoyed many ties of marriage and business with the South. Although Philadelphia was a major stronghold of abolitionists, they were a "despised minority," whereas Jones, in his medical school environment, belonged to the majority: most medical students were southerners.[39]

Nonetheless, Jones was obviously much more likely to encounter antisouthern sentiments in Philadelphia than in Savannah, and he was very aware of the multiplying criticisms of southern society—particularly from the presses of New England—ranging from attacks on the institution of slavery to disparagements of the South's literature and culture. The towering pride of Massachusetts was particularly hard for Jones to bear, despite (or because of) the state's position in the forefront during the colonial period and, especially, the Revolutionary War. Massachusetts, birthplace of the first of the state historical societies in 1791, had produced historians who, many southerners thought, had written volumes of "boastful eulogy" that suggested that the history of America was, basically, the history of New England. Against such attacks and assumptions, Jones probably felt called upon to defend his "country" (as he called the South) and his heritage. Even conversations about history and literature at Penington's bookshop could take a sudden sectional turn, for though southerners brought the bookseller much of his business, New Englanders, including Charles Sumner, were also drawn to his shelves.[40]

To Jones, one of the most provoking aspects of the assaults on the South was that there was no defense from some of the criticisms. If he himself thought the South was making contributions to history and literature (and contributions *were* being made), his library did not show it. Whether or not he wanted to admit it, an underlying vexation was the sad truth that, despite the efforts of a small cadre of southern historians and litterateurs, southerners were largely indifferent to intellectual matters. This was a major reason for both the weakness of southern publishing and the circumstance of Georgia and other southern states having their histories "illustrated by strangers," like William Bacon Stevens, who was "amazed at how much history Georgians had made and how little of it they had written." Nonetheless, Jones felt that even northern writers who showed an intelligent appreciation of southern history were "insulting the present race, while exalting the past."[41]

Since the northern houses had a near monopoly on publishing and even some southern histories were being written by northerners, it seemed to

Jones that the South could at least serve as place of copyright for works produced there. As one who had steeped himself in the arcana of printing and publishing and copyright, Jones knew that a book's place of printing did not dictate its place of publication. And the society understood this as well, for, though printed in Boston, both volumes of the *Collections* listed Savannah as the place of publication on their title pages. The rub for Jones was that both volumes displayed a statement, on the verso of the title page, that the books had been entered for copyright purposes in the district court of Massachusetts. As Jones knew, the pertinent law allowed the copyright to be secured in the book's state of origin—southern authors using northern printers routinely secured copyrights in the South—and, as he noted, there was no necessity for such books as the *Collections* to be copyrighted at all. It was "a disgraceful stigma," he wrote, that "even our historical collections must be entered in the court of another state." Did "the deliberations of *Georgians*," he inquired, "terminate in such foolery?"[42]

He soon had an answer. On April 7, 1846, only four days after the appearance of Agricola's essay, the editor of the *Georgian* announced that Agricola would not "have the field all to himself." In an adjacent column, Agricola's opponent (calling himself "Toma Chi Chi," after Oglethorpe's Indian ally) decried the fact that "any person however closely veiled by his anonymous signature, should be so reckless in his assertions." There followed some assertions at least equally reckless, along with much slinging of Latin (though Toma Chi Chi disparaged Agricola's use of classical quotations). Proceeding at first with more passion and injured feelings than accuracy, Agricola's critic made several incorrect statements, relatively trivial in themselves: he misquoted from a title page of the *Collections* and confused the copyright law with the U.S. Constitution. He charged as well that Agricola did not know the difference between a printer and a publisher (all the while demonstrating his own confusion in the matter). Regarding Agricola's complaint about the Georgia Historical Society's having sought copyrights in New England, he maintained that the copyright was legally binding whether secured in Massachusetts or Georgia—showing that he had missed the point. Nonetheless, he as much as admitted that Dr. Stevens, as agent for the society in these printing and publishing matters, had been left to suit his own convenience in the matter of the copyrights.[43]

Printing the *Collections* in the North, however, made good economic sense: "A book can be issued from the press at the North, at about two thirds the cost that it can be done here." And he further explained that no third volume had been issued because the society's available money was being invested in obtaining transcripts of early Georgia records from the State Paper Office in London; pleas to the General Assembly for financial assistance with this project had gone unheeded.[44]

Toma Chi Chi's conclusion was more calm and constructive. He provided an excellent summary of the society's achievements to date, filling a full column of the paper with the organization's many good works. He included the two volumes of *Collections* (in which, he pointed out, such Georgians as Thomas Spalding of Sapelo had "illustrated" the history of the state), the winter lecture series that had been offered for six years, the several pamphlet publications of historical discourses and orations that had been offered, and the "large sums" that had been spent in the preparation of Dr. Stevens's history.[45]

Agricola's response, printed two weeks later, showed little contrition or mercy. His opponent, he wrote, having assumed "the name of a wild Indian," had "written in the style of one." There followed a discussion of several of the mistakes and misunderstandings of the "princely savage." But Agricola protested that he had not intended to be a malicious critic of the society. His objective, "though forwarded only by the limited means of a private individual," coincided with that of the society: both sought "to promote the welfare of Georgia, to diffuse knowledge of, and to increase the interest in, her history." He wished earnestly that the organization's "existence [would be] prolonged, its sphere of usefulness enlarged, and its honors increased." His criticism, he emphasized, had been directed to a "*particular proceeding*" of the society to which he had justly objected. His main question remained, Why could not the book have been entered in the district court of Georgia? He ultimately received an answer of sorts, for the next volume of the *Collections,* issued in 1848, was printed cheaply in New York but not copyrighted there.[46]

Almost a year would pass before Agricola's next (and last) appearance in the *Georgian.* A flood of news about the war in Mexico had intervened since the last essay, and Jones's absorption in his studies in Philadelphia had probably also reduced his leisure for controversy. But it was the same censorious Agricola who wrote the seventh essay, which was published on February 5, 1847, unnumbered and untitled.[47]

Others had previously criticized the abundant errors in Captain Hugh

McCall's *History of Georgia*. Agricola in his last essay demonstrated that McCall had also extensively plagiarized Alexander Hewat's history of South Carolina and Georgia. Plagiarism was commonplace in the historiography of the time; many books, like McCall's, were to a great extent cobbled together from other sources with neither attribution nor comment. What most provoked Agricola, however, was McCall's elaborate attempt to disclaim the benefit of any predecessors in writing the history of the state. "Without map or compass," McCall had written in his introduction, he had "entered an unexplored forest, destitute of any other guide than a few ragged pamphlets, defaced newspapers, and scraps of manuscripts." How, then, Agricola inquired, could one explain the failure to mention Hewat's "work in 2 volumes, containing together seven hundred pages, printed in London, with good type and on good paper"? In case anyone doubted that McCall had copied from Hewat, Agricola supplied lengthy parallel columns that proved the plagiarism beyond any doubt.[48]

Mindful of William Hunter Bulloch's earlier disapproval of his criticisms of the late Thaddeus Harris, Agricola was at pains to defend himself from charges that he was attacking another defenseless dead man, McCall. He admitted that some would say that "the fact of an author's being defunct entitles him to immunity from blame." For him, he declared, the maxim would not be the one Bulloch had quoted against him at that time—*De mortuis nil nisi bonum* (Speak only good of the dead)—but his own: *De omnibus nil nisi verum* (Speak only truth of all).[49]

One fact, only suggested in previous pieces, became very clear in this last essay. From his wide reading, young Jones had become well acquainted with Georgia history, but his knowledge of the recent past of Savannah and its people was limited. He admitted that he had no knowledge of McCall "except what his title page affords"; indeed, he made a half-humorous guess that McCall must have been British. Yet McCall was very well known to older Savannahians. Along with Dr. George Jones, he had been a founder of the Savannah Library Society in 1809; he had died just over a score of years earlier, having served for almost two decades as the town's jailer (though much confined to a "roller chair"), and was buried in the Old Cemetery. Jones had obviously not yet sought out—or had not had the opportunity to exploit—many living sources of history, particularly in Savannah. This lack would be remedied.[50]

The essays Jones wrote as Agricola, though intrinsically interesting, are also valuable for what they say about the young author. He began them at age eighteen and finished them at nineteen, but many passages seemed like the work of a much older, more mature mind. He would never abandon his conviction (perhaps partially explained by his medical training) that history should be written with the care and exactitude demanded by science. But the writer's youth betrayed him most noticeably in episodes of posturing, in his combination of idealism and iconoclasm, and in those passages where his passions outran his discretion; as a more mature man he would be more deliberate and certainly more charitable. For now, he displayed the unshakable certitude of the young.

Predictably enough, Dr. William Bacon Stevens was among those who wondered who Agricola was; he asked his friend and admirer Bulloch to secure the author's permission for Stevens to learn his identity and write to him. Jones consented and in mid-March 1847 received a letter from Stevens complimenting the recently concluded series of essays, which he said "evinced so much critical knowledge of the history" of Georgia. Furthermore, he expressed the hope that their correspondence would lead to "an enduring personal friendship."[51]

Stevens's first letter of a dozen or more was much the most charming and diplomatic of the lot. In it he by turns complimented his correspondent and attempted to overawe him. He wrote of his own well-stocked library— including the imported folio volumes (recently increased to thirty at a total expense of over $7,000)—while also asking whether Jones might have (and share) some sources that still eluded him. Stevens agreed with Jones on McCall's plagiarism but said that he himself had made the discovery in 1840. And he admitted that his late friend Harris's Oglethorpe biography was "full of errors & many of them important" but disclosed that only Harris's death had prevented the two of them from preparing a planned second edition, corrected and otherwise improved.[52]

Having used his first letter to discuss subjects they agreed on, Stevens differed with Jones in several of the communications that followed, sometimes condescendingly. His tone ranged from fatherly to magisterial, though only a dozen years separated the two men in age. In some instances Stevens revisited passages in the Agricola essays, in others he corrected what he saw as minor errors of fact or interpretation in both Jones's essays and letters. These were not always corrected gently, but neither was Jones always diplomatic. He once clearly exasperated Stevens by referring to the two volumes of *Collections of the Georgia Historical Society* as mere "advertisements of the Society's existence."[53]

It was obvious from Stevens's letters (particularly from the numerous titles he quoted) that he had indeed been supplied with an extraordinary library for his project and that he had discovered a considerable number of sources on his own. To his credit, Stevens was generous with his materials; he took the trouble and expense to have a copyist prepare for Jones excerpts relating to Noble Jones from his bound manuscripts and passed along other information on the Jones family that he encountered. An elderly parishioner of his, for instance, had recollections dating back to the Revolution. She remembered Noble Wimberly Jones and his family—particularly that Jones's son John had been killed in the streets of Savannah when the British had taken the city in 1778 and that N. W. Jones's brother Inigo Jones had been a Loyalist.[54]

Jones responded to Stevens's generosity with unselfish acts of his own. His first letter to Stevens invited the historian to visit him in Philadelphia to consult his library, which contained at least two of the books Stevens still sought. Later, at his own expense, he had an engraving made of Noble Jones's rendering of the Orphan House at Bethesda for use in Stevens's book and supplied Stevens with two thousand plates from it. He did likewise with an engraving of Oglethorpe that the English engraver William Greatbach had executed for him (including his name, as having commissioned it), even though Jones had meant it to illustrate a "proposed work" of his own, probably a biographical sketch of Georgia's founder. Stevens accepted both contributions gratefully and used the portrait as the frontispiece for his first volume.[55]

In the fall of 1847 the two finally met. Stevens arrived in Philadelphia in late September, on his way to the General Convention of the Episcopal Church in New York City the next month, and visited Jones in Portico Square. There Stevens examined the splendid library that the young man had collected. Having seen the Georgia books of Israel Tefft and others in Savannah and presumably also having been given entry to the libraries of coastal grandees (and society members) such as Thomas Spalding and James Hamilton Couper, he bestowed high praise: no private collection of which he had knowledge, he wrote, was more complete in books relating to Georgia than that of Jones.[56]

But Stevens's very presence in Philadelphia foreshadowed a breach with

Jones, as well as strained relations with other friends and supporters. Much of the reason lay behind in Georgia. Stevens's Athens rectorship had apparently not been what he had hoped it would be. After preaching for a while at City Hall, he had finally moved into the newly constructed Emmanuel Church, a small, steepled wooden structure with some forty pews. There Stevens never had more than three dozen communicants (as compared to the 150 he had worshiped with in Savannah's Christ Church), and no more than eight came to him in his other church at nearby Lexington, where he preached once a month. Additionally, his chances for moving up in the Georgia diocese seemed problematic, his experiences at the college were not notably happy, and his time-consuming labors on his history were only half complete.[57]

Stevens was, however, beginning to be courted by congregations in large cities in other states, both north and south. His oratorical skills, which had helped him win his position as historiographer, were particularly admired. One congregation that showed deep interest in Stevens was that of St. Andrew's Church, near Portico Square, a crosstown rival of the Smiths' and Joneses' Christ Church on Second Street. Currently without a rector, St. Andrew's was nonetheless equipped with a prosperous congregation of 236 families and had a reputation for pampering its ministers. Since he was in Philadelphia, Stevens consented to preach to this shepherdless flock.[58]

Patterned after the Temple of Bacchus at Teos, St. Andrew's Church was a slightly larger, more ornate counterpart of Savannah's Christ Church, "with heads of Medusa, indefinitely multiplied, adorning the iron fence in front." Inside Stevens found a golden, harp-shaped organ and a "lofty pulpit" flanked by towering Ionic columns and emblazoned with "outstretched gilded wings." After ascending to the pulpit by a hidden flight of stairs, Stevens spoke at length to an admiring throng. A deputation of the church's vestrymen soon followed him to New York City and presented him with a call to be their rector. He declined, but on his way home he revisited St. Andrew's and, as he noted later, "preached all day." A few months later another St. Andrew's deputation pursued Stevens to Athens and told him that, after a period of fasting and prayer (prescribed by Stevens), the congregation was still resolved to have him. He then accepted their call.[59]

Stevens's departure from Athens was marked by his being hanged in effigy by some of his students, and the attitude of several of the university's trustees toward the reverend doctor was little better. His communicants, however, were pained at his departure, as was his patron Bishop Elliott, over such a "sad loss." The bishop—having essentially sponsored him as priest and professor, while also supporting him as historian—expressed his feelings with some ambiguity. He spoke of the "rupture" of Stevens's "connexion with Emmanuel Church and the University" and characterized the decision as Stevens's "having believed himself to see the guiding hand of the Holy Ghost" in the St. Andrew's call. That this was the case, said the bishop, "[might] well be so."[60]

Stevens's decision to move to Philadelphia confirmed Jones's worst suspicions. A few months earlier—in December 1847, when the first volume of his *History of Georgia* finally appeared—Stevens had denied to Jones that he had any intention of leaving Georgia. This was his second such disclaimer, for St. Andrew's interest in Stevens had become well known the previous August. At that time, Stevens had mentioned St. Andrew's to Jones while assuring him that he had no plan to leave his adopted state. "Georgia is my home," he had written, "and its soil will probably be my grave." St. Andrew's formal call in October had prompted Eliza Jones to take the extraordinary step of writing Stevens to advise him, for reasons unknown, to refuse the call. That December, through her son, Stevens had assured Mrs. Jones that he was not leaving Athens. He reiterated that Georgia was his home, adding that it was a "privilege to labor for it & in it, for so noble a State is worthy of all my energies."[61]

In December 1847 Stevens also arranged to have Jones sent an "elegantly bound" copy of his history. In March he wrote somewhat plaintively, "You have never yet expressed your opinion of my first volume, and I begin to fear that it does not meet your favour." Indeed it did not, as Stevens was later to learn unmistakably. But, for the time, Jones withheld judgment, waiting for Stevens's intentions regarding St. Andrew's (and thus, to Jones, his true character) to become clear.[62]

Meanwhile, Jones had been occupied with publications of his own. The first, which appeared in late 1847—a month or so before Stevens's history—was *Observations upon the Effects of Certain Late Political Suggestions*. A new edition in quarto of a rare pamphlet, it illuminated an obscure incident relating to Georgia's fortunes in the waning days of the Revolution. A copy was duly sent to Stevens in Athens. So was a copy of the second publication, a slender octavo printed for Jones in Philadelphia in December 1847, *Theory Concerning the Nature of Insanity.*[63]

But Jones did not send the second book until May, by which time Stevens's acceptance of St. Andrew's call had become known. No letter accompanied the gift, and Stevens wrote back, unsure whether Jones had answered his last letter in March. Almost sheepishly, he informed Jones that, bidden by "ministerial duty," he was moving to Philadelphia. "This decision so unexpected to me," he wrote, "was made in view of the developments of God's Providence in such a manner that I should have felt that I was running upon the 'thick bosses of Jehovah's buckler' had I refused." He looked forward, however, to "being near" Jones and "having access to [his] valuable library."[64]

Stevens had nothing but praise for Jones's book on insanity, calling it "one of the most chaste and elegant ever produced on this side of the Atlantic." And though he could not subscribe to "all the points" advanced in the text, he felt that the writing was characterized by "clearness, beauty & in several passages with true eloquence." More "than a bud of promise," it represented "an earnest of those rich stores of learning" yet to be developed by Jones's "industrious mind."[65]

Jones perhaps considered this praise perfunctory. In any case, this volume was the last of Jones's publications to be presented to Stevens, and no further works would be printed until the next year, after Stevens had bidden a final farewell to Georgia. Jones's next two publications arrived in Savannah in mid-November 1849, almost a year after Israel Tefft had informed the young man of his election to membership in the Georgia Historical Society. Each of these volumes created a stir in its own way. Both were discussed at the society's November meeting, held just off Monument Square in the society's new hall, a two-story Gothic structure bristling with crenellation and lighted through pointed arches and diamond panes. Attending the meeting was a small but august assemblage of eight officers and members, including the society's president, James Moore Wayne, associate justice of the U.S. Supreme Court, as well as Israel Tefft, Dr. Arnold, William B. Hodgson, and A. R. Lawton. Tefft, as corresponding secretary, was directed to tender the society's thanks to the absent Jones for his "splendid" contribution of a "valuable and rare work . . . printed at his own expense": John Gerar William De Brahm's *History of the Province of Georgia*. The members of the society were delighted to receive a copy, for they had coveted the rare manuscript on which it was based for several years.[66]

A copy of the other publication—though presented by no one and with no author's name on the title page—nonetheless garnered its own share of discussion. It finally and unambiguously answered Stevens's query of two years before; he would now know Jones's opinion of the first volume of his history. A handsomely printed pamphlet of twenty-eight pages, *Observations on Dr. Stevens's History of Georgia* had been widely but quietly distributed in Savannah a day or so before the scheduled meeting. A wittily sarcastic attack, the *Observations* relentlessly hammered Stevens's book. Even the pamphlet's title page had been used as a weapon; it featured a deadly epigraph from the book-burning episode in *Don Quixote:* "What overgrown piece of lumber have we here? cried the curate"—a characterization to make any serious historian shudder.[67]

The reviewer proceeded on the same principle to which Jones had subscribed in his earlier attack on McCall, Georgia's first historian: "The publication of a book necessarily and properly subjects it to criticism." The critique ranged widely and was expressed with force and humor, as the critic lampooned stylistic lapses, ridiculed breaches of logic, and ruthlessly exposed factual errors.[68]

The critic first established that six years had given Stevens more than sufficient time and resources to make his book "accurate in statement and correct in style," then commented that the preface had a tone of "presumptuous egotism." The remainder of the book was "marked by shallowness and incapacity," as well as a foolish tendency "to talk nonsense with the air of one uttering wisdom." Indeed, the observer noted, "a serene self-satisfaction pervades the whole performance."[69]

Nonetheless, the unknown reviewer argued, the book was not entirely without merit. In a way it had supplied the want of a history of Georgia: "But how? Rags have been stuffed into the broken window, and the hole is no longer open. The tempest is kept out, but so is the light." Ironically, the reviewer argued, Stevens's failure was in itself the salvation of his sponsor, for had he succeeded in completing an "accurate and well-written history of Georgia," the society would no longer have had a function or a reason for existence, and it would have "degenerate[d] from the dignity of a Society down to a mere club of Jonathan Oldbucks."[70]

This single merit, however, was overwhelmed by deficiencies. Stevens's style was "pompous," "corrupt," and "grotesquely incongruous with the simplicity of the subject" and his diction "ambitious . . . not infrequently rising into nonsense." Hopelessly prolix, Stevens had padded even the most commonplace observations to absurd length so that "sense is often lost in the diffuseness of phraseology."[71]

In his endless digressions, Stevens had "tortured" numerous topics "into some relation with the history of Georgia" and had filled fifty-five pages with "*Ante-colonial history*," that is, "*history before there was* any State, and consequently before there was any history." Such introductory matter was fair game, for it had been lampooned to good effect decades earlier by Washington Irving in his *Diedrich Knickerbocker's A History of New York*. Therein he described "introductions to American histories" as "very learned, sagacious, and nothing at all to the purpose" and devoted the introductory book of his history to such subjects as the "Creation of the World."[72]

So far, the critic was on safe ground, and Stevens's book obligingly provided many laughable examples of the faults that had been listed. But it was undeniably a scholarly and extensively documented work. And when the reviewer provided a "few specimens" of Stevens's factual errors (not, he stressed, a "*list*," for he singled out only those mistakes that "present themselves on a cursory perusal"), they were relatively minor: of the dozen or so offered, several were obvious mistakes in dates; others were misstatements and misinterpretations. Some did suggest a lack of understanding of the historical context of the Georgia story. This was particularly true of the last one supplied, which showed that Stevens did not know his British history (or his Sir Walter Scott) well enough to distinguish between the Old and Young Pretenders to the British throne—an unusual error, given Stevens's emphasis on the Oglethorpe family's connections to the exiled Stuarts. Interestingly, however, only one of these errors (and that a very debatable one) related specifically to Georgia history; the others were mistakes concerning European historical matters. Apparently, Stevens had at least mastered his voluminous Georgia sources well enough to forestall criticism of that vital aspect of his book.[73]

Before he finished, the reviewer inserted a few more skewers, as he reached "two inevitable conclusions" regarding Stevens:

> First.—That he cannot write History.
> Second.—That he cannot write English.
> But we have compassion upon his inexperience; and shall therefore repeat some advice, which he would do well to profit by.

"Whenever you have written anything which you think particularly fine—strike it out."

Observance of this advice will certainly diminish the bulk of his volumes, and cannot diminish their value.[74]

There was one more parting blow. Appended to the text was a brief excerpt from a review of Stevens's two volumes of the society's *Collections;* it had appeared the previous August in the *Augusta Constitutionalist.* The lines quoted informed the society how it could have best served the people of Georgia. The organization should have collected original materials in the form of manuscripts and printed sources; chosen from among them the best of the manuscripts for publication; issued "a few of the rarest and most curious tracts," in the style of Peter Force, once the best and rarest manuscript materials were in print; called for essays on particular subjects from the state's history and published the best of them; and then, and only then, selected someone "to digest these copious materials in one historical work." Unfortunately, the excerpt ended, the "Society's action has been the reverse of this: it has begun where it should have ended." [75]

The author of the *Observations,* though anonymous, was probably readily identified by some members of the society, and soon it became an open secret that Jones was the author. Certainly the voice of the *Observations,* as well as that of the anonymous critic in the *Constitutionalist,* seemed to be the voice of Agricola. Characteristics of style and quotation also suggested the identification, as did some of the material the *Observations* omitted from the original newspaper review, including a complaint about the *Collections'* Massachusetts copyright.[76]

There were as well some interesting lines from the conclusion of the Augusta paper's review essay, which obviously came from someone (though there were no doubt many) who had heard Stevens protest too much that he had been transformed for life into a Georgian: "For the Society," the critic had written, "as it at present exists, we entertain the most profound respect; nor do we feel aught but good will towards a single one of its members who calls himself a Georgian. We will say no more. We do not like professions. Experience has taught us to distrust them." [77]

Probably more society members secretly enjoyed the *Observations* than had appreciated Agricola's essays, having long since lost patience with Stevens, but many were genuinely proud of Stevens's work and placed the most positive construction on his decision to leave Georgia. Consequently, at the November meeting, the society sprang to Stevens's defense by passing resolutions regarding the "rather bitter pamphlet." The society chastised Stevens's anonymous critic as having been motivated by spite, asserting (with some justice) that the pamphleteer had shown "more personal feeling and dislike than fair and allowable criticism." In a separate attack, one member said of the reviewer that, "as he dabbles in the classics, he may perhaps with a slight blush recollect that Zoilus was a critic as well as Longinus; and he may try whose judgment cap fits him better." The members also renewed their avowals of "respect and regard" for Stevens personally and declared that his *History* had done "him and the Society credit" and was "altogether worthy of the confidence and patronage of the people of Georgia." The society ordered copies of the resolutions sent to Stevens and also had them published in the Savannah newspapers.[78]

Though most of Jones's barbs had found fair targets, his criticism had an undeniable personal thrust. He obviously regretted his brief friendship and collaboration with Stevens. And he no doubt repented of having contributed so conspicuously to the first volume of Stevens's history, particularly when he found that the book clashed jarringly with his conceptions of style and historiography. But even before the book's publication, Jones's opinion of Stevens may have changed for the worse, principally because of their personal encounters, late and few though they were. Stevens's personality, as revealed in his letters, could be somewhat overbearing, but in person it was perceived as "repellent" by many of his Athens students, Jones's contemporaries. Ultimately, Jones saw Stevens, in leaving Georgia, as violating his word, abandoning his responsibilities, and spurning the honors Georgians had conferred on him. And in case it seemed that Jones was reacting as strongly against Stevens as if "the Historiographer" had seduced and abandoned a woman, the *Observations* made the implication plain: "Poor Georgia! Hers is a woman's name, hers has been a woman's fate! Trusting—yielding—deserted." Jones saw Stevens's actions as stereotypical Yankee calculation and shrewdness, aggravated by an unbecoming claim of having merely submitted to divine providence.[79]

Critical opinion of the departed historian's book was mixed. Not surprisingly, William Hunter Bulloch's praise was unstinting: he found that Stevens had "invested the dry details of the early settlement of the colony with an interest which his glowing style and matured research could alone impart to them." And a respectful review, replete with summaries and extracts, appeared in the *North American Review*, with the suggestion that the chapter on slavery could "be read profitably by all parties." But William Gilmore Simms, writing anonymously in the *Southern Quarterly Review*, objected to "an excess of particularity, an occasional awkwardness in style, and to something of a coldness in details in regard to matters that might seem provocative of warmth." He regarded the four chapters of "ante-colonial" history as worth no more than a glance. Nonetheless, excepting errata and numerous printer's errors, he found much to praise as well.[80]

As for the "patronage" of Stevens's history by Georgians and others in purchasing the books, there were difficulties in selling both the first volume and its companion, which did not appear until 1859. That year William Gilmore Simms commented privately that Stevens's mistake was in presenting too much detail for the general reader, despite Simms's warning against being too "copious." Instead, Stevens "was ambitious of giving as many volumes to the 100 years of Georgia" as William H. Prescott "had assigned to the Conquest of Mexico & Peru. The consequence was that nobody bought his first vol. and after 10 years, the [society] is trying to raise the funds to print the second."[81]

With the passage of years, the esteemed bibliographer Joseph Sabin would describe *Observations on Dr. Stevens's History of Georgia* as a "severe and able criticism." And Stevens's successor as historian of Georgia would appear before the Georgia Historical Society and give favorable notice to the "caustic" *Observations*, while mentioning the *History of Georgia* in deprecating terms. Stevens's work, he noted, "partial in its scope, did not gratify public expectation . . . and does not appear to have commended itself to general favor."[82]

CHAPTER 3

Book-Madness

Lo, all in silence, all in order stand,
And mighty folios first, a lordly band;
Then quartos their well-order'd ranks maintain,
And light octavos fill a spacious plain.
—GEORGE CRABBE

B etween 1847, when George Frederick Tilghman Jones began corresponding with William Bacon Stevens, and 1849,
when Jones's scathing critique of the first volume of *A History of
Georgia* appeared, Jones underwent a transformation. When the
metamorphosis was complete, George Frederick Tilghman Jones
was no more; in his place stood George Wymberley Jones of
Wormsloe. Jones adopted this modification of his birth name in
late 1847, apparently in anticipation of reaching his majority the
next year. "Tilghman" disappeared entirely, as did his uncle Frederick Campbell-Stewart's forename; but he would occasionally
employ a similarly hyphenated surname: G. Wymberley-Jones.
"George" remained, through filial devotion—but often only in
the form of its initial, and not, as it had been, as the name by which
he was known to family and friends: from this point on they would
call him "Wymberley." [1]

In its original spelling—"Wimberly"—this name had been
borne by both George Wymberley Jones's grandfather, the first

Noble Wimberly Jones, and by Wymberley's older, deceased brother, the father of George Noble Jones. The name had also been given to the Jones Plantation north of Wormsloe on the Isle of Hope, parcels of which would be among George Wymberley Jones's first purchases after he came into his inheritance.[2]

The change in the spelling was probably partly fanciful, partly done to distinguish his branch of the family from the other one. The works of Sir Walter Scott may have been an inspiration: the name "Wymberley" suggests Scott's *Waverley*, whose pages contain not only the title character but another called Everard, the name Jones would give to his second son. Jones no doubt appreciated the archaic look of Wymberley as well; its elaborate spelling was similar to that found in the title of one of the books in his library: the fifteenth-century work *Treatyse of Fyshynge wyth an Angle*. Moreover, he had something of a model in the way that the English bibliophile Egerton Bridges had come to spell his surname "Brydges."[3]

At the same time, Wymberley also modified the Jones arms by substituting a new motto for his branch of the family. In retrospect, the choice would have served as a warning to William Bacon Stevens, for Jones's new bookplate bore the Latin words *Haud impune laesus:* Not provoked with impunity. This motto was perhaps a nod to the Philadelphia Smiths and their Scottish forebears. It seems to be a variation of the motto of the kings of Scotland, *Nemo me impune lacessit* (No man provokes me with impunity), and is also reminiscent of *Haud obliviscendum* (Not to be forgotten), the motto of the Redgauntlet family in one of Scott's Jacobite novels.[4]

Why Jones made the changes in his name is a matter of speculation. But thoughts of his own family's history certainly preoccupied him as his twenty-first birthday and the end of his medical schooling approached. He seems to have pondered over his own position in the Jones family and to have felt the necessity of clarifying for himself his familial rights, priorities, and responsibilities. Part of defining who he was, however, depended on how he defined his father. A major step in this process occurred after Jones reached his majority in July 1848 and began living at Wormsloe. That December, he moved his father's remains (along with those of his sister) from the cemetery in Savannah to a more appropriate location.[5]

Though it was the final resting place of many of Georgia's early leaders, the Old Cemetery had become something of an eyesore and been closed to further interments. At the same time, parklike rural cemeteries, such as

Philadelphia's Laurel Hill, were increasing in popularity. They not only fulfilled their most obvious purpose but were also "places of resort," whose picturesque settings expressed "noble sentiments and refined taste." For Savannah, the most appropriate spot for such a cemetery was a wooded peninsula that projected into the Wilmington River: Bonaventure, long a much-visited scenic attraction. Somberly beautiful, its groves of mossy oaks created a sort of natural shrine that was perfect for its new role.[6]

Here Jones purchased secluded lots on the edge of the newly opened cemetery that was closest to Wormsloe and had a crypt constructed in the sandy soil. Sealing it forever was a broad marble monument to "GEORGE JONES OF WORMSLOE." On the reverse an inscription read:

THIS MONUMENT WAS ERECTED BY
GEORGE WYMBERLEY JONES.
MDCCCCXLVIII.

The shade of George Jones might have been mildly surprised to find himself identified with a *nom de terre*, particularly since Newton had been the plantation most associated with him; Wormsloe, despite its ancestral allure, had mainly been the country place of his old age. To his son, however, such an identification was important in several ways. With more than one George Jones still alive, it was useful to bestow on the patriarch of their clan a distinction similar to that employed by such notables of the revolutionary era as the long-lived Charles Carroll of Carrollton, who had died during the previous decade: Carroll had also found it necessary to distinguish himself from similarly named kinsmen by means of his landholdings. And having provided George Jones with such an identification, the son had by extension provided a means of distinguishing himself, for the legal documents to which he affixed his seal for many years to come would accompany the signature "George Wymberley Jones of Wormsloe." As a final step, he had made the ancestral estate his own by changing the spelling of its name from "Wormslow" to "Wormsloe."[7]

Simultaneously, Jones was acting to distinguish himself in an even more obvious sense—partly to ensure his privacy—by experimenting with variations of his surname. For many years George Noble Jones had been called George Jones, Jr. This bred a certain amount of confusion among some of those wishing to make contact with the son, rather than the grandson, of Dr. George Jones, since the younger man and his older nephew were both called

George. Because both men owned property in and around Savannah (and both also made frequent use of Newport, Rhode Island, as a resort), there were abundant chances of each man's mistakenly receiving the other's mail, a circumstance particularly embarrassing to one of as private a nature as George Wymberley Jones. One means of differentiating himself more clearly was being called "Wymberley" by family and friends, instead of "George," and when he signed himself "G. Wymberley Jones," as he often did in correspondence, he made the confusing "George" all but disappear. Moreover, his occasional use of a hyphen between "Wymberley" and "Jones" suggests that he was also attempting to remove himself from the same alphabetical order as Jones, by using Wymberley-Jones as his surname.[8]

If he was seeking some distinctiveness, "Jones" was also a problem; it was, after all, the second most common British name. Mark Antony Lower, whose works on heraldry and family nomenclature had their place in Jones's library, perhaps best expressed the young man's predicament: "The commonness of some surnames . . . renders the bearers of them, though of good family, undistinguishable from the *ignobile vulgus*" (undistinguished masses). According to Lower, however, the Joneses of Denbigh in Wales were of good descent, and a general armory of 1842 assigned them armorial bearings very similar to those found on Noble Jones's bookplate; it was asserted that the great architect Inigo Jones was of this Denbigh line.[9]

In Lower's words, "the *name* is *essential* to the *man*," and he may have given Jones the idea for the eventual change in surname—to De Renne— that seems finally to have satisfied him, though he waited almost two decades to make this ultimate legal change. Lower noted "many cases on record of the sons of great heiresses having left their paternal surnames for that of their mothers," among them the Nevilles and the Percies. Although Eliza Jones could probably not be classed among the "great heiresses," and her British surname, Smith, was the only one more widespread than Jones, Jones's maternal grandmother's surname was distinctive. Since Wymberley's infancy, there had hung in the Smith home in Philadelphia Charles Willson Peale's regal portrait of Letitia Van Deren Smith, an abbreviated crown of flowers in her hair. With some imagination Van Deren could be altered to the dignity and stateliness of "De Renne," a name that could have been borne by one of Scott's paladins. It also would not be out of place on the Continent; in Jones's copy of the letters of Madame de Sévigné, in fact, there was a reference to a "Monsieur de Rennes," and removal of the "s" removed identification with the French town. "De Renne" may also have signified an affinity for the impressive name of one of the eighteenth-century authors whose work Wymberley published: J. G. W. De Brahm, for, eventually, George Wymberley Jones of Wormsloe would become G. W. J. De Renne. Such a distinctive name made a territorial designation superfluous, and "of Wormsloe" then disappeared from his signature.[10]

But the change to De Renne was years in the future. In the early months of 1849, following the transfer of his father's remains to Bonaventure and the placing of the monument there in 1848, Jones came into his inheritance. The estates of both his father and sister were finally settled, and the sizable legacy he received would make it unnecessary for him to practice medicine. With careful handling of his assets, he could look forward to a life of relative leisure such as his uncle Washington Smith enjoyed.[11]

In those winter months of early 1849, Jones took another step toward deciding who he was. As part of the settlement of the estates, some of the plantation lands were sold, along with many of the slaves that had for decades been chattels of the Jones family. The most important of those properties now passing from the Joneses was Leta's Newton Plantation, which was sold to Jacob Motte Middleton, a scion of the eminent South Carolina family. Since Leta had died intestate, her assets were liquidated and the income divided among Wymberley Jones and other heirs. Dean Forest Plantation was retained by George Noble Jones, however, as were Wormsloe and Poplar Grove by George Wymberley Jones. Since acquiring land was his overriding interest, Wymberley kept relatively few of the approximately 150 slaves that were his portion of his father's estate. Essentially, he kept all of the Wormsloe slaves (excluding four who had been left to George Noble Jones) and a dozen from Poplar Grove, plus the two most valuable household servants, Mode and Jim. This gave him a total of thirty-five slaves.[12]

Wymberley Jones did not record his thoughts on becoming the owner of human property, the fourth generation of his family to hold slaves since Noble Jones had first brought bondsmen to Wormsloe in the 1750s. But he seems to have had some initial reservations. It would be several years before he would take any particular interest in planting; in his cryptic words, he was at first "averse to agriculture." The practical effect of his aversion was that for a time some of his slaves were concentrated near Savannah at his

Lincoln's Inn Chapel (*center*), attributed to Inigo Jones, where the marriage of Noble Jones and Sarah Hack was solemnized in 1723. (*Lincoln's Inn, the Chapel, and Old Hall, London,* c. 1730, artist unknown, Yale Center for British Art, Paul Mellon Collection.)

London: The Thames from Lambeth Palace, 1746–47, by Canaletto (1697–1768), from the Roudnice Lobkowicz Collection, Czech Republic. Completed over a decade after Noble Jones embarked for the New World, this panorama shows several sites associated with his youth and early manhood in London: St. Paul's Cathedral (*extreme right*), near which Jones was born, with (*just to the left*) the vicinity of Lincoln's Inn Chapel, where he was married; *right foreground:* Lambeth Palace, London residence of the archbishops of Canterbury, and the most considerable structure in the parish of Lambeth, where Noble Wimberly Jones was born; *left of center:* an important cluster of buildings—the tallest,

Westminster Abbey, where Jones apparently worked as a builder; St. Margaret's Church (with flag), where he sometimes worshiped; and gabled Westminster Hall, marking the vicinity of the Houses of Parliament. Between the Hall and the Abbey was Old Palace Yard, where were located James Oglethorpe's house and the offices of the Trustees for Establishing the Colony of Georgia in America. Construction of Westminster Bridge (*right of center*) did not begin until several years after the departure of the Jones family and was not entirely completed at the time of the painting. (The structure to the extreme left is St. John's Church.)

Catalogus Remediorum

Bolus Anti-Dysentericus
1. R. Philon. Roman. ℈ß
   Rhabarb. pulv. ℈ß
   Syrup. q. f. Misce.

Cataplasma Sinapinum
2. R. Farin. Semin. Sinapin.
   Avenae. ana
   Acet. q. f. Misce.

Collyrium e Vitriolo
3. R. Aq. Fontan. ℨviij
   Vitriol. Alb. ℈ß Misce.

Decoctum Anti-Emeticum et Febrifugum
4. R. Sal. Absinth. ℨvj
   Coq. in Aq. Fontan. ℔ iij
   Despuma, deinde instilla gradatim
   Sp. Vitriol. q. f. ad Saturationem, et adde
   Aq. Alexeter. spirit sacch. alb. aa ℨiij M.

Decoctum Peruvianum
5. R. Cort. Peruvian. pulv. ℨij. Nitr. ℨß
   Coq. in Aq. Fontan. ℔ iij ad Dimidias
   et Cola.

Decoctum Serpentariæ
6. R. Rad. Serpent. Virginian. contus. ℨiij.
   Aq. Fontan. ℔ j Coq. ad Medias
   Colatur. add. Tinctur. Thebaic. gutt xxx
   Spirit. Sal. Vol. Oleos. ℨj
   Syrup. e Cortic. Aurant. ℨß M.

Electarium Astringens
7. R. Pulv. e Bol. cum Op:o
   Nuc. Moschat. tost ana ℨj
   Syr. e Mecon q. f. Misce.
   Cap. e ℨß ad ℈ij cum Julap. Cretae.

Electarium Alexeterium
R. Pulv. Contrayerv. Comp. ℨij
Rad. Serpentar. Virgin. pulv. ℨj

Electarium Balsamicum
9. R. Conserv. Ros. rubr. ℨiij
   Balsam. Locatell. ℨij Syr. q. f. M.
   Cap. ℈ß urgente Tussi. Add. pro re nata
   Balsam. Sulph. Terebinth. ℨß.

Electarium Diaphoreticum
10. R. Pulv. Contrayerv. comp. ℨij
    Nitr. depurat. ℨj Syr. Aurant. q. f. M.
    Cap. ℈ß. sexta quaque Horâ.

Electarium ad Gonorrhoeam virulentam
11. R. Elect. Lenitiv. ℨij
    Rad. Jalap. pulv. ℈ iij
    Nitr. depur. ℈ß
    Cap. ℈ß primo manè et Horâ Somni.

Electarium ad Gonorrhoeam post Inflammationem
12. R. Elect. Lenitiv. ℥j Balsam. Copaiv. ℨ ß
    Pulv. Rhei. Gum. Guajac. Nitr. dep. ana ℈ iv
    Syr. e Cort. Aurantior. q. f. M.

Electarium Hæmorrhoidale
13. R. Elect. Lenitiv. ℨij Flor. Sulph. ℨß.
    Nitr. depurat. ℨj Syr. Aurant. q. f. M.
    Cap. ℨj bis in die.

Electarium Hydropicum
14. R. Gambog. pulv. ℨjß Sem. Sinap. pulv. ℨj
    Zinzib. pulv. ℨß. Syr. alb. q. f. M.
    Cap. ℈ß. primo mane.

Electarium Jalapi
15. R. Rad. Jalap. pulv. ℨij Zinzib. pulv. ℨj
    Syr. Aurant. q. f. M.
    Cap. ab. ℨ ß. ad ℈ij primo manè.

Electarium Ictericum
16. R. Sapon. Castiliens. ℨiij
    Rhei pulv. Spec. Hier. Picr. ana ℨß

Medical notes in Latin in the hand of Noble Jones, from a notebook that drew on
John Theobald's "compendious dispensatory" *Medulla Medicinae Universae*,
1749, and other sources. (De Renne Collection, Hargrett Rare Book and Manuscript Library, University of Georgia Libraries.)

N. W. JONES.

The "Morning Star of Liberty," Noble Wimberly Jones. A mid-nineteenth-century line engraving by the English portrait engraver Henry Robinson (fl. 1827–1875) based on a Charles Willson Peale portrait, c. 1781. (De Renne Collection, Hargrett Rare Book and Manuscript Library, University of Georgia Libraries.)

George Jones, physician, judge, and United States senator, from a portrait, c. 1822, by Rembrandt Peale. (Telfair Academy of Arts and Sciences, Savannah, Georgia.)

Left: William Smith, D.D. (1727–1803), first provost of the University of Pennsylvania. (From an engraving, based on an 1800 portrait by Gilbert Stuart, used as the frontispiece to volume 2 of Horace Wemyss Smith's *Life and Correspondence of the Rev. William Smith, D.D.,* 1880.) *Right:* Thomas Smith (1745–1809), delegate to the Second Continental Congress and associate justice of the Pennsylvania Supreme Court. (From a miniature, c. 1781, in the possession of Eudora De Renne Roebling.)

Left: Letitia Van Deren Smith (1759–1811), whose maiden name suggested the surname De Renne. (From a portrait by Charles Willson Peale, c. 1780, Telfair Academy of Arts and Sciences, Savannah, Georgia.) *Right:* Eliza Smith Jones in old age. (De Renne Collection, Hargrett Rare Book and Manuscript Library, University of Georgia Libraries.)

Left: Silhouettes of
George Frederick
Tilghman Jones and
Letitia Georgina
Telfair Jones, 1830s.
(Wormsloe Collection,
Hargrett Rare Book
and Manuscript Li-
brary, University of
Georgia Libraries.)

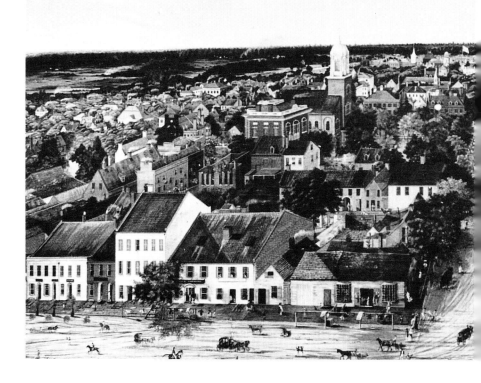

Firmin Cerveau's Panorama of Savannah, 1837, from the tower of the City Exchange near the river. Bull Street bisects the painting, running south toward George Jones's Poplar Grove Plantation, on the horizon. The flag just below the horizon, left of center, marks Oglethorpe Barracks; just to the right of the flag are the steeples of the Unitarian and Presbyterian churches, respectively. In the left foreground is a three-story building behind which can be seen the ruins of the Custom House, whose lot would soon be the site of the Hall of the Georgia Historical Society. South of the ruins rises the Bank of the State of Georgia, with its white-trimmed windows, and, south of it, the steeple of Christ Church, replaced the next year by a Greek Revival structure. In the right foreground, farthest right in the central row of lighter-colored buildings, is the entrance to the bookstore of William Thorne Williams. (Georgia Historical Society.)

MAP 1. Environs of Savannah, Georgia, mid-1800s, Showing the Principal Land-holdings of the Decendants of Noble Jones

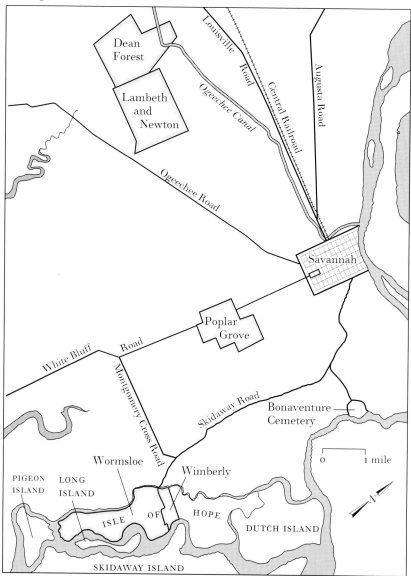

Sources: Charles G. Platen, *Map of Chatham County, State of Georgia,* 1875, Georgia Historical Society, Savannah; Edward A. Vincent, *Subdivision Map of the City of Savannah,* 1853, Office of the City Engineer, Savannah; O. M. Poe, *Map of Savannah and Vicinity . . . 1864,* National Archives, B G 77: N 70; Edward J. Thomas, *Map of Poplar Grove,* 1897, Hargrett Rare Book and Manuscript Library, Box 33, Ms. 2819.

Panorama of Philadelphia from the State House Steeple, Looking East, 1838. The Delaware River is in the background, with the steeple of Christ Church to the extreme left. Just right of center is the Library Company of Philadelphia, with the statue of Benjamin Franklin in its niche. (From Ellis Paxson Oberholtzer's *Philadelphia: A History of the City and Its People,* 1912.)

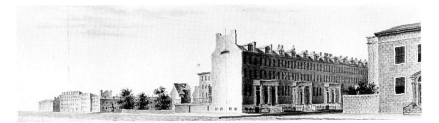

Portico Square, Philadelphia. (Historical Society of Pennsylvania.)

The University of Pennsylvania, Philadelphia, as it appeared in 1839. (From Ellis Paxson Oberholtzer's *Philadelphia: A History of the City and Its People,* 1912.)

Books from the antebellum library of George Wymberley Jones. (De Renne Library, Hargrett Rare Book and Manuscript Library, University of Georgia Libraries.)

John Penington's bookstore was the "centre of the *elite litterateurs*" of Philadelphia in the mid-1800s. (From a business card, based on Carl Spitzweg's *Der Bücherwurm, um 1850*, Edward Carey Gardiner Collection, Historical Society of Pennsylvania.)

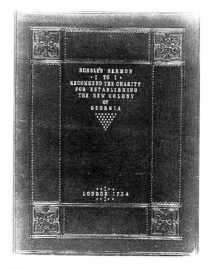

The cover of one of the antebellum library's leather-bound eighteenth-century sermons, preached in support of the colony of Georgia. (De Renne Library, Hargrett Rare Book and Manuscript Library, University of Georgia Libraries.)

Left: Thomas Frognall Dibdin (1776–1847), "Bibliomaniac Extraordinary." (By permission of the Houghton Library, Harvard University.) *Right:* Alexander A. Smets, Savannah bibliophile. (Hargrett Rare Book and Manuscript Library, University of Georgia Libraries.)

Left: Israel K. Tefft, Savannah's nationally known collector of autographs and manuscripts. (Georgia Historical Society.) *Right:* Peter Force, creator of a "noble library" of history in the District of Columbia. (Library of Congress.)

Left: Horace Walpole, fourth Earl of Orford (1717–1797), eminent English collector, printer, and connoisseur, whose works and letters fascinated George Wymberley Jones. (Drawing by William Daniell for his 1808 engraving, after the 1793 crayon drawing by George Dance the Younger. Courtesy of the Lewis Walpole Library, Yale University.) *Right:* George Washington Smith, Easter 1874. (De Renne Collection, Hargrett Rare Book and Manuscript Library, University of Georgia Libraries.)

Left: Winthrop Sargent VI. (Hargrett Rare Book and Manuscript Library, University of Georgia Libraries.) *Right:* Hugh McCall, author of *The History of Georgia,* two volumes, 1811–16. (Hargrett Rare Book and Manuscript Library, University of Georgia Libraries.)

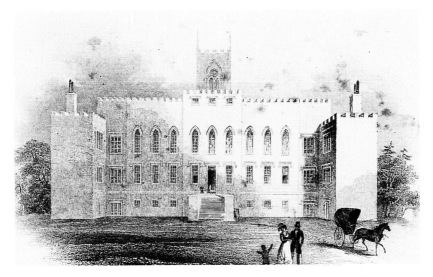

The State House, Milledgeville, where many of the primary sources of Georgia history reposed for most of the nineteenth century. (Hargrett Rare Book and Manuscript Library, University of Georgia Libraries.)

Left: Dr. Richard Arnold. (From Richard H. Shryock, ed., *Letters of Richard D. Arnold, M.D., 1808–1876,* Seeman Press, Durham, N.C., 1929.) *Right:* Dr. William Bacon Stevens, the Historiographer, shown in later life. (Georgia Historical Society.)

Above: Stephen Elliott, bishop of Georgia, from an antebellum photograph. (Hargrett Rare Book and Manuscript Library, University of Georgia Libraries.) *Right:* The image of James Oglethorpe produced in England for George Wymberley Jones by the portrait and figure engraver William Greatbach (1801–c. 1885). (De Renne Collection, Hargrett Rare Book and Manuscript Library, University of Georgia Libraries.)

The first of the "Agricola" essays. (Georgia Department of Archives and History.)

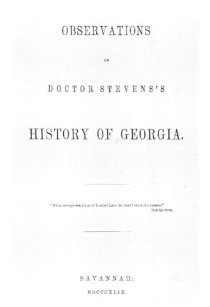

Left: The title page of *Observations on Dr. Stevens's History of Georgia,* 1849. (De Renne Library, Hargrett Rare Book and Manuscript Library, University of Georgia Libraries.) *Right:* Bookplate of Noble Jones. (De Renne Collection, Hargrett Rare Book and Manuscript Library, University of Georgia Libraries.)

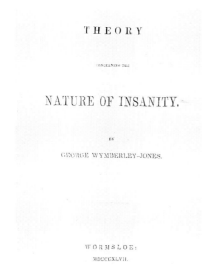

Left: Title page of *Theory Concerning the Nature of Insanity,* 1847. (De Renne Library, Hargrett Rare Book and Manuscript Library, University of Georgia Libraries.) *Right:* Bookplate of George Wymberley Jones. (De Renne Collection, Hargrett Rare Book and Manuscript Library, University of Georgia Libraries.)

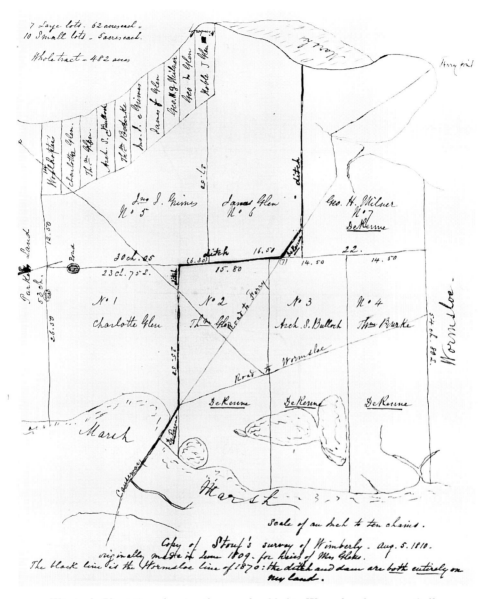

Wimberly Plantation, showing the parcels added to Wormsloe, from a postbellum
tracing by George Wymberley Jones De Renne. (De Renne Collection, Hargrett
Rare Book and Manuscript Library, University of Georgia Libraries.)

Top: George Wymberley Jones, from an antebellum photograph. (De Renne Collection, Hargrett Rare Book and Manuscript Library, University of Georgia Libraries.) *Bottom:* Signature of George Wymberley Jones. (De Renne Collection, Hargrett Rare Book and Manuscript Library, University of Georgia Libraries.)

Johann Wilhelm Gerrard de Brahm
of
Coblenz and Philadelphia
Aged 73.

Left: George Walton. (Hargrett Rare Book and Manuscript Library, University of Georgia Libraries.) *Right:* Silhouette of De Brahm, showing a variant of his name. (Courtesy of the Library of the Society of Friends, London.)

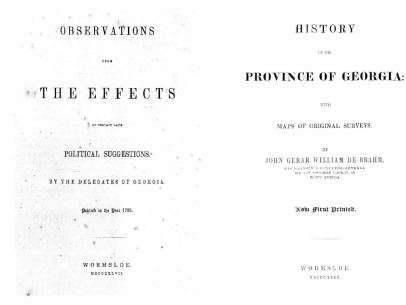

OBSERVATIONS

UPON

THE EFFECTS

OF CERTAIN LATE

POLITICAL SUGGESTIONS,

BY THE DELEGATES OF GEORGIA.

Printed in the Year 1781.

WORMSLOE.
MDCCCXLVII.

HISTORY

OF THE

PROVINCE OF GEORGIA:

WITH

MAPS OF ORIGINAL SURVEYS.

BY

JOHN GERAR WILLIAM DE BRAHM.
HIS MAJESTY'S SURVEYOR-GENERAL
FOR THE SOUTHERN DISTRICT OF
NORTH AMERICA.

Now First Printed.

WORMSLOE.
MDCCCXLIX.

Left: Title page of *Observations upon the Effects of Certain Late Political Suggestions,* 1847. (De Renne Library, Hargrett Rare Book and Manuscript Library, University of Georgia Libraries.) *Right:* The title page of *History of the Province of Georgia,* 1849. (De Renne Library, Hargrett Rare Book and Manuscript Library, University of Georgia Libraries.)

Left: Harriott Pinckney Holbrook. From a miniature. (Courtesy of Mrs. S. Henry Edmunds, Charleston, South Carolina.) *Right:* Winthrop Sargent IV, 1753–1820. From a portrait, c. 1805, by Gilbert Stuart. (From *Dictionary of American Portraits,* Dover Publications, 1967.)

JOURNAL AND LETTERS

OF

ELIZA LUCAS.

Now First Printed.

WORMSLOE.
MDCCCL.

DIARY

OF

COL. WINTHROP SARGENT

ADJUTANT-GENERAL OF THE UNITED STATES ARMY

DURING THE CAMPAIGN OF MDCCXCI.

Now First Printed.

WORMSLOE.
MDCCCLI.

Left: The title page of *Journal and Letters of Eliza Lucas,* 1850. (De Renne Library, Hargrett Rare Book and Manuscript Library, University of Georgia Libraries.) *Right:* The title page of *Diary of Col. Winthrop Sargent,* 1851. (De Renne Library, Hargrett Rare Book and Manuscript Library, University of Georgia Libraries.)

A
Bachelor's Reverie:

IN THREE PARTS.

I. SMOKE — *Signifying* DOUBT.

II. BLAZE — *Signifying* CHEER.

III. Ashes — *Signifying* Desolation.

BY

Ik: Marvel.

WORMSLOE.
MDCCCL.

Left: A Bachelor's Reverie, 1850, one of the personal leather-bound copies of George Wymberley Jones. (De Renne Library, Hargrett Rare Book and Manuscript Library, University of Georgia Libraries.) *Right:* The title page of *A Bachelor's Reverie*. (De Renne Library, Hargrett Rare Book and Manuscript Library, University of Georgia Libraries.)

Geo. Wymberley Jones.
of Wormsloe.

Left: Bookplate of George Wymberley Jones of Wormsloe. (De Renne Collection, Hargrett Rare Book and Manuscript Library, University of Georgia Libraries.) *Right:* Donald G. Mitchell ("Ik Marvel"). (Courtesy of Robert Heffner, Jr., Fairmont State College, Fairmont, West Virginia.)

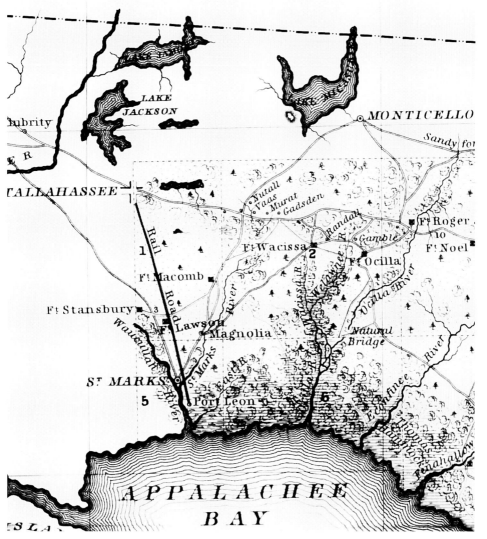

Middle Florida. El Destino Plantation is in the upper center, east of Tallahassee, marked *Nutall*. (A detail of *Map of the Seat of War in Florida . . . by Capt. John Mackay and Lieut. J. E. Blake, U.S. Topographical Engineers [1839]*, Hargrett Rare Book and Manuscript Library, University of Georgia Libraries.)

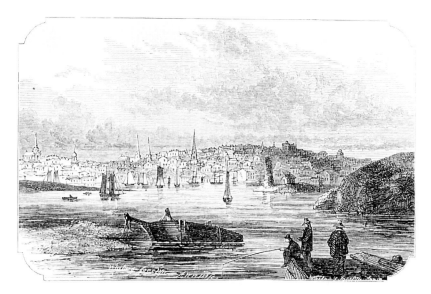

Newport from Brenton's Cove. (From George C. Mason's *Newport Illustrated, in a Series of Pen and Pencil Sketches,* 1854.)

The George Noble Jones Cottage, Newport, Rhode Island. From a watercolor by Richard Upjohn, c. 1840. (Avery Architectural and Fine Arts Library, Columbia University.)

George Noble Jones, from a postbellum carte-de-visite. (Courtesy of Eudora De Renne Roebling.)

Left: Mary Savage Nuttall Jones. (De Renne Collection, Hargrett Rare Book and Manuscript Library, University of Georgia Libraries.) *Right:* Mary Wallace Nuttall, from a daguerreotype taken in Newport in 1851. (Wormsloe Collection, Hargrett Rare Book and Manuscript Library, University of Georgia Libraries.)

Left: William Brown Hodgson, diplomat, antiquarian, and Orientalist. (Courtesy of Eudora De Renne Roebling.) *Right:* Mary Nuttall Jones, after her marriage to George Wymberley Jones. From an antebellum carte-de-visite. (Courtesy of Eudora De Renne Roebling.)

The children of George Noble Jones and Mary Savage Nuttall Jones

Left: George Fenwick Jones. (Courtesy of Eudora De Renne Roebling.) *Right:* Wallace Savage Jones. (Courtesy of Eudora De Renne Roebling.)

Left: Noble Wimberly Jones III. (David McCord Wright Papers, Georgia Historical Society.) *Right:* Lillie Noble Jones. (Courtesy of Eudora De Renne Roebling.)

Left: Wormsloe House, north front, 1870s. From a stereograph. (De Renne Collection, Hargrett Rare Book and Manuscript Library, University of Georgia Libraries.) *Below:* Wormsloe House, south front, 1870s. From a stereograph. (De Renne Collection, Hargrett Rare Book and Manuscript Library, University of Georgia Libraries.)

Wormsloe slave cabins. From an 1899 photograph. (Courtesy of Eudora De Renne Roebling.)

The well house at Wormsloe. From a postbellum stereograph. (De Renne Collection, Hargrett Rare Book and Manuscript Library, University of Georgia Libraries.)

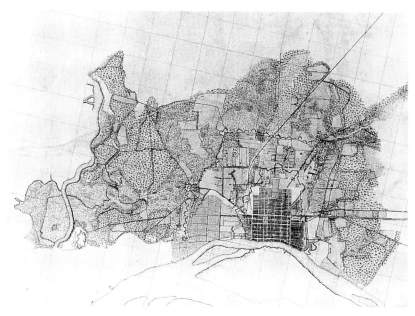

Confederate Savannah. From a previously unpublished manuscript map. (National Archives.)

Montpellier, France. An early nineteenth-century view. (Courtesy of Direction des Services d'Archives de L'Hérault, Montpellier.)

Top: G. W. J. De Renne. Portrait, 1894, by Carl L. Brandt (1831–1905), from a photograph taken in London in 1866. (Courtesy of Eudora De Renne Roebling.) *Bottom:* Signature of G. W. J. De Renne. (De Renne Collection, Hargrett Rare Book and Manuscript Library, University of Georgia Libraries.)

G. W. J. De Renne.

DE RENNE

Left: Bookplate of G. W. J. De Renne. (De Renne Collection, Hargrett Rare Book and Manuscript Library, University of Georgia Libraries.) *Right:* One of the smaller De Renne bookplates, shown enlarged. (De Renne Collection, Hargrett Rare Book and Manuscript Library, University of Georgia Libraries.)

The "Old Fort" at Wormsloe. (From *Art Work of Savannah,* 1893.)

Leta, Kentwyn, Wymberley, and Everard De Renne, Paris, July 1869. From a carte-de-visite. (Courtesy of Eudora De Renne Roebling.)

A wax impression of the De Renne
seal. (De Renne Collection, Hargrett
Rare Book and Manuscript Library,
University of Georgia Libraries.)

Savannah in the early 1870s. (Detail of A. Ruger's *Bird's Eye
View of the City of Savannah, Georgia*, 1871, Georgia Historical Society.)

1 De Renne Block and Wharf
2 Hall of the Georgia Historical Society, 1849–71
3 Christ Church
4 Hall of the Georgia Historical Society, 1871–75
5 The Telfair Mansion
6 The Stoddard House (later the Barrow residence)
7 The De Renne residence, Liberty Street
8 Oglethorpe Barracks (later site of the Hotel De Soto)
9 Northwest corner of Liberty and Drayton Streets
(later site of the De Renne Apartments)

Top: The De Renne residence on Liberty Street, Savannah. (Georgia Historical Society.) *Bottom:* The garden of the De Renne residence. (Georgia Historical Society.)

Colonel Charles C. Jones, Jr. (*right*), and his brother Dr. Joseph Jones, a founder of the Southern Historical Society, on the front lawn of Montrose, c. 1885. (Special Collections, Howard-Tilton Memorial Library, Tulane University.)

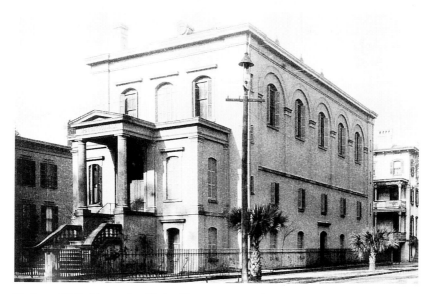

Hodgson Hall. (From *Art Work of Savannah*, 1893.)

The library in Hodgson Hall, 1876. (From an engraving that appeared in *Harper's New Monthly Magazine,* January 1888.)

The binding of the presentation copy of *The Dead Towns of Georgia* given by Charles C. Jones, Jr., to G. W. J. De Renne. (De Renne Library, Hargrett Rare Book and Manuscript Library, University of Georgia Libraries.)

The Confederate Soldier, 1879. From a stereograph of the bronze sculpture by David Richards (1829–1897), taken in Forsyth Park before installation atop the Confederate Monument. The Chatham County jail, 1845, appears in the background. (De Renne Collection, Hargrett Rare Book and Manuscript Library, University of Georgia Libraries.)

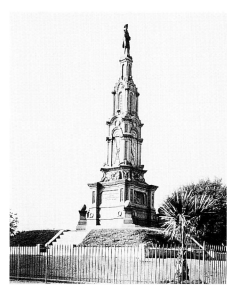

The Confederate Monument, Savannah, with *The Confederate Soldier*, surrounded by the wrought-iron fence that was the gift of Mary De Renne. (From *Art Work of Savannah*, 1893.)

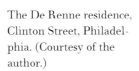

The Pennsylvania Company for Insurances on Lives and Granting Annuities, 431 Chestnut Street, Philadelphia. (Library Company of Philadelphia.)

The De Renne residence, Clinton Street, Philadelphia. (Courtesy of the author.)

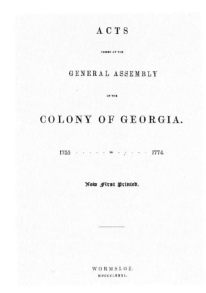

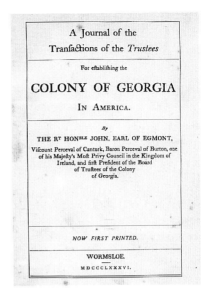

Left: Title page of *Acts Passed by the General Assembly of the Colony of Georgia, 1755 to 1774,* 1881. (De Renne Library, Hargrett Rare Book and Manuscript Library, University of Georgia Libraries.) *Right:* Title page of *A Journal of the Transactions of the Trustees for Establishing the Colony of Georgia in America,* 1886. (De Renne Library, Hargrett Rare Book and Manuscript Library, University of Georgia Libraries.)

Left: Colonel Charles C. Jones, Jr., who prepared the *Acts* quarto for printing. (Hargrett Rare Book and Manuscript Library, University of Georgia Libraries.) *Right:* Sir John Percival, first Earl of Egmont, 1683–1748. From the portrait by Hans Hysing, 1733. (Courtesy of Oglethorpe University.)

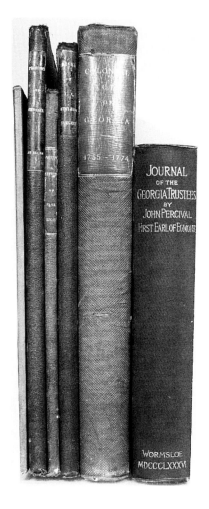

The Quartos Completed, 1886. Copies from the De Renne Gift. At fourteen pages the Walton quarto (*far left in plain cloth binding*) could not support a label on its spine. (De Renne Library, Hargrett Rare Book and Manuscript Library, University of Georgia Libraries.)

F. G. de Fontaine. (Hargrett Rare Book and Manuscript Library, University of Georgia Libraries.)

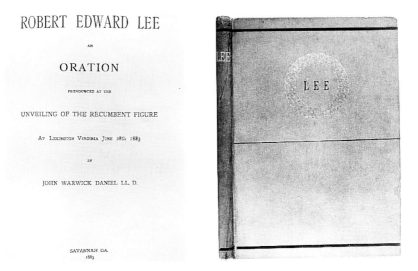

*Detail of the Permanent Constitution of the Confederate States of America.
(Facsimile of the last four lines and signatures, from* Catalogue of the Wymberley
Jones De Renne Georgia Library, *1931.)*

ROBERT EDWARD LEE

AN

ORATION

PRONOUNCED AT THE

UNVEILING OF THE RECUMBENT FIGURE

AT LEXINGTON VIRGINIA JUNE 28th 1883

BY

JOHN WARWICK DANIEL LL. D.

SAVANNAH GA.
1883

Left: Title page of *Robert Edward Lee: An Oration,* 1883. (De Renne Library,
Hargrett Rare Book and Manuscript Library, University of Georgia Libraries.)
Right: Spine and front cover of *Robert Edward Lee: An Oration.* (De Renne
Library, Hargrett Rare Book and Manuscript Library, University of Georgia
Libraries.)

Top: Mary De Renne, c. 1885. (Courtesy of Eudora De Renne Roebling.) *Bottom:*
Signature of Mary De Renne. (De Renne Collection, Hargrett Rare Book and
Manuscript Library, University of Georgia Libraries.)

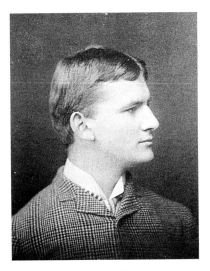

Leta De Renne. (Courtesy of
Malcolm Bell III.)

Kentwyn De Renne. (Courtesy of
Eudora De Renne Roebling.)

Dr. Everard De
Renne. (Courtesy
of Eudora De
Renne Roebling.)

The Georgia State Library in the State House, Atlanta, which received the G.W.J. De Renne Georgia Historical Collection in 1894. (Atlanta History Center.)

The Confederate Museum, showing the south portico. Katharine C. Stiles (1832–1916), longtime custodian of the Georgia Room, marked its location on this photograph with the upper cross and noted that the lower one marked the room where the ladies of the Confederate Memorial Literary Association had their meetings. The basement's bookcases held those volumes of the Mary De Renne Confederate Collection that were not displayed upstairs. (De Renne Collection, Hargrett Rare Book and Manuscript Library, University of Georgia Libraries.)

The Georgia Room of the Confederate Museum, c. 1906. (Eleanor S. Brockenbrough Library, Museum of the Confederacy, Richmond, Virginia.)

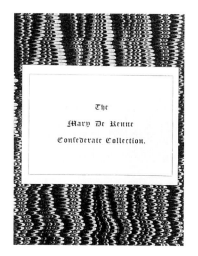 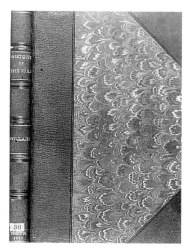

Left: Bookplate of the Mary De Renne Confederate Collection in Roussillon's *Puissance militaire des États-Unis d'Amérique d'après La Guerre de la Sécession, 1861–1865* (Paris, 1866). (Eleanor S. Brockenbrough Library, Museum of the Confederacy, Richmond, Virginia.) *Right:* Front cover and spine of Edward A. Pollard's *Southern History of the Great Civil War in the United States* (Toronto, 1863). From the De Renne Confederate Collection. (Eleanor S. Brockenbrough Library, Museum of the Confederacy, Richmond, Virginia.)

Covers of a leather-bound copy of *Sermons of Bishop Elliott* in the De Renne Confederate Collection. (Eleanor S. Brockenbrough Library, Museum of the Confederacy, Richmond, Virginia. Photography by Katherine Wetzel.)

Poplar Grove plantation, where they did little more than produce provision crops, while the remainder worked at Wormsloe, which produced nothing but butter and calves until the mid-1850s.[13]

If his views of slavery and its importance to the South resembled those of his close friend William B. Hodgson, he believed that the "long years of peaceful industry" under the regime of slavery formed the basis of all values in the South: "Land, houses, Bank & railroad stocks, Corporate and State Bonds. . . . Not only the interest . . . but the accumulated capital, itself, derived from labor & economy." This capital, in turn, (inherited by people such as young Jones and his cousin Margaret Telfair, whom Hodgson had married) created in the South an important leisure class—for without leisure, there could be "no intellectual progress, no civilization." According to Hodgson, himself the author of several books, "Letters are cradled in ease and Leisure. So is all science, human and divine."[14]

In any case, Jones did not divest himself of his slave property; instead, he joined the planter class to which his ancestors had belonged. It may have seemed to him that to do otherwise would have been a repudiation of his forefathers and that to do as he did was an affirmation of his membership in the class to which they had belonged. Since he was never dependent on the income of his plantations, however, he could have certainly sold his slaves, let his acreage lie fallow, and confined his life to Savannah and Philadelphia. But the responsibility of Wormsloe was apparently decisive. And Jones seems to have decided, whether sooner or later, that, in the world that he inhabited, Wormsloe's preservation and maintenance would depend in some measure on slave labor.

By the late 1840s, when he began spending all of his autumns and winters at Wormsloe, Jones had already begun to preserve his ancestral estate in another fashion. While in medical school he had begun printing a series of books which, like those produced in the eighteenth century by Horace Walpole's Strawberry Hill Press, bore the name of his country estate as place of publication—though Jones's productions were actually printed in Philadelphia.[15]

Of the two Wormsloe editions that appeared in late 1847 to inaugurate the series, the least typical was *Theory Concerning the Nature of Insanity*. The only work that Jones ever published under his own name—given on the title page as "George Wymberley-Jones"—this slender octavo was printed by the Philadelphia firm of C. Sherman, in a limited edition of forty-eight copies (the number no doubt representing the next year of the century, when Jones would reach the age of twenty-one). The young author dedicated the work to his friend Winthrop Sargent "as a slight token of admiration for his talents, esteem for his character, and of personal attachment."[16]

Other than Sargent, recipients of presentation copies included three of Jones's professors: Reed, Jackson, and Gibson; also presented copies were two prominent Charleston doctors: John Edwards Holbrook—an alumnus of Jones's medical school and founder of the Medical College of Charleston—and Benjamin Huger. And William Bacon Stevens was not the only Episcopal clergyman to receive a copy of the book; a presentation was also made to Paul Trapier, rector of Charleston's St. Michael's Church from 1840 to 1846.[17]

Ever the classicist, Jones prefaces his study with a Latin epigraph from *The Consolation of Philosophy* of Boethius: *Vulgus ista non respecit* (The common sort do not consider these things). In his text, Jones proceeds with the same confidence he had shown as Agricola:

> Among the various sciences whose pursuit affords employment to the human intellect, there is scarce any so profoundly interesting, and at the same time so abstruse, as that which relates to psychological phenomena. The nature of spirit, its modes of existence, the conditions of its connexion with matter, its manner of action upon material substances and upon other spirit—are questions which gave scope to the brilliant speculations of ancient philosophers, exercised the ingenuity of medieval metaphysicians, baffled the investigations of modern inquirers, and are at the present time as interesting and unexhausted as the most novel discovery.[18]

Though admitting that his subject is in some respects "trite," he asserts that its importance derives from its relation to a matter of great import: "the separate existence and immortality of the human soul." He denies, however, the "tripartite person" (body, soul, mind) posited by some philosophers; he embraces instead a dualistic theory: man is constituted of two elements, a material body and "an immaterial essence, called indifferently mind or spirit" (though Jones sometimes uses these terms, together with "soul," synonymously). He describes the brain as the "agent, or instrument, wherewith the mind, during its alliance with the body, is compelled to work"; the mind's relation to the brain, he states, is "somewhat analogous to that of an engineer in a steamship," an updated metaphor from Plato.[19]

In simplest terms his theory is that insanity—which he defines as a single disease characterized by a variety of forms, differing only in degree—is a problem of the brain, not the mind. One piece of evidence supporting this view, he feels, is hereditary insanity. Though he makes no mention of it, he had the opportunity to observe some of the inmates and speak to some of their physicians at the Department of the Insane of Pennsylvania Hospital on the outskirts of Philadelphia.[20]

His metaphysical meditation suggests deep reading in numerous sources, from Plato and Descartes and George Berkeley to Robert Burton's "quaint" *Anatomy of Melancholy*. Characteristically, the production is carried off in fine style, with vigorous, self-assured prose prodding the reader through some of the more questionable passages. Some of Jones's assertions are debatable. He declares earnestly, quoting Horace, that all people are mad to some extent. And he refuses to be bound by the idea that the soul is restricted to the body. Instead, he argues, it "may have its abode in the regions of upper air, it may wander through the vast vacuity of space, it may hover above that earthly being with whose course its destiny is so intimately interwoven, and by whose deeds its doom will be determined. But so long as it breathes the breath of life, that terrestrial form is the centre whither the spirit always wends its returning ways, and to which it is drawn by an irresistible attraction."[21]

His most dramatic passage takes its departure from some lines of Lucretius suggesting "that the mind is begotten along with the body, and grows up with it, and with it grows old." He disagrees:

But what is it, which is thus declared to have a commencement, a maturity, and a termination?—The human soul. Behold then the resurrection of the ancient and unanswerable Epicurean argument against the soul's immortality; which, incapable of refutation, sat like an incubus upon the mightiest spirits of antiquity—mocking at their futile attempts to bring the doctrine of their delight within the reach of demonstration—confounding their imaginings—crushing their aspirations—overwhelming their hopes—and leaving no refuge to their despair but in the embrace of a gloomy and sensual infidelity, or in the bewildering mazes of profitless speculation. . . . But, in the process of time, Christianity revealed to the world the existence of a human spirit, whose attribute was eternal life. . . . The decay of the intellectual powers, which proved a stumbling block to so many honest inquirers, instead of indicating the decrepitude of the spirit, and foreboding its final annihilation, only marks the progress of functional infirmity or organic dilapidation, while the spirit's vigour is not diminished nor its viability enfeebled.[22]

The Christian beliefs that informed Jones's philosophy are nowhere as clearly shown as in this passage, and, not surprisingly, it was at about this time he also wrote, at an aunt's request, a brief pamphlet on the need for the wide distribution of inexpensive copies of the Book of Common Prayer. "The extension of the Church," he writes therein, "depends in no slight degree on the dissemination of the Prayer Book. The seed will not more surely produce the plant after its kind, than will the Prayer Book engender a love for the Church and fire its distinctive doctrines, discipline, and worship." But he asserted that wealthy Episcopalians—whose prayer books were "clothed in rich morocco" and glistened with "profuseness of gilded decoration"—most needed to contribute toward the distribution of "the same Prayer Book in humble dress."[23]

In *Theory Concerning the Nature of Insanity,* Jones's self-confidence, skepticism, and youthful iconoclasm are all in evidence, along with his strong religious beliefs. But this would be his only printed venture into the realm of metaphysics. Afterward, Jones would, with one notable exception, restrict himself to printing historical materials. And he would follow his own advice to the Georgia Historical Society, for he would mainly print manuscripts.[24] Since the rallying cry of the antiquarians of the period was "to rescue from oblivion" endangered historical sources, he reasoned that the most vulnerable materials should be rescued first. Unique manuscripts should obviously have priority, but extremely rare publications also deserved consideration.[25]

In this Jones was apparently inspired in part by Thomas Frognall Dibdin, who had suggested that book-madness could be cured (or at least rendered more useful) through "the reprinting of scarce and intrinsically valuable works." The Roxburghe Club, founded by Dibdin and others in 1819, had begun a series of such reprints, and its example had been followed by other English printing clubs, some of whose publications Jones owned. These "learned associations" were formed for "the preservation of such rare information," literary or historical, that was in danger of "loss or destruction by reason of its being in a unique copy."[26]

Though the Georgia Historical Society's first two volumes of *Collections* had contained interesting and intelligently selected reprints, almost none of the publications reprinted were actually in danger of loss. Jones felt the society was emphasizing the least important of its aims by choosing diffusion over preservation. In 1848 his friend William Brown Hodgson had put the society back on what Jones considered the proper course by printing as the third volume of the society's *Collections* a manuscript of the Indian agent Benjamin Hawkins, "A Sketch of the Creek Country in the Years 1798 and 1799."[27]

For Jones's first historical publication, an influential model was Peter Force's *Tracts and Other Papers Relating Principally to the Origin, Settlement, and Progress of the Colonies in North America*, which preserved "many of the *rarisimi* of early American history"; the first volume, published in 1836, included the texts of five eighteenth-century pamphlets with colonial Georgia as their subject. Here, in Jones's eyes, was a project worthy of emulation. Consequently, at about the same time his *Theory* appeared, he produced the first of his own historical series, the Wormsloe Quartos, four of which would appear from 1847 to 1851.[28]

The unearthing of a forgotten controversy of the American Revolution inspired Jones's first quarto. Since his principal guide to eighteenth-century publications on Georgia was Rich's *Bibliotheca Americana Nova*, he was pleasantly surprised to discover a Georgia pamphlet that had not been listed in that source. He made his find near Independence Hall, in one of Philadelphia's most beautiful Palladian structures—the Philadelphia Library, founded by Benjamin Franklin, whose marble statue, clad in a toga, occupied a niche above the door. The institution, also known as the Library Company of Philadelphia, had increased its holdings by purchases and through bequests to become the second largest library in the United States. Among the treasures on its shelves were the seven thousand volumes gathered by the collector William Mackenzie, whose portrait surveyed one of the rooms.[29]

Coincidentally, the rare pamphlet Jones discovered had originally been printed only a few blocks away "in Market Street, three doors above the Coffee-House." Titled *Observations upon the Effects of Certain Late Politi-*

cal Suggestions, it had been written and published in early 1781 by several of the Georgia delegates to the Second Continental Congress, principally George Walton. The pamphlet is a reaction to persistent rumors that Great Britain would offer peace to its rebellious American colonies on the basis of an *uti possidetis:* each side would retain the territory it then controlled. Consequently, Great Britain would keep the occupied provinces of Georgia (certainly) and South Carolina (probably), both of which contained numerous Loyalists. Arguing strongly against this idea, the pamphleteers stress the strategic importance of Georgia to any postwar American union. They also bolster their claims of Georgia's commercial value to its fellow states with a table showing the growth of Savannah's trade from 1755 to 1772.[50]

Delegates other than those from Georgia considered the threat of an *uti possidetis* to be serious, but British military reverses elsewhere in the southern theater—and the final achievement of a union under the Articles of Confederation—soon removed the Georgians' fears. Jones, however, noted that James Madison of Virginia had been an opponent of the Georgians.[51]

As Jones pointed out in the preface to his printing of the *Observations,* the original pamphlet was so "exceedingly rare" that the library's copy was the only one he had "seen or heard of." His reprint was not to be much less rare, for he noted that there were "but twenty-one copies printed" of his edition, a number presumably suggested by his approaching majority. Jones clearly visualized this quarto and those that were to follow as a series of manufactured rarities. Unlike the productions of Peter Force—to whom he sent copies of all his quartos—the Wormsloe editions would not be offered for sale. Instead, Jones would present them only to friends, fellow bibliophiles, and students of history, as well as to certain favored libraries.[52]

Jones set a pattern with the first quarto that he would follow with all the others. He would print only works produced in the eighteenth century. Editing would be minor and the number of copies printed always small—never more than forty-nine. The printing would be nothing less than superior, with the typography based on typefaces designed by the English punch-cutter Richard Austin. Catchwords would end each page of text (an eighteenth-century convention), but, unlike some other private printers of works of the 1700s, he would not employ the "long s." The paper used would be of better than average quality—some copies of each quarto were printed on heavy "plate paper," with the remainder either on "fine" or "C. H.—English paper," the last-mentioned apparently from the papermaker Charles Harris of Countess Weir Mills, near Exeter. The binding would be durable and attractive but inexpensive; the quartos were "simply put up in cloth," as Jones described it, with the titles in gilt on leather labels so that recipients could have the books rebound, if they wished, to match those in their own libraries.[55]

Jones's remaining three quartos were all based on manuscripts and consequently had the words "Now First Printed" on their title pages. The second of the series, brought out in 1849, was arguably the finest—and certainly the largest: $14^{15}/_{16}$ by $10^{15}/_{16}$ inches. Its source was a report that had been presented to George III a few years before the Revolution: "History of the Three Provinces, South Carolina, Georgia, and East Florida," prepared by John Gerar William De Brahm. A military engineer who had come to Georgia from Germany in 1751, De Brahm had later rested briefly on one of the more distant branches of the Jones family tree. Submitted in 1773, De Brahm's report, beautifully illustrated by him with maps and plans, was based on numerous surveys conducted for the Crown.[54]

The particular manuscript version of De Brahm's report that Jones edited and published in 1849 had been bought the previous year by the Harvard College Library, the nation's largest. Costing a little over £12, the manuscript had been purchased from Henry Stevens, an American-born book dealer in London, then beginning a long career as an expert supplier of Americana. Through Jones's friend William Brown Hodgson, the Georgia Historical Society had known of De Brahm's work since at least 1845; Dr. William Mackenzie, searching for Georgia records for Hodgson and Israel Tefft, had remarked of the British Museum's copy of the report: "I don't see how you can get along without De Brahm's History of Georgia." Now another copy had turned up suddenly in the United States, and Jones had it carefully transcribed by the Harvard Library's assistant librarian, John Langdon Sibley.[55]

To inspect the De Brahm manuscript, Jones had to travel to Cambridge, Massachusetts. There Harvard's library was housed in the medieval splendor of Gore Hall, whose exterior was patterned after King's College Chapel in the English Cambridge. Inside, to either side of the hall's soaring rib-vaulted nave, were alcoves where the books were kept. Because he was seriously interested in historical matters, Jones was allowed by the librarian the liberty of visiting the alcoves himself. There, among other treasures, he could consult that vast collection of Americana purchased in 1830 from bibliographer and dealer Obadiah Rich, the library's longtime supplier.[56]

For his edition of the De Brahm manuscript, Jones deleted those portions pertaining to South Carolina and East Florida—well over half of the whole—and printed only the Georgia information from the original reports survey, together with some of De Brahm's general prefatory material. He titled this abridgment *History of the Province of Georgia*. One of the richest sources of information on provincial Georgia, the report offers information on numerous aspects of Georgia life during the 1750s and 1760s, including a table of products exported during the administrations of the three royal governors. There is also information on the province's navigable streams, its climate, various settlements, and Indian tribes, as well as its "African servants" (which had grown in numbers from around three dozen in 1751 to thirteen thousand in the early 1770s).[57]

De Brahm also discusses several other subjects of particular interest to Jones and his family: Savannah wharfage (which had helped make the Jones family's fortune) and two of the family's perennial enthusiasms: gardens and libraries. Of the latter De Brahm writes:

> There is scarcely a House in the Cities, Towns or Plantations, but what have some Choice Authors, if not Libraries of religious, philosophical and political Writers. Booksellers endeavour to import the newest Editions, and take Care to commission the best, well knowing they will not incumber their Shops long, but soon find Admirers and Purchasers, besides that many of their Books they write for are commissioned by the Inhabitants. The Province was scarce thirty years settled, before it had three fine Libraries in the City of Savannah, the fourth at Ebenezer, and a fifth 96¾ miles from the Sea upon the Stream of Savannah. In these Libraries could be had books wrote in the Caldaic, Hebrew, Arabec, Siriac, Coptic, Malabar, Greek, Latin, French, German, Dutch and Spanish, beside the English, viz' in the thirteen Languages.[58]

Jones illustrated the text with fine engravings by the Boston map engraver G. W. Boynton, based on six of De Brahm's eight ink drawings, themselves characterized by "extreme beauty and excessive minuteness." Jones deleted, as "possessing neither interest or importance," two of De Brahm's plans of the lots in the Salzburger settlements near Ebenezer.[59]

In explaining his editorial policy, Jones wrote that the quarto was "printed with the exactest adherence to the original, as well in the spelling as in the construction of sentences," though both are "occasionally faulty" because his "design [was] simply to produce the work as it is, not to show how it might have been better." To him, correcting the "uncouthness of a quaint old writer, be his style ever so ungainly," was "like whitewashing a ruin." [10]

His attitude was in stark contrast to that of the man who had given him permission to publish the manuscript, the historian Jared Sparks, then president of Harvard; he had used whitewash by the gallon in his edition of the papers of George Washington and would soon be at the center of a great controversy because of his practices. Sparks's editorial method, however, was not uncommon, and editors such as he normally made no apology for "improving" the papers they prepared for the press—no more than did historians who, without attribution, transferred passages from other historians' books into their own. Both practices were anathema to Jones. [11]

In 1850 appeared *Journal and Letters of Eliza Lucas,* Jones's third quarto, the first of two not directly related to Georgia history. Its printing was the happy outcome of one of Jones's most cherished friendships. He had spent time in the South Carolina low country in the 1840s, visiting Charleston, where his family had formed connections during the time that Noble Wimberly Jones and George Jones had practiced medicine there. Northeast of Charleston on "the Neck" was Belmont, the plantation of Dr. and Mrs. John Edwards Holbrook, where Mrs. Holbrook's family, the Pinckneys, had lived since colonial days. Though the original house had been burned by the British during the Revolution, there was a cottage on the site, with a "low, deep piazza . . . shut in by vines and roses," that the owners used as a country retreat. [12]

The Holbrooks often entertained friends at Belmont, which was known as "a centre of stimulating and cultivated social intercourse, free from all *gêne* or formality." Dr. Holbrook, famed as a naturalist in the realms of herpetology and ichthyology, was "a silent man with a talent for making others talk." His wife, Harriott Pinckney Holbrook, to whom Jones had presented a copy of the De Brahm quarto, was a remarkable woman with strong literary and theological interests. The Swedish novelist Fredrika Bremer found her spellbinding; to her, wandering through Belmont's myrtle groves in Mrs. Holbrook's company was an "intellectual feast." Another of her admirers noted that she had "rare mental qualities, which had been developed by an unusually complete and efficient education. The wide and various range of her reading, the accuracy of her knowledge in matters of history and literature, and the charm of her conversation, made her a delightful companion. She exercised the most beneficent influence upon her large circle of young people, and without any effort to attract, she drew to herself whatever was most bright and clever in the society about her." [43]

Such a lady would be a magnet to Wymberley Jones under any circumstances. But among her other distinctions, Mrs. Holbrook was also the great-granddaughter of another extraordinary woman, Eliza Lucas Pinckney, who had successfully introduced indigo culture to the low country in the 1740s and was remembered as well as the mother of Charles Cotesworth Pinckney and Thomas Pinckney—famous as generals, diplomats, and statesmen. When she died in Philadelphia in 1793, President George Washington served as one of her pallbearers, an indication of the esteem in which she was held. [44]

In Mrs. Holbrook's possession were her great-grandmother's letterbook and other papers, none of which had been printed. Jones was not only fortunate enough to be allowed to examine these treasures but was also successful in persuading Mrs. Holbrook to edit a selection to be printed as one of his quartos. [45]

Apparently Mrs. Holbrook's views were consistent with Jones's in regard to reproducing historical manuscript materials, for she presented her great-grandmother's text as it appeared, preserving peculiarities of capitalization, spelling, and abbreviation, along with such practices as elevating the terminal letters of some contractions. For passages deleted, she used a string of asterisks. Just over thirty pages in length, the Lucas quarto was limited to nineteen copies, making it the rarest of the series, as was symbolized by its diamond-shaped colophon. [46]

Born in the West Indies and educated in England, Eliza Lucas had come to South Carolina in 1738 at the age of fifteen, the daughter of a British army officer who owned three plantations in the province. Most of the quarto's selections alternated her letters with journal entries from the years 1740–44, when, in her father's absence, she had the responsibility of running his Wappoo Creek Plantation near Charleston—a tract of six hundred acres worked by twenty slaves—and she supervised his other two plantations as well. This portion of the book concludes with a letter announcing her coming marriage to Charles Pinckney; she is his widow when the letters resume for a brief final section, 1759–62. [47]

The early 1740s, though the years when Eliza Lucas was engaged in her experiments with the indigo plant, were also a time of war. Her first journal entry, written during the War of Jenkins's Ear, mentions General James Oglethorpe's failure at St. Augustine in 1740, and she later comments on the attack by the "Spainyards" against the general's outpost at Frederica. Her final letter, written in 1762 during another international conflict, hopes for peace; it would finally come the following year, when the Treaty of Paris ended the Seven Years' War.[48]

Throughout the book, the excerpted passages vividly present "the varied activities, hopes, and fears of an energetic, intelligent, and imaginative eighteenth-century woman." Eliza Lucas's prose is clear and vigorous and her subjects always interesting, whether she is reporting war news, passing along party gossip, or giving her commonsensical appraisal of Samuel Richardson's *Pamela*. The day-to-day incidents and events at her Wappoo Plantation are a frequent subject; she reports not only her endless tasks but her pleasures as well: her "little library," her "Musick and the Garden." Rumored slave revolts receive mention, as do her efforts to teach some of Wappoo's slave children how to read. In the 1760s—worried that the province would be left open to the depredations of the Cherokees ("Barbarians," in her estimation)—she applauds the coming of those English allies the Mohawks ("very fine men . . . looked upon by the rest of the Indians with both dread and respect").[49]

Jones used imported English paper for the first time for some copies of the Lucas quarto. Of all the books he printed, it alone contained parchment presentation pages, which were used for the copies presented to Mrs. Holbrook, Winthrop Sargent, George Noble Jones, and the Philadelphia bibliophile Robert Morris.[50]

Before printing the last of his four quartos, Jones in 1850 made the first of several transatlantic trips, this one his equivalent of the Grand Tour. He took with him a letter from U.S. Secretary of State John M. Clayton to the "respective Diplomatic and Consular Agents of the United States in Europe," identifying him as "a gentleman of leisure, fortune, and high character." Clayton concluded, "At the instance of his uncle, George W. Smith, Esq., of Philadelphia, I take the liberty of introducing Mr. Jones to you, and of bespeaking for him, during his stay in your neighborhood, such attentions as you may find it convenient to extend to him."[51]

In Europe from May through July, Jones spent most of his time in England and France, though he also visited Belgium, Germany, and Switzerland. Although his French sojourn centered in Paris, he also visited his expatriate aunts, Maria Campbell-Stewart and Juliana Smith, at Montpellier, west of Marseilles near the Mediterranean.[52]

He made acquisitions for his library during the trip, particularly in London. Obadiah Rich, the bibliographer and longtime dealer in Americana, had died the previous January, but there were numerous other shops to attract young Jones. Writing of this general period, the Vermonter Henry Stevens commented that during those "happy days . . . on a July morning one might run down a hundred brace of rare old books on America in London at as many shillings a volume as must now be paid in pounds."[53]

Stevens's activities had probably reduced the number of rarities available. He had for some time been supplying books, chiefly Americana, to a long list of buyers, including Peter Force, Jared Sparks, George Bancroft, Francis Parkman, John Carter Brown, and James Lenox, not to mention purchases for the Library of Congress. For Antonio Panizzi, librarian of the British Museum, he had "run down" ten thousand books on American history in one eighteen-month period.[54]

Stevens had no shop at the time because he was acting as a purchasing agent, but antiquarian bookshops were numerous. One establishment at 77 Picadilly had Americana in its stock, as well as happy associations for Jones. It belonged to one of his favorite publishers, the English Aldus, William Pickering. Jones took this opportunity to add to his extensive collection of Pickering imprints.[55]

Following his return to America, Jones prepared to print the last of his quartos, this one almost entirely unrelated to Georgia history. Appearing in 1851, the book was another token of Jones's friendship for Winthrop Sargent. *Diary of Col. Winthrop Sargent, Adjutant-General of the United States Army During the Campaign of MDCCXCI* was based on a manuscript diary of Winthrop Sargent IV (1753–1820), in the possession of his grandson, Jones's friend, the sixth in his family to bear the name. Jones extracted from the diary passages relating to the earliest and most disastrous of the United States Army's losses to the Indians: the defeat of the expedition of General Arthur St. Clair in 1791, unavenged until "Mad" Anthony Wayne's victory at Fallen Timbers three years later.[56]

The diary's author, a veteran of the Revolutionary War, was a personal friend of General St. Clair. Despite his civilian status, Sargent had been handpicked by the general to serve as the army adjutant general on the expedition. St. Clair's army—composed principally of unreliable militia and footloose levies—was to mount an offensive against an alliance of hostile Indian tribes that was then stirring the Northwest Territory into a dangerous state of unrest. The Indian alliance had routed another American army the previous year, and President Washington was sending St. Clair to pacify the area, combining a show of force with the construction of a string of forts from the Ohio River to Lake Erie.[57]

St. Clair was to have even worse luck than his predecessor. Less than a hundred miles north of his base at Fort Washington on the Ohio, just before dawn on November 4, 1791, St. Clair's force was struck by more than one thousand warriors under the command of the Miami chief Little Turtle. According to Sargent, defense of the camp was embarrassed from the start by "the most ignominious flight of the militia," who rushed "helter skelter" into the defensive lines formed by the regulars. Sargent assumed that the U.S. force had been surrounded at the time of the attack and, having only "raw and undisciplined Troops" (though at least equal in number to the Indians), did well to fight for two hours before deciding to retreat. Along with the regulars, the female camp followers did their part: they "drove out the skulking Militia and fugitives . . . from under waggons and hiding places," writes Sargent, "by firebrands and the usual weapons of their sex," but in the end most were "inhumanly butchered."[58]

St. Clair's retreat was not creditable: according to Sargent, it was "in a most supreme degree disgraceful." Artillery and baggage were sacrificed, along with some of the wounded. The Indians did not attempt a concerted pursuit, partially, Sargent surmises with some delicacy, because the "unfortunate men . . . we were compelled to leave behind must for a time have engaged their attention." As another survivor notes, the deserted field was littered with dead American soldiers, their scalped heads smoking in the cold dawn light. Hurried along by such sights, the retreating troops covered the thirty miles to the nearest fort by seven o'clock that evening. The day's loss had been staggering: "Of Regular Troops and Levies in non-commissioned officers and privates [there were] five hundred and fifty killed and two hundred wounded; and of commissioned officers, out of ninety five we had in the field, thirty one were killed and twenty four wounded. The Militia had four officers killed and five wounded, and of non-commissioned officers and privates, thirty eight killed and twenty nine wounded."[59]

The Sargent book was the last quarto whose printing was personally supervised by Jones. He again commissioned G. W. Boynton to prepare engravings; these two illustrations were based on "original drawings" by Sargent: "A Plan of the Encampment and Sketch of the Action" and "Order of Battle, March and Encampment." The book's distinctive colophon, whose black-letter text formed a fatal hourglass, noted that forty-six copies had been printed. Jones reserved five of these copies for his friend Sargent, who in turn made presentations of his own, including one to Jared Sparks.[60]

Between 1847 and 1851, then, Jones had produced four quartos on historical subjects; the first reprinted a rare eighteenth-century pamphlet, and the others represented the first printing of significant manuscript material from the same general period, roughly 1740 to 1790. His other writings to reach print included a précis of his medical dissertation, a brief religious tract, a metaphysical essay, and an anonymous pamphlet review of the first volume of William Bacon Stevens's *History of Georgia*. But one additional work was printed during the period. It belonged to none of the other categories and existed in so few copies that it was to be the rarest of all the productions to bear the Wormsloe imprint.

This unique creation was based on a contemporary literary work, compared by some to one of the more charming sketches by Washington Irving. In any case, it appealed strongly to the young bibliophile at this stage of his life. In the September 1849 number of the *Southern Literary Messenger*, Jones found to his pleasure a sentimental essay on the subject of bachelorhood and marriage titled "A Bachelor's Reverie" by Ik. Marvel.[61]

The narrator, a twenty-six-year-old bachelor, sits in his rustic farmhouse retreat, musing before a fire of oak and hickory. His reveries on the possibility of leaving his bachelor state follow the progress of his fire. The green wood first only smokes, prompting him to consider that "smoke . . . always goes before a blaze; and so does doubt go before decision." His doubts about marriage are manifold. Will it not mean losing "respectability, independence, comfort"? What of the "plaguey wife's relations"? What of her annoying habits, whether "forever talking" or "provokingly silent"? What if her appearance becomes slatternly after she is safely married? Or—given that she keeps her looks—what if she turns "shrewish"? Perhaps most frightening, what if she is a danger to your books? "Your copy of Tasso, a treasure print of 1680, is all bethumbed and dog's-eared, and spotted with baby gruel. Even your Seneca—an Elzevir—is all sweaty with handling." But soon thereafter, the smoking logs burst into a blaze, representing cheer.[62]

The bachelor's cheerful thoughts are as relentlessly optimistic as his doubts were morose. The lady's person is enchanting:

> [Her] hair parted to a charm over a forehead as fair as any of your dreams,—and if you could reach an arm around that chair back, without fear of giving offence, and suffer your fingers to play idly with those curls that escape down the neck, and if you could clasp with your other hand those little white, taper fingers of hers, which lie so temptingly within reach,—and so, talk softly and low in presence of the blaze, while the hours slip without knowledge, and the winter winds whistle uncared for;—if, in short, you were no bachelor, but the husband of some such sweet image—(dream, call it, rather,) would it not be far pleasanter than this cold single night-sitting—counting the sticks—reckoning the length of the blaze, and the height of the falling snow?[63]

Could she be a comfort? "Your sister . . . is dead—buried. The worms are busy with all her fairness. How it makes you think earth nothing but a spot to dig graves upon!

"—It is more: *she*, she says, will be a sister; and the waving curls as she leans upon your shoulder, touch your cheek, and your wet eye turns to meet those other eyes—God has sent his angel, surely!"[64]

What of children? ". . . no, they do not disturb you with prattle now—they are yours." What of sickness? ". . . no lonely moanings, and wicked curses at careless stepping nurses. . . . The soft, cool hand is upon your brow." What if your illness is your last? "Kind hands—none but *hers*—will smooth the hair upon your brow as the chill grows damp, and heavy on it; and her fingers—none but hers—will lie in yours as the wasted flesh stiffens, and hardens for the ground. *Her* tears,—you could feel no others, if oceans fell—will warm your drooping features once more to life; once more your eyes lighted in joyous triumph, kindle in her smile, and then. . . ." The blaze suddenly dies and becomes "nothing but a bed of glowing embers."[65]

The bachelor reflects that "ashes follow blaze, inevitably as Death follows Life." What is *she* becomes sick? What if there comes a time when there is no money to see to her wants and needs? What if the children die young? What if they are followed by their mother: "There is a smell of varnish in your house. A coffin is there; they have clothed the body in decent grave clothes, and the undertaker is screwing down the lid, slipping round on tip-toe. Does he fear to waken her? . . .—Another day. The coffin is gone out. The stupid mourners have wept—what idle tears! She, with your crushed heart, is gone out!" [66]

At last the bachelor comes back to full consciousness:

> The embers were dark; I stirred them; there was no sign of life. . . .
>
> I dashed a tear or two from my eyes—how they came I know not. I half ejaculated a prayer of thanks that such desolation had not yet come nigh me; and a prayer of hope that it might never come.
>
> In a half hour or more, I was sleeping soundly.
>
> My reverie was ended. [67]

Jones was not the only reader enthusiastic about Marvel's work, for an expanded version—*Reveries of a Bachelor: A Book of the Heart*, containing three additional meditations on love and friendship—was soon to become a mid-nineteenth-century best-seller. The first, and only, book printing of the original reverie, however, was that of George Wymberley Jones. [68]

He had been alerted to the impending, expanded publication of the piece in book form by a note that accompanied a reprint of the reverie in the first volume of *Harper's New Monthly Magazine*. Recruited to assist him with his plans was Winthrop Sargent. At Jones's request, Sargent wrote to Donald G. Mitchell, who used "Ik. Marvel" as his pseudonym:

> Sir:
>
> An odd, bibliomaniacal friend of mine having some time ago perused an article over your *nom de plume*, entitled "A Bachelor's Reverie" . . . desires me to address you this note. In common with every person of taste who has seen it, he has read the article with exceeding delight—and is desirous, in his enthusiasm, of preserving it in a more elegant and worthy dress than it would receive from an American Publisher. Having some experience as a private printer of rare American M.SS., . . . he wishes to print privately, for distribution among his friends & for his own gratification ten copies of the "Reverie," and requests your consent thereto.
>
> The tale will, you understand, be privately printed—not published—and the edition limited to ten impressions. The paper, ink, and typography shall all be of the most beautiful and costly description—and should you make no objections to his *project*, he will be happy to show you one of the most exquisite passages in the whole range of English Literature, in a garb unexcelled, and probably unequalled by any book *published* in America. Should you yield this assent, he begs me to desire your acceptance of a copy of his edition, and his and my sincere thanks. [69]

With Mitchell's consent, the *"project"* proceeded as described, with the difference that the number of impressions was increased to an even dozen. Certainly the binding of the slim octavo volume was "unexcelled," for unlike the simple cloth of the quartos, the Wormsloe edition of *A Bachelor's Reverie* was leather-clad, with the title stamped on the spine in gold. Different colors of leather were employed: one volume, for example, was bound in green, while another combined a blue backstrip with red covers. The typography was superb as well, with a dignified Gothic for the title and a combination of Gothic with other typefaces for the headings of each of the three parts, as well as for the colophon.[70]

Other than the copy destined for the author, only eight copies of *A Bachelor's Reverie* were distributed. Winthrop Sargent, inevitably, received one, as did George Noble Jones. Only two women were recipients: one was married—Mrs. Holbrook—the other, a spinster: Jones's kinswoman Mary Telfair. But the young woman who occupied the reveries of bachelor George Wymberley Jones was not—and could not appropriately be—considered for a presentation copy. Nonetheless, she had ready access to the Wormsloe edition of *A Bachelor's Reverie:* with her own charmingly parted hair and "waving curls," Mary Wallace Nuttall was a member of the family of George Noble Jones, who had married her widowed mother ten years before.[71]

CHAPTER 4

Ancestral Fields

He determined in his own mind that there was no condition more truly
honorable than that of a country gentleman on his paternal lands.
—WASHINGTON IRVING

In 1828, Mary Nuttall's Virginian father went to the Florida
frontier to make his fortune. William B. Nuttall was not a lone
adventurer, however, for his father and a brother had preceded him
and begun buying up land in territory that only a decade before
had belonged to Spain. The place they chose, known as Middle
Florida, was rich land between the Apalachicola and Suwannee
Rivers; their tracts, east of the capital in Tallahassee, lay principally
in Jefferson County, which stretched all the way from Georgia's
southern border to the Gulf of Mexico. Land speculators were rampant, and the Nuttalls speculated with the best of them. They acquired extensive acreage, including a large plantation called El
Destino, and worked it with a force of fifty-two slaves transferred
from their Virginia plantation.[1]

Though essentially the overseer of El Destino at first, Nuttall
was a lawyer by profession, a graduate of Connecticut's esteemed
Litchfield Law School. His was an advantageous calling in a time
when knowledge of the legal technicalities of land acquisition was
at a premium. And he involved himself in politics as well, forging

several beneficial alliances, the foremost with Richard Keith Call, of whose political cabal, the "Nucleus," Nuttall became a member. The Nucleus could hardly have had better connections, for among Call's friends was a man who had already made a name for himself in Florida: Andrew Jackson, who in 1829 would begin his first term as president of the United States. Call himself was an influential friend to have, for from the time of Nuttall's arrival in Florida, Call held an important position in the state land office; he would become territorial governor of Florida in 1836.[2]

Another of Nuttall's alliances was matrimonial: on June 20, 1832, in Savannah he married Mary Wallace Savage. She was the daughter of the Georgia planter Thomas Savage, who had died at Silk Hope, his Bryan County plantation in October 1812, just over a week after Mary, his only daughter, was born. Savage had traits that seem to have been transmitted to some of his descendants, for he was described as "an accomplished gentleman, and finished scholar, of great dignity of deportment, . . . more devoted to books than society." Among his other legacies, he left to his daughter "a half-interest in fifty-four slaves as well as other property," which she shared with her mother and namesake, the daughter of Savannah's sometime British consul John Wallace and his wife, Mary.[3]

Accompanied by the bride's mother, the Nuttalls made a wedding trip to the North, where they spent most of their time at the increasingly popular resort of Newport, Rhode Island. Seeing them there, an acquaintance wrote, "Mary looks very well & pretty & I think Mr. N. an uncommonly fine looking man."[4]

The year that William Nuttall married, his father died. William purchased El Destino from the estate and used his wife's slaves and money to develop the plantation. There, in their large, plain plantation house, "embowered in vines and shrubbery," the young couple entertained lavishly, particularly by frontier standards. Mary Nuttall made such a striking impression in those days that she dominates her passage in *Florida Breezes*, which was woven by Richard Keith Call's daughter from her father's reminiscences. The book describes Mrs. Nuttall as "very handsome, large, and grand looking," possessing a "countenance more expressive of all that is beautiful in womanly character; intelligence and active amiability gave character to more than ordinary beauty." One character, a gentleman, comments, "Oh, no; there is nothing provincial about her; she would grace a queen's drawing room." In fact, she did grace the parlor of a "princess" at least, for among her friends in the Tallahassee area were the Achille Murats—the prince, nephew of Napoleon I, was for a time William Nuttall's law partner.[5]

Florida Breezes contains a vivid description of a costume ball at El Destino in the early 1830s at which there was "revelry, but all was decorous as merry." As champagne flowed, waltzes were danced by such costumed merrymakers as Cleopatra, Bluebeard, Marie Antoinette, and Falstaff. Outside, slaves fed a belt of fire that encircled the house at a "distance of fifty or sixty yards," ostensibly to "prevent a surprise from Indians"—though neither host nor guests "seemed to be apprehensive of attack."[6]

Such merriment at El Destino was counterbalanced by cares and sadness. The Nuttalls' first child, a daughter, died not long after her birth in May 1833, and Nuttall soon became entangled in financial difficulties. He was gladdened, however, by the birth at Newport on May 16, 1835, of another daughter, Mary Wallace—sometimes called "Molly"—a plump child who grew quickly and was soon playing happily with the slave children in the dust of the plantation house yard.[7]

Though both Mary and her future husband, Wymberley Jones, would hold strong feelings about the plantation homes of their youth, Mary's were destined to be almost entirely negative; to her, El Destino was little more than a "snake hole and alligator pond." The fashionable watering places of the country would always be more congenial to her, particularly her birthplace, Newport. Not yet one year of age, she was there with her mother in the spring of 1836 when word came that William Nuttall had fallen dead of apoplexy at El Destino on April 20, 1836. Only two weeks earlier, his friend Richard Call had taken his oath of office as governor of Florida.[8]

Nuttall had left no will, and his financial affairs were in a very murky state; it would be almost a decade before everything could be sorted out. Meanwhile, the widow Nuttall would be pursued by a variety of suitors, from her husband's business partner to the recently widowed Governor Call, who was greatly "cast down" at his lack of success. The widow, whose financial adviser had "deluded her with the belief that her affairs were most prosperous," may have wondered whether her hand or land was most sought after. In any case, the suitor who would lead her to the altar would not be from Middle Florida but from Georgia and would be someone she had apparently met at Newport: George Noble Jones. Since it had been summertime, he was probably in residence there when her trip to Newport was cut short by her husband's sudden death; if so, he himself was in mourning for his wife, whom he had also met at Newport, and who had died only a few months before the death of William Nuttall.[9]

Delia Tudor Gardiner—the first Mrs. Jones—came from an old Maine family whose seat, Oaklands, was at Gardiner, near the Kennebec River, some miles south of the capital at Augusta. Delia Gardiner's father, Robert Hallowell, had assumed the surname Gardiner to meet the terms of a will that left him an "ample fortune," including much land. He had raised his children in much the same way as had George Jones, with an emphasis on the Episcopal faith and a rigorous education, which two of Delia's brothers had received at Round Hill, as had George Noble Jones; in 1842 one of her brothers, Robert Hallowell Gardiner II, would wed Sarah Fenwick Jones, sister of George Noble Jones.[10]

As had Dr. George Jones, Robert Gardiner spent some time in Philadelphia, but it was at Newport that his daughter met George Noble Jones and "formed an acquaintance . . . which ripened into affection." In doubtful health at the time of her courtship, Delia Gardiner married George Noble Jones at Gardiner on September 9, 1834, less than a month before a catastrophic fire destroyed Oaklands. The newlyweds spent their first winter together in Georgia, mostly at the Jones plantation in Jefferson County, just north of the old state capital at Louisville; perhaps in honor of the new bride, the plantation was named Oaklands.[11]

When the couple returned to Maine in the summer of 1835, Mr. Gardiner was distressed to see a "hectic flush" in his daughter's cheek; examination by a physician showed that her lungs had become diseased past any hope of recovery. It was her father's sad duty to tell her the worst. She and her husband then moved into the cottage where the Gardiners were living until Oaklands could be rebuilt, and there she died on January 8, 1836, aged twenty-four. After the death of his grandfather Dr. George Jones two years later, George Noble Jones would commence a decade as executor and administrator of the two estates, a role he fulfilled for several other family members as well.[12]

Perhaps anticipating the bequests of his grandfather and of the $10,000 he would earn as executor of his estate, George Noble Jones decided in 1839 to abandon Newport's boardinghouses and have a Gothic Revival cottage built in the country south of town. The architect Richard Upjohn, who had been hired by the Gardiners to draw the plans for the new Oaklands, did the drafting. Though Oaklands had been designed as a massive Gothic structure of hammered stone, the "cottage orne'" designed for George Noble Jones was more delicate and fanciful and was of faux stone—wood covered with a mixture of sand and paint and scored to resemble building blocks. Unlike some resort cottages, it was not to be closed up for part of the season; instead, Jones had it well insulated so that his mother, Sarah Campbell Jones, could live there year-round. A lover of Newport, she died there in 1843 and was buried in the churchyard of Trinity Church.[13]

By this time, George Noble Jones and the widow Nuttall had become man and wife. But her business affairs were in such a state of confusion at the time that the fate of El Destino, as well as of Chemonie Plantation—which she had acquired on her own in 1840—was uncertain. Her late husband's indebtedness, it transpired, was almost $87,000, and his estate was "nearly or quite insolvent." Consequently, George Noble Jones acquired El Destino at a foreclosure sale, along with almost seventy slaves, soon after his second marriage. For the rest of his life his fortunes would be as closely linked to Florida plantation lands—more than sixty-four hundred acres of them—as had been those of William Nuttall.[14]

But Jones would be an absentee planter, spending less time in the South than in Europe and the North, where his principal residence was his cottage in Newport. Kinship and hospitality drew Wymberley Jones there, and there he would meet and marry Mary Nuttall, George Noble Jones's stepdaughter, thus placing another family of Joneses in the Newport orbit.[15]

An island town, accessible only by water, Newport had a resident population of twelve thousand and was more than a "resort of fashion." Attesting to this status were its "three sugar refineries, seventeen factories of sperm oil and candles, five ropewalks, one brewery and twenty-two distilleries for the manufacture of rum." Nonetheless, visitors could put all this behind them when they left their accommodations in town for the rural regions to the south.[16]

There, where a few houses and cottages (and, later, hotels) hosted some of the island's visitors, the terrain was picturesque. It rolled toward the sea, arriving variously at beaches, cliffs, and stony promontories. Much of the rugged coastline was rockbound, though—Anthony Trollope noted—it was unequal to the scenic pleasures of the waterfronts of Dieppe and Biarritz, French resorts that in the future would figure in the itineraries of both families of Joneses. Inland there were placid pools and woody dells, suitable destinations for outings on horseback, as were the many overlooks that offered vistas of sea, coves, and islands. For those who enjoyed fowling, like George Noble Jones, there were reedy ponds to furnish ducks for the table. And there was food for the intellect as well, for it was boasted that Newport had "as much culture as Boston." In general, the resort offered its visitors an air of leisure and refinement, along with that "cosmopolitan atmosphere" common to some ports.[17]

Like Philadelphia, Newport welcomed southerners. It had done so for decades, beginning in the 1700s, when slaves still worked some of the island's farms. During those years there had been an annual summer influx, particularly of low-country Carolinians, seeking refuge from southern heat and insects. Some were invalids and convalescents, and Newport was indeed healthful for the sick, as well as very pleasant to the healthy. Its temperate climate combined sea air with thermometer readings that permitted bathing on its several beaches. And many considered its famous mists both romantic and good for the complexion.[18]

Southern slave owners like George Noble Jones were not hindered from bringing their house slaves with them to Newport, and there was little controversy about such things until the late 1850s. An example of the resort's evenhanded approach to sectional matters could be seen in the Redwood Library (a principal attraction to such southern bibliophiles as Wymberley Jones); its walls displayed portraits both of Daniel Webster and of John C. Calhoun.[19]

Savannah was the setting for the marriage of George Noble Jones to Mary Savage Nuttall. The wedding took place at 8:00 A.M. on May 25, 1840 (the groom's twenty-ninth birthday), at the lately rebuilt and newly consecrated Christ Church, with the church's rector (and groom's cousin) the Reverend Edward Neufville officiating. The bride wore a "light colored" dress of French muslin, with a veiled silk hat—"very simple and suitable for traveling." She won the praise of the groom's family, who admired her beauty and poise, as well as her stature; it was good, one remarked, to have someone of height "in a family of so many little ones." Little Mary Nuttall had shown herself unwilling to share her mother's attention with Jones and thus had not been advised of the purpose for the gathering—she thought the Reverend Neufville was preaching a "small sermon." When the five-year-old child heard the couple pronounced man and wife, she broke loudly into a "flood of tears." The weather matched her outburst: a hard rain drove the newlyweds under umbrellas as they dashed for a carriage to take them to their ship; a short voyage took them to Charleston, where they spent their honeymoon, to be joined within a week by Mary and her grandmother Mrs. Savage for their trip to Newport.[20]

Upon their return, the Joneses stayed in a rented house while their Gothic cottage was being constructed, saddened by the illness of the new bride's mother, Mary Savage, who succumbed to cancer on December 1, 1840. As the cottage's construction continued, the Joneses spent much of the next year in Savannah and New York, partially because Mrs. Jones, expecting a child, "was unwilling to return to the house in which her Mother had died." Soon after the first anniversary of Mrs. Savage's death, Mary Savage Nuttall Jones was delivered of her first son, who was called George Fenwick Jones.[21]

When the family returned to Newport, their "rustic Gothick" cottage awaited them, already occupied by George Noble Jones's mother and some of his Campbell cousins. Structures, like people, have ancestors, and Wymberley presumably noticed with approval that the Jones cottage, with its pointed arches and crenellation, was a descendant of Horace Walpole's Gothic fantasia, Strawberry Hill. Though the house had seven bedrooms, it was destined to be crowded with visiting friends and relations. Young Mary had been provided with a second-story bedroom with a large, diamond-paned double window that offered a distant view of the sea. The window, which looked onto a narrow battlemented balcony, was flanked by matching window closets to accommodate her books, as well as flowers from her own plot in the garden. There was also a letter recess in one wall, perfect — it was suggested — for use as a bedchamber for her dolls, and there was a pillar at her entrance to the hall, convenient, she was told, for playing "Here we go round the Goose Berry bush" with young playmates such as her neighbor Annie Middleton. And, though the cottage had been built in an entirely rural area, the Ocean House, a vast hotel, was soon constructed (and soon destroyed by fire and rebuilt) just across the street. The young girl was no doubt attracted by the comings and goings there. As one observer noted, the "air of retirement" of the Jones cottage contrasted sharply with the "busy human hive on the other side of the road."[22]

There were numerous comings and going at the Jones cottage as well, as the varied and numerous friends and relations of George Noble Jones arrived and departed, enjoying his hospitable table and cellar. Certainly among them were "Mr. Hodgson and his two ladies," as they were described. A diplomat by profession and an Orientalist by taste, William B. Hodgson had served the Department of State from 1824 to 1842 in various capacities, at such posts as Constantinople and Tunis. In 1842 he had married Margaret Telfair, a cousin of George Noble and Wymberley Jones, and moved into his bride's ancestral mansion on St. James Square. His sister-in-law Mary Telfair continued in residence at the mansion; the Hodgsons had no children, and the three always traveled together on both sides of the ocean. Absorbed by scholarly pursuits as was Wymberley Jones, Hodgson also supervised the Telfair business interests and managed the sisters' vast plantation lands, from Sabine Fields near Savannah to considerable cotton acreage in Burke and Jefferson Counties.[23]

Another visitor whose company Hodgson enjoyed was Wymberley's uncle Washington Smith. The two shared an interest in North Africa and the Middle East, and both were masters of several languages. One description of Smith serves as fittingly for Hodgson: he had "conversational powers and ease of manner which made him welcome at all gatherings of savants." When Smith went to North Africa in the late 1850s to pursue his interest in the Jugurthine War, he no doubt found it helpful to have conferred with Hodgson, who had served in the region.[24]

More siblings joined Mary Nuttall and George Fenwick Jones: two brothers—Wallace Savage Jones in 1846 and Noble W. Jones III in 1852—and a sister as well—Sarah Campbell Jones, born in 1843, who would later rename herself Lillie Noble Jones. She would soon inherit Mary Nuttall's distinctive bedroom, for Mary grew to maturity quickly. Increasingly a lover of driving and, especially, riding, Mary turned her attention from the gardens to the fashionable barouche and the horses of the Jones carriage house and stable, which had been built to resemble a Gothic chapel.[25]

There is no record of when Wymberley first noticed that George Noble Jones's stepdaughter had reached womanhood. But her change would have been difficult to ignore, for she had left her childlike plumpness behind and had grown slender and tall—by sixteen taller than her mother (and therefore taller than her future husband). Privately educated, Mary had become a lover of reading as well as riding. The hopeful suitor, then twenty-five and not alone in his aim to make the young Mary Nuttall his wife, implored Mrs. George Noble Jones to give a final and favorable answer to his request for her young daughter's hand:

Wormsloe Jan. 24th, 1852

My dear Mrs. J: Lady Oaklands, d'El Destino, friend, cousin, Mother,
    whichever you like best to be called.

I am in that particular state of suspense, of which hanging is an inferior degree, vibrating between hopes and fears, uncertain how long I'm to be miserable, when I'm to be made happy, and dependent on your considerate kindliness for an early issue to this tantalizing period of expectation.

Your ladyship has been arbitress of the destinies of so many poor fellows, and has been constrained to be cruel so often, that I permit myself to hope you may incline to mercy in the present case, if for no other reason, at least to indulge the fancy of your sex for change.

But I have other causes for hopefulness. You are all-powerful. The decision you make is final—there's no appeal—no contesting it—nothing but submission.

By a different disposition this unrestrained authority might be severely used; but I am willing to believe that your generosity is equal to your power—that you are as indulgent as you are absolute. Your ladyship's temper is, if I mistake not, quite Roman in its nobleness—not to say divine. I may not quote Latin to a lady, but the English of a famous line describes what I think is your habit "to resist the proud but be gracious to the humble" and yield to supplication what you'd refuse to demand.

Your ladyship has in your late cousin a supplicant most humble, and beyond doubt sufficiently lowly. He acknowledges your power with dread; but finds consolation in the memory of your kind heartedness. He implores you to terminate his harassing doubts as speedily as your wisdom will allow your compassion—to fix some definite period to his suspense—some end to his uncertainty; and he relies upon your gracious sympathy that it be not too long.

In fact there is limit to the powers of endurance even when there is none to the willingness to endure, and we know that saints as well as sinners sometimes cry "How long, O Lord? How long?"

My dear Cousin, you have dealt kindly with me; deal kindly with me now also. I would you could know how entirely absorbing this one charming idea is to me. My mind, thoughts, my whole attention are concentrated upon one subject with an exclusiveness which without exaggeration, is almost painfully intense. Nothing will divert them. You are philosopher enough to know that this state of things cannot last long without material injury. I pray you therefore my cousin, that it may not last long.

The Spaniards have a proverb which prays God to deliver them from a man of one book. You will readily understand that devotion to one single subject unfits a man for general—perhaps for any companionship.

You may say that this is foolish, unreasonable, absurd, and to be corrected. If it had been in my power to have controlled my feelings, I should not have troubled you with a letter as tedious and so importunate.

Once more, my cousin I pray you be kind, if it be possible. But at all events tell me your decision very soon in pity, if not in love.

Will you give my love to Mary, and accept the poor remnant yourself, and believe me faithfully yours

G.W.J.[26]

Mrs. Jones was sure to be charmed by this mock-chivalric epistle and re-assured by its entirely serious undertone. In any case, the mother gave her blessing. The following year a marriage contract was drafted, establishing what the bride would bring to the alliance. It showed Mary to "possess in her own right" nine slaves; around thirty others ("with the future issue and increase of the females") were to come to her at her mother's death, along with an "undivided interest . . . in common" (with her half-siblings) in approximately sixty other slaves, which would come to them after the deaths of Mr. and Mrs. George Noble Jones.[27]

The wedding of Mary Wallace Nuttall to George Wymberley Jones took place on October 21, 1852, in Newport's Trinity Church, long attended by the Jones clan. Its two high tiers of arched windows lighted a formal interior, with hanging galleries on three sides and "square high-backed pews." Its tall, three-decked pulpit, "located directly and most inconveniently in front of the chancel," had drawn many eminent divines, including George Berkeley, bishop of Cloyne. Fittingly for a young man so intensely interested in the Loyalist cause as Wymberley, the church was reputed to be the only one left in the former colonies to have a symbol of the English king atop its steeple—and, below the steeple, a bell given by "Good Queen Anne." The groom's Philadelphia relations were not the only citizens of the Quaker City to attend, for the marriage service was conducted by Alonzo Potter, the bishop of Pennsylvania.[28]

Within a month the newlyweds were in Europe, enjoying a much more extensive tour than Wymberley's of two years before. They spent from November 1852 until May 1853 traveling from England through France to Italy, Austria, Czechoslovakia, and Germany. Going by private coach and always accompanied by a Swiss courier and a French maidservant, the young couple first stayed two weeks in Paris, during which, among other entertainments, they enjoyed the opera and a masked ball. Mary fell in love with the city; it would always be "her Paris." [29]

After traveling southward to visit his relatives near Montpellier, the two took a boat from Marseilles to Genoa and traveled throughout Italy during January and February 1853, going to Florence and Rome, Perugia and Naples, and, of course, Venice; there, visiting the church where the body of Aldus Manutius had lain in state, his books stacked around him, was more obligatory than the gondola rides the couple took. Vienna, Prague, Dresden, Leipzig, Frankfurt, and Cologne were also on their itenerary, but they eventually returned to Paris and spent most of April there. [30]

Returning to London in early May, the Joneses stayed for a time at the Clarendon Hotel, then went to Liverpool and boarded an America-bound steamer. Their return came on the day of the celebration of the bride's birthday, May 16, by which time it was obvious that within a few months there would be another birthday. The couple went back to Newport for the lying-in; there, on September 23, 1853, Mary presented her husband of eleven months with a son and heir. Perhaps since his own infant form had been so burdened with Christian names, Wymberley decided to make the baby boy's christening a simpler matter: he would be called Wymberley Jones. His parents had been married by a bishop and young Wymberley would be christened by one — Stephen Elliott, the bishop of Georgia — with water from the River Jordan brought back from the Holy Land by the Lynch expedition. [31]

Until 1860 Wymberley and Mary spent most of their springs and summers in Newport. Mary joined her mother in the Queen of Clubs, which met weekly, on Tuesdays, from 11:00 until 2:00. The meetings were held in members' houses, with the hostess serving refreshments "of the simplest character." The club excluded men and "had no AIM, beyond fun and laughter. One of its 'Regulations' required . . . an 'original composition,' to be read aloud and commented upon at the meeting." When this became too burdensome, the women occasionally enlisted the aid of the men, but "the masculine effusions were apt to be too classical, too full of Thalia and Melpomene, and side-saddles upon Pegasus." [32]

Slightly preceding the Queen of Clubs, the Newport Athenaeum and Reading Room was founded on December 12, 1853; the names of both Wymberley Jones and George Noble Jones were on the list of the forty-four original stockholders. Books and magazines were available for the members, as were billiard tables, playing cards, and backgammon and chess boards. There were, however, stern rules against wagering more than $5 on any game of billiards or cards. One Newport woman conjectured that the Reading Room's actual purpose was as "a refuge for men, where they [were] safe from female intrusion." [53]

On numerous occasions, of course, Wymberley, Mary, and others socialized together. Young married couples particularly enjoyed riding, and at the George Noble Jones cottage there was a love of amateur theatricals. There were also excursions to New York City for entertainment, including the opera. Historian and Newport friend George Bancroft reported seeing Mrs. Wymberley Jones at the Academy of Music at a performance of Bellini's *Norma*, "radiant in loveliness and beauty," inspiring Madame Grisi and Signor Mario "to do their best." William Brown Hodgson and others gave "grand banquets" at such hotels as the Atlantic House (the favorite stopping place of the southern enclave), and there were balls and "hops" as well in the ballrooms of the great hotels such as the Ocean House. [54]

Despite the attractions of Newport, the decade of the 1850s was the period when Wymberley Jones's life centered at Wormsloe, though his progress toward becoming an actual planter there was slow and reluctant. From 1838 through 1848, while the estate of Dr. George Jones was being administered by George Noble Jones and Wymberley was being educated in the North, the slaves at Wymberley's legacies of Poplar Grove and Wormsloe had been employed mainly in producing cotton and provision crops. The plantation's annual net incomes for the period were low, very far behind the sums being produced by the estate's lucrative properties in Savannah. [55]

In 1849, when Wymberley came into possession of his thirty-five slaves, he had three additional slave houses and a servants' hall built at Wormsloe, where his mother held a life tenancy. But he made no move to continue cotton planting; instead, Wormsloe's seventy dairy cattle provided the only income, annually producing for sale about $150 worth of butter and calves from 1850 through 1853. During the same period, Poplar Grove, most of whose slaves had been sold when the estate of Dr. Jones had been settled, produced a small annual crop of provisions for sale (and for consumption by the slaves), including corn, peas, potatoes, and watermelons; timber and sheep were sold as well.[56]

The best that could be said of the farming and livestock operations on the two plantations, however, was that they helped sustain the slave corps and that they usually turned a small profit. But this profit dwindled steadily from around $700 in 1850 to a loss in 1852, then to little more than a gain of $150 in 1853. That same year the profit from one of Jones's inherited town properties alone exceeded the total profits of both plantations from 1850 to 1853. Admittedly "averse to agriculture," Jones placed the plantations' operations in the hands of a part-time, nonresident overseer. The young owner's lengthy summer sojourns in the North, as well as his time in Europe, caused him to "neglect [his] plantation affairs even more."[57]

Beginning in 1854, the year after the birth of his son, Wymberley began to view Wormsloe as his home rather than as a winter residence and to take more interest in the estate as a plantation. He moved his library to Wormsloe in 1854 and the same year spent the entire summer there for the first time in his life (though Mary did not forsake Newport). And apparently for the first time, he took part in the semiannual ritual of distributing clothing to his slaves, which always marked the beginning of the summer and winter seasons.[58]

In 1857, through the sad fact of his mother's death of pneumonia in Philadelphia, Wormsloe became his alone. He was at the plantation when word came to him and reproached himself as an inattentive son; he felt he had devoted too much of his time to business and planting affairs in recent years and not enough time to his mother. His aunts attempted, with little success, to console him. They pointed out that his mother had forbidden them to bother him with news of her illness—that his place was with his wife and young Wymberley; thoughts of the child had cheered her last days. The Smith aunts also assured him that his mother had been "ripe for heaven" and that her deathbed, like young Leta's, had been very inspiring and "instructive." Wymberley searched out the date of his mother's death in his plantation journal. It had otherwise been a day of no incident; there was no notation except for the temperature, 44° at 8 A.M. Around the date, January 14, he scratched a broad black box in ink.[59]

The news of his mother's death coincided almost exactly with an event he had awaited with pleasant anticipation: the sale of his first cotton crop. The previous year, 1856, Wymberley had studied the yields of Wormsloe from 1838 to 1848 and found that the cotton crops had annually grossed almost $800 on an expenditure of $250, a reasonable return. After conferring with other planters, including George Noble Jones and William Brown Hodgson, he decided to "abandon Poplar Grove," partially because of "its proximity to town"; instead, he determined to rent it out and to gather all of his slaves at Wormsloe, erecting there "suitable plantation buildings for cotton-planting" and other purposes. Much of the construction occurred in 1856 and 1857, using bricks and lumber brought by water from Savannah and carpenters from the town as well: principally two free men of color, Prince Golding and Bruno Deziray. To accommodate Amos Henderson, his first full-time overseer, a house and kitchen were built near the slave quarters, and also constructed were a gin house, cotton house, mill house, well house, pea barn, and poultry house, along with stabling for horses, mules, and cows.[40]

Soon Wymberley had six more slave houses constructed — two single-family and four double-family dwellings. Some of these were to house the "Savage negroes" — slaves who had once belonged to Mary's uncle William Savage and had been destined to come to her at her mother's death. Though they had been part of the work force at George Noble Jones's Florida plantations, he had decided to reduce his planting interests and offered to send Mary these twenty-seven slaves, as well as two that she owned "in her own right." On receiving the offer in early 1856, Wymberley responded that, though he knew "little of negroes and less of cotton-planting," he would "receive them with pleasure." Anything they made "would go simply to augment Mary's pin-money," for he intended "not to benefit in any way by either the income or the principal of her property."[41]

In the mid-1850s, then, the bibliophile became a planter in more than name, and for half a dozen years, Wymberley devoted much of his energy and many of his thoughts to his agricultural pursuits. Nonetheless, he continued to read widely, to add books to his library, and to enjoy visits at Wormsloe from such congenial friends as Israel Tefft, Dr. Richard Arnold, and William Brown Hodgson. Despite his initial reluctance, he pursued planting with increasing enthusiasm, drawn by the almost mystical pleasure of producing crops from seeds planted in ancestral fields. His pride and delight were evident in journal entries such as one recorded during his first summer on the plantation: "Wormsloe, 28 July [1854], corn stalk 14 ft. high, 5 1/2 inches in circumference."[42]

There is no mystery as to why the printing of quartos was suspended while he was engaged in planting at Wormsloe. In the summer of 1855, Peter Force received a letter from young Jones, requesting his aid in securing something other than books on Georgia's history: he wanted instead the series of agricultural reports printed by the commissioner of patents. Jones explained, "Since the printing of Sargent's Diary of the Campaign of 1791, I have not been able to find material for another 'Wormsloe quarto' and in the mean time, am occupying myself in agricultural experiments." The "mean time" would be lengthy; over two decades would pass before he again ventured into printing.[43]

The change from printing to planting seems a jarring one indeed, and the explanation Jones offered seems incomplete. It does, of course, make sense that a young gentleman of fortune would want to occupy himself more thoroughly, not only to stave off ennui but to make himself "useful" as well. He may also have been committing himself to southern civilization as Hodgson saw it: a world with a lettered and leisured aristocracy at the apex of a pyramid supported by the broad base of plantation agriculture, characterized by two vital elements, "*continuous* labor" and "*small compensation.*"[44]

A further spur, however, was probably his intention to provide a fuller patrimony for his growing family, which was increased with the addition of a second son, Everard, in 1857 and the birth of a daughter, Letitia, three years later. But money from Wormsloe's crops would never make a vital contribution toward maintaining the Jones fortune. Instead, it was other investments, in property and stocks, that made his "agricultural experiments" possible, for his other ventures produced 95 percent of his annual income. In an indirect way, however, he was providing a patrimony of a different type: he loved Wormsloe, and it had been his father's wish (as well as his grandfather's and his great-grandfather's) that Wormsloe be held and maintained by his posterity; it would be difficult to foster a love for Wormsloe in his own children if they never lived there.[45]

Another reason is probably found in his reaction to one of his own legacies: if he were to keep his slaves, they should not be idle. In any case, he wrote to George Noble Jones in early 1856: "I shall plant cotton with my own people here this year for the first time—of course, like a genuine planter, have plenty of hope—and can give excellent reasons (based too upon *figures!*) why I *ought* to make a crop. But there is so wide a difference between seed just bought and cotton just sold —between seed-time and harvest—that I do not venture to calculate upon results until they are accomplished, nor count my bales before they are packed. At all events, 'twill give me occupation, and the place will be kept up—whether it helps to keep me up or not." [46]

Results of the first year of cotton planting were somewhat discouraging. The twenty-five bushels of cotton seed (costing $62) that his slaves planted produced a crop that when ginned and packed into nine bags equaled 2,295 pounds of white Sea Island cotton, with an additional 315-pound bag of stained cotton. With the white cotton bringing 50¢ a pound (the highest amount he would ever get) and the stained 15¢, Jones's first crop grossed $1,194.75. Though this was well above the average gross at Wormsloe for 1838–48, it was below the average number of bags produced during those years: 11⁷⁄₁₁. He also noted with some disappointment in his journal that the "amount of clean cotton in 100 lbs. of dry seed-cotton was only 20 lbs., and the product of clean cotton per acre was but 41 lbs.—attributable to drought and a storm." [47]

This was indeed a "miserable yield," as he termed it, but it was only his first attempt. Over the next several years, he steadily improved his output of cotton, from 3,979 pounds in 1857 to 7,056 pounds the next year, and 1859 was best year of all: 10,155 pounds produced, for 135 pounds per acre. This last was in the average range for Sea Island cotton plantations, normally 120 to 150 pounds per acre. Every crop other than 1859's, however, produced a below-average yield because cotton seems never to have been grown on less than 55 or more than 75 acres at Wormsloe during the 1850s. [48]

The Wormsloe cotton crops of 1856–60 sold for an average of $1,900, which Wymberley thought satisfactory. Obviously, each of the crops could have failed entirely and had little effect on his financial well-being: cotton planting to him was essentially an avocation, never a livelihood. But there seems no doubt that cotton would have been produced at Wormsloe as long as slavery lasted because he continued to expand and improve his operations. In 1859, for example, Wymberley purchased four additional field hands, and in 1860 he exchanged his horse-powered gin for an expensive steam-driven model. [49]

Wymberley's fascination with cotton culture was enduring; long after he had sold his last bag of cotton he continued to gather information on Georgia's great staple crop, and he found evidence in England of its cultivation as far back in time as Oglethorpe's colony. But he also got great satisfaction from the edible produce of Wormsloe, including the stock and poultry he raised (and tried to improve by bringing in Newport cocks, Newport bulls, and Spanish merino rams). There was also natural bounty: fish and oysters from the marsh-flanked tidal river, with its scent of salt and sulfur. And in the fields, he made numerous experiments with food crops, particularly corn, including such varieties as Wyandot, Maryland white, and Rhode Island yellow flint.[50]

He had a lively appreciation of the productivity of his plantation, as he noted at Thanksgiving time in 1856: "We have of eatables—the produce of this place—this month, the following: oysters, crabs, shrimp, fish (whiting), wild ducks, turkeys, chickens, eggs, milk, butter, English walnuts, hickory nuts, persimmons, pomegranates, hominy, sweet potatoes, Irish potatoes, tanyahs, turnips, carrots, beets, cow peas, Lima beans, egg plant, tomatoes, okra, peppers, lettuce, spinach, besides benne & arrowroot, and syrup from the Chinese sugar cane—to say nothing of cabbage & pumpkins. We had also as fine a *watermelon* as I ever tasted on the 11th of this month."[51]

Wymberley Jones was also closely attuned to the natural beauty of his portion of the Isle of the Hope and to the rhythms of the seasons. He recorded the simple pleasures of witnessing the greening of his willows in February, the return of the swallows in April, and the blooming of yellow jasmine in December. Days in June could be faultless: "cool, not a sand fly or musquito or nuisance of any sort—high tide, the blue water fringed by green meadow." But not all days were so benign. Summer air was normally hot and heavy with moisture, and the house held the strong odor of camphor melting to ward off biting insects. There were violent thunderstorms, with hailstones "as big as strawberries," and winter squalls that threw snow thickly against Wormsloe House; the mercury would plummet, pipes would burst, and panes of ice would form in the creeks at the Isle of Hope causeway. Like other planters, Wymberley had a passion for the thermometer and recorded the temperatures each morning and evening, noting whether a fire had been necessary in the house. Use of a fireplace was not always required, as a notation for 7:00 on an August morning indicates: "85°!"[52]

Wormsloe House itself was a source of pride and pleasure. Over the years the simple cottage erected by Dr. George Jones had grown into a commodious, somewhat austere Greek Revival mansion, rising three wooden stories over a tabby-walled basement. Although his father's house had faced the river, the expanded structure faced north toward Skidaway Road and entirely enveloped the original house; the cottage's forty-foot front had become the narrow side of a rambling structure whose face stretched almost seventy feet in length. The first floor had double parlors separated by a wide hall from the dining room and its adjoining spacious pantry; in the southwest corner, a large study contained Wymberley's desk and bookcases. Bedrooms for family, guests, and servants occupied the upper floors. As a convenience for enjoying the view of the oaks and willows and palmettos—along with the transplanted Deodar cedars and Cherokee roses—and as a cool refuge on warm days, a piazza was constructed to run the length of the back of the house.[53]

Looking south from the piazza in the direction of the "Old Fort," Jones could see the screen of trees that hid the slave quarters, separated from the house by several hundred yards and a bridged creek. No doubt the people there had a vastly different perspective on Wormsloe than did the family in the big house, but they could not have been unaware of the beauties of their surroundings and shared to some extent in the bounty of Wormsloe; they were almost as much a part of the plantation's traditions as the tabby ruins, for Noble Jones had brought his first seven slaves to Wormsloe in 1750. Frustrated at their inability to produce a profit at Wormsloe, Jones had requested and received other land grants—rice acreage on the Ogeechee—and the land policy of the day had encouraged him to buy more slaves, for the more slaves a landowner had, the more land he could get.[54]

In the time of Noble Jones's great-grandson, Wymberley Jones, Wormsloe Plantation's work force seems to have averaged around forty field hands, and some two hundred acres were planted in a variety of crops. The cultivated land at Wormsloe consisted of four main fields, whose sandy gray soil was annually enriched with thousands of pounds of Peruvian guano. Just northeast of the front of the residence was the "Creek Field"; the "Palmetto Field" was farther north toward Skidaway Road. South of Wormsloe House, near the ruins of Noble Jones's fortified residence, was the "Fort Field," below which was the largest of the fields, the 75¼-acre "Point Field," which the slaves normally worked for cotton, while the other fields were planted with corn, cowpeas, sweet potatoes, and groundnuts. Other open land provided pasturage for cattle and sheep, horses and mules.[55]

The quarters that awaited the slaves at the end of their day were single and double cabins, raised from the ground as was recommended (some by brick "underpinnings"), with fireplaces and glazed windows. The women were tasked with keeping the cabins clean, and Wymberley rewarded those who were the best housekeepers by giving them extra clothing, looking glasses, and furniture. For a time, he tried to increase the slaves' productivity in the fields with a money reward to the overseer for increases in cotton gathered. This did not seem to work, so Wymberley began offering presents to the field hands, normally quantities of herring. Their regular diet, like that of most slaves, ran heavily to pork, whether bacon or middlings, and was supplemented from the plantation's provision gardens and fields.[56]

Clothing and medical care for Wormsloe's slaves was typical for the region. "Negro cloth"—coarse osnaburgs—clothed both men and women, and they received new clothing twice a year. In the warmer months straw hats were also distributed, and shoes and blankets were handed out as winter approached. The physician responsible for maintaining the slaves' health was the same one who cared for the Jones family: Dr. Phineas M. Kollock.[57]

Wymberley Jones seems never to have committed to paper his precise thoughts on slavery, although, once the slaves had been freed, he aided them in material ways. His initial aversion to becoming a planter may or may not have had anything to do with a disinclination to own slaves. There is no evidence, however, that he had any powerful political or intellectual commitment to slavery. He cast no votes during the 1850s, as the slave question loomed ever larger and as such friends as Hodgson and acquaintances like James Henry Hammond became more active in championing slavery.[58]

Jones's library contained little to suggest his attitude on slavery. It had no copies of such polemics as *The Pro-Slavery Argument* and only two books bearing on the controversies of the time. One related to the illegal slave trade—*Captain Canot; or Twenty Years of an African Slaver*—and was a late addition to his library. Based on the embroidered memoirs of Theodore Canot, it did, however, have an agenda. Aside from Canot's adventures, the book pictured the Middle Passage as an "Atlantidean idyll," with slaves frequently allowed up on deck to take the air and dance gaily. The man responsible for its publication "believed that the Abolitionists were insane . . . and liked to think that the problem of slavery could gradually be solved by shipping the negroes to Africa." Jones's library also contained an ethnological defense of slavery, Samuel George Morton's *Crania Ægyptiaca*, but its pres-

ence on the shelves may have had more to do with William Brown Hodgson's enthusiastic promotion of the book than any deep personal interest on
Wymberley's part. Opposing views of slavery appeared in some of Jones's
books, including Bishop Samuel Wilberforce's contention that the "curse"
of slavery was a "degradation" to both master and slave because it used
"persons as things" and treated "redeemed men as soul-less chattels." [59]

Jones's chattels, like the slaves of other masters, represented both labor
and capital. But unlike most masters, he kept the bulk of his capital in real
estate, with a sizable portion in bank and railroad stocks (particularly of the
Central of Georgia Railroad). These investments produced most of his income. Just as slave owning was part of the legacy of his family's founder, so
was ownership of Savannah riverfront property; some of it Wymberley inherited, other parcels he bought, such as wharf property purchased in 1849
that had belonged to Noble Jones. He bought real estate in other sections of
the city as well and took pains to maintain and improve what he owned, displaying a civic concern that his mercantile properties be creditable to him
and to the city. Rents from his wharves and warehouses on the river, along
with other commercial properties on or adjacent to Bay Street, contributed
the largest share of his income, over 50 percent. By 1860 he was in the top
2 percent of Savannah's real estate owners, having in ten years increased the
value of his property from just over $41,000 to just below $88,000. [60]

But he would learn unambiguously several times during his life that
preservation of such tangible symbols of his family's heritage as Wormsloe
depended in great part on the existence of a family fortune. In 1857 he experienced the first in a series of incidents that showed him that those who
had more acres than dollars would be at risk of losing their land.

The road that ran past Wormsloe was called Skidaway Road for a reason;
it led to a ferry that provided access to Skidaway Island. The island had been
partially owned by the Jones family during the 1700s—Noble Jones and his
son Inigo, in particular, had for a time held part of the island's acreage—
though of the early settlers John Milledge was most closely associated with
the island; his plantation Modena had occupied its northern acres. [61]

In nature's scheme, Skidaway, like outlying Wassaw Island, helped protect Wormsloe, forming a barrier between the Isle of Hope and storms that
swept in from the Atlantic. In man's scheme, however, Skidaway would
from the first be more of a threat to Wormsloe than a blessing. Once Skidaway's settlers took the island from nature, they came to see the southern

half of the Isle of Hope mainly as a docking point for their boats, a ferry crossing point, or a bridgehead to provide convenient access to Skidaway Island.[62]

Only a few years after the death of Noble Jones, Wormsloe's privacy had been invaded by Skidaway residents, who, "greatly to the annoyance and incommodity" of those at the plantation, found it convenient to use Jones Point—the southern tip of the Isle of Hope—as a landing place, as it had been during the Spanish War. Temporarily, the ferry from the end of Skidaway Road had not been in operation. But once ferry service resumed, James Bulloch (husband of Noble Jones's daughter Mary) placed a notice in the Savannah newspaper warning the islanders that such trespassing would no longer be tolerated.[63]

Among Wymberley's earliest purchases of land had been the two 62½-acre tracts through which Skidaway Road entered the Isle of Hope. These parcels had been part of his grandfather's Wimberly Plantation, more than 480 acres north of and adjacent to Wormsloe. By 1852 he had reclaimed through purchase a total of around 250 acres—over half of Wimberly—so that almost all of Skidaway Road passed through his property to reach the ferry point, located on a promontory that now was also his. In 1856, he purchased Long Island, a marsh-bound islet east of Wormsloe (formerly the property of Noble Jones) to which the ferry ran and from which a short bridge led to Skidaway. These additional tracts increased both his acreage and his privacy on the Isle of Hope.[64]

In 1857, however, the islanders determined to construct a bridge from the Isle of Hope to Long Island to give access to Skidaway and decided that the best route for the road to the bridge would be through Wormsloe, to a point south of the residence. This would have made Wormsloe all but untenable as a family estate. Wymberley noted that, given his plantation's long and narrow shape, "the proposed road, running nearly through its whole length, would greatly injure its value by the quantity of fencing required to enclose the long narrow strip of land—to say nothing of the damage to a plantation of being cut up by a thoroughfare, or the nuisance to a private residence of having its privacy destroyed."[65]

The islanders argued that the public's right and necessity had a superior claim over private property rights. But Wymberley asserted that the road was not for the benefit of the public but for the convenience of "half-a-dozen" Skidaway residents. " '*The public*,' " he wrote, "are not concerned in the matter: the point at issue is, Can a man's property be taken from him, without his consent, by *private individuals?*" Had Wymberley not had the money to employ adequate legal counsel, the answer might not have been to his liking, but he prevailed in his case, and Wormsloe was safe for the time being. The matter would surface again in his time, however, and in that of his children and their children's children. The islanders, for their part, subscribed to have an eleven-hundred-foot bridge constructed to Long Island from the ferry site. It was built there from April to July 1857 and opened with much fanfare.[66]

Only a few years later, Wormsloe was threatened much more seriously, far beyond what legal counsel could remedy, for the plantation became the site of military operations between elements of two great powers.

The southern world of Wymberley Jones's youth and early manhood was destined to be swept away by forces that he only partially understood. He could see no reason why the social and economic structure of the Georgia that he had always known could not continue to exist. Like Noble Jones a man of substance and, unsurprisingly, of conservative thought, he realized that any sudden, radical change to his accustomed world would have a destructive effect on the fortunes of those such as himself. But he and Mary had little idea of how likely and how imminent was a convulsion in the country's social, economic, and political systems. Their half-years spent in the North gave them no inkling of how close the storm was to breaking, probably because their northern acquaintances were as conservative and insulated as they were. A few months after the war ended, Mary took up her pen and attempted to describe the republic as the two of them had seen it just before the cataclysm. But she found herself unequal to the task of concluding her narrative by revisiting in her mind those wartime scenes that had affected her so strongly.[67]

Nonetheless, her fragmentary recollections gave insight into the couple's opinions on the momentous issues of 1860 – 61. The secession of the various states, she noted, was a move they "regretted deeply, having friends and interests in both sections, and being in the habit of dividing the year between them. We felt no wrongs," she wrote, "and sought no redress, such as might not have been obtained in the Halls of Congress, had the Southern members but held together, and by voting in unison made themselves a powerful minority." Having stated their opposition to secession, however, she added that she and her husband were convinced of the *right* of secession, and she found a powerful argument for it in the opening words of the Declaration of Independence.[68]

Likewise, they had a low regard for Abraham Lincoln's objective of forcing the seceded states back into the Union: "A baser or more tyrannical act has never been committed in ancient or in modern times." Indignation over this coercion, coupled with "interest to protect the bulk of [their] property," led (or "compelled," as Mary termed it) the Joneses to side with their seceded state. Nonetheless, they thought the Confederate leaders misguided in their action at Fort Sumter; the bombardment, she wrote, was a "fatal mistake," a "cowardly" action given the inferior numbers of the enemy garrison. The firing on Sumter, she asserted, put the Confederacy "in the wrong" and "allowed the enemy to say that we began the war."[69]

Though much of Confederate Georgia would be safe from enemy incursions for months or, in some cases, years, it was plain from the start that the Georgia coast and its major port city would be vulnerable targets of Union naval forces. Wormsloe, situated as it was between two of the major water approaches to Savannah, was hardly less strategic than it had been during the time of Noble Jones and was, as it happened, much more in harm's way. After the outer defenses of Savannah (including batteries on Skidaway Island) had been completed, Wormsloe became part of the inner line of defense.[70]

In the northeast corner of the plantation, flanking Skidaway Road, battery emplacements were prepared to protect the long bridge that connected Skidaway to the mainland. And when in 1862 the "New Exit," a makeshift alternate bridge for the Skidaway troops, was constructed, it stretched from Long Island to Wormsloe, to a point south of the residence. Further southward at Jones Point, massive earthworks were constructed to help guard the approach from the Vernon River, and their guns repulsed probing Federal gunboats on at least one occasion. From the early days of the war, when the white tents of the Chatham Artillery sprang up at Captain Joseph Claghorn's Wymberly Plantation, to the final months, when a siege train was kept in readiness to haul artillery to a variety of vulnerable points, the Isle of Hope would be an armed camp.[71]

Whether Wormsloe's master would become a soldier was never seriously in question. Poor health decisively overruled any such consideration. Though thirty-four in April 1862 — when the First Conscription Act sought to gather white males between eighteen and thirty-five into the Confederate army—Wymberley had already been found unfit to serve. Two doctors had given certificates of disability in March 1862, and other certificates were issued in April and November of the same year; an official certificate of exemption followed in September 1863.[72]

Chronic nephritis was his major ailment. The first stage of the disease apparently began in the early 1850s and time only increased its severity. For the remainder of his life, Wymberley was intermittently but increasingly an invalid, "often unable to give proper attention to [his] private affairs." Consequently, his major contribution to the Confederate war effort was making monetary donations to such local military organizations as the Coast Rifles.[73]

In one extraordinary instance, however, Wymberley did temporarily volunteer, under circumstances that would make it impossible for him and his family to continue living at Wormsloe. While summering in Greenville, South Carolina, like many other low-country refugees, the Joneses received news of the Battle of Manassas, which they considered "more to [the] credit" of the Confederate forces than the attack on Sumter, as well as "an everlasting shame to the army of the U.S." But soon after they returned to the coast in the fall of 1861, the Joneses found that the war was almost literally on their doorstep. The calamity came upon them suddenly. Forty miles northeast of Savannah, the Union fleet bombarded the Confederate works protecting strategic Port Royal Sound, shaking Wormsloe House "from cellar to garret." These cannonades, wrote Mary, "were the signal guns of distress, and the ship of our peace and prosperity went down to the sound of them."[74]

Panic spread through Savannah, whose citizens feared that the city would surely be captured, despite its ring of fortifications. Wymberley "resolved on the spot" to send Mary, then expecting their fourth child, into the interior with their young sons and daughter, her "Infantry," as she called them. They made up part of an anxious crowd swelling the Savannah train station but were soon traveling toward safety in Augusta. Mary was preoccupied, however, with those she had left behind, particularly a weak and ailing husband determined to help defend Savannah and, if fate allowed, to "endeavor to save and send" to Augusta some of their belongings. "I can never forget the last time I saw my home," Mary wrote, "and the dreary afternoon upon which I left it for a nine mile drive to the city to take the train, and the agony of the moment when I parted from my husband and Father, and left them to meet I knew not what danger."[75]

The Federals made no direct attempt to take Savannah at the time, but for the remainder of the war, the Joneses would make their home in a succession of hotels, except for those periods that they spent at Oaklands, the plantation of George Noble Jones near Louisville. The Planters Hotel accommodated them in Augusta, where the Jones family had long had property interests and where such relations as the Campbell family lived. In April 1862, the Joneses' third son and last child was born in Augusta, and his cherubic beauty immediately captivated Mary Telfair, who, with her sister Margaret and brother-in-law William Brown Hodgson, was always part of the Joneses' circle. The infant Kentwyn resembled "one of Raphael's angels," Miss Telfair wrote, "—such beautiful dark blue eyes and mouth, with a dimple in his right cheek, and a skin fair as the unsunned lily that opens near the rill. If babies could be sold at auction, I should be the highest bidder for him. He is really too lovely for earth."[76]

Mary Telfair (and probably Mary Jones) was less impressed with Augusta—"not an aristocratic place"—and felt that it suffered from a surfeit of democracy, not to mention the fact that its leading men seemed mainly to be shopkeepers. She was more in her element at Flat Rock, North Carolina (long a summer refuge for low-country grandees), where on at least one occasion she was hostess to Mary Jones, visiting from nearby Greenville.[77]

This South Carolina town, nestled in the foothills of the Blue Ridge, came to be as much of a home to the Jones family as any during the war, for they spent the summer months of 1861, 1862, and 1863 there (and there the older Jones children, "Wymbey" and "Evey" received their earliest education). The family lived at the Mansion House, a three-story brick hotel that had long been a resort for wealthy travelers and—because of its position in the center of town near the courthouse—lawyers and politicians as well (John C. Calhoun had favored Room 92). Famous for its tiled lobby, winding staircases, and superior dining room (as well as the crystal chandelier that drew gawkers to the bar), the Mansion House also had a spacious parlor that "extended the whole depth of the building," requiring "the unique feature of having two fireplaces." The hotel was obviously a pleasant retreat. Moreover, Greenville was readily accessible by rail from Savannah, and—nestled as it was in the foothills of the Blue Ridge, with the Saluda Mountains rising in the near distance—offered a much more healthy climate than the Georgia coast.[78]

When his health permitted, Wymberley stayed on the coast, managing his properties in Savannah and the affairs at Wormsloe, where the slaves were now farming four hundred acres, profitably producing food crops (principally corn and peas) and hay (some of which was supplied to the local artillerists for their teams). Commanding the loyalty of the slave force seems to have been less a problem than securing a dependable overseer, but despite problems with supervision, the plantation netted $20,000 Confederate in 1863 alone because of the rise in prices for farm products. But because of "the derangement of the currency and of all values," Wymberley did not bother to make out full accounts for the period 1861–65. His Savannah rents, for example, "were reduced one half nominally; but being paid in Confederate currency, really amounted to almost nothing." Since neither proceeds from his northern investments nor financial help from the Smiths was available to him, however, every dollar mattered.[79]

If Wymberley had not removed his library to safety at the time of the Port Royal affair, he surely must have done so in March 1862, when the Confederates abandoned the Skidaway works and Union troops reconnoitered on the island. The next month, Fort Pulaski was captured, ending Savannah's importance as a Confederate port. It also ended any chance of shipping the library to safety; most of it remained stored at R. Habersham and Sons on the riverfront. Other boxes of books, together with manuscripts and heirlooms, were sent up the Central of Georgia Railroad and hauled to George Noble Jones's Oaklands Plantation near Louisville.[80]

Unlike some of their friends and relatives, Wymberley and Mary made no attempt to travel to Europe to wait out the war, apparently because of poor health and the necessity of seeing to his business affairs—or a simple determination to stay in their country. They decided, however, to send young Wymberley, then ten, through the blockade to Mary's mother to be schooled on the Continent like his Jones cousins.[81]

The three younger children stayed with their parents, sharing their nomadic existence. In late 1864, they had apparently planned to be far out of harm's way in the solitude of El Destino in Florida. But for whatever reason, Wymberley and his family chose instead to stay with George Noble

Jones at Oaklands, where, in late November, they found themselves in the path of Union general W. T. Sherman's left wing in late November. Other than calling November 28, 1864, "one of the most terrible days of my life," Mary left no record of what happened, but the combination of fear, miserably cold weather, and a pillaging army on the march, fresh from its occupation of Georgia's capital at Milledgeville, must have been terrible indeed.[82]

In early 1865, not having seen Wymberley since the Savannah Campaign began, William Brown Hodgson wrote to Washington Smith, giving a brief account of what had happened to his nephew and his family at Oaklands. Upon reaching George Noble Jones's plantation, Hodgson reported, Union general Judson Kilpatrick's cavalry "burned all his cotton, took off his Horses & Mules, and ransacked his house." More damage probably would have been done but for the timely arrival of Rebel cavalrymen. They skirmished with the Federals near the plantation house and maintained an active presence in the area for several days. With some understatement, Hodgson commented that "Wymberley & his family must have been agitated."[83]

As often happened along the line of Sherman's march, many of the Oaklands slaves followed the columns marching toward Savannah. As the Federal army closed on the town on 19 December, the Confederates evacuated their Isle of Hope line and joined the other Rebel troops the next night, while Confederate general W. J. Hardee's tiny army escaped from Savannah. Among the relatively infrequent acts of looting by the Union soldiery that rushed into the city the next day was "the sack of Habersham's store," as Wymberley later termed the incident, and the destruction or theft of his books stored there. Hodgson, knowing how grieved Wymberley would be over losing his "rare & valuable library," tried to recover as many of the books as he could, but his efforts met with little success. And though the remainder of the library had escaped destruction in November, many books—along with historical manuscripts, valuable autographs, and several family heirlooms—would be lost four months later in an unexplained fire at the Jefferson County plantation.[84]

As Federal garrisons were sent to Savannah's outlying fortifications, Wormsloe underwent pillaging similar to that visited on Oaklands. Though the circumstances are unclear, the furniture at Wormsloe and most of the family silver were lost, and a certain amount of vandalism was carried out by Federal troops at Wormsloe House, including the defacement of the fine marble mantels in the house's parlors. As a reminder of the turmoil of the war, the mantels were never repaired.[85]

With Confederate defeat all but an accomplished fact, it became a point of great concern whether Wormsloe would be lost. In January 1865, while Wymberley was still at Oaklands, Sherman's Special Field Order No. 15 was issued. It provided the procedure for transferring plantation land along the Georgia coast to the freed slaves, giving them parcels on the rice plantations in the tidewater regions, as well as on the sea islands—a "*mauvaise plaisanterie*," thought Hodgson. He believed the freedmen incapable of "settling such places" and asserted that Sherman had "destroyed but cannot restore [a social order] or introduce a Substitute."[86]

Only a small part of Wormsloe seemed at risk since most of the plantation—because of its location on the Isle of Hope (actually a mainland peninsula) and its character as a cotton rather than a rice plantation—were not within the terms of the order. The Long Island portion of the plantation, however, was surrounded by saltwater. Consequently, during the period between April and August 1865, the island was split into plots of from twenty to forty acres and divided among four freedmen: Charles Steele, Prince Jackson, Bristol Drayton, and Linnius Howell.[87]

Striking into the Carolinas from Savannah in January 1865, Sherman left behind him a military garrison with orders not to allow the city's inhabitants to communicate with anyone outside the city; those who entered occupied Savannah from the Confederacy had to stay, and those who left for the Confederacy were forbidden to return. The Joneses, observed Hodgson in 1865, were better off where they were because the plantation at least provided such necessities as firewood, whereas in Savannah, chilblains and "raw food" were as common as wood was scarce. The same month a much-feared eventuality came to pass: black troops became part of the Savannah garrison. Even had there been no privation in Savannah, however, two other circumstances would have kept the Joneses where they were. An invalid, "much confined to bed" by this time, Wymberley would have encountered difficulty traveling. And although he and his family would have been permitted to travel to Philadelphia from Savannah, they had "no resources" for traveling.[88]

But as Hodgson wrote to Washington Smith, there was, despite present

discomfort and anxieties about the future, one consolation: "You will recollect that when all the evils flew out of Pandora's Box, Hope alone remained
for Humanity. That is all that is now left, and so, we hope for Peace."[89]

By April, peace came into sight when the Confederate armies surren-
dered, and during the first week of May, war governor Joseph E. Brown sur-
rendered himself and the Georgia state forces to General James Harrison
Wilson. Of the principal cities of Georgia, Augusta had been the least damaged by the war; it was there that the Joneses went when Wymberley could
travel, and there that Wymberley swore his oath of allegiance to the victo-
rious U.S. government. Under President Andrew Johnson's recently issued
amnesty proclamation, Wymberley was presumed to be in the thirteenth
exception: those of the propertied class who had holdings worth more than
$20,000, a category that—according to the latest tax rolls—included him
and more than twelve thousand fellow Georgians. He and many others no
doubt questioned what they were worth, given their losses and the unprecedented instability created by military conquest and emancipation. But they
had been caught up in the "twenty-thousand-dollar dragnet" that President
Johnson intended to use to punish the planter class.[90]

By mid-June Wymberley was finally back in Savannah, attempting to
salvage or preserve as much of his property as possible. There was much
confusion, frequent "depredations," and "the peril of famine and anarchy."
Just the previous month a petition had been addressed to the president de-
crying the lawless state of Chatham County: it was feared that a crop could
not be raised because of the turmoil, which was in danger of "terminating
in a destructive collision between the races." As far as anyone at the time
knew, all property could be confiscated then or later, and there was talk that
all former slave owners might have to subdivide portions of their land to
give homesteads to their former slaves. But Wymberley's property, though
not confiscated (with the exception of Long Island), was occupied by the authorities. Since March, Wormsloe had fortunately been in the temporary
occupation of someone Hodgson considered a "very good man," who would
take care of the plantation and try to raise a crop for the next season. Dealing with the provost court during June, Wymberley first succeeded in gain-
ing permission to rent Wormsloe and Poplar Grove and then was also given
the right to control his town property, though he had to pay legal costs for
repossession. Wormsloe, now with four hundred acres under cultivation,
was then rented to the firm of John W. Teeple and Robert T. Smillie, north-

erners both, in mid-June. But by the time Wymberley was able to leave for Philadelphia in early July, he had been forced to place "the persons occupying Wormsloe" under court order not to destroy property there.[91]

Postwar Philadelphia displayed a stark contrast to Savannah's poverty and continuing martial array: there was "untouched wealth and prosperity on every side," and the streets "were thronged with men in citizen's clothes and beaver hats." Uniformed soldiers appeared "seldom, if ever." At last, Wymberley was reunited with his uncle Washington Smith in the house on Clinton Street, where the Smith family had lived since 1848. There the old gentleman had been alone since the previous July, when Williamina Smith had died.[92]

One of Wymberley's first actions in Philadelphia was to apply to President Andrew Johnson on July 19, 1865, for a pardon. "[As] my property once did and may now exceed $20,000 in value," he wrote, "I am told that your pardon is necessary to enable me to acquire a proper legal status—and as we are assured that your intention is not to punish those who have been the victims not promoters of secession—I therefore solicit from you a pardon which may restore me to my former rights—declaring that it is my purpose hereafter to continue a quiet, law-abiding citizen—a course which the state of my health, as well as my inclination, binds me to." One must assume that Wymberley was indifferent to whether his political rights would be restored—he had not exercised them for some time before the war—but it was imperative that he have a pardon if he was to resume his "right to engage in normal business." Having heard nothing by August 28, he mailed Johnson a certified copy of his amnesty oath and again asked for a pardon, noting that he considered himself with the thirteenth exception only "by implication; contrary to the actual facts of the case." His pardon was issued on August 29, 1865, even before his second request arrived, for he had received the support of staunch Unionist and fellow Savannahian James Moore Wayne of the U.S. Supreme Court.[93]

Returning to Savannah in December, Wymberley began to arrange his affairs so that he could travel to Europe, where he had already sent his family. Among the pieces of business that engaged his attention was legally changing his surname, and those of his wife and children, to "De Renne," a European name for a new life in Europe. Perhaps, one day, the family could return. But he was uncertain what the social, economic, and political conditions of Savannah would be in the future, so complicated had the position of the South become. Into the roof of one of the trunks that traveled with him, Wymberley—now George Wymberley Jones De Renne—pasted a card on which he had transcribed some verses from *Punch*, dealing with the anom-alous situation of his state:

> *Says Johnson, to hold that the states of the South,*
> *Were e'er out of the Union is sin.*
> *Says Congress, Wa'al, guess if they never were out,*
> *There ain't no call for letting them in.*[94]

Wymberley and his family had been refugees throughout the war. They would continue to be refugees in the postbellum world until some hope arose that they could safely return to the country of their forebears.

CHAPTER 5

The Noblest Road

Dreams, books, are each a world; and
  books, we know,
Are a substantial world, both pure and
  good.
—WILLIAM WORDSWORTH

L eaving behind the wreck of the life he had known, G. W. J. De Renne traveled to the ancient French town of Montpellier. Its survival through centuries of war and turmoil offered him some consolation. Once, the town had been haven for a famous survivor of another civil war: the Earl of Clarendon had lived several happy years in Montpellier two centuries earlier, reflecting on his life as he wrote his autobiography. There, in the time-worn walled capital of the Languedoc region, De Renne could see numerous examples of survivals of the past, from the medieval cathedral, with its solemn stone faces peering down at observers, to the gallery of statues in the Jardin des Plantes. A major cultural center, Montpellier was famous for its medical university and other educational institutions, its excellent art museum (the Musée Fabre), and its salons. For many years a resort for invalids, particularly from England, the town offered a mild climate and an abundance of physicians, a wonderful combination for the ill. And there were many renowned hotels to accommodate sightseers, convalescents, and invalids.[1]

De Renne had relatives from both sides of his family in residence in and around Montpellier. Though his aunts had moved from the town after decades of living there, they were still nearby at their Château Mirabel. And after a time in Nice, the family of George Noble Jones had also found a haven in Montpellier and maintained a sunny apartment in the town, while the Jones children (along with young Wymberley De Renne) were educated there and in Switzerland and Germany.[2]

The town and its environs boasted multiple attractions and distractions as well. From its popular Promenade citizens and tourists enjoyed views of the surrounding hills, distant mountains, and—six miles south—the Mediterranean. Nearby were salubrious baths and springs, as well such interesting destinations for day trips as the old Roman town of Arles and historic Avignon. For those tired of culture and sightseeing, there were seats for viewing the town's many restful, decorative fountains and its placid pools with their gliding swans.[3]

For one as fascinated with the eighteenth century as was De Renne, there was much to stir interest, for many of the most prepossessing of Montpellier's buildings and monuments had been constructed in the 1700s, when France approached its own cataclysm. Emblematic of the ancien régime were a massive equestrian statue of the Sun King and a triumphal arch in his honor. Such features, along with mid-eighteenth-century additions like the city's magnificent *château d'eau* and the ornamental aqueduct that stretched across the valley to feed it, led Henry James to write in 1882 that the combination of attractions was "worthy of a capital, of a little court city. The whole place, with its repeated steps, its balustrades, its massive and plentiful stonework, is full of the air of the last century."[4]

Montpellier emphatically lent itself to reflection on the past, and it was here that Mary De Renne began the brief memoir of her war experiences, but her husband left no record of his own ruminations. Though his health was lost, never to be appreciably regained, his situation could have been much worse. He could have had nothing left but devastation, as was the case with many of his class in Georgia and in the South at large. Among his friends, Dr. John E. Holbrook of Charleston in particular had suffered much by the war, although losing "most of his fortune" was one of his lesser tragedies. His wife had died "toward the close of the Confederate war, broken-hearted at the ruin of her country." And during the Federal occupation of Charleston, Dr. Holbrook's specimen collections were discarded, his manuscripts destroyed, and his books stolen; he never recovered his fortune or his spirit. And not only southerners would be harrowed by the war. In Philadelphia, De Renne's old friend John Penington was all but broken by the conflict and its aftermath because so much of his trade had been with southern bibliophiles, many now dead or impoverished.[5]

Peter Force had lived in Abraham Lincoln's Washington during the war and had not lost his library, but the hostilities almost fatally complicated his negotiations, begun in 1859, to sell it. In 1867 the Library of Congress finally purchased Force's books for $100,000 and hauled them away in wagons. The process was "watched with careful interest" by Force, "who was left to his desolated shelves, and often lamented that he never again felt at home without his old companions around him." He died within a year, and over his grave his children placed a monument with a shelf of books carved on its face.[6]

Of all of De Renne's friends, Winthrop Sargent had been the closest, and the terrible misfortune the war had brought to him was difficult to contemplate. Even before the war, Sargent's life had been sad, resembling too much one of the gloomier passages from *A Bachelor's Reverie*. His wife of one year had died after giving birth to a son, and Sargent's own health soon slipped into an irreversible decline. Though Wymberley's own mischance in losing almost all of his books and manuscripts was a bitter one, and the depredations at Wormsloe and elsewhere were hard to absorb, Sargent had suffered a much more tragic visitation. After the Federal troops had taken Natchez, a party of plundering soldiers had broken into Gloster Place and shot Sargent's father on the stairs. He "lingered in great agony" before dying three days later. Sargent's grief-stricken mother was soon reunited with her husband in the family plot near the mansion, and Sargent himself was broken by the tragedy. His health shattered, he would die a consumptive's death in Europe in 1870; his great project of creating a *catalogue raisonne* of American historical works would never be completed.[7]

Wymberley's own health was an increasing concern, but his prosperity seemed less and less to be so—despite the uncertainties at Savannah—for, as the sole surviving heir of the children of Justice Thomas Smith, he stood to inherit a considerable fortune. But those riches would necessarily rob him of his remaining Smith relatives in Philadelphia and abroad. His bereavements began little more than a year after his arrival in Europe. His aunts, their health failing, had to leave their château and move closer to medical attention in Montpellier; there they took rooms at the Hôtel Nevet, a huge but hospitable establishment with "brown, labyrinthine corridors." Maria Campbell Stewart died there on January 30, 1867, aged eighty-two, and was followed a week later by her seventy-six-year-old sister, Juliana Smith. The black-bordered announcement of death noted that "Monsier Georges De Renne; Madame Georges De Renne et leurs enfants" were in Montpellier at the time. Wymberley and his uncle, who, with the assistance of George Noble Jones, would administer the sisters' French estate, had the two women buried side by side. They marked the grave with an ornate monument that displayed memorials to each on either side, accompanied by verses from Romans and the Revelation of St. John.[8]

With the generous bequests he received, along with the continuing profits from his investments and the steadily rising rental income from his Savannah properties, Wymberley could have used his time in Europe to begin collecting a new library similar to the one he had lost. For the rest of his life, however, he was seldom to purchase replacements for his vanished rarities; De Renne's postbellum collection held few volumes that would have won a second glance from Thomas Frognall Dibdin, and De Renne would not even replenish his assortment of the handsome nineteenth-century publications of William Pickering. In almost none of its categories would his new library approach his old one, and in only one subsection, that relating to Georgia history, would the new collection surpass the one he had lost.[9]

Ultimately, De Renne's decision not to attempt to recreate his destroyed collection was more a matter of the heart than the purse. He would not attempt to replace the irreplaceable: a collection that over decades, from his youth, had been gathered book by book and manuscript by manuscript, many accompanied by valuable memories. Though he would always surround himself with books, in both time and temperament he was far from the days of book-madness.

Ironically, had De Renne been as deeply engaged in collecting as earlier, the immediate postwar years would have been the perfect time for him to create a remarkably extensive library. Both Israel Tefft and Alexander Smets died during the war, and both of their collections—the one heavy with manuscripts and autographs, the other with printed rarities—made their way to the auction block in New York City in 1867 and 1868. When these books and manuscripts were brought to the hammer, they were in many cases sold at embarrassingly low prices and could easily have been secured by De Renne's agents while he was abroad, in the same fashion that they conducted his other business. But he seems to have made no move, even toward purchasing such particularly tempting volumes as those that Smets had owned that were associated with Horace Walpole, one of which included notes in Walpole's hand. Perhaps the decisive point was that the collections were the Tefft Collection and the Smets Collection: personal achievements that De Renne would not feel comfortable adding to his own shelves, particularly en bloc.[10]

But in collecting, De Renne's attraction to the history of his state remained undiminished, if not increased, during the postwar years. He continued to gather transcripts of original Georgia colonial sources, printed and manuscript, apparently beginning his researches in London in the waning months of 1866 and continuing during the 1870s. As always, he was fortunate that his interest in his family's heritage and his interests in Georgia as trust colony and royal province intertwined. Researching either, he frequently turned up information of interest on both. For printed materials, the British Museum's magnificent circular reading room awaited him, along with Americana purchased over several decades by Henry Stevens.[11]

De Renne was also fortunate that, since the state of Georgia and the Georgia Historical Society had first begun to gather records from the State Paper Office, it had been subsumed into the Public Record Office (PRO), which was increasingly enhancing the arrangement and accessibility of its records. The PRO's papers were stored in a massive mock-Tudor pile that overshadowed Lincoln's Inn Chapel, where Noble Jones had wed Sarah Hack. This mammoth government edifice was like a great fireproof hive; its unconnected seventeen-by-twenty-foot manuscript storage rooms had iron ceilings and door frames and shelves of slate; each room opened onto a brick hallway. From these rooms the bound papers were carried to a circular reading room for study and transcription.[12]

At the PRO, De Renne was aided by W. Noel Sainsbury, editor of the *Calendar of Colonial Papers* and tireless assistant to all Americans who came to London to gather information about their country's past. Perhaps most famous of these researchers had been Wymberley's friend George Bancroft. Between 1866 and 1880, De Renne would make other trips to London to carry out his researches, occupying himself making copious notes while keeping the clerks busy making lengthier transcriptions for him. In this fashion he amassed a significant amount of manuscript material, some of which would eventually see publication.[13]

For five years after the close of the war, De Renne spent most of his time in Europe, Newport, or Philadelphia and depended on reports from his agents in Savannah to keep him apprised of the situation there, though he occasionally traveled to the city himself. Thomas Lloyd (law partner of George Fenwick Jones, eldest son of George Noble Jones and himself one of Wymberley's lawyers) was one of his principal agents and attorneys, and he also kept Major William Starr Basinger on retainer as confidential counsel. Basinger in particular kept De Renne informed of the ebb and flow of the political and social readjustments of Reconstruction.[14]

Much of the news from postwar Savannah was not encouraging. Major Basinger became certain in 1867 that a revolution by the freedmen was at hand. And Dr. Richard Arnold judged Savannah to be in "a terrible state" in early 1868; by the end of the year there was murder, riot, and, increasingly, "the fear of the torch." Then came the alarm of the so-called Ogeechee Insurrection of early 1869. But by 1870 the situation had finally become more stable, and the death of Mrs. George Noble Jones in Dieppe, France, the previous year had broken the tie that kept Mary De Renne in Europe. Her husband became optimistic that he and his family would be able to return to Savannah and live there with some hope of peace and safety. As the most convincing evidence of his confidence in Savannah's future, De Renne purchased in 1870 over $110,000 worth of city real estate.[15]

The De Rennes' Savannah homecoming did not, however, include a return to living at Wormsloe; it would instead become their country retreat. There were several reasons for this decision. Most important, Wymberley's health made it unwise for him to be distant from medical assistance. Moreover, the labor situation made it difficult to imagine returning Wormsloe to agricultural production in the foreseeable future. Teeple and Smillie had proved as much in their unsuccessful attempts to grow cotton with paid labor from 1866 through 1868. In addition, conditions on Skidaway Island in the late 1860s and after made living at Wormsloe less than secure. After an early period of orderly cultivation of the land, the Skidaway freedmen, many of them dispossessed when their land was returned to its previous owners, earned a reputation for lawlessness: in one violent incident, Negroes armed with rifles had fired on fishing boats with white crews, allowing only boats with black crews to pass. Probably because of this and other incidents Wymberley considered the Skidaway Negroes "the most disreputable in the county." [16]

Another reason for his deciding not to live at Wormsloe, however, was probably the resurgence of the Skidaway Bridge matter in 1871; it again brought into question whether the plantation could survive intact. The long bridge to Skidaway, damaged during the war, had been crudely repaired a few years afterward. Then, in 1870, by act of the General Assembly, the Skidaway road and bridge had been made "a part of the public roads" of the county. [17]

But several of the Skidaway residents apparently hoped to enhance access to Skidaway and thereby make the place more attractive to development, either as a resort (such as the nearby village called Isle of Hope had become) or otherwise. They decided that the county should change the course of the Skidaway Road (for which Wymberley had given the right-of-way across his portion of the old Wimberly tract in 1858) so that it crossed the original Wormsloe grant, with a new bridge to be built one mile south of the existing structure, at the site of the temporary "New Exit" (or "military causeway") constructed by Confederate engineers during the war. [18]

It was argued that the county now had the responsibility for maintaining the existing road and bridge as part of the public road system under the act of 1870. The case for a new bridge seemed bolstered, however, when the ramshackle old bridge was swept away in October 1871. After this incident, the General Assembly passed a law in December 1871, allowing the county to change the course of Skidaway Road and build a bridge elsewhere. The Skidaway men, apparently emboldened both by Wymberley's long absence and their argument that Wormsloe was in "a state of decay," hoped to get the county officials to take their side, regardless of what their representative termed Wymberley's "plea of special private rights." [19]

Wymberley responded that he claimed no right except "simply to be protected in the use of [his] property and not to be sacrificed to a few speculators in wild lands on Skidaway, who call themselves 'the public.'" As for Wormsloe being in a "state of decay," he noted that he had spent $2,000 in the last year making repairs, building fences and hanging gates, and having the property resurveyed and planted with stone markers. Throughout the 1870s he continued to improve Wormsloe, clearing more of the land, expanding the gardens, repairing and maintaining the residence, and erecting handsome gateposts (of Georgia granite from Stone Mountain) at the entrance to the oak avenue that followed the river toward Wormsloe House.[20]

His lawyers kept him posted on the matter, and he himself, spending the summer of 1871 in London—when the initial attempt to reroute the road was made—wrote sending them advice. As he noted, the new road would be of great expense to him, necessitating the erection of over four miles of fencing to separate his land from the new public road. And the road itself would come so near his "settlement" that its privacy and security would be destroyed, particularly since the "disreputable" element from Skidaway would be using it. His main hope seemed to be to make the bridge-building project prohibitively expensive for the county by charging for the existing dams in his marshland (scheduled to be used in the construction of the bridge), as well as charging "for the earth to raise it to the proper size." He would try to make them pay other damages as well so that it would be cheaper to rebuild at the original spot.[21]

Unfortunately, this gambit at first succeeded in Pyrrhic fashion: though the road commissioners did indeed report to the ordinary that a bridge and causeway at the proposed Wormsloe site would be too expensive, they suggested a better, cheaper route, with the bridgehead "beyond the settlement of Mr. De Renne . . . near the old fort," an even more egregious violation of the privacy and security of Wormsloe. The next grand jury of the Chatham Superior Court, however, was not enthusiastic. Despite the recent legislation, they questioned whether the county was "*legally and constitutionally* bound for this expensive work," which they calculated at "upwards of six thousand dollars, a very large amount for the county to expend for the benefit of a few individuals." Though they left the decision to the "good judgment of the Ordinary," they made it obvious that they opposed the project, and the ordinary ultimately did not lend his support. There were additional alarums and excursions regarding the matter throughout the 1870s, and the General Assembly passed more than one bill dealing with the bridge. But despite the continued threat of action, Wormsloe would be safe for G. W. J. De Renne's lifetime, though, in one way or another, the "Skidaway matter" would resurface for generations to come.[22]

During their visits to Savannah in the late 1860s and during their lengthier stays beginning in 1870, De Renne and his family had occupied rooms at the Pulaski House, but hotel life proved unsatisfactory. Once they returned to Savannah for good, the De Rennes decided to maintain their principal residence in the city proper. Consequently, in early 1871, Wymberley purchased one of the town's most celebrated mansions, an Italianate residence that had been built in 1849 by John S. Norris for Joseph S. Fay. Several years after its construction, the Fay residence, located on Liberty Street at its intersection with Bull, had been the only dwelling house in Savannah that a national periodical would class as "very handsome" among the city's homes. Though some might have disputed this characterization, it was certain evidence of the structure's exceptionality.[23]

De Renne would make the house and grounds even more impressive, buying adjacent property so that when he was done his lot had a frontage of 150 feet on Liberty Street and 100 feet on Bull, with a carriage house and servants' quarters adjacent to and west of the house. To the rear of the structures he created a formal garden, lush with camellias and roses and enclosed by a high brick wall, with a greenhouse in one corner and a screen of cypress trees along Bull Street. Among the gardeners employed to care for this urban oasis was J. J. Cadogan.[24]

Setting the precedent in Savannah for transplanting large trees from the countryside to ornament his lot, De Renne had palmettos brought from Wormsloe to be placed between his house and the streets. Transported for planting behind the residence were tulip and other trees: "magnolia, cypress, sweetgum, and olive." These additions were watched with much interest by the local press. De Renne also brought Wormsloe to the Savannah residence in another way. He had J. N. Wilson take numerous photographs at the plantation, designed for viewing through a stereoscope. These detailed and three-dimensional images displayed the natural beauty of Wormsloe—the river, the oaks and palmettos, the clusters of Spanish bayonet—as well as the tabby ruins, covered with vines, and Wormsloe House itself, appearing weathered but resilient. Two of the women of the place were shown at the old well near the house, documentation of the transition from slavery to tenantry.[25]

The massive, rather plain facade of the Savannah residence concealed an interior that was "one of the most handsomely fitted up in town." The large front door opened onto a hall with a frescoed ceiling lit by a brass chandelier. To the left of the wide hall was a double drawing room, similar to that at Wormsloe House but with pocket doors and fireplaces with marble mantels six feet across, topped by French mirrors stretching to the high ceiling. To the right, near the end of the hall and the door to the piazza, was the dining room, upon whose walls were portraits of Noble Wimberly Jones and William Smith. These and the other principal rooms had cornices carved from English walnut and large windows, each of whose sashes contained one large pane of glass, an unusual feature for the time. A stately mahogany staircase led to the two upper floors, which were supplied with water closets and bathrooms, along with clothes closets for the seven bedrooms. The basement below accommodated a large kitchen (accessible by brick steps that descended through the wooden floor of the wide piazza), as well as a servants' washstand and water closet, various storage rooms, and, by the late 1870s, an "Allegretti Refrigerator N° 6 with 200 lbs ice, and 75 lbs daily to supply the loss by melting."[26]

Such was the De Rennes' love of books that several rooms were required to hold their acquisitions. Rooms on several floors were furnished with bookcases, and an assortment of them was needed to accommodate Leta's library. Wymberley's study, which housed his postbellum collection, was located on the first floor, adjacent to the dining room.[27]

Dr. George Jones had been a connoisseur of fine wines, and not only his taste but, happily, his cellar had been among his legacies to Wymberley, who had expanded the selection judiciously. After years of experimentation at Wormsloe and in the Liberty Street house, Wymberley decided that his wines should be stored according to their place of origin. Consequently, those from cold lands like Germany were consigned to two wine cellars in the cooler regions of the basement, while the products of warmer countries, such as his cherished Madeiras, were stored in a warm, dry room on the house's third floor.[28]

Compared to Wormsloe, the town house offered expanded opportunities for entertaining guests and was particularly convenient for his city friends, and De Renne became well known for offering "the choicest hospitality." Several times a week, guests were invited for dinner, either in groups of up to a half a dozen or, occasionally, tête-à-tête. Luncheon and dinner guests were assured of a splendid dining experience, likely to include such diverse items as okra soup, fresh figs and strawberries, ice cream, and, in season, oysters brought in from Wormsloe. The meals were always complemented by a generous selection from the wine chests, as well as fine cigars for the gentlemen, from Purdy and Nicholas of New York. Guest bedrooms awaited family members—such as George Noble Jones and, more frequent visitors from El Destino, his sons Wallace and Noble—and family friends, like John W. Beckwith, Stephen Elliott's successor as bishop of Georgia.[29]

Often De Renne's guests were fellow connoisseurs of wine, and this occasionally led to competitive wine tastings to determine whose palate was sophisticated enough to identify particular wines. In April 1879, one of the best of the Madeira men, William Neyle Habersham, was put to the test at a dinner attended by Bishop Beckwith, General Henry R. Jackson, General A. R. Lawton, and Dr. William S. Lawton:

> [The test] on the boards of the dining room table (custom forbade table cloths when Madeiras were served) consisted of nine unlabeled decanters of wine set before Mr. Habersham. He was to taste, and identify. One by one he called the names of the wines to the interested guests. Trinity Sherry, Hurricane Madeira, Painted Pipe, Chillingsworth Madeira, Leacock Sercial, Margade Madeira—and at the next decanter, Mr. Habersham hesitated. "I can identify this wine, except that I know De Renne has none." He named the two remaining wines and came back again to the one put aside. "This wine," said Mr. Habersham, "is Molyneux Sherry and it has been away from Savannah for some years, and only recently returned." He was absolutely correct, the wine, having spent some time in Washington, Georgia, [had been brought that day by General Lawton].[30]

On other occasions, De Renne's hospitality took the form of an excursion. On a memorable Saturday in the spring of 1880, with the weather "charming," De Renne hosted a luncheon party at Wormsloe for twenty-year-old Leta and ten of her friends. They traveled from Savannah on the Isle of Hope railway and were then taken by carriage to the plantation, where the garden had recently been enlarged. Three cooks prepared—and a like number of waiters served—a meal that included "Oysters on the shell, Boned turkey truffled, sandwiches, crab salad, ice cream and orange sherbet, cakes, strawberries, oranges, apples, Prunes, Dried ginger, . . . Burnt almonds, sugared almonds, [and] chocolate caramels," with sherry, champagne, and coffee; all but the last mentioned were served cold.[31]

A more elaborate jaunt in the spring of 1878 had taken the De Rennes and eighteen companions—including Mr. and Mrs. John L. Stoddard, Mr. and Mrs. William Neyle Habersham, Mr. and Mrs. J. L. Hardee, N.W. Jones III, and the artist Carl L. Brandt—to Daufuskie and Tybee Islands, attended by six servants. Traveling on the steamer *Centennial,* which Wymberley had chartered for the day, the group left the wharf at 9:15 A.M. Upon arrival at Bloody Point on Daufuskie, Wymberley and several of his guests (along with his gardener Cadogan) accompanied Stoddard on a visit to the gardens of his family's Melrose Plantation, while the others stayed at the point. At two, the party began the crossing to Tybee, "lunching en route." The meal included "boned turkey, roast chicken, sandwiches, rolls, crab salad and chicken salad, orange sherbet, strawberries, and strawberry ice cream, snowball pound cakes, 6 bottles champagne, two sherry, 2 of whiskey; lots of ice." For the ladies' comfort, bamboo rocking chairs had been brought from the Liberty Street house. Arriving at Tybee landing, the party took the train to the nearby beach and hotel, where they spent the rest of the day, returning to Savannah at 6:45 P.M. In his journal, Wymberley summed up the day with satisfaction: "The weather was perfect, and nothing untoward happened." [52]

Although living in Savannah rather than at Wormsloe afforded additional opportunities for participating in the political, religious, and social life of the city, De Renne chose not to take advantage of the first mentioned at all—declining a seat as a city alderman offered him by the mayor—and his activities at Christ Church did not include accepting a proffered post as a vestryman. [53]

Christ Church and the Diocese of Georgia in general did have a large place in his thoughts, however, and both were recipients of his benefactions, known and unknown. Among those that came to the attention of the communicants of Christ Church were his purchase of a pew for the sole use and convenience of the bishop and his family and the mounting of an early nineteenth-century plaque in a prominent position on the church's rear facade. The inscription noted that the church had been "destroyed by fire" in 1796, "refounded on an enlarg'd plan" in 1803, "partially destroyed in the hurricane of 1804," and again rebuilt in 1810. [54]

In one case in which his identity was to remain unknown, De Renne offered "seed money" for a worthy cause. In 1876, he instructed his cousin the lawyer William Hunter to approach the annual convention of the Diocese of Georgia to broach an anonymous proposal. De Renne would personally donate $5,000 "to aid in creating a permanent fund for the support of the Episcopate," if within a year others in the diocese would contribute a total of $20,000. If the contributions reached $40,000 or $80,000, he would contribute $10,000 and $20,000 respectively. As he once wrote, it had been his experience that people appreciated something more if it cost them something. The Standing Committee of the diocese issued a request that the vestry of each parish "act as a local committee to obtain contributions; suggesting that from those not finding it convenient to give cash they accept any good securities that may be offered." At the end of the year, however, the Standing committee reported, "No Vestry has, up to this time, 'reported results' or 'remitted collections,' in answer to this appeal." [55]

Living in town, Wymberley was necessarily thrown more into society than during his relatively reclusive time at Wormsloe before the war. He began to take a greater interest in various organizations in the city, including the Youth's Historical Society and the Society for the Prevention of Cruelty to Animals (of which he was an officer), but most of his dwindling energy was devoted to the Georgia Historical Society. [56]

Although he had been a member of the society since 1847, there is no evidence of his active involvement in its work until the 1870s. By that time, of the triumvirate that had created the organization, only Dr. Richard Arnold remained; Israel Tefft was dead, and William Bacon Stevens, now bishop of Pennsylvania, was still in Philadelphia. Wymberley was on good terms with Dr. Arnold, and another mainstay of the organization was his close friend William B. Hodgson. Presiding over the society at the time of De Renne's return to Savannah was Edward J. Harden, the biographer of George M. Troup, whose son William Harden had been elected as the society's librarian in 1869 and would remain at his post until well into the next century. Throughout the 1870s Wymberley took a close interest in the society and made numerous contributions of books and, occasionally, artifacts, to its holdings. He was also instrumental in reviving the society's series of *Collections*—whose last volume had been published by Hodgson in 1848— with the preparation of two additional volumes; afterward publication would again be suspended for over two decades. [57]

Sadly for Wymberley, his new life in Savannah had hardly begun when William Brown Hodgson died. When leaving Savannah in the spring of 1871, Wymberley had noticed that Hodgson "did not seem as well as usual," but he was shocked to receive in Munich a letter from George Noble Jones informing him of Hodgson's death and acquainting him with its particulars. From the description, Wymberley concluded that Hodgson's medical treatment had been the main cause of his death. Then seventy-one, Hodgson—

unaccompanied by his two ladies—had gone to New York City by steamer on a business trip. He arrived sick, complaining of having had a chill on the boat, and was diagnosed as suffering from double pneumonia. Wymberley decried the fact that circumstances had placed his friend in mortal danger without the presence of his physician, Dr. Phineas Kollock. "The stimulant method of treating inflammatory disease," he wrote to George Noble Jones, "is generally fatal and whatever chance of life he may have had from his natural vigor of constitution was destroyed by his physicians. It is a pity he could not have been attended by Kollock—who was acquainted with his constitution, and would not have been misled by the appearance of exhaustion—probably rather nervous than vital." [58]

"His loss will be severely felt in many ways," he continued, "not only by Mrs. Hodgson and Miss Telfair, but by the community, where he was a most public-spirited and useful citizen. Mary and I will both miss him greatly: he was so kind and attentive, and had so many sympathies in common with us: and was more with us than any of our friends. Indeed for more than twenty years there has been a sort of parallelism in our experiences, which, together with similar thoughts on many subjects, tended to make and keep us intimate. There is no one to fill his place, and Savannah will be a dull place to me without him." [59]

His heart went out to Hodgson's survivors, for whom he could imagine no solace: "We feel the profoundest sympathy for the ladies: what they will do without him, simply as their most useful friend, it is hard to say. But when we think of Mrs. Hodgson's devotion to him and the loneliness of her life deprived of his society, and gloom of the two survivors shocked at the sudden break in their small circle, it is really deplorable." Even the conventional comforts of religion failed him at this prospect: "There is no consolation in such a case—and no hope." [40]

Since Hodgson died just as the final reconstruction of Georgia was coming to a close, there is no way of telling whether, absent the passions of the time, he would have revised his views on the freedmen, as Wymberley was to do. In his 1868 lecture "The Science of Language," Hodgson asserted that the "doctrine of *race* is involved in that of language," and, "for the races speaking the Aryan tongues," he claimed a position of "political, ethical, and social supremacy." This supremacy, he argued, was "of God's ordination," though "man now proposes to overrule, by the bayonet, in favor of the exotic, inferior, race. . . . Such a sacrilegious attempt to degrade the nobler race will be punished by the eternal law of retributive justice." [41]

Wymberley may or may not have agreed with his friend, but his only recorded postwar words on the subject have a different tone. In 1878, he decided to give to the local Board of Education the Scarborough House, a historic Regency mansion on West Broad Street. As he explained in an affidavit,

> Considering that the people called of African descent came among us not of their own motion nor for their own gain, and that they have, as a people, been faithful, docile, and laborious during their sojourn in this land; that by their sudden emancipation they have been left helpless save for their labor, of which they have need for their daily bread; that it is wise and right that there should be means of communication other than verbal between them and the people among whom they live, and that there is no other way to establish such communication but by enabling them through education to read and write the English tongue,

he granted to the Board of Education the property described "*for the education of colored children of African descent exclusively.*" This was only the most conspicuous of his philanthropic acts directed toward the freed slaves and their descendants and was, by his wish, followed by the contribution of another building, across town on East Broad Street, to be used for the same purpose. [42]

Two years after Hodgson's death, the Georgia Historical Society published the successor to his 1848 volume of the *Collections*, based on Wymberley's research in England. Having learned in 1870 that he was to visit the Public Record Office in London, the society had appointed De Renne its representative, empowering him to "examine and obtain from the public offices of her Britannic majesty's Government copies of all papers and records relating to the history of Georgia." Though this sounds as sweeping as the task given the Reverend Charles Wallace Howard in the 1840s, there was an important restriction: he was to spend no more than twenty-five to thirty pounds sterling. [43]

When he surveyed the seventy-eight volumes bearing on Georgia during the colonial period—both from the Board of Trade papers and from the America and West Indies papers from the Colonial Office—De Renne suspected that there were many letters of General James Oglethorpe that had not been copied for the state government in the 1840s. At his request, William Harden, the society's librarian, secured a list of those Oglethorpe letters in the State Library in Atlanta and sent them to him in London. As De Renne noted to Harden, the many letters of Oglethorpe he had discovered were "quite interesting, both as showing his own energetic temper, and the dangers and difficulties of the Spanish campaigns: but I don't wish to have any of them copied, until I know first what they have in Atlanta." Having prevented any duplication, he had Oglethorpe's letters copied, along with a selection from the correspondence of royal governor James Wright, 1774 through 1782, "omitting such as were merely formal." Noel Sainsbury saw to it that the copies were precise and that all were identified exactly as to source, including volume and page numbers. De Renne had the transcripts bound into two volumes and presented them to the society in January 1872. As an addition to the Wright volume, he donated to the society a transcript of a lengthy report on conditions in Georgia in 1773, sent by Sir James Wright to Lord Dartmouth.[44]

In an accompanying letter, Wymberley noted that he considered the Oglethorpe letters "to be of value, not only for the light thrown by them on our early history, but also by their illustration of the character of an eminent man—one of the few whom Lord Bacon's rule places in the highest rank. 'The true marshalling of the degrees of sovereign honor are these: In the first are conditores Imperiorum—Founders of States and Commonwealths.'" He added, in an oblique reference to the Oglethorpe biographies he had attacked long ago, "Much has heretofore been written about him—in these letters he speaks for himself."[45]

In his explanation for providing the selection of Governor Wright's letters, he made plain that another of his earlier enthusiasms was still alive. He noted that he had particularly wanted to include letters from the British occupation of Savannah during the Revolution so that there would be a source at the society's library for the viewpoint of the Loyalists, a group "which like all the vanquished has received scant justice from the conqueror historians."[46]

The following November the society decided that De Renne's volumes deserved more than placement in the library and voted to publish all the transcripts, along with an appendix of other material, at the society's expense, as part of its series of *Collections*. Though dissimilar to the Wormsloe Quartos in format (octavo), length (368 pages, exclusive of the unrelated appendix), and number of copies (one thousand), this volume was in spirit a continuation of De Renne's earlier work. In actuality, it represented Wymberley's keenest interests even more than the books he had printed himself, since it dealt with his twin passions for Oglethorpe and the Loyalists. Moreover, the volume followed the guidelines Wymberley himself had suggested to the society for its publications decades before. And it conformed as well to his views on the presentation of such material: the Publishing Committee's members noted that they had "carefully abstained from any alteration of the copies in their possession, the copies themselves conforming closely as possible to the originals." [47]

By the time the book was published in late 1873, a related event had brought De Renne into a conspicuous public position for the first and only time in his life. In the preface to the Oglethorpe/Wright volume, the Publishing Committee had noted that the publication was based on the researches of "Mr. G. W. J. De Renne, of this city, a gentleman who has devoted much time to historical inquiry" and who had also recently been elected the society's president. This event had occurred after the death in office of Edward J. Harden and was arranged with a certain amount of diplomacy, as well as some harmless subterfuge. Assuming rightly that De Renne's sensitivities would not allow him to accept the position if he thought that his election had left another, perhaps better, candidate disappointed, the society's representative wrote to him in Philadelphia that he had been elected unanimously. Technically, this was true, but the unanimous election had followed an initial balloting in which Wymberley had outpolled Solomon Cohen by a large majority, as was later admitted to him by one of his friends. [48]

This tactful ruse worked, and Wymberley accepted the post, agreeing to take the president's chair in the society's new headquarters in Armory Hall. De Renne was touched by being called upon to head the organization he had both supported and assailed in his youth. "Circumstances have made me a nomad," he wrote W. Grayson Mann, "and the common results have followed of lessening local prejudice, and likewise enfeebling the feeling of local obligation. . . . This election has pleasantly reminded me of the claims a community has upon its members, however errant, and I ought to recognize the gentleness of the rebuke:—— for it is not often that a man is recalled to duty by such a compliment." His hope of completing the remaining eight months of Harden's term, however, was wrecked by a decline in his health so precipitous and alarming that he began to perfect elaborate plans for the disposition of his estate. He had the General Assembly pass a special law for him in 1875, allowing his estate to be handled in unprecedented fashion. For most of his term, consequently, De Renne's place was occupied by a substitute, while he remained sick at home. And when time came for a full term, he declined reelection. In his place, the presidency was put in the capable hands of General Henry R. Jackson, and almost a quarter-century passed before the president's chair would be draped in black at Jackson's death.[49]

De Renne served in other capacities in the society, most notably as one of the seven curators who helped manage the society's business and as a member of the Finance Committee. And, oddly enough, the year following his retirement from the society's presidency found De Renne more than usually engaged in its affairs. At the December 1875 meeting, at which more gleanings from his research were contributed to the society, a letter was read from Samuel V. Niles—grandson of Hezekiah Niles of *Weekly Register* fame— to Georgia governor James M. Smith, who had transmitted it to the society. Nile requested that a suitable person be found to contribute an article on revolutionary Georgia to be included in the centennial republication of his grandfather's *Principles and Acts of the Revolution in America* (1822).[50]

Almost inevitably, the society requested that De Renne produce the article as the person "most eminently fitted by his special knowledge of our early history." What was expected of the grandson of the "Morning Star of Liberty" may be imagined; what was furnished was something else altogether. In making his selection, De Renne put aside the old Georgia Whigs in favor of the colony's last royal governor: extracts from several of Sir James Wright's letters, 1774–76, drawn from the latest volume of the society's *Collections,* were submitted for Niles.[51]

In his letter to Governor Smith transmitting these excerpts, De Renne defended what might have been considered an inappropriate choice and enunciated most clearly his attitude toward the Loyalists of the Revolution:

As the events of the Revolution of 1776, seen from the Rebel point of view, are to be found described in several well known books—it has seemed good to the Society, in complying with your Excellency's request, to give a glimpse of the comparatively unrepresented opinions of the Loyal men of that day—

supporters of the Government and Constitution—whose characters and aims have not yet recovered from the obloquy of defeat.

Scant justice is ever obtained by the vanquished: the American Loyalists have received none at all from the historians of the triumphant Rebellion. But perhaps time and experience may have taught our countrymen that even the Revolution had two sides; that men equally pure, highminded, and devoted to duty were to be found among Tories as among Patriots; and that the virtues were not monopolized by the winners. If they should learn that success is not the sole test of Right, something may be gained for wisdom as well as for charity.[52]

The society's reaction to the submission may be inferred from a discussion during the January 1876 meeting as to whether the "article was such as Mr. Niles desired," and the matter was referred to a committee that reported, over a month later, that "after mature consideration of the whole subject," it recommended "the adoption of the paper as prepared." Niles, in his introductory note to the Georgia section of his book, duly thanked all concerned for the "interesting extracts." It seems, however, that the society also suggested an additional excerpt, for, along with a 1776 speech of Archibald Bulloch (the sole Georgia entry in the 1822 volume) and the Wright passages, there was an extract from McCall's history regarding Sergeant William Jasper, a patriot hero who had fallen during the siege of Savannah.[53]

As De Renne continued and expanded his research into Georgia history in the 1870s, Charles C. Jones, Jr., was becoming increasingly conspicuous as Georgia's foremost historian; in time, he would be identified with the history of the state in unprecedented fashion, entirely eclipsing his predecessors McCall and Stevens. Not surprisingly, Jones would forge a collaboration with De Renne; in one sense, it was destined to extend past the latter's death.[54]

Though both men had been born with the surname Jones, they were not related and seem not to have been well acquainted until the last days of Reconstruction. Colonel Jones, as he was invariably styled after the war, came from a family descended from Puritan emigrants who had come to the Georgia coast from South Carolina in the mid-1700s. Bringing their slaves with them, they had settled between the Ogeechee and Altamaha Rivers and soon covered coastal St. Johns Parish with rice plantations. In the 1770s their revolutionary zeal had put them in the forefront of the Whig cause, leading to their parish's becoming part of a county called Liberty.[55]

Like Wymberley De Renne, Colonel Jones had divided his life between the North and the South. His father, the Reverend Charles Colcock Jones, was a nationally known Presbyterian divine whose calling had led his family to several northern cities, including Philadelphia, and he had seen to it that his son received his undergraduate education at Princeton, followed by a Harvard law degree. The family's roots (and plantations) were in the Georgia tidewater region, however, and there both father and son returned in the 1850s. The father won fame as minister to the coastal slaves, and the son practiced law in Savannah, whose citizens elected him mayor in 1860.[56]

The previous year Jones had auspiciously begun his career as an orator and historian with *Indian Remains in Southern Georgia*, which was delivered to the Georgia Historical Society as its twentieth anniversary address and afterward published by the society in pamphlet form. This initial work was followed in later years by scores of books, pamphlets, and articles. Though archaeology, particularly relating to the southeastern Indians, always exerted a strong pull on Jones, the events of 1861–65 greatly changed his direction and emphasis as a historian. Many of his postbellum productions would have as their subject the War Between the States.[57]

In that conflict Jones had served as an artillery officer, beginning with Savannah's Chatham Artillery; when stationed for a time on the Isle of Hope, he became familiar with Wormsloe. By war's end, with his father recently deceased and his patrimony almost entirely depleted, Jones had joined that band of southern expatriates who moved north in an attempt to restore their war-wrecked fortunes. While practicing law in New York City, he availed himself of every resource and opportunity to gather materials for his numerous historical works. His prolific pen, his printing projects, and his collecting activities (in the areas of books, manuscripts, and autographs) drained rather than supplemented his income, and the fees from his legal work were strained to maintain his family in comfortable style and underwrite his expensive avocations. His lack of a "long purse" would be a constant regret to him.[58]

Throughout the years, Jones had maintained his ties with his earliest patron, the Georgia Historical Society, but had been unable to persuade the society to publish any of his lengthier works. He had, for example, offered for publication his magisterial *Antiquities of the Southern Indians*, which D. Appleton and Company ultimately brought out for him in 1873, in a handsome illustrated edition of over five hundred pages. The society, which at the time had opted instead to publish De Renne's Oglethorpe/Wright volume, seemed loath to publish any original historical works of any length, perhaps in part because of the stark example of Stevens's *History of Georgia*. In any case, had the society attempted to print Jones's prodigious output, its treasury would soon have been emptied.[59]

Jones had little alternative except to have his works privately printed, not published, in a manner resembling that chosen for the Wormsloe editions. The press of John M. Cooper of Savannah, for example, printed only twenty copies of Jones's *Ancient Tumuli on the Savannah River* in 1868. More often, Jones used the press of Joel Munsell. A printer and antiquarian based in Albany, New York, Munsell was an admirer of William Pickering's publications and considered himself an American disciple of Aldus; he had an enviable reputation as a printer whose various historical works were distinguished by their beauty of typography and had served many scholars of note, including Winthrop Sargent and George Bancroft. By 1871, Munsell had printed Jones's *Historical Sketch of the Chatham Artillery* (1867), *Historical Sketch of Tomo-Chi-Chi* (1868), and an edition of *Reminiscences of the Last Days, Death and Burial of General Henry Lee* (1870) that was limited to 125 copies.[60]

The gift of a copy of this last-mentioned book, which recounted the death of Robert E. Lee's father on Georgia's Cumberland Island, inaugurated Jones's friendship with G. W. J. De Renne in November 1870. De Renne—who found the book "beautifully printed" and "an interesting addition to our biographical literature"—could see that he was dealing with a kindred spirit. Jones would find in De Renne a collaborator and sometime patron who viewed his work with admiration and his printing efforts with sympathy and understanding.[61]

Four years De Renne's junior, Jones approached him with an attentiveness and diplomacy that outweighed his uncanny superficial resemblance to William Bacon Stevens, for he was a tall, physically imposing man with a tendency toward pomposity. But it was also helpful that Jones was a southerner by birth and allegiance, and the mellowing of years had probably also served to temper Wymberley's perspective.[62]

The Lee offering was the first of many thoughtful gifts—both books and autographs, including one of J. G. W. De Brahm's—that increased as the decade of the 1870s waned. "Your courtesy," De Renne wrote Jones in 1875 in thanks for a book, "is like a never-failing spring—and you know how grateful that is to dwellers in our climate." He appreciated Jones's contributions to what he called "the ruins of a collection"; the colonel's offerings would come to make up a sizable percentage of De Renne's Georgia books, whether gifts of others' books or presentation copies of Jones's own works.[63]

The friendship of the two was firmly based in their mutual historical interests, for after the death of William Brown Hodgson in 1871 De Renne had increasingly missed his conversation and companionship. Though Jones could never replace Hodgson in this regard—particularly since he never returned to live in Savannah—De Renne was grateful to have such a friend as a correspondent and occasional guest. Upon receiving Jones's translation of a French account of the 1779 siege of Savannah, De Renne wrote, "Apart from the gratification of receiving so valuable an addition to my Georgia books, it is a real pleasure to find that you take an interest, as rare as it is earnest, in a subject very attractive to me."[64]

It was not only eighteenth-century Georgia that attracted the two, however, for Jones and De Renne were fellow Confederate Jacobites regarding the Lost Cause of 1861. Wymberley particularly admired the roster of the Confederacy's civil and military leaders that Jones had compiled for publication by the Southern Historical Society, which his brother Dr. Joseph Jones had helped found in 1869. A "most valuable contribution to our History," De Renne called the roster, and he relayed to Jones complimentary remarks on his works from his Philadelphia friend, former Union officer John Page Nicholson, a noted collector of publications relating to the Civil War.[65]

De Renne realized that Jones's attempt to win recognition as a man of letters in the South was foredoomed, as had been that of William Gilmore Simms and others, and that he was most likely to attract a discriminating audience in the North. As he wrote to Jones: "You must look, my dear sir, to our late enemies for appreciation of your historical and literary work. . . . It is useless to blink the fact that our people are a century behind a right sympathy with such studies. A scattered few admire understandingly your loving labors:—the rest have no care for these things. You are writing for a distant posterity of our people, but for our contemporary enemies at the North: and to receive hostile praise is certainly a great achievement."[66]

By 1876 Jones and De Renne had formed a lasting friendship, and one of its fruits would be a remarkable book. But the centennial year would in many ways be a time of great sadness; death made sudden, severe inroads in the circle of friends and relatives that had already been sadly diminished by the death of Hodgson in 1871 and those of Mrs. Hodgson and Miss Telfair in 1874 and 1875. Indeed, 1876 had begun with the dedication of Hodgson Hall, the new headquarters of the Georgia Historical Society, built by Hodgson's ladies to honor his memory, a gesture apparently suggested by De Renne, as was Miss Telfair's bequest of the Telfair mansion as a museum and academy of the arts, under the trusteeship of the society.[67]

The De Rennes attended the dedication of Hodgson Hall with some anxiety. This was not because of the inclement weather, even though a rainy day had turned into a stormy night, and crashes of thunder periodically rattled the hall's high windows. Instead, there was some unease regarding Dr. Richard Arnold, who had been asked a year earlier to be one of the speakers; it was feared that he would create an incident of some sort. He had long carried an animus toward Hodgson. Even months earlier, he had been reported by General Moxley Sorrell to have been *"raving"* over the possibility that the gift of the hall would lead to Forsyth Park being renamed for Hodgson. General Henry R. Jackson hoped that De Renne would be able to quiet Arnold, but it seemed doubtful that the doctor would subside.[68]

The new building, however, left nothing to be desired. The work of Detlef Lienau, its lofty-ceilinged library chamber was approached by a long flight of steps that ended at tall double doors sheltered by a portico; its frieze bore the words "W. B. Hodgson Hall." Inside, chairs had been placed to face a temporary platform for the speakers, opposite the doors. Behind the platform was the draped portrait of Hodgson and, in the gallery above, a small choir, accompanied by a piano. The society's books, in their thousands, lined the shelves of the main floor and gallery, and numerous portraits hung from the wrought-iron gallery railing along both sides of the spacious room. Despite the awful weather, not only the hall floor but the gallery was filled, "a practical demonstration," said the *Savannah Morning News*, "of the interest felt . . . by our cultivated and literary citizens."[69]

Music—Donizetti's solemn "Mighty Jehovah" and Verdi's "Spirit Immortal"—was followed by prayer, and then the moment came for the building to be formally conveyed to the society. General Jackson, president of the society, received the official documents and turned to speak. He admonished the members to remember that as recipients of the hall "the conditions of [their] trust [were] sacred; moist with a widow's and a lonely sister's tears, none the less copiously because silently shed." A eulogy to Hodgson followed, praising him as a diplomat, a scholar of the Orient, a recipient of numerous literary distinctions, and a philanthropist. Noting that he was self-taught, having "never taken the degree of Bachelor of Arts from any institution of learning," General Jackson observed that Hodgson "owed his education and all of his opportunities, and all of his attainments and honors, to his own efforts, and to the Library. In the Library, then, does his image find its appropriate place." So saying, he turned and drew apart the curtains concealing the portrait. The rapt gathering saw for the first time the life-sized "striking likeness" of Hodgson, painted in vivid colors by Carl Brandt: the linguist and scholar standing in his own library in the Telfair mansion, surrounded by Oriental books and manuscripts.[70]

De Renne found Jackson's speech "perfect . . . absolutely poetic, and admirably delivered." But the ceremony did not end with the general. Dr. Arnold—only thirty when he, Tefft, and Stevens had founded the society—was at sixty-eight the organization's oldest curator and only six months from death. His opening remarks concerning Hodgson and the ladies were brief, curious, and somewhat ambiguous; with more enthusiasm, he proceeded to the subject he had chosen for his address: Israel Tefft. One interpretation of his remarks was that simple wealth rather than personal merit had led to this handsome memorial hall being dedicated to Hodgson and that the impecunious Tefft, the source and origin of the society, would have been a more appropriate recipient of the honor of having the hall named after him. Arnold's remarks—"singularly malapropos," thought Mary De Renne—were politely received and were followed, after a chorus from "Lucrezia Borgia," by the benediction.[71]

To De Renne, the ceremonies seemed gratifyingly conclusive. His friend's image was now enshrined in a handsome building dedicated to historical and literary uses, while the elegant mansion where the De Rennes had often been entertained by their closest friends was now transformed into an academy of arts and sciences, supported by a $100,000 endowment provided by the last of the Telfairs—a splendid perpetuation of the family name. Hodgson would be fittingly remembered, and his monument would face the spacious park that in the 1840s he had "conceived" and "enclosed at his private expense." For a time the pine-shrouded "pleasure grounds" had appropriately borne the Hodgson name, and it had been disappointing to De Renne (and other members of the society) when the city had renamed the area Forsyth Park. De Renne's attempts after Hodgson's death to restore his name to the park had been unsuccessful (as future attempts by him and the society would be), but now there had at least been a measure of justice.[72]

In March 1876, a little over a month after the hall's dedication, George Fenwick Jones died suddenly at age thirty-five; he was soon followed in April by his father: George Noble Jones was felled by a stroke at El Destino, as had been William Nuttall four decades earlier. Then, in May, Washington Smith died unexpectedly, and Wymberley's last link with his mother's family was broken.[73]

As had been the case at Eliza Jones's death, De Renne was not present when his uncle died, and, had his sons not been at school in New York, no family members would have been at the funeral. Sadly, De Renne's last communication from his uncle had been an inquiring letter: Why was he tarrying so long in fever country when he should be in Philadelphia? De Renne's loss and self-reproach were such that he could have felt little consolation in the fact that he stood heir to an estate valued at half a million dollars. As had been the case with his becoming master of Wormsloe at his mother's death, the cost of this good fortune was too high.[74]

Against this backdrop of bereavement, Colonel Jones requested that De Renne read a new work of his, *The Lost Towns of Georgia;* he wanted an opinion of its merits, as well as permission to dedicate the book to him. One of Jones's most original and well-researched studies, the new work traced the founding, decline, and disappearance of several once thriving Georgia settlements, including the Salzburgers' Ebenezer, General Oglethorpe's Frederica, and the Puritans' Sunbury. Jones's aim was to "gather up the fragmentary memories of towns once vital and influential within [Georgia's] borders, but now covered with the mantle of decay, without succession, and wholly silent amid the voices of the present."[75]

In the book's final section, where he offered a miscellany of various towns and plantations, Jones displayed an appreciation of one old settlement that had so far defied oblivion: Wormsloe. Unlike the other colonial plantations the colonel listed, Wormsloe had neither "passed into the ownership of strangers" nor "lost all traces of primal occupancy." After presenting several eighteenth-century descriptions of Wormsloe, Jones provided his own picture of the Wormsloe of the 1870s and then passed on to a meditation on continuity:

> With all its wealth of magnificent live-oaks, palmettos, magnolias, and cedars; with its quiet, gentle views, balmy airs, soft sunlight, inviting repose, and pleasant traditions, this beautiful residence has at all times remained in the possession and ownership of the descendants of the original proprietor.

Mr. G. W. J. De Renne now guards the spot with all the tender care and devotion of a most loyal son, and to the memories of the past has added literary and cultivated associations in the present, which impart new charms to the name of Wormsloe.

In this youthful country, so careless and indifferent to the memories of other days,—so ignorant of the value of monuments and the impressive lessons of antiquity,—where no law of primogeniture encourages in the son the conservation of the abode and heirlooms of his fathers,—where new fields, cheap lands, and novel enterprises at remote points are luring the loves of succeeding generations from the gardens which delighted, the hoary oaks which sheltered, and the fertile lands that nourished their ancestors,—where paternal estates are constantly alienated at public and private sales,—landed acquisitions are placed at the mercy of speculative strangers, and family treasures, established inheritances, and old homesteads are seldom preserved. Thus it comes to pass that ancestral graves lie neglected, abodes once noted for refinement, intelligence, virtue, and hospitality lose their identity in the ownership of strangers, and traditions worthy of transmission are forgotten amid the selfish entanglements of an alien present.[76]

Jones knew firsthand how perfectly Wymberley represented the diligent preserver of family heritage. He was aware that in the old colonial cemetery in Savannah, Wymberley had taken steps to preserve the memory of Noble Jones, to whom he had erected a cenotaph on the site where the vault of Dr. George Jones had once stood. In the shape of a gable-lidded coffin, the monument was designed to suggest the previous century, with the archaic look of its lengthy inscription and the armorial emblem of a lion rampant. Nearby was the original Jones family vault, where Noble Jones lay with other relations; this vault De Renne had refurbished, cleaning the upright marble slab to the memory of Noble Wimberly Jones that had been placed there by George Jones. At Wormsloe, near the tabby ruins, now buttressed with masonry for their preservation, Wymberley had marked the first resting place of his people, not all of whom—like Noble Jones—had been moved to the city cemetery. These remains had been committed to the earth beneath a great oak that was old even at their interment but still remained. To keep this spot forever sacred and inviolate, he had ordered a massive stone monument of almost six tons, which required six teams of draft horses to haul to Wormsloe. On its top, a cross stood out in bold relief; to one side of it was inscribed

George Wymberley Jones De Renne
Hath Laid this Stone
MDCCCLXXV
To Mark the Old Burial Place of
Wormsloe
1737–1789
And to Save from Oblivion the Graves of his
Kindred.[77]

Colonel Jones's sincere compliment to De Renne's efforts to preserve the past could not help but please the recipient, and De Renne was probably drawn as well by such an eloquent articulation on his views. But as someone familiar with the available source material, he was also much impressed by Jones's spadework in uncovering such a mass of detail on these abandoned settlements. "Though aware of the thoroughness and accuracy of your knowledge of Georgia history," he wrote Jones, "I yet could hardly have supposed you would have been able to give such full accounts of the unlucky old towns, or have made the narrative of their sad fate so attractive." [78]

In his initial response to Jones, which accepted the dedication "with thanks for the compliment it implies," De Renne had noted that Jones's idea for the book was "excellent:—if we have lives of dead men, why not Memoirs of Dead Towns." Subsequently, Jones changed his book's title to *The Dead Towns of Georgia* and accepted De Renne's suggestion for a suitable epigraph, based on Hebrews 13:14: "For here have we no continuing city." As someone conversant with much of the literature Jones was mining, De Renne also suggested several other promising sources, shared some facts of which Jones was unaware, and happily loaned Jones the Ebenezer engraving made for the De Brahm quarto to assist with the illustrations.[79]

The gestation period for the book, 1876–78, was fairly lengthy by Jones's standards. The year 1877, however, saw the colonel's return to Georgia from the North for good, and he was much occupied by the responsibilities of concluding his New York legal business and of moving. Instead of returning to Savannah, Jones chose to set up his practice upriver in Augusta, and he purchased a stately mansion, Montrose, in the healthful, forested sandhills above the city. Continuing to make additions to the manuscript and find new illustrations, he waited for his legal practice to provide him with a large enough fee to commit his book to the printer.[80]

De Renne offered to bear the costs of printing himself and, surprisingly, wrote to suggest that he arrange for it to be issued as the fourth volume of the *Collections of the Georgia Historical Society.* Though beyond the scope of what he previously had thought the society should print, he considered the book remarkable enough to be worthy of such an honor. He recommended further that the book be printed in either Augusta or Savannah, for he thought Georgia the most appropriate place for its histories to be printed—particularly since the Morning News Press of Colonel John H. Estill had done a respectable job with the previous volume of the *Collections.* Despite state pride, however, De Renne was forced to admit that Georgia had no adequate facilities for photolithography, and the work on the illustrations was assigned to the capable hands of Julius Bien of New York. Jones was pleased and flattered to have De Renne's patronage for his book and especially delighted that one of his books was finally to appear under the auspices of the society. "As you have generously consented to stand sponsor for the child," Jones wrote De Renne, "I trust the Society may be persuaded to allow the christening."[81]

Jones was soon pleased to hear that General Henry R. Jackson, the society's president, "heartily endorsed" De Renne's plan. But the colonel was somewhat disappointed to find that his book was not to appear alone. It had been the practice of the society to make the printed collections just that, miscellanies including both primary and secondary works; Hodgson's volume (published at Hodgson's expense) had been the only exception of the volumes previously printed. The society concurred with De Renne's suggestion that *The Dead Towns of Georgia* be accompanied by a scarce printed source, which Jones had quoted extensively in his description of Wormsloe: *Itinerant Observations in America,* an anonymous piece from an English periodical of the mid-1740s, later recognized as the work of Edward Kimber. Sensing Jones's disappointment, De Renne arranged to have five hundred copies of the Jones and Kimber works printed as the *Collections* volume and then paid to have five hundred additional copies of each produced separately, without the society's title page. Jones's five hundred copies of *The Dead Towns of Georgia* were put at his disposal, with De Renne's assurance that he would have as willingly provided him with two thousand.[82]

As the volume neared publication, Jones wrote: "My earnest hope is that it will not prove entirely unworthy of your goodness, and I am much complimented by the favorable opinion you have been pleased to express of the labor. . . . In regarding this volume as our joint contribution to the Georgia Historical Society, and in finding my name thus associated with yours, I experience sincere pride and special gratification." De Renne also found himself thanked publicly in the book's graceful dedication:

To
GEORGE WYMBERLEY-JONES DE RENNE, ESQ.,
OF SAVANNAH,
WHOSE INTELLIGENT RESEARCH, CULTIVATED TASTE,
AND AMPLE FORTUNE HAVE BEEN
SO GENEROUSLY ENLISTED IN RESCUING FROM OBLIVION
THE EARLY MEMORIES OF GEORGIA,
THESE SKETCHES ARE RESPECTFULLY AND CORDIALLY INSCRIBED.[85]

The notice of the book in the *Savannah Morning News* gave high praise to the whole enterprise. It noted that no one could have anticipated that, after the previous volume of collections had been printed five years before, another would appear so soon. The reviewer also observed that such a circumstance would have been impossible without the "curious coincidence" that brought together the "historic interest and the literary taste" of Charles C. Jones, Jr., and "the public spirit and the State pride" of G. W. J. De Renne. "Both of these gentlemen . . . are alive to the honor of their State, and whether resident at home or abroad, they have never forgotten her historical traditions. Both have done much to preserve these traditions, and in this beautiful volume they are and ought to be forever associated."[84]

For the next few years, Jones brought out no lengthy works, but in 1879 he was finally able to realize his dream of traveling to England to conduct research at the Public Record Office, the British Museum, and elsewhere. Though he and De Renne continued to correspond and Jones visited the Liberty Street house when in Savannah, there was no further collaboration. Jones went on to produce more articles and short monographs, but he was apparently busy building his Augusta legal practice and gathering materials for his magnum opus on Georgia's history, not to appear until 1883. Meanwhile, De Renne was at work on a magnum opus of his own, a large volume that would gather between two covers all those rare colonial laws which the General Assembly had passed but whose manuscripts had gone unprinted.

It was to be the fifth of the Wormsloe Quartos, and again Noel Sainsbury would assist De Renne in the Public Record Office, where the principal research was done in the summer of 1878.[85]

While in London, De Renne also made an effort to learn more about his family's obscure English past. He placed an advertisement in the *Times* that read "INFORMATION WANTED.— IN WHAT COUNTY AND PARISH IS A PLACE CALLED WORMSLOW? LIBERAL REWARD.–D.E.R." The *Times* office sent him numerous responses. The most tantalizing was from Wales, near the Herefordshire border: "Mrs. Stephens begs to inform D.E.R. that Wormsley or *Wormsloe*, the latter being the old fashioned name of a parish sometimes called 'Wormsley'—... is situated six miles and a half from Weobley, another ancient village in Herefordshire. . . . There is a residence called Wormslow Grange—in this place or village—sometimes called 'Wormslow'—or the older name still *'Wormsloe.'* " Also intriguing was an offer of help if he would contact a gentleman in London named W. J. Noble. What, if anything, De Renne made of these and other responses is unknown, but he apparently decided they were more suggestive than definitive. After his death, the letters were found among his papers, along with some of his commonplace books, in which he had carefully recorded the information.[86]

In the later 1870s, most of De Renne's backward glances were, as usual, directed at the eighteenth century. But in 1878 he took steps to memorialize the more recent past. His interest in the War for Southern Independence increased with time; he had an abundance of reminders, particularly at Wormsloe, some of whose earth was still gathered into Rebel fortifications and whose residence's marble mantels would always bear traces of the vandalism of Union soldiers. Once De Renne moved permanently to Savannah, his circle of friends and acquaintances became heavily represented with former Confederate officers, particularly generals, including Alexander R. Lawton, Henry R. Jackson, and Joseph E. Johnston. The last mentioned had lived in Savannah in the 1870s, in a brick row house near De Renne, with whom he was on friendly terms. Johnston and De Renne attended the same church and occasionally shared meals and carriage rides; both were elected Christ Church vestrymen on the same day (on which day both declined). And that most urbane of Confederate generals, Moxley Sorrel, lived near De Renne and was often a dinner guest. Under the circumstances, the Confederacy was often in De Renne's thoughts.[87]

Others in Savannah, principally the Ladies' Memorial Association, had sought to preserve the memories of the Confederacy and its soldiers. In 1875 the association had unveiled a fifty-foot-tall monument to the Confederate dead, designed by Robert Reid, with the poignant inscription "COME FROM THE FOUR WINDS, / OH, BREATH, / AND BREATHE UPON THESE SLAIN / THAT THEY MAY LIVE!" Atop the gray sandstone monument, and within a canopied niche, were white marble statues of robed, mourning women, one "with her finger to her lips indicating silence." But, as one Savannahian later noted, "It was a conception of one . . . who had not entered fully into the spirit or the aspirations of those who sought a memorial that would unmistakably illustrate those who had gone forth to fight, to suffer, and perchance to die. It did not meet with popular approval." In April 1878, De Renne proposed to the association that the marble statuary be removed, the open niche filled, and the pedestal surmounted by a bronze statue of a Confederate soldier; De Renne would absorb the cost of both the design and the statue. His suggestion and offer were gratefully and immediately accepted.[88]

At the time, Confederate monuments featuring representations of Confederate soldiers were seldom seen, and De Renne was determined that his statue would be a distinctive and accurate portrayal of the fighting man to be memorialized. In keeping with his aim, he secured the assistance of Captain Hamilton Branch of Savannah, a thrice-wounded Confederate veteran of the war. Branch gathered several other veterans who had the necessary qualifications to serve as models: "courage and firmness during the entire war . . . always in the ranks . . . either on the march, in the camps, or in the fight—except when absent wounded."[89]

From these men, Major A. S. Bacon was chosen to be photographed in a composite uniform, described for De Renne by Branch (who himself was photographed to show the sculptor how the hat was worn and whose face— including imperial—was depicted on the statue):

The hat . . . is a regular Confederate hat and was worn by myself (then a private in the [Oglethorpe Light Infantry]) during the 1st year of the war and at the 1st Manassas. The coat was worn during the last year of the war by a gallant soldier now dead and the pants are the ones issued to the Georgia troops the last year of the war by the Georgia Relief & Hospital Association and as you can see are all scorched out at the ankle by standing too close to the log fires[;] the seat is a great deal worse worn and the [pants] are fastened with a peg instead of a buckle. The gun was made at [Cook and Brother Armory,] Athens, Georgia, during the war and was used by a noble gallant boy.

Branch apologized for the "U.S." on the belt clasp and cartridge box but noted that Georgia troops often used such Union accouterments, though they changed them by cutting the "U." into a "C.," which he suggested the sculptor do. He was most disappointed that he had not been able to find any shoes dating from the war, "for it would have looked so natural to have seen the flesh and stockings between the old worn out shoes and the short, burnt-out breeches." Branch concluded, "I think the pictures good and that they are just like the boys looked during the war whilst in the field. I could have had it look much nicer for I have a nice uniform, but I thought you wanted it as he looked when he marched and fought and not when he danced and fluted at home."[90]

Once satisfied that his preparations and investigations were complete, De Renne employed the Welsh sculptor David Richards (whose later patrons included Cornelius Vanderbilt and Jay Gould) to sculpt a small clay model. It would serve as the basis for the bronze statue to be cast by Maurice J. Power's National Fine Art Foundry in New York City. To assure accurate detail, the photographs that had been made as guides were accompanied by the clothing, accouterments, and rifle that had been used.[91]

From the foundry, Power reported that the completed bronze statue attracted much admiring attention from many veterans, North and South, including Generals Mansfield Lovell and Gustavus Woodson Smith. General Smith, who had spent the last year of the war in Georgia commanding the state militia, was particularly impressed with the accuracy of the depiction of the Georgia soldier. He was also among the first to voice the major complaint about the work: he felt that its "motive, its historical—or rather archaeological—correctness" merited "a place near the eye of the spectator." To some extent, De Renne counteracted this criticism by having two bronze castings made from the mold of the original twenty-eight-inch sculpture before it was destroyed: one for himself, the other presented to the Telfair Academy for display. And he also gave large photographs of the statue to various institutions and individuals in Savannah so that, in the late nineteenth century at least, the meticulous detail of the work was widely known, even though the life-size monumental bronze itself loomed fifty feet above its viewers.[92]

Its height was not a problem when the statue arrived in Savannah in April 1879 and was taken for exhibition to the Armory of the First Volunteer Regiment near Forsyth Park. There, while Savannahians flocked to examine it, the statue was under the military charge of Captain Branch's Oglethorpe Light Infantry and the Savannah Cadets. Finally, in the early morning hours of May 22, 1879, with "no fanfare," the bronze soldier was hoisted to the top of the shaft.[93]

In tendering the statue to the ladies of the Memorial Association, De Renne gave his personal view of Richards's Confederate soldier:

> It represents him as he was—marked with the marks of service, in features, form, and raiment; a man who chose rather to be than to seem, to bear hardship rather than to complain of it; a man who met with unflinching firmness the fate decreed for him to suffer, to fight and to die in vain.
>
> I offer the statue as a tribute to the men of the Confederate army. Without name or fame or hope of gain they did the duty appointed them to do.
>
> Now, their last fight fought, their sufferings over, they lie in scattered graves throughout our wide Southern land, at rest at last, returned to the bosom of the loved mother they valiantly strove to defend. According to your faith believe that they may receive their reward in the world to come.
>
> They had none on earth.[94]

The ladies of the association were suitably grateful, and to their thanks of 1879 they added a presentation the next year: an "engrossment of the papers relating to the bronze Confederate Soldier statue—so skillfully made, and so cunningly ornamented, as itself to be a work of Art." In thanking the ladies of the association, De Renne meditated further on the statue: "Whatever success the statue may have had, seems to me to be largely owing to causes which I do not wish forgotten. First among them is the *attitude*, originally suggested to me by Mr. H. M. Branch—himself a true Confederate soldier, faithful unto the end. It is that which, technically called 'parade rest,' has moreover an absolute significance: for it indicates submission to the inevitable, without excluding the idea of a manly struggle to avoid it." He added, too, the obvious contribution of the "plain Welshman, Richards," whose "successful representation of the Georgia Soldier's face and form" was such that "the men themselves should accept it as typical."[95]

The statue, then, was as successful as De Renne could have wished, and it satisfied the association, the veterans, and the general public. Even a northern art critic, T. H. Bartlett, would pay it some reluctant compliments. "That it has more character than any figure of a soldier in the whole country is saying very little in its favor," Bartlett wrote, eight years after the statue was installed. "It is more direct and complete in its conception, and has more individuality than any statue in the United States, the Jefferson, by David d'Angers, barely excepted. As a soldier, he is worn out, and conquered. As a man, he faces the future with a sad but firm countenance. The upright modesty of the body, the uncertainty of the action of the arms and lifeless hands, and the unaffected general position of the whole figure, make it a Confederate soldier, and nothing else. . . . It is also a symbol. The rude shoes and the tattered and overworn clothes have a true and appropriate force. It is really the only statue that has come out of the Civil War." [96]

A few weeks after corresponding with the Ladies' Memorial Association, De Renne began perfecting plans for more personal memorials. It seemed inevitable that the Old Cemetery in Savannah would soon be broken up and all the bodies exhumed and transported to other city or family cemeteries. He determined to transfer all the Jones remains to a new vault at Bonaventure and to leave behind (temporarily) only the monuments to the memories of Noble Jones and Noble Wimberly Jones. [97]

Having accomplished most of this by May 18, he bade farewell the next day to Mary and Leta, who left for Philadelphia on their way to spend the summer in Europe, a trip that his middle son, Everard, would join; Wymberley, his eldest, was in Texas, and the youngest, Kentwyn, was still at school in the North. Mary had occasionally crossed the Atlantic without him; a few years earlier, for example, she had spent several months in Paris and London, where she had sat for an almost life-size canvas by the society portraitist Louis DesAnges. [98]

After Mary, Leta, and Everard sailed, De Renne journeyed to Philadelphia. He had been "much occupied" by business in Savannah, but, once having dealt with the most pressing matters, he was bound for the Quaker City, where, he commented with some asperity, he had matters that he had "long wished to attend to, but hampered by a family, could not." These words were addressed to his oldest son, who arrived in Philadelphia after his mother's departure for the purpose of getting married—a step that would prove to have many ramifications. In any case, young Wymberley and his bride would be gone from Philadelphia before his father's arrival there. [99]

Notwithstanding his complaint about being "hampered" by his family, De Renne by 1880 had much reason to be well pleased with the children that he and Mary had raised in peace and war. Wymberley, the eldest, had followed years of education in Europe with a tour of the Orient before returning to the United States to earn a law degree. Surprisingly, he thereafter had almost immediately headed for the frontier to make his fortune, a move similar to that made by his Nuttall grandfather decades earlier and one that his parents viewed with a mixture of misgivings and hope.[100]

Closest to De Renne in interests and sympathies was his second son, Everard, who—after schooling at the Rectory School in Hamden, Connecticut; St. John's School in Ossining, New York (an unusual Episcopal military academy); and Princeton University—had followed De Renne in earning a medical degree, though at the City University of New York, not his father's alma mater. Genealogical research attracted Everard almost as much as it had his father, and he had compiled a small book of family history. It contained much information gleaned from the family archives his father had accumulated, but he had enriched it with other materials as well. Likewise, he shared his father's passion for fine wines and pleased him by traveling to the bodegas of Spain and sending back tales of his adventures among the winegrowers there, including a tour of vineyards in a coach drawn by a splendid pair of matched white horses. He loved Europe and was a dauntless traveler, though he was grateful that his father's distinctive name could open doors for him in London.[101]

The youngest boy, Kentwyn, had always been paired with Everard at school and shared his enthusiasm for athletics: both were prize-winning gymnasts. Though all of the De Renne children had seen their education disrupted by the war and the travels that followed, Kentwyn had encountered the most difficulty in making up for time away from the schoolroom. After receiving most of his education at the same places as Everard through Princeton, he left that institution to complete his education at the Rensselaer Polytechnic Institute at Troy, New York.[102]

More than any of her brothers, Leta displayed a hunger for reading, and though her formal education was sporadic at best, she set herself to master numerous subjects for the sheer sake of learning. Unlike her robust siblings, she was often unwell and suffered the first throes of heart disease when still quite young. Nonetheless, her demeanor was always cheerful and her pleasant personality attracted many friends in Savannah, at Newport and Montpellier, and elsewhere. She most closely matched her father in love of books and in her spiritual concerns and shared more than the others in her mother's passion for all things French.[105]

In her father's commonplace book, one of the more whimsical entries presented a few verses from Mary Howitt's "The Seven Temptations":

Saving up money—
Is labour and care:
All you have toiled for
Is spent by your heir!

Whatever his actual view, De Renne took great care in crafting a last will and testament. Drafting its most recent version was among the matters he saw to in Savannah, the day after his son had been married in Philadelphia. De Renne had in 1875 taken the unusual step of having Georgia's General Assembly pass a piece of special legislation for him that authorized Philadelphia's Pennsylvania Company for Insurance on Lives and Granting Annuities to act as executor and trustee of his estate, "as if [the company] was a natural person resident within the State of Georgia." He had determined that his wealth and property would not be distributed among his wife and children after his death. Instead, excepting certain special bequests, his money, stocks, and real estate would be kept in a generation-skipping trust, and the interest paid on his considerable capital would serve to pay handsome annuities to his survivors for the rest of their lives. Only when the last of his survivors died would the corpus of the estate be divided among his surviving grandchildren. If there were no grandchildren, the entire estate would be used to found the De Renne Hospital for Incurables in Philadelphia.[104]

His exact reasons for handling his estate in this manner are unknown. He left no explanation. But it is probable that he observed various shortcomings in his children that made him uneasy to the point that he could not in good conscience leave a fortune to them. And a fortune it was, consisting not only of his own carefully husbanded wealth but of the considerable legacies of the Smiths as well. At the time he wrote his will, Wymberley, his eldest, seems to have been his chief concern; the young man had abandoned the law for ranching in Texas, after enjoying a life in Europe and the Orient that his father may have considered too colorful, and his marriage had not met his parents' hopes. His speculations in Texas land and livestock were already leading him to borrow considerable sums from his father, who noted them carefully in the will and subtracted them from what Wymberley and his children, if any, would receive from the estate.[105]

Neither Savannah nor the Georgia Historical Society were to receive any largess, though, in fairness, both had long profited from De Renne's benefactions. Obtuse in the matter of Hodgson Park, the city's government, as well as some of its citizens, had occasionally acted as if they were victims rather than beneficiaries of De Renne's philanthropy. The reasons for his omission of the society are unknown, but the survivors of William Brown Hodgson had, at least partially at De Renne's suggestion, put the organization on better footing than it had ever enjoyed, and he would have considered it inappropriate to seem to be competing with Hodgson's memory.[106]

Though De Renne's health had not been good for many years, his wife would never have made her trip to Europe if she had harbored any fears that his illness was approaching a critical stage. But by the time De Renne was ready to leave for Philadelphia in July, he had suffered an alarming decline: he was "in very delicate health and exceedingly weak, so much so that some of his most intimate friends urged him to take a companion in the event that anything should happen to him." De Renne refused to take this precaution; he thought his increased weakness only temporary and imagined that the change in climate and locale would improve his health. Instead, after arriving in Philadelphia, his health deteriorated even more rapidly, apparently because of renal failure. By the end of the month, he could hardly write, and his usual graceful hand had degenerated into an unsteady scribble. The beginning of August found him completely bedridden in the house on Clinton Street. At six on the morning of August 4, his condition worsened dramatically and he sent the servant girl downstairs for coffee, which to him was "a greater stimulant than brandy." When the girl returned, De Renne was prostrate on the floor. By the time she could lift him back into bed, he was dying.[107]

His bankers, Biddle and Company, cabled Mary with the news of his death; she responded that the remains should be kept until her return. They also notified Kentwyn, who reached Philadelphia on the evening of his father's death, and young Wymberley, who was advised that there was no "absolute necessity" that he return east.[108]

Unfortunately, the only way that De Renne's body could be kept until the family's return was embalming, a procedure then not frequently employed. To a person as private as De Renne, this could only have represented the ultimate violation of privacy. Kentwyn, already distraught, went to view the body, and though the features were composed, the boy was appalled at the clear evidence of his father's final sufferings.[109]

The body was sent by express train to Savannah, but Mary, Leta, and Everard did not join Kentwyn there until the last Saturday in August, and young Wymberley did not join them at all. The funeral was held the next day, August 29, from the residence on Liberty Street, where the "metallic coffin, cased in black cloth," had been placed. Bishop Beckwith, who had left his sickbed to bury his friend, "said in private the Burial Service of the church over the remains." The members of the Georgia Historical Society, identified by badges, arrived at the residence in a body and formed part of the long cortege that wound its way to Bonaventure. There the services were completed at the new family vault; De Renne had ordered it prepared across the sandy lane from his father's plot, next to that of George Noble Jones.[110]

There had been much regret but little surprise in Savannah at De Renne's sudden death at age fifty-three, and the local newspapers did their best to satisfy public interest in his passing and burial and in the disposition of his estate. The *Savannah Morning News* made an interesting attempt to describe and define De Renne for its readers and printed an obituary that was almost as distinctive as the life it tried to summarize. Readers would have to wait for the first week in September for a comprehensive appreciation of De Renne's life—sent to the paper from Augusta by Colonel Jones—that did more justice to De Renne's literary contributions and noted also that his "benefactions were without ostentation . . . judicious and thoughtful."[111]

In its attempt to characterize De Renne, the *News* noted his patronage of the Georgia Historical Society and his support of public education. He was, the article observed, "a gentleman of peculiar characteristics," a person of "a retiring nature and especially sensitive regarding the amenities of life, which characteristics caused many to form an erroneous impression of him, but withal he possessed a kindly heart, and the numerous noble deeds he had quietly performed came accidentally to general knowledge and showed him as he was . . . as he was loath to speak of his own actions." In fact, the paper noted, "any publicity of his charitable or generous deeds was particularly repugnant to him."[112]

Ironically, the retiring nature and dislike of publicity that had characterized De Renne in life made it difficult after his death for the members of the Georgia Historical Society to honor his memory as they wished. They felt that conventional resolutions of regret, no matter how heartfelt and sincere, would be insufficient in his case and ordered a committee of three—including General Moxley Sorrel—to choose an orator for the annual address the coming February; the speaker's "theme and subject" was to be the "life and character of [their] departed friend."[113]

Upon hearing of the society's planned eulogy, Mary wrote immediately to General Sorrell: "While we thoroughly appreciate the very high compliment intended, we, my children and myself, earnestly beg that it may not take the form proposed. You, as well as Mr. De Renne's other friends, know how he always shrank from appearing before the public; therefore you will understand why we deprecate the proposed tribute to his memory, and have ventured to appeal to your kindness, feeling sure that you will use your influence to carry out our wishes." General Sorrel assured Mrs. De Renne that the society would modify the action taken and reassured her of its "sincere admiration of [her husband's] high character and varied attainments." The society members voted that the committee "be requested not to suggest to the anniversary orator a subject for his address." This finessed the entire matter and honored both their duty and Mrs. De Renne's feelings, for the orator selected was Charles C. Jones, Jr., and the title of his address was "The Georgia Historical Society: Its Founders, Patrons, and Friends."[114]

The address, delivered in Hodgson Hall on February 14, 1881, was one of the best efforts of Colonel Jones, "eminently discriminating and truly historical," as the society's minutes described it. After having spent a third of his speech tracing the actions of the society's founders and delivering a litany of its foremost patrons, Jones, as a matter course, came to the first of De Renne's major contributions to the society: the Oglethorpe volume of the *Collections*. Then, after a dramatic pause, he continued, "And here, my friends, permit me . . . to place a memorial wreath upon the new-made grave of one who, since our last annual meeting, has left our companionship and fallen on sleep." There followed a graceful eulogy of G. W. J. De Renne, occupying the middle third of the speech, recounting his life and displaying his character with all the detail and sympathy that could be expected from such a friend as Jones: his northern birth and education (and unwavering allegiance to the South), his love of books and scholarship, his contributions to historiography and printing, his love of Wormsloe.[115]

From a historian of Colonel Jones's self-esteem, the praise bestowed on De Renne's qualities as a scholar, historian, and writer was extraordinary:

We have no hesitation in expressing the opinion that in a thorough acquaintance with the history of Savannah, and of Georgia,—both as a Colony and as a State,—he was excelled by none. Often have we hoped that he would have undertaken a general history of our State; and more than once did we commend the suggestion to his favorable consideration. Such a work, from his capable pen, composed in that spirit of truth and characterized by that patient research and philosophical analysis of men and events which distinguished all his investigations, would have proved a standard authority.[116]

Of De Renne's philanthropic acts, Jones provided a dexterous and stylistically complex summation:

> Of the public spirit which characterized Mr. De Renne as a citizen of Savannah,— the public spirit of a high-toned, independent gentleman solicitous for the general welfare, yet counting neither personal advantage nor political preferment,— of the sterling qualities which he exhibited in the business affairs of life and in the administration of his ample fortune,— of the active and intelligent interest he manifested in everything promotive of the material and intellectual progress, the ornamentation and the civilization of this City,— of his many charities, unheralded at the time of their dispensation, I may not speak. They are fresh in the recollection of us all. Were he here, he would tolerate no eulogium, and now that he is dead, as his friend I will do no violence to his known wishes.

Jones could not forbear, however, from mentioning De Renne's two most well-known benefactions: his donations of the Confederate statue and the West Broad Street School.[117]

Mrs. De Renne was happy with Colonel Jones's presentation, to which she had given her blessing in advance. Indeed, Jones had secured her help in locating and confirming certain facts, and he was diplomatic enough to assure himself that there was nothing in his oration that would offend her. To the contrary, she distributed copies of the printed address to friends and was gratified two years later when the *Southern Historical Society Papers* printed that portion of the address concerning her husband. She herself, however, could not rest until she had done more to save his name from oblivion.[118]

CHAPTER 6

The Altar of Memory

To live in hearts we leave behind is not to die.
—THOMAS CAMPBELL

Mary De Renne now found herself in much the same bereft state that had been Mrs. Hodgson's lot at her husband's death, for she had lost both husband and friend, one on whom she had long been dependent. Oppressively, "the sorrows and shadows of life" closed "thickly" about her; there seemed little consolation or hope. But Mrs. De Renne was not childless, as Mrs. Hodgson had been, and she had other advantages as well. Bishop Beckwith, to whom she turned for spiritual solace, seems to have found her grief somewhat excessive. But he understood that her husband's previous attentiveness to her and his protection of her from the pressures of business would necessarily make Mrs. De Renne's new status disagreeable, no matter how comfortable her financial status.[1]

She would have much to occupy and distract her, however, principally estate matters and her own collecting and printing ventures. But there would be heartaches as well: an estrangement from her eldest son (whom she rejected at what must have been great personal cost) and Leta's rapidly declining health. Along with her father's intellectual interests, Leta had inherited his delicate constitution, and her remaining years would be "terribly overshadowed."[2]

Mrs. De Renne's own health also deteriorated. She had always been a large woman, but the effects of several pregnancies and her enjoyment of fine dining had brought her to a state of corpulence that her doctors knew was life-threatening. As had her mother, she began to have difficulties walking, aggravated by her heaviness; ultimately, she would have to wear a brace. But her physicians' efforts to bring her to a healthier style of life through various regimens (including forbidding her Madeira and its happy associations) were unavailing.[3]

Despite the increasing pressures of business and personal matters, Mrs. De Renne felt that she had to bring to the press her husband's final project, the publication of the fifth quarto: a collection of all of the acts of the colonial legislature of Georgia from 1755 to 1774 that had "received royal sanction" but had never been printed. All of the transcripts had been completed with Noel Sainsbury's help, but they needed to be arranged, annotated, and indexed.[4]

Fortunately for Mrs. De Renne, Colonel Jones stood ready to assist her. He, more than most, understood the tragedy of a lengthy project ended prematurely by its author's death. And as a lawyer—as well as a historian and writer with expertise in Georgia history—he was arguably better fitted for completing the task than any other living person. Additionally, he had been privy to the project since its inception, and the book had formed the subject of conversations and correspondence between Jones and De Renne. They had agreed, for instance, that there was no need to include the few laws that the Trustees had formulated: only those laws passed during the administrations of the three royal governors should be printed. In a sense, then, the Acts quarto marked the final collaboration between De Renne and Jones.[5]

The colonel worked quickly, for the manuscript that came to him from Mrs. De Renne in January 1881 was in its finished form by August, the first anniversary of De Renne's death. Titled *Acts Passed by the General Assembly of the Colony of Georgia, 1755–1774*, the work was monumental in size as well as intent. It matched the De Brahm quarto in height and exceeded all the previous Wormsloe Quartos in number of pages: none of the earlier volumes had exceeded sixty pages, but the *Acts* contained over four hundred. It was printed on specially prepared, super-calendered paper, and, after the impression of forty-nine copies, its type, never before used, was melted down.[6]

Mrs. De Renne had intended the book to be "the finest specimen of a privately printed book which [had] yet appeared in America" and had hoped to have it issue from the press of Joel W. Munsell, a "genuine disciple of Aldus" as Colonel Jones termed him. Unfortunately, she found, Munsell had died the same year as her husband. Consequently, she used the Philadelphia firm of T. K. Collins, which sent the proofs to Colonel Jones for checking and correction. Although Mrs. De Renne deferred to Jones in most matters connected with producing the book, she herself composed the dedicatory note. Printed in black letter at her direction, it read:

> The materials for this work were obtained from the Public Record Office in London, by the late George Wymberley-Jones De Renne, who intended himself to prepare them for the press.
>
> At the request of his Widow the task has been accomplished by Charles Colcock Jones, Jr.; and the book is a Tribute to the memory of one whose profound love for Georgia and interest in her History ceased only with his life.[7]

The binding was left to another Philadelphia firm, that of Mrs. De Renne's friend (and fellow collector of books on the late war) Colonel John Page Nicholson. He used blue-gray cloth as the standard presentation binding, with a red morocco label on the spine, its letters and border stamped in gold. Special editions, such as the one Mrs. De Renne had prepared for Colonel Jones's library, were bound in leather, as was the massive manuscript of the book, whose sheets of pale blue Public Record Office transcripts were interleaved with the cream-colored paper of Colonel Jones's notes.[8]

Colonel Jones assured Mrs. De Renne that there was in America "no finer expression of the printer's art . . . than appears in the pages of the [*Acts* quarto]. It is a monument alike of your generous devotion, and of the refined patriotism of him who conceived the work and conducted it even to the verge of completion." For his labors, Colonel Jones received from Mrs. De Renne a "valuable" check and five copies of the quarto, four bound in cloth (for his distribution, subject to her approval) and one—for his own library—bound in half levant. The cost to Mrs. De Renne of printing the forty-nine copies was just over $1,200.[9]

In his plan for printing the colonial acts, De Renne had intended to pro-

vide complete texts of those colonial laws that had not been printed con-
temporaneously by the Savannah printer James Johnston—either individually or gathered together in pamphlet form as legislation of particular sessions of the General Assembly—and had not been included later in the two
extensive digests of Georgia laws, those of Robert and George Watkins in
1800 (second edition, 1801) and Horatio Marbury and William H. Crawford
in 1802. In determining what had not seen print, De Renne was guided by
the digests and by a bound collection of printed legislation. Subsequently,
he had located the unprinted laws in manuscript at London's Public Record
Office and had them copied, "largely under his personal supervision." [10]

Jones apparently eliminated some of these copies (reducing the total
number to just under seventy); he accomplished this with the assistance of
another collection of printed acts, privately held, that had been the property
of William Ewen, first president of Georgia's Council of Safety (and, therefore, Jones contended, first governor of the state of Georgia). The colonel
also prepared a brief but comprehensive prefatory note for the volume, describing the nature of Georgia's colonial government, its legislative pro-
cesses, and its apparatus for securing the Crown's sanction for its laws. Along
with a three-page index, Jones also provided numerous marginal glosses to
explain "the scope of other legislation by the General Assembly of the
Colony of Georgia upon kindred topics." [11]

In filling "a hiatus in the printed legislative enactments of Georgia,"
Jones wrote, the quarto had "no little historical value." In a published assessment of De Renne's compilation, Jones cited the historical importance
of legislation addressing such varied subjects as "those regulating the militia, the finances, the police, the commerce, the judiciary, the highways, the
defense, the land titles and the slaves of the Province." To satisfy De Renne's
interest in his family's history, the quarto also preserved numerous references to that ubiquitous royal official Noble Jones and to his sons as well. [12]

With Colonel Jones's assistance, Mrs. De Renne completed a list of recipients for the presentation copies of the fifth quarto. Near the top of the
list, of course, was Noel Sainsbury, who had assisted De Renne in gathering
the unpublished acts. Several of the libraries that De Renne had favored,
including Newport's Redwood Library, the Lenox Library, and the library
of Harvard College, also received copies. Several state historical societies
were on the list as well, along with the Southern Historical Society, emblematic of Mrs. De Renne's burgeoning interest in books and relics associ-

ated with the Lost Cause. Additionally, copies were sent across the Atlantic to the Bodleian Library and to the Bibliotheque Imperiale de France.[15]

As Colonel Jones observed, the fifth quarto could "be properly regarded as the concluding volume of the series of *Wormsloe Quartos*." But the first step toward the publication of the sixth and truly final quarto was made only a few months after publication of the *Acts*. Mrs. De Renne had been intrigued to read of the sale of a two-volume manuscript journal of the Earl of Egmont, preeminent trustee after Oglethorpe. In the summer of 1881 the bound manuscripts had been offered for sale in London by the redoubtable Henry Stevens, still the nonpareil of dealers in rare American-related sources. According to Stevens, these folio volumes—numbered "2 & 3" and "very closely written, mostly in the neat small round hand" of the Earl of Egmont—were the "Sibylline leaves of Georgian History." This was a treasure that would have certainly captured the imagination of Mrs. De Renne's late husband. Colonel Jones, who had tried to persuade the Georgia legislature to purchase the volumes, discovered for Mrs. De Renne that the buyer had been Junius Spencer Morgan, an American banker and collector, residing in London, whose son J. Pierpont Morgan was destined to transcend him in acquiring rare books and artworks.[14]

There the matter rested until September 1885. During the time intervening, both Colonel Jones and Mrs. De Renne continued their correspondence, but both were much occupied by other projects: he was completing his magnum opus, *The History of Georgia;* she was assiduously gathering her collection of Confederate books, manuscripts, and relics. Of the two, hers was the more fulfilling experience, for the collection that was to bear her name increased rapidly in both quantity and quality.[15]

Colonel Jones—though he had in 1883 produced two peerless volumes of his Georgia history (only the first half of a projected four-volume history)—found the research and publication expenses of his venture too great to bear comfortably. He was embittered that the members of the General Assembly would not assist him; they refused his request that the state subscribe for a generous number of the volumes, to be distributed gratis to educational institutions throughout Georgia. In the end, the legislature's lack of support not only left Jones financially injured by the cost of his history's first two volumes, but it also led to his abandonment of the work's two concluding volumes—slated to cover "Georgia as a Commonwealth" and to carry the state's history "down to a period within the memory of the living." As Joel Chandler Harris sympathetically described Jones's situation, the colonel "felt the influence of cold neglect from every source that might have been expected to afford him aid and encouragement" and also had "reason to know that, at the end of his task, public inappreciation was awaiting him." [16]

Mrs. De Renne, however, had been someone to whom he could confidently turn for "material aid." As he readied the first two volumes for publication, she personally subscribed for ten of the books, and she had also given him "generous assistance in the use of copies of valuable documents collected by Mr. De Renne," as well as the gift of hundreds of frontispiece plates for both volumes, prepared by Colonel Nicholson from the engravings of Oglethorpe and Noble Wimberly Jones that her husband had commissioned decades before. Mrs. De Renne was impressed by both volumes and no doubt gratified by the numerous quotations from the Wormsloe Quartos and from the published correspondence of General Oglethorpe and Sir James Wright. She brought the colonel's masterpiece to the attention of her friend George Bancroft, who was inspired to give Jones the sobriquet "Macaulay of the South." [17]

Another gift proved almost as pleasing to the colonel. In 1885 Junius Morgan generously presented the Egmont journal to the state of Georgia, and, as a mark of appreciation, Mrs. De Renne sent Morgan a copy of the *Acts* for his library. Morgan, commented Jones, had done what the "niggardly, utilitarian spirit" of the legislature had prevented the state from doing for itself. Nonetheless, some of Jones's allies in the legislature saw to it that the journal was placed in his hands on "special loan" so that he could assess its historical worth. As he confided to Mrs. De Renne, he intended, as far as his means would allow, "to give publicity to such portion of [the journal] as will minister to our fuller knowledge of the Colonial history of Georgia." He noted that if the manuscripts "share the fate of many others in our State Archives, they will lie neglected." [18]

Having secured and examined the journal, he reported to Mrs. De Renne. As records in Egmont's own hand, he wrote, they ranked "among the earliest and the most precious memories of Georgia." Unfortunately, they were "liable to loss and destruction" because they existed only in the original manuscripts. Henry Stevens had noted that the journal was "ready for the press at once, and is *all* well worth printing." But Jones was certain that the General Assembly would not bear the expense of preserving the manuscripts through publication, given what he saw as the insularity, narrow-mindedness, and lack of cultivation of all but a "chosen few" of its members:

> Unfortunately, [he wrote,] nine out of ten of [Georgia's] legislators have little thought beyond a mess of "bacon and greens," reinforced by a modicum of sweet potatoes and corn dodgers. With them the sun rises "just over the branch," and sets "on the other side of the cow-pen." The "country store" is the commercial mart, and their thoughts travel not beyond the neighborhood gossip as retailed at church, courthouse, or camp-meeting. What care such persons for the memories of the past or the traditions of the elders? They have no part nor lot in such matters, and education has not yet exerted its ameliorating influences.[19]

Mrs. De Renne determined that the Egmont manuscripts would be preserved without the General Assembly's assistance. "I cannot bear to think of the fate of the Egmont Journal unless put into some permanent shape," she wrote Colonel Jones, and authorized him to make inquiries regarding the cost of such a project. The cost would have to be a consideration, for she had found that her annuity would not support her as comfortably as she wished without certain economies. Consequently, she at first intended a smaller publication, not in quarto form; instead she planned to issue the journal in two volumes octavo, like Colonel Jones's history of Georgia. "In the matter of the Colonial Acts," she wrote, "there was a sentiment which made the cost a minor consideration, but this is a different affair and I cannot undertake heavy expense."[20]

Despite Mrs. De Renne's sentimental preference for having a Philadelphia firm print the book, Colonel Jones was able to persuade her that the printer of his Georgia history—H. O. Houghton & Company of the Riverside Press at Cambridge, Massachusetts—would provide the lowest estimate and do the best work. "There are comparatively few printers who possess the experience and the ability requisite for the intelligent and accurate accomplishment of the task," he wrote. He also was able to convince her to have the book brought out as a small quarto, thus bringing the Egmont book into the series of Wormsloe Quartos.[21]

Mrs. De Renne was impressed to receive from the press's proprietors a tastefully designed specimen page, with margins in the "antique style," and was pleased by their thoroughness: in preparing their proposal, they had examined the *Acts* quarto in the Harvard library. The press's estimate of $800 for the work, including binding, persuaded her that it would be possible to add the book to the quarto series economically but without any decrease in quality. Consequently, she decided to print the book as a "Memorial, and to preserve an Historical Record which surely must perish in its present form." Also, she thought that producing the book would allow Georgia to "show herself not ungrateful for Mr. Morgan's generous contribution to her history, and that all of her citizens are not represented by her legislature!" [22]

At the end of January 1886, Mrs. De Renne notified Jones that she would accept the Cambridge firm's proposition, with the exception that she insisted that the binding be done by Colonel Nicholson in Philadelphia, who used medium blue cloth, with the title stamped in gold on the spine. She reminded Jones, however, that there had to be the "best of everything," for the "Dedication cannot be put into any volume wherein one single thing falls short of the highest standard." The Riverside Press accepted her challenge, assuring the colonel that the quarto would "be printed on a very superior quality of laid paper, with good ink and best presswork." [23]

The firm did mention, however, that it might be necessary to increase the estimate by having a copy made of the journal so that more than one compositor could work on the project at the same time, as well as "to preserve the original copy clean and free from any injury or defacement." To save time and additional expense, Colonel Jones suggested instead "taking the book[s] apart, and placing the leaves before the compositors." This was done, and the manuscripts were placed in the company's safe when not in use. [24]

Preparing the Egmont journal for publication required much less time and labor from Colonel Jones than had the *Acts* quarto. The manuscripts required no more from him than some penciled notations of the material to be omitted, in this case an index to material in the missing first volume of the journal. Indeed, the text lived up to the high praise of Henry Stevens, who had written that "it speaks for itself, being full, concise and to the point, exceedingly well written, clear, honest, and convincing." [25]

Mrs. De Renne's instructions were simple: she wished Jones to act for her in the matter, and, as he suggested, to prepare a prefatory note (to which the press appended his flourishing signature in facsimile). After having been sent the prefatory note for her blessing, Mrs. De Renne approved most of it but held back the final page in which Jones had apparently written of the De Rennes' contributions to history. There was "no need" for this, she wrote, for "the Dedication and the Colophon tell the story sufficiently." The other pages, she thought, were "eminently adapted to explain the Journal to ignorant people like me who know very little of the Earl of Egmont." [26]

The prefatory note did indeed provide a lucid and informative introduction to Egmont and his journal. Coupling him with Oglethorpe as the most important of Georgia's founding fathers, Jones noted that while Oglethorpe crossed the Atlantic to promote the Trustees' enterprise, Egmont, "with equal zeal, devoted his attention and substance to the administration of the Trust in England," where he was the young colony's "moving spirit and steadfast friend." Of the importance of Egmont's journal, Jones commented that its "historical value . . . may not be questioned." Apart from its intrinsic value, he noted that the journal admirably supplemented various other printed primary sources on the Trustees' colony, including the Georgia Historical Society's edition of De Renne's Oglethorpe letters, which covered much the same period as the journal, 1738 to 1744. [27]

When the forty-nine copies of the quarto arrived in the summer of 1886, Mrs. De Renne was more than pleased with the look of them. Among other things, the Riverside Press had created an exceptionally handsome title page. The title chosen—*A Journal of the Transactions of the Trustees for establishing the Colony of Georgia in America. by the R^t Honble John, Earl of Egmont*—was set in various styles and sizes of type (some including the antique "long s"), and the words were arranged on the page with very attractice symmetry. [28]

Mrs. De Renne sent copies to much the same group of individuals, libraries, and historical societies as she had done with the *Acts*, being particularly sure that Junius Morgan received a copy. She also had Colonel Jones (who received three copies but apparently no check) present a copy to Henry D. McDaniel, governor of Georgia. And she received a large measure of gratification from sending a copy to former Confederate president Jefferson Davis. When in Savannah in early May 1886—while the Egmont journal was at the printer's—Davis had paid a visit to the Liberty Street house, where Mrs. De Renne's hospitality had included a glass of the Hunter Madeira of 1796 (a "divine tipple," observed Colonel Jones). Upon receipt of his copy of the journal, Davis thanked Mrs. De Renne for "the magnificent volume recording the early history of Georgia. It is really an edition de luxe rarely equalled by bookmakers in this country." On a personal note, he continued, "I vividly remember the gracious reception accorded to me by yourself and your brilliant Daughter, and have so described it to my wife as to increase her regret for not having accompanied me." [29]

Though the final two volumes of the Wormsloe Quartos were Mary De Renne's most conspicuous memorials to her dead husband, their preparation, printing, and distribution occupied only a few months in 1881 and 1886. For her, most of the decade of the 1880s was devoted to another species of memorialization: a careful attempt to gather into one collection an impressive array of relics, manuscripts, illustrative materials, and printed sources relating to the War for Southern Independence. It was said that the impetus for her collection was her ire at a northerner who was traveling through the South buying up southern relics of the war. But this project was not unconnected to her husband, for figuring prominently in her remembrance of her last year with him was his planning and presentation of *The Confederate Soldier*, which she enhanced and protected in early 1882 by donating a fence of wrought iron. But her idea of creating an array of Confederate mementos was her own and would lead to her being recognized as a discriminating collector in her own right. [30]

All evidence indicates that Mrs. De Renne came late to Confederate collecting, particularly of books. In late 1864—when her friend Colonel John Page Nicholson was enriching his collection by sending Georgia imprints home to Philadelphia from captured Atlanta—Mary was isolated with her family at Oaklands Plantation, in the path of Sherman's left wing. In 1865, while her life remained in turmoil, such northern historians as Francis Parkman descended on Richmond and left with boxes and crates packed with books and papers. Dealers began to offer Confederate collectibles through catalogs, such as one that offered a "Confederate Miscellany, comprising battle reports, manuscripts, autographs, letters of prominent Confederate generals and statesmen, Confederate bonds of different characters, Confederate notes of rare and scarce issues, and many other valuable papers and documents"— exactly the kinds of materials that would later constitute the Mary De Renne Confederate Collection. But for Mrs. De Renne the end of the war ushered in a period of dislocation, travel, and near exile that in one sense did not end until late 1871, when she moved into the Liberty Street house in Savannah. Even then, what collecting she may have done was desultory for most of the next decade, for only in 1881 did she be-

gin the seven-year period of collecting in earnest that would produce a wonderfully comprehensive collection, all the more remarkable for the speed
with which it was assembled.[51]

Her collecting was promoted by more advantages than the obvious ones
of time and money, for her connections in the field she chose were of the
highest order. Several of Georgia's Confederate generals—among them
Porter Alexander and Moxley Sorrel—located autograph letters for her, as
did the Reverend J. William Jones, editor of the *Southern Historical Society
Papers*. And as the premier Georgia collector of Confederate books and
manuscripts, Colonel Charles C. Jones assisted her throughout the period
she was collecting and donated many books, autographs, and other materials. One of her earliest and largest single accessions was a gift from Jones
that included ten Confederate imprints: their diverse points of publication
ranged from Mobile and Macon to Columbia, Raleigh, and Richmond; their
subjects embraced fiction, official reports, religious tracts, and school texts.[52]

Among the last mentioned was Mrs. M. B. Moore's rare *Primary Geography Arranged as a Reading Book*, whose maps were rudimentary and
crudely colored. In an accompanying letter, Jones directed attention to the
question-and-answer section in the back that had made the book famous:
the response to a question regarding the major "drawback" to Confederate
trade identified it as the "unlawful blockade by the miserable and hellish
Yankee Nation." He quickly added, as counterpoint to the levity: "Behold
the maps. They tell a tale of sadness and of poverty which quickly converts
our smiles into tears."[53]

Both Colonel Jones and Mrs. De Renne considered their gathering of
these materials as a very serious, almost religious activity. They considered
their collections "souvenirs" (as Jones explicitly called them) in the strictest
definition of the term, remembrances of a righteous cause that had fallen to
a mightier but not worthier foe, badges of sacrifice representing thousands
of southern boys and men whom the war had maimed or killed, reminders
of a society and culture gone without hope of resurrection. Jones wrote that
he hoped that Mrs. De Renne would "look gently" upon these materials,
"stained and moth-eaten as some of them [were]," in consideration of the
hopes, the trials, the aspirations, the privations and the disappointments of
a dead past."[54]

As the former Confederate capital, Richmond irresistibly beckoned collectors of the remains of the Lost Cause. There was always the hope of

locating treasures still hidden by families in their trunks and attics. But ready money could secure less elusive prizes from a variety of sources: the shops of the city's dealers in old books and manuscripts, the crowded emporium of C. F. Johnston (Richmond's single dealer in things confederate when Mrs. De Renne's collection began), and the occasional dispersal of private clusters of Confederate materials.[55]

In tapping all these sources, two friends of Colonel Jones gave Mrs. De Renne much assistance and their friendship as well. Robert A. Brock, himself well on the way to winning fame as a Confederate collector, assisted Mrs. De Renne while he was corresponding secretary of the Virginia Historical Society. He located for her assorted Rebel "flotsam," as he called it (including Confederate imprints and autographs and letters of such Confederate notables as General Robert E. Lee), and guided her in making purchases by advising her whether collections being offered for sale were worth the price asked. He recommended that she use John Bartlett's *Literature of the Rebellion* (1866) as a guide and also gave her the sound advice (though unusual in the South at the time) that the *Official Records*, published by the U.S. government beginning in 1882, should form part of her collection. Mrs. De Renne showed her gratitude to Brock in various ways, including presenting him with copies of the Wormsloe Quartos.[56]

As a member of a prominent Savannah family, Colonel Jones's close friend Katherine Clay Stiles was already well known to Mrs. De Renne. Miss Stiles became Mary's most trusted supplier of materials and soon gave to her searches the thoroughness and enthusiasm of an admiring friend. Her mother had died during the first year of the war and her only brother had been killed in action near Front Royal, Virginia, during the war's last months. A maiden lady who spent most of her life in Richmond, she would later become one of the Vestal Virgins of the Cause, devoting most of her time and energy to memorializing the Confederacy. An invaluable ally in Mrs. De Renne's quest for "souvenirs," Miss Stiles possessed a vast knowledge of Confederate collectibles; she suggested, for example, that John Esten Cooke's *Surry of Eagle's Nest* was desirable—even if Mrs. De Renne did not want postwar Confederate fiction—because it contained wonderful sketches of Confederate soldiers by Winslow Homer. She searched out families who were finally ready to part with wartime heirlooms and knew from what connections to get items ranging from autographs to wartime numbers of newspapers, as well as such relics as locks of hair from the Confederate chieftains.[57]

Among the last were samples from Robert E. Lee and Jefferson Davis. A story current at the time had it that Mrs. De Renne, grateful to have secured such rare mementos, was determined that the locks be accorded the respect they deserved and not fall victim to substitution and theft. Consequently, she had the jeweler who set the hair into lockets do the work under her eyes and those of one of her sons and a hired policeman, as all four sat in the De Renne carriage outside the jeweler's shop.[58]

Though Mary De Renne's collection was not restricted to books, it would be her Confederate library that would earn the most notice from posterity. Selected with "rare judgment," her books included postwar publications and, more important, Confederate imprints, from government publications and tactical manuals through histories and fiction to newspapers, songsters, and other works—a catholic collection that was a veritable history of the Confederacy told through the heterogeneous output of its scattered presses. The Confederate publications were normally left as they were, to tell the pitiable story of a depleted Confederacy. As one commentator noted, they demonstrated by the "dingy hue of the paper and the indistinctiveness of the print and further by the binding (in some instances of wallpaper) the dire straits" in which the Confederacy spent its entire existence. Almost without exception, Mrs. De Renne had her postwar publications bound in the finest style, as she did for a few of her most treasured Confederate imprints such as her one-volume collection of the sermons of Stephen Elliott, Episcopal bishop of Confederate Georgia. Her collection also included books on the Confederacy published in Canada, England, and France. Among the last mentioned was a family curiosity: an extract from *The Prison Life of Jefferson Davis* rendered into French by her half-brother Wallace Savage Jones.[59]

In one sense, Mary De Renne's Confederate collection contained books almost incidentally, for it was astonishingly rich in relics of the battlefield, the camp, and the home front: fragments from regimental flags and generals' tents; displays of uniform buttons (at R. A. Brock's suggestion); hats worn by officers when they were mortally wounded; drums and tent pegs; cannonballs (one that had been found near where an officer fell and was "presumed to have given the death wound"); and weapons: sabers and swords, bayonets and pistols, and bullets fired at various battles embedded in tree trunks and branches. From northern prisons there were rings cut from buttons, as well as carved candlesticks and chess pieces. From southern firesides came cotton yarn, linsey-woolsey, homespun, and woven flannel; a soldier's trousers, made by his mother from "cotton and cow's hair"; wrapping and writing paper; and Confederate money of all types, from paper money to needles, "used as currency during the war, in Habersham County, Georgia." [10]

Manuscripts and documents were also in abundance: everything from ships' logs, originals of military orders, scores of autographs of Rebel luminaries, correspondence between Confederates both famous and obscure, and official letters from various departmental commands, along with circulars, permits to leave camp, and certificates of death. Among the most impressive of the collection was a book containing "the last two orders of the Confederate government." [11]

It was in the category of manuscripts that Mrs. De Renne's collection most surely outstripped any rivals, for in 1883 she was able to purchase the undisputed supreme collectible of the southern Confederacy: the Permanent Constitution of the Confederate States of America, a vellum sheet over two feet wide and twelve feet long, "beautifully engrossed." Securing this prize brought her into contact with a notable former Confederate, the journalist and publisher Felix de Fontaine, "Personne" of Civil War fame, whose *Marginalia* (1864) was among her books. [12]

De Fontaine had taken possession of the document at war's end. The fleeing remnant of the Confederate government had jettisoned numerous boxes of papers at a South Carolina whistle-stop called Chester, where de Fontaine had moved with his printing press after the burning of Columbia. Having commandeered a wagon and a four-mule team, de Fontaine rode to the town depot, then being pillaged. With the bodies of several shot looters lying nearby, he loaded some boxes onto his wagon, hoping they held enough blank stationery to allow him to continue printing his newspaper in makeshift fashion. Reaching home, he found that he had indeed salvaged scores of reams of stationery, as well as some worthless receipts. But there were also many important manuscripts, bound and unbound, including the bound opinions of the Confederate attorneys general and both the Provisional and Permanent Confederate Constitutions. [13]

De Fontaine kept many of these documents until early 1883, when financial difficulties prompted him to begin offering some of his most valuable pieces for sale. His newspaper connections assisted him in printing an article titled "Two Relics of the War" in the *New York Sun* of March 26, 1883. Though framed as a news item, this piece (it would soon be clear) was essentially a prospectus; de Fontaine was preparing to offer for sale facsimiles of the Provisional Confederate Constitution, and apparently (if the price was right) the document itself. Much of the article traced the history of de Fontaine's acquisition of his Confederate trove, in his own words, but his name did not appear; he was simply identified as an "ex-Confederate." The only person named was the owner of the second of the two relics of the title, Brevet Brigadier General Ely S. Parker, the Seneca Indian who was U. S. Grant's protégé before, during, and after the war. Parker (also financially troubled and presumably seeking a buyer) wrote of the gold pen, given him by Grant, "with which the articles of surrender were signed" at Appomattox.[14]

The *Sun* article attracted the attention of many readers, including Mrs. De Renne, who wrote to General Parker in early April asking for the name and address of the owner of the Confederate documents. She was soon in touch with de Fontaine, to whom she sent a copy of Colonel Jones's eulogy of her husband, along with an expression of interest in acquiring some of the facsimiles (one apparently to be presented to the Georgia Historical Society) as well as one or both of the actual constitutions—for in his article de Fontaine had also revealed his possession of the "permanent" document. He informed Mrs. De Renne that W. W. Corcoran, a millionaire banker, philanthropist, and collector (and also, incidentally, an officer of the Southern Historical Society) wished to buy the "original" Constitution of the Confederate States but that he had "declined the proffer." Several flyers that de Fontaine enclosed, along with a copy of the *Sun* article, made it plain that what he described as the "original" constitution was the provisional version signed February 18, 1861. But since de Fontaine did not invariably use the terms "Provisional" and "Permanent" (or their dates of signing) to describe the constitutions, he contributed to confusion that would persist for decades.[15]

In his response to Mrs. De Renne's inquiry, de Fontaine feigned indifference regarding a sale, sounding as if he thought Mrs. De Renne would be most satisfied with the lithographs: perhaps a framed facsimile for presentation to the society and one in bound form for her parlor. As for the "original," "it will not knowingly and with my consent pass into the hands of anybody who did not in some way help to defend it, and give to it the same character that is illustrated by the monument of the Confederate soldier presented to the ladies of Savannah." He said this in the face of his own article: it had decried the inability of southern historical societies, as well as the descendants of the instrument's signers, to purchase the document, and despite having suggested that he would sell to the British Museum or (to many southerners, worse) the government in Washington. He did, however, mention the figure of $5,000, while suggesting that he would probably retain the documents, consigning them to the protection of his wife, as he had done for the last eighteen years.[16]

His stratagem proved to be a tactical error, for Mrs. De Renne considered his letter entirely too artful. She realized that he wished to make a sale and was trying to increase the price by playing her against Corcoran; consequently, she determined it wisest not to respond at all. Her assessment was correct. Two months later, she received a lengthy letter from Mrs. de Fontaine, who had discovered that she was summering in Newport. Mrs. de Fontaine's communication unfolded a woeful story of a dangerously ill but still proud husband who was being forced by straitened financial circumstances to part with his most treasured possession, the original Confederate Constitution. "If this precious relic *must* be sacrificed," Mrs. de Fontaine wrote, "I want a *Southerner* to have the benefit of the sacrifice. I will know then, that it will not become a *target* for the *taunts* of the *victors*, who were victors only from force of circumstances." The wife would not mention to her husband the letter to Newport until Mrs. De Renne responded.[17]

Events were picking up speed, however, for on the day that Mrs. De Renne responded, she received a letter from attorney George T. Hanning in New York City. He informed her that he was attempting to sell the original Confederate constitution for a client, Mrs. L. H. Barnard, who held it as collateral for a loan of $800 made to de Fontaine. His next letter named a price—$1,000—and revealed that Corcoran had offered only $2,000 for the document last winter and now refused, without explanation, to offer anything. In less than a week, Hanning telegraphed for permission to visit Mrs. De Renne in Newport on fourth of July, bringing the document with him.[18]

Mrs. De Renne consented, and the lawyer arrived as agreed at her sprawling Queen Anne cottage, rented, as it happened, from the family of the late Francis Lieber, first custodian of the U.S. government's "Rebel Archives." Hanning brought with him a letter from (oddly enough) Mrs. de Fontaine in which she stated that to her and Mrs. De Renne ("us at the South"), the Constitution's value "could not be measured by figures," yet she realized that the original price specified was "a large one to be contributed by a single individual." She suggested that $2,500 would be a fair price. More-over, she had sensed, "since the perusal of the pamphlet . . . referring to the noble work" of G. W. J. De Renne, that Mrs. De Renne, "among all the women of the South," was the "proper custodian of this precious relic—our Magna Charta, around which are clustered so many sad, heroic, and event-ful memories." [49]

Despite the price Mrs. de Fontaine mentioned, Hanning's instructions from her husband—not Mrs. Barnard—were to get as much as possible for the document but (unknown to Mrs. De Renne) no less than $900. De Fontaine also instructed the lawyer to secure permission to repurchase the Constitution later for the selling price plus 10 percent. Faced with this bizarre turn of events and the obvious urgency with which Hanning was trying to dispose of the document, Mrs. De Renne offered $1,500, with the understanding that she would immediately be given all legal papers neces-sary to prove her title to the relic, as well as a certification that upon her pay-ment of the money she would receive the Constitution "free from all claims, liens & demands whatsoever"—including any option for de Fontaine to re-purchase the Constitution at a later time. By the sixth of July all of her terms had been met, and she had become owner of the "original Constitution of the Southern Confederacy." [50]

According to a long-lived anecdote (that Mrs. De Renne's friends at least hoped was true), she was approached in New York City shortly after her pur-chase of the Constitution by two men purporting to be acting on orders from the government at Washington, who offered her a large sum of money for her document. She was reported to have said that the federal government "had not money enough to get it from her." Giving some credence to this probably apocryphal story, the U.S. government had indeed paid large prices for some Confederate documents, including, most conspicuously, the Confederate State Department collection known as the Pickett Papers. [51]

Mrs. De Renne had a large book prepared to preserve the correspon-dence and legal documents relating to her momentous purchase and soon was being assisted by Colonel Jones with her idea of filling a large folio with autographs of all the signers of the Confederate Constitution ("*our Decla-ration of Independence*," as he called it), in much the same way that col-lectors were gathering autographs of the U.S. Constitution's signers. This was a novelty much admired by R. A. Brock when Mrs. De Renne wrote him of it. [52]

There was, however, a sequel to Mrs. De Renne's dealings with de Fontaine. During the period in their negotiations when she was letting de Fontaine wonder why she had not responded to his letter, she was approached by the bookselling and publishing firm E. J. Hale & Son of New York City. As agents for the anonymous owner, they offered her the "Opinions of the Department of Justice" of the Confederate States for $4,000. She saw the fine hand of de Fontaine behind this offer: the *Sun* article had established that the volume being offered had been among his finds at Chester. As in the case of the Constitution, she was told that another party was very interested—in this case, the U.S. attorney general, Benjamin H. Brewster—and that the government would probably pay $5,000 or more for it. The owner, however, would prefer that it go "to Southern hands." Mrs. De Renne was not uninterested, but her coolness toward the price quoted brought a rejoinder from Hale that the firm considered the price "an ample equivalent for a document of such historic value" but that "the gentleman in question" had given them authority to invite a "proposition" from her. Hale had probably already gone too far, but he added more: "It is known in the book trade that your agent purchased at auction the small slip of a quartermaster ordering the last official payment of the Confederacy, but this volume . . . must be infinitely more valuable to one who desires to hold in trust for her state, the most precious relics of the Confederacy." Mrs. De Renne did not answer.[53]

Nonetheless, in May 1884, a few months after selling the Provisional Confederate Constitution to W. W. Corcoran, Felix de Fontaine himself appeared in Savannah, remarkably recovered; among his baggage was the volume of attorneys general's opinions, priced for sale.[54] He was assisted by the Georgia Historical Society, which distributed, under its seal, a subscription list in an attempt to raise enough money (at $5 a subscription) to buy the volume for the society, which allowed it to be deposited temporarily at Hodgson Hall. If the plan was still to induce Mrs. De Renne to purchase the volume, those involved could not have proceeded in a more inept fashion, particularly given the subscription circular's curious opening: "To the Citizens of Georgia: By the contribution of a noble lady whose name is well known to all Georgians, there has been secured to the State the Original Permanent Constitution of the late Confederacy. An opportunity now occurs for obtaining *a document that is even more historically valuable* [emphasis added], namely THE OFFICIAL OPINIONS OF ALL OF THE

ATTORNEY GENERALS AND LEGAL ADVISERS IN THE CABINET OF
PRESIDENT DAVIS FROM APRIL, 1861, TO MARCH, 1865." The sub-
scription drive failed, as did de Fontaine's eventual direct proposal that
Mrs. De Renne purchase the volume for the society, and it would not be sold
until 1897—a year after de Fontaine's death—when the New York Public
Library purchased it from his son for $500.[55]

The year 1883 was a remarkable one for Mrs. De Renne's Confederate interests, for reasons other than her purchase of the Permanent Constitution.
While her negotiations with Hanning were under way, one of the most
heartfelt celebrations of the Lost Cause was enacted in Lexington, Virginia.
There, Robert E. Lee had spent the last years of his life as a college president and had there died and been entombed in a crypt below the college
chapel. On June 28, a throng of over eight thousand people gathered on the
campus of what was now Washington and Lee University for ceremonies
marking the unveiling in the chapel of Edward Valentine's fine recumbent
figure of Lee. The principal orator, Confederate veteran John Warwick
Daniel, delivered a lengthy address "celebrating Lee's military genius and
personal character."[56]

In honor of the occasion, Mrs. De Renne had a handsome memorial volume printed in November 1883; it included not only Daniel's speech but
three illustrations as well: a frontispiece ("in the finest style of photogravure") of a detail of Matthew Brady's immediate postsurrender study of
Lee, another photogravure of the recumbent statue, and a plate displaying
the obverse and reverse of a medal that had been struck to commemorate the
unveiling. The edition was limited to one hundred copies, twenty-five quartos on large paper and seventy-five copies in octavo size. Mrs. De Renne had
the twenty-five quartos produced for presentation to her closest friends and
most favored institutions. They were not of the series of Wormsloe Quartos:
the title page for the books, which were printed in Philadelphia, gave Savannah as place of publication. All of the copies were bound by Colonel
Nicholson in "cadet blue pebbled cloth" with the cover imprinted with the
name "Lee" encircled by a golden laurel wreath.[57]

Mrs. De Renne's publishing and collecting activities provided some of the
most pleasant and rewarding moments of her years of widowhood and no
doubt provided welcome distraction from the perplexities and problems
that increasingly beset her. Though his good intentions cannot be doubted,
her husband had framed a will that left Mrs. De Renne and her children

peculiarly dependent on lawyers. Fortunately, De Renne's friends and advisers in the legal profession—notably Henry R. Jackson, A. R. Lawton, and William Starr Basinger—provided her with excellent counsel. Their earliest and most important suggestion was that the Pennsylvania Company be empowered to appoint their firm—Jackson, Lawton, and Basinger—to act as the company's agents in Savannah. With her business in the hands of longtime friends who would take a personal interest in her welfare, Mrs. De Renne found her life much simplified. The firm gave the estate's business and properties its intelligent attention and management and would through its successor—Lawton and Cunningham—be the Savannah agent for the Pennsylvania Company when the estate was finally settled thirty-six years after G. W. J. De Renne's death.[58]

Still, the will created many burdensome complications, particularly for someone who had always been sheltered from all business affairs. At their father's death, Leta and Kentwyn were legally "infants," under twenty-one years of age, and had to have guardians. The trust officer for the Pennsylvania Company agreed to assume Leta's guardianship for the few months that remained before she reached her majority, and Mary was, after initial resistance, allowed to become Kentwyn's guardian until he reached twenty-one in 1883. A petition was granted for funds for "maintenance and support" of Mrs. De Renne and her minor children for the year beginning with De Renne's death: $20,000 (of which $7,000 was to be deducted to give them possession of her husband's wines and other spirits, then calculated at over two thousand bottles, including Madeiras, sherries, French and German wines, port, brandies, whiskeys, and liqueurs).[59]

The family was also given use of the Liberty Street house and all its furnishings, with the same privileges accorded at Wormsloe. For the next decade, Everard and Kentwyn frequented Savannah more than at any other time of their lives. They participated in various organizations, including the Savannah Yacht Club (Wormsloe was handy to one of the club's main racing areas), the Georgia Hussars, and the Oglethorpe Club (which was located in one of the properties of their father's estate). Kentwyn in particular was singled out in the newspaper for a benefaction relating to Bethesda, reminiscent of the philanthropy of his father. But both brothers seem at times to have taken their father's pleasures in the amenities of life farther than he would have thought prudent, and one of the few traces that they left behind in the Savannah gossip of their day was that they were "very fast."[60]

Kentwyn never married. And young Wymberley had conducted his courtship and arranged his engagement and marriage in a fashion that was more romantic than pleasing to his parents. But Everard proceeded to the altar with every respect for the proprieties of the time. The period of his engagement to Jeannette Sterling of Cleveland, Ohio, allowed Mrs. De Renne ample time to conduct the gentle investigations due such an important undertaking as marriage. She found that the young woman was an heiress, the second child and only daughter of Frederick Augustine Sterling, one of Cleveland's wealthiest merchants, and his wife, Emma. Jeannette was present at the Academy of Music in New York City in early March 1882 to see her fiancé receive his diploma as a doctor of medicine, making him the fifth generation of his family to become a physician.[61]

In his marriage and other ways Everard made his mother extremely proud. He was the most accomplished scholar of the family; his four years at Princeton, 1875−79, had been followed by a year as Boudinot Fellow in Modern Language before he began his medical training at New York University. There he had studied assiduously, taking several private courses in addition to his regular course of instruction, and had received practical training in the wards of Bellevue Hospital and in the Chambers Street Clinic. Though no less a personage than Ward McAllister, New York society's *arbiter elegantiarum*, had offered to sponsor him, Everard followed his own social path.[62]

After his graduation in March 1882 Everard had entered into the demanding societal rounds, in New York City and Cleveland, that preceded his wedding in May of that year. The evening ceremony took place at the home of the bride's parents on Euclid Avenue, in the presence of more than one hundred guests, with more than two hundred attending the reception that followed. Among the gifts was an "exquisite" floral parasol, sent by Mrs. De Renne. Following the reception, the couple, "in traveling attire," was "off for the cars" for a trip that included Chicago, St. Louis, and Nashville. That October, after visiting Mary and Leta at Newport, they traveled to Europe. They intended spending time in France, Switzerland, and Italy, after which they were to live for a time in Vienna, where Dr. De Renne was to "perfect his medical studies" at the Allgemein Krankenhaus.[63]

Their European travels were very pleasant and made even more so by the news that their first child would be born during their stay in the Old World. Then, in late March 1883, while they were visiting Milan, Everard was suddenly taken very ill with typhoid fever. Within an hour of the diagnosis, his resourceful wife had him on a train and, without the attending physician's "knowledge or advice," had begun the twenty-two-hour trip to Vienna, where she hoped superior medical care would save him. She did not sleep throughout the journey, instead sitting beside him, feeding him "cracked ice and milk." In Vienna, she had two doctors attend him at the house she rented and hired nurses to be with him constantly. She herself seldom left him and had the nurses wake her every two hours during the night.[64]

For a time it seemed that all her exertions had been in vain. A telegram was sent to warn Mrs. De Renne of her son's critical illness, but by April 7, Everard was somewhat better, though very feeble. At the same time, however, an even more virulent form of the fever struck Jeannette De Renne, who sank rapidly, rallied encouragingly, then suffered a "sudden miscarriage" and died. Among her last words were, "Poor Everard, poor boy, how he must have suffered." Everard De Renne would never remarry or pursue the medical career he had intended. It would be noted of him that he "practiced little," had "independent means and traveled much." In New York City, his home for the rest of his life, Delmonico's and the Racquet Club would figure prominently in his weekly itinerary.[65]

Jeannette De Renne left no will, only a memorandum written during her last days. In it she left Everard her ruby pin as a remembrance and noted that she wished Leta to have the pin that Everard had given to her, as well as the wedding silver the De Rennes had presented them.[66]

By this time the elaborate will of G. W. J. De Renne was taxing the inventiveness of the family's lawyers. They found that a certain amount of creativity would be necessary to protect the interests of both the survivors of the testator and the inheritors to come. It was soon discovered, for example, that the will made no provision for selling and reinvesting any stocks or for disposing of any of the estate's real property, even though some of it might become a financial burden and eat away at the corpus of the estate. The apparatus that the lawyers first devised was to have the family file a complaint against the Pennsylvania Company in the Chatham County Superior Court, relating to whatever transaction was contemplated. As a consequence of the action, the judgment in the case would provide authorization to the Pennsylvania Company (the defendant) to carry out whatever transaction was considered most beneficial.[67]

In an early example of this strategy, in 1881, the lawyers advised selling some of the estate's stock in the Central of Georgia Railroad, which they knew that De Renne had not intended as a permanent investment. At the time that the suit over this matter commenced, the value of each share had reached "the extraordinary amount" of $147 per share, "without any probability of an increase in the dividends." Through the suit it was authorized that the shares be sold and the amount reinvested in Georgia state bonds.[68]

In 1883 her lawyers advised Mary De Renne that a bank building on Johnson Square had become a burden on the estate. This structure, Israel Tefft's workplace when it was the Bank of the State of Georgia, had been one of De Renne's last purchases. Since his death had prevented him and his partners from setting up the business they had planned (the Savannah Trust and Safe Deposit Company), the building had been rented, but it brought in only $300 per annum. As in the case of the Central of Georgia Railroad shares, General Lawton decided that it would be best for the De Rennes to go through the formality of suing the Pennsylvania Company so that the property could be sold. This was done successfully, and $25,000 was added to the estate. In most other cases, the lawyers would work around the will by filing petitions with the Chatham County Superior Court.[69]

Almost unthinkably, thoughts also turned to whether the Clinton Street house in Philadelphia might have become too expensive to maintain. But it was kept, to some extent because of its link to the past and no doubt partially because of its convenient proximity to Dr. Jacob da Costa and Leta's other Philadelphia physicians.[70]

These doctors did not consider Philadelphia a suitable place for Leta to spend her summers, however. Since she was becoming progressively weaker with heart disease, the doctors normally advised sea or mountain air and a change of scene. Leta was too weak to withstand a transatlantic voyage, and, consequently, Mrs. De Renne would never again see Europe. Instead, she and Leta spent time among the natural splendors of the Catskill Mountains and enjoyed the bracing salt breezes of Sea Girt, on the Jersey shore. The doctors also approved Newport as a suitable vacation residence, fortunate since it was Leta's favorite resort, where she had many friends.[71]

Since Leta could not be well, it was Mrs. De Renne's foremost concern that she be as cheerful as possible. As her mother's "constant companion," Leta, simply through her presence, forestalled Mrs. De Renne from expressing her grief or voicing her worries and concerns—these had to be poured out to friends in letters. For her part, Leta in her own illness and be-reavement found much more solace in her religious faith than did her mother, who found little consolation anywhere.[72]

One summer place that had not figured prominently during Mrs. De Renne's married life had taken on increasing importance during her widowhood: Litchfield, Connecticut. There lived the Ritchies, relatives of the Telfairs, to remind her of that happy but now broken circle, and there her father had attended Tapping Reeve's law school before moving to the Florida frontier. And there in Litchfield Mary De Renne died suddenly of an apoplectic stroke on the morning of August 31, 1887, a few months after her fifty-second birthday and just over seven years after her hus-band's death.[73]

Though sudden, her death could not have been entirely unexpected be-cause of her increasing corpulence since her husband's death. By 1884 she had realized that, as one of her sons later wrote, "her coffin [would be] too large to pass the aperture" of the family vault at Bonaventure, and she had prepared a separate brick vault in a corner of the lot. Following her instruc-tions, her survivors and friends met her remains at the Savannah railway depot and formed a cortege that took them directly to Bonaventure for her interment.[74]

In reporting her death, the *Savannah Morning News* noted that she was "well-known not only as the widow of a former prominent and wealthy citizen, but also for many noble qualities. She was a liberal contributor to every charity and did much good with the large fortune in her keeping. By her death Savannah has lost a citizen who took a pride in everything that tended to advance its prosperity."[75]

In the sadness felt by the survivors, Leta, as the child closest to and most dependent on Mrs. De Renne, had a special part. Colonel Jones understood this in writing to her of "the sacredness of her great grief." Remembering his patron, he wrote, "She was so generous, so patriotic, so full of good works, and so replete with everything that was refined, attractive, and ele-vating, that the memory of her many virtues will be cherished by all who were so fortunate as to enjoy her confidence and friendship.[76]

In her will Mary De Renne had divided her considerable personal es-tate—valued at more than $70,000—among her three youngest children (with the proviso that Chatham County's Episcopal orphanage would re-ceive her estate if the three predeceased her); her eldest son, Wymberley, was not named in the instrument. She made a special bequest, however, of one hundred shares of railroad stock to George Nuttall, who had long served her family in slavery and freedom and had been the butler at the De Rennes' Savannah residence.[77]

Leta continued to occupy the Savannah house for part of the year but was unable because of her poor health to take much advantage of Wormsloe, now kept up by caretaker Brutus Butler, one of the former slaves of the plantation. In the North, she seems to have stayed almost exclusively in Philadelphia, where a house on Walnut Street became her principal residence. Toward the end of the decade of the 1880s, she brought to Philadelphia for schooling the two young daughters of the late George Fenwick Jones, who were there when she died in February 1890.[78]

Leta's brothers had spent some time with her in Savannah after their mother's death, but with the loss of their sister they no longer needed the Liberty Street house; it, along with Wormsloe, now reverted to the estate. It was decided to sell the residence because rental income could not keep pace with taxes and upkeep. Consequently, the mansion was sold to the Georgia Hussars several months after Leta's death; it became a very opulent armory and headquarters. At about the same time the house was sold, the brothers also disposed of much of the family furniture, as well as Leta's extensive library and some of the books that had belonged to their parents, a total of over thirteen hundred volumes.[79]

Not to be dispersed were the family's jewelry, *objets de vertu*, portraits, and other heirlooms; the wines and spirits; and the historical collections, along with the voluminous Jones–De Renne archive gathered by their father. Everard had the most interest in these things and had been singled out for the most important bequests in his mother's will, including Charles Willson Peale's portrait of Noble Wimberly Jones. Kentwyn's death at twenty-eight, just over a year after Leta died, left Everard in total control of the family's possessions and, in large part, its history and heritage. At the time of Leta's death, he seems to have known that Kentwyn had only a short time to live, for, though they remained close, he omitted Kentwyn from his will in mid-1890. No one of his blood, in fact, was mentioned in the document. And since he had never remarried, no descendant would participate in the division of the estate when he and all of his siblings were dead.[80]

Between the time of his mother's death and Leta's, Everard had taken from the Liberty Street house most of the books so lovingly collected by his parents, as well as his mother's Confederate relic and manuscript collection. These he identified in his will as the "Mary De Renne Georgia Historical Collection" and the "Mary De Renne Confederate Collection," although the former was for the most part the library of his father. Strangely, Everard at first decided to will these collections to a family friend, Margaret E. Ritchie, a relative of the Telfairs and sometime resident of Litchfield, Connecticut, who had assisted with the settlement of Leta's estate. In December 1893, however, he wrote a codicil to his will that was more logical in all respects, given the interests of his parents. The Mary De Renne Confederate Collection was to be given to the Ladies' Hollywood Memorial Association, then organizing (through the Confederate Memorial Literary Society) the Confederate Museum in Richmond, Virginia; the State Library of Georgia was to take possession of the rest of the books, now more fittingly to be called the "G. W. J. De Renne Georgia Historical Collection."[81]

When Everard died in early 1894, less than three months after writing the codicil, the books were distributed as he had directed. All the rest of his belongings, including some of the heirlooms and all of his personal papers, were divided among three of his friends, who were empowered to sell them if they wished. Whether intentionally or not, he had left the family archive and the most valuable of the heirlooms in a large vault in Savannah's Germania Bank and did not stipulate that they were part of his estate.[82]

Following a March announcement of its bequest, the State Library in June 1894 gratefully received the De Renne books, more than two hundred volumes, as well as assorted maps, photographs, and engravings. By some accident, however, it received a copy of Everard De Renne's original will, without the codicil, and consequently gave his mother's name to the collection, as the original instrument had dictated. Located in the new capitol building in Atlanta, the State Library was in need of accessions, for it had sustained heavy losses in late 1864. At that time the capital was at Milledgeville, and the library had been extensively vandalized and pillaged by Sherman's troops.[83]

Accepting the books for Georgia was the state librarian, John Milledge, descendant and namesake of one of Georgia's first colonists, whose family had long ago owned Modena Plantation, near Wormsloe on Skidaway Island. Milledge, a lawyer and Confederate veteran, had no library training; his was essentially a political appointment. When the boxes of books arrived from New York, he immediately (and idiosyncratically) cataloged them by alphabet (putting titles beginning with "The" in the "T" section, for example) and placed them in a new glass-fronted bookcase purchased to accommodate them. Having begun to buy other books, "touching on the early history of Georgia, South Carolina, and Alabama, and other works of an historical character," he stood them, numbering some fifty-odd, in a second bookcase, placed near the De Renne collection, separate from the law books that made up a great proportion of the library's holdings.[84]

To acquaint the citizens of the state with its new acquisitions, Milledge had his bibliography printed in a twenty-page pamphlet, titled *The De Renne Gift*, that contained the De Renne titles as well as a separate list of the other books relating to southern history. He also furnished a brief introduction explaining how the books had come to the state and applauding the generosity of Dr. De Renne's bequest. The De Renne books, he noted, were "of great value" and included the "transcript in manuscript . . . from the original record in England of the Colonial Acts of Georgia," along with ten of the quartos of the same title and eleven copies of the Egmont quarto.[85]

As readers of the catalog noted, the collection also contained multiple copies of all the Jones–De Renne publications, including an astonishing three copies of the rarest of them, *A Bachelor's Reverie*. As might be expected, there were also numerous eighteenth-century books and pamphlets relating to Georgia's colonial period, G. W. J. De Renne's best-loved subject. There were as well several examples of historical works by Colonel Charles C. Jones Jr., some of which—users noted—were finely bound for presentation and included a beautiful copy of *The Dead Towns of Georgia*, half-bound in red leather.[86]

Over the years, with the De Renne collection as its nucleus, the state library continued to expand, drawing researchers who were preparing books and studies on the history of Georgia. The De Renne books, always kept separate from the others in the library, were an irresistible draw to those knowledgeable of such rarities, for several of its titles could be found nowhere else in the state. Unfortunately, some came not to read but to steal, and by the turn of the century some of the most valuable books had disappeared.[87]

This was not the case with the Mary De Renne Confederate Collection because those books, manuscripts, and relics were displayed, beginning in 1896, in the Confederate Museum. There they were under the constant, jealous care of a group of the unsalaried faithful, who maintained the building, the former Richmond residence of the president of the Confederacy, as a vast and inviolable reliquary. Women representing each of the former Confederate states were assigned an area or room for the display of relics and mementos of the Confederacy. Appropriately tasked with the care and maintenance of the Georgia Room and its De Renne collection was Mrs. De Renne's good friend Katherine C. Stiles, who had helped her to collect the array of books and relics and who for two decades would be the room's custodian.[88]

To Miss Stiles, the Mary De Renne Confederate Collection (which she had apparently helped persuade Everard De Renne to donate) was the sine qua non of the museum. The collection had been willed at a perfect time, she asserted, because adding the books in March 1894 gave strength to the Confederate Memorial Literary Society's titular claim and, in June of the same year, helped prompt the Richmond city government to deed the former Executive Mansion of the Confederate States to the organization for use as a museum. Though her participation in the keen competition among the various "state" rooms may have led Miss Stiles to exaggerate, the collection was immediately adjudged "the finest and most extensive collection of Confederate relics ever made" and required much wall space, a large glass-topped mahogany display case, three bookcases, and numerous leaves of revolving "glass album" stands.[89]

The collection's excellence and extensiveness no doubt helped assure its place of honor in the Confederate Museum. For many years visitors were led through a vestibule to the stately Solid South Room, from which they entered the Georgia Room, located to the right. Looking onto the house's back portico, this large corner room — the western drawing room during Davis's occupancy — shared the first floor with only two other states, Virginia and Mississippi, while the rooms of all other states were distributed in the two upper stories. As visitors entered the Georgia Room, they faced a fireplace over whose mantel was a portrait of John McIntosh Kell, one of Georgia's foremost Confederate naval officers, surrounded by other images and assorted relics, which were displayed in profusion on all of the walls. Large "presses" contained the bulk of the De Renne collection; most of the De Renne books occupied the press to the left, on the portico side of the room. As the 1898 catalog's introduction the collection stated, Mrs. De Renne had "spared neither effort nor expense in gathering books, papers and all that added to their value. [She] soon found that persons were glad to put together what made history, when isolated relics or papers told so little. The result now tells an absorbing story."[90]

By the early 1900s the Confederate Museum had begun to receive nationwide recognition through such articles as "Where Southern Memories Cluster" in a 1906 number of the *Ladies' Home Journal*, which featured photographs of all the display rooms of the museum and noted that the Georgia Room contained "the famous Mary De Renne Confederate collection of books, papers, pictures, and specimens of war-time ingenuity." Increasingly, the museum had begun to attract scholars as well as sightseers and followers of the Lost Cause, having "gained an international reputation as the foremost research facility on the Confederacy." This reputation was enhanced by a young local scholar, Douglas Southall Freeman, who prepared a guide to the museum's print and manuscript collections: *A Calendar of Confederate Papers, with a Bibliography of Some Confederate Publications.* Freeman's guide appeared in 1908, during which year the American Historical Association met in Richmond and was favorably impressed with the facility.[91]

To later generations, who until the 1970s could visit the museum in something approaching its original state, it had somewhat less appeal, and the overcrowded rooms, full of all manner of exhibits, often gave an impression of loosely organized clutter. Nonetheless, this prodigious jumble appealed strongly to the nineteenth-century mind, which seems to have enjoyed being overwhelmed, and most particularly, to the southern mind, with its dislike of abstractions.[92]

Though Henry James looked at the museum's displays and saw only "sorry objects," many southerners saw instead the Cause made real; to a conquered people, the seemingly numberless artifacts served as potent symbols of valor and aspiration. When interpreted by one of the museum's guides, these objects had the power to bring surprisingly sympathetic reactions, even from northerners who had come to scoff.[93]

Although in his musings on the Confederate Museum Henry James would seem almost incapable of anything but a profound misinterpretation of what he saw, even he ultimately viewed these "documentary chambers" with some understanding, as an example of the "Southern state of mind [relating to its] heritage of woe and glory": "The collapse of the old order, the humiliation of defeat, the bereavement and bankruptcy involved, represented, with its obscure miseries and tragedies, the social revolution the most unrecorded and undepicted, in proportion to its magnitude, that ever was; so that this reversion of the starved spirit to the things of the heroic age, the four epic years, is a definite soothing salve."[94]

By 1894 the collections lovingly gathered by Wymberley and Mary De Renne had been launched into a new existence. They would perpetuate the names of their collectors, serve as lodestones for scholarly research, and act as nuclei about which other books would accumulate. By the same year, however, the De Rennes and three of their four children were dead, including the two who had shown the greatest promise of carrying the family's "illustrious traditions" into the next century. But, ironically, 1894 also found Wormsloe rejuvenated, with the second Wymberley De Renne as its master. Though his name had not appeared in the will of his mother or in those of any of his siblings, it was now — and would be until his death — inscribed on a lease to Wormsloe. And, more important, for the first time in Wormsloe's history, the 1890s would find children born with the surname De Renne riding and playing beneath the old plantation's oaks.[95]

PART TWO

A Promise to the Ashes, 1853–1916

CHAPTER 7

Wandering Scion

Who can tell when he sets forth to wander, whither he may be driven by
the uncertain currents of existence; or when he may return; or whether
it may ever be his lot to revisit the scenes of his childhood?
—WASHINGTON IRVING

On the night of December 3, 1863, the blockade runner *Fannie* left the Confederate port of Wilmington, North Carolina. Penetrating the U.S. naval blockade, it sped toward Nassau with a large cargo of cotton and a small number of passengers. Among them was Wymberley De Renne, aged ten; in the care of his young uncle George Fenwick Jones, he was bound, ultimately, for France. Though this was his first extended voyage, it threatened to be his last: his ship was soon hotly pursued by the heavily armed USS *Rhode Island*. Her captain, Stephen Trenchard, had many Rebel prizes to his credit, as well as a reputation for chasing his quarry into British waters, if necessary. Trenchard's target, however, had a reputation of her own; she was wonderfully elusive and normally brought her owner, the Importing and Exporting Company of South Carolina, a profit of over $100,000 for each successful round-trip. During this routine December run, the *Fannie* lived up to her reputation; she easily outran the *Rhode Island*, whose shells fell harmlessly in the blockade runner's wake.[1]

This episode under fire proved to be the most dangerous portion of young De Renne's journey, which had begun weeks earlier, after his parents had decided to accept Mrs. George Noble Jones's invitation for her grandson to join her in France. The invitation had been hand-delivered (and been made practicable to accept) by Mrs. Jones's eldest son, George Fenwick Jones. A recent graduate of the University of Heidelberg, Jones had for a time been an aide to the Confederate envoys to Europe and had been through the blockade before, apparently as an unofficial courier. Accompanying his uncle on his return trip, Wymberley could travel to Europe to pursue his studies in a less haphazard manner than he had previously. Before the war, his schooling had been minimal, whether during his annual half-year in Newport or while he and his family spent their yearly six months at Wormsloe. After the war began, his education had suffered even more. Though he had recently attended classes taught by a woman in Greenville, South Carolina, he asserted that he "did not learn anything by it." Without question, he would have more educational and cultural opportunities in the Old World, and Bellerive, the Swiss institution to which he was bound, was well known on both sides of the Atlantic, as was Professor Edouard-Frederic Sillig, who had founded the school in 1836. Among other Americans who sent their children there was Junius Spencer Morgan, whose son Pierpont attended in 1854. Mr. and Mrs. George Noble Jones had sent their two older sons to Sillig in 1855, and Mrs. Jones felt her youngest, Noble Wimberly — now in attendance there and only a year older than Wymberley — had made much progress during his time at Bellerive.[2]

Consequently, Wymberley prepared to depart for the Old World. First, however, came a leisurely round of trips to visit those members of the family he was leaving behind. Accompanied by his uncle Fenwick, he traveled first to see his grandfather George Noble Jones at Oaklands Plantation near Louisville. There he passed a pleasant week, mostly in the saddle, before spending a similar stretch of time with his father at Wormsloe. Then he visited briefly with his mother, brothers, and sister in Augusta, just before his departure for Wilmington. He and Fenwick Jones had spent several days in the port while the uncle arranged for them to leave the Confederacy.[3]

Once their eventful voyage landed them in Nassau, the two rested for a week before sailing to Havana, Cuba. There they booked passage on a large Spanish steamer, the *Infanta Isabella*, which deposited them in Cádiz during the first week of 1864. Wymberley was particularly glad for the crossing to end, for, despite the steamer's great size, the voyage had not been a smooth one, and he had been constantly seasick.[4]

Finally, on January 10, after sailing to Marseilles and taking the train for the Côte d'Azur, the two travelers arrived at the coastal resort town of Nice, where they were warmly welcomed to the rooms shared by Mary Savage Jones and her daughter Lillie. Not having seen Wymberley since his infancy, Mrs. Jones wrote teasingly to her daughter Mary that he had "excellent manners and keeps himself quite clean, which is a great improvement since I saw him in Newport." The boy who stood before her was, despite his long voyage, "perfectly well," his health, if anything, improved by his experience, and his complexion clear. Mrs. Jones's only regret was that the rest of Wymberley's family had not accompanied him, for only then could she be truly happy.[5]

Though "much surprised" that her grandson now bore the surname De Renne, she felt that it was "judicious" that he change it "so early in life." She noted that even though "Allyn Izzard put off his change very late . . . no one recollects his name as *Smith.*" She also understood that there would be less room for confusion with a more distinctive surname (as opposed to that of her three sons, who, she commented, "have only been known by the illustrious cognomen Jones"). She was also alive to the fact that a name such as *De Renne* would suggest aristocratic lineage to class-conscious European society. Moreover, experimenting with names could not surprise her, for her husband and all her children would make changes in their Christian names at least once, as in the case of her daughter, Lillie Noble Jones, born Sarah Campbell Jones.[6]

Though delighted with her newly arrived grandson, Mrs. Jones had only a brief time to enjoy his company (though long enough to judge him "very bright, good"). Fenwick Jones brought with him instructions from Wymberley's parents that he be enrolled in school as soon as possible, so, after a few weeks' visit, he was taken to his new school by another uncle, Wallace Savage Jones. A graduate of the University of Paris who was then enjoying a vacation from the French military academy at St. Cyr, Wallace, like his elder brother Fenwick, had enjoyed several years at Bellerive, particularly the opportunities for lengthy jaunts into the Alps.[7]

Located in the village of Tour-de-Peilz, adjoining the town of Vevey, Bellerive was on the northeastern shore of Lake Geneva between Montreux and Lausanne. The institute was set in a region of extraordinary natural beauty. Like all others who saw the area, Wymberley was no doubt impressed by the splendor of the encircling, snowcapped mountains and by the incredibly blue waters of Lac Léman. He may have noticed, as had Henry James, Vevey's similarities to "an American watering-place"; its ambience reminded James of Newport. In particular, the Trois Couronnes, a hotel frequented by American tourists, evoked for James the Ocean House, the mammoth hotel that stood opposite the Joneses' Gothic cottage.[8]

As the town nearest Bellerive, Vevey also had much to recommend it, given its cluster of associations with history, literature, and the fine arts. First a Celtic village and then a Roman town, Vevey had in its time been in the hands of assorted Goths, Vandals, and Burgundians. A fragment of a white Roman altar stone was to be found in the Hôtel De Ville, and construction excavations periodically exposed Roman ruins. The town's setting among extensive vineyards, thick with white grapes, prompted festivals "at uncertain periods, chosen usually during years of peace and abundance." These celebrations followed a distinctly classical theme, featuring a thousand costumed revelers, many attired as "Fauns, Satyrs, and Bacchantes," with their leaders masquerading as Bacchus, Ceres, and Silenus.[9]

In the seventeenth century, Vevey had offered refuge to several of the Englishmen who had sent Charles I to the block, including Andrew Broughton, who had read the king his death sentence; a black marble tablet to Broughton's memory stood in Vevey's largest church, its lofty square tower spiked with turrets on each corner. The town had been the setting for Rousseau's *La Nouvelle Heloise,* and across the lake could be seen another literary landmark, the château of Chillon, made famous by Lord Byron's poem. And opposite the only church that held English services was the hotel where Charles-François Gounod had a few years earlier composed his opera *Faust.*[10]

Bellerive's staff of instructors could be depended on to stress Vevey's historical and cultural associations (and those of smaller La Tour-de-Peilz, which had its own Roman past and its medieval castle), but for Wymberley and his schoolmates, the area's recreational opportunities were most seductive. The institute allowed the boys free time for such activities as ice skating, an exercise that had not been a part of Wymberley's Savannah winters, and there was a large stable of horses as well. Edwin Sillig, the founder's son and successor-to-be, also took the boys on periodic excursions; Wymberley was particularly captivated by a "course" to the Great Saint Bernard Pass.

Among the boys, in class and out, he was popular and was awarded two nick-names: "Red Rufus" (for his auburn hair) and "Jupiter," presumably be-cause he had already developed the air of command that would be one of his most salient adult characteristics.[11]

Wymberley made an auspicious start at Bellerive: during his first full month of work he took courses in religion, penmanship, arithmetic, and drawing and received satisfactory (or better) grades in all but the last mentioned—though he would later compile a record of resisting the finer points of penmanship. During his first year at the school, however, his conduct brought him a number of *marques de désapprobation* ("very few" in his grandmother's interpretation), for such offenses as class disturbance, obstinance, and immature behavior, though, as Mrs. Jones also noted, "his manners [were] much commended." If he possessed (or developed) a marked propensity for indiscipline, he had arrived at a place well equipped to deal with it. Sillig was renowned, in America particularly, as some-one whose rigors would be "the solution in cases of recognized wildness"; though he "[dispensed] an education all of milk and honey and edelweiss and ranz-des-vaches," it was "combined with his celebrated firmness."[12]

Wymberley's initial stay at Bellerive lasted for over a year. He made good progress in his studies, particularly in learning French, which he spoke with "an excellent accent." Generally, he enjoyed himself for, as his grand-mother noted, he and Noble had "a variety of pleasures and amusements and [were] never homesick." During one of his short vacations, he went to visit his great-aunts at Château Mirabel, their new residence near Montpel-lier. Their spacious "English" flower garden doubtless appealed to him less than the bluntly medieval aspect of the thirteenth-century structure, long associated with the Chevalier Bayard. Its defensive moat, the set of square machicolated towers that had been deadly to attackers, and many other as-pects of the chateau and its environs were redolent of the Middle Ages. Close by Mirabel, for example, was a "peculiarly elevated" tumulus—the resting place, it was said, of seven knights who had dared measure themselves against the chateau's lord, a landmark perfectly suited to the young boy's imagination.[13]

During the spring of 1865 word finally came that the war had ended. By this time Mrs. Jones and Lillie had tired of Nice and moved to Montpellier. All along, Mrs. Jones had hoped that with the conflict's end, her husband and the De Rennes would remove to France permanently, and (perhaps in anticipation of their coming) she had the boys transferred from Bellerive to the Lycée Impérial at Montpellier. Wymberley was not pleased with the move, even though the Lycée seems to have been less demanding in both studies and conduct than Sillig had been.[14]

Reunited, the De Rennes lived together for a time in Montpellier, where all four of the children received some of their education—the boys at the sprawling, neoclassical Lycée, and Leta at the Pension Hammer. Lillie Noble Jones took much of the responsibility for them, and the young De Rennes grew very close to her during this period. Living near their grandparents, the children took occasional meals with them and were sometimes on hand when they received visitors from America, such as Georgiana King, an old friend from Newport whose family had purchased the Jones cottage and renamed it Kingscote. Georgiana King loved the Joneses' Montpellier residence and remembered particularly its sunny views and the oranges that she enjoyed there in February.[15]

Before Wymberley's parents returned to America permanently in 1871, they sent Everard to attend Bellerive for a period of time. But soon Wymberley was the only member of his family remaining in the Old World. The Joneses had returned to El Destino, with the exception of Fenwick, who had moved to Savannah to practice law. Mrs. Jones had died at Dieppe in 1869, before the French Empire itself expired at the close of the Franco-Prussian War.[16]

In the fall of 1868, Wymberley had returned to Bellerive for three additional years of study. In his advanced courses, he displayed a conspicuous facility for languages and was marked "Very satisfactory" in Greek, Latin, and German and "Totally satisfactory" in French. He also did well in penmanship (at last) and in geography and history (the latter, in a sense, attended Bellerive in the form of one of his classmates, the Prince Victor Napoleon). He achieved the highest grades possible in mathematics (in both "application and progress" and "conduct in class") and, unsurprisingly, riding—always one of his passions. As he matured physically, so did his conduct, leading to a disappearance of the *marques de désapprobation.* At the time he left Bellerive for good in June 1871, Sillig wrote that Wymberley had "distinguished himself above all for his zeal for studying and for the sustained efforts he made to join the top ranks in terms of conduct. Consequently, we remember him as a good student, and he received the affection of all who devoted their attention to him."[17]

Wymberley's next educational experience would be far different, for he was leaving the placid environs of Lake Geneva for a university education in Germany. He was now eighteen, and most of the pressures of the previous eight years were suddenly gone. James Morgan Hart, who attended the University of Göttingen in the 1860s, provided a detailed description of the dramatic change that Germany university novices experienced. Like other incoming German university students, according to Hart's general descriptions, Wymberley had suddenly become his own master and was no doubt somewhat unsettled by his new freedom. He had changed his place of residence and could now live alone if he wished. He had some choice both in deciding his schedule and in determining whether to attend lectures; he had formed new associations and been brought into contact with "unwonted temptations. A new life [had] suddenly dawned upon him." Consequently, according to Hart, it was not unusual for a young man entering the university to spend at least a semester "undergoing the process called in German *ausrasen,* called [in America] 'sowing wild oats.' But if there [was] in him the making of a man, the dream [would] not last forever." [18]

Wymberley's attendance at the university, however, had the backing of his father. Before returning to America in 1871, G. W. J. De Renne had visited several universities in the newly forged German Empire, with a view toward enrolling Wymberley in one of them. His choice was the University of Leipzig. Dating from the early fifteenth century, it had during this period an enrollment of over twenty-five hundred (among them fewer than fifty American students). Among its alumni were numbered Johann Wolfgang von Goethe (a fitting predecessor for a young man now embarked on living a *Bildungsroman* of his own) and Leopold von Ranke, father of scientific historiography, whose ideas would energize many historians of Wymberley's generation, much as Scott had inspired the romantic historians of G. W. J. De Renne's day. [19]

The university was set in a large city of over one hundred thousand people. Leipzig's name strongly evoked Napoleon's disaster at the Battle of Nations, but the city's cultural eminence was closely related to its early commitment to the printing of books. Dominated by the medieval tower of the Pleissenburg—"a mighty, rugged thing"—the city, in its more ancient sections, emanated "an intimate, Old-World, human flavor": narrow streets wound through steep blocks of aged buildings, lighted from above by a ribbon of sky. In the environs of the university all was spaciousness and neoclassical formality, particularly in the wide Augustus-Platz, bounded on the west by the dignity of the university's Augusteum. Wymberley was to study in Leipzig for two years, in one of the most celebrated European cultural centers, attending lectures in such courses as philosophy, logic, and international law. But one of the most memorable aspects of his university education had little to do with education or culture, at least in their most widely accepted senses.[20]

In his father's library was a book titled *The Student-Life of Germany;* its title page featured a crude but lively woodcut of a group of students brandishing duelling swords, and it was this subculture of the duellists that captivated young De Renne, formed some of his most enduring associations, and forged many of his most cherished memories. In the most literal sense, none of his other educational experiences would mark him as permanently. It would be interesting to know what Wymberley's grandfather George Jones—as one of the founders of the Savannah Anti-Duelling Association—would have thought of this enthusiasm for swordplay, though, unlike the Savannah duels, the death of one of the combatants was normally an unfortunate and unintended consequence of the contest, not its raison d'être.[21]

The young duellists organized themselves into corps—fraternities of the sword—and were as famous for hard drinking as for fighting. "The cardinal sin of the students is excess in drinking," wrote Hart. "They all drink, and nearly all drink too much." Hart qualified his statement, however, by noting that everyone in Germany drank "as a matter of course" and that their beverages of choice, beer and wine, were "much less injurious to the health than the gin and whisky of America," which "[waste] the tissues and nervous energy." More hopeless sots, he asserted, could be found in an average American village than in a German town like Leipzig.[22]

Most of the corps-students' songs had to do with drinking, including a popular one in which a young man tells his fellows what to do with him when, "faint with gout and palsy," he nears death. His summons having come, he is to be placed in a "Rhenish cask" instead of a coffin, and the cask topped off with wine. Once he is buried, his gravestone is to say:

This man was born, grew, drank, and died,—
And now he rests where he imbibed
In lifelong joy the purple tide.

The dueling corps were expressions of the class system in Germany, open mainly to the upper social tiers, particularly in the sense that membership

Bellerive, Switzerland. Lithograph by J. Jacottet. (Musée historique du Vieux-Vevey.)

Château Mirabel, France. (De Renne Collection, Hargrett Rare Book and Manuscript Library, University of Georgia Libraries.)

MAP 2. Western Europe, 1870s

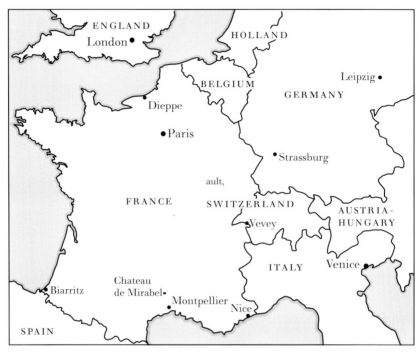

Sources: Alexander Keith Johnston, *Europe,* 1879; maps in the Archives Départementales de l'Hérault, France.

Leipzig, Germany. An early nineteenth-century view showing the Pleissenburg, the city's medieval citadel. (Library of Congress.)

The duellist: Wymberley De Renne in Leipzig, 1873. (Courtesy of Eudora De Renne Roebling.)

German corps-students duelling. (De Renne Collection, Hargrett Rare Book and Manuscript Library, University of Georgia Libraries.)

A Japanese temple, as pictured in a souvenir photograph from Wymberley De Renne's visit to Japan. (De Renne Collection, Hargrett Rare Book and Manuscript Library, University of Georgia Libraries.)

MAP 3. Texas and the Concho Country, 1870s–1880s

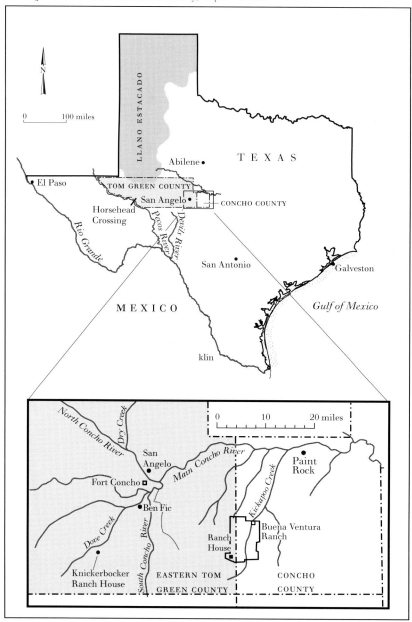

Sources: *The Buena Ventura Stock Ranch, Tom Green County, Texas,* 1891, privately held; *Buena Ventura Stock Co.,* Hargrett Rare Book and Manuscript Library, University of Georgia, Box 17, Ms, 1964; Leona M. Ross Clemens, "The Concho Country [map]," in *The Concho Country,* by Gus Clemens (San Antonio, Texas, 1980); William Elton Green, *Land Settlement in West Texas: Tom Green County, A Case Study, 1874–1903* (Ph.D. dissertation, Texas Tech University, 1981), 97, 270; A. Ray Stephens and William M. Holmes, *Historical Atlas of Texas* (Norman, Oklahoma, 1989), map 4.

Joseph Tweedy of the Knickerbocker Ranch. (Fort Concho National Historic Landmark, San Angelo, Texas.)

Fort Concho, Texas, with the North Concho River in the foreground. (Fort Concho National Historic Landmark, San Angelo, Texas.)

San Angelo, Texas, c. 1880s. (Tom Green County Historical Society, West Texas Collection, Angelo State University.)

Sheep shearers at work near the Knickerbocker Ranch. (Tom Green County Historical Society, West Texas Collection, Angelo State University.)

Laura De Renne.
(Courtesy of Eudora
De Renne Roebling.)

Buena Ventura Ranch. Home Ranch—Looking East. (De Renne Collection,
Hargrett Rare Book and Manuscript Library, University of Georgia Libraries.)

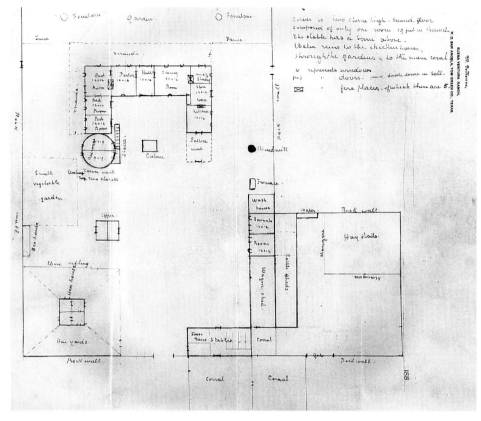

Wymberley De Renne's plan of his ranch house and outbuildings at Buena
Ventura, done on ranch stationery showing San Angelo's spelling at that time.
(De Renne Collection, Hargrett Rare Book and Manuscript Library, University
of Georgia Libraries.)

The central hall of the Buena
Ventura ranch house, looking into
the dining room. The door beyond
is a modern alteration. (Courtesy
of Mr. and Mrs. A. H. Denis III.)

The ranch house tower. (Courtesy of
Mr. and Mrs. A. H. Denis III.)

The grave at Buena Ventura.
(Courtesy of Mr. and Mrs. A. H.
Denis III.)

William Vernon
(1856–1913) with
his wife and child.
(Tom Green
County Historical
Society, West
Texas Collection,
Angelo State
University.)

Certificate of the Buena Ventura Stock Company, with signatures of the partners.
(De Renne Collection, Hargrett Rare Book and Manuscript Library, University
of Georgia Libraries.)

Biarritz, France.
(De Renne Collec-
tion, Hargrett Rare
Book and Manuscript
Library, University
of Georgia Libraries.)

Wymberley De
Renne at Biarritz.
(Courtesy of Eudora
De Renne Roebling.)

Elfrida De Renne. (Courtesy of Malcolm Bell III.)

Villa Constance, Biarritz, birthplace of Wymberley Wormsloe De Renne. (Archives d'Architecture de la Côte Basque, Biarritz.)

The original Oak Avenue (the "Old Avenue") at Wormsloe, May 1, 1895. (Courtesy of Eudora De Renne Roebling.)

The gate to the Old Avenue, from Skidaway Road, April 1909. (De Renne Collection, Hargrett Rare Book and Manuscript Library, University of Georgia Libraries.)

The Hotel De Soto. (From *Art Work of Savannah and Augusta,* 1902.)

Westport Inn on Lake Champlain, c. 1903. (Courtesy of the Westport Library Association.)

Wymberley Jones De Renne, Germany, 1896. (Courtesy of Eudora De Renne Roebling.)

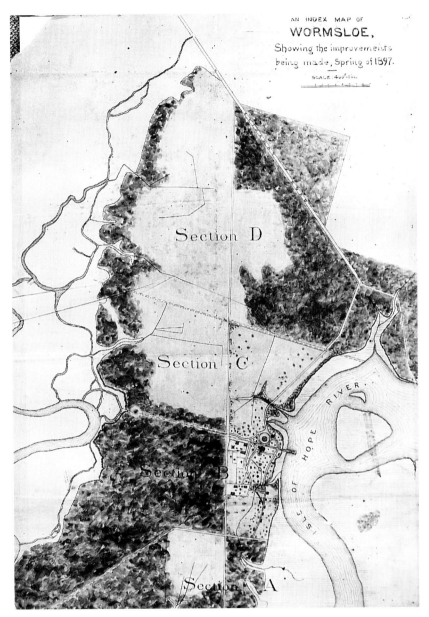

A portion of Wormsloe Plantation in 1897. (De Renne Collection, Hargrett Rare Book and Manuscript Library, University of Georgia Libraries.)

MAP 4. Wormsloe Plantation, Chatham County, Georgia, early 1900s

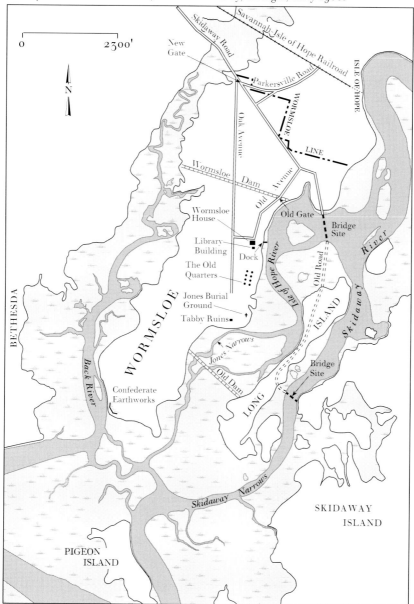

Sources: W. O'D. Rockwell, *Map of Wormsloe and Vicinity Compiled from Authentic Maps,* 1908,
Hargrett Rare Book and Manuscript Library, University of Georgia, oversize drawer, Ms. 2819;
Marmaduke Floyd *A Map of Wormsloe* [1927], Hargrett Rare Book and Manuscript Library, Univer-
sity of Georgia, Box 24, Ms. 2819; Thomas and Hutton, Engineers, *Map of Wormsloe and Vicinity
Compiled from Authentic Maps and Aerial Photographs and Plat Showing Portions of Wormsloe,
Chatham County,* 1960, Superior Court Records, Chatham County, Georgia, Plat Record Book L,
Folios 118 and 119.

Top: Wormsloe House, north front, 1899. (De Renne Collection, Hargrett Rare Book and Manuscript Library, University of Georgia Libraries.) *Bottom:* Wormsloe House, south front, 1899. (De Renne Collection, Hargrett Rare Book and Manuscript Library, University of Georgia Libraries.)

The first-floor hall in Wormsloe House, 1899. (Courtesy of Eudora De Renne Roebling.)

The dining room in Wormsloe House, 1899, showing the 1873 portrait of Mary De Renne by the English society portraitist Louis William DesAnges (1822–1887). (Wormsloe Collection, Hargrett Rare Book and Manuscript Library, University of Georgia Libraries.)

Top: The stables, cottage, and water tower at Wormsloe, 1899. (Courtesy of Eudora De Renne Roebling.) *Bottom:* W. J. De Renne, children, and stable hand, May 1, 1895. (Courtesy of Eudora De Renne Roebling.)

Wormsloe House, south front, 1901, showing the newly added servants' wing and second-floor boudoir, next to the tower. (Courtesy of Eudora De Renne Roebling.)

Wormsloe House. Architect's sketch of the north front. (De Renne Collection, Hargrett Rare Book and Manuscript Library, University of Georgia Libraries.)

Wymberley, Elfrida, and Audrey De Renne, c. 1893. (Courtesy of Eudora De Renne Roebling.)

W. J. De Renne at the Jones burial ground, Wormsloe, 1899. (Courtesy of Eudora De Renne Roebling.)

The Oak Avenue at Wormsloe. (Wormsloe Historic Site.)

Wormsloe arch and gate. (Wormsloe Historic Site.)

Sketch of the Wormsloe arch and gate, 1912. (De Renne Collection, Hargrett Rare Book and Manuscript Library, University of Georgia Libraries.)

The Georgia Hussars at Wormsloe, February 22, 1895. (Courtesy of Eudora De Renne Roebling.)

Left: Detail of the cover of *Address of Colonel John Screven,* 1892. (Hargrett Rare Book and Manuscript Library, University of Georgia Libraries.) *Right:* J. G. B. Bulloch (1852–1934). (Courtesy of Eudora De Renne Roebling.)

Burton A. Konkle, biographer of
Thomas Smith. (Courtesy of William
C. Fischer.)

Presentation copy of *The Life and
Times of Thomas Smith*, 1904, given
by Burton Konkle to W. J. De Renne.
(Courtesy of Eudora De Renne
Roebling.)

Martha Lumpkin Compton.
(Hargrett Rare Book and Manuscript
Library, University of Georgia
Libraries.)

Left: Wilson Lumpkin, governor of Georgia, 1831–35. (Hargrett Rare Book and Manuscript Library, University of Georgia Libraries.) *Right:* The Lumpkin manuscript volumes and the book that came from them, *The Removal of the Cherokee Indians from Georgia*, 1907. (De Renne Library, Hargrett Rare Book and Manuscript Library, University of Georgia Libraries.)

The receipt for the Lumpkin manuscripts. (De Renne Collection, Hargrett Rare Book and Manuscript Library, University of Georgia Libraries.)

THE REMOVAL
OF THE
CHEROKEE INDIANS
FROM
GEORGIA.

BY
WILSON LUMPKIN.

INCLUDING

His Speeches in the United States Congress on the Indian Question, as Representative and Senator of Georgia; His Official Correspondence on the Removal of the Cherokees during his two terms as Governor of Georgia, and later as United States Commissioner to the Cherokees.

1827-1841

Together with a Sketch of His Life and Conduct while holding many Public Offices under the Government of Georgia and the United States, prior to 1827, and after 1841.

VOLUME I

PRIVATELY PRINTED
WORMSLOE
1907

DODD, MEAD & COMPANY
Publishers — New York

The Birth of the Confederacy

Jefferson Davis taking the Oath as First President at Montgomery, Ala., February 18, 1861.

Left: Title page of *The Removal of the Cherokee Indians from Georgia.* (De Renne Library, Hargrett Rare Book and Manuscript Library, University of Georgia Libraries.) *Right:* Cover illustration of *A Short History of the Confederate Constitutions,* 1909. (De Renne Library, Hargrett Rare Book and Manuscript Library, University of Georgia Libraries.)

William Harden (1844–1936), librarian of the Georgia Historical Society from 1869 until his death. (Hargrett Rare Book and Manuscript Library, University of Georgia Libraries.)

Douglas Southall Freeman, 1910.
(Dementi Foster Studios, Richmond,
Virginia.)

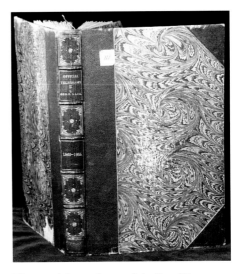

The surviving volume of the Lee Dispatches. (Special Collections Library,
Duke University.)

LEE'S DISPATCHES

Unpublished Letters

of

General Robert E. Lee, C.S.A.

to

Jefferson Davis and the War Department of
The Confederate States of America

1862–65

From the Private Collection of

WYMBERLEY JONES DE RENNE

of Wormsloe, Georgia

Edited with an Introduction by

DOUGLAS SOUTHALL FREEMAN

G. P. PUTNAM'S SONS
NEW YORK AND LONDON
The Knickerbocker Press
1915

Title page of *Lee's
Dispatches*, 1915.
(De Renne Library,
Hargrett Rare Book
and Manuscript
Library, University
of Georgia Libraries.)

Left: Bookplate of W. J. De Renne, as it appears in his copy of *A Bachelor's Reverie*, bound by Launder of New York. (De Renne Library, Hargrett Rare Book and Manuscript Library, University of Georgia Libraries.) *Right:* The Wormsloe Quartos, bound "in green crushed levant morocco, gilt" by Launder for W. J. De Renne. (De Renne Library, Hargrett Rare Book and Manuscript Library, University of Georgia Libraries.)

The Alpha and
Omega of the
De Renne
Georgia Library

Left: McCall's *History of Georgia*, the first Georgia title purchased by W. J. De Renne. (De Renne Library, Hargrett Rare Book and Manuscript Library, University of Georgia Libraries.) *Right: Charters of North America*, the last Georgia title purchased by W. J. De Renne. (De Renne Library, Hargrett Rare Book and Manuscript Library, University of Georgia Libraries.)

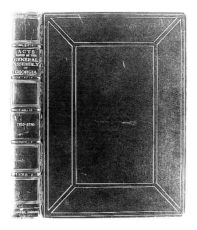 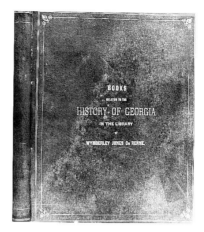

Left: The William Ewen volume of Georgia session laws, bound by Launder. (De Renne Library, Hargrett Rare Book and Manuscript Library, University of Georgia Libraries.) *Right:* The first catalog of the De Renne Georgia Library, 1905. (De Renne Library, Hargrett Rare Book and Manuscript Library, University of Georgia Libraries.)

List of Books Wanted

by

Wymberley Jones DeRenne,

Savannah, Georgia.

ÜRLSPERGER, SAMUEL, Amerikanisches Ackerwerk Gottes oder zuverlässige Nachrichten den zustand der Amerikanish Englischen und von Saltzburgischen Emigranten erbauten Pflanzstadt Ebenezer in Georgien betreffend. Augsburg, 1754-1767 4to.

BOTH SIDES OF THE QUESTION, or a Candid and Impartial Enquiry into a Certain Doubtful Character, in a Letter to a General Officer, remarkably acquitted by a C——t M——l. London, J. Meebell, 1749, 8vo. pp. 28. Relates to Georgia and South Carolina.

THE GENERAL ACCOUNT OF THE MONIES AND EFFECTS, received and expended by the Trustees for establishing the Colony of Georgia, in America, London. 1786 folio. pp. 29.

PROCEEDINGS OF A COUNCIL OF WAR, HELD AT BURKE JAIL, GEORGIA, June 14th. 1779, with a narrative of the subsequent proceedings, and the proclamation issued by Lieut. Col. James Ingram, Edited by Paul Leicester Ford, Brooklyn, N. Y. Historical Printing Club, 1890, 12mo. pp. 20. Edition 250 copies. Worthington Chauncey Ford. Cong. Lib. in Wash. Now first printed from the original mss. detailing much in the Revolutionary Contest unnoticed by all writers. It relates to a military movement in Georgia, early in 1779, and contradicts the historians of that state in a most essential point.

CURSORY REMARKS ON MEN AND MEASURES IN GEORGIA. Anonymous pamphlet 1784.

GOV. CLARKE'S PAMPHLET AGAINST CRAWFORD, TAIT AND MITCHELL, 1819

WHITEFIELDS WORKS, (Ed. Chas. Daily?) London 1772. for letters to the Orphan House and Reports.

An account of the Foundation and Establishment on the Golden Islands, South of Port Royal (in Carolina) London 1820.

An act for the better regulation of the Indian trade, 1735.

Journal of the Proceedings in Georgia, by William Stephens Esq. vol. III. 1748.

One of W. J. De Renne's want lists. (De Renne Collection, Hargrett Rare Book and Manuscript Library, University of Georgia Libraries.)

The Wormsloe House study: Audrey, W. W., and W. J. De Renne, 1899. (Wormsloe Collection, Hargrett Rare Book and Manuscript Library, University of Georgia Libraries.)

The library building at Wormsloe, as proposed in an original sketch by Henrik Wallin, 1907. (De Renne Collection, Hargrett Rare Book and Manuscript Library, University of Georgia Libraries.)

The library building at Wormsloe under construction. (De Renne Collection, Hargrett Rare Book and Manuscript Library, University of Georgia Libraries.)

The library building at Wormsloe. (De Renne Collection, Hargrett Rare Book and Manuscript Library, University of Georgia Libraries.)

Top: The library building at Wormsloe—interior, facing west. (Wormsloe Collection, Hargrett Rare Book and Manuscript Library, University of Georgia Libraries.) *Bottom:* The library building at Wormsloe—interior, facing east. (Wormsloe Collection, Hargrett Rare Book and Manuscript Library, University of Georgia Libraries.)

Elfrida De Renne Barrow in her wedding gown. (De Renne Collection, Hargrett
Rare Book and Manuscript Library, University of Georgia Libraries.)

Dr. Craig Barrow in the Liberty Street house. (Wormsloe Historic Site.)

W. J. De Renne, working beneath a silhouette of his son. (Courtesy of Eudora De Renne Roebling.)

Audrey De Renne and W. W. De Renne, early 1900s. (Courtesy of Eudora De Renne Roebling.)

Audrey De Renne
Coerr. (Courtesy of
Eudora De Renne
Roebling.)

Virginia, Frederica,
and Wymberley
Coerr. (De Renne
Collection, Hargrett
Rare Book and Man-
uscript Library, Uni-
versity of Georgia
Libraries.)

Charles Edgeworth
Jones, 1867–1931.
(Special Collections
Library, Duke
University.)

Julius L. Brown.
(Hargrett Rare Book
and Manuscript Li-
brary, University of
Georgia Libraries.)

Left: Telamon Cuyler at Wormsloe, April 1909. (De Renne Collection, Hargrett Rare Book and Manuscript Library, University of Georgia Libraries.)
Below: W. J. De Renne, U. B. Phillips, and Alexander McC. Duncan in the portico of the library building at Wormsloe, April 1909. (De Renne Collection, Hargrett Rare Book and Manuscript Library, University of Georgia Libraries.)

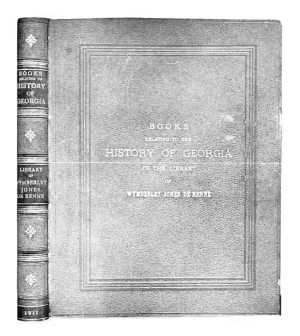

The second catalog
of the De Renne
Georgia Library, 1911.
(De Renne Library,
Hargrett Rare Book
and Manuscript
Library, University of
Georgia Libraries.)

Left: Robert Preston Brooks. (Hargrett Rare Book and Manuscript Library, University of Georgia Libraries.) *Right:* Leonard L. Mackall, bibliophile and bibliographer. (Hargrett Rare Book and Manuscript Library, University of Georgia Libraries.)

Herbert Putnam, Librarian of Congress for forty years, 1899–1939. (Library of Congress.)

One of the last photographs of W. J. De Renne. (Courtesy of Eudora De Renne Roebling.)

Top: W. J. De Renne, the 1915 portrait by Gari Melchers (1860–1932). Wearing a boutonniere of yellow jessamine, De Renne sat for Melchers in his library at Wormsloe. (Courtesy of the Wormsloe Foundation.) *Bottom:* Signature of W. J. De Renne. (De Renne Collection, Hargrett Rare Book and Manuscript Library, University of Georgia Libraries.)

The turreted Hotel Netherland, New York City, with, in the foreground, left of center, Augustus Saint-Gaudens's *Sherman*, unveiled in 1903. (Cityana Gallery, New York.)

was expensive. The duellists were always a minority of students, but, as one authority noted, "being well organized and comprising nearly all the stirring, aggressive elements, they shaped things pretty much to suit themselves." [23]

Meeting rooms of the duelling corps were usually conveniently located above restaurants and taverns; the walls were hung with swords, as well as "coats of arms and colors, trophies, ornaments, photographs of members past and present." In this atmosphere, the corps-students gathered convivially for talking, smoking, and drinking. Wymberley's organization was the Saxonia Corps, which had been founded in 1812. He particularly gloried in writing his corps' elaborate monogram after his name; it was composed of the initial letters of the corps' motto: *Virtuti Semper Corona*—"Valor Is Always the Crown." [24]

Along with proving one's courage (and capacity for suffering wounds manfully), there were other reasons for corps-students to fight duels, including the redress of insults or simple boisterousness (as in "renowning," picking fights through insolent actions). But Wymberley felt that the most honorable cause for duelling lay in fighting representatives of rival corps so that victories with the blade would shine in the corps record book (and on the duelling ribbons) of the duellist and do "honor to his individual record." [25]

Whatever the reason for a duel (known as a *Mensur*), it always took place in some secluded area (whether a room, an enclosed yard, or a forest clearing) and proceeded in a severely regulated manner. In addition to spectators and duellists waiting their turn, there were always two seconds, two witnesses, and an umpire and a surgeon; the last mentioned was equipped with basins of water, linen bandages, and curved needles for stitching. The duellists were fitted out in a special costume that protected the upper body: a gorget of thickly wound silk to protect the neck arteries, a cuirass of leather or quilted cloth that stretched from neck to thighs, and quilted detachable sleeves (much thicker on the sword arm), with a heavy fencing glove for the sword hand. The duellist could partially protect his free arm by gripping a tag of leather that projected from the back of the cuirass, thus partially shielding the arm behind his trunk. Though the face was meant to be the vulnerable area, some concession was made by protecting the eyes with heavy iron goggles. This allowed the student to receive a coveted scar with relatively little risk of losing his sight—a scar that would win from men an admiration for his courage and would prove attractive to the opposite gender as well. In sum, it was thought to be "a convenience to carry the record of one's valor upon the countenance."[26]

The contest, restricted in area and movement, was fought between two lines twelve feet apart, and the combatants were required to remain rooted a yard from each other. They had to use great economy of movement, confining the motion of their bodies mainly to their wrists and waists, and had to employ the extremely tiring "hanging guard," which kept their sword hands elevated above their heads. Consequently, they did not use the downward cut employed for sabers but a "short, quick whipping motion, whereby the swordsman . . . lets the sword revolve with the hand on a free wrist . . . and tries to cut over or under his adversary's guard." The opponents were forbidden both to move their heads to avoid approaching blows and to use the riposte. As Wymberley saw it, the duellist should have "no other advantages . . . than those a skilled wrist can give."[27]

The weapon used, called a *Schläger*, had a basket hilt. Since the swordplay was based on slashing instead of thrusting, the three-and-a-half-foot blade was blunt at the end; its cutting edge, fresh from the grindstone, ran twenty inches from the square tip. After the seconds used their swords to place the weapons of the combatants together, the command "*Los!*" ("Apart!") was shouted, and the duel began, with strokes directed toward the head, arm, and chest.[28]

Whenever one of the duellists received a wound (usually to the face or scalp), the fighting was stopped so that a surgeon could determine whether the cut was serious enough to end the fight. Such wounds could include the loss of a nose or ear or a cut that reached the bone; some slices across the cheek were known to expose the jaw teeth. If dangerous wounds were not inflicted, the fighting continued for a maximum of fifteen minutes, not counting the pauses for examining injuries. Combatants sometimes received several cuts before the period was over, and if both held out for the maximum time their valor was proven, and the surgeon began his work. For winning a duel (normally, delivering a cut that ended the match before the fifteen minutes expired), the swordsman was given a sash of corps colors to wear. After his third successful duel, he was under no necessity to fight again, though many continued to volunteer. Since the scars were seen as tributes to the owner's courage and stoicism, some young men became quite disfigured.[29]

When Wymberley left Leipzig in the fall of 1873 he had both a certificate of studies completed and a large duelling scar that crisscrossed his left temple. The scar did not look out of place in Germany. Among its soldier and professional classes, it was not uncommon to see faces marked by duels; indeed, one commentator of the 1880s went so far as to say that there was "scarcely a German of prominence whose face [did] not bear witness to encounters of this sort; and these reminiscences of student days may be seen engraven upon the faces of judges and senators and advocates, the same as upon officers of the army."[50]

But there was much negative comment about duelling both in books and in the press; about all the good that most critics could say of it was that it prevented street brawling. At its worst, it was called mere savagery or a ridiculous spectacle. Novelist Jerome K. Jerome, who witnessed a corps-student duel, called it a "successful attempt to combine the ludicrous with the unpleasant." Since the scar was so important to the duel, one commentator argued that the "combats were not really duels at all, but elaborate ritualistic facial operations." Yet duelling to the death also went on in the Europe of that day, and public opinion seemed to support the duel in all forms. As one critic wrote, "Here are hundreds of youths . . . all more or less imbued with the notion that it is right and honorable to resent an insult, all at that age in life when passion runs highest, sustained and even urged on by the general opinion of the community, that looks upon a *Mensur* as a venial youthful escapade, and a *Schläger* scar as something to boast of in afterlife."[51]

During his years of such revelry and diversions at Leipzig, Wymberley had also done a certain amount of studying. In any case, he received a certificate from the university showing attendance in several courses, together with a notice that "considering his moral behavior, nothing adverse has happened." During 1873–74 Wymberley continued his law studies at the university in recently besieged Strassburg, near Germany's border with France; the University of Strassburg, had, in fact, been a French university until the end of the Franco-Prussian War. Nonetheless, compared to Wymberley's time in Leipzig, his stay at Strassburg must have seemed sedate.[52]

Having spent a decade on his continental education, Wymberley at last prepared to return to the country he had left at age ten, but his parents determined to give him a Grand Tour before he settled down to his degree work at Columbia University. Since his years in France, Switzerland, and Germany had offered numerous opportunities for traveling in Europe, it was decided that he would be sent on a tour of the Far East.[53]

Ironically, the 1875 trip to the Orient also presented an opportunity for

Wymberley to become somewhat better acquainted with the United States during his week-long rail journey from New York City to San Francisco. As he crossed the country, he found little to impress him until he passed Omaha, Nebraska, and first experienced the vast western plains. Huge expanses of grassland had been set aflame by settlers, and Wymberley was astonished by the sight of such a conflagration by night. By day he was amused by the teeming villages of prairie dogs and awestruck by desert whirlwinds that took the sand "right up in the air like a column of water blown up by a fountain." Crossing the Rockies, he marveled at the engineering and construction skills that had cut roadbeds through the mountains and was appalled by a spectacular three-locomotive accident brought on by a careless telegrapher.[54]

Upon arriving in San Francisco, he judged it delightful, particularly because it reminded him of European cities he had known. Well supplied with letters of introduction to local citizens (including representatives of Savannah's far-flung McAllister clan), he dined out several times, visited clubs, and secured additional letters of introduction to various Americans living in the Asian cities he was to visit.[55]

Wymberley began his journey to the Far East in mid-May 1875 on board the *City of Peking*, a "very fine ship of 5500 tons." Among the amenities of travel were large staterooms and pistols—all the passengers had been armed in case of a mutiny by the Chinese sailors. The Chinese waiters in the dining room presented different problems: "They sometimes bring you red pepper when you ask for cauliflower & chocolate when you ask for stew." A letter of introduction to the captain, however, soon had Wymberley placed near him at table, where such confusion could easily be set right.[56]

During the three-week voyage, Wymberley mainly amused himself by reading and was careful to keep a journal of his activities, which he would mail to his mother and father as opportunities allowed. Though he wished that he had the power to send them "an account better than the Comte de Beauvoir's," he feared his descriptions were instead a "miserable barbouillage." While other passengers spent their time, day in and day out, in card playing (for which Wymberley admitted he had an enthusiasm), he had made certain solemn promises to his parents before leaving, and card playing was one of the pastimes he had been persuaded to deny himself. Most of the Chinese crew, he noted, spent much of their time gambling belowdeck; they normally came topside only on days when cattle and other stock were brought up to be slaughtered so that they could lay claim to the intestines.[57]

Wymberley's decktime amusements were confined mainly to walking and watching the play of dolphins and porpoises. He also learned from the captain how to "take the time" sailor-fashion, as well as other practical skills such as splicing rope. Late in the voyage he and some of his fellow passengers also tested their firearms on the bosun birds that flew over the ship, trying to make one fall on the deck so as to get its long red tail feathers. To the marksmen's disappointment, all birds that were hit fell into the sea.[38]

At one point, Wymberley's knowledge of French was called upon in a bizarre fashion. A peculiar youth began to vex his fellow passengers by speaking to them continuously in what seemed to be some form of French. Confronted by Wymberley and questioned in French, the boy became nonplussed, claiming that he did not speak the kind of French that Wymberley was using. He was quiet for the rest of the trip and his former victims thanked Wymberley for their deliverance.[39]

All told, Wymberley found the crossing very pleasant. During his voyage, he had no recurrence of the seasickness that had troubled him in his first Atlantic crossing, even though the passage was unusually rough. The Pacific, the captain explained, had won its name from its character in the lower latitudes, not from its rowdy behavior along the thirty-seventh parallel.[40]

When the ship sailed into Yokohama, Wymberley paid Tokyo Bay the compliment of comparing it to a Swiss lake and gazed admiringly at the grandeur of Mount Fuji in the distance. He was fascinated by the contrasts of the various shades of green in the lush foliage and in the fields that met his eye. As his ship proceeded to its anchorage, he closely examined the striped sailed junks and numerous sampans.[41]

His joy at finding the Grand Hotel's boat ready to take him ashore was tempered by finding that the hotel resembled a prison. During a subsequent rickshaw tour of the town, he was startled to find that the buildings never exceeded one story because of the danger of earthquakes. Though he was surprised at the number of Japanese men he saw wearing European clothes and hairstyles, the emperor (a young man his own age) had been Westernizing his country at a rapid rate. Japan had been opened to the West only some twenty years earlier (at which time Yokohama had been built southwest of Tokyo), and Wymberley found some aspects of the cultural transformation that had followed to be unfortunate, particularly the presence of inferior European furniture in Japanese homes and palaces.[42]

During his stay he sampled the pleasures of the English Club and took several tours of the local shops, viewing with interest the bronzes, porcelain, lacquer work, and silks they displayed. He conserved his funds, however, by purchasing little beyond standard tourist souvenirs and packets of seeds that his mother had requested for the garden at the Liberty Street residence. His happiest time was spent on a horseback tour of various nearby sites, most already famous as tourist attractions. Guides were available to take visitors to the most popular statues, temples, and shrines, but Wymberley had not intended to employ the boy who offered his services: he was on foot. The young guide insisted that he could keep up easily for twenty miles and more, however, and was as good as his word.[43]

The sites the two visited combined scenic beauty with historical and cultural interest. Of the many places Wymberley saw, he was most taken by Kamakura, ancient seat of shoguns, with its immense bronze Buddha and its Shinto temple. The statue sat in a valley, with the mountains to its back, facing the valley's opening, its various gradations of pale green patina complementing the lush vegetation that surrounded it.[44]

Kamakura's temple, Wymberley discovered, was dedicated to the war god Hachiman. Following a flight of stone steps, the young traveler found a shrine displaying reputed relics of the god, including his helmet, armor, and saddle, as well as an array of Japanese swords that Wymberley inspected respectfully. "They are really terrible weapons," he wrote, adding that he thought that he "under[stood] something about such things." His father was particularly interested in all of his descriptions, for he had long been fascinated with Japan and would probably have made a visit himself, if not for poor health and his "dread of the sea."[45]

Wymberley's excursion was broken several times, with mixed results, when he sought refreshment at teahouses. One incident left his reputation for good manners intact, despite severe provocation. Unknown to the young man, his horse's hooves had flecked his face with mud. After entering the teahouse and exchanging preliminary bows and compliments, he was shocked when his hostess "spat on a clean cloth she had & commenced wiping the mud off my face. It was a great compliment & kindly meant so nothing was left me but to thank & bow."[46]

Fortuitously, one of Wymberley's shipboard acquaintances had proven to be a Japanese nobleman, who added to the trip by arranging to take him on a tour of the Summer Palace. Having by this time visited numerous sites, the young man was less impressed by the royal establishment: "The gardens were very beautiful but I expected more." He was struck favorably, however, by two huge porcelain lanterns standing ten feet tall, as well as by one of the chambers, whose walls were covered with forms "painted up quite fantastically." After the tour, the nobleman asked Wymberley to dine with him at a "first class restaurant." Wymberley accepted but begged that the meal "be entirely Japanese & nothing foreign about it." His wish was granted, and the two reclined on mats and were brought pipes before the meal began. Sake was served, and he was taught how to use chopsticks (by "*une jolie demoiselle*" he confided in some detail in a letter in French, for Everard's eyes only), though he admitted he did not use the "*deux bâtons*" as gracefully as his host. He enjoyed all his courses, "all on little plates & saucers . . . with delicate little morsels of all kinds of compositions" that he found indescribable. He also liked the entertainment that was offered by the dancing and singing of the geishas. While in Yokohama he enjoyed more conventional meals as well, dining with local Americans and Englishmen to whom he had introductions, and he also treated the ship's captain to a meal, in recognition of his courtesies aboard ship.[47]

Reluctantly, Wymberley brought his time in Yokohama to a close. The Japanese had impressed him as a people as very proud and gracious, their aristocracy gratifyingly similar to that of France. He would always have an admiration for the Japanese country and culture. Sailing down the coast toward Nagasaki, he found the scenery incomparable, particularly the hundreds of islands, "all rising precipitously out of the water," their green expanse occasionally broken by cultivated fields.[48]

A terrifying typhoon marred the ship's arrival at Nagasaki, a town he found beautiful, "surrounded on all sides by high mountains all covered with rich green foliage." Leaving Japan, however, he left behind the most pleasant part of his tour; until he sailed up the Suez for Cairo in August, his travels would be an ordeal. Upon arriving at Shanghai, he found nothing to like about the Chinese or their city, in marked contrast to his admiration for almost everything Japanese. His opinion was probably partially based on seeing them through Western eyes, for their attempts at Westernization had been unsuccessful. In any case, he perceived the Chinese as dirty and cowardly and was indignant that their only term for foreigners such as himself, whether they meant to be insulting or gracious, was "strange devil." Though impressed by the fields of superior cotton he saw, as well as the handsome villas of the foreigners, surrounded by gardens, his major impression of China from his brief visit to Shanghai was one of barbarity. He wrote of seeing "the wells in which Chinese women throw their children. One was full & was barred up & a new one was dug just next door." Along a roadside where he was walking he saw a pole topped by a human head—that of a soldier whose grumbling had caused his commander to make an example of him.[49]

So disappointed was Wymberley with his brief encounter with China that he wished to leave immediately. When he found that it would be a week before he could take a decent ship, he booked passage on the *Amoy*, a freighter bound for Kowloon, so that he could depart from the major port of the Celestial Empire at once. His farewell was of a piece with his initial impression: sailing down the Yangtze he was tormented by clouds of mosquitos and made even more miserable by the "close, heavy atmosphere." Though his ship offered facilities for bathing, he found that his fellow passengers were three hundred sheep and that the vibrations of the boat's powerful screw propeller constantly jarred his bones.[50]

After five days' sailing, the *Amoy* arrived before dawn for a brief stopover at the island of Hong Kong. Wymberley immediately left the ship to have a look at the town of Victoria. A "delicious walk" took him on an upward path through "dense foliage" filled with singing birds. When he emerged on the hilltop, he found that it gave him a fine view of the sleeping city below. Returning to the ship, he stayed on deck for the trip across Victoria Harbor to the Kowloon peninsula, which Great Britain had acquired from China only fifteen years before. He was unimpressed by the vista of "ragged hills" and flooded rice fields that met his view as they approached their destination, the Kowloon Walled City, which remained a part of China. During his visit, he found the city infernally hot; the coolest residence he saw was that occupied by the "holy pigs." Among the other sites he visited were the Temple of Three Buddhas, the Temple of the Five Hundred Geniis, and various pagodas. One was so peaceful that he climbed to the top; there a concessionaire offered him refreshments, and he spent a period in quiet reading while his guide drank numerous cups of tea.[51]

Again, however, incidents of barbarity struck him most indelibly and increased his antipathy toward the Chinese. He ventured into the Temple of Horrors, which displayed graphically the punishments to be meted out to the wicked in the afterlife: dismemberment, flaying, and boiling in oil were conspicuous among them. He also encountered a bloodstained executioners' ground, "a small place by a high wall." On its slope, potters were drying their wares, oblivious to the numerous heads that had rolled to rest along the wall's base. He was told that what he saw represented only a very small percentage of the annual number of executions, which approached fifteen thousand. Wymberley was also stunned by the contrast of wealth and squalor he saw in Kowloon, from the resplendent mandarins to the long-haired mendicants, and was annoyed by the crackling discharge of fire-crackers, "day and night." Although he did not find the city as dirty as Shanghai, he noted that "the smells as you passed along the street were many & strongly flavored" and that "a Christian should not go through them without Cologne or segars." [52]

Eager to take his final leave of the Celestial Empire, he boarded the *Glaucus* to travel to Singapore, beginning the most dangerous leg of his journey. Out of port, the wind rose and "the sea boiled," sending a continuous wash of waves over the ship, breaking the panes of all the windows and tearing away their shutters. In his cabin, Wymberley found himself drenched and his effects floating in three feet of water. The ship began to lurch so heavily that it was feared it would split. But after one final smashing wave the sea began to subside, and, after a day of bailing and drying, the *Glaucus* was able to proceed on its way. [53]

Sailing from Singapore past India and through the Suez Canal, Wymberley arrived in Cairo, where he more than matched his parents' fondness for the culture of the ancient Egyptians. This would not be his last trip to the Land of the Pharaohs, for he had an abiding interest in its ancient civilization. Although Palestine was also to have been part of his itinerary, he had become so enervated by the heat during his travels that he resolved to visit the Holy Land during some future winter. He had suffered a surfeit of days when he had been able "fairly [to] wring [his] clothes out." [54]

After traveling to London for a brief visit, Wymberley set sail for America. Arriving in New York after having circumnavigated the world by rail, passenger ship, and freight steamer, he found America's metropolis a trifle commonplace but nonetheless welcoming. In the fall of 1875 he set about completing his education at the law school of Columbia University, attending classes there until his graduation on May 17, 1876; a week later he was admitted to the New York bar and seemed on the brink of beginning the career in law that his parents wished him to pursue. But America's centennial year was to mark something very like Wymberley's own decla-ration of independence, from both his mother and father and from much they held dear.[55]

Wymberley's return to New York marked the beginning of the second and last of those brief periods when he was thrown together with his sib-lings. Leta was nearby at Miss Haynes's school in Gramercy Park, so the two spent some time together when they could spare it from their studies. To-gether they made social calls on such family friends as Mr. and Mrs. Theodore Roosevelt (though Wymberley would nurture a lifelong dislike of their son, the future president). Although Wymberley's brothers were be-ing educated at no great distance from New York, it would take a family be-reavement—the death of Washington Smith in the spring of 1876—to bring all the children together. Because his father was detained in Savan-nah by illness, Wymberley was his family's major representative at his great-uncle's funeral and acquitted himself well. G. W. J. De Renne was pleased to hear that his Philadelphia friend W. H. Drayton had judged the eldest of the De Renne children "a gentleman and quite intelligent" and had presented him to his family; all were "delighted with him."[56]

Several weeks earlier Wymberley had impressed his father even more. Prompted by a temporary decline in the income from the lucrative Savan-nah wharf properties, he asked his father to decrease his allowance and let him move to less expensive lodgings, hoping that these cutbacks would be of assistance. His mother wrote him that his father, though pleased by his suggestion, wanted him to continue as normal, though if he wished to make "any little economies," he should use the extra money to purchase for himself "articles of permanent value." She added, "Your Father has spoken more than once of the considerateness, disinterestedness and good feeling of your proposal. The identification of your own interest with that of the fam-ily, and your willingness to share in the economy if economy was necessary, was particularly gratifying to him, for he has a very strong family feeling, and has always been willing to give up personal pleasure to promote the family prosperity; so keep the money he allows you."[57]

After Wymberley's graduation, however, money—and how he was to ac-quire it—became a more pressing concern. Other than a small allowance from his father, he was apparently expected to support himself as a lawyer in New York City, where he lived the life of a young gentleman about town, dining at Delmonico's and spending leisure hours at the patrician Union Club. For a brief time, he was associated with a Manhattan law firm, but there is no sign that he had any great love for lawyering.[58]

There is evidence, however, that Wymberley was desperately seeking an alternative to the life that stretched unalluringly before him. He probably contrasted his lot with that of his father at his age. By twenty-five, G. W. J. De Renne had come into his fortune, had abandoned the profession for which he had been educated, had begun to pursue the life of a gentleman farmer and antiquarian, and had become a married man. His father had been unrestricted in choosing what to do, but Wymberley felt hedged around with restraints, including his father's apparent reluctance to see him married in the immediate future.[59]

Part of this reluctance may have been based on an idea that his son was not yet a steady enough man for the responsibilities of marriage. Wymberley described himself in the mid-1870s as presenting the appearance of "a thoughtless, light-headed fellow who had not an idea beyond the morrow." Beneath this devil-may-care exterior, however, he was seriously seeking another life. As early as 1877 he seems to have decided that his future had to lie far from the world of Manhattan, with its desultory legal work and monotonous social obligations, brightened mainly by feasts at Delmonico's and cards at the Union Club. Like many other young men his age, he saw the Great West beckoning to him; unlike most of them, he answered the call.[60]

He was no doubt moved to some extent by his father's "windfall," as the Philadelphia newspapers termed it, in being the sole legatee of Washington Smith's considerable estate. Part of the estate included that of Smith's sister Rebecca, who had died in 1855 and whose will had stated that after her brother's death, her bequest was to be passed along to G. W. J. De Renne and his children. Since Wymberley wished to make his own fortune but needed capital to make a start, he asked his father in 1877 to buy his interest in the Rebecca Smith estate for its value at the time, almost $4,000.[61]

Unknown to his parents, it was also at about this time that he made the first steps toward matrimony. In Philadelphia, he had met a young widow, Laura Camblos Norris; her husband, lawyer William Pepper Norris, scion of one of Pennsylvania's oldest and most distinguished families, had died of typhoid in 1876, a little over a year after their marriage. For the moment, the conventions of the time would prevent their marrying, but in the meanwhile Wymberley hoped to make a beginning of his own. The delay also suited him because he did not want it thought that he was marrying a wealthy widow for her money.[62]

By the fall of 1878 Wymberley had arrived in Texas, determined to seek his fortune there. His arrival in the West could be traced in part to the striking impression that the Great Plains had made on him during his transcontinental train crossing in 1875. But the allure of the West had also been all around him in Germany, which had for decades been inundated with literature seeking to lure German emigrants to the prairies. And he would have had to have been a hermit not to notice the pervasiveness of western themes, both in European and American popular fiction and in the fascinated accounts by journalists, printed in the press the world over.[63]

Exactly what he was to do in the West became the object of close personal inquiry, guided mainly by what he thought would produce the income necessary to support him and his future wife in style, while also promising a more pleasant and interesting future than a life in courtrooms and attorneys' chambers. One of the most attractive aspects of Texas life, of course, was that horses would be intimately involved in most activities of work, play, and transportation, since his family's traditional love of horses and riding was particularly strong in him.[64]

Soon after his steamer passage to Galveston, Texas, he took a rail trip to San Antonio. His entry into the old Spanish city in October 1878 was soon followed by an encounter with someone he had known in New York, and this meeting in turn led him to Joseph Tweedy, another New Yorker, just four years Wymberley's senior. Tweedy was soon heading northwest (in a relatively comfortable ambulance wagon) for his ranch in the Concho Valley, at the raw edge of the Texas frontier. He agreed to let Wymberley accompany him on his two-day journey.[65]

The two travelers at first seemed to be a total mismatch. Though Tweedy had not been in Texas a great while, he had already become a successful sheep rancher, and, taciturn by nature, he also had the sheep man's proverbial disinclination for talk, particularly about his business—which was the subject Wymberley wanted most to discuss. Wymberley's constant questions about the frontier, cattle herding, and sheep raising brought curt answers or none. Despite his incommunicativeness, Tweedy failed to stem Wymberley's incessant talking. Apparently operating under the notion of giving confidences in hope of receiving others in exchange, Wymberley also told Tweedy more than he wanted to know about his antecedents and his life up until that point, including his experiences of "the world."[66]

It is questionable how well his past experiences had prepared young De Renne for the world he was now entering. In some ways Tom Green County and its principal town and county seat, the mail and stage station called Ben Ficklin, must have been welcoming; both were named for former Confederates, and the "father of the county," F. C. Taylor, was a Georgia-born former Confederate colonel; there was a strong southern presence among the men who had moved there. The population as a whole, though much more cosmopolitan, presented few problems for Wymberley; the plains were thick with Englishmen, Frenchmen, and Germans. And Wymberley's facility with languages soon gave him a working command of Spanish; it would be invaluable in dealing with the largely Mexican working force, just as his lawyer's training would be helpful in mastering the legal arcana involved in buying and keeping land on the frontier.[67]

But the frontier itself was unlike anything he had encountered, particularly in its scale. Tom Green County, created in 1874, was one of the largest counties of the nation's largest state; eventually, a dozen other counties would be carved from it. There land was sold not only in acres but in larger parcels, called sections, that comprised 640 acres and equaled one square mile. Another young southerner in Texas at the time, William Sidney Porter, later wrote (as "O. Henry") that in Texas "Tom Green County was once the standard of measurement." Though confessing he had forgotten "how many New Jerseys and Rhode Islands it was that could have been stowed away and lost in its chaparral," it was a considerable number—one and a half and ten, respectively. So large was the county that it was easiest to express its size in terms of meridians and parallels: roughly wedge-shaped, it stretched from the 100th to the 104th meridian of longitude and from the 31st to 32d parallel of latitude.[68]

But Tom Green County's position with respect to the 100th meridian was most significant, for this had long been considered the line past which no intelligent settlers would go; the land on the west side of the line was judged a forbidding wilderness—an exaggeration, as it turned out, but one with a basis in fact. For to the northwest stretched the trackless, featureless grasslands known as the Llano Estacado—the "Staked Plain"; its distinctive name was said to have come from early Spanish explorers who held that prudent men did not enter it without leaving behind a trail of stakes to lead them out. Shortly before Wymberley's arrival, a detachment of soldiers and scouts had not treated the Llano with sufficient respect, and some had not lived to regret their foolhardiness.[69]

But even in this unforgiving land, the frontier was disappearing. The decade of the 1870s saw a boom in buffalo hunting (in which Wymberley participated), and the beasts were soon overhunted into extinction. Most of the Indians who had depended on them likewise vanished during the decade, though a few remained to rustle livestock and give meaning to the continued existence of the frontier forts. Though the famous Goodnight-Loving cattle trail of the immediate postwar years had passed through Tom Green County (as had other trails), rail lines had by the mid-1870s extended close enough to the Concho Valley to make the great trail drives unnecessary.[70]

Oddly, the most untamed and dangerous section of this frontier when Wymberley arrived was probably the town of San Angelo, located on the north bank of the North Concho River, three miles north of the South Concho town and county seat of Ben Ficklin. San Angelo was just above Fort Concho, an unstockaded collection of limestone barracks and stables noted for the excellence of its post hospital. Compared to Ben Ficklin, San Angelo's population and orientation were much less southern; the nearby fort was under the command of Colonel Benjamin Grierson, who had won fame during the war leading a raid that helped General U. S. Grant capture Vicksburg. His command was the black Tenth Cavalry, the celebrated "Buffalo Soldiers," among whom was Henry Ossian Flipper. The town's major citizen was the Yankee merchant (and, later, banker) W. S. Veck, whose supporters had been bested by Colonel Taylor's forces in an 1875 election to determine whether Veck's or Taylor's town would become the Tom Green county seat.[71]

San Angelo in its early years existed mainly because of the fort, with which, by most accounts, it had a harmful, parasitic relationship. The year of Wymberley's arrival, the town was described by one of the fort's surgeons: "[San Angelo] is full of human sharks, and as every inducement is held out there to soldiers to spend money, the nights succeeding pay day are hideous. There are so many gamblers, cut-throats, murderers, [and] horse thieves living and finding harbor [there that] it is never considered safe to pass through there at night, and no officer ever thinks of leaving the garrison after dark."[72]

Though cattle remained a big business in the Concho Valley, particularly in the areas where the land was flat and the grass abundant, sheep had been introduced to the country in 1877, the year before Wymberley arrived. Sheep raising quickly spread throughout the region, especially in those areas of rolling hills and short grass that were not as hospitable to cattle. Joseph Tweedy was one of the pioneers of the area's sheep business; with several fellow New Yorkers (E. Morgan Grinnell, Lawrence L. Grinnell, and J. Barlow Reynolds), he owned the Knickerbocker Ranch, which would in time grow to over one hundred thousand acres.[73]

Wymberley was invited to stay at the Knickerbocker spread during his first trip to the Concho country, and he soon became good friends with Tweedy and his partners; they found him both excellent company and reliable help, "full of spirits & always good natured." Consequently, during the two years Wymberley spent "knocking about" in Texas and learning the ways of ranching, he had a standing invitation to visit at the ranch. He was judged a splendid horseman, bareback or otherwise, for he often dispensed with the "bore" of saddling up. When the day's work was done, the ranchers often worked together on their Spanish and frequently shared a convivial glass or two; in later days Tweedy happily recalled his and Wymberley's mutual enjoyment of Texas "red eye." Sometimes at night there were also political discussions, and since the Knickerbocker was a hotbed of Republican northerners, sparring with such a confirmed southern Democrat as Wymberley was always lively.[74]

Mr. and Mrs. De Renne were no doubt astonished at the turn their eldest child's life had taken and were not entirely pleased with the state where that turn had taken him. The phrase "Gone to Texas" covered a variety of emigrants (and sins), and for every venturer like Wymberley there were several drunkards, spendthrifts, and other ne'er-do-wells. Though concerned that their son was living in such a "rough state of society," his parents also viewed his situation with some amusement (particularly his protest that he felt "suffocated" back east), but they showed parental concern by sending buckskins and corduroys and boxes of medicine and notions. During the two years he spent traveling in Texas, "learning the ropes" before settling down, he sent his mother—in whose "special charge" his father had placed him—accounts of his activities and adventures. These included close calls with Indians, shoot-outs he had witnessed, and descriptions of hunting expeditions to such remote spots as Devils River near the Rio Grande. With his rifle he often brought down antelopes and wild pigs (and also brought a motherly admonition that he should eat all that he shot and never kill for sport).[75]

Unsurprisingly, in her letters—often filled with news of the family and of Savannah or Philadelphia society—Mrs. De Renne occasionally dispensed maternal advice. She warned Wymberley most forcibly that of all the schemes he considered for making money, he should never contemplate running a saloon. He himself had written her as much, recognizing that "to keep a bar was impossible for a gentleman, or a man with any idea of honor." But she felt that, considering his situation, she should remind him of "the true principles of thought and action . . . lest [he] get bewildered by [his] surroundings." Consequently, she underlined her point: "Labor is honorable, but never liquor selling, and whatever your companions may say about the fact of money being all important, and the way it had been got of no consequence, a man's antecedents always become known, and the keeper of a dram shop can never be respected." [76]

It was not saloon running but sheep raising, however, that Wymberley had chosen for his livelihood. After examining sheep ranches at various points in Texas, Wymberley determined that the Concho Valley would be the best location for his ranch. Finally, in May 1880, he took up the task of convincing his father to lend him the money he needed to make a start. Following his father's instructions, Wymberley made his plans and then wrote directly to his father so that he could then decide whether—or to what extent—to help his venturesome son.[77]

Wymberley made a persuasive case. He insisted that his views were not simply theoretical, just "gathered from description & superficial inquiry amongst sheepraisers . . . or from books or papers." Instead, he had discovered that "practical experience in all the details of the *manner* of managing sheep here was necessary for success, also that those who succeeded best were those who paid most attention to the *details* of the business." Consequently, he had "entered practically into *all* the *work* of a sheep ranch & met men whose success especially seems to be due to their attention to *management* and *detail*." [78]

Though Wymberley's father had kept sheep at Wormsloe, their numbers had been few, and he would have been astonished by the amount of work and care necessary to maintain the great flocks of West Texas. Though a man might purchase cattle and leave them to their own devices to a certain extent, sheep could never be treated so. They demanded constant watching and care from herders to save them from themselves because they seemed to have no instinct for survival. Their reputation for stupidity was honestly earned, but they had the virtue of being stupid in predictable ways. Their annoying (and apparently mindless) bleating was actually an indication of contentment; silence from the sheep was a clue of danger. The ewes were notoriously uncommitted to motherhood and their lambs practically suicidal.[79]

Under the circumstances, all the energies devoted to ensuring the sheep's survival throughout the year were burdensome and, not least, included either getting them to ranges for grazing or, if not, providing hay for them. But every spring an unprecedented round of activity began. At this time, the past year's investment in time, money, and energy would finally pay off, when itinerant shearers were brought in to take the wool. Other tasks at this time—necessary to ensure the next year's profit—included branding (normally done with paint on the exposed skin so that it would grow out with the new wool), docking (clipping the ewes' tails to facilitate breeding), and wethering (castrating rams destined for the table rather than fatherhood). The details of the last-mentioned procedure, and the rancher's part in them, would have appeared brutally medieval and repellent to the De Rennes. But had they known all the details that Wymberley discreetly withheld, they would have realized that the business that he was entering with open eyes and due reflection was far from an easy one.[80]

It could not be denied that he had followed his father's advice to "commence at the foot of the ladder." But now, he wrote, "I want to settle in Tom Green Co.—1—because the range is good—2—I have been through two winters & know what provisions to make in the way of shelters & hay—3—I know a great many of the Mexicans & who to depend upon—4—I think sheep do better here than down south."[81]

Wymberley intended to rent a ranch on the North Concho above San Angelo and buy his sheep there to save the cost and danger of having flocks driven to him. He estimated that he would need $8,000 to commence sheep raising. Having this amount, he could afford to take a loss if necessary during the first year of rental and still rent for a second year, meanwhile looking for ranch land to purchase. Instead of taking a partner, as he had once thought best, he felt that he should run things alone until he discovered which of his employees had the intelligence and trustworthiness to be made ranch manager. He would then have his manager take "his pay in sheep" so that he would have "an interest in their welfare." He appealed to his father to give him "the power of asserting [him]self in life (if only as a successful sheepraiser)," something that he had been unable to do during his "hitherto aimless life."[82]

On May 24, 1880, G. W. J. De Renne ordered his Philadelphia bank, Thomas A. Biddle & Company, to allow Wymberley to draw funds to his credit "for a sum not exceeding five thousand dollars." By August 1, he had made other funds available totaling something over the $8,000 requested in his son's letter. Consequently, on May 29, Wymberley rented for $200 the ranch on the North Concho that he desired — over two thousand acres, with a creek and some pecan groves, as well as a three-room adobe house — with the option of renting it for an additional two years at the same price.[83]

In his letter to his father requesting the $8,000 (and in one of the same date to his mother), Wymberley had also broached a more personal matter: he finally revealed his two-year courtship of Laura Camblos Norris and announced their engagement, as well as their intention of marrying "as soon as possible." The announcement took both parents off guard, particularly since Mrs. De Renne's planned trip to Europe would make it impossible for her to attend the wedding (or to inquire about or meet the young lady's family). Both parents reacted with coolness to the news but made no attempt to dissuade Wymberley from his plans. His letter had strongly suggested that any objections would be futile.[84]

He had pointed out to his father that, with his approval, he had led a "life of contact with the world in all its matter of factness." Surely, then, he wrote, he could "appeal to [him] as [his] father" to agree that he was capable of giving "calm & mature consideration to the question." He struck the theme of maturity with his mother as well, asserting, "Reflection has matured me more in the last eighteen months than ten years could of the life I used to lead."[85]

Nonetheless, he feared that he would incur their displeasure, particularly because one of his father's friends had met a sad fate through the mistake of "poor men marrying rich women." He himself knew of numerous similar examples in New York, but he was certain his own case would be different, and, in any event, his happiness depended on the match. His fiancée knew that he was "penniless," and he had explained to her the "hardships & privations" of ranch life. Yet she still wished to marry him and had inquired whether hardships "would not be easier to bear if . . . shared . . . together." She had argued as well that "if [he had] nothing, she at least would be of no expense to [him] as she [was] very well off in her own right," and though she had hinted that he would not have to work, he had "immediately declared [his] intention of making [his] own way in the world," to which she had agreed. In sum, he wrote, "she is the one woman I have ever loved & cared to marry." He would be "a fool to dash away the cup & be forever afterwards devoured by regret & soured for life." Such arguments allowed few rejoinders.[86]

As shocked as they were by their son's news, the De Rennes may have been even more disappointed by comments he made to his mother: they amounted to a near rejection of his heritage. From a flippant line, explaining why he knew little of Laura's antecedents ("Family histories are not my forte"), he expanded his comments to detail vividly what his experience in the West signified to him regarding the value of coming from an eminent family line. "Life has a very different meaning & appearance to me now. I know that I have to make my own living & position & I mean to do it. In a country like this home prestige is of 'no account.' Every man no matter what his antecedents may be is every other man's equal or superior according to his capabilities. Business aptitude & not social status is enquired into. If you are a successful man you carry social prestige with you. If you are poor and you may be a lineal descendant of Charlemagne your opinions would be of no weight & you would be utterly disregarded." Having started so strongly, he came to a rather odd conclusion, which seemed to suggest that family name would have been more acceptable with a share of the family fortune: "Poverty may not be degrading in the abstract but the surroundings are. I intend then to rise by my own exertions for I hold that any man is poor who does not succeed himself or has not from his ancestors the wherewithal to associate with his equals."[87]

After Wymberley had rented his ranch and purchased his sheep, he traveled to Philadelphia for his marriage, set for June 22. Upon his arrival, he wrote to his father, prompting a frosty response from sultry Savannah, dated June 18. Without salutation it began, "It would have been in accordance with ordinary business usage, as well as the rules of common politeness, if you had written before leaving Fort Concho to inform me what was the date and amount of your draft on . . . Biddle & Co., and whether you sold it at a premium, at par, or at a discount, and to whom." With some understatement he added, "I learn from your letter from Philadelphia of the errand you are on there." By this time he had presented Wymberley with $500 for his wedding journey and returned to the subject of the impending marriage: "Say to your wife, with my compliments, that to give you the ordinary wedding rubbish would be of no use to either:——I propose therefore that my present to you shall be a cottage, house, or ranch, whatever you call it, and to her the furniture of it, when you get your land and are ready to establish your home. In the meantime and henceforth, I say, in old English phrase which covers everything, Good luck to you both."[88]

The wedding took place at the bride's family's home in Chestnut Hill, a suburb of Philadelphia, near the falls of the Wissahickon. The comfortable, spacious residence where the ceremony was performed was far removed in quality and distance from the adobe ranch house near Dry Creek to which the couple was soon bound. In late July 1880, soon after taking up residence, they had an unexpected visitor, a sheep herder returning from a mail run to town. Hoping to get some bread and milk, he stopped by, thinking he would be welcomed by the cattleman who had treated him in the past. Instead,

> But what was my surprise [he wrote] on stepping to the door to see a spruce looking couple setting down to the table for dinner, and a huge *black* niggar for waiter; the gentleman gets up and welcomes me while the Lady greets me with a smile, he forceing me into a chair by the table opposite the lady, which I afterwards found out was a bride direct from Philadelphia. My plate was filled with nice roast mutton, new potatoes with trimmings, soda biscuit, and coffee. I was so embarased that I can't tell whether the coffee was on my plate or in a cup. And the niggar was ordered to bring a glass of milk which was offered me, and which I politely refused, something I never was knowed to do before since being in Texas. The refusal being about the first words I had spoken since my arrival, and I had disposed of the first plate full, and had got well along on the seckond before it occured to me to introduce myself, which I done amediately, and then found out I was dining with Mr. and Mrs. De Renne, bride and groom just arrived from the Quaker City. Mr. De R., being as the paper states it, one of our most prominent sheep men. After the introductions embarisment wore off I had a very socible time, and upon leaving, received a very cordial invitation to call again.[89]

By this time Wymberley had received two letters from his mother. They were very gracious, particularly since she had not known with certainty when the marriage was to take place and had learned of it in a letter of

June 14 that she received in Munich in early July. Consequently, she wrote, "It only remains for me to offer my best wishes for your happiness and that of your wife, in which Leta and Everard beg to join." Her second letter was even more affectionate, recalling fondly a past family outing in the Alps: "I enclose a photograph showing the cross to which you climbed. I thought you might wish to tell your wife of your youthful feat, and [I enclose] a little sprig of Alpenrose such as you brought down. We shall be very glad to get her photograph—you must give her my kind regards and tell her so."[90]

At about the time his mother's letter arrived, Wymberley received two other communications. One was a brief note from his father in Philadelphia, written in a surprisingly enfeebled hand: "Thank your wife for her photograph, and say that I don't wonder you succumbed to such charms. You may draw on the Biddles for thirty four hundred dollars." The other was a telegram, telling him that his father had died on the fourth of August.[91]

All was changed. The will showed that he would no more be "penniless," that indeed with care he could be comfortable for life, with no necessity for work, in much the same way his father had been. The children that he and his wife expected to bring into the world would have the chance of being provided for even more handsomely, for his father's entire estate would be split among them and any cousins that his siblings provided. He did not rejoin his family to attend his father's funeral, though there was ample time for a trip east. Instead, he did as he had told his parents he would do and went to work to become a successful rancher.[92]

In October Wymberley paid $2,000 for a spread along Kickapoo Creek, southeast of San Angelo. This would be the beginning of the ranch of his dreams. With the winter celebrations of Thanksgiving, Christmas, and New Year's Eve impending, he prepared to act as host to his friends, inviting them to the North Concho Ranch that he would soon leave behind. Although the accommodations were so limited that Tweedy and three other friends had to sleep on the floor, the guests thought that the De Rennes' hospitality more than made up for it.

It was a very pleasant affair [Tweedy wrote]. Mrs. DeR had been North on a short business visit, & brought back with her a younger sister (unmarried) [Margaret Camblos]—so you may be sure we all had on our best "bibs and tuckers" and our best behavior. . . . Altogether it was a very swell affair for Texas—De Renne, since coming into his property, has launched out quite extensively in his household arrangements—the table itself would be no disgrace anywhere—white cloth napkins & the pretty set of china & glass ware Mrs. DeR had brought down with her—in the eating line, which perhaps went as far to win our approbation as the table, we had an excellent soup, followed by some delicious terrapin stew (also imported)—beef, game, vegetables & for dessert pies & cakes followed by excellent coffee & Dutch cheese—It was a novel sensation to sit down at table with ladies but altogether agreeable—& we flatter ourselves we did the thing up in very good style as if it were a daily occurrence.[93]

The Knickerbocker Ranch returned the compliment before Christmas, and the all-male establishment went through "a great scrubbing and cleaning up." The one-room structure where the men ate and slept was blocked with a partition at one end to make a bedroom for the ladies, who were seated with their backs to the stove before the meal, "for fear that their appetites should suffer from seeing the dinner prepared." Soon after eating, the sisters retired, and the men had a turn at the cards. But a torrential rain blew in overnight and drove the visitors home the next morning. For New Year's, the festivities switched back to the De Rennes'.[94]

The celebrations at the end of 1880 masked genuine sorrow at the death of Wymberley's father, though, had the young man been in Philadelphia rather than on the Texas frontier, more conventional practices of grief would have been followed. It was his living parent, however, that most concerned him. Mrs. De Renne's initial complaisance regarding the marriage had been closely followed by her husband's death, and by October 1880 she had drastically changed her opinion of the match. Indeed, her son had written her a plaintive note that month hoping that she would allow Laura to call on her in Philadelphia while she was in town on her pre-Thanksgiving business trip. The meeting seems not to have taken place.[95]

Apparently, Mrs. De Renne, at last able to make inquiries, had made certain discoveries about her daughter-in-law that gravely displeased her, and she may have questioned whether her son had been entirely frank with her regarding his intended. Consequently, she may have entertained doubts as to whether his announcement of the engagement and coming marriage had so closely coincided with her European trip by accident or design. That Laura had been considered a suitable match for a representative of so prominent a Philadelphia family as the Norrises seems to have allayed any of Mrs. De Renne's initial suspicions. And apparently there was no insurmountable objection to the bride's family—her late father, Charles C. Camblos, though a first-generation American, had been a banker and a member of the board of the Philadelphia Stock Exchange.[96]

But it became plain that the new Mrs. De Renne had not only been married to William Pepper Norris but had presented him with a son, then in the care of his Philadelphia relations, with whom he would remain throughout his minority. The omission of the fact of the child's existence could have been tolerated, particularly since its most basic significance was to suggest good hopes for a De Renne heir. But there was additional information: Norris had been Laura's second husband; her first she had divorced in 1872 while Wymberley was still a student in Europe. It was true that Laura's first husband, a young Irish-born lawyer named Austin C. Maury, had deserted her. But the temper of the times did not inquire after the reasons for terminating a marriage; the fact that a woman was a divorcée was enough in itself to cast grave doubt on her social standing. As if this were not enough, it was rumored that, before her first marriage, Laura had at least briefly appeared on the stage.[97]

Though his mother's rejection of his wife may have seemed a sufficient calamity, it was eventually followed by her estranging herself from him and disinheriting him as well. This rupture may have had its origins in earlier incidents that had been tolerated or overlooked at the time but had in retrospect loomed much larger, such as Wymberley's failure to join his family in Savannah at the time of his father's funeral. But matters were possibly brought to a head over a case involving the liquidation of some of the estate's Central of Georgia Railroad stock. General Lawton and, apparently, Mrs. De Renne, began to have second thoughts regarding the transaction; Wymberley did not. In any case, the Central stock matter was a major topic of discussion in Mrs. De Renne's letter dated May 12, 1881 — the last of her letters that he kept. By 1883, Mrs. De Renne's Savannah lawyers, when writing to her, were making a careful distinction between her "sons, Everard and Kentwyn," and a person identified only as "Wymberley De Renne." Wymberley would not be included in his mother's will or in those of his siblings, and, whatever the complete series of familial complications and grievances had been, he would later remark that he had been all but disinherited because of his marriage.[98]

He was not, however, without what could be classified as a grievance of his own, though he seems not to have been at any pains to define it as such. As was known to anyone who was familiar with his father's will, $2,100 was to be deducted each year from Wymberley's annuity as interest on money loaned him by his father. His father's will stated, "I have already advanced, and am about to advance, to him in cash various sums of money, the interest on which is about equal to said deduction," an amount which he identifies later in the will as $30,000. Wymberley claimed, and the records of the Biddle Company confirmed, that although G. W. J. De Renne may eventually have intended to advance such a sum, at the time of his death he had provided only $8,400. And so it remained an unfulfilled intention, like the wedding gift of a ranch house and furniture. As long as any of his siblings lived, Wymberley paid the $2,100 a year, and, after Everard's death, his heirs unsuccessfully tried to continue to have the money paid into his estate.[99]

During the fall of 1880, while the De Rennes were still living at the North Concho ranch, Wymberley began to make purchases of land and sheep that would result in the creation of his Buena Ventura Ranch. To facilitate his land acquisitions, he soon became licensed to practice law in the county. Though the Buena Ventura, a vast holding of around thirty thousand acres, equaled about one-tenth the area of the Georgia county where Wormsloe was located, there was little in Wymberley's land to remind him of his family's plantation. Although there were oaks among the scanty tree life on his acreage, they were stunted, wizened, dry-country cousins of the stately oaks of the Georgia coast. Mesquite trees were much more abundant. And though a spring rose near the site he chose for his house, the wide, shallow stream that it formed, luxuriant by some West Texas standards, paled in comparison to the brackish but expansive Skidaway River. Unlike the sandy acres of Wormsloe, his soil at Buena Ventura was extravagantly rocky, its short, pale grass littered with bonelike shards of the limestone shelf that everywhere lay beneath a thin coating of dirt. In place of the lush gardens at Wormsloe were clumps of various short-blooming wildflowers such as coreopsis and the prickly agarita bush with its powdery perfume. But on the essentially seasonless Buena Ventura Ranch, the surest sign of the arrival of spring was not the sprouting of flowers but the sudden appearance of rattlesnakes.[100]

Nonetheless, living at Buena Ventura exhilarated Wymberley. His wife, however, was taken aback, having known life only in one of America's most comfortable metropolitan areas, where the closest thing to a wilderness was Fairmount Park. Wymberley did his best to see to her comfort, and in the winter of 1881–82, he had parties of workmen quarrying limestone and hauling sand and water to construct their Texas home. When completed it resembled many ranch houses, with its low cedar-shingled roof and wide veranda, but it was not the customary rectangle. Instead, wings on either side created a U-shape, within which was a courtyard. To add a fanciful touch, De Renne had his German masons construct a crenellated tower at the end of one wing, inaccessible from the house. Projecting above the roofline, it contained four bedrooms (so that such friends as Tweedy would no longer have to resort to pallets on the floor) and an attic, with a trapdoor to the roof, which provided an excellent vantage point for surveying the approaches to the settlement. The house's walls were a foot and a half thick, plastered on the inside; its rooms, cross-ventilated by numerous windows, were tolerably cool in the prevailing hot weather and were heated in winter by fireplaces. The tower wing contained the bedrooms, the other held the kitchen and pantry. A wide central hall, with doors to both the courtyard and the long veranda, was flanked by a large dining room and a roomy parlor.[101]

The customary dependencies were to the tower side of the dwelling, many of them limestone as well, and included a barn, stables for Wymberley's numerous horses, a chicken yard, an apiary, and a spacious two-room privy (marked as the "Office" on his plan). A windmill near the house pumped water from recesses in the limestone below, while a hidden cistern carved through the solid rock of the courtyard collected rainwater through a subterranean pipes; it could also be filled with water hauled from the nearby springs and creek and then be brought up by a hand pump.[102]

By the standards of the country this was all lavish indeed, and many women transplanted from the East did well with much less. But it is questionable whether Wymberley's Philadelphia wife could have remained happy in this remote and cheerless spot, with its unfriendly terrain, its ubiquitous snakes, and its often unpleasant, occasionally brutal weather, marked by windstorms that sometimes created clouds that blotted out the sun. She had her domestic responsibilities and had reading to divert her, but outside, always, the land seemed to roll away, almost endlessly, toward bleak horizons.[103]

Just after construction of the house began, it became clear that the first child of the marriage would soon arrive there. Although there had been rumors as early as the summer of 1881 that the De Rennes were going to sell out and return to the East, the news of the impending birth of an heir seems to have ended them. The De Rennes had been in residence several months by the time the baby was due, but the circumstances of the birth, and whether a doctor was present, are uncertain. Nonetheless, the proud father reported that all was well and announced to friends the birth on July 31 of a son, named George Wymberley Jones De Renne after his late grandfather. The mother and child, however, soon became gravely ill and were seen at least once by Dr. S. L. S. Smith. By this time the doctor had among his other patients Lillie Tweedy, who had married De Renne's friend the previous fall. He delivered her first child, a son, on August 20, 1882, and left the same day to check again on Mrs. De Renne and her child. As the doctor's wife described it, he "cut across country through the muddiest road you can think about to Mr. De Renne's and found her a little better, but the baby upon whom so much depended dead and buried." [104]

For the bereaved couple the death of the second G. W. J. De Renne was fraught with almost as much consequence as that of the first. The mother herself had come perilously near to dying, to the point that one of her sisters was summoned from Philadelphia. She brought with her Laura's young son, Charles Camblos Norris, who it was supposed would be seeing his mother for the last time. Though she survived, she "never regained her former health," Norris later wrote. Nonetheless, Laura De Renne was to endure three more pregnancies. Those who knew her in later years agreed with Norris's assessment of her broken health, and some pointed to the effects of her ordeal at Buena Ventura as the source of an increasing reliance on pain-relieving medications.[105]

In a wooded draw down the slope from the ranch house, the De Renne infant's small coffin was buried and covered by a raised stone. Its inscription read—in French, English, and Latin—"CI GIT [Here Lies] / THE FIRST BORN / of / W. De Renne / and / Laura C. his wife / Born / July 31, 1882 / DIED / AUGUST 20 / 1882 / FATUM [Such is Fate]." In the florid style of some novels of the time, it could be said that Wymberley's Texas hopes and aspirations were buried in the same grave, and in this instance, melodrama approached reality. As a final irony, Buena Ventura suggested a Spanish form of Bonaventure.[106]

Almost immediately, the De Rennes' anguish found distraction, for their personal tragedy was followed closely by an immense natural catastrophe. The rains that had muddied the roads traveled by Dr. Smith to reach Buena

Ventura continued to fall in profusion until the tributaries of the South Concho began to swell. As the river flooded Ben Ficklin, its adobe structures "melted like sugar" in the rushing waters, and the town was almost totally destroyed, with great loss of life. Wreckage, human corpses, and animal carcasses were carried as far as thirty miles downstream, and afterward it was not unusual to see animal and human remains hanging in treetops. Not too immersed in his own anguish to feel sympathy for others, Wymberley generously helped the Ben Ficklin survivors with money and provisions. But the town would never be rebuilt, and San Angelo became the new county seat.[107]

Eventually Paint Rock, the county seat in adjoining Concho County, claimed much of Wymberley's attention because a large portion of the Buena Ventura Ranch lay across the Tom Green County line in Concho County. Because some of Wymberley's interests and much of his business centered in Concho county, he qualified to run for one of the county commission posts and won his seat in November 1882. He was thus the first of his family to be elected to political office since his grandfather George Jones had become a member of the Georgia legislature in the late 1700s.[108]

Wymberley's sheep business had been running well, and his ranch and flocks had expanded since the fall of 1880. He had been able to follow fairly closely the plan he had outlined to his father, even down to hiring a ranch manager, which he was able to do earlier than expected. The man he chose, W. J. Skinner, not only gave excellent service managing the ranch but offered sincere personal allegiance as well, as Wymberley would soon have reason to appreciate.[109]

Having earned something of a reputation as a sheep man, particularly for his attention to detail, Wymberley was especially noted for his constant battle against the disease called scab that afflicted many flocks. His commission merchants in San Antonio, the firm of Staffel and Vogel, stocked a celebrated sheep dip that Wymberley used with such success that he wrote a letter in praise of it. Printed with other endorsements in an advertisement in the San Antonio periodical the *Texas Stockman*, it would be the closest he came to leaving a written record of his time as a sheep rancher:

> For the benefit of wool growers, I herewith give you my experience in the use of Little's Chemical Fluid. About the 7th of January, 1883, I bought 2000 head of sheep, very poor and fearfully scabby. The winter was a very hard one,

and it was predicted by all who saw them that if they were dipped more than half would die. It was, however, Hobson's choice. Some had hardly a handful of wool on them. . . . That night the thermometer went below the freezing point, and a northeast wind set in. The sheep were driven under a bluff, and brush that had been previously piled up on the north side set on fire. We only lost about 40 sheep, who died through exhaustion, they hardly being able to get to the vat, much less out of it. The others improved from that day, and that one dipping cured them completely of the most aggravated case of scab I ever saw. The sheep are to-day free from scab and in very good condition.[110]

Since his efforts at ranching had required much money during its first years, cash outlays had been considerable, and much of each of his quarterly annuity payments had been plowed into Buena Ventura. Since his annuity payments were not always available when he needed them or sufficient to cover certain purchases, he also secured loans from the banker John Twohig in San Antonio and from other sources. Increasingly cash poor, Wymberley began by early 1883 to cast about for a partner to share in both the expenses and profits of his enterprise.[111]

He chose his partner from the flood of British gentlemen that inundated the Texas frontier during the period: a young bachelor named William Frederick Cuthbert Venables-Vernon, known familiarly as Will Vernon. Like De Renne, he was in Texas with a certain amount of money to invest, courtesy of an affluent and scholarly father. At the family's ancestral seat at Sudbury Hall, there was a massive library, and the family had a passion for Italian literature, particularly Dante, that went back for generations; the fifth Lord Vernon's three-volume translation of the *Inferno* had been brought out by the Chiswick Press in a "sumptuous and comprehensive edition" in folio, 1858–65; the printing of the last volume had been supervised by the sixth lord, Will Vernon's father. During the time De Renne and Vernon were forming their partnership to operate as a firm called De Renne and Vernon, Lord Vernon suddenly died, and Will Vernon returned for a time to England. There his eldest brother was to assume the title, along with estates in Derbyshire and Cheshire, comprising over nine thousand acres and worth £24,000 per annum. It would therefore be a new, seventh Lord Vernon who would oversee Will Vernon's Texas venture.[112]

The Buena Ventura Ranch, though in need of cash at the time the partnership began, was an impressive empire for a young man just turned thirty to have created. On the ranch's thirty thousand acres (several sections of which were purchased by "L. C. De Renne") were more than thirteen thousand sheep (value estimated at over $55,000), as well as the stone house and other improvements, including a rock-walled horse pasture that enclosed the house and over a square mile of land, to give the ranch a total value of over $180,000. Such a rapid expansion since the fall of 1881 had not been without risks, however, and the expected infusion of $20,000, to be paid by Vernon for a quarter interest in the ranch, was vital. Vernon, however, paid only $16,500 by mid-August 1883, when Wymberley and Laura went to Philadelphia to see to pressing affairs relating to her property there. While detained in Philadelphia for months, Wymberley saw his financial situation in Texas deteriorate further, and it seemed that the partners might have to sell. The power of attorney that Vernon had assigned to Wymberley in May 1883 was revoked, and Vernon was given power of attorney and authorized by the De Rennes to sell the ranch lands.[115]

Nonetheless, Wymberley was astonished to receive a telegram on December 1, 1883 in which Vernon proposed selling the ranch for $60,000. Even an "auction under foreclosure," Wymberley wrote Vernon, "would fetch more & leave us the sheep to sell over & above." It would be far better, he advised, to secure a loan that would enable the firm to pay most outstanding debts and continue running the ranch for two more years; this would allow them time to get patents on other lands they held and would meanwhile increase the value of their sheep, which were being bred into a more profitable category. In two years, the ranch would bring at least $200,000, he reasoned. For the time, he asserted, "We are simply embarrassed on account of the variety of our debts and compound interest." If Vernon needed advice on how to proceed, he was counseled to go to Joseph Tweedy, who, in De Renne's estimation, stood highest among the stockmen of the Concho country.[114]

The partnership, now known as the Buena Ventura Stock Company, foundered unpleasantly over a disagreement on what to do next; Vernon apparently suggested that he buy out Wymberley's portion, and Wymberley demanded that Vernon bring the firm's books east to be examined. Wymberley assured the ranch manager, Skinner—who took De Renne's part in the dispute—that he would take care of him, regardless of the outcome. In reference to Lord Vernon, then visiting New York and soon to become deeply involved in the matter, Wymberley wrote Skinner that Will Vernon, "through his brother commands money & is squeezing me, so I have put the whole matter in able hands," those of Winthrop Smith, a Philadelphia stockbroker.[115]

By Christmas almost all was settled, though there would be some delays born of lawyerly caution on the part of Lord Vernon's attorneys. Of the settlement taking shape, Wymberley wrote Skinner:

> All the ranch debts & my personal debts will be paid immediately; this is part of the trade. So no one will suffer but myself, & that I do very cheerfully, because I do what I promised to. . . . Lord Vernon originally would have lent us money at 6%, which would have tided us over our present difficulties; gradually, though, seeing I could not raise money anywhere else & Vernon crying down Texas securities made him change his mind & finally he bought me out, agreeing to pay all the . . . debts & to give me $19,200 cash. So it is all over, old man, & the good old days are gone. I wish you every luck and happiness possible [and] wish you would accept my San Antonio horse . . . & my double-barrelled shot gun, in remembrance of me, & that you will think kindly of me when you use them.

He also offered Skinner lands that he had purchased on the Rio Grande and offered to lend him several thousand dollars if it would be helpful.[116]

Wymberley apparently never saw the ranch again. Skinner collected all the possessions that the De Rennes requested and sent them east and sold their livestock and other belongings and forwarded the money they brought. Despite early misgivings, Skinner stayed on as Vernon's ranch manager and was still on the Buena Ventura in 1891, when Vernon sold the ranch to Sarah E. Chambers for $100,000. Over a century later, the ranch was still essentially intact and Mrs. Chambers's descendants were still living in the towered limestone ranch house.[117]

But a more immediate, personal indication that all his efforts had not been for nothing came to Wymberley in a letter in 1894, written by W. J. Skinner. After reporting that he and his wife now had five children, he wrote: "I am getting along very well. I left [Buena Ventura] last July and am on my own ranch on the head of Crow's Nest Creek. I have 600 head of good cattle and 100 head of horses and 12000 acres pasture. 3000 acres I own; the balance under lease. I have it very well improved. What I have I am indebted to you for—you ware the one that hope me to start."[118]

In the winter of 1883–84, crowded as it was with anxieties and disappointments, there was, nevertheless, a very happy event, for in Philadelphia on January 7, 1884, the De Rennes became parents of their second child, a daughter, who was named Elfrida. As with the birth of children always, she brought with her "forward-looking thoughts" at a time when they were much needed. And soon it was decided that the family would return to live in Europe, where Wymberley had spent a third of his life and some of his happiest years.[119]

In 1864 he had spent his first European days on the Côte d'Azur, but it was on the Côte Basque, in the French resort town of Biarritz, that he and his family would live during his second stay in the Old World. The surroundings he chose were as different as possible from the Texas of his last several years. The countryside all around was verdant with farms and forests. The town occupied a bluff that dropped precipitously to the sea, with the dim outline of the Pyrenees rising to the south. Whereas water had normally been a scarce commodity at Buena Ventura, at Biarritz the sound of tons of it churning against the rocky coast was omnipresent and during the swells of winter could be heard twenty miles inland. Though there were great rocks at the shoreline, carved into fantastic shapes by the force of the tides, the major beach, the Grand Plage, was celebrated for its soft, pebble-free sand. It was popular with children, as well as that portion of society that chose to take a turn on the beach or to occupy beach chairs during the clearly defined social hours in the morning and afternoon. Bathers also frequented the beach, often with attendants: the frequent roughness of the water made bathing an activity to be conducted cautiously, while sailing was a dangerous (some said suicidal) pastime.[120]

There were amusements enough in town, however, not least among them the simple pleasures of sightseeing. The great variety of coastal views drew people constantly, and many spent hours simply gazing seaward or following the numerous paths, often flanked by stone walls or tamarisk trees, that led up and down the rocky bluff. Two of the most popular vantage points were at either end of the Grand Plage: to the east the white column of the lighthouse drew sightseers who paid a franc to climb the tower's 256 steps for a panoramic view of the area; to the west, a shaft of rock, its wide base hollowed into a picturesque tunnel by the waves, supported a much-venerated statue of the Virgin Mary. There sightseers often ascended steps to an iron balustrade that enclosed the statue's base. For those drawn to opulent man-made attractions, there was the imperial palace, begun for the Empress Eugénie in 1854.[121]

Tennis and croquet were very popular, though Wymberley was more likely to be found on the golf links; and the casino offered indoor entertainment of a less rigorous nature, with rouge et noir a favorite. The distinctive cuisine, French heated with a dash of Spanish, drew tourists and residents alike to the several restaurants and more particularly to the tables d'hôte at the numerous hotels. Wymberley took many meals at a favorite haunt, the British Club on the Avenue du Palais, where there was also a library stocked with books, newspapers, and magazines.[122]

Nearby towns had notable attractions as well: the fishing port of St. Jean-de-Luz to the south; Bordeaux, nestled in wine country to the north; and, a short distance inland, Bayonne, with its popular bull ring. Paris was five hundred miles northeast by train, and the spa of Baden-Baden, known to Wymberley since his days at Strassburg, was not much farther. All of Europe was very accessible to the De Renne family.[123]

For a dedicated angler and hunter like Wymberley, the environs of Biarritz offered trout streams to be fished as well as good sport in shooting chamois in the nearby hills. His companions, on the links and in the hunt, often became his friends. Among the last bonds forged in Biarritz was one with Duncan Pringle, who became Wymberley's closest lifelong friend. A bachelor from an old South Carolina family (and, ironically, a descendant of "Ik. Marvel"), he lived at the Villa Pringle with two spinster sisters and a variety of dogs.[124]

In later life, Wymberley would remember his time at Biarritz as his happiest period, but his mother probably saw his presence at the popular resort as confirmation of a fear that he would simply live off his annuity, leading a life of amusement and inconsequence. The birth of her granddaughter had not mellowed her. Indeed, to Mary De Renne the main effect of the child's birth was that she had her will redrawn, making it clear that none of her personal estate was to go to Wymberley or any child of his. When a codicil was drawn up later, it likewise made no provision for the child. Mrs. De Renne remained relentless and unappeasable toward her eldest son until her death.[125]

In 1889, two years after the death of Wymberley's mother, another daughter, named Audrey, was born to the De Rennes. Laura arranged to be back home in Philadelphia for this birth. The children's aunt Letitia, then in the city as well (though with only four months of life remaining), seems to have taken no notice of the De Renne children.[126]

During their stay in Biarritz the De Rennes occupied several of the villas that could be rented furnished in various parts of town, but they lived longest at the Villa Constance on the Rue de France. They usually had at least two servants in their employ. Despite his later preoccupation with books, Wymberley—after eight years in Biarritz—owned a small collection of books worth only $150, while he had $400 in "Guns, rifles, fishing rods, sticks, pistols."[127]

At the beginning of 1891, when Laura was expecting another child, Wymberley finally decided to return to Wormsloe to reclaim his heritage. Since his sister's death, Everard (himself terminally ill) had been renting the plantation from the estate. In one of the few agreements of their later lives, the brothers apparently determined that Wymberley would move to the family seat and rejuvenate it. Nonetheless, the rapprochement was very limited; when Kentwyn died a few months later, Wymberley was not informed of the fact by his surviving sibling but had to get the news from the family's Savannah law firm. The lawyers also advised him of Everard's intention to move the furniture from Wormsloe to a warehouse in Savannah. When Everard died three years later, he left his entire personal estate outside the family; fortunately, his heirs agreed to allow Wymberley to purchase some of the wine, objets d'art, and heirlooms that had belonged to the De Rennes.[128]

On his return to Savannah in 1891, Wymberley found many changes. The town was much larger than when he had last spent appreciable time there; the early 1860s population of some twenty thousand had almost tripled, but the town remained an unusual combination of the provincial and the cosmopolitan. The two houses he remembered best from his youth were no longer homes; his parents' Liberty Street residence was now the armory of the Georgia Hussars, and, at the Telfair Mansion, he, like other visitors, was greeted by five "heroic stone statues," indicative of the other works of art waiting in the galleries within. In the country, down Skidaway Road, the village known as Isle of Hope had also grown as Savannahians had moved to such coastal resort areas, known as the "salts." Frame cottages proliferated under the trees, and the masts of pleasure craft projected above the river banks. But at the end of the old oak avenue that followed the river, Wormsloe remained in its own world. Still embowered by its oaks and palmettos, the house still stood, though needing paint and repairs. So did most of its outbuildings, including the latticed well house and the old slave cabins. Nature had regained much ground since the death of Wymberley's father a little over a decade earlier, but these encroachments could soon be reversed.[129]

Wymberley spent little time in Savannah before returning to France for the birth of his last child: finally, another son. His first name would match his father's, but his middle name would honor the family's ancestral estate—Wymberley Wormsloe De Renne. But before he left Savannah for France, De Renne completed two errands. He went to Bonaventure Cemetery and bought three adjoining lots for the construction of a large family crypt. And he revisited Wormsloe, with all its associations of a happy and illustrious past and its memories of an extraordinary father and mother and of everything that they had valued and been unwilling to let perish. Enclosed by the same walls that had harbored them, on land long ago granted by the king to the patriarch of his clan, Wymberley sat with a small blackbound journal. In it he had begun to record information about his forebears, beginning on the first page with his father's epitaph for the monument of Noble Jones. Opposite this inscription, on the book's paste-down, he wrote a line of Latin below which he signed himself with a new name—not "Wymberley De Renne," as he had been known to his instructors in Europe, or "W. De Renne," as he had inscribed it in Texas, but "Wymberley Jones De Renne," with the place and date below it: "Wormsloe year 1891." The Latin he chose was very fitting: *Servata fides cineri*—"The promise made to the ashes has been kept."[130]

CHAPTER 8

Master of Wormsloe

To be a cosmopolite is not, I think, an ideal: the ideal should be to be a
concentrated patriot.
—HENRY JAMES

The return of Wymberley Jones De Renne and his family to
Wormsloe was not abrupt. Instead, there was a transitional
period of several years, during which his wife and children remained in Biarritz and he traveled. De Renne journeyed to various
points in Europe, to Savannah (where he normally stopped at
the Hotel De Soto, next door to the old De Renne mansion), and
to New York City. Wormsloe could not be prepared for family
life overnight. And if Wymberley intended to resume one family
tradition—using the old estate as a residence six months out of
the year—he would have to enlist a work force to tend the place
year-round.[1]

He intended to return Wormsloe as fully as possible to the
status of a working farm and determined to defray the expenses of
labor, production, and upkeep with money earned from what
Wormsloe could produce. Though he did not plant cotton, he grew
food crops for the table and for sale and provender for the livestock
as well. A herd of dairy cows was once again pastured under the
oaks, and eventually Wormsloe cream would be a byword in Savannah provision stores. De Renne's pleasure in the plantation's

productivity would rival his father's and would embrace Wormsloe's oyster beds, fabled since colonial days. He leased them out for harvesting and renewal, with the proviso that a certain number of bushels be regularly delivered for the table at Wormsloe.[2]

As farm hands, he carefully selected a force of Negro laborers, some of whom had been among Wormsloe's tenantry since Reconstruction days; others lived in or near the hamlet of Sandfly, just over the causeway on the road to Savannah. De Renne would be a stern and demanding taskmaster, not easily satisfied. Consequently, those who worked for him feared his displeasure and highly valued his praise and respect.[3]

To manage this work force De Renne needed not only a black man who was a leader but one who was literate, for he would have to make his reports by mail for six months of the year. Jesse Beach, longtime Wormsloe tenant and former employee of G. W. J. De Renne, fit the position perfectly. A diligent worker himself, he earned the respect of those who labored under his direction, as well as that of his employer, who recognized him as uncompromisingly honest and conscientious. Additionally, Beach had a sincere devotion to Wormsloe; as his employer commented, "all his interests for life are centered in the place."[4]

Jesse Beach was tasked with running the farm on a day-to-day basis, much as the plantation's overseers had done in antebellum days. He saw that De Renne's orders were carried out—which field to plow and what to plant—and as time went on he and his workers cleared more and more rampant undergrowth, until Wormsloe once again had spacious expanses of fields and pastures, with fencing repaired, replaced, or built anew. Clearing vegetation was far from a onetime job in the semitropical climate of coastal Georgia, for nature fought tirelessly to reclaim the entire estate, and many man-hours were also required to keep the grounds properly drained with a system of ditches.[5]

Others on whom De Renne depended were Abram Miller and, increasingly, Frank Jenkins, who began as stable boy and rose to the position of butler, despite De Renne's original intention of having only French house servants. Jenkins would devote himself to the estate for over half a century and, like Jesse Beach, eventually died at Wormsloe.[6]

The staff and hands at Wormsloe could depend on steady work at good wages, including loans and advances when needed (plus the various amenities of having such a refuge as their workplace). But Christmas at Wormsloe was a festive occasion for the estate's servants and laborers, when De

Renne displayed his appreciation in special ways. In the servants' hall in the western end of the residence a huge tree was decorated with ornaments and presents; candles were placed around the room to be lighted on Christmas Eve as the procession of servants to the tree began. The white servants came first, to receive presents of money ($8 to $12). Their wives and children accompanied them and received candy and other gifts. After some time of conversation with the De Rennes, the white staff departed as the black servants were welcomed by the family. Led by Jesse Beach (and in later years by Abram Miller and Frank Jenkins, respectively), the workmen received their Christmas bonuses in the form they most preferred—gold or silver coins in amounts from $5 to $10; their wives received boxes of candy. The Negro children were taken to the tree, where gifts were cut from the branches and presented to them. Ophelia Dent, who as a child witnessed the servants' yuletide celebration, remembered it as "a very moving scene."[7]

During the six months that Jesse Beach directed his workers independently, De Renne spent part of his time in Europe, at least for the first decade after his return. His annual Carlsbad cure continued to draw him to Europe, and his trips were occasionally enlivened by the company of friends and fellow Savannahians, like J. Florance Minis, and other coastal Georgians, including James T. Dent, of the Altamaha River plantation Hofwyl. De Renne apparently bore up under the cure better than his comrades, though his daughter Elfrida did not envy him the Carlsbad water: "tepid, awful stuff!" as she described it, quoting Eugene Field. Also often on De Renne's agenda while in Europe was a visit to Duncan Pringle and his sisters at Villa Pringle, or at Pau, or wherever else they happened to be residing. Whether in America or Europe, De Renne, as a person of social consequence, saw his comings and goings noted in the local press.[8]

De Renne's hunting trips continued, though the locale shifted almost entirely to the New World. In his early days De Renne even tried the Southeast: he and some friends set up their own hunting club near Asheville, North Carolina, in 1894 and observed with interest the mammoth construction activities at the Vanderbilt estate. But more often De Renne traveled much farther north, including trips to Canada. He was a life member of the Tourilli Hunting and Fishing Club in Quebec Province, where he shot caribou and moose, and he also fished for salmon at the Tobique Salmon Club near the Maine border. Occasionally, he would make trips to such remote spots as Yellowstone in the American Northwest.[9]

During the decade leading to the Great War, De Renne went to Europe less frequently and made New York State his home away from home. He enjoyed the social and cultural attractions of New York City as well as sampling rural pleasures at Westport, "the Gateway to the Adirondacks," on glinting Lake Champlain. In the metropolis he spent much time at the Union Club and stayed for years at the Buckingham Hotel but finally was drawn permanently to the turreted grandeur of the Hotel Netherland, despite its unfortunate (to him) location, directly across the street from Augustus Saint-Gaudens's heroic equestrian statue of General William T. Sherman. In Westport, De Renne regularly enjoyed the breeze-cooled rooms and spacious lakeside verandas of the Westport Inn.[10]

At Westport and elsewhere the post would bring communications from Jesse Beach, bearing the news of Wormsloe: whether the hens were laying, how many acres had been planted in peas and how many in corn, and whether there was a rising demand for milk and cream. Beach's letters also included reports on the activities of the Wormsloe bull, described like all else with great dignity, discretion, and decorum. Always the letters ended with the good wishes of all at Wormsloe and courteous inquiries regarding the health of Mr. and Mrs. De Renne and family.[11]

The children were usually hearty, though young Wymberley was more likely than his sisters to suffer from ill health and had to wear spectacles from an early age. Nonetheless, he was an active child and particularly enjoyed summers in the New Hampshire mountains and at Lake Champlain, where he had his own tiny motorboat. Like his sisters, he loved to ride; all were very active. Mrs. De Renne was less fortunate in her health and always had the services of at least one attendant. The children were always in the care of a nursemaid, although Elfrida, the oldest, bore some of the responsibilities of caring for her younger siblings and, increasingly, took on other adult tasks as well.[12]

Shortly after his return to Wormsloe, De Renne began to make plans not only to refurbish Wormsloe House and reclaim the grounds but to transform them entirely, and before long the estate had become a noted showplace. Just as Dr. George Jones's simple cottage had disappeared into his son's massively austere Greek Revival residence, that rambling structure in turn underwent a metamorphosis into a tour de force of late Victorian excess, with the abundant architectural flourishes so beloved toward the end of the nineteenth century. Since the death of Everard De Renne left Wymberley's surviving children as the only heirs of G. W. J. De Renne—and thus inheritors in common of Wormsloe and all other remaining De Renne property — the Pennsylvania Company bore the expenses of renovation, using funds drawn from the estate. Following established practice, petitions were submitted to the Chatham County Superior Court, and favorable judgments were secured for a variety of improvements to Wormsloe House, as well as for the construction of necessary outbuildings.[15]

By 1897 De Renne had widened the front portico and placed a roofed balcony above it, added a two-story veranda on the river side of the house, and built second- and third-floor balconies that stretched the length of the garden front above the piazza. Abutting the piazza at the southeast corner of the house, another of his towers appeared, this one resembling a slender Alpine campanile; projecting far above the roofline, it enclosed a wrought-iron spiral staircase that gave access to the eastern verandas. A latticework railing now enclosed the flat roof, where a flagpole was centered. Never before accessible from the garden, the piazza was supplied with a wide central stair, covered by a glass roof, that led down to a Gothic porte cochere. On the west side of the house, De Renne constructed a narrow three-story addition that provided bathrooms for each level of the house, as well as service stairs, and extended the basement level westward with a brick kitchen; from it, there was access by a dumbwaiter to the pantry adjoining the first-floor dining room.[14]

Renovating the inside of the house in 1894, De Renne "pretty well ripped out" the original interior and remodeled "after the modern style of architecture and finish," with the new wood finished in hard oil. He expanded the dining room so that it became the largest room in the house, eighteen by thirty-six feet; a bay window, as well as large mirrors over the twin fireplaces, enhanced the effect of spaciousness. There he hung Des-Anges's immense portrait of his mother, as well as other family portraits, against a background of ornately designed wallpaper. The intricately patterned carpet chosen for the room was hardly less ornamental than the decorated ceiling above it.[15]

Within a decade the room had been redone in an Egyptian motif, complete with bronze statuary (originally owned by his parents) and wall hangings that evoked the Land of the Pharaohs. This effect was heightened by newly installed mantels of red Numidian marble, shaped like pyramids and decorated with bronze statues of sphinxes, with a wide band of brass surrounding the fireplace. Above the two mantels were murals depicting the

Valley of the Kings. Across the wide hall, the northeast parlor—now with its own bay window and settee—became De Renne's study, lined with custom-made bookcases, while the southeast parlor continued its original use. In the hall itself, a terra-cotta fireplace, reminiscent of the Basque country, was installed near the front door, and a new oak staircase was constructed near the door to the piazza.[16]

In 1900 De Renne extended the house westward over forty feet by constructing a service wing: it included an expanded pantry and a two-story octagonal servants' hall. In the addition's basement was a spacious new kitchen and servants' dining room, with a built-in refrigerator beneath the stairs; the first and second floors each contained three bedrooms, a bathroom, and a sitting room for the servants. There was access from the service wing to the basement of the residence, which was devoted to wine cellars and a world of wine-related paraphernalia. Down at the river, a lengthy pier stretched eastward to a large screened concrete pavilion, itself something of an engineering marvel.[17]

The house had for many years been painted white, with dark shutters, but the expanded residence was covered with more dramatic hues. The colors chosen for the painting that was done in 1906, for example, combined what must have seemed acres of vermilion with white for trim and Orient green for the blinds.[18]

Obviously, such a commodious showplace was built for hospitality, and numerous guests visited the family during the fall and winter. Much like De Renne's other bachelor friend, Duncan Pringle of Biarritz, Captain Alexander McCrie Duncan of the Georgia Hussars became the closest of De Renne's friends in Savannah and visited Wormsloe often, sometimes staying with the family for weeks at a time. A Confederate veteran with a long white beard, "Sandy" Duncan resembled an attenuated Santa Claus; he was a favorite of all the children but particularly close to young Wymberley. Other gentlemen of martial aspect also visited, including some with scarred faces and heavy Teutonic accents, come to see their old comrade at Wormsloe. De Renne's fellow members of such local organizations as the Georgia Historical Society and the Sons of the Revolution also made the trip to Wormsloe, as did the De Rennes' circle of friends in Savannah—including Mr. and Mrs. J. Florance Minis and Mr. and Mrs. George Owens—who enjoyed Wormsloe's hospitality in its various forms.[19]

Such an establishment obviously required a large staff, and in the early days the servants were exclusively white and often French or English. In 1895 Wormsloe House had both a head butler and an underbutler, as well as a chef (Alex Bedart), a kitchen maid, two chambermaids, and a washerwoman. At the stables, there were a coachman, a groom, a stable man, and several stable hands. A governess and a nurse were also in residence, as well as an attendant for Mrs. De Renne. In relation to the residence, there were also, among the black laborers directed by Jesse Beach, two woodcutters who worked constantly to provide fuel for cooking and heating.[20]

On such occasions as formal dinners, De Renne's table emulated the legends of his father's time, as did the De Renne cellar; its fabled reputation grew with the years and with the increasing number of bottles acquired and enjoyed. There were many that had been passed down (some even from the time of Dr. George Jones) and purchased from the estate of Everard De Renne, others collected during the stay in Biarritz, and still more shipped in the mid-1890s from the Bordeaux firm of Geo. Regis & Charpentier.[21]

As in Wymberley's father's day, meals, whether en famille or otherwise, were always very formal affairs, and the children were often required to speak French at table. Punctuality for meals was particularly stressed. This trait, however, was not among Mrs. De Renne's virtues, and her husband was often left impatiently standing, consulting his pocket watch as he awaited her tread on the stairs. Often appearing only at lunch and dinner, Mrs. De Renne spent almost all her day in her second-floor bedroom, usually reading novels and plays; her sanctum was eventually expanded by the addition of a boudoir that enclosed a portion of the second-story balcony. Increasingly, her children saw her only in her bedroom. Twice a day—between nine and ten in the morning and just before bedtime—they would enter her preserve, a spacious chamber full of the fragrance of cut flowers and the scent of sandalwood, and troop to her bedside table for a chocolate.[22]

Beyond Mrs. De Renne's windows were Wormsloe's gardens. Celebrated since the days of Noble Jones, they benefited from unprecedented planning, maintenance, and expansion after the return of Wymberley Jones De Renne. Though in past years the major garden had been south of the house, De Renne had flowering plants and shrubs planted to the front of the residence and along all approaches to it. He added a greenhouse, employed a gardener, and in 1897 had maps carefully drafted showing the location of all flowers, shrubbery, and trees, complete with genus and species. To the front and rear of the house, circular pools were constructed, both equipped with fountains, both with graceful bronze waterbirds rising from their centers.[23]

Past the gardens, the grounds south of the residence were fenced into numerous lots and pens for the livestock, and many dependencies were constructed, from ample stables and cow houses to hen coops. Looming above the stables was a water tower and tank, constructed in 1897, which was filled by ram pumps. Just west of the residence, De Renne had a story-and-a-half cottage constructed for Jesse Beach.[24]

Not surprisingly, De Renne took steps to make Wormsloe a pleasant and interesting place for riding. He had bridle paths cut through some of the forested areas of the estate for himself and his children; Audrey, as she matured, proved to be the most exuberant and tireless of the young riders. For racing, De Renne had an oval half-mile track constructed in the late 1890s near Skidaway Road. Soon it would accommodate another kind of horsepower, for the father and his children were fascinated by automobiles. In 1905 De Renne held an Automobile Gymkhana at the track, allowing "Large Machines," "Runabouts," and "Electric Machines" to compete for prizes.[25]

Elfrida, since she had lived in Biarritz longer than the others and had begun her schooling earlier, saw less of Wormsloe than did the younger children during the 1890s, but she loved the estate as much. Her father sent her numerous Wormsloe mementos, including photographs depicting each new renovation and view. Her fellow students in New York, studying the pictures, understood why she preferred to go home rather than abroad during the holidays.[26]

Though they saw more of Wormsloe than Elfrida did, Audrey and young Wymberley did not see nearly as much of it as they wished. Even during the months normally set aside for living at the estate, some of their time was spend in the North with their mother and a complement of servants, while De Renne traveled. His family's principal northern residence from the mid-1890s through the early 1900s was the resort village of Lakewood, New Jersey, just sixty miles by train from New York City. Some who frequented Lakewood, like President Grover Cleveland, owned cottages there, but Laura De Renne and the children always stayed at the Laurel House, one of the resort's "commodious, home-like hotels," and took advantage of the area's convenient schools. Since Lakewood became rather warm in the summer, the Laurel House closed for the season, but its companion resort—the Jefferson, in New Hampshire's White Mountains—had cottages awaiting refugees from the New Jersey heat. The De Rennes sometimes occupied the Cherry Cottage there, and at the Jefferson the children would often see their father, who enjoyed his membership in the Waumbek Golf Club there and arranged lessons for all the young ones.[27]

Wherever his travels took him, De Renne was always pursued by letters from his children, with the younger two—and Audrey in particular—constantly asking when they could go to Wormsloe. They normally wrote the name of the estate in all capitals, often over an inch tall, and sometimes printed "WORMSLOE" in letters that occupied a whole page. Nature had given the place multiple attractions for the young, but De Renne had added to them, making the family estate a place of enchantment for the children. Not least among the allurements was the stable with its waiting ponies, Wymberley's Rob Roy and Audrey's Jumbo, ready to take the two down shadow-dappled trails. But there were also small pools near the house, haunts for statuettes of elves and gnomes, figures that also appeared at various other points in the gardens south of the house. Tiny decorative bridges crossed some of the pools and the creek, and a narrow cement stairway led to the welcoming fork of one of the massive trees. Near the residence, a large one-room playhouse also stood, with its own stove for heating in winter and a wide array of cooking utensils, games, and toys.[28]

Though indulging the coming generation, De Renne was not unmindful of generations past. The old family burial plot was cleared of undergrowth, as was the old tabby ruin. And soon after he returned, De Renne improved the old trace that ran due south to the tabby ruin from Skidaway Road, covering the thoroughfare with crushed oyster shells. He then lined it with oaks on both sides, partially inspired, it was said, by an old French custom. It held that such a stretch of timber should be grown in honor of the first-born son, to be presented to him at his majority so that he could harvest the trees and receive the profit of their sale. The custom was somewhat modified, however, since the trees were not meant to be cut down; to the contrary, they and the avenue (and a monumental arched gateway) were to be dedicated in the son's honor when he reached twenty-one. Consequently, the intent was closer to that described by Washington Irving: they were planted so that in time they would come to symbolize "the long settled dignity, and proudly concentrated independence of an ancient family."[29]

The new Wormsloe arch, equipped with iron gates, opened onto a re-routed Skidaway Road that promised to end decades of controversy over the bridge to Skidaway Island. The bridge matter had resurfaced in 1894, just as De Renne was beginning his renovation and expansion of Wormsloe House. The Skidaway Islanders engaged in several years of litigation, attempting to have the bridge rebuilt at the original site. They based their case on the earlier legislation that had made the road and bridge public and insisted that the county commissioners had an inescapable obligation to construct and maintain the bridge. Though Wormsloe was less threatened by this proposal of the 1890s, De Renne's lawyers brought pressure to ensure that the new span, if erected, would have a central drawbridge that would allow boat access to Wormsloe.[50]

There was little public support for the new bridge in any case. It was pointed out that the structure would cost the taxpayers of Savannah and Chatham County over $10,000, which was more than the taxable value of Skidaway Island: it annually yielded only about $50 in taxes. Nonetheless, in 1897 the Chatham County Superior Court issued a mandamus absolute for construction of the bridge. The following year, however, when the county commissioners took the case before the Georgia Supreme Court, the justices unanimously reversed the decision of the lower court. With the passage of ten more years, the commissioners were able to abandon the old Skidaway Road entirely for a new one that avoided the bridgehead and instead ran northeast to the village of Isle of Hope; Skidaway Island was now accessible only by boat. With the road's abandonment by the county in 1908, De Renne wrote "Finale" to the bridge matter—somewhat prematurely it would transpire, though the controversy was indeed dead for his lifetime.[51]

The abandonment of Skidaway Road seemed to open the way to a further expansion of the Wormsloe lands. The new Skidaway Road followed the southern border of Wymberly, the largest remnant of N. W. Jones's Wimberly Plantation, formerly owned by the Claghorns and now the property of the widow of Colonel John H. Estill. Since the new road threatened the privacy of Wymberly House, Mrs. Estill offered the residence for sale, along with ninety acres of highland and eleven and a half acres of marsh, together with nearby Burnt Pot Island. De Renne negotiated for the property for over a year, attempting to secure the Wymberly House furnishings in the bargain, but was ultimately unsuccessful.[52]

Nonetheless, abandonment of the road had increased Wormsloe's privacy, and De Renne was able to enhance it further in 1912. The only portion of the old road still in use was that leading to the Parkersville Road. To induce the commissioners to abandon it, De Renne offered them land for a new road—a strip that followed the northern border of Wormsloe—and when the officials accepted, all public thoroughfares vanished from Wormsloe. Additionally, in 1913, De Renne purchased five lots of the old Dupon property opposite the new Wormsloe gates; now there could be no construction by outsiders on the parcels across from the estate's entrance.[53]

By this time De Renne had also helped enhance the value of the other De Renne plantation, Poplar Grove, which was destined to be engulfed by the southward expansion of the city of Savannah. By the late 1880s the city had opened several streets in the area. One called De Renne Avenue (later renamed) formed the northern border of Kensington, a subdivision adjoining Poplar Grove. Though mostly flat land, Poplar Grove suffered from poor drainage, despite the deep ditch known as the De Renne Canal. In later years, De Renne feared that the tract's drainage problems would detract from its value, so he employed Frederick Law Olmsted to examine the area and submit a proposal on how best to remedy the situation. In any case, the development potential of Poplar Grove was greatly increased in 1907, when the Pennsylvania Company allowed a new De Renne Avenue to be constructed through the southern portion of the tract, linking Middle Ground Road, to the west, with Waters Road, to the east. This enclosed most of the old plantation within a rectangle that had Estill Avenue (later renamed Victory Drive) as its northern border.[54]

At Wormsloe, the new oak avenue led for a mile and a half from Skidaway Road to the tabby ruin of Noble Jones's bastioned house. One of the oldest military sites on the Georgia coast, it was usually called simply the "Old Fort" by De Renne. Fittingly, he sometimes made that area of the estate available for excursions and exercises by the Georgia Hussars. This elite coastal cavalry unit counted Noble Jones as an eminent predecessor because of his status as first commander of colonial Georgia's First Troop of Horse, and the Hussars elected his descendant Wymberley Jones De Renne as an honorary member. On more than one occasion De Renne hosted the troop at Wormsloe, sometimes holding shooting matches for them.[55]

The Georgia Hussars were among the first Savannahians to visit newly renovated Wormsloe House in the spring of 1895. Mounted on a "great bay horse," De Renne met the troopers at the gate to the old oak avenue and led them along the river to Wormsloe House. During the course of the day, the Hussars "gloriously won" a match with a visiting northern team. Writing De Renne afterward, William W. Gordon thanked him for his "courteous welcome at the entrance to Wormsloe, the gracious introduction to the ladies & to the mansion house, the excellent management for the contests, & the banquet served throughout the day. . . . We appreciated also your kindness in making our guests, the New Jersey Riflemen, your personal guests, & rejoiced that they participated in an entertainment, given by an Hussar, which was so eminently calculated to impress them with pleasant memories of the South & of our Troop." [56]

Other military organizations also benefited from De Renne's generosity. The Oglethorpe Light Infantry, in which De Renne also had an honorary membership, received from him a handsome silver cup; an engraving on one side depicted its members marching in Forsyth Park, with the Confederate Monument in the background. And the Savannah Military Rifle Range Association was recipient of an elaborate silver pitcher, deeded as the "De Renne Trophy." It was to be the prize in marksmanship contests, restricted to "military small arms," held annually in Savannah; the winning team would have the privilege of keeping the trophy for one year. Though the most prominent feature of the pitcher was a winged statue of Fame, there were also echoes of De Renne's days in Texas: a "bas-relief of the 'Alamo,'" and, supporting the body of the vessel, representations of the prickly pear cactus. [57]

Of all of Savannah's elite military units, the Hussars were foremost in De Renne's estimation, partially no doubt because of his friendship with Captain Alexander McC. Duncan. On the fiftieth anniversary of Captain Duncan's joining the Hussars, December 14, 1908, De Renne staged a splendid "entertainment" for him at Wormsloe, complete with marquee-covered trestle tables loaded with food and drink. There were also speeches and exhibitions of marksmanship, while many of the younger Hussars, resplendent in their uniforms and on handsome mounts, showed why it had been said that cavalry added tone to any military proceeding. But illness and death had greatly thinned the ranks of those Hussars of Duncan's age. One elderly trooper, who had been recruited by Duncan before the war, sadly sent De Renne his regrets, noting, "Prepare to dismount! is our order coming down the column." [58]

De Renne was also drawn to another organization that had martial aspects: the Sons of the Revolution, one of many hereditary patriotic associations that sprang up during the 1880s and 1890s. Founded in New York City in 1883, on the centennial of the British evacuation of the city, the SR, as it was called, was a very conservative organization. Its constitution resembled that of the Society of the Cincinnati, and its membership was restricted to male descendants of those who had taken part in the revolt against the Crown, either on the battlefield, in the Continental Congresses, or in state assemblies. For some years the SR had discouraged the formation of branches in other states, but just a year after a General Society was created in 1890, a Georgia branch appeared. Though open to members throughout the state (State Librarian John Milledge of Atlanta was a member, for example), Savannahians were the driving force behind the creation of the Georgia branch and composed most of its membership.[39]

The organization, not yet a year old when De Renne joined in January 1892 (as great-grandson of Noble Wimberly Jones), was headed by one of his father's old friends and close contemporaries, Colonel John Screven. The vice president was De Renne's cousin Dr. J. G. B. Bulloch, a great-great-grandson of Noble Wimberly Jones and the most prolific of Georgia's genealogical writers of the period. Other members included relatives such as Wallace Savage Jones and friends J. Florance Minis and George Owens.[40]

One conspicuous offshoot of De Renne's membership in the SR was his first venture into printing. At the group's first annual dinner, held at Savannah's De Soto Hotel on February 8, 1892, Colonel Screven presented an address that De Renne thought worthy of preservation. Screven observed that if there was "anything true or good, anything great or exalted, in the motives and actions of the revolutionary sires, their sons [had] a right to claim them, not with misplaced or insolent boasting, but with 'secret joy' and a grateful sense of potent obligations to recognized good examples."[41]

De Renne had the address printed as a thin volume, restricted to forty-five copies—the "number of members subscribing to the dinner." The presswork for the book was done in Philadelphia, as well as the binding, which included a ribbon marker and, on the front cover, a gilt medallion in relief. At the end of the book there was a list of the toasts given, as well as the menu for the evening, which included four wines. The dinner began with soft-shell crabs, proceeded—through boiled red snapper with pommes parisienne, saddle of venison with mushrooms à la crème, filet mignon, and stewed terrapin à la Maryland—to roast quail bardes on toast, and ended with Nesselrode pudding, petits fours glacé, fruit, charlotte russe, and coffee.[12]

That the Sons of the Revolution was organized during the year of De Renne's return to Wormsloe was a fortunate coincidence. His membership immediately propelled him into the society of the city of his forefathers and also introduced him to like-minded men from Macon and Atlanta. The SR also reinforced his growing interest in his antecedents. Genealogical research was enjoying a heyday in the early 1890s, and De Renne would find the lure of his ancestry all but inescapable. This was particularly so since, for the first time as an adult, he was faced with living in a place where numerous people could make claims of kinship on him. His family had been so long established and its alliances with other old families were so complicated that he found it difficult to sort out all of the intricate interrelationships with which he was surrounded.[13]

Happily, a kind of primer was at hand. In 1892 his kinsman Dr. J. G. B. Bulloch published *A History and Genealogy of the Families of Bulloch, Stobo, De Veaux, Irvine, Douglass, Baillie, Lewis, Adams, Glen, Jones, Davis, Hunter, with a Genealogy of Branches of the Habersham, King, Stiles, Footman, Newell, Turner, Stewart, Dunwody, Elliott, with Mention of the Families of Bryan, Bourke, Williams, Wylly, Woodbridge, and Many Other Families.* It included a chapter titled "Memoirs of the Noble Jones Family"—illustrated with an armorial bookplate provided by De Renne—that presented a rough outline of the Jones–De Renne line. The family genealogy was in fact imperfect: De Renne made numerous pencil corrections in his copy of the book (saving, however, the blackest ink for a strike-through of Bulloch's presumptuous designation of the Reverend James Bulloch, Esquire, husband of Mary Jones, as having been "of Wormsloe"). Nonetheless, Bulloch's book was a start, and it seems to have spurred De Renne's interest in the far-flung net of his relations, for he began to draft genealogical tables—some of them massive—in an attempt to clarify his lineage in his own mind. One of the charts, written on sheets of foolscap pasted together, was over a yard wide and stretched over eight yards in length. Incredibly, it covered only the descendants of Sarah Jones Glen, the daughter of Noble Wimberly Jones.[14]

De Renne seems to have recognized Bulloch's strengths as a genealogist—particularly his capacity for hard digging for information and his knowledge of source materials—but he seems to have understood his limitations as well. Bulloch was a credulous researcher, guided too often by wishful thinking, if not fantasy, and often transformed into fact whatever happened to make sense to him. He had no qualms about tracing Noble Jones back to the Royal House of Wales or even further back to various Romans. And he posited that Noble Jones's wife had Wimberly as her maiden name (it would prove to be Hack), presumably since that was the middle name of her eldest son. There was no documentation for his assertion, though he did trace a likely Wimberley family to Scotland.[15]

The research that Bulloch conducted for De Renne included a foray into the background of the Jones family in England, and among the subjects he attempted to investigate was the lineage of Noble Jones and the authenticity of the arms displayed on the bookplate and seal traceable to him. De Renne warned Bulloch that he had already heard from genealogists who offered "to make up, publish & record any kind of pedigree" he wanted, and he had no interest in such trifling. But he soon realized as well—after Bulloch made preliminary inquiries with several English genealogists and at the College of Arms—that probing into the history of a family with the surname Jones would, in all likelihood, be prohibitively expensive in time and money, with no guarantee of certain results. Despite De Renne's financial investment and support, Bulloch turned up little on the Jones family, armorial or otherwise. In the case of the arms, De Renne, like his father before him, ultimately took the lion rampant on faith.[16]

De Renne carried out some research of his own in the late spring of 1895, when he withdrew the family archive and portraits from the vault at the Germania Bank to inventory them. Among the papers gathered by his father, there were manuscripts, portraits, and relics enough to contribute significantly to a book-length biographical account of only one of his ancestors. Oddly enough, that forebear was neither the "Companion of Oglethorpe" nor the "Morning Star of Liberty" but Justice Thomas Smith, his great-grandfather, whose wife's maiden name had suggested the surname De Renne.[17]

Though not looking for a biographer, De Renne in 1902 came across one anyway, in the person of Burton Alva Konkle. This Indiana-born scholar, eight years De Renne's junior, was then historian of the Pennsylvania Bar Association. During his research on members of the Continental Congress, Konkle had heard that De Renne had a likeness of Justice Smith, and he wrote requesting that a copy be made for display in Independence Hall. He also inquired whether there was a biographical sketch of Smith among the De Renne papers, but soon found that—though there was important material in Savannah—his own Smith materials (gathered as protégé of Hampton L. Carson, historian of the Supreme Court of the United States) were much more extensive. Prominent among these Smith papers in Pennsylvania was a series of letters, dated 1785–86, between Smith and the famous gentleman for whom he acted as attorney, George Washington. At De Renne's request, Konkle provided him with typescripts of these Washington-Smith letters. In reviewing these copies, De Renne saw that in making them Konkle had employed the scientific approach, favored by the new generation of university-trained historians and identical to that which G. W. J. De Renne had championed. In contrast to such earlier compilers as Jared Sparks, Konkle had made copies that were as far as possible exact duplicates of the originals and had reproduced "commas, bad spelling, abbreviation, and so far as possible, the general appearance of the page."[48]

Assuming correctly that De Renne would be interested in having a biography of Thomas Smith appear, Konkle sent him propositions in July and August 1902: with De Renne's financial support, he would prepare an "extended biography" of Justice Smith for between $1,200 and $1,300, and he would have it published, within a year, in an edition of five hundred copies, for between $500 and $600.[49]

Further letters followed, and by September the biographer and his patron had come to an arrangement. De Renne admitted to being "much impressed" by some of the statements in Konkle's letters, in particular his avowal that he wanted to "make a useful work to historical students, not a mere memorial," and that he wished to "reconstruct the environment, state & national, in which Justice Smith worked." Consequently, De Renne accepted Konkle's offer, with one major financial stipulation: De Renne would not be responsible for more than $2,000 for expenses. If, however, Konkle could persuade a publisher to carry the book, he was welcome to whatever percentage of the profits the publisher offered. De Renne also specified that he "reserve[d] the privilege of passing on the illustrations, paper, printing, & form of volume."[50]

Konkle worked quickly on the manuscript of what was his first book. He took advantage of De Renne's generosity in sending him valuable manuscript materials and illustrations, a "wealth of material," wrote Konkle, that filled him with "great pleasure and great anxiety." Soon after beginning his work in earnest, Konkle arranged with the Philadelphia publisher Campion and Company to bring out the volume, and W. H. Campion of that firm began to correspond with De Renne about the project. Konkle also wrote to De Renne frequently and conferred personally with him more than once during his patron's stays in the North.[51]

By August 1903 Konkle had sent De Renne a draft of the text and solicited his corrections and suggestions. De Renne was pleased with what he saw and offered only a few corrections of misspellings of family names (though some such errors remained in the published version). In answer to Konkle's request that he be allowed to dedicate the work to him, De Renne declined but suggested that Konkle might perhaps wish to dedicate it to the subject of the biography, "explaining how you were struck by his personality when reading Pennsylvania history & were thereby induced to make further researches & finally to write his own history." This Konkle did not wish to do, saying he had covered that territory in his preface; instead, he dedicated the book to his young daughter Winifred.[52]

Though this failure to accommodate him may have been an indication to De Renne that other things might not go as he hoped, he was unprepared for what he found in the introduction to the finished volume. Seeking to honor both his Pennsylvania mentor and his Georgia patron, Konkle had invited Hampton Carson to write the introduction, to which De Renne had lodged no objection. Carson—a busy man at the best of times—had recently become more so, having been appointed Pennsylvania's attorney general; the publishers, delayed by waiting for Carson's contribution, had to postpone publication of the book. As Konkle admitted, Carson's ultimate submission was not what either of them had wished: Carson "was desirous of writing a far longer Introduction, but in his efforts to find time for it, he delayed so long we were compelled to ask for whatever could be done at once." Konkle himself made an ill-considered suggestion that Carson incorporate into his introduction a lengthy anecdote regarding Justice Smith, written by one of his contemporaries, Horace Binney. De Renne, of course, had no opportunity to read the introduction until late February 1904, when he received the first copy of the book, titled *The Life and Times of Thomas Smith, 1745–1809, a Pennsylvania Member of the Continental Congress.*[53]

De Renne saw that the Binney anecdote took up more than a page of Carson's perfunctory three-page introduction and that Binney described Smith as "rough and bearish in his manners, uncouth in person and address, and . . . incapable of raising the skin by a reproof without making a gash." There was also a strikingly extraneous passage, jarring as part of the introduction to a book, that depicted Smith's arrival at a friend's for dinner after a hot July ride: "His hat was then in his hand, but on his head was a mass of paste made by the powder and pomatum, a part of which had run down in white streams upon his face, as red in all the unplastered parts as a boiled lobster."[54]

Writing to Konkle about the book, De Renne first favorably assessed the work as a whole. He predicted that "historically" the book would "make its mark" and commented that its style was good and its general appearance attractive. (In these assessments, he would later be joined by most of the book's reviewers.) But his displeasure with the introduction was severe:

> It should never have been printed & would not have been had I seen it. Mr. Binney's opinions and sarcastic criticisms . . . are his own personal views, & brought in at the proper place in the text would bear the weight they deserve. But to use Mr. Binney's description of Judge Smith as the highest and best that could be said of him & introduce him by it to the public, shows a want of common sense or a shirking of his duty on the part of the writer. He did not take the trouble to write a suitable introduction, based on the book itself or knowledge of the subject.
>
> The introduction leaves a bad taste in your mouth, which the most diligent & careful reading of the book can not wholly obliterate. . . . I am sorry that you subscribed to that Introduction.[55]

At first, Konkle was abject in his apology, dictating from a sickbed an immediate response to De Renne's letter: "I now frankly confess, with much chagrin, that I lost my grip on matters of taste in this instance." While defending the historical necessity of including the anecdote, he admitted that he had hoped that Carson would place it better in context and qualify it in some manner. Later Konkle pleaded his case more elaborately and tried to bolster it with commendatory reviews that had given no notice to the introduction, as well as appeals to De Renne's "historical spirit." But he had not helped himself with an observation that suggested that only someone with "a personal relation to the subject" could have viewed the anecdote so unfavorably.[56]

De Renne replied:

> I can read with perfect equanimity the failings of great men not related to me, even with a spice of pleasure & I do not doubt that the public will do so in case of Judge Smith.
>
> The book was written by you for yourself & for the public, of course, but would never have been written by you, unless I had made it possible for you to do so, so my feelings on the subject of the publication of any personal anecdotes, should at least be entitled to some consideration where you were responsible.
>
> Generally, authors avoid mentioning personal anecdotes derogatory to and not necessary to the history of their heroes, especially if they have any regard for their family. General [Ulysses S.] Grant's weaknesses & misfortunes were not laid bare to the ridicule of the public, nor were Abraham Lincoln's.
>
> I have written the above to clear your mind of the idea of my changing mine. My [earlier] letter . . . should have done that; as it did not do so, I have had to be more explicit.[57]

The contretemps over the book's introduction did not entirely sour the relationship between Konkle and De Renne, nor did the book's failure to sell well. In 1905 De Renne offered the historian the hospitality of Wormsloe and put him on the trail of the elusive manuscripts of Edward Langworthy (1738–1802), presumed author of the first history of Georgia, of whose book all had been lost but a newspaper notice. Though provided with financial support by De Renne, Konkle made little headway with his quest, and a later researcher would make the only significant discoveries relating to the Langworthy papers (though Konkle did eventually publish an article on Langworthy). By 1906 the futile search for the Langworthy papers had effectively ended the association between the two, for De Renne did not encourage Konkle's suggestion in 1913 that he prepare a "life and times" of Noble Wimberly Jones similar to the Thomas Smith biography.[58]

Konkle contained his career of composing and publishing sketches of Pennsylvania legal and political figures, most notably books on James Wilson and Benjamin Chew. For the rest of his life he engaged in productive research and was a highly respected figure at the Historical Society of Pennsylvania for over half a century.[59]

Having published such a thorough study of one his Smith forebears, De Renne in 1905 showed that he was not unmindful of his Jones ancestors.

In that year he was approached by A. B. Caldwell, managing editor and publisher-to-be of an elaborately organized project for producing a seven-volume biographical compendium titled *Men of Mark in Georgia.* It was slated to publish its first volume in 1907 with former governor W. J. Northen as editor in chief and an array of Georgia historians and journalists as the contributors of the hundreds of sketches. Included were those Georgia historical writers most noted at the time, including Joseph T. Derry, Lawton B. Evans, William Harden, and George Gilman Smith. The last mentioned, who had recently published a voluminous history of Georgia, was one of De Renne's correspondents and admirers. In regard to the proposed biographical entries on Noble Jones and Noble Wimberly Jones, Smith had suggested that De Renne was "better fitted for [their] preparation . . . than anyone else." Caldwell agreed and also hoped that, along with the sketches, De Renne could furnish steel engravings of his subjects.[60]

De Renne responded that both an engraving of Noble W. Jones (the one produced for his father) and an excellent biographical sketch of him (written by Colonel Charles C. Jones) were available, and these were indeed used by Caldwell. But Noble Jones was a different matter. Neither an engraving, nor indeed a likeness of any kind, was known to exist, and the closest thing to a biographical sketch was the extended epitaph prepared by De Renne's father for the Noble Jones monument. There were, however, original sources aplenty among his father's manuscripts, for one of G. W. J. De Renne's lifelong pursuits had been tracking down all traces of Noble Jones. And in De Renne's rapidly expanding library were many printed sources that shed further light on the founder of his line in America.[61]

De Renne entered wholeheartedly upon what was to be his lengthiest, and most scholarly, appearance in print. He marshaled his sources well, quoted extensively, and provided prose of his own that was direct and forceful. He prepared several drafts of his essay, averaging about forty manuscript pages—in black ink on thick paper—and carefully furnished his footnotes and source citations in red.[62]

In addition to providing a comprehensive account of Noble Jones's multifaceted career as officer of the Trustees, royal official, and military man, De Renne provided a rebuttal to a charge made against his great-great-grandfather over a century earlier by James Habersham. This accusation had provoked G. W. J. De Renne, who had recorded it in one of his notebooks and provided evidence that proved it baseless. Habersham, while acting governor of the Georgia province in 1772, had written to the Earl of Hillsborough making serious accusations against Noble Jones and his son, Noble Wimberly Jones—"as ardent a patriot," De Renne noted, "as [his father] was a thorough royalist." De Renne suspected that Habersham, "embittered" at being unable to "punish the son, brought his spleen to bear upon the father." Noble Wimberly Jones, Habersham wrote, "was several years First Lieutenant and Surgeon in a company of Rangers paid by the Crown, and in these capacities met with great indulgence. His father is the King's Treasurer, and if I am not mistaken reaps very considerable emoluments from it by his accounts having never been clearly stated and examined by any Assembly that I know of: and such an inquiry may not be agreeable." [63]

To the contrary, De Renne cited one such audit of Noble Jones's accounts, approved by Governor James Wright—stating that the accounts were regular—as proof that they had indeed been checked. He further noted that Habersham must have "either found out that the accounts had been audited, or that an investigation was unnecessary, as there is no record of one having taken place—and as Noble Jones continued Treasurer until the day of his death, which occurred three years afterwards, it would seem reasonable to suppose that Mr. Habersham's fears were groundless." [64]

As had his father, De Renne quoted Habersham's letter from its manuscript source in the Georgia Historical Society, for in the printed version—published in the sixth volume of the society's *Collections* (1904)—the offending passage had been conspicuously deleted. De Renne's correction showed great discernment, particularly since the marks of elision in the printed source were likely to draw some readers to the misleading manuscript. In any case, De Renne made it less likely that some future historian would take the canard at face value because he put Habersham's remarks in proper context and then exploded them. De Renne ended his sketch with his father's Noble Jones epitaph, but he could as well have concluded with his father's motto, "Not provoked with impunity." [65]

Having done such a thorough job on the sketch of his family's founder, De Renne awaited its publication with pleasant anticipation. But when the first volume of the series arrived in 1907, he was appalled to discover that all of his source citations had been omitted. He immediately wrote of his displeasure to editor Caldwell: "We in the South are reproached by Northerners & Europeans of writing history without giving authorities; consequently, our books are not considered. In the case of Noble Jones's sketch,

I gave you my authorities carefully written in red ink & expected to find them as is usual at the bottom of the page—My sketch as it stands printed . . . will not be considered anywhere as based on authorities any more than the other sketches," which he described as mere unsupported "narratives." He predicted that other lovers of Georgia history would be as disappointed as he to find the lives of the state's great men printed in such unscholarly fashion.[66]

Nonetheless, he recovered from his disappointment to the extent of providing a short sketch of Dr. George Jones for the second volume of *Men of Mark*, published in 1910. He was careful, however, to provide a textual reference to his main source, the eulogy that had appeared shortly after Dr. Jones's death; De Renne quoted it in its entirety so that it took up the lion's share of the space allotted. Providing only a few lines of his own, mainly of introduction and conclusion, De Renne ended his account of his father's father by calling him "a worthy descendant" of Noble Jones and Noble Wimberly Jones, the "three having devoted their lives to Georgia, Colony and State, for more than one hundred years." The essays on the three Joneses would be reprinted in 1913 with little change in the biographical volume of William Harden's *History of Savannah and South Georgia*. Appearing as the first section of the book, under the title "Ancestors of Wymberley Jones De Renne," these biographical accounts were accompanied by a concluding essay, Colonel Jones's sketch of G. W. J. De Renne.[67]

De Renne's final appearance in print came in 1913. Two years previously the historian Lucian L. Knight, Georgia's compiler of state records, had requested that De Renne provide a description of Wormsloe, plus photographs, for his forthcoming two-volume work, *Georgia's Landmarks, Memorials and Legends*. De Renne's "Wormsloe," posted to Knight in late November 1911, formed chapter 17 of Knight's first volume and was illustrated by a photograph of the "Old Fort." The sketch, colorful and succinct, traced the history of the plantation from the time of Noble Jones and noted that "the present incumbent" had "laid out live-oak tree avenues and arranged native trees and plants in groups and lines, thus developing the natural beauties of the place."[68]

By 1905, the year after the publication of the Smith biography, De Renne had begun amassing a matchless collection of books on Georgia history and had already filled his shelves with five hundred titles and issued his first catalog. But at the same time he was also seeking original, unprinted source material. In particular, he was engaged in the discreet pursuit of one elusive batch of papers; he was certain that they would prove invaluable in delineating one of the most momentous periods of early nineteenth-century Georgia history. These manuscripts—consisting mainly of an autobiography and correspondence—had no more to do with De Renne's coastal Georgia heritage than had the raw materials of the Smith book. Instead, they dealt with Georgia's last frontier and in large part chronicled the Indian expulsion that cleared northwest Georgia for white settlement. The manuscripts had been written by Governor Wilson Lumpkin, a prime mover of the Cherokee exodus, and were privately held in the university town of Athens. Their presence there was an open secret. But sadly for those who wished to consult them, the papers were in the custodianship of Governor Lumpkin's surviving daughter, Martha Lumpkin Compton, a decidedly unusual septuagenarian.[69]

Fittingly, Mrs. Compton lived in the massive three-storied stone residence built by Lumpkin between 1842 and 1844. It occupied the summit of a hill due south of the University of Georgia, whose buildings clustered on a neighboring eminence across a deep valley. When built, the Lumpkin house was surrounded by the governor's farmland, which sloped eastward to the banks of the Oconee River. But by 1905, she had sold most of the extensive acreage, parcel by parcel. Long widowed, and surrounded by antiques and memories, she occupied the old house, attended by a single servant, the daughter of a former slave of the Lumpkins.[70]

The trove of manuscripts within the house's two-foot-thick stone walls had not only attracted De Renne's interest; it had also drawn the attention of many of the scholars across the valley, including Mrs. Compton's greatnephew David C. Barrow, soon to become the university's chancellor. Mrs. Compton's father, the author of these coveted papers, had been Georgia's governor from 1831 to 1835, and a major struggle of his administration had been the fight to remove the Cherokees from Georgia and to settle their lands. Following the end of his term, Lumpkin had served as a commissioner during the preparation of treaties with the Indians and afterward had served in the U.S. Senate (1837–41), fighting all who tried to have the treaties set aside. Viewing the final removal of the Cherokees in 1838 as the "capstone" of his career, he had in 1843 retired to his plantation at the edge of Athens. That same year the state had indirectly honored another of Lumpkin's efforts to open "Cherokee Georgia" to settlement and commerce: his contributions toward constructing the state-owned and operated Western and Atlantic Railroad. Consequently, the southern terminus of the railroad was named Marthasville after his daughter Martha Wilson Lumpkin, then in her early twenties.[71]

To Governor Lumpkin's displeasure (and to the deep chagrin of Marthasville's namesake), the town's name was changed permanently to Atlanta within three years. But by the time the Lumpkin manuscripts were drawing scholars to her Athens home, Mrs. Compton had long been claiming that the city's new name was based on her middle name, Atalanta, given her by her father during her childhood because—like the mythological runner—she had been "fleet of foot." As proof, she would show skeptics the family Bible, where the name had been inserted above hers in a hand suspiciously resembling her own. Despite incontrovertible evidence to the contrary, gullible reporters gave this tale currency in various Georgia newspapers for many years.[72]

Extremely protective of her father's reputation and his place in history, Mrs. Compton showed his manuscripts to very few of her inquiring visitors. One of the more successful was U. B. Phillips, whose knack for charming "dowagers and maiden aunts" was fast passing into legend. His major success, however, after five years' courtship, was simply to be allowed to look at the papers and to take some notes from them that could be quoted in print. As he wrote in 1905 to a friend, advising him of the presence of the papers in the hands of the "rather eccentric" Mrs. Compton: "You'll have to wheedle her if you get a peep at the documents. I am quite in her good graces; but I've been begging for five years in vain for permission to have it published. She has a great idea of its money value—and thinks that a mere glimpse is not to be lightly conceded."[73]

Obviously, De Renne's task of securing these papers would not be easy. From reports similar to those of Phillips, he had decided that it would be folly to identify himself as a bidder for the papers, lest Compton form ideas from his customary (though inaccurate) description in the state press as the "Savannah millionaire." The man he chose to act as his confidential agent, C. S. Hook, had already filled part of the study at Wormsloe with printed treasures and was regarded as one of the more astute southeastern dealers in rare books and manuscripts. Despite his wide experience in making such purchases, Hook would find the cunning Mrs. Compton a very challenging opponent.[74]

By late October 1905, Hook had visited Mrs. Compton and attempted to gauge what she would take for the manuscripts; since he had not been allowed to see them and form an opinion of their worth, his bid was deliberately low. Nonetheless, Compton was sufficiently interested by Hook's inquiry to correspond with him and give him a more thorough description of what she was offering for sale. But a subsequent letter alarmed Hook: it suggested that rather than accept less than $600 for the papers she would burn them. As Hook wrote De Renne, Mrs. Compton had told him previously that "her physician, to prevent her sitting up nights, reading the old letters, 'to save her life' as he declared, took two large cases of letters into the adjoining woods and burned them." If the story was true, wrote Hook, this was a "crime that deserves punishment." [75]

By the time Hook returned to Athens on November 25, armed with $600 provided by De Renne, Mrs. Compton's evaluation of her manuscripts had "gone skyward" to $750, apparently because her nephew, Professor David Barrow, had lately paid her several visits and entered into the competition. Or at least so Hook was told. As he confessed to De Renne, "She is so infernally erratic that it is difficult to plan a line of argument that would be safe. One moment she will exclaim that 'her father's thoughts and sentiments' (or his 'soul') should leave the world with her, and the next she will say, "I wish I had $10,000, so that I could invite three people who profess to be my friends, and who hope to '*acquire*' these papers, to see a little fire started in my grate with them." [76]

Despite his best efforts, Hook still had not been allowed to examine the papers, and he advised De Renne against paying even $100 for them on speculation, sight unseen. He had assured De Renne that he could "readily detect, if given a fair opportunity," whether the papers had been "bungled, jumbled or slighted for want of time," and in that event he would "decide against the purchase at any price." When he again asked to see the papers, Mrs. Compton advised him, "They are all locked up with the letters, ready to send away, and it would be a great inconvenience to unpack them when there is no prospect of your paying me what I want for them." Since the figure she mentioned was $750, Hook retired from the field, promising that he would come to "bid her good bye" in two days, on his way out of town. [77]

Instead, he returned suddenly at ten the next morning and, "after a siege of four hours," left with the manuscript autobiography, bound in two volumes, as well as "37 letters, written by and to the Governor," with a receipt for the $600 he had paid for them. Presumably, he used in part a strategy described earlier to De Renne: "I have a plan of argument," he wrote, "that may induce her to let me examine the papers, and if it succeeds, and they are satisfactory, I will put $600 in cash down on the table and tell her that is all I have to invest, and that if she knows of any person who is ready to pay more, let him have them." [78]

Though now in possession of the prize, Hook continued to proceed cautiously, not willing to wind up having wasted his efforts "under circumstances so provoking, where the whims of an old woman—suspicious of everybody—had to be overcome, by humoring her, and giving her plenty of play." Consequently, he sent the heavy package by express from Athens to another party in Savannah and mailed De Renne an order on this person for the parcel, by registered mail from Atlanta. Knowing that there would be "a 'stir' in a day or two," after Mrs. Compton told Professor Barrow that she had disposed of the manuscripts, Hook did not want anyone "look[ing] the matter up at the express office" and finding that De Renne was the recipient. Mrs. Compton had noted, without explanation, that she did not want the papers "to go in certain directions at any price," and Hook had assured her that he was buying them for himself (though without adding that he then intended "selling" them to De Renne). He suggested that when De Renne sent him his check for $68.20 (for his $50 commission and $18.20 travel and expenses) he enclose for Hook's signature a receipt "for $668.20 or a higher 'even' amount if you prefer. Your ownership could not then be disputed, and the 'faculty' of the University could fret and fume as much as they pleased." [79]

De Renne, however, did not intend to have his purchase of the Lumpkin manuscripts create any breach between him and Professor Barrow. In fact, their work together in preparing the manuscript for publication was probably one of the most important of several factors that led to a mutually valuable relationship between De Renne and the university, which would enjoy De Renne's patronage for the rest of his life. [80]

The two volumes that De Renne received from Hook were weighty foolscap folios that would have looked at home in any courthouse vault. Twin buff-colored leather books labeled "RECORDS," they contained over thirteen hundred pages written in Wilson Lumpkin's hand. Divided into twenty-two chapters and accompanied by various appendixes, the account bore the title "Incidents connected with the life of Wilson Lumpkin, illustrated by selections from his speeches and official writings and compiled by himself in the seventieth year of his age. 1852." To De Renne, it was for the most part an absorbing, enlightening account that richly merited publication. Lumpkin provided "interesting and valuable" information that De Renne had not found elsewhere, particularly on the subject of the Cherokee removal. There was also, however, much relatively unimportant incidental matter, as well as many advisory, aphoristic passages directed to his children and a chapter of family history. These De Renne determined to delete.[81]

During the summer of 1907 De Renne wrote to now chancellor David Barrow (whose nephew Dr. Craig Barrow had married Elfrida De Renne the previous year). Telling him of his plans for publication, he added, "I venture to ask your aid, first as a descendant of [Governor Lumpkin], and secondly as a student of the history of Georgia." He wished in particular that Barrow would signal his approval or disapproval of the cuts he had made in the manuscript and suggest more if necessary. If Barrow would assist, De Renne wished to send him by express both volumes, accompanied by the introduction he had written for the proposed book.[82]

"Compared with my interest," Chancellor Barrow responded modestly, "my information [on Georgia history] is very poor." But he nonetheless consented to review the manuscript and returned it to De Renne in November 1907. He approved De Renne's deletions and De Renne's introduction (which he liked "very much") and suggested the deletion of three other chapters that contained official gubernatorial correspondence and details of Lumpkin's senatorial career. De Renne was delighted to have Barrow's assistance, which also included furnishing two portraits of Lumpkin to serve as frontispieces for the two-volume book.[83]

De Renne decided to have the book printed in a limited edition of five hundred sets, at a cost of around $1,100. In keeping with his commitment to use Georgia printers for his books whenever possible, he had the volumes, which he titled *The Removal of the Cherokee Indians from Georgia*, printed by W. S. Pottinger's Morning News Book and Job Printing firm, which had printed the 1905 catalog of his library; the use of a Savannah firm made the book's title page notation ("PRIVATELY PRINTED / WORMSLOE") more geographically correct than had been any of the earlier Wormsloe editions. Though printed by the Morning News firm, the book was published by Dodd, Mead of New York City, which agreed to manage sales and marketing for a $2 commission on the book's $6 price.[84]

Other than Barrow, De Renne's other major collaborator in the project was William Harden, librarian of the Georgia Historical Society and fellow member of the Sons of the Revolution. Harden, who was most responsible for the book's furnished form, began editing after De Renne and Barrow had made their deletions. He made numerous (though minor) changes and created a text that, though not unfaithful to its author, was made more accessible to general readers: he corrected grammar and punctuation and occasionally added or deleted words to improve transitions and speed the flow of the narrative. Though G. W. J. De Renne would scarcely have approved of this method, it represented a middle way between exact transcription—which some scholars were beginning to find pedantic—and the more casual style of presentation common during the 1800s. Harden also read proofs, wrote the advertising circular, and prepared the index.[85]

Although the publication year on the title page was listed as 1907, Pottinger and his printers apparently were unable to have the first installment of the books prepared and shipped to New York before the spring of 1908. De Renne had hoped for an early announcement of a specific date of publication and that the printer would meet it. He noted that if the publication date remained "vague" it would provoke "uncharitable remarks about the dilatoriness of Southern business methods & less attention [would] be paid to the circular."[86]

Unfortunately, De Renne found that the book would receive little attention under any circumstances. Its lack of success could not have been the result of its appearance, for it was published as a handsome large octavo (patterned after the Smith biography) and was bound in maroon cloth with uncut pages and was also available unbound, for binding to order. Nonetheless, fewer than two hundred sets of either kind seem to have been purchased by 1911 (when De Renne literally wrote "Finis" to the project), and though several schemes were tried during his lifetime to dispose of the remaining books, hundreds remained with Pottinger's firm after De Renne's death.[87]

Popular tastes in 1908 would give such books as *Anne of Green Gables* and *The Trail of the Lonesome Pine* sales exceeding 750,000 copies, but there was obviously no demand for a printed original source such as the Lumpkin book, from either the general public or from libraries and historical societies; upon these last De Renne had counted heavily (and toward them he had directed his advertising circulars). Though De Renne had not expected to reap huge profits from his printing venture, neither had he expected to lose money. If he had broken even, he at least would not have drained money away from his library purchasing fund, as was the case. All in all, this major venture into historical publishing had left him dissatisfied; even his own major contribution to the book—the introduction—he described in later years as "not a success." [88]

The Life and Times of Thomas Smith and the *Men of Mark* and Wormsloe sketches had come from De Renne's own family manuscripts, and the Cherokee book had sprung from his purchase of papers from another family. Each had produced its share of disappointments. But his initial venture into collecting, made soon after his return to Georgia, would produce a book as well: one, in fact, that of all his books would enjoy the widest appeal and receive the warmest reception.

CHAPTER 9

Maecenas

Show me the man you honour; I know by that symptom, better than by
any other, what kind of man you yourself are.
—THOMAS CARLYLE

S oon after his return to Georgia, most likely in the winter of
1892–93, Wymberley Jones De Renne received an invitation
to Summerville. There, on the healthful heights above the city of
Augusta, Colonel Charles C. Jones had made his home since returning to Georgia in 1877 from his northern sojourn. Jones's estate, known as Montrose, seemed to suit its owner perfectly, from
the stately, spacious columned mansion, with its gardens—distinguished by more than two hundred varieties of roses—and its orchard of fruit trees, to the ancient ivy-wreathed fieldpiece that
commanded the old artillerist's front lawn. There was also a shallow cistern near the back steps, where recently acquired Indian
artifacts lost their coating of earth. Inside, visitors found that, although there was a room called a library, most of the house's rooms
fulfilled a library's purpose; bookcases and cabinets were spread
throughout the structure, and mantelpieces often served as shelves.
No other collection of books in Georgia held as much of the state's
printed history, and Jones's manuscript collections excelled all others in Georgia in private hands.[1]

During the postwar period Jones had continued to uphold the culture of antebellum days and had defended his region's agrarian economy against the encroachments of industrialism; he had wasted little time in answering Henry W. Grady's "The New South" with a ringing oration of his own titled "The Old South." But De Renne found the old warrior much changed from the robust, leonine presence whom he had known in the Wall Street lawyer's chambers that Jones had shared with John Elliott Ward. The ravages of Bright's disease had diminished his once solid frame and weakened his stentorian voice. And years of living well and constantly acquiring (or printing) books and buying manuscripts and autographs—without the "long purse" he desired—had brought his financial affairs into disarray. His money worries had been compounded by disasters at his plantations, which yielded minimal profits at the best of times. Worse were sieges of sickness in his household; they had affected not only the colonel himself— now only months from death—but his wife's mother, who had died in 1889, and his beloved wife, who had died the year following.[2]

Since Mary De Renne's death in 1887, Jones had unsuccessfully attempted to interest Everard De Renne in his literary labors, and now, his days of writing all but over, he hoped that Wymberley would make a purchase from him to help relieve his pressing financial concerns. He offered his fabled collection of bound Confederate manuscripts, "beyond doubt the finest in existence." The array proved irresistible to De Renne: volume after splendidly bound volume—over a dozen in all, ten of them a generous twelve by sixteen inches—with such titles as "Confederate States Generals" (with each officer "traced through all his grades"), "Confederate States Senators," and "Deputies to C.S. Provisional Congress; Members of C.S. Provisional Congress," along with volumes devoted to "the President and his military family," all the Confederate governors, and the signers of the Confederate Constitution. Colonel Jones had filled these unique books with letters and reports and autographs of all the prominent Confederate political and military leaders, embellished with their likenesses, so that there was a complete pictorial record of the Confederacy's principal soldiers and statesmen. Paramount among these matchless tomes was one that had no need of illustration: a two-volume set of letters and telegrams of General Robert E. Lee. But there were masses of official correspondence of President Jefferson Davis as well, including many letters from Benjamin H. Hill,

Davis's chief ally in Georgia's congressional delegation. A price was agreed on, and De Renne became owner of one of the choicest such collections ever assembled, a trove that because of its value and nature he would closely guard and long keep secret.[3]

Four years after this momentous acquisition from Colonel Jones, De Renne received an unusual addition to his Confederate collection. It came to him in a very curious fashion, and, with the colonel's expertise gone with him into the grave, diligent inquiry would be required before it gave up its secret. Ultimately, the process of investigation would provide several significant and unexpected sequels.

In January 1897, W. M. Davant, a newly installed official of the Merchants National Bank of Savannah, completed a survey of the bank's vault. In a space above the safety deposit boxes, he found "a neat package bearing wax seals, which from outward appearances one would say . . . contained a roll of papers." Since his surname was written on the package's exterior, De Renne was notified of Davant's discovery and soon came to collect the mysterious parcel.[4]

Inside the package was a large document; when unrolled, it appeared to be the Constitution of the Confederate States of America, though De Renne was unsure what to make of it. Over the next several years, he would display the long, beautifully engrossed roll of vellum only to close friends, normally after securing the viewer's agreement to keep the existence of the document secret. Nonetheless, its exact nature was a matter of speculation: a version of the Rebel Constitution it certainly was, but what version? Richmond's Confederate Museum, opened in 1896, had during its inaugural year publicized the presence in its valuable Mary De Renne Collection of "the original Constitution of the Confederate States." How did this document relate to that treasure?[5]

De Renne apparently did not begin an intensive effort to identify the document fully and to trace its history until 1905. That year, in his first published library catalog, he revealed his possession of what a brief entry called "The Constitution of the Confederate States. Original engrossed document, duly signed and authenticated. 'Vellum sheets 28 inches by 31. Whole document 28 inches by 148½.'" To forestall questions and inquiries (and to increase the book's value as a gift to his friends), he had a facsimile prepared and bound opposite the entry; it included the last four lines of the instrument, with the place and the date signed and all the signatures.[6]

Nonetheless, the state of Confederate historiography was so feeble at the time that De Renne's claim was met with skepticism, and he was spurred to gather information to support what seemed to him to be a self-evident identification. Among the first sources from whom De Renne requested information on the document was Major William Starr Basinger, who had acted as one of the De Renne attorneys in the 1870s and 1880s. Basinger supplied an account of the Constitution's acquisition, derived partially from his wife; as a friend of Mrs. De Renne, she had been shown the document shortly after its acquisition. He voiced the opinion that the document was the Provisional Constitution. "A. L. Hull [of Athens], the Treasurer of the University, married a daughter of Genl. Tom Cobb, who was a member of the Convention which adopted the Constitution," he explained, and Mrs. Hull had "a great many, if not all, of her father's papers, among which is one which purports to be the original draft of the permanent Constitution, on which the vote of adoption was taken." [7]

Unsatisfied, De Renne probed further. By the spring of 1907 he had convinced himself that he possessed the "original Constitution of the Confederate States," formerly the property of Felix de Fontaine; consequently, he dispatched his friend Captain Alexander McC. Duncan to "discover the line of transmission . . . from its proper owner." Duncan soon tracked de Fontaine's son, Wade Hampton de Fontaine, to New York, where he ran an investment brokerage firm. Apprised of de Fontaine's whereabouts, De Renne paid him a visit, and by the end of the summer de Fontaine had written to confirm in essence the story that had been printed earlier in "Two Relics of the Confederacy," a copy of which De Renne had obtained, and to give independent confirmation that Mary de Renne had purchased one of the Constitutions from his father. Since it had to be assumed that the document had been in Richmond for most of war, having been transferred there when the capital was moved from Montgomery—and having reached de Fontaine's hands shortly after Richmond's evacuation—the chain of transmission seemed complete, and the document, with its telltale date, seemed confirmed as the Permanent Constitution which Mrs. De Renne bought from de Fontaine. [8]

From the first De Renne had determined that once he had satisfactorily identified and traced the provenance of the Permanent Constitution he would publish a brief account of the document to silence any further questions. He was confirmed in this course when news came from Richmond in late 1908 that his mother's copy of the Constitution had been "found" there. A newspaper article in the *Richmond Journal,* widely reprinted, presented a sensational account suggesting that the Constitution that Mary De Renne had purchased in 1870 [*sic*] for $25,000 [*sic*] had been discovered accidentally in "an old cupboard" in the cellar of the Confederate Museum, "much the worse for wear, and . . . considerably soiled as it has lain neglected for decades." The invaluable document, said the account, had been given by Mrs. De Renne to the Southern Historical Society and had been handed over by the society to the Confederate Museum when it had opened; unfortunately, it had been "overlooked or forgotten" ever since.[9]

Here was a story garbled almost past redemption. On 30 December, 1908, however, the *Richmond News Leader* published a marginally more accurate version, clearing the Confederate Museum of any negligence. It reported that the document had been found by a young historian, Douglas Southall Freeman, who had recently canvassed the museum's collections for the Confederate Memorial Literary Society. The organization had published in October 1908 *A Calendar of Confederate Papers,* based on Freeman's work among the museum's books and manuscripts, but the calendar had made no mention of a manuscript copy of the Constitution.[10]

There was a good reason for this omission. Though unmentioned by the *News Leader,* the Constitution in question had actually not arrived at the museum until February 1908, several months after Freeman had completed his research for the *Calendar.* The document had been sent by the Southern Historical Society, along with other manuscripts, to join others donated by the organization to the museum in the mid-1890s. The *News Leader,* however, contained to misidentify the Provisional Constitution— presented by W. W. Corcoran to the Southern Historical Society in 1884— as the Constitution purchased by Mary De Renne. And though understanding that it was the Provisional, not the Permanent, Constitution, the newspaper made the questionable claim that it was the third most valuable document in the country, after the Declaration of Independence and the U.S. Constitution. The *News Leader* also added that the instrument was to be put on display the following week for the convention of the American Historical Association.[11]

De Renne, knowing that Katherine C. Stiles was still in charge of the Confederate Museum's Georgia Room, had his attorney (and their mutual friend) George W. Owens write her to see what she could make of the matter. Unfortunately, her account was also confused and riddled with incorrect assumptions, such as one that Mary De Renne had arranged to have facsimiles of her Constitution made. This was an obvious reference to de Fontaine's photolithographs of the Provisional Constitution, of which Mrs. De Renne had indeed purchased and distributed several copies. Miss Stiles also asserted that the tube containing the Constitution was addressed to the former secretary of the Southern Historical Society, the Reverend J. William Jones (undoubtedly true), from Mrs. De Renne (impossible); she added that the Reverend Jones, still living, remembered nothing of this valuable accession. She did, however, agree to ask the young historian Freeman for a solution to the problem of the two Constitutions; and she was apparently provided by De Renne, for Freeman's use, a copy of his facsimile of the last portion of his Constitution.[12]

Freeman's three-page response was a model of organization and clarity. He noted that comparison of the Confederate Museum's document with the facsimile of the De Renne Constitution showed by their dates that though both were "original" documents, the first was the Provisional Constitution of February 1861 and the latter the Permanent Constitution of the Confederacy, signed in March the same year. He had, however, searched the available printed and manuscript records in an attempt to find the reason for the confusion, consulting both de Fontaine's "Two Relics of the Confederacy" and the 1884 number of the *Southern Historical Society Papers* that had printed the correspondence relating to the Corcoran gift. He had also made use of a massive volume in the Mary De Renne Collection; it contained all the correspondence and other documentation relating to Mrs. De Renne's purchase of the Permanent Constitution, a volume whose very presence helped explain part of the misunderstanding; only one Constitution was in the museum, and Miss Stiles well knew that Mary De Renne had purchased one.[13]

Freeman concluded: "If I might be allowed a surmise in the premises, I would suggest that de Fontaine, while financially embarrassed, sold the Provisional Constitution, secretly . . . and then sold the Permanent Constitution to Mrs. De Renne, without mentioning the fact that he . . . had sold another. If you will read de Fontaine's second letter to Mrs. De Renne, you will observe that he speaks of the 'MSS' and of the 'Constitutions,' but, before he closes, he mentions 'the original.'" The archivist of the Virginia State Library, Hamilton James Eckenrode, Freeman added, "agrees completely with my conclusions.[14]

Owens was satisfied that this concluded the matter, and De Renne himself considered the authenticity of his own document established, but he wanted additional information. Who was Freeman, he asked, and could Eckenrode supply his thoughts on the matter? Also, did Miss Stiles have any objections to any of her correspondence in the matter being published, and would she secure copies for De Renne of his mother's correspondence, mentioned by Freeman?[15]

Freeman, she answered, "is a young man of this place, a fellow of the Johns Hopkins University, whose life, I think will be given up to literary work." Though sending a formal certificate of authenticity for the Constitution, signed by both Freeman and Eckenrode, Miss Stiles hoped that De Renne would publish nothing, for, thinking of the newspapers' hurtful suggestions of the Confederate Museum's negligence, she was afraid that additional publicity might "do us a great injury." She had been quick to correct Owens's own comment about the Constitution having been found in the "cellar," for, as she noted, "there is no cellar to the house, & the *basement* room . . . is finished off like the rest of the house, with book cases with glass doors, & drawers that lock in which papers are kept." She was already having copies of Mrs. De Renne's correspondence transcribed by a discreet person. Her only regret, she wrote Owens, was that she had not known earlier that the correspondence related to the document in De Renne's possession: "I would have said nothing here, but sent it to him—Now it would bring a perfect howl."[16]

De Renne was apparently able to persuade Miss Stiles that nothing he printed regarding the Constitutions would be injurious to the museum, and at any rate the two printed accounts he finally sponsored were innocuous. In late May 1909 there appeared both a lengthy *Savannah Morning News* account of the Constitutions, based on De Renne's information, and his *Short History of the Confederate Constitutions of the Confederate States of America, 1861–1899.* Why he chose 1899 as the ending date in his title is a mystery; that year is not mentioned in the text, is not the date of any sources cited, and was not the year that he found that he possessed the Constitution.[17]

A quarto printed in an edition of 150 copies (100 on handmade paper), the book was bound in thick paper, appropriately gray; it displayed on its cover a woodcut based on the photograph of Jefferson Davis's inauguration in front of the Alabama State House. Under the illustration there were three lines in black letter-"Gothic" type, the most conspicuous of which read "The Birth of the Confederacy," which some people took to be the book's title. Only eight unnumbered pages long (plus a folding plate displaying the concluding lines of the Constitution, with the signatures underneath), the book included few of De Renne's own words; instead it contained a selection of quotations from Jefferson Davis, A. L. Hull, and Felix de Fontaine, demonstrating the differences between the Corcoran, Cobb, and De Renne Constitutions. It brought much-needed clarity to a murky controversy and explicitly defined De Renne's Constitution as preeminent of the three, shielding him from any further questions from doubtful inquirers. As Captain Duncan wrote on receipt of his copy, "It is well I think that you have put beyond disputation the genuineness of the original which you hold, & I feel assured no one can successfully combat your claim to the possession of the 'Original.' I beg to offer my congratulations upon the surcease of . . . that [which] very naturally occasioned some annoyance." [18]

The *Savannah Morning News* article had brought the Constitution to the attention of Georgians, and the 1905 catalog and De Renne's *Short History* had made it known to his circle of friends (and to certain libraries and the antiquarian book trade as well). But De Renne took a final step in 1909 that brought the document to national attention: he acceded to a request by the Library of Congress that the Permanent Constitution be lent for exhibition in the nation's capital.

For some years De Renne had enjoyed cordial relations with the library's Manuscript Division. Upon learning of the Constitution from the catalog De Renne presented him in 1905, Worthington C. Ford, the New Yorker who was chief of the division, wrote that he "could not forbear to suggest that such a document belongs in only one place, and that is in the Library of Congress by the side of the Declaration of Independence and the Constitution of the United States. Now that the bitterness of the War has subsided, and the right of both sides is being recognized, the document deserves to take its place with the great historical documents of our history." De Renne had no intention of donating or selling the document, of course, but several years later, when Librarian of Congress Herbert Putnam proposed an exhibition of the Constitution, De Renne assented. His restrictions on the loan were few: he wished to send the document by express and to be there when the package was opened, and he also forbade the making of a facsimile; otherwise the library was free to do as it pleased.[19]

When he traveled to Washington in mid-June 1909 as had been agreed, preparatory to the Constitution's display, De Renne greatly enjoyed his visit. Though a previous visitor, he was impressed anew by the magnificence of the building, opened just a dozen years earlier, with its soaring ceilings, spacious chambers, and the rich ornamentation of mosaics, frescoes, and statuary. Unlike most who came to the library, he was welcomed like visiting royalty, not only by Gaillard Hunt, new chief of the Manuscript Division, but also by Herbert Putnam, both of whom spent most of a day with him and afforded him "very pleasant entertainment & courtesies."[20]

Soon thereafter Hunt sent De Renne a report on the condition of the document, which had been inspected and cleaned by the library's manuscript repairer. He disclosed that although certain stains on the vellum could not be removed (probably because they were caused by "the melting of fat in the skin"), the Constitution was in "a state of admirable preservation, and will undoubtedly remain so, long after you and I have lost earthly interest in it. It has been placed in one of [the Manuscript Division's] large cases, with a placard, stating that it is a loan from you." Almost a year later, Hunt reported, "Your noble loan is in good condition, in the exhibition case, gazed at by thousands." Only in December 1914, when his deteriorating health became a matter of grave concern, did De Renne terminate the loan and have the Constitution returned (insured at $10,000) to its Savannah vault.[21]

Having published four books from 1904 to 1909, with varying degrees of satisfaction, De Renne began to make plans in 1910 to have part of his Jones Confederate Collection examined, with a view toward producing yet another book. This one would be entirely different from the diverse works he had printed earlier; it would be a compendium of wartime letters from Robert E. Lee, most of them directed to Confederate president Jefferson Davis or the Rebel War Department.

By 1910 Lee's excellence as a commander and his nobility as a man had increasingly become a major source of pride in the South, and many in the North had come to admire him as well. Appreciations of him had come into print before the end of the war, and as the turn of the century approached, scholarly biographies had begun to appear, foremost among them an estimable study "written throughout from original sources" by Henry A.

White, a professor at Washington and Lee University. Only a few years before De Renne decided to bring his Lee collection into print, Lee's son and namesake had published *Recollections and Letters of General Robert E. Lee* (1904), soon followed by *Life and Letters of Robert Edward Lee, Soldier and Man* (1906) by the Reverend J. William Jones and *Robert E. Lee, the Southerner* (1909) by Thomas Nelson Page. Around the same time, De Renne's friend (and eminent Lee panegyrist) Senator Thomas M. Norwood had suggested that Lee and other southern heroes be memorialized in more fitting ways, including the building of a pantheon to them.[22]

A volume of Lee letters, previously unknown to historians, would be another appropriate memorial, and the fortunate few to whom De Renne had shown his treasured Lee manuscripts had already suggested to him that his collection contained numerous unpublished communications. With the comparatively recent completion of the publication of *War of the Rebellion: Official Records of the Union and Confederate Armies*, a voluminous source lay at hand to check De Renne's Lee letters against those in print.[23]

With his state pride to the forefront as ever, De Renne hoped that Georgia's most prominent young historian would undertake the task of editing the Lee letters. But U. B. Phillips, though eager to appear in print as often as possible, admitted that this particular project was not within his expertise. It was only logical that De Renne turn next to Douglas Southall Freeman, then in his mid-twenties and much less well known than Phillips, but fated to achieve greater popularity and renown. Freeman had offered competent assistance in the case of the Confederate Constitutions, and in his *Calendar* had also paid graceful compliments to De Renne's mother and her collection. On a visit to Freeman in Richmond in June 1910, De Renne revealed the existence of his Lee manuscripts and his desire to see them prepared for the press. Would Freeman consider taking on the project? "I assure you," Freeman soon responded, "that nothing will give me more pleasure than the co-operation in an undertaking which bespeaks so much patriotism on your part and which will be of such great value to the people of the South."[24]

In the early fall of 1910, De Renne invited Freeman to visit him at his retreat at Westport, on Lake Champlain. There, in an environment more evocative of the French and Indian War than the War Between the States, the two discussed at length the purpose and practicality of creating the book that De Renne envisioned. Freeman was impressed by De Renne's reason for offering the letters to the public: "Altogether apart from what they showed of General Lee's military character, they were worth publishing for the light they threw on the man." And, as it happened, Freeman idolized Lee and had long cherished a hope of writing the history of Lee's Army of Northern Virginia, in which his revered father had served. The project could not have suited Freeman better.[25]

Soon the Lee volume of letters—splendidly bound in three-quarter morocco—rested safely in a vault at Richmond's Planters' National Bank, subject to Freeman's call. As the project began in earnest, typescripts were prepared for Freeman's use from the manuscripts. Captain Robert E. Lee, Jr., gave his blessing to De Renne's venture, and Richmond's "final authority on Confederate history," W. Gordon McCabe, came aboard as an adviser to Freeman. McCabe's assistance was particularly crucial during the task of comparing the letters to those in print, for he had earlier compiled a checklist of published Lee letters, including sources other than the *Official Records.*[26]

Freeman's research soon showed that of the 242 letters, a majority (136) had not seen print, suggesting that they were originals of which no copies had survived. To Freeman's eyes, the most important of them dealt with three major campaigns: the Seven Days, Gettysburg, and Petersburg. Though somewhat disappointed that there were not more original letters, he consoled himself with the idea that the letters previously unprinted were much more interesting than those in the collection that were already in print: the dispatches that "told a thrilling story were the ones which had escaped the previous editors." In any case, Freeman calculated, the finished book would approach two hundred pages.[27]

Approaching the firm of Dodd, Mead (which had handled his Lumpkin book), De Renne was gratified to find the publishers "strongly disposed" toward publication of a Lee volume. Further, they would stand all expenses and pay De Renne a 10 percent royalty on all books sold. Sadly, the firm's reaction upon actually sampling the letters sent by Freeman was much cooler: "They seem to us to be merely in the nature of reports and would be technically interesting perhaps to military strategists, but would not . . . appeal to the general public." Freeman faced a daunting task in settling the publisher's doubts.[28]

By June 1911 Freeman had made much progress and done a great deal of annotation on the letters. They were "so detailed," he wrote, "and refer to so many minor matters that, without copious notes, they are practically a sealed book. On the other hand, to secure information which will make them easily understood is an enormous task. . . . In some cases I have worked every night for a week on a single letter."[29]

Freeman noted further that the discovery of several ostensibly unprinted letters in some published sources had reduced the total number unprinted to 125 (they would finally be reduced to 114). Consequently, Freeman had decided that it would be best to publish and annotate the entire collection of 242 letters, both unpublished and published. Surprisingly, De Renne chose this time to offer an additional complication: he disclosed the existence of his other volume of Lee materials, heretofore unmentioned. Freeman found that among these 295 official telegrams, fewer were in the general's hand than was the case with the letters; but they were "valuable," nonetheless, and a few were "of very great importance." Like the letters, they now had to be transcribed and compared to those in print, and the 90 that survived the process would prove—through their often inscrutable brevity—even more difficult to decipher and annotate.[30]

By the spring of 1912, it had become obvious to De Renne that the Lee book could not soon be published. Freeman had said as much: "While I do not want to alarm you as to the outcome of the Lee publication, I must tell you that neither of us had any idea of the extent of the undertaking when we began. The telegrams have proved a veritable mine of new truth and with the notes, the whole collection will make two volumes. . . . I was of the opinion that the telegrams would not long detain me, but they offer some very interesting problems which must be solved. I am giving the work the best scholarship of which I am capable and trust to make the finished task worthy of the writer of the letters and of the distinguished owner of them." Despite the burdens of his task, Freeman was exhilarated by the challenge of working with the dispatches; with his expenses paid by De Renne—whom he compared to Maecenas, patron of Horace and Virgil— the young scholar exulted that he was in "about the Paradise of the historical student."[31]

De Renne found himself in a less Edenic situation. He would have to wait for more than four years from the project's inception to his receipt of the completed typescript. In his experience, this time span between the projection of a book and a manuscript's completion was unprecedentedly long, and he found the delay difficult to accept. Death made inroads in those around him and those connected with the book: Mrs. De Renne died, as did Captain Robert E. Lee and two of De Renne's friends (including Senator Norwood), "who were most anxious" to see the letters in print. During 1913 and 1914, De Renne's own health began to suffer a rapid and irreparable decline. As he later admitted to Freeman, "I myself commenced to despair of living to see [the book] published."[52]

Freeman's own serious health problems and the financial difficulties they caused him (while working at several jobs) caused the delay. When Freeman and De Renne first met in 1910, the young Virginian was on the staff of the *Richmond Times-Dispatch*, but he left journalism temporarily the same year, returning to join the editorial staff of the *Richmond News Leader* in 1913. In the interim he worked with the Virginia Tax Commission, the Virginia Anti-Tuberculosis Association, and the Virginia State Board of Health.[53]

Not long after beginning his work on the dispatches, Freeman had worked himself to the point of exhaustion and had fallen prey to crippling attacks of paralysis and rheumatism. Upon recovery, he had to postpone his marriage and repair his finances by "work[ing] overtime on those things which brought immediate return." The Lee papers had had to be set aside, and, to complete the book in a more timely fashion, Freeman had finally suggested (and De Renne approved) omission of all the previously published letters and telegrams (even though most of the former had already been supplied with extensive annotation). This hastened the editing process by giving Freeman a smaller book to prepare.[54]

In May 1914 De Renne gladly received the typescripts of the dispatches and had the manuscript "carefully paragraphed and corrected" by William Harden, using the bound volumes that had been returned to Wormsloe in December 1911. Meanwhile, De Renne and Freeman completed other plans relating to the book: the frontispiece would be William Marshall's engraving of one of Julian Vannerson's photographs of Lee, and, though De Renne vetoed supplying facsimiles of particular letters as illustrations, he later approved as essential the preparation of a map of Lee's area of operations.[55]

De Renne's long wait was finally rewarded in early September 1914: "Perhaps you have despaired of ever receiving this letter," Freeman wrote, "but here it is: the papers are finally and completely done, [and] are in the bindery so that they can be forwarded to you in proper form. . . . I hope you will be pleased with the editorial work. I have done 'my durnest' on it and am not ashamed of it." Soon after the letter, the bound typescript arrived, with a detailed cover letter explaining many of the decisions Freeman had made. Finally seeing for himself the prodigious amount of work that Freeman had done, De Renne was astounded that the book had been completed as soon as it had been.[36]

As a title Freeman had chosen *Lee's Dispatches,* inspired, he noted, by another series of military letters, *Wellington's Dispatches;* given the importance of the Lee papers, he did not feel the title "too pretentious." Freeman showed himself very protective about his lengthy introduction—and rightly so—for it was masterfully researched and written. He explained to De Renne that he had sought to show "why letters of General Lee's are important and worthy of publication at this time" and to explain "the new and important evidence" provided by the dispatches. Freeman also wished to stress, echoing De Renne's own opinion, that the letters were "deemed especially interesting in that they illustrate, adequately but concisely, the splendid character of the great man who wrote them." Further, he wanted to show how Lee's character had continued to develop "in the ordeal of battle"—as Freeman put it, "Noble he was; nobler he became." The introduction concluded with a "brief account of the history of the letters, their preservation, and the method of their presentation."[37]

The history of the letters had been told more briefly than Freeman wished. He felt that the dispatches' previous ownership should be cited to provide the provenance for the papers and had requested De Renne's "theory . . . as to how these letters came into the possession of Col. Jones." De Renne demurred: "I do not know how Colonel Jones secured the letters, and I see no reason to mention that I bought them from him. You could say if you want that I bought them among others in a collection of MSS of southern military men and statesmen." A quarter-century later Freeman would have the mystery solved for him by Dallas Irvine, in a magisterial essay titled "The Fate of Confederate Archives," and Freeman would ultimately reveal part of what he knew of Colonel Jones's secret in his classic *The South to Posterity* (1939).[38]

De Renne found the manuscript's introduction "explicit and forcible," but he did suggest a few deletions. Freeman, realizing that he lacked objectivity regarding Lee's postwar nemesis James Longstreet, asked De Renne's opinion of the "wisdom of the criticisms" that he had elaborated "somewhat frankly" in his opening. Among other statements, De Renne discovered a phrase regarding Longstreet's "attacks of self-important dotage." Freeman followed De Renne's suggestion that this and a few similar passages be modified or deleted.[39]

De Renne let stand the preface's brief complimentary remarks about himself in which Freeman described him as "an historian and collector to whose patient and discriminating labor the South owes a debt not yet fully appreciated." He continued, "The editor could but hope that the future of Southern history were in the keeping of men like Mr. De Renne who combine means for publication with reverent regard for historical accuracy." But the dedicatory epistle that Freeman offered was a different matter:

To
W. J. De Renne
Master of Wormsloe

My dear Mr. De Renne:

If ever a book should be inscribed to a man this should be to you. Through years when others neglected Southern history, you preserved it. In days when others were too busy to save the annals of the South, you collected them. While others waited for the coming of some great Southern historian, you prepared the way for him. As I have turned the pages of your great Lee collection,—may I say it,—I have thanked Heaven that the South boasted a man rich enough and wise enough to preserve such treasures.

We owe you a debt, Sir, which one of the humblest of Southern historical writers cannot hope to pay, even in part, by inscribing to you a work you have made possible.

But as it is, will you accept it as a token of esteem from

Douglas Southall Freeman[40]

De Renne was no more disposed to accept a dedication from Freeman than he had been from Burton Konkle. And his comment was apt: he found the dedication, though sincere, "too flattering. . . . It jars very much with the real value and good sense of the rest of the book, and you certainly give me enough undeserved recognition in the introduction." Though disappointed, Freeman acquiesced.[41]

De Renne was impressed by Freeman's method of presenting the letters and telegrams. They were arranged in chronological order by numbers rather than dates; since some of the dispatches shared dates, Freeman's system prevented confusion in the cross-references. Footnotes, often lengthy, bridged the several gaps in the correspondence and explained the dispatches with satisfying thoroughness; indeed, one scholar later commented that the notes could "stand alone as a condensed history of Lee's active command." Finally seeing the notes, De Renne found them extraordinary, and he admitted that they had required "much more work than [he had] supposed." [12]

All in all, De Renne was deeply pleased by Freeman's work, and Freeman "rejoiced" at De Renne's approval. He admitted that he could have finished much more quickly (and have written as many notes in one night as he had in one week) had he substituted for "microscopic analysis the easier style of general notes," which he decried with a tactical metaphor as "written in the air." In Freeman's opinion, the more comprehensive notes, with their abundant source citations (90 percent of them to the *Official Records*, "the only documents fit to rank with those we print"), would be valuable to the research of both historians and the descendants of the men Lee had led. [13]

Thus what Freeman had called their "joint labor" was winding toward its conclusion. But ironically, the collaborators' exchange of congratulations was premature, for in mid-October Dodd, Mead informed De Renne of its final decision that "it would not be wise . . . to undertake this book, interesting as it is." The Great War was raging in Europe, of course, but, Freeman commented: "Despite the unsettled condition of the bookmarket, [Dodd, Mead's] action is somewhat surprising. The widespread interest in military matters at this time and the remarkable similarity of some of Lee's campaigns to those of [French general Joseph] Joffre render this a peculiarly suitable season for the publication of letters from the great Confederate commander." [14]

De Renne determined immediately that the book would be published, even if he had to pay for publication himself—which turned out to be the case. G. P. Putnam's Sons (which Freeman had suggested because it published "more of this kind of work than any other American house") agreed to publish and offer for sale five hundred copies of the book, "in dignified and suitable form," for a little over $1,000, with further impressions of five hundred copies from the same plates for $300. From the books sold, they would pay De Renne 50 percent of the retail price of $3.75. Final costs would be somewhat higher, mainly because of De Renne's insistence on the finest quality—for example, the use of a photogravure rather than the more economical half-tone for the frontispiece and the expansion of the campaign map from page size to a 12½ × 17-inch pullout, with march routes in red.[15]

But De Renne was less concerned with this additional outlay than he was with having to await the 1915 publication date. "If the book could have appeared in London on King Edward's death or on King George's coronation [May 1910 and June 1911, respectively]," he declared, "it would have been bought in large numbers by British officers & scattered to the four corners of the earth. Now the new war interests everyone to the exclusion of all other matters."[16]

A further disbursement was necessary to pay the debt De Renne felt that he owed Freeman. Though Freeman's expenses had been paid and there had been no formal agreement regarding any further payment, De Renne sent Freeman a check for $1,000 "to compensate . . . in some measure for the time . . . devoted to the work. Although he realized that the young historian had labored "con amore & not for gain," De Renne knew that Freeman "could ill afford" the time expended. "Allow me," he ended, "to contribute my mite to the work."[17]

Freeman responded: "It is useless for me to attempt to express the feelings with which I received your letter. I am afraid if I attempted the task, you would not understand what I meant. Only a man who has fought his stubborn way in letters and has grappled with the wolf on the very threshold of his home can understand what a thousand dollars means. It is more money than I ever had in my life and it is to be put away to lay the foundations of a house for me and mine. Perhaps I can best express my thanks by saying that I could never never, perhaps, have hoped to own a home had it not been for this money." He concluded: "Do not fail to call upon me and believe me when I say that no association of my life has been more pleasant than that which marked the editing of this book. Would that all patrons of letters were like yourself; there would then be no Grub Street."[18]

Freeman continued to shepherd the book through the press; no detail was too small to escape his notice. He made suggestions regarding the typefaces to be used and proposed the form of the index. He also composed several descriptions to be used by the publishers in announcing the book's publication and in marketing it. The lengthiest of these compositions revealed—concisely and dramatically—the editor's view of the book's most important revelations:

Should "Stonewall" Jackson have assumed the offensive and invaded Pennsylvania after his famous valley campaign? Should the charge of Pickett's division have been ordered? Who was responsible for the failure of that bloody day? Was it safe to remove Johnston and to place Hood at the head of the army facing Sherman? How soon was the true objective of Grant's famous "left flank" movement discovered by his great opponent? Why did Lee order the costly assault on Fort Stedman? These and many other questions—the most vital in the military history of the war—are asked and answered by General Lee himself in this striking contribution to the literature of the war.[49]

During the winter of 1914–15, Freeman finished correcting the book's galleys—complimenting the carefulness of Putnam's proofreaders—and corrected and returned the page proofs. From this point, the project was entirely out of the hands of De Renne and Freeman, and the elder man, his health continuing to decline, did not wait patiently. He had hoped to receive notice of the book's impending arrival in the early spring of 1915. Consequently, a communication he received from Putnam's in mid-May provided a seriocomic footnote to De Renne's prolonged wait.[50]

The firm's elderly president, a Civil War veteran who signed himself "G. H. Putnam, Late Major, U.S. Vols.," noted that in Henry A. White's biography of Lee, which he had commissioned, an advertisement for a biography of Ulysses S. Grant had appeared. "It is our general idea," the major wrote, "that the citizens of the present generation who are interested in studying the characters of the leaders in the Civil War period would want to have before them the records of the leaders from both sides of the line." Consequently, he inquired whether De Renne would object to an ad for the letters of Grant appearing in *Lee's Dispatches*.[51]

Already displeased that his book had not been issued earlier in 1915—which "might have assured its success"—De Renne was in no mood to countenance any tampering with his project, particularly when it involved a matter of taste. "I do not think that I could ever conciliate an advertisement, for no matter what reason, appearing in a book published by me. An advertisement included in a book takes away the dignity of the book as I look at it."[52]

Nonetheless, in only a few more weeks, the book was in De Renne's hands. Having been heartily satisfied by Freeman's work, he was gratified to be able to applaud Putnam's labors as well. The stout octavo volume, bound in maroon cloth with the top page edges gilded, was a delight to him. "I congratulate you on the appearance of 'Lee's Dispatches,'" he wrote the firm. "The book is neat and complete in all details. The paper makes itself felt as you lift the volume. The different types are in proportion & easy to read. Altogether it is attractive and dignified." [53]

The majority of the reviews echoed De Renne's enthusiasm for the work of Freeman and Putnam's. The most significant of the early reviews, printed on the first page of the June 27, 1915, issue of the *New York Times Review of Books*, hailed the book as "one of the literary surprises of the season" and stressed the volume's revelation of Lee's character, as De Renne and Freeman had intended. The dispatches, noted the reviewer, "add still another cubit to [Lee's] moral stature. Nowhere, even when facing the bitter certainty of final surrender, does he pen a querulous sentence, a word of complaint, a breath of censure of anyone else." Other reviewers would second the opinion of the great value of the introduction and the notes, which "bear witness to much patient research and are written with a good taste as unfailing as is the admiration they breathe for General Lee." [54]

De Renne himself earned plaudits for having the volume published and thus sharing his valuable Lee collection with the reading public. As might be expected, the mysterious provenance of his collection provoked comments and queries. But decades would pass before anyone's curiosity would be satisfied on this score, particularly since De Renne himself had no knowledge of how the dispatches had been gathered, and Colonel Jones's son and heir, when asked by De Renne, reiterated that he did not know his father's source for the dispatches. [55]

The critics' favorable reception of the book overjoyed Freeman, who congratulated De Renne that "the newspapers confirmed the judgment you expressed to me these years agone, that the Lee papers were valuable and deserved to be in print." He added a hope that, given the glowing reviews, book buyers would join in the enthusiasm and that De Renne would "upset all historical precedents and actually make some money" from the book. [56]

Financial profit was far from De Renne's mind, but the book did sell well, certainly better than any of De Renne's other publications that had been offered for sale. Within six months of publication, only 60 books remained on hand, so a second impression of 514 copies joined the 506 originally published. By early 1918, royalty payments, deducting miscellaneous expenses (such as insurance, circulars, and advertising in newspapers and maga-zines—including $40 for an ad in the *Confederate Veteran*), totaled over $1,000, although prepublication expenses, plus outlays for publishing and binding, had approached $3,000.[57]

Nonetheless, De Renne considered his expense negligible in relation to his satisfaction in preserving the dispatches in printed form and in spread-ing Lee's fame through their publication. He was gratified as well in know-ing that nothing he could have published would have pleased his mother more. And though the critical applause and book buyers' expenditures were pleasing to him, the response of a narrow segment of the reading public was even more important. He gave numerous presentation copies to the historians, archivists, friends, and relatives who had watched his collect-ing and publishing activities with interest and admiration. Soon, letters of appreciation from many of the grateful recipients—including Chancellor David Barrow, Worthington Ford, and U. B. Phillips—made their way to De Renne.[58]

Most cherished of them all was one posted from the Via Po in Rome. There resided Lillie Noble Jones, the last of his links to the long-past golden days in Newport and Montpellier. This grand and regal lady had lived abroad for years but nonetheless had known many of the major figures of the Civil War. Fittingly, she enclosed with her letter a copy of the "last photo taken of Gen Lee, 'in gray,'" given to her many years before by the general's daughter Mildred. "'Lee's Dispatches' have arrived," she wrote, "& last night I read the admirable introduction & up to Gettysburg. How fortunate you were in your selection of Mr. Freeman! How well he writes, & how competently, & how he loves Gen Lee!" The ultimate compliment followed: "The book is worthy of the De Renne collection & I am sure your Father would have approved of the paper, print, binding. It must prove a success.[59]

Freeman also sent thanks for his presentation copy:

> You are a modest man, who declines compliments and spurns flattery. But now that you are reading and cannot stop me from saying it, I must tell you that the South owes a debt to you for the reverent manner in which you have handled the precious correspondence of your great chieftain. Have you no-ticed—of course you have—that all the reviewers emphasize the very point you made in your talk to me about the letters the day on Lake Champlain—that . . . they were worth publishing for the light they threw on the man?

Personally I owe you a debt that could not be paid you if I had done a piece of editorial work that would be a classic. I am in your debt because, in a sense, you have enabled me to pay a debt. You will pardon me if it sound[s] sentimental, but we have in Richmond near my house a very handsome statue of General Lee—it is the Mercié, the best I think. I walk by it almost daily and I confess that for years I have felt like apologizing for never having done anything to perpetuate the fame of that great man. But now, thanks to you, I can walk by the statue and say to myself, "I'm not the man he would have Southerners be, but thank God, I've done a little something to keep alive his fame!" That was my debt: you have enabled me to pay it, in part at least.[60]

It would be to decades before Freeman paid the next installment of his debt to the general: his definitive four-volume biography, *R. E. Lee*. But his agreement with Charles Scribner's Sons to produce a Lee study came close on the heels of the publication of *Lee's Dispatches;* the book brought him to the forefront as an articulate and exceptionally able interpreter of Lee's military career. In this sense, then, De Renne had indeed, as Freeman had written, "prepared the way" for a "great Southern historian": ultimately, Freeman's monument to Lee would be built in part on De Renne's two splendid volumes of dispatches.[61]

CHAPTER 10

A Befitting Temple

Libraries are not made; they grow.
—AUGUSTINE BIRRELL

T he nucleus of the matchless Wymberley Jones De Renne
Georgia Library was provided in large part by De Renne
himself. Though Wymberley's return to Georgia in 1891 and his
lease of Wormsloe from his father's estate signaled that he was in
earnest about preserving the De Renne legacy in all its forms,
Everard De Renne appears to have remained unconvinced. Although Everard did not deny the family archive to the brother who
seemed fated to be his generation's last survivor, he left the libraries
of their father and mother outside the family, as memorials. Sent to
fill bookcases in Atlanta and Richmond shortly after Everard's
death in 1894, these collections were lost to Wymberley forever.
And all that the surviving son was left of his parents' printing endeavors were the few copies of quartos and octavos given to him
during their lifetimes, along with several more found in the De
Renne vault in the Germania Bank.[1]

In truth, as late as 1894 (when De Renne's sizable library was
moved into its specially designed cases in the study of Wormsloe
House), he possessed relatively few books that related to Georgia
history. Those volumes that he had accumulated up to the time of

his marriage—a general collection made up of English and American literature, as well as a selection of books relating to American history—had
apparently been warehoused in America during his stay in France; after
eight years' residence there he possessed only a small number of books,
which he valued at $150. Some that seem to have been European acquisi-
tions would have appealed to his father: a late seventeenth-century edition
of La Bruyere's *Caractères*, for instance, that seems to have been one of his
purchases during his stay in Biarritz. An 1896 inventory De Renne made of
his personal property at Wormsloe—which presumably includes the books
shipped from France and those brought from storage, as well as titles purchased in America and Europe up until that time—values his books and
maps at $1,500; additional purchases made from 1897 through 1899 added
only $500 worth of books. Nonetheless, a letter of the period indicates that
he did consider himself to be collecting books, though in a general, rather
desultory fashion.[2]

The rough catalog that De Renne made of his approximately nine-hun-
dred-volume library in around 1898, however, shows that he was making
a substantial beginning in collecting Georgiana. Indeed, in quantity the
five dozen titles listed exceeded the forty-odd "Books relating to Carolina
& Georgia" listed in his father's antebellum catalog. And in some areas
there are attempts toward completeness, particularly in gathering all the
nineteenth-century general histories of Georgia, including the handsome
two-volume leather-bound set that he later recalled as the first Georgia
title he ever purchased; ironically, it was Hugh McCall's history, which had
so offended Agricola. But these books were almost all easily accessible; of
scarcer eighteenth-century printed sources, such as had excited the envy of
William Bacon Stevens, there were only two, though these were nicely balanced: a glowing account of the Georgia colony issued by the Trustees and
the "second opinion" offered by the arch-malcontent Patrick Tailfer.[3]

In later years, it would be thought impressive that De Renne had
amassed his Georgia library in just a quarter of a century, the period of time
between his return to Wormsloe and his death. Actually, his intensive collecting of Georgia books (as opposed to his earlier collecting of autographs
and manuscripts) actually spanned a decade less than that, beginning in
earnest only around 1902.[4]

In that year he celebrated his forty-ninth birthday, and, though his
health seemed good, he had already enjoyed a dozen years more of life than

his longest-lived sibling and was within four years of the span of his father, longest-lived of the family to that point. If he wished to leave a more extensive and distinguished "record of usefulness' than had heretofore been the case, his time might be limited. Indeed, though he was to live more years than any of the other members of his family, the peace of his deathbed was fated to be disturbed by thoughts of a monument left incomplete.[5]

His early acquisition of the Jones Collection of Confederate Manuscripts had had a mixed effect on the growth of De Renne's Georgia library. The fact that the volumes were essentially bound autograph collections, similar to many other such collections that Colonel Jones had created, seems to have channeled De Renne's early collecting activities into accumulating autograph signatures and holographs of documents and letters. In so collecting, of course, De Renne was following the example not only of Colonel Jones but of G. W. J. De Renne as well, who had remarked that "the destruction of [his] papers during the war" had "finished another old storehouse of oddities—and certainly made autographs of Georgians rare." This type of collecting, pioneered in America by Israel Tefft, was particularly widespread in the 1800s—understandably so because it lent itself to the popular biographical interpretation of history and allowed the historical enthusiast to own something with an intimate, personal connection to historic figures. But autograph collecting was in essence antihistoriographical: at worst, it sometimes led to the mutilation or destruction of letters for their signatures alone; at the least, it promoted the dispersal of sometimes important and almost always unique manuscripts, often into private collections—too frequently a near equivalent of that oblivion against which the antiquaries and historians of the nineteenth-century had fought so fiercely. And it seemed oblivion indeed, as far as the scholarly community was concerned, because the removal of such items from their context made them all but impossible to trace and locate.[6]

Autograph collecting could also be costly, as De Renne soon discovered. For example, the $155 he paid for an interesting and significant letter written to General Nathanael Greene by Jonathan Bryan in 1781 was a sum that could have bought a considerable number of books from the same century. As his collecting came to focus almost exclusively on Georgiana, he seems to have realized that his books merited priority, and he began to dispose of those parts of his autograph collection that had no particular tie to Georgia—such as a letter of George Washington's that he sold for $800—or as he did with a George Walton holograph; though linked with Georgia, it was more valuable in money (and book) terms from its association with one of the signers of the Declaration of Independence, at a time when collections of the signers were very popular. De Renne was also willing to exchange autographs for Georgia books he lacked.[7]

Significant as an early expression of De Renne's historical interests, his autograph collecting helped lead him toward the more useful and less destructive avocation of assembling collections of manuscripts. And as a collection, his autographs—whether signatures, letters, or documents—represented an accumulation heavy in Georgiana at a time when his library reflected no such emphasis. The manuscript catalog that he made of his collection in 1896 shows that he was collecting intelligently and purposefully, particularly in holograph material from Georgia's colonial and revolutionary periods, using the published catalogs issued by various American autograph dealers. In De Renne's collection, each of Georgia's three royal governors was represented by letters, as were most of the early chief executives of the state, including the redoubtable James Jackson, several of whose letters from the revolutionary period were present. Military activities in the Savannah vicinity during the Revolution were well represented by letters, as well as by an order book of General Benjamin Lincoln and an anonymous French journal, both containing much information regarding the attack on Savannah in late 1779 by the allied French and American force and its subsequent siege of the town.[8]

There were some nineteenth-century manuscripts as well, including deeds and slave documents and some Civil War letters (exclusive of the Jones Collection, which he did not list) but they did not compare in quality or quantity with those of the late 1700s. Indeed, the most interesting items of the 1800s were the most parochial: letters from the 1830s and 1840s by Israel Tefft, William Brown Hodgson, and William Bacon Stevens that provided background on the infancy of Georgia historiography.[9]

In 1903, however, as De Renne began to concentrate almost exclusively on collecting printed Georgiana, he stated explicitly that he no longer had any interest in autographs and letters. Nonetheless, the future would yet bring a few holograph purchases of note. Most exceptional was the voluminous Anthony Wayne–Nathanael Greene correspondence, for which De Renne paid $3,500 in 1911, the largest (and one of the last) of his manuscript acquisitions.[10]

Though he seems to have followed no particular guide in collecting his autographs and manuscripts, De Renne used several references and bibliographies as he gathered books for his library. He had been methodical in choosing titles for his general collection (including his collector's items), using such sources as Putnam's *Book Buyer's Manual* and the three massive volumes of Kegan Paul's *Bibliographica*. For his Georgia collection, he had much more detailed guides, including, on the most personal level, his father's manuscript catalog of the antebellum library and John Milledge's pamphlet *The De Renne Gift*. Much of Colonel Jones's vast knowledge of the materials of early Georgia history was contained in an essay following his "English Colonization of Georgia, 1733–1752," in the fifth volume of Justin Winsor's *Narrative and Critical History of America* (1887), with voluminous additions by Winsor, often including cross-references to other pertinent works such as Joseph Sabin's *Bibliotheca Americana, or A Dictionary of Books Relating to America* (1868–92) and the *Bibliotheca Americana* (1870–71) of the John Carter Brown Library, a collection that was rich in works relating to eighteenth-century Georgia.[11]

The catalogs of book dealers who specialized in Americana also often contained scarce information about certain items, even if the items themselves were long sold. Particularly helpful were catalogs of the firm of the late Henry Stevens of Vermont, whose family was still doing business in London, under the firm's name of Henry Stevens, Son & Stiles, in Great Russell Street, opposite the British Museum. Though De Renne occasionally dealt with other members of the constellation of British book dealers, including the famous Bernard Quaritch, his first major supplier of early Georgia volumes was the Stevens company; it combined a vast expertise with decades of experience in securing a wide range of titles and demonstrated an enjoyment of the book trade that was far removed from dry financial transactions. Like a few of his other suppliers, the Stevens firm had warm relations with De Renne; its representatives not only valued him as a customer but admired him as a collector, priding themselves on the part they were playing in the growth of his collection. From one of his earliest Stevens purchases (a portion of the rare third volume of William Stephens's *Journal of the Proceedings in Georgia* [1742]) to his last, De Renne and his favorite English firm enjoyed a very special relationship.[12]

De Renne forged a comparably cordial and mutually beneficial link with the American dealer C. S. Hook, who secured the Lumpkin manuscripts for him. This was a closer relationship, for the two actually met face-to-face frequently in the early 1900s, and Hook was several times a guest at Wormsloe. Though a book dealer in Savannah when the two first met, Hook eventually moved to Charleston, South Carolina, and then to Staunton, Virginia; he was, however, such an indefatigable finder of books that even his removal several states away did little to stem the flow of material he sent to Wormsloe. He had a particularly fine nose for auctions and estate sales and was likewise adept at finding decayed southern families who were eager to liquidate ancestral libraries. His gifts also included a knack for finding complete runs of early Georgia newspapers and "nests" of session laws—the printed records of the legislation passed during the annual sessions of the General Assembly that were one of De Renne's passions.[13]

As he later described it, Hook spent decades as a wandering dealer (and sometimes as a "wholesaler" to other dealers). These years were filled with "all hardships of the road, including the awful hotels in the small towns of Georgia and the South generally." But he was well-equipped—during his early days at least—with "a cast-iron stomach, built especially for one who intends to hunt elusive books in the wilderness." Like the representatives of the Stevens firm, he enjoyed his relationship with De Renne and was no doubt even more willing occasionally to forgo a large profit. As he explained after De Renne's death, "I always pleased to do him a favor, and his being a man of means did not prevent his getting rare items at a reasonable figure when I could afford it." As a case in point, Hook had found the first five volumes of an early Georgia newspaper in the possession of a carpenter near Athens, who charged him $50 for the set. Though the volumes were "worth possibly $1500," Hook sold them to De Renne for $100.[14]

Hook bought much on speculation at auctions, including thirty-two thousand pounds of old papers from the Baltimore Customs House, some of which were of interest to De Renne because of his interest in the early Georgia historian Edward Langworthy, whose signature appeared on many letters.[15]

Hook also bought at a Georgia auction a "book of surveys of coastal Camden County"; this purchase led to a comedy of errors. County officials "seemed at first to be interested in it," then stopped answering Hook's letters on the subject. When he sold it to De Renne for $20, Hook promised to "stand good for the amount paid," commenting, "I don't think anybody will care for it as much, or as well, as yourself." Interestingly, the county officials resumed their interest in the book two years after it entered the library at Wormsloe; De Renne was contacted in quick succession by, first, the chairman of the county commission and, second, the county lawyer. Having no intention of keeping the book under the circumstances, De Renne presented it, with his compliments, to the county. The officials sent their thanks in a much more dilatory fashion than they had seemed to threaten legal action.[16]

Each new acquaintance De Renne made among the booksellers seemed to have other acquaintances who stood ready to be useful to a collector; Hook was no exception. As he explored Hook's and others' contacts, De Renne's network grew larger and larger. Among other sources, Hook was responsible for De Renne's becoming acquainted at an early date with legal scholar and publisher T. L. Cole, of the Washington, D.C., Statute Law Book Company; Cole also sold early session laws and was to provide much of De Renne's law-related desiderata not available from Hook.[17]

If one portion of his collection could be singled out as providing De Renne the most personal satisfaction, it would have to be those imprints relating to Georgia laws. They had a threefold attraction for him: they related closely to the profession in which he had been trained; they had been the focus of his father's last project; and the printed laws themselves represented the earliest specimens of Georgia printing. Though De Renne's only librarian, Leonard L. Mackall, deprecated "arithmetical rarity" as a reason for the pursuit of certain imprints (stressing instead that the criterion should be intrinsic historical value), most of the early law items met both standards.[18]

De Renne's relationship with C. S. Hook led to the publication of another limited edition. Though it was printed by T. L. Cole, it could not have appeared as Cole planned it without De Renne's help. Unfortunately, heavy-handedness on Cole's part almost ended his acquaintance with De Renne before it began. He needed De Renne's assistance with an undertaking that was essentially the opposite of what G. W. J. De Renne had planned for his last quarto (the first printing of unpublished colonial laws). Cole wished to print, in photo-facsimile, all of the early session laws that *had* been printed, 1755–70, issuing them separately as small folios, in editions of thirty copies each.[19]

Only three collections of these laws were then known. None included all of the laws; each contained some the others lacked. Cole owned one collection; the other two were in the hands of the Georgia Historical Society and

Wymberley Jones De Renne. Cole wrote De Renne, requesting his assistance in dealing with the society, which was loath to allow its rare volume of acts to be shipped on loan to Washington. Not hearing from De Renne as soon as he wished, Cole composed a somewhat coercive follow-up letter that irritated De Renne. "I have been hoping to hear from you," Cole wrote, "in regard to my application for the loan of either your copy, or the Georgia Historical Society's copy, of the Ga. Laws, 1755–1770, which I am reprinting." If he did not receive the assistance from Georgia he required, Cole "would be obliged to make an apologetic statement" in the reprint's introduction, explaining the reason why his project was not "entirely satisfactory."[20]

De Renne delayed in responding in part because he had been devising a method that would allow Cole to have the use of *both* the volumes from Georgia. De Renne intended to lend Cole his copy and had also persuaded the society to lend its, after Cole had finished with De Renne's volume; the De Renne laws could then be lodged at Hodgson Hall as security for the society's copy. The tack that Cole had taken, however, jeopardized the plan: "Your letter . . . does not encourage me," De Renne wrote. "I am doing this solely to be obliging, as I care nothing for the matter & am not amenable to threats. . . . Unless I hear further from you I shall drop the matter."[21]

A letter soon arrived from Cole; it was conciliatory but not entirely convincing in its protests that no threat had been intended. In any case, he was allowed the use of the two Georgia copies, though the society's curators declined what they described as De Renne's "generous offer" to deposit his volume with them. They did see to it, however, that Cole stood the expenses of shipping the book round-trip, insuring it for $1,000. As a mark of his gratitude, Cole provided De Renne and the society photo-facsimile copies of the laws missing from their collections.[22]

Cole's edition of the laws (1905–6) was almost immediately rendered incomplete by De Renne's 1907 acquisition of an even finer trove of Georgia colonial laws, the so-called William Ewen collection, which contained other uncollected laws. Though it had been used by Colonel Jones in weeding out printed laws from the manuscript of the fifth quarto, it had apparently dropped from sight soon thereafter. One of the most prized of De Renne's acquisitions, it was soon sumptuously bound in full blue morocco by the Launder Bindery of New York City, the firm De Renne always used for clothing his most treasured volumes. Nonetheless, an agreement was apparently made for De Renne to lend the Ewen volume as well. In consideration of the loan, De Renne was to be given the 1905–6 edition of Georgia's colonial laws, "complete in every particular."[23]

Around 1902, when De Renne began his concentrated campaign to gather Georgia books, he drafted a manuscript catalog of his library. It showed that he had collected almost 150 Georgiana titles, more than doubling the number in his 1898 list. By 1905, when his first published catalog appeared, his Georgia books exceeded five hundred.[24]

De Renne compiled the seventy-four-page 1905 catalog himself, titling it *Books Relating to the History of Georgia in the Library of Wymberley Jones De Renne, of Wormsloe, Isle of Hope, Chatham County, Georgia.* He had no expert assistance and was guided principally by what he could glean from a few bibliographical aids; the book is obviously the work of an intelligent and enthusiastic (though hurried) amateur. But as he explained in March 1906, the catalog "was printed in great haste, so as to attract the attention of dealers who would not consider my claims as a collector seriously. It succeeded admirably in doing that, as I have added more than 600 books, maps, pamphlets & mss to my collection & they are still coming. The catalogue is faulty, printer's errors, my errors & not as complete as I would wish it. When I publish my next, I will recall my old ones to destroy & send the new ones to replace them."[25]

Considering the circumstances, his initial effort was no cause for shame. A large quarto bound in blue paper wrappers, its entries were grouped under thirty headings in rough chronological order. The first, "Early History of Georgia," gave separate sections to George Whitefield, John Wesley, and the Salzburgers, among others. As would be expected, given his own and his father's major field of interest, the lion's share of the books related in one way or another to eighteenth-century Georgia.[26]

The "Wormsloe Editions"—the six quartos only (though all but the Egmont journal are listed as folios)—appeared second on his list, followed fairly closely by a section of the works of Georgia's premier nineteenth-century historian, Charles C. Jones, Jr. To this were appended five titles by his son, Charles Edgeworth Jones, who, with the colonel's surviving daughter, Ruth Jones Carpenter, occasionally made valuable gifts of books to the De Renne library.[27]

Publications from the Civil War era appeared, at first glance confusingly, under the heading "1861–1864," the inclusive dates of the five Confederate imprints listed. (These were all Georgia-related imprints, his numerous non-Georgia titles having been omitted.) Other than two books of the post-war period relating to the war, there was no other entry except the very impressive first one: the engrossed manuscript of the Permanent Confederate Constitution, the last few lines of which—plus delegates' signatures—were reproduced as a folding plate.[28]

The bibliographical information that De Renne provided was fairly complete: the book's full title, with its size and format (sometimes incorrect), number of pages, and place and date of publication, along with occasional notes by the collector. A brief introductory passage said of his collection: "The Books & Pamphlets are all well bound, (unless marked otherwise). Some very handsomely. Missing pages & maps are recorded. Torn pages likewise. Portraits, letters & signatures of famous men are inserted in their proper places."[29]

At the time that he issued the 1905 catalog, De Renne also began to distribute to dealers in America and abroad printed lists of his wants, often supplying a copy of the catalog as well, a practice he continued until 1911. That year the last of his lists appeared, disguised as an appendix to the elaborate 1911 catalog. Most of the earlier individual lists ran to several pages, with the black letter heading "List of Books Wanted by Wymberley Jones De Renne," and ended with the request, "Please report as this list is sent to all prominent dealers." Several lists specify that prices and full descriptions of the books be provided, along with "whether half title is missing, leaves missing, torn, water marked or written on.—Binding unless very good is immaterial." There were at least four numbered lists, whose contents and printers varied; some were printed in Savannah, others in Westport, New York—both being locations where De Renne wished to be contacted. De Renne's lack of any complete bibliographic source to consult shows in the occasional imprecision of both titles (some of which are conjectural) and supporting information, while the spelling often reflects a lack of care by either writer or printer.[30]

The distribution of the 1905 catalog (showing what had been gathered) and the want lists (showing what was needed) was very effective in expanding the library. But the desiderata that headed the first list—the missing manuscript journals and letters of the Earl of Egmont—were never to come to Wormsloe, though they were targets of as much searching as had been the Langworthy papers. Other elusive wants included the extremely rare copy of the Georgia constitution printed by William Lancaster in Savannah in 1777 (only two copies of which were known to exist) and a Savannah pamphlet of 1770, an early product of the press of James Johnston, whose existence was known only from its presence in the antebellum catalog: *An Account of the Remarkable Conversion of Jachiel Heishel from the Jewish to the Christian Religion,* which Philadelphia collector and dealer A. S. W. Rosenbach continued to search for fruitlessly years after De Renne's death.[51]

Still, though the De Renne Georgia Library would be very much a work in progress at its founder's death, the want lists, when compared with the 1911 catalog, show that he succeeded in getting most of the books for which he advertised—from the 1741 *Resolutions of the Trustees . . . Relating to the Grants and Tenure of Lands* to the Reverend Charles C. Jones's *Religious Instruction of the Negro* (1861) and Joseph Hodgson's *Cradle of the Confederacy* (1876).[52]

De Renne's increasing numbers of books required more space. For the 1894 renovation of Wormsloe House, the architect Henry Urban had designed for the study a series of glass-fronted, black walnut bookcases. Glowing with brass fixtures, the glossy cabinets surrounded the room; each was over five feet high, and they contained approximately ninety feet of shelf space. Nonetheless, they were soon filled, and by 1899 De Renne had installed an immense matching bookcase, eight feet wide and eight feet tall, which blocked the passageway to the southeast parlor.[53]

Still, as the library and its value increased, so did De Renne's anxiety for the safety of his books and manuscripts. A kitchen accident, a faulty fireplace, or a bolt of lightning could quickly turn Wormsloe House into an all-consuming inferno that would leave no trace of the myriad books and papers so lovingly gathered. Even the large safe, which had been installed along with the bookcases to protect his most valuable acquisitions, could not have saved them from such a conflagration.[54]

De Renne's solution to the problem was to construct a fireproof library building a short but safe distance from the house, a structure that would be both convenient and secure. And following De Renne's suggestions, as interpreted by the Savannah architects Henrik Wallin and Edward Warren Young, it would also be beautiful and dignified. The Ironic style chosen lent itself well to the fireproof materials that had to compose the building: concrete and marble, tile and plaster.[55]

Just southeast of the residence, near the river, the narrow, columned front of the rectangular library building turned seaward. The only entrance was up the wide marble steps to the portico, through a tall double door bound in iron. Before the door, the De Renne coat of arms, in colorful mosaic, was set into the white tile floor. Beyond the door was the spacious library chamber, twenty-six by thirty-eight feet. Naturally lighted by a fixed transom window—as well as three screened casement windows on either side, stretching toward the lofty twenty-foot ceiling—the room was floored with tiny marble tiles: white for most of its expanse, with a golden mosaic border trimmed with thin lines of gray and maroon and blue tiles, the work of James Pelli.[56]

At the far end of the room there rose a dramatic departure from the classical motif: facing the door was a fireplace with a massive hooded mantel in the Gothic style; "WORMSLOE" was carved on the face of the mantel proper, which seemed supported by double columns on either side of the fireplace. Above the columns' capitals were four statuary figures of medieval aspect, appearing to bear the mantel on their backs. At the highest point of the mantel, near the ceiling, two monkish figures flanked a dedicatory tablet reading

To
Noble Jones
Owner of Wormsloe
from
1733 to 1775

To either side of the mantel were doors leading to two smaller rooms, joining by a communicating door: one was a water closet, the other fit for a small lounge, office, or storage room. Into the floor of the room to the left, a small vault was sunk, covered with a marble slab.[57]

The shelves, purchased from a New York firm, were metal painted with dark-green enamel and could be affixed to their wall supports at various heights. The original range of shelves was confined to the walls to either side of the great door, with the upper shelves accessible by a long ladder. Map cases held De Renne's cartographic items and larger documents, and there were several filing cabinets as well. In addition there were safes of various sizes and types. Comfortable chairs were distributed about the room, which also contained a desk and a large mahogany work table.[58]

Upon the walls, each of the previous four generations of the family was represented. Above the fireplace, there was the tablet dedicating the library and its treasures to the memory of Noble Jones. To the left was hung Charles Willson Peale's portrait of Noble Wimberly Jones; to the right was his son Rembrandt Peale's study of George Jones. Above the door, facing the tablet and portraits, De Renne placed a portrait of G. W. J. De Renne, painted by his father's friend Carl L. Brandt, who based it on an 1866 photograph and his memories. Near the door on a pedestal was G. W. J. De Renne's bronze statuette of *The Confederate Soldier*.[39]

Construction of the library began in the summer of 1907, and the building was completed by spring of the following year. Late in April 1908, several of De Renne's friends and acquaintances received an invitation in black letter, requesting the pleasure of their company at a "private view" of the library. "Conveyances to Wormsloe will meet the car leaving the city at eleven-thirty from Fortieth Street," it stated, arriving at the Isle of Hope at noon." As Leonard Mackall noted of the impressive building, it was "merely a casket" for its "wonderful treasures," and the library's first guests could not have failed to be impressed by the hundreds of volumes lining the building's eastern wall. Most of them had been bound in leather by Launder of New York: roan was used for law books and the large newspaper folios, red for histories, and green for books of description and travel. After being introduced to the wonders of the building and its contents, the New York bookman Joseph F. Sabin described the library perceptively to De Renne as "a monument both externally and internally to your family, your State, and the nation."[40]

Mackall understood that the library was to De Renne a "holy of holies." He spent many happy hours there, reading widely, researching matters that had captured his interest, and assisting friends and visiting scholars who came to do the same. His familiarity with his holdings made it possible for him to find information on many subjects quickly, both because of his knowledge of his collection and because of finding aids that he created himself. One such guide was a detailed, personal key to the poorly indexed volumes of *The Colonial Records of Georgia*. On many cold, rainy winter afternoons he worked quietly at his desk in the library, the firelight dancing along the gleaming golden spines of his wall of books, drawn by him to Wormsloe from both sides of the Atlantic.[41]

De Renne's relatively rapid success at creating a library of such excellence was not because he had or spent unlimited funds. He never had the resources to purchase all he wanted, whatever the price, as was the case with such plutocrat-collectors was J. Pierpont Morgan, for whom, at one level, collecting was merely a form of conspicuous consumption. At least partially for this reason, De Renne's collecting ventures consistently engaged his interest and attention. He had to use care and planning to make his available funds go as far as possible; never were De Renne's resources lavished on his collection at the expense of his family. Unquestionably, however, he was in an enviable position: no matter what became of his own money, his children would be very well provided for by his father's will. Nonetheless, he cheerfully spent much of his annuity on his son and daughters and in maintaining Wormsloe and developing its grounds as part of his own legacy to them. What he had left from family expenditures, including travel and investments, was not inconsiderable, but his library purchases, he once remarked, kept him "poor," and, to accomplish what he did, he had to "strain every resource." [42]

By 1908, the year his Georgia library was moved into its handsome new home, all of De Renne's children had reached young adulthood. The eldest, Elfrida, had attended a finishing school in New York City, in the charge of a Charlestonian, Meta D. Huger. Her boarding school was near Central Park and also handy to De Renne's Union Club, so the father could frequently take the daughter to dinner, plays, and the opera. Elfrida matured into a young woman of stately beauty; though not lacking in humor, she had a fundamental seriousness and dignity that suggested the De Renne grandfather she had never known. She had attracted several suitors, including an Italian count (whom she found somewhat ridiculous), but she ultimately married Dr. Craig Barrow. Raised in Athens, he had been educated at the university there, where he was "prominent in both scholastic and athletic activities." He then pursued medical studies at the University of Maryland, followed by postgraduate work at the German university of Breslau, and began practicing in Savannah in 1902. One of Elfrida's earliest memories of Dr. Barrow, however, was her delight in beating him at billiards on the Wormsloe House table. Dr. Barrow's sense of humor appealed to her, as did the enthusiasm he shared with her for both automobiles and horses. [43]

The wedding of Elfrida De Renne to Dr. Craig Barrow took place at Wormsloe on January 3, 1906. It was apparently the first such ceremony to be conducted at the plantation, and De Renne made certain that it would be a memorable occasion, "characterized by extreme simplicity in arrangement" but "exquisite in every detail." The ceremony was conducted in an improvised chapel—a prie-dieu with a background of palms—at the northern end of the wide hall of the residence. The hall and surrounding rooms were decorated with a "profusion of bamboo," along with "many handsome palms." The only flowers used, American Beauty roses and Easter lilies, had been placed on the mantels and were also tied in clusters along the staircase, which the wedding party descended.[44]

As an orchestra stationed on the third floor played "The Wedding March," the bride, dressed in white chiffon and satin, descended with her father; they were preceded by two flower girls, dressed in pale blue, and Audrey, the maid of honor, in a "pretty girlish gown of white liberty silk." Waiting below was the bride's mother, wearing "an elegant costume of black silk net over cloth of gold." The groom, with his brother, the lawyer David Barrow, as best man, stood beneath a wedding bell of white hyacinths, where the service was performed by the Reverend Francis Alan Brown, rector of Christ Church.[45]

After a wedding trip to the North, the Barrows moved into a house her father owned on Liberty Street, within sight of the old De Renne mansion; there in October 1906 she gave birth to a son, who was named for his father. Another son, Wymberley Jones De Renne Barrow, was born in March 1908, as his grandfather's collection was being moved into the new library. Sadly, as had been the case with the child De Renne had named for his own father, Wymberley Barrow soon died. But during the next several years, young Craig was joined by two sisters, Elfrida and Muriel.[46]

De Renne greatly admired Dr. Barrow, who in his early years in Savannah was associated with both the Georgia Infirmary and the Telfair Hospital; by 1917 he would become chief surgeon of the Central of Georgia Railway and Steamship Company. An early advocate of preventive medicine, Dr. Barrow expanded services to the company's employees by bringing to reality his dream of creating a modern company hospital in Savannah. He also added civic responsibilities to his professional activities and served several years as a Savannah city alderman. De Renne reposed considerable trust in his son-in-law, often counting on him to take care of important business dealings as well as sensitive family matters.[47]

But De Renne was not as pleased with Audrey's choice for a husband,

Frederic Coerr, a New Yorker and also a doctor. Audrey, handsome, viva-cious, and impulsive, with a mass of auburn hair, was less prone to book-madness than horse-madness, though she, like her sister, had attended Miss Huger's school. She had made an enviable name as a fearless horsewoman not only in the Chatham Hunt Club but in European cross-country riding as well. A surviving picture of Dr. Coerr reveals one probable reason Audrey was attracted to him: he looked magnificent in the saddle. The two were married in New York City on November 20, 1912, in the Chapel of St. Bartholomew's Church, "in the presence of a few relatives and friends." Since the couple was leaving on their wedding journey immediately after the ceremony, Audrey was married in "a traveling suit of dark lavender velvet," with a matching hat, "topped with plumes." For the first years of their marriage, the Coerrs lived in New York City. In 1913 Audrey had her first child, a son, named Wymberley Jones De Renne Coerr and called "Pym"; he was to be joined by three sisters, one of whom, named for her mother, died in infancy. The arrival of a Coerr grandson reconciled De Renne to Audrey, and he was a doting grandfather to all of the grandchil-dren but saw more of the Barrows because they also saw more of Wormsloe. Young Craig, for instance, learned to ride on the "war saddle," kept at the estate, that had belonged to Captain Alexander McC. Duncan's brother Dr. William Duncan.[48]

Young Wymberley would not marry during his father's lifetime. His frail health kept him long at school, but his father was pleased that he loved books and reading, as befitted one who would fall heir to one of the coun-try's great private libraries. In 1907, Worthington Ford received a letter from the elder De Renne, alerting him to expect a visitor at the Library of Congress: "You may some day before the Xmas vacations see a lanky boy with spectacles who will introduce himself as W. W. De Renne. He has a de-cided taste for books. All his pocket money goes into good editions of stan-dard authors. He is very thoughtful & reads thoroughly what he does read. Any courtesy you may show him will always be remembered by him & per-haps encourage him on the good road." Ford soon wrote De Renne of his and Librarian of Congress Putnam's pleasure at meeting young Wymberley and of their telling him "to call whenever he passes through that we may show him material in which he is interested." [49]

Because of his frequent illnesses, it was thought that the bracing climate of Newport, Rhode Island, would be good for Wymberley, and this proved to be the case. This was far from his father's more rustic Newport, however. Now there were "the villas, the palaces, the lawns and the luxuries," with "something like the chink of money itself in the murmur of the breezy little waves at the foot of the cliff." The young man spent several years at St. George's School in Newport, enjoying literature particularly and participating in orchestra and debate; he also composed and had printed a twenty-six-page pamphlet, *My Knowledge of Some Rules in Grammar Books.* Soon Wymberley displayed what would be a lasting love for journalism, serving as an editor for the *Dragon,* one of the school periodicals, and contributing such articles as "The International Races at Savannah." In 1913, soon after reaching his majority, he would be issued press credentials to cover the inauguration of Woodrow Wilson.[50]

In 1910 young Wymberley became the first of the family to attend the University of Georgia. There he went from the freshman to the junior class in one year; one of his professors noted that "his only shortcoming (!) [was] his desire to do too much. He naturally finds his courses easy—so thorough has been his preparation—and is tempted to crowd into the week too many recitations." A member of Chi Psi fraternity, he was also on the staff of the *Georgian,* the university magazine; he acted as business manager and contributed occasional articles.[51]

Wymberley next attended Columbia University, as had his father, but earned a degree in journalism rather than law. Somewhere along the way, he became friends with another young student, George S. Kaufman, with whom he co-authored a play, an amusing curtain-opener titled *That Infernal Machine;* it was copyrighted in 1915 but never performed.[52]

Since Wymberley Jones De Renne's responsibilities to his children and grandchildren pleasantly expanded during the last decade of his life, it was well for his library that he chose and spent wisely and often dealt with people who wanted to make their own contribution to his work. Sometimes they were dealers, who offered good prices, or, for expensive items, allowed him to pay in installments. More often than might be suspected, however, the distribution of his catalogs and his want lists would lead friends and admirers in Savannah and elsewhere to make outright gifts of items he needed to help him with his labors.[53]

Georgia institutions, both governmental and educational, also assisted him, for De Renne was prescient enough to realize that he should gather for his library such official publications relating to the state's public affairs as reports and bulletins. In writing to Georgia's comptroller general to request copies of some of his office's reports for De Renne, A. R. Lawton noted that the library at Wormsloe was "a source of pride and gratification to every Georgian" and that it was "a labor of love and patriotism to help" De Renne. Among Georgians at the national level who admired and assisted De Renne with their own (and other) publications were U.S. senator A. O. Bacon and U.S. Supreme Court associate justice J. R. Lamar, who christened the library the "Little Greek Temple by the Sea." [54]

Fellow collectors—and particularly fellow Georgians—were also generous with suggestions regarding titles and subjects to be added and offered gifts of books and manuscripts as well. The most celebrated Georgia collector of the late 1890s and early 1900s was no exception. Julius L. Brown, eldest son of Georgia's Civil War governor, had retired from a profitable law career in 1890 and had soon begun collecting; before long he had filled his rambling, chateauesque mansion near the center of Atlanta with a wildly eclectic accumulation of books, manuscripts, coins, antiques, and objets d'art. Consequently, when he played host to President Grover Cleveland, he was able to seat him for dinner in a thronelike chair formerly the property of Napoleon I, at a table covered with a cloth that had belonged to the unfortunate Emperor Maximilian of Mexico. Like most collectors, Brown was not without his eccentricities, and he once entertained a group of Atlanta ministers at a "Dinner to Death," in which "the tablecloth was black, the hangings of the room were black, and everything of the sombre hue of death." [55]

Seeing Brown's collection in the early 1900s, U. B. Phillips was unimpressed, so singled-minded was he in his quest for manuscripts relating to southern history. Instead, he was shown, as a most prized possession, Thomas Moore's manuscript of his Oriental romance *Lalla Rookh*, which, wrote Phillips, "all must worship." Though there were certainly items that would have interested Phillips, the chaotic arrangement of the various collections would have made finding any particular item very difficult: every room of the cavernous mansion was "literally lined with books of all descriptions"; they occupied "scores of bookcases," lay "piled in orderly confusion on a score or more of tables," and "filled to overflowing every niche in the big house." [56]

Five years De Renne's senior, Brown died in 1910 and became acquainted with De Renne only during the last few years of his life. Despite his poor health during that period, he was at least once a guest at Wormsloe. A friend of Captain Alexander McC. Duncan, Brown was a fellow veteran as well, for as a teenager he had been among the Georgia Military Institute cadets who had contributed to the unsuccessful resistance to Sherman's March to the Sea. Brown had also been a friend of Colonel Charles C. Jones and had once swapped him a collection of Indian relics for a copy of the Egmont quarto. A bon vivant, Brown appreciated social occasions where ardent spirits were available in generous amounts, and he invited De Renne to bring Captain Duncan on a visit to his "great big barn of a home" in Atlanta, promising the captain they would "lay him out." All three men looked askance at the growing prohibition movement in Georgia. Fittingly, one of Brown's gifts to De Renne was bottled, not bound—a vintage from "the time of Oglethorpe." [57]

Among the books Brown presented to De Renne were complete, bound sets of the pamphlets recording his most famous court cases, the majority of which were defenses of railroad interests. But he was also a good source of material relating to Georgia's two governor Browns, since the first— Joseph E. Brown, governor from 1857 to 1865—was his father, and the other—Joseph M. Brown, whose first term began in 1909—was his brother. The rich material relating to Julius Brown's father was essential to De Renne's library since he had been a major figure in late antebellum politics in Georgia, as well as in the state's Civil War, Reconstruction, and Bourbon eras. [58]

Though less prolific of political writings than his father, Joseph M. Brown was himself a published author—his Civil War sketch, *The Mountain Campaigns in Georgia*, was one of De Renne's early acquisitions, and his historical novel *Astyanax*, one of his later ones. As chief executive of Georgia during part of the time De Renne was collecting, Governor Brown was instrumental in De Renne's receiving some of the voluminous state publications that were to be an integral part of the library. [59]

De Renne's association with Julius Brown was a cordial one, as their correspondence attests. They complimented each other on various acquisitions, and De Renne loaned some of his rare items so that Brown could have typescripts made in Atlanta. [60]

Strictly speaking, Julius Brown was not a competitor of De Renne's, though the other major collector of the early 1900s was, at least in the early days. Unlike De Renne's close contemporary Brown, Telamon Cruger

Smith Cuyler was over two decades younger, and he would introduce De Renne to the most eminent of his own contemporaries, U. B. Phillips. By profession Cuyler was a lawyer, with business interests—mainly related to cotton—in Atlanta and Savannah. Though interested in books, he was drawn most strongly to autographs and manuscripts. De Renne's collection of these materials irresistibly drew Cuyler. Slender and dark-haired, with a somewhat piratical, upcurling mustache, the young man first visited Wormsloe in 1903.[61]

At that time Cuyler had recently married a California heiress and was still known by his birth name, Telamon Cruger Cuyler Smith, though his surname gave him no joy. No doubt the earlier metamorphosis of Jones to De Renne was part of his inspiration for legally changing his last name in 1905 to Cuyler, the surname of his mother's family, which by that time had no descendants in the male line. Also in 1905 Cuyler engaged in another sincere form of flattery by issuing the first of his "Beverwyck Quartos," large pamphlets, limited to fifty copies, that were said to have taken their name from the first place the Cuyler family had settled in America after emigrating from Holland.[62]

Part dilettante and part poseur, Cuyler had a broad but shallow knowledge of Georgia history, though he proclaimed himself the successor of Colonel Jones as Georgia's premier historian. His major asset was not his knowledge but his charm, for he was an engaging companion (though prone to excessive talking) and could be extremely entertaining, particularly on brief acquaintance and in short stretches. In the long run, his charm had a tendency to pall, particularly when his endlessly plausible statements began to contrast with reality.[63]

During the early part of his acquaintance with Cuyler, De Renne found the young collector's knowledge of Georgia history and its sources impressive. Moreover, Cuyler's connections with dealers and collectors could not be gainsaid; and he occasionally provided De Renne with coveted materials that had been troublesome to find, such as pamphlets on Georgia's Yazoo land scandal of the 1790s. By 1905 De Renne still valued Cuyler's opinion to the extent of seeking his input into the plans for the library catalog soon to be issued. But by 1910, the relationship had all but run its course. Part of the problem was surely that, as De Renne's expertise in Georgia matters grew, his estimation of Cuyler's knowledge diminished.[64]

But another factor was Cuyler's lack of discretion. He was among those few who had been admitted to the secret of the "steel box" that contained much of the Jones collection, with its multitudinous bound Confederate manuscripts, alternating with inlaid engravings of their authors. In 1910 Cuyler wanted De Renne to divulge the box's contents (except the Lee volumes) to an English friend, A. S. Broadley, who was writing a book on autographs. Believing that the book would make De Renne's reputation, Cuyler wanted De Renne to write a history of his collection and send a catalog of his books (only the latter of which he did). Though Cuyler promised Broadley's book would be definitive, its own title (*Chats on Autographs*) seemed to question that assessment. And though the book quoted from Cuyler slavishly and with total credulity, an embarrassed Broadley was distancing himself from Cuyler by the time of its publication.[65]

Also in 1910, while living in Paris, Cuyler made another attempt at exploiting the Jones volumes when he asked De Renne (unsuccessfully) to have all of the engravings of the Confederate officers photographed for him so that he could have a local artist execute them in red chalk for posterity. This scheme was only one of hundreds that seemed constantly to be spun from Cuyler's teeming brain, most of them having little merit or practicability. And the longer that De Renne or anyone else was acquainted with Cuyler, the more obvious it became that for all his voluble talk, he accomplished few of his aims.[66]

Early in his friendship with De Renne, for example, Cuyler said he was working on a study of the Wormsloe editions for the American Historical Association. De Renne provided him with as much information as possible, only to see the project stillborn like most others. And though Cuyler confided to the publisher A. B. Caldwell that he had literally scores of books awaiting the publisher in manuscript form, almost none of them ever saw print. In fact, during a long life, Cuyler mainly published reminiscences (in the *Atlanta Georgian*) and columns in the *Journal of Labor*, together with some privately printed ephemera, including an adulatory sketch of himself, *Telamon Cuyler: Sportsman, Historian and Man of Letters*, which he wrote in the third person. Not until the 1930s would his most useful work be issued (by the Work Projects Administration): collections of Georgia land grants and colonial wills.[67]

By mid-1909, Captain Duncan was writing to De Renne, "I have *another, awful* epistle from our good friend T. C. S. Cuyler which I wish I could inflict upon you." Such importuning letters steadily decreased the number of Cuyler's friends.[68] But he did have friends in high places, at least for a time. In 1905, Cuyler was appointed Georgia's agent in England for gathering materials relating to the colonial history of Georgia, but most of the work was done by the London firm B. F. Stevens & Brown. Later, when Cuyler sought the recommendation of De Renne and others to be appointed compiler of state records, he was repeatedly passed over.[69]

Cuyler's notoriety increased over time. Though he had been enthusiastically lampooned during his ultimately successful effort to have his name changed, De Renne, of all people, could sympathize with that predicament. But in 1912 and 1913, Cuyler's marriage unraveled in spectacularly public fashion in the newspapers. His wife accused him of general faults, including gross immorality, and very specific ones, such as flourishing a pistol at her in their London suite while they were viewing the funeral procession of Edward VII. In an apparently unrelated headline, he was reported to have become demented and thrown himself from a train in South Carolina (though he explained he was merely in a hurry to send a telegram). A variety of factors, then, effectively ended the relations between De Renne and Cuyler; his absence from the presentation list for *Lee's Dispatches* indicated most tellingly his fall from grace.[70]

Cuyler's own collection, of which only the manuscripts were of considerable value, was a vast trove. A great number of the manuscripts show clear evidence of having been at one time part of Georgia's state archives, though exactly how or when Cuyler secured them is a matter of conjecture. The most charitable interpretation of his collecting activities holds that he gleaned most of his collection from papers that had been abandoned in Milledgeville when the capital was moved in 1868. But he was present in Atlanta during most of the decade of the 1890s, during which the state's records, already stored carelessly, were moved from the old capitol to the new, with no improvement in their custodianship. As late as 1903, the group of papers from which many of Cuyler's antebellum and Civil War manuscripts seem to have come was stored in an overflow document room on the third floor of the capitol building, with no security or supervision, and "not visited as often as once a year." At the time, it was noted, their classification was such that they "might almost as well have been in a promiscuous heap upon the floor." Worse was to come, however, for by 1917, this room had been broken up, and many of its manuscripts were bundled into the basement rooms of the capitol, where some were consigned to the furnace. Only in 1918, after much prodding by Lucian L. Knight and others, did the state create the Department of Archives and History; with Knight as the department's first director, the state's records were safe for the first time in decades.[71]

Whatever Cuyler's source or methods, he secured many state manuscripts—correspondence and otherwise—and they joined his other papers, many presumably purchased during the period of his marriage, when his disposable income was greatest. Happily, the bulk of his manuscript collections, many of his books, and his extensive personal correspondence would eventually go to the University of Georgia Library.[72]

In some of his acquisitions, Cuyler represented a type of collector best described in 1915 by De Renne's friend Worthington Ford. Though Ford's description is exact, he was premature in thinking that the species under inspection had become extinct:

> I have a high admiration for the old-time collector, while thankful that the breed has died out. He took anything without perplexing his mind with questions of right or fitness. He thought nothing of borrowing from private and State offices, and training his memory to forget the fact of borrowing. . . . According to his lights he was correct in his position, for he sought to counteract the neglect of others, and in default of any other recognized custodian he constituted himself keeper of the rolls. No doubt much has been saved which would otherwise have been lost, and for this he should have full credit. But much was also lost through his ignorance, lost actually and geographically, for what he got so cheaply, he scattered with a lavish hand and never appreciated the advantage of keeping great collections intact. His actions, entirely well intentioned, were unmoral, and rarely did he rise to so high a plane as to merit our gratitude unmixed with real regret that he should have been permitted to have his way.[73]

Nonetheless, it was through Cuyler that De Renne first became acquainted with U. B. Phillips, then beginning his career as a historian; Cuyler had completed his flamboyant tenure at the University of Georgia in 1893 just as Phillips was commencing his studies there. Despite their friendship, Phillips seems to have had no knowledge of Cuyler's massive hoard of state manuscripts (if he had gathered it by that time). At least, Cuyler's manuscript collection is not mentioned in Phillips's survey of Georgia historical manuscripts, published in 1905 by the American Historical Association, which was then promoting the "scientific study of Southern history" through "the collection of manuscripts, the care of archives, and the publication of bibliographies." Also in 1905, De Renne sent Phillips, then teaching at the University of Wisconsin, a copy of his newly printed library catalog, as well as an invitation to visit Wormsloe. Though Phillips could not come to Savannah for some time, forces were already at work that would lead to a mutually beneficial relationship between De Renne, Phillips, and the Georgia Historical Society.[74]

Of all the Savannah organizations, the society would seem to have been the best placed to enjoy De Renne's support from the time he returned to Georgia in 1891. Like other local groups, it courted him, electing him to membership in February 1893. His frequent traveling prevented him from attending most meetings, but he occasionally presented the society's library with books, including some of the Wormsloe Quartos. Fuller participation seemed assured when, in February 1896, De Renne was elected one of the society's curators. After delaying his response so that William Harden could explain to him what his duties would be, he wrote, "I now accept the honour, which I appreciate all the more as I know I owe it to 'Virtutis avorum premium [The reward of my ancestors' virtue].' "[75]

But De Renne resigned his curatorship by May of the same year, pleading his "absences abroad." These were surely a factor, but another consideration may have been the state of the society in the 1890s. No volume of the *Collections* had been published since his father's of 1878, and the organization had been channeling its dwindling energies toward "the maintenance and management of its library," which had become "in effect a circulating library," with members paying $5 a year for borrowing privileges.[76]

In 1899 new leadership under Colonel John Screven (whom De Renne revered) revitalized the society and renewed De Renne's interest in it, though Screven was to die in 1900. Nonetheless, De Renne now found himself among those who wanted the organization rejuvenated and made his own contribution: when the fifth volume of the society's *Collections* was finally published, in two parts, 1901–2, De Renne paid for the publication of Part Two. It consisted of the order book of General Samuel Elbert, 1776–78, and Elbert's letterbook for 1785, the first year he served as Georgia's governor.[77]

Though the society's resumption of publishing was laudable, nothing short of a rigorous reorganization could return it to its original mission. De Renne and others demanded change, following the leadership of such men as A. R. Lawton, Henry C. Cunningham, and George J. Baldwin. In early 1903, they waged a campaign to bring the society back to the "objects of its creation, as indicated in its charter." The society had to "return to its original purpose of being purely an historical society," argued Cunningham, "in which membership shall be a distinguished honor instead of being merely a library subscription right. Let the Society separate its historical documents and books, valuable for the true purposes of the Society, from the ordinary run of books, turning over the latter with a portion of the building to a library board . . . entirely separate from the Board of Managers of the Georgia Historical Society."[78]

With financial support from the city, the transformation of Hodgson Hall from a subscription library, supported by dues, to a free public library soon became a reality. But the changes made were to go farther: membership in the society was restricted to one hundred, and residents of Georgia towns other than Savannah were accepted, for it was the "desire of the Society to extend its membership throughout the entire State." Under the old subscription library system, the society had four hundred members, who payed $5 per annum. With the newly restricted membership, dues would be raised to $25 a year to "provide an ample fund for all of the true purposes of the Society, such as the purchase, publication, or reproduction of historical publications, books, valuable documents and other matters of historical interest." To guarantee the society "from loss in making the improvement," De Renne and twenty-four others each promised a maximum of $100 per annum to make up any shortfall.[79]

Far away, at his teaching post at the University of Wisconsin, U. B. Phillips heard of these developments with great interest. Such signs of life cheered him; he had feared that the society was "moribund." And he was glad to see the society making an attempt to include Georgians beyond Savannah in its membership, for he had considered the organization to be the Savannah Historical Society in all but name and had cherished the "dark design of agitating for a real Historical Society to be established at Athens or Atlanta" if he returned to the state. But he was also very intrigued by the new emphasis on publications. Like William Bacon Stevens and Charles C. Jones, Jr., before him, he saw the society as an appropriate diffuser of his own work; his first book, *Georgia and State Rights*, had been published in 1902, but he already had several other historical studies in the working and planning stages.[80]

When one of his friends in the society contacted him, however, it was to secure his advice on what was being planned as one of the earliest of the new society's publications: a bibliography of Georgia history. Phillips understood the pitfalls of embarking on such a project, but he gave the society some good advice, along with the titles of the best of current bibliographies: his own ten-page listing, contained in *Georgia and State Rights* (for the first half of the nineteenth century), and, as a model, the Alabama bibliography compiled by his friend Thomas McAdory Owen, publisher of the *Gulf States Historical Magazine.* Phillips suggested that Owen would be a suitable consultant to the society.[81]

The young professor hoped as well that the society could arrange to take charge of the publication of *The Colonial Records of Georgia.* Phillips did not believe this project could be decently accomplished by the elderly, half-blind compiler of state records, Allen Candler, whom he considered a well-meaning but essentially ignorant political appointee. The records, Phillips asserted, should be prepared by the state's historical society, with scientifically trained historians as its agents.[82]

Phillips had some aspirations to be involved in these activities, for he suggested himself as the society's new secretary/historian/librarian. He assured George Baldwin that he could lecture for only five months of the year (to which his university had no objection); in the months remaining, he could be a very active secretary for the newly energized society and would "look after its interests and make search for historical material all over the state." Obviously, he could not "always be at hand in Savannah," for while he could "easily act as librarian of the public library," he could not "always be present at the loan desk." Though the society displayed some initial interest in Phillips's proposal, it was ultimately decided that there was a need for someone who could work for the organization full-time. Phillips was disappointed, of course, but he assisted the society with some of its plans and publications, including helping to edit the sixth volume of the *Collections* (the edition of the letters of James Habersham, printed in 1904) and evaluating the letters of Manuel de Montiano, which he recommended be translated and published.[83]

Neither Phillips nor the society fully understood that the growing De Renne Georgia Library—as an attempt to gather everything significant in print that related to the history of the state—represented the best hope for a definitive Georgia bibliography. Since De Renne's library predated, and was independent of, the society's bibliographical aspirations, and since he would have no substantive discussions with Phillips until 1909, it was manifestly De Renne's own experiences that had shown him the need for such a bibliography, as well as the importance of his own collecting to that end. As early as 1905, he informed George Parker Winship of the John Carter Brown Library that the development of a bibliography of Georgia history was a major goal of his collecting. Winship, like several other librarians, applauded his aim and provided him with a list of his institution's Georgia titles.[84]

By 1909, when the society was again reorganizing and once more recruiting new members, De Renne was entering his most active period of membership. A. R. Lawton, now the society's new president, realized that its success and effectiveness rested on intelligent planning, and he hoped for assistance from U. B. Phillips. By this time teaching at Tulane University, and well known as a rising young southern historian, Phillips was obviously the best choice to come and meet with the society for an extensive planning session. As Lawton explained to Phillips, the 1903 attempt to establish the society on "a new basis," including a limit of one hundred members, had failed; membership never reached more than sixty-five, and "this dwindled to thirty-five." Lawton had concluded, sadly, that in Savannah (and elsewhere in the state) there were not enough men who would pay $25 a year "for purely patriotic and public purposes." Consequently, membership restrictions had been withdrawn, dues had been reduced to $10, and seventy new members had been elected.[85]

The 1903 reorganization had not been a total failure, however. The society had reclaimed its books and manuscripts and separated them from the general collection of the new, successful public library in Hodgson Hall. It had also gotten out of debt and, having published the Habersham letters, was preparing to publish "the manuscript journal and letters of Montiano, the Spanish commander at Saint Augustine during the period of Oglethorpe's siege in 1745," as Phillips had recommended. As Lawton noted, because the society was "no longer a circulating library association, it behooves it to devote itself exclusively to its historical work."[86]

In drawing Phillips to Savannah, Lawton presented Wormsloe and its library as a major inducement, noting that De Renne's "splendid collection" would be placed "entirely at [Phillips's] disposal." He warned Phillips, however, that he had one danger to face from De Renne's hospitality: "over-

feeding." Phillips soon agreed to come ("with the most pleasant anticipa-
tions") and secured permission for his visit from Tulane's president and
dean. He notified his hosts that he would arrive by train at the Savannah
station on April 4, 1909. "To identify myself," he wrote, "I am six feet, three
inches and will be wearing a gray suit and a soft black hat." On reading
Phillips's letter, De Renne commented, "6 ft. 3 inches—Rien que cela
[Only that much]! Georgia ought to be proud." [87]

All involved were satisfied by Phillips's visit. His address "The Plantation System in the Old South," delivered to the society members and their
guests, was well received, and Phillips used his time in Savannah to gather
more information and manuscripts on his topic and also arranged to borrow
pertinent books, pamphlets, and plantation records from the Telfair Academy's collections, with the society's permission. [88]

But apparently the most vivid memory Phillips carried with him back to
New Orleans was of Wormsloe. He had enjoyed several days' hospitality at
Wormsloe House and worked pleasantly for extended periods in the newly
opened library building. One day Telamon Cuyler was on hand with his
camera and took several photographs, including one of Phillips standing in
the portico of the library with De Renne and Captain Duncan. Decades
later Phillips wrote appreciatively of De Renne's generosity—of his "two
tables, one loaded with delicious food and wine of rare vintage; the other
laden at command with the choicest manuscripts." [89]

On Phillips's last day in Savannah, he met with the society's officers at
Wormsloe and presented his suggestions for the organization's future
course. Most were based on his earlier ideas, though he was emboldened to
add that the society could increase its numbers by offering ("at a lower rate
of dues") associate memberships to "women of Savannah, to young men of
Savannah, say not above twenty-five years old, and to non-residents of the
City." In regard to the society's library, he was so impressed by the growing
De Renne library and the force of its owner's personality that he assumed
the library would be as permanent a fixture in Chatham County as the society itself. Consequently, he recommended that the organization expend no
funds in duplicating any of the books at Wormsloe. [90]

In keeping with his earlier concerns, Phillips made a plea for the society
to expand beyond Savannah by establishing affiliated societies elsewhere in
the state, particularly in Athens and other college and university towns. The
benefit, he thought, would be more in "moral support and in the increased

influence upon public opinion than in pecuniary assistance." For future publications, Phillips saw among the society's holdings "scant" material—other than some remaining manuscripts of Indian agent Benjamin Hawkins—but suggested that the society branch out by publishing other available manuscripts, including some correspondence of William H. Crawford and others, with which he had been working. He made a case as well for the society to solicit and print original monographs from scholars at large and from some of its members—a bibliography of Georgia by De Renne, he suggested, or a "history of the reorganization of the Central of Georgia Railroad" by Colonel Lawton. Incredibly, Phillips seems to have been offered the opportunity to "undertake the preparation of a History of Georgia, with the Society's financial support." Nothing came of it, however, nor of his suggestions regarding manuscripts. And for lack of funds, the society would not be able to accede to his 1913 request that his life of Robert Toombs appear as one of the volumes of the *Collections*. But by 1914, for whatever reason, the society had more than 130 members, about two dozen of them women, and 9 members were from Augusta, Atlanta, and elsewhere. Soon, however, the idea of an affiliated society at Athens would take a strange turn, with great consequence for the society's future.[91]

Although there were other factors at play, the visit of U. B. Phillips certainly helped to energize the society, and the intelligent appreciation of his library by the young professor was a tonic to De Renne. He agreed with Phillips on much, but particularly with one of his previously stated views, to which De Renne's father would also have heartily subscribed: "The history of the United States has been written by Boston and largely written wrong. It must be written anew before it reaches its final form of truth, and for that work the South must do its part in preparation. New England has already overdone its part. There have been antiquarians and chroniclers at work in the Southern field, but few historians—few thinkers—and thought is the all-essential." In future books Phillips would show that he had used the De Renne library well, and his grateful acknowledgments (and presentation copies) would bring his good wishes back to Wormsloe for the rest of De Renne's life.[92]

Beginning in 1909, the year of Phillips's visit, De Renne became deeply involved in one fashion or another in the publication of five more of the books in the society's series of *Collections*, the last of which would appear in 1916. This was an unprecedented output for the organization and entirely in keeping with the aims expressed in 1903. Most of the books published contained illustrative material from De Renne's library. Moreover, he would be concerned with two other society publications that did not come from the society's holdings. De Renne provided the primary materials for one of them, a companion to the society's earlier publication of the letters of Montiano, which had been based on transcripts gathered in the 1840s by William Brown Hodgson. For the 1913 edition of *The Spanish Official Account of the Attack on the Colony of Georgia*, De Renne secured copies of documents from the Archives of the Indies in Seville and paid to have them translated by Major C. De Witt Willcox, a professor at West Point. Afterward, the archival transcripts—copied in ink onto heavy, cream-colored paper—were placed in the files of the Wormsloe library.[93]

The other publication was unlike any other the society had undertaken. Planning for a suitable monument to James Edward Oglethorpe had begun in Savannah in 1901 and reached fruition in 1910 with the placement of the heroic bronze statue by Daniel Chester French in the center of Chippewa Square. To commemorate the event, the society decided to publish, as part of the *Collections,* an illustrated account titled *A History of the Erection and Dedication of the Monument to Gen'l James Edward Oglethorpe.* Though De Renne contributed $500 of the considerable sum that was required for the monument, he made another contribution that afforded him a transatlantic adventure.[94]

While his library contained a source that stated authoritatively that Oglethorpe had been born in 1696, many other printed sources disagreed—Colonel Jones, for example, had "honored" 1689 "as most reliable"; not until 1932 did one of Oglethorpe's biographers cite the date correctly. It appeared that an incorrect date was set to appear on the monument, and, as De Renne noted, "a monument should be properly dated, for if not it is bound to draw the ridicule of somebody sooner or later." He offered to travel to England to verify his information.[95]

Arriving in London in mid-May 1910, De Renne found the city unusually glum. "King Edward by dying when he did ruined what promised to be the greatest London season ever," he reported, "and people here are very much depressed." Pushing on nonetheless, De Renne found that a just-published volume of the *Dictionary of National Biography* contained a lengthy sketch of Oglethorpe, giving his birth year as 1696. It also mentioned that Oglethorpe had been baptized at the London church of St.

Martin-in-the-Fields and had died at the village of Cranham. De Renne immediately visited both places, securing a witnessed extract from the register of baptisms at one and a copy of Oglethorpe's "extravagantly long" epitaph at the other. Having received a Savannah newspaper declaring that the monument was finished, he cabled to stop the inscription: "Oglethorpe Born 1696. Bringing proofs. De Renne." One of the proofs, the register extract, would appear as an illustration in the book, but, in the end, no date was placed on the monument.[96]

As De Renne's purchases filled more shelves of his library, his dissatisfaction with the 1905 catalog increased. In 1910, the year after Phillips's visit to Wormsloe, De Renne began making inquiries in an attempt to find someone who would produce a scholarly new catalog for him. It would have to reflect several years of additions and would certainly serve as a more suitable basis for a Georgia bibliography than had the previous one. De Renne, was, however, under no misconception that this second effort would be definitive, for, at the rate he was buying, another catalog could not be far in the future. When completed in 1911, the second catalog recorded a total of around twenty-two hundred titles, showing that some seventeen hundred titles had been acquired since 1905. After the second catalog appeared, the rate of purchases accelerated even more, as the deluxe new volume attracted the attention of an increasing number of dealers and fellow collectors.[97]

The 1911 catalog was prepared by Oscar Wegelin, a Manhattan book dealer and bibliographer, who stayed at Wormsloe for a few weeks in 1910 working in the library. Though his work was a great improvement over the original catalog in some ways, it suffered from hurried composition and inadequate time among the books themselves. This was partly De Renne's fault, for, with the library expanding so rapidly, he valued speed of production over lengthy study and painstaking accuracy. The next catalog, he promised himself, would be exactly what he wanted; the 1911 version was necessarily a stopgap measure.[98]

It was, however, an elegant expedient, on larger paper than the original and bountifully illustrated with thirty-four facsimiles of rare title pages, with a photograph of the library building as frontispiece. The number of copies was actually fewer than that for the 1905 catalog, 200 rather than 250. The number of subject headings, however, was increased to include, among other new sections, one that listed the works to date of "Ulrich Bonnell Phillips, Ph.D.": eighteen volumes, "handsomely bound." All but two of these had been presented by the author, and one of the presentation volumes was the rarity *Deletions,* consisting of pages omitted from Phillips's *Plantation and Frontier Documents* (1909). As Phillips noted in an inscription, "Before the distribution of the type, four proofs of the deletions were made at my request. The present one I have given to Mr. W. J. De Renne, of Wormsloe." [99]

The better known De Renne made his library, the more requests he received from laymen and scholars who wanted to make use of it. These ranged from interested society members in Savannah who wished to research areas that particularly interested them to out-of-state graduate students such as Luther Anderson. As De Renne recalled, Anderson, a student at Yale in 1906, "wrote that at the Lenox Library he had been told that I had the best collection on Saltzburgers known in America, and asked to visit it, as he had a thesis to write on the Saltzburgers of Georgia. He came a total stranger & I was so impressed with his earnestness, that he was invited to stay with us. For three weeks he worked diligently & on his return wrote his thesis. He now has the chair of Modern European History in the Imperial University of Pekin." Other researchers included university professors like Phillips and another native Georgian, C. Mildred Thompson, who found at Wormsloe many obscure pamphlets for use in her study *The Reconstruction of Georgia* (1915). No person who demonstrated a need to use De Renne's books was turned away from Wormsloe. [100]

Distinguished from other academics who used the library was Robert Preston Brooks, the first and only De Renne Professor of Georgia History at the University of Georgia. A native of Milledgeville, Brooks had been schooled at the university and then gone on to become Georgia's first Rhodes scholar. His first major work was a study of conscription during the Civil War. In 1907 Chancellor Barrow wanted to employ Brooks as a professor of Georgia history, a very new concept indeed, and De Renne was an obvious choice to help endow the professorship. De Renne, particularly delighted that Brooks was a native Georgian, agreed to assist with the endowment, but he later stipulated that the funding would continue only as long as the position was held by Brooks, whom De Renne had come to admire. In 1914, with De Renne now contributing the entire endowment, Brooks became De Renne Professor of Georgia History, by vote of the trustees. [101]

Brooks spent a good deal of time at Wormsloe, but not as much as he wished. ("As you are no doubt aware," he wrote De Renne in 1907, "the [university] library is practically without books on Georgia history.") To anyone wishing to use De Renne's treasures there was always the major, insuperable barrier that the library was closed for half the year. This was a special trial to a college professor like Brooks, since the library was not open during the summer, when (despite the less than comfortable conditions of the sweltering Georgia coast) he could have made optimal use of it. Nonetheless, he used De Renne's collection whenever he could and, at other times, De Renne himself answered Brooks's queries by mail.[102]

After his first visit to Wormsloe in December 1907, Brooks wrote. "I feel that I can take up my study of Georgia History with much greater enthusiasm now that I have 'seen the backs' of some of your books. . . . I believe I got most profit from conversing with you and your friends & catching some of the spirit with which you are imbued." Brooks continued to enjoy the hospitality of Wormsloe whenever possible and was stimulated by long conversations with De Renne on a wide range of topics. Occasionally, Brooks sent De Renne books that he had enjoyed that were unrelated to history, including Arthur C. Benson's *Upton Letters*.[103]

Unsurprisingly for the period, some of the conversations between De Renne and Brooks at Wormsloe centered on race; the topic was all but inescapable because part of Brooks's mandate as De Renne professor was to look into the "Negro problem." Apparently because of this subject of common interest and Brooks's particular responsibilities relating to it, the library at Wormsloe had books on the Negro as the largest subsection of works not specifically related to Georgia history. Several of Brooks's articles during his period as De Renne professor would have race as their subject.[104]

Another of the publications of the university's professor of Georgia history was a 1913 history of Georgia for use in the public schools; predictably, it drew from the De Renne library for both sources and illustrations. A brief bibliography of Georgia was also one of Brooks's products during the period.[105]

Brooks was to be on hand for the last of De Renne's grand entertainments at Wormsloe. With the Georgia Historical Society's seventy-fifth anniversary approaching in February 1914, De Renne and the other officers planned numerous festivities for their many important guests. As their keynote speaker, they determined upon J. Franklin Jameson, president of the American Historical Association. A deputation of society members, excluding De Renne—who was too ill to travel—went to Charleston, where the association's 1913 convention was being held, and attempted to persuade Jameson to join them for the coming celebration. Lawton noted that, as had been the case with U. B. Phillips, one of their most persuasive stratagems involved an invitation to explore the library at Wormsloe. Though initially reluctant to commit to a speaking engagement, Jameson was soon won over.[106]

As would be expected at such an important anniversary, the society arranged a splendid banquet at the De Soto for the evening of February 12, 1914, complete with addresses by four distinguished speakers. But perhaps the choicest entertainment was provided earlier that day, at a noon reception at Wormsloe. Given the great interest in the recent Savannah automobile races, De Renne had his 150 guests, who included Georgia governor John M. Slaton, brought to Wormsloe along the public roads that had been used as the racecourse. Upon arrival, Jameson and the others were given a tour of the house, the library, and the "Old Fort" and then served luncheon "out-of-doors on the tennis courts." The meal "consisted of almost everything seasonable and numerous sorts of flowers and evergreens furnished the decorations." Because Jameson's address was set for the Lawton Memorial Hall that afternoon at four and the other orations scheduled for the banquet, the Wormsloe reception was "rather informal and neither speech nor toast-making was indulged in." [107]

There were some gratifying remarks regarding De Renne at the later banquet, however. As was reported in the press, "Governor Slaton . . . spoke of Mr. De Renne as the foremost citizen of the state. Usually compliments paid in after-dinner speeches are like the bubbles of the wine, but the words spoken of Mr. De Renne were like the very spirit of the wine. No man in all of Georgia's broad domain is doing more for her than the modest, unassuming but scholarly and dignified gentleman who is building up a great historical library at Wormsloe." Jameson thoroughly enjoyed his time on the Isle of Hope and left Savannah with a great respect for De Renne and his work. The library at Wormsloe remained for him a very vivid memory.[108]

Herbert Putnam, Librarian of Congress, was never able to accept his standing invitation to visit Wormsloe, though De Renne wrote him that the "contrast [between the Wormsloe library and the Library of Congress] would please & interest you, I am sure." But during the years De Renne was amassing his collection, Putnam followed the Georgian's efforts, applauded them, and did much to further his aims. Their meetings in Washington and their communications were not confined to the subject of the Confederate Constitution—so long on loan to the congressional library—but centered more on Georgiana and how the two facilities could best aid each other. For his part, De Renne presented several gifts to Putnam's library, including a copy of Georgia's earliest almanac. He also on occasion sent duplicates of some of his books, for which he was allowed credits for purchasing some of Putnam's duplicate copies, and the two sometimes made exchanges as well. De Renne also allowed the Library of Congress's map expert, P. Lee Phillips, to visit Wormsloe to examine and document some of the Wormsloe library's rarest cartographic items.[109]

Worthington C. Ford, whom De Renne first knew as head of the Library of Congress's manuscript department, kept in touch with the Georgian after becoming librarian of the Massachusetts Historical Society. Ford, incidentally an uncle by marriage of U. B. Phillips, took a great interest in De Renne's doings, as he himself made history in publishing several of the most important document collections of his day. Something of a southern partisan, despite his New York birth and the location of his headquarters, Ford was a great admirer of both the De Renne Constitution and *Lee's Dispatches*.[110]

Despite many years of cordial relations, it was to be the lot of Worthington Ford and Herbert Putnam to deliver to De Renne the most crushing disappointments that he would suffer as a collector. In fairness to Ford, however, he was only the bearer of bad news. The Massachusetts Historical Society held the only known full run of James Johnston's *Georgia Gazette* (1763–70), a gift of Savannah's Dr. Lemuel Kollock; oddly, his presentation had been made at a time when the Georgia Historical Society existed and would have been grateful for the gift. De Renne proposed to purchase the newspapers from the society at a high price, a type of transaction not unknown during that period. As De Renne pointed out, with Ford's agreement, Savannah was a more appropriate location for the papers because they would certainly be of more interest, and consequently of more use, on the Georgia coast. The Boston board's decision was negative, however, a fact decried by Ford; as a consolation, he worked to have the newspapers photographed and bound for De Renne. Two sets were created, each "an admirable facsimile reproduction, bound in seven handsome volumes, of a unique set of the first 346 numbers": one for the library at Wormsloe and the other for Hodgson Hall.[111]

The disappointing news that Putnam delivered offered no such solace, particularly since it came during the last months of De Renne's life. De

Renne badly wanted the Library of Congress's copy of the rare printing of the Georgia Constitution of 1777 (the "Lancaster Constitution"). He offered in exchange an item not only rare but unique, a map which the Library of Congress wanted very much. Putnam wrote:

> We have considered this suggestion with appreciation, and with a disposition to adopt it, if we could do so without injustice to the Library. I am sorry to say that, as the matter now appears, we do not seem able to. . . . The exchange would involve our relinquishment of an item which, from a bibliographic standpoint, is, if not unique, nearly so; and of which in this form the prospect of our obtaining a duplicate seems practically nil. We should not even have the excuse of transferring this to the custody of a public authority or institution.
>
> Irrespective of legal authority, would you yourself, in my place, feel the exchange to be warrantable?[112]

De Renne, though deeply disappointed, found this letter all but unanswerable, as well as very kind. He pointed out, however, that though his was a private, not a public, library, the Lancaster Constitution would be perfectly secure. Like many collectors, he feared what his own passing might mean to his books and manuscripts: "Death bursts among them like a shell, / And strews them over half the town." Consequently, he had fashioned a will to protect the library. "I have taken every precaution," he wrote Putnam, "to preserve my collection as a whole after my death."[113]

De Renne's letter was unavailing, but meanwhile Leonard Mackall had argued on his behalf in the matter, though unknown to De Renne and without success. Mackall, a late but extremely important player in the story of the development of the library at Wormsloe, was its first and last librarian. In vain he pointed out to Putnam the excellence of the library, the unselfish work of De Renne, and—always an important consideration to Mackall in such matters—the sheer logic of the placement of such an item as the Lancaster Constitution where it best belonged, would get the most use, and would be most appreciated. This was an idea that he often put into practice himself, whether buying from his own pocket items that he felt belonged in the De Renne library or, as in the case of a rare volume of Gibbon (which by luck he found and bought cheaply), sending it as a gift to the foremost Gibbon scholar, a man personally unknown to him.[114]

Mackall's family had been well known to De Renne for years—Mackall was a nephew of General A. R. Lawton and brother-in-law of the painter Gari Melchers, then artistic director of the Telfair Academy. He had been schooled in America and Germany and was an expert on Goethe, as well as a bibliographer of note. His generosity with his time and expertise often led to his taking on projects that he should have refused, but, as a lifelong bachelor, his room for maneuver was considerable. In any case, he had offered to catalog the Telfair's collection of the books and manuscripts of William Brown Hodgson. He did a painstaking, intelligent job and presented to De Renne and the other society officers a cogent report of his activities. De Renne knew at once that circumstances had finally delivered to him the perfect collaborator for completing his library and recording its contents.[115]

De Renne's rapid decline in health made it impossible for him to attend to the library's business and correspondence as closely as he wished, and there was already a need for another catalog. Mackall's celebrated instincts for tracking down obscure titles and elusive volumes would make it possible for the next catalog, De Renne hoped, to be truly complete, even if some of the titles would have to be listed as still missing from the library. Having published two catalogs that failed to satisfy him wholly, De Renne at last had a bibliographer on hand who could produce a comprehensive source that would benefit from both the latest compiler's expertise and his immersion in the collection that was to be listed and described.[116]

To gather as much information as possible for the planned catalog, Mackall began a detailed inventory of many of the library's books, often recording information that would have been lost at De Renne's death, for the dying collector spent many of his last days in the library with Mackall. The new librarian also began a tireless correspondence with the American, British, and German dealers from whom De Renne had purchased books and wrote to pertinent institutions as well. It was very seldom that he did not get the information he wanted, for he was prepared to go to any length—pleading, cajoling, hectoring, shaming—to get what he wanted. He was not successful with all institutions; the Historical Society of Pennsylvania, for example, could not bring itself to comply with Mackall's request to return to Wormsloe all of its copies of the Wormsloe Quartos.[117]

To De Renne, Mackall's presence in the Wormsloe library—and his indefatigable, loving labors with the collection that he had created—gave hope that this would be his "monument more enduring than bronze." He became progressively aware of his own mortality and of the "uncertainties of life." His wife had died suddenly of heart failure in February 1913, some months after they had arrived at an informal agreement to live apart. Mrs. De Renne, who at Wormsloe had become an increasingly unsettling presence to her husband and her children, had planned to live at the Hotel Touraine in New York City, supported by a generous quarterly payment. Instead, she soon died there, of chronic heart disease and pneumonia, and became the first to occupy the plain, massive crypt designed by Wallin and Young as one of their last projects for De Renne: a flat expanse of granite squares, the grated opening to the vault covered by a large raised slab with "De Renne 1913" carved on its face. By the year of his wife's passing, De Renne himself had already received from his doctor a diagnosis of diabetes mellitus, an almost certain death sentence in those days before the isolation of insulin.[118]

In New York City in mid-1914, De Renne crossed the street outside the Hotel Netherland and then found himself too weak to return to the hotel. His doctor, Francis W. Murray, had attended both of De Renne's brothers (and had signed both their death certificates, a task that he would perform for De Renne). He found his patient's diabetic condition aggravated by heart and liver complaints and suggested a course of medication (without complete abstention from alcohol), along with rest and slight exercise, such as riding in his horse-drawn phaeton at Wormsloe.[119]

During the subsequent winter of 1914–15 on the Isle of Hope, De Renne's children prevailed on him to sit for a portrait by Gari Melchers. The finished product was striking: De Renne, hair snow-white, complexion still florid, a study in ravaged dignity.[120] The following winter, his last at Wormsloe, De Renne's days were enlivened by Mackall's productive activity in the library, but there was also the shock in November 1915 of the sudden, unexpected death of Captain Duncan.[121]

When his own death came, De Renne was not at Wormsloe but in his suite at the Hotel Netherland. There, his thoughts still turned to Wormsloe. In one of his last letters to Mackall in the spring, he wrote, "Wormsloe must be beautiful." Mackall had at least seen to it that De Renne was able to add one final elusive volume to his library before he died: *The Charters, etc., of the Provinces of North America* (1766), "a magnificent copy of a rare and valuable volume." A week after this final purchase, on the day he died, De

Renne—all three of his children at his side—solemnly compelled them to make him a last promise, that they would see to it that the final catalog be published as he had intended. Returned to Wormsloe, his body lay in state in the library before the hooded mantel, with his thousands of books arrayed nearby, suggesting, very literally, some lines soon to be published: "*Ses livres veillaient et semblaient pour celui qui n'était plus, le symbole de sa resurrection.*" For his funeral service, De Renne's friends from Savannah crowded the book-lined room, as did dignitaries from elsewhere, including Chancellor Barrow and Professor Brooks, down from Athens.[122]

Brooks soon did the same service for De Renne that Colonel Jones had done for his father in 1880, publishing a suitable eulogy in the press. He noted, in part, that in De Renne's death

> the state suffered the loss of a gentleman who rendered Georgia and the South services of a unique and most valuable character. In other sections of the country it is not unusual for men of large means to devote their time and financial resources to various forms of unselfish social betterment, but in our section the small, wealthy, leisure class have not as a rule, been noteworthy for this sort of activity. In Mr. De Renne's case, the cause to which his life was devoted was one which made appeal to only a limited portion of the community, while, furthermore, the unostentatious manner that characterized his benevolence served to keep his deeds concealed from the general public.[123]

In a memorial eulogy printed later, a committee of De Renne's friends at the Georgia Historical Society also took special note of his passing. One section focused on his striking individuality:

> In character Mr. De Renne was a man of strong personality, and, if a seeming paradox is pardonable, he might fitly be described as a democratic aristocrat. By birth, taste and family training he was an aristocrat, but, in his appreciation of merit and in his admiration for true manhood—he was a democrat. It might be said of him that he combined the highest accomplishments of a Georgia gentleman with the best characteristics of a Texas ranch man. In matters of etiquette, he was punctilious to a fault with his social associates, but on the other hand, he was always ready to extend the right hand of fellowship to any man, whatever his social position might be, who showed an inclination to improve and develop the talents with which nature had blessed him. And, thus, it would happen that Mr. De Renne would resent, as an act of discourtesy, a typewritten reply by one of his acquaintances to an invitation

to dinner, but would welcome at Wormsloe as his guest the humblest individual who showed an interest in Georgia history and desired to avail himself of the treasures of the Wormsloe library.[124]

But perhaps Douglas Southall Freeman evoked De Renne best in the fewest words, in a telegram of condolence to the collector's son and heir: "I grieve with you and the South in the loss of a father whose high patriotism accorded well with his kindly spirit, and whose services to Southern history were excelled only by his loyalty to his friends. He set you a lofty example of manhood." [125]

PART THREE

Inheritors,
1884–1970

CHAPTER 11

Mortmain

We possess nothing certainly except the past.
—EVELYN WAUGH

With the death in 1916 of Wymberley Jones De Renne, the time had come at last for his father's estate to be divided, and the three grandchildren that G. W. J. De Renne had never known finally became his heirs. The Pennsylvania Company of Philadelphia, with the law firm of Lawton and Cunningham as its Savannah agent, had husbanded the estate well. It had bought and sold stocks, collected rents, disposed of unprofitable properties, purchased other property and constructed new buildings, maintained existing properties (including spending $20,000 to improve the mercantile block adjacent to the De Renne Wharf), lent the Georgia Hussars $10,000 for improvements on the former De Renne mansion on Liberty Street, and transformed Wormsloe House into a residence of princely style. The company had also handsomely maintained G. W. J. De Renne's survivors; since 1880, his last surviving son had received over a million dollars in annuities. Nonetheless, the three heirs would share a substantial fortune.[1]

Careful financial management would be a continuing necessity, however, for the heirs would never have an income approaching that enjoyed by their father as an annuitant, and they would not have the luxury of counting on large quarterly checks; extravagance could easily lead to catastrophe. Changes in the local economy and tax structure—manifest even twenty-five years earlier, when the De Renne mansion had passed from the estate—continued and increased in number. Some real property—which G. W. J. De Renne probably thought would be of permanent benefit—would leave the hands of his grandchildren when rents could not keep pace with maintenance costs and property taxes. The national and world economies were changing as well under the rigors of the Great War, raging now for the last two years. What the postwar world would be was past anyone's imagining.[2]

For the sake of convenience, the G. W. J. De Renne estate was subdivided into a Pennsylvania Account, made up mainly of securities (many of which had been the legacy of George Washington Smith and his sisters), and a Georgia Account, principally the extensive Savannah property holdings amassed by G. W. J. De Renne in the middle decades of the previous century. Though it was determined that the securities would be divided among the three siblings so that they could keep or liquidate them as they saw fit, Wymberley Wormsloe De Renne and his sisters decided to hold the Savannah property as tenants in common, leaving Lawton and Cunningham to oversee and maintain their holdings and to distribute the monthly profits among them. Wormsloe, however, was to be held individually by Wymberley, to whom his sisters transferred their interests.[3]

Aside from their grandfather's legacy, their father's personal estate provided handsome bequests for the three, particularly in ready cash (which De Renne had begun to distribute generously in the months before his death), and gave them certain real estate as well. Unlike the equal sharing of their grandfather's estate, however, their father's bequests more closely resembled primogeniture than those from any previous Jones–De Renne will. Of the over $93,000 in property and bonds, Elfrida De Renne Barrow and Audrey De Renne Coerr received the family silver (valued at about $2,000), the family jewels (over $10,000), and the house and lot on Liberty Street where the Barrows lived ($15,000—presumably the only bequest destined for liquidation since the other items were heirlooms), for a total of over $27,000 worth of property to be divided by the sisters. Of the almost $85,000 in cash and insurance, however, Mrs. Barrow and Mrs. Coerr divided over $67,000.[4]

Wymberley, on the other hand, was left the library (its value very conservatively estimated at $45,000); the four "Dupon" lots immediately north of Wormsloe ($100); some silver, furniture, and other property at Wormsloe (over $4,000); and almost $17,000 in bonds: a total of around $66,000 (roughly 40 percent of his father's estate) plus a $2,400 commission as his father's executor; his total share (including his portion of his grandfather's estate) was around half a million dollars.[5]

Wormsloe, of course, was part of the legacy of G. W. J. De Renne, theoretically to be shared by the three siblings. But the sisters honored their father's wish that his son become the master of Wormsloe. By this time Audrey had left Savannah for good, joining her physician husband in New York City, where they lived for a time before traveling to Europe. Elfrida soon purchased Audrey's half-interest in the frame house on Liberty Street where the Barrows were making their home, though they would soon move to a larger house on Chippewa Square. When Wormsloe was conveyed to Wymberley on February 17, 1917 (the same day that his sisters took possession of their bequests), he purchased the house and grounds for "Ten Dollars . . . and other valuable considerations . . . paid at or before the sealing." Any additional transactions between the brother and his sisters were not explicitly detailed, but by the end of February, Wymberley had given Elfrida a check for over $25,000, and Audrey one for $2,300. Whether this transaction related to his coming into the ownership of Wormsloe is a matter for speculation; the plantation had been valued at only $20,000 in 1880, and in 1917 the residence was insured for only $16,500. Events would show that a reasonable money value for Wormsloe at the time would have been only about $30,000. Nonetheless, Wymberley's recollection, for which no documentation has been found, was that he had paid his sisters $100,000, which, in his words, "was supposed even then to be a nominal value between heirs."[6]

Audrey Coerr, for all her love of Wormsloe, would see little of it for the rest of her life. She and her family spent much of their time in Europe, staying in such familiar resorts as Biarritz, Bagnor, Lausanne, and Vevey, and did not return permanently to the United States until 1923. Then, despite her youthful antipathy toward Philadelphia, she and her husband settled just west of the city at Ardmore, where they purchased Broadsteps, a "nice, comfortable, old place." Nearby, "on its high wooded ridge," was Fairhill — the Gothic stone mansion of her half-brother, Dr. Charles Camblos Norris—and, she noted happily, Wanamaker's Department Store in downtown Philadelphia was also within an easy drive.[7]

Wymberley Wormsloe De Renne entered upon his inheritance at a time when his life had been marked for several years by exploration and change, losses and challenges. Only in 1911, after Wymberley had begun studying for his university degree, had his father become satisfied that he was finally free of the chronic illnesses that had troubled his childhood and adolescence. The next year Audrey had married and moved from his orbit, and the year after that—after her permanent departure from Wormsloe—his mother had died. Then, only weeks after Wymberley graduated from Columbia on June 7, 1916, came his father's death. The remaining months of 1916 and the early months of 1917 found the young man absorbed in settling his father's estate, of which he and his father's lawyer friend George Owens were the executors.[8]

When Congress declared war on Germany in April 1917, Wymberley began a series of attempts to join the armed forces. Ultimately, he was accepted into the Army National Guard and was in training from the summer to the early fall of 1917. In November 1917 he was commissioned a second lieutenant, but soon thereafter he was injured in an automobile accident. After a brief hospitalization, he was sent home on leave until February 1918. During this furlough, he met a Savannah beauty, Augusta Gallie Floyd, and fell immediately in love; after a seven-week courtship, he proposed and was accepted.[9]

Augusta Floyd was from an old Georgia family. One of her most famous ancestors was Major General John Floyd, an Indian-fighting general of the Creek War, as well as a wealthy planter, owner of Bellevue in Camden County, with its unique plantation house, a masonry structure shaped like an anchor. Augusta's widowed father, Thomas Bourke Floyd, was in the cotton business in Savannah, as was her brother Marmaduke.[10]

Since Wymberley was attached to the Sixty-second Infantry Brigade, Thirty-first Division, as aide-de-camp to Brigadier General Robert E. Steiner, he found himself bound for France. Consequently, he and Augusta decided to marry as soon as possible. The wedding was "quietly solemnized" by the Reverend John Durham Wing at Savannah's Christ Church on Saturday, March 9, 1918, with the groom in his uniform and General Steiner in attendance. Dr. Charles Camblos Norris stood as best man, and Augusta's sister Frances was maid of honor, while Dr. Barrow and George

Noble Jones II served as ushers. Since the Lenten season had begun, there were no decorations.[11]

Before the embarkation, Wymberley was posted to Camp Wheeler near Macon, Georgia. Consequently—after a brief wedding trip to Washington, D.C., and New York City—the couple extended their honeymoon; officers were allowed to find billets in town, so the De Rennes, along with such amenities as the wedding silver, moved into a suite at the Dempsey Hotel. Soon Wymberley, now a first lieutenant, was sent across the Atlantic on the USS *Hamburg* and during the voyage took his turn as a lookout for U-boats. Meanwhile, Augusta went to the Finch School in New York City to take some courses, but she was back in Savannah by December. There she spent her first Christmas at Wormsloe, receiving detailed instructions from Wymberley on how the holiday festivities were to be conducted for all the staff and workmen and their families.[12]

Some of the ferocious battles that broke the Kaiser's army were fought after Wymberley arrived in France, but his "Dixie Division" was safely in the rear in a support capacity. As liaison officer, he had some leisure time for reading and for writing letters, and, in fact, spent much of his time at the moated Château Malicorne near Le Mans, where General Steiner was headquartered. Wymberley's knowledge of French greatly helped the general, who used him as an interpreter. All told, Wymberley was stationed in France for only three months, and, by January 1919, honorably discharged, had returned to Wormsloe.[13]

As only the second De Renne to be full master of the estate, Wymberley continued several traditions, two of the most important of which concerned the Georgia Historical Society and the De Renne library; in a sense, for him the two had become intertwined. As had been the case with his grandfather many decades earlier, during the year he reached his majority Wymberley had received notification of his election as a member of the society. And at the death of W. J. De Renne, the society had immediately honored the son with his father's seat on the Board of Curators. Wymberley served actively, working, as had his father, on the Committee on Publishing and Printing. Sixteen years later, his services were gratefully noted when the society elected him to one of the few honorary memberships it ever conferred.[14]

Following his father's example, Wymberley appeared in such disparate places as the fitting rooms of Brooks Brothers, the hunting trails of the Tourilli Club, and the convivial fastness of the Union Club. For a brief time in early 1917, before spending half the year in training camp, he had first performed the various duties that fell to Wormsloe's master (including replenishing the flowers and expanding the shrubbery), and he also had a gatehouse built at the end of the new oak avenue, just southwest of the Wormsloe arch.[15]

From the time of his father's death, Wymberley worked to assure that his father's "monument," the De Renne Georgia Library, be completed and cataloged. Interested parties—mainly librarians and book dealers—received an engraved notice, dated July 10, 1916, which, over Wymberley's signature, announced in black letters:

> Wymberley Jones De Renne, founder of the Wymberley Jones De Renne Georgia Library of books, manuscripts and maps relating to the State of Georgia, died on June 23, 1916. He bequeathed all his collections to his son, Wymberley W. De Renne.
>
> These collections will be maintained and added to as heretofore. Mr. De Renne's friend, Leonard L. Mackall, who has been in charge of the Library since he entered upon the preparation of a new Catalogue in March, will continue the work.
>
> Communications should be addressed to the Wymberley Jones De Renne Georgia Library, Post Office Box 1166, Savannah, Ga.[16]

Wymberley gave Mackall carte blanche to fill as many voids as possible in the Georgia collection so that the library itself—and the catalog that was to make it more accessible to historians—would be as complete as possible. This was a necessity, for, as rich as the library was, it still lacked many volumes and could have given its assembler pleasant challenges for decades into the future. As it was, over $10,000 was spent in making additions. In 1917 Wymberley also hired the Yale-educated antiquarian William Price to work as Mackall's assistant. The same year young De Renne moved to correct one of the library's most serious deficiencies, the lack of ready, systematic access to the family archive. Consequently, Wymberley employed Savannah accountant Chipley R. Setz, treasurer of the city of Savannah, to arrange and catalog the library's voluminous Jones–De Renne family papers.[17]

All who were concerned in the library effort—but Mackall in particular—knew how much it had meant to W. J. De Renne that his collection be completed and suitably cataloged as quickly as possible. De Renne's original idea could have been realized fairly rapidly; he had thought of simply issuing a supplement to the Wegelin catalog of 1911, following its pattern, while listing additions and correcting errors.[18]

But an early publication date was precluded by the model that De Renne had ultimately chosen: the voluminous five-volume E. D. Church catalog of Americana, published in 1907. Church, a wealthy New York business-man born a decade after De Renne's father, had not begun collecting un-til the 1880s, when he purchased numerous books from the estate of Henry Stevens. These titles had formed the beginning of what would be-come a choice collection of some two thousand volumes relating to the his-tory of the Americas, published from 1482 to 1884. Generously illustrated with hundreds of title-page facsimiles (most of them actual size), the Church catalog had brought to reality Henry Stevens's dream of a "photo-bibliography" and included detailed information for each book, including collation by both signatures and pagination (with complete title-page in-formation, separated by division lines), as well as copious annotations, including locations of other copies and bibliographical references. The Church catalog thus laid claim to being the first comparative bibliography, facilitating the identification of "imperfect or variant copies." [19]

Mackall, with the Church catalog as his guide, began the process of tran-scribing all necessary information from the books onto large note cards, with William Price as his assistant for a year and a half (1916–17). Work-ing with the 1911 catalog particularly, Price corrected and expanded its en-tries and also worked on cards for more recent acquisitions. At the same time Mackall directed a steady stream of correspondence toward dealers and librarians across the country, in search of information on the library's most significant volumes, and also began building a peerless collection of pertinent bibliographies to support his research.[20]

Though he felt fully confident when dealing with nineteenth- and twen-tieth-century volumes, Mackall decided that someone with more expertise should describe the earlier volumes. Who better than George Watson Cole, compiler of the Church catalog? By that time Cole had seen the Church col-lection purchased for over a million dollars by the railroad magnate Henry Edwards Huntington, who had hired him to catalog the rest of his bur-geoning collection, preparatory to its removal to his recently completed mansion in San Marino, California. Nonetheless, Cole—assisted by his col-league Herman Ralph Mead—was allowed to travel to Wormsloe and la-bor there for most of the steaming August of 1917, while Wymberley was away for basic training. It seemed possible that the new catalog, which reportedly would resemble the Egmont quarto in appearance, might indeed be published by the end of 1917, as one published report indicated.[21]

By year's end, however, Mackall's halcyon days at Wormsloe were drawing to a close. Wymberley, having allowed the expenditure of thousands of dollars as Mackall filled in the gaps on the library shelves, at last ordered a retrenchment. With his marriage imminent (as well as his probable assignment to the American Expeditionary Force bound for France), the young heir determined to postpone further work on the catalog and in January 1918 suspended further purchases for the library. The same month, however, as Mackall continued his labors, he received expert assistance with the library's colonial laws from T. L. Cole, who worked for a week at Wormsloe with the extensive collection of legislative acts and related legal works, lending his authority to that series of cards. But for 1918 and 1919, Mackall would have only this temporary but crucial assistance. William Price was gone, and there was no one to take his place. The only other significant help that Mackall would enjoy was from the lawyer-historian Edgar L. Pennington, a friend of Wymberley's from his university days, who had been editor of the *Georgian*. For a few days in 1919, Pennington worked on the more recent additions to the library and prepared annotations for some of the travel volumes in the collection.[22]

Perhaps the most remarkable of Mackall's labors in 1918 was his preparation of an absorbing paper that "[placed] permanently on record as much concrete information as possible on the history and scope of the Library." Delivered as a lecture before the Georgia Historical Society in May 1918, it was published in the *Georgia Historical Quarterly* the next month, with abundant annotations and a frontispiece of the library building. Having completed the production of the cards that would be the basis of the catalog, as well as having written a comprehensive history of the library while its wonders were fresh in his mind, Mackall then moved to New York. There he wrote a regular column on books for the *New York Herald Tribune* and continued to make a name for himself in scholarly circles.[23]

It would fall to the new master of Wormsloe, recently returned from France, to perfect plans for his library's catalog. He visited New York's celebrated American Art Association, which, despite its name, was also involved in cataloging and selling libraries, among them those of Henry Ward Beecher and the collector of Americana S. L. M. Barlow. Wymberley made an arrangement to complete Mackall's work with Azalea Hallett Clizbee, the association's head cataloger (and a devoted bibliophile herself). She was well qualified to finish the project by converting the mass of cards into a useful reference. Miss Clizbee received the cards and her instructions in 1920 but almost immediately was forced to put her work on hold: severe business reverses left Wymberley unable to finance her labors. Over a decade would pass before her work could be completed and the catalog published.[24]

Wymberley was unable to bring the project to a timely conclusion because of catastrophic financial problems. While he had followed the family tradition of bibliophily, he had also chosen to mirror his father in another, more dangerous respect, expanding on his father's limited ventures into real estate and business. Young Wymberley took his business interests so seriously that, in a sense, he let them define him. Whereas his father and grandfather had described themselves in the nineteenth-century manner, which differentiated between "quality" (in their case, "gentleman") and "profession," Wymberley proudly listed himself in modern fashion as a "capitalist."[25]

For his first major capitalistic endeavor, Wymberley emulated his father, who in 1906 had persuaded the Pennsylvania Company to construct two three-story apartment buildings on Liberty Street, just east of the De Soto. Popularly known as the De Renne Apartments, they were actually named Frederica and Sunbury after fortified colonial towns of the Georgia coast. Respectable additions to G. W. J. De Renne's estate, the apartment buildings produced a decent monthly sum for the heirs until they sold them in 1920.[26]

At the end of the war, however, there were numerous reports in the press and elsewhere regarding the number of people, veterans and others, who would soon be moving to Savannah and looking for a place to live. Wymberley determined to create an even larger apartment building on Liberty Street at Drayton; it would quite literally overshadow the original apartment complex associated with the family name. This venture was far from risk-free, however, and the lawyers at Lawton and Cunningham argued forcefully, though without success, against Wymberley's undertaking such a mammoth project in uncertain times. He forged ahead nonetheless and spent over $142,000 in 1919 and 1920 just buying up property for the building's construction and for later developments that he planned for its immediate vicinity. Some of his capital came from the proceeds of the heirs' sale of several of their Savannah properties—the De Renne Wharf, for instance, was sold for over $60,000 in 1919 (though the adjacent De Renne Block would long remain at least partially owned by the family). In financing the project, he offered, through the Citizens and Southern Bank, "6 per cent. bonds, amounting to $225,000, to be secured by a first mortgage on the apartment building." The announcement of the bond noted that the apartment building would represent "an investment of approximately $500,000." Not mentioned was the fact that this sum closely approximated De Renne's entire inheritance.[27]

The building itself, designed by Henrik Wallin and constructed by the Artley Company, was an impressive masonry structure of eight stories and forty-four apartments, each of which had French doors leading to recessed balconies. High above the pavement, a frieze of colored tiles decorated the area between the top windows and the parapet roof. Justly called "an ornament to Savannah," the Georgian Revival building also deserved its description as "the last word in comfort and elegance." The structure was U-shaped, its open end pointing toward Liberty Street, where residents and visitors entered its spacious courtyard through a colonnade. Across the top of its square central arch were the words *De Renne Apartments*, beneath an elaborate cartouche of a palmetto tree. Behind wide glass doors was the lobby, from which halls led to various offices available for rent and to the elevator. Upstairs the elevator opened onto halls whose doors led to the apartments' own private halls, a new feature in Savannah apartment buildings. Such colors as old ivory, buff, and pale gray predominated in the rooms. Amenities unusual for the time included many built-in conveniences: spacious closets for the bedrooms, medicine chests for the bathrooms, and gas ranges, refrigerators, and garbage disposals for the kitchens. The De Rennes themselves planned to use one of the apartments, making it their Savannah stop, much as Wymberley's father had used the De Soto.[28]

Others in Savannah joined De Renne in participating in the building boom; indeed, it was estimated that construction in Savannah during the time the De Renne Apartments were being built jumped 900 percent. Ready to compete with the De Renne Apartments by the fall of 1920, for example, were the Forsyth Apartments, six stories and sixty apartments, adjacent to the park near Hodgson Hall. In any event, there was soon a housing surplus instead of a shortage, accompanied by a sharp lowering of rents.

And by the end of 1920, there came "the most drastic price collapse in cotton history," a portentous event for the city and port of Savannah.[29]

Even in the early months of 1920 there had been a steep rise in the cost of living, attributed by one of the Savannah newspapers to the excesses of an "era of dizzy optimism" in which many Savannahians had lived since the end of the war. The conflict's end had indeed brought on a "period of unexcelled prosperity." But according to an editorial, "the strange thing is that nobody seems to realize that the only remedy for the high cost of living is simpler living and careful economy. There has never been an era of greater extravagance in this country. Everybody is spending. Money has fallen into hands that never held it before and it is slipping through very rapidly. Those who have always lived with a certain degree of comfort and elegance are keeping to their accustomed habits while paying three or four times what they have formerly paid." The solution offered was "self-restraint and economy," but the paper noted that instead everyone preferred "to keep up a dizzy hopefulness that somehow and in some way everything will come out all right."[30]

The majority of the units in the De Renne Apartments had been rented in January 1920, long before the building's opening the following September. But the excessive costs of purchasing property and constructing the towering structure—along with other investments—had all but absorbed Wymberley's fortune. By the end of 1920 he had mortgaged Wormsloe, one of the few properties not held with his sisters as tenants in common. This mortgage of the ancestral estate, without consulting Audrey or Elfrida, was a step that would have momentous repercussions; it set into motion an inexorable progression of events that would have agonizing consequences. Presciently, Audrey, always his champion, had written Wymberley to impress upon him that whatever happened, Wormsloe should never be mortgaged "out of the family"—that, in short, Wormsloe was to be considered "absolutely *sacred.*" Unknown to her, Wormsloe had been mortgaged at the time she wrote.[31]

For a while, Wymberley was able to fend off his creditors by liquidating stocks and by selling or borrowing on some of the properties he had purchased in his own name, as well as selling his one-third interest in some of the family properties and using funds generously lent to him by Audrey Coerr. And in 1925 he secured a loan of $225,000. But as his financial situation continued to deteriorate, he had to make arrangements to sell his portion of Poplar Grove, the largest property held jointly by the siblings. Consequently, in 1928 Wymberley arranged with his sisters for a partition of the old plantation, and before long the idea of holding the family properties as tenants in common was abandoned. Finally, in 1929, Lawton and Cunningham turned over the management of the remaining family properties to a real estate agency.[52]

In addition to De Renne's manifold worries regarding his general financial situation, there were concerns about maintaining Wormsloe itself, house and grounds, as well as the paramount responsibility of caring for his wife and two young sons: Inigo Jones De Renne, born in 1919, and Kentwyn Floyd De Renne, who had arrived four years later. Wymberley tried to make money with measures of varying practicality and success, including speculation in Florida real estate and the expansion of Wormsloe's dairying operations, later leased to Foremost Dairy Products. But it became obvious that another expedient was desperately needed. Thus came a new manifestation of Wormsloe, which would make the estate's name much more commonly known than before, not only in Georgia and the Southeast but beyond: Wormsloe Gardens.[53]

In their earliest years at their plantation home, the De Rennes had occasionally hosted events for the benefit of favored organizations: Wymberley's Georgia Historical Society and Augusta's Colonial Dames in particular. Invitations to Wormsloe were widely coveted, and visitors often bemoaned that the beauties of the De Rennes' Eden were shared with others so infrequently. Beginning in 1925 annual one-day spring tours were conducted, with the proceeds given to the Colonial Dames. By this time, some South Carolina plantations had begun to welcome paying tourists on a regular basis. And in 1926, the *Atlanta Constitution* publicized Wormsloe—though still a very private estate—as one of Georgia's "Seven Natural Wonders"; the article made special mention of the plantation's historic importance and of the presence there of "the world's finest collection of books on Georgia."[54]

Thus the De Rennes decided to open not only the gardens but the Old Fort and the library as well during the day of the 1927 annual tour. The visitors' response encouraged them, and they soon announced that in future years Wormsloe would be open to the general public during the entire azalea season, with a nominal entrance fee charged. By the last week in June 1927, however, the gardens were open on a daily basis. And by September, Wormsloe and its various attractions were being advertised in tandem with the opening of the Owens House, a Regency mansion designed by William Jay that graced Oglethorpe Square; both, following "a custom . . . adopted during the last few years by Charleston and other Southern cities," would be open to tourists during the winter of 1927–28. But Wormsloe Gardens had evolved into a year-round attraction and would be promoted aggressively by Wymberley, the Savannah Board of Trade, and, later, the Savannah Chamber of Commerce.[55]

The genesis of the plantation's gardens could be traced back to the 1760s, in the time of Noble Jones, when the Savannah press had begun noticing Wormsloe's horticultural richness. Later, G. W. J. and Mary De Renne had expanded the gardens significantly, and their eldest son had brought them to near perfection. Augusta De Renne, during her first winter at Wormsloe (1918–19), had begun her own additions, beginning with a small flower garden near the library. She next created a formal garden opposite the south front of the residence, beginning in the late summer of 1925.[56]

The formal garden—actually a complex of three adjacent gardens—developed over several years into an L-shaped arrangement of mellowed brick walls and flagstone walks, with parterres containing everything from fountains, birdbaths, and graceful bronzes to whimsical terra-cotta gnomes. Also incorporated were elements from other coastal historical sites, including four impressive Ionic columns from the ruins of Thomas Spalding's Sapelo and handsome wrought-iron grills, salvaged after a twentieth-century renovation of the old De Renne mansion on Liberty Street.[57]

The first of Mrs. De Renne's three interconnected gardens centered around the extant circular pool and fountain, with its handsome bronze waterfowl, that lay just south of the porte cochere and dated from the late 1890s. She made the pool the center of a rectangular garden that paralleled the house's south front, bounded by a two-foot-high brick wall surmounted by a wrought-iron fence. Arbors thick with climbing roses occupied the corners and the center of the east wall; two other arbors enclosed gateways that broke the north and south walls opposite the fountain. Inside the wall and following its perimeter, a herbaceous border grew in a narrow band toward the flagstones. Flanking the fountain were four beds, filled with cypresses, azaleas, and roses, along with snowdrops, brought from Bellevue, the coastal plantation of Mrs. De Renne's ancestors. At the garden's western border, the Sapelo columns were ranged "after a Pompeiian manner." Just beyond the south wall, in the direction of the library, stood a tall dovecote with a steep, pointed roof similar to those of the tower and porte cochere; it was equipped with small mirrors for the amusement of the preening tumblers and fantails that resided there and "added greatly" to Mrs. De Renne's enjoyment of her creation.[58]

In 1928, Augusta De Renne completed her work by adding a sunken garden immediately west of the original garden and a gnome garden at a right angle to the south, forming the short leg of the L-shaped design. The sunken garden was the simplest and most private of the three, with a solid, ivy-covered wall to the west, fitted with a cypress door in its center; a small circular grill set into the south wall afforded a view into the adjacent gnome garden. The remaining two walls were more open, with grillwork flanking the wide opening in the east wall; there three steps led down into the garden, with rock gardens running in both directions from the sill, surrounding a grassy central area. Various kinds of greenery dominated this garden, which contained four beautiful bronzes, including an exuberant interpretation of Robert Browning's "Pippa," along with a pensive girl. And there were as well two graceful female nudes: one held a ewer over the central well-like pool; the other grasped a water lily whose stem pointed to the hour on a sundial in the statue's base.[59]

The gnome garden, sometimes called the brownie garden, displayed the De Renne mansion grillwork in its western wall and held an old iron fountain that dripped water, "in the Moorish manner," into a brick-encased pool that was decorated with iron water lilies. On the brick ledge around the pool, yellow calla lilies grew from a collection of jugs and jars. In the parterres surrounding the fountain sat the imported German gnomes, particular favorites of younger visitors. The entire effect of the gnome garden, wrote Mrs. De Renne, was that it be "quaint though formal." From her second-story bedroom, Augusta De Renne had a fine view of all three components of her garden, laid out below her like roofless adjoining rooms.[40]

Greatly admired by those who saw it, the formal garden was not just a pleasure to Mrs. De Renne's friends and guests but also brought her the recognition that such work deserved. Among her most treasured plaudits was one reported in 1932, in *The Garden Club of Georgia Yearbook:* "The real achievement of Mrs. De Renne's garden at Wormsloe has been recognized," it noted, "as is shown by her election to the Garden Club of America."[41]

The formal garden was complemented by a thick wilderness of azaleas and camellias that spread under the oaks to the front and, particularly, the rear of the residence. Instead of grass, Algerian ivy covered most of the ground in open spaces. Oyster-shell paths led through the flowered masses of vegetation, whose blossoms were reflected in the still waters of pools; one focal point was a spring that flowed in a thin stream from a large, ornamental stone acorn. Here and there stone benches awaited those who wished to rest and admire the magnificent surroundings.[12]

Wormsloe Gardens also offered other attractions to lure enthusiasts of history as well as lovers of natural beauty. There was, of course, the fundamental appeal of visiting the oldest estate in Georgia to be continuously owned by the same family. But to that attraction was added an opportunity to venture out on automobile side trips further south into the plantation, after completing the garden tour. One of the slave houses, for example, was opened for sightseers. Filled with utensils, tools, and artifacts appropriate to the late antebellum era, the structure eventually also housed an aged woman said to have been born into bondage there. Nearby was the old slave cemetery, with its low, projecting markers, carved from oak, and, just beyond, the massive granite monument of the ancient family plot. Two other stops allowed visitors to view fortifications built over a century apart: the crumbling tabby walls of the old fortified residence of Noble Jones's day and the clearly distinguishable Confederate earthworks at Jones Point, accessible by a narrow road that wound through the pine woods.[13]

A typical tour of Wormsloe Gardens began just off Skidaway Road at the arched gateway, where tickets were usually purchased. Tourists proceeded down the stunningly picturesque oak avenue and parked under the trees near the gardens' entrance on the east side of the avenue; if none of the guides came to meet them, tourists could ring the plantation bell at the entrance gate to gain admittance. Behind the gate, Ermentra Williams (who also served as governess at Wormsloe House) presided in a log cabin built for receiving visitors; on one wall was a beautifully detailed eight-by-twelve-foot map of Wormsloe, the work of Mrs. De Renne's brother Marmaduke Floyd. For a time, the cabin also housed a tearoom, operated by the Savannah Junior League. After Miss Williams welcomed them and took their tickets, tourists were provided with a guide, normally one of about a dozen black youths from the nearby hamlet of Sandfly. Occasionally, during the peak of the season, some visitors were escorted by the dignified major domo of Wormsloe House, Frank Jenkins, who was pressed into service when crowds were particularly large.[14]

The guides delivered a lengthy speech, prepared by Wymberley; it covered such subjects as the history of the plantation, the age of its structures, and the varieties of its flora and fauna. Among the trees particularly commended to notice was an ancient mulberry, a relic of the days of colonial Georgia's silk culture. In one of the outbuildings was a display of hundreds of stuffed animals. One of W. J. De Renne's lesser-known collections, it included examples of all the birds and mammals indigenous to Chatham County. The walls of this "fauna room" were decorated with photographs and etchings of the plantation. And postcards were available for purchase, featuring views of the natural and man-made attractions of Wormsloe; some came from photographs, either tinted or sepia-tone, while others displayed the artwork of the Savannah artist Christopher Murphy, Jr.[15]

The walking tour featured the gardens at the back of the house, including the formal garden. At the height of the blooming season, the vistas were almost overwhelming, with the dark, dense foliage providing the perfect backdrop for the multicolored petals of the azaleas and camellias—the most popular and abundant of the gardens' flowering shrubs—as well as for the delicate flower clusters of the climbing wisteria.[16]

At some times, the first floor of the residence itself was open for tours; the twin pyramid mantels were a popular attraction. A guidebook of the period also reports that it was possible to mount the "tortuous stair" to the roof for a panoramic view of the estate and the river and islands beyond. The library was usually open, at least to allow visitors either to peer through its screen door, or, if more fortunate, to enter the chamber and view the collection from behind a barrier set up just past the entrance. On special occasions, the Confederate Constitution, transported from its vault in town, was displayed before the hooded mantel. Later, to provide more suitable (yet still secure) exhibits, Wymberley placed glass-topped display tables just beyond the barrier near the door. Particular volumes and other items of interest could be viewed without endangering them, though tourists were never allowed access to the shelves. At various times, however, the library was again made available to scholars who wished to work there. Among them were Amos A. Ettinger, who did research there for his exhaustive 1936 Oglethorpe biography; John Donald Wade, who consulted the library's sources for his biography of Augustus Baldwin Longstreet; and Haywood J. Pearce, Jr., who tapped the Jones Confederate Collection for his life of Benjamin H. Hill.[17]

A particular attraction of the library, beginning in 1933, Georgia's bicentennial year, was a collection of artifacts excavated from the tabby ruins (called "Fort Wymberley" in the gardens' promotional literature). The assorted bottles, plates, and metal implements had been recovered by Augusta's brother Marmaduke, a keen amateur archaeologist, who dug several trenches through the old site.[48]

During the eleven years the gardens were open year-round to the public, they attained great popularity, despite the fact that the Great Depression began only two years after the 1927 opening. The representatives of the Board of Trade in Savannah were fully aware of the importance of this and other attractions to the financial health of the city and county, particularly given the area's location on the Atlantic Coast Highway; a valuable conduit for the increasingly lucrative tourist trade, it pushed "further north every year." By 1928, Savannah's "hotels were filled, the garages crowded, and the . . . route filled with trippers.[49]

The Central of Georgia Railway recognized Wormsloe Gardens as a uniquely attractive destination for spring excursions, and it helped Wymberley with promotion, particularly by sponsoring a March 1929 visit to Wormsloe by Georgia journalists and photographers. This visit, during which Wymberley's guests were afforded the finest hospitality, resulted in a plethora of newspaper coverage. Consequently, that year's azalea season at Wormsloe Gardens was inaugurated with reams of free publicity: articles, most of them detailed and often generously illustrated, appeared in Georgia's major newspapers and in many minor ones as well. Moreover, the gardens also appeared on celluloid in 1929, in a segment of a Metro-Goldwyn-Mayer newsreel.[50]

The master of Wormsloe worked tirelessly to attract visitors to the estate, generating a barrage of correspondence that inundated local and out-of-state newspapers, as well as scores of automobile and tourist associations and numerous proprietors of other southern attractions. Their good words and conspicuous display of Wormsloe materials, including postcards and decorative maps, sent numerous readers and guests to Wormsloe. Wymberley's constant efforts made Wormsloe Gardens a rival to Magnolia Gardens and Middleton Place in neighboring South Carolina and won it mention in all lists of Georgia's natural and historic attractions.[51]

People came in droves, particularly during the spring blooming season. But no doubt the historical attractions were important in making Wormsloe Gardens a viable concern in what otherwise would have been the off-season, when the oaks and the luxuriant green foliage were the principal natural attractions. By the late 1920s there was widespread, increasing evidence of attempts by public and private owners of historical attractions across America to lure tourists with the "improving" aspects of travel; and in the same period numerous roadside historical markers began to dot the southern landscape.[52]

Among the many visitors to Wormsloe Gardens were the famous and celebrated of the day, including Henry Ford, who drove up from his Georgia estate at nearby Richmond Hill. There he was having his own Confederate earthworks, Fort McAllister, restored. Indeed, more than anyone else Ford would be given credit for the growing popularity of such attractions as Wormsloe Gardens, since his automobile had "democratized travel" and made many "out-of-the-way natural wonders and historic sites accessible."[53]

Writers came to Wormsloe as well, including Herschel Brickell, who wrote a graceful appreciation for the *North American Review* in 1933. Brickell compared Savannah favorably to Charleston, noting that the Georgia port had "as much Revolutionary history as Charleston, but less pride"; the quaint old town, he noted thankfully, was "wholly uncommercialized and likely to remain so unless it is put into a successful novel and sets out to imitate art." As impressed as he was by Savannah, Brickell wrote, "There is nothing in or near it so fine as Wormsloe, the plantation home of the De Renne family, with a library housing the most complete collection of documents and books relating to the history of Georgia in existence, the work of three generations of collectors, and great oaks covered with Algerian ivy, and japonicas of large size and brilliant color, and all the other flowers that make the gardens of this part of the South worth crossing oceans to see."[54]

The popular novelist Ben Ames Williams visited Wormsloe in the late 1920s; his 1930 novel *Great Oaks,* set on a coastal Georgia plantation, seemed to draw part of its inspiration from Wormsloe, just as Fanny Heaslip Lea's *Good-bye Summer* (1931) certainly did. As the New Orleans-born novelist admitted, her fictional plantation Riversedge, with its rambling riverside house, tabby ruins, and slave graveyard, was based on her memories of a visit to Wormsloe. She was enchanted by the estate, which she called "the loveliest bit of the true South I have ever seen," a phrase that would be used to describe Wormsloe for decades.[55]

Savannah's most famous expatriate son of the period, Julien Green (1900–1998), came to see Wormsloe, and details of the house and landscape were to appear in some of his novels in coming years; *Each Man in His Darkness* would even use the name Wormsloe for one of Green's fictional plantations. In January 1934, Green visited the De Rennes and committed a detailed, rather eldritch description of the estate to his diary. "Wormsloe," he wrote, "is an old house hidden in the heart of a dusky park. It is protected by ghostly oaks; these giant trees are covered with Spanish moss that hangs in gray tatters continually stirred by the breeze, and nothing can be stranger than the light that filters through this sort of airy, funereal fabric." Of Wormsloe House he noted, "Its name would have delighted Poe, its name and all the shadow that moves through the low-ceilinged, silent rooms." [56]

Many other newsworthy figures of the day also visited Wormsloe Gardens, not only from the world of literature and the arts but from the realm of politics and diplomacy as well. In the spring of 1929 the *Atlanta Constitution* reported that in the "library's visitors' register are found the names of Ruth Draper, Walter Damrosch, James Stevens, of Dublin; DuBose and Dorothy Hayward; George S. Chappell, of *Vanity Fair*; Cyrus H. K. Curtis, of the *Saturday Evening Post*; former Governor Al Smith of New York; Julia Peterkin; S. Claudel, French ambassador to the United States, and many others of prominence." [57]

Wormsloe's visual wonders also attracted artists and photographers. Savannah's Christopher Murphy, Jr., became most firmly identified as an interpreter of Wormsloe; he executed a series of evocative drawings and etchings of the gardens, house, and library, which he exhibited in both the North and the South. Cornelia Cunningham, of Savannah and Atlanta, produced her own pen-and-ink interpretations of similar views, including the only image of the slave cemetery that has survived. And Bayard Wootten, famed photographer of the low country, did a series of views of the house and library, the river and the gardens, which she incorporated into her popular lantern-slide and lecture presentation on gardens of the coastal South. The work of Murphy and Wootten appeared in two of the several series of postcards that were offered at the plantation gift shop and elsewhere, and Cunningham's sketch of the Wormsloe arched gateway served as the cover illustration for a 1937 booklet, produced for sale at Wormsloe Gardens, titled *Wormsloe: An Historic Plantation Dating from 1733.* [58]

Though the great flood of publicity for the gardens in 1929 went unmatched, mentions in the press were frequent and favorable. The second most prominent and extensive notices came with Georgia's 1933 bicentennial celebration. Bicentennial organizers and political and literary figures, as well as dignitaries from across the state, came to Wormsloe on the afternoon preceding Georgia Day in February 1933 for the ceremonial opening of the bicentennial. Among the events was the cutting of a multitiered birthday cake in the dining room of Wormsloe House. Among the guests were the aged historian Pleasant A. Stovall—biographer of Robert Toombs and head of the Bicentennial Commission—and the Reverend Charles Colcock Jones Carpenter, grandson of the colonel. Governor Eugene Talmadge was the featured speaker at a later round of celebrations in April, which also included what Mrs. Talmadge remembered as a "wonderful visit" to Wormsloe. At the major banquet held in Savannah, Mrs. De Renne was accorded a place of honor at the governor's table.[59]

Both De Rennes produced contributions to mark Georgia's two hundredth birthday. Following Wymberley's specifications, Cornelia Cunningham drafted a colorful historical wall map of Georgia; in muted pastels it illustrated major events from the past of colony and state. He also issued sheets of Georgia Bicentennial Souvenir Stamps, which featured Oglethorpe, Tomochichi, Bethesda, and Fort Wymberley. Augusta produced a bicentennial calendar whose heavy cardboard leaves highlighted important events from Georgia's history.[60]

At about the same time, Wormsloe received extended treatment in two landmark books on southern gardens: *Garden History of Georgia, 1733–1933*, published in the latter year by Atlanta's Peachtree Garden Club, and the Garden Club of America's *Gardens of Colony and State* (1934). Both books contained numerous photographs and other illustrations of Wormsloe, including artwork by Augusta's brother Marmaduke Floyd. The *Garden History* featured his pen-and-ink rendering of the formal gardens, and both books printed his striking map of Wormsloe. *Gardens of Colony and State* also helped perpetuate an anecdote of unknown origin and doubtful authenticity, found in promotional literature for Wormsloe Gardens: "At one time a party of Indians and Spaniards made an attack on Fort Wymberley when [Noble Jones] was away from home. Mary Jones took command and successfully defended the fort. In recognition of her courage on that occasion, Wormsloe has always been left to the widows and unmarried daughters of the house, the fee to be vested at death in the male heir."[61]

During its final days in the late 1930s, Wormsloe Gardens was visited by writer Hal Steed, who described it appreciatively in his book *Georgia:*

Unfinished State, published in 1942. By the time of Steed's visit, the family had experienced the tragic loss of one of the De Renne boys and, soon after, the birth of a daughter. In November 1928 Inigo De Renne, aged ten, had died suddenly of diptheria; after the example of his grandfather's funeral, his small casket had been placed in the library for the burial service. He had been a promising child, handsome and well liked, and the outpouring of sympathy to the family was remarkable, even by the standards of such heartrending events. Augusta De Renne had been all but inconsolable and would perhaps have proved entirely so without the birth of her daughter, Eudora, less than two months after Inigo's death. The woman who had acted as nurse-governess to the children became hopelessly distraught after Inigo's death and left Wormsloe. In her place came Ermentra Williams, "a fine elderly talkative soul," who arrived in 1930 to care for Eudora.[62]

Young Kentwyn De Renne, painfully bereft by his brother's death, was overjoyed at the birth of a sister. A serious, artistic child, Kentwyn had inherited some of his great-grandfather De Renne's fascination for printing and was absorbed by such works as Douglas C. McMurtrie's *The Golden Book: The Story of Fine Books and Bookmaking—Past and Present*. He owned a succession of small job printing presses; his print shop was in a room of Wormsloe House's now all-but-abandoned servants' wing. Despite learned claims to the contrary relating to the Wormsloe Quartos, Kentwyn's press was the first and last to be located at Wormsloe. Assisted by young Frank A. Jenkins, Jr., Kentwyn made his own contribution to the family finances. He printed for sale such items as stationery, labels, and postcards, as well as "over one million circulars advertising Wormsloe Gardens." Also, during the summer of 1936, he and a friend put out several numbers of a miniature newspaper, the *Isle of Hope Weekly*.[63]

When Georgia journalist and author Hal Steed made his visit to Wormsloe in the late 1930s, he encountered both the young De Rennes. In his somewhat fictionalized account, he and two friends "entered the Wormsloe estate through a mile-long lane. This was lined with liveoaks and moss which formed an arch over us." Coming to the entrance to the gardens, he "tapped the bell and two beautiful children responded, a boy of twelve and a younger girl. He explained that he was acting for the regular gatekeeper who was temporarily off duty, and took my fee. He felt his responsibility and showed it. . . . His manner and speech were English. The girl said nothing, but was smiling and happy."[64]

Steed took the full tour and left one of most complete descriptions of a visit to Wormsloe Gardens, including a description of his young black guide, "his manner grave and courteous beyond his years." But as Steed noted, he returned to his friends, "more interested in the family than the gardens." One of his friends agreed:

> It's a remarkable family all right. . . . There's an old expression: "from shirt-sleeves to shirt-sleeves in three generations." The first generation shucks its coat, if it has one, and makes the money for the second to spend. The third returns to shirt-sleeves, dead broke. There have never been any shirt-sleeves in the Noble Jones line. They kept their coats on for two centuries. Not only their coats, but their shirts too. There have been but few American families who have lived for two hundred years on one piece of ground.[65]

Perhaps unknown to Steed, the seemingly perpetual continuity of ownership of Wormsloe had been in question for some time. In fact, De Renne had lost title to Wormsloe in 1929, as had been reported in the Savannah newspapers. By the early 1930s, Wormsloe Gardens, along with the dairy operation, had become the major source of income for the De Rennes in attempting to continue in residence there. For easing financial strain on the family, the approximately $5,000 that Wormsloe Gardens netted annually, coupled with the dairy rental, at least made it possible for them to make ends meet and take care of their most pressing obligations, as long as they kept their living expenses at around $250 a month—an economy that helped make clear Edith Wharton's phrase "the squalid compromises of poverty." Kentwyn recalled a particularly grim Christmas after a banking crisis had further complicated the family's predicament; his father "brought home a case of canned tomatoes and a sack of rice, saying these would have to feed the family" for the duration.[66]

But to restore his fortunes and create circumstances that would free Wormsloe from danger, De Renne would be required to raise a considerable sum. It seemed that his best, if not only, hope lay in selling the library whose catalog had been an on-again, off-again project for most of the 1920s. De Renne's lack of money had postponed the project almost immediately after its inception in 1921, but, luckily for all concerned, Azalea Clizbee, his choice as compiler, continued to make herself available and worked patiently and sometimes without timely compensation for much of a decade. She would be largely responsible for the catalog's ultimate success, from the quality of its entries to the impressive and dignified appearance of the massive three-volume set.[67]

Though the catalog was in limbo in the early 1920s, while Audrey Coerr was in Europe, upon her return she made its completion her main concern. She supported the project financially and otherwise, for after her removal to Philadelphia, she often went to New York to confer with Miss Clizbee. Work resumed in 1923, with Mrs. Coerr's backing and financial support. Wymberley and Audrey wished their sister Elfrida to become financially involved in the project but found cumbersome her insistence on meticulous planning and strict business procedures.[68]

Elfrida Barrow was the least impulsive of the three, and she also benefited greatly from her husband's counsels; on her own, she could be direct, uncompromising, and exacting in business dealings, whereas the other two tended to approach such matters more casually and trustingly. Mrs. Barrow had shown her independence from the outset, when the heirs had received their inheritance. Regardless of the expectations for her gender, she would allow no one to act for her without her express consent and would honor no arrangement that had not had her approval. An old lawyer friend of her father's had found this out the hard way, when, without securing her consent, he had told Wymberley that he would represent the three siblings in settling the estate. When he presented Mrs. Barrow the bill for her percentage of his sizable commission, she refused to pay it, on the grounds that she had not retained him to represent her. She also was not pleased when she heard that her brother was taking the lawyer's side in the affair.[69]

Mrs. Barrow thought the catalog project needed to be brought to a timely and respectable conclusion, in accordance with their father's wishes and in a manner befitting his expectations and honoring his labors. But she recognized the imprudence of entering into such a project without all concerned reaching a full understanding regarding the amount of money to be spent and exactly what that money was to buy. Regardless of its importance, she was not in favor of making the project an open-ended arrangement in which the compiler and printer were given both carte blanche and blank checks.[70]

Once the three siblings had reached an informal accord, De Renne attempted to push the project back on course. Acting for his sisters, he approached Miss Clizbee regarding the probable cost of her work and that of the printer. She had preferred Douglas McMurtrie of the Condé Nast Press of New York over a Baltimore printer championed by Leonard Mackall, and the siblings had wisely supported her. McMurtrie, who almost immediately left Nast to form his own printing firm, had already made a name for himself as both a printer and a bibliographer; he offered not only impressive expertise but the best value for the money as well. In any case, as De Renne explained to Miss Clizbee, the catalog had to be "as creditable as possible, and we should overlook no detail, however small." It seemed from the proposal that Wymberley submitted that the catalog, estimated at six hundred pages (and now to resemble less the Church catalog than that of the John Carter Brown Library), could be produced for a total of $10,000. The sisters subscribed for the full sum, paying equal shares, with the understanding that their brother would repay them his share when he was able.[71]

With $10,000 on deposit, Wymberley was authorized by his sisters to deal with Clizbee and McMurtrie and pay their bills. Unfortunately, it soon became clear that the sum quoted to the sisters as the total amount covered only the printer's work, not other items such as the engravings, the author's corrections, and the compiler's continuing labors. Further delays ensued, and Mrs. Coerr—concerned that because of failing health she might not live to see the catalog completed—made provision in her will to ensure that her father's dying wish regarding his catalog would be honored.[72]

Azalea Clizbee's contribution was in large part to arrange the catalog cards, previously prepared by Leonard Mackall and William Price, organizing them chronologically (and by subject in some cases), and to check them for accuracy. Unfortunately, she herself was never able to visit the library at Wormsloe, so the only books she was able to check against the cards were those shipped to New York for preparation of the title-page engravings that were to be used as illustrations. She also, however, checked as many of the cards as she could against matching editions in various bibliographies and in several New York libraries.[73]

Miss Clizbee proposed appending all information regarding the newspapers, maps, and engravings at the end of the last volume in their own chronological section, and this suggestion was approved by Wymberley and his sisters. Her proposals that handmade paper be used was accepted as well, as was her suggestion that the title-page illustrations be uniformly printed in a half-page format; she considered this format more aesthetically pleasing (and more economical) than the Church catalog's precedent, which called for printing as many title pages as possible at actual size. She also persuaded the heirs to include frontispieces in the gravure medium so that the three volumes included, in ascending order, a detail of the Melchers portrait of the founder, a view of the library's exterior (highlighting the portico), and an interior view taken during the lifetime of Wymberley Jones De Renne, in which the statuette of *The Confederate Soldier* and the hooded mantel were conspicuous.[74]

Before the catalog could be published, there were other changes and complications. Audrey Coerr's marriage had ended in divorce, and in 1929 she had married Stanley Howland, a railroad executive, of Asheville, North Carolina. Douglas McMurtrie left the firm he had founded, just as Azalea Clizbee left her employer, the American Art Association, to become co-owner of a bookshop. But Leonard Mackall, now long a resident of New York, where his "Notes for Bibliophiles" appeared weekly in the *Herald Tribune*'s Sunday supplement, agreed to write the catalog's introduction, an excellent and appropriate fifteen-page essay, based in part on his earlier article for the *Georgia Historical Quarterly*.[75]

Ultimately, McMurtrie's former firm, its name changed to the Plandome Press, did its job well, and by the summer of 1931 it began sending presentation copies. The catalog—three stout royal octavo volumes, limited to three hundred sets—contained around fourteen hundred pages in Caslon monotype, with over one hundred illustrations. Its dedication read:

To the Memory of
WYMBERLEY JONES DE RENNE
the Founder and Collector of the Library
this Catalogue is Dedicated
by his Children

Recipients of presentation copies were requested to forward acknowledgments of receipt to Stanley Howland in Asheville.[76]

Regular purchasers could send orders for copies to Azalea Clizbee and, later, to Wormsloe. The four-page "Announcement of Publication" offered the catalog at a prepublication price of $100, with discounts for libraries. The catalog—"bound in full buckram, gilt lettered, with gilt top, other edges uncut"—could be "bound to order in half or full morocco" as well and could also be "delivered *unbound*, for special binding."[77]

The catalog was very well received in the specialized community for which it was designed. Fittingly, the reviewer chosen to describe it for readers of the *American Historical Review* was someone who knew the library well from his own visits there: U. B. Phillips. He spoke from personal experience of the joys of conducting research in the library and gave a brief history of the growth of the collection, including its inspiration in the "notable collection of Georgiana" amassed by the first De Renne. Wymberley Jones De Renne, he wrote, wanted to "make his possessions better known to the historical craft" and published two catalogs himself, but "the technique of these did not suit him, and he died with a purpose of a thorough, collated catalogue unattained." His aim had now been fulfilled by his children, who, "cherishing the library and their father's memory," had produced a catalog that was "monumental" and left "nothing to be desired unless it be the price of a hundred dollars at which sets are for sale. To an historian, however, it may be more tantalizing; for its extremely copious listing of books, newspapers, maps, and manuscripts makes one hanker for not a mere visit but a sojourn at Wormsloe where these riches of print and pen very safely but remotely wait." [78]

Among the other reviewers, the New York book dealer and bibliographer Charles F. Heartman (1883–1953) spoke most articulately and appreciatively from the perspective of a bibliophile in an essay for his periodical the *American Book Collector.* "It is a fact," he noted, that "some wonderful collections have been made in America in the last eighty years, but with the exception of the John Carter Brown Library, we can not quote other worthwhile instances where a great collection became a family tradition." This was a major reason he welcomed the catalog so warmly, for he admired its traditional inspiration as well as other characteristics that he found distinctively southern, including "cultured education, refined leisure, and a greater sense of *noblesse oblige*" than was found "anywhere else." [79]

Heartman provided a lengthy description of the library's contents and complimented all who had allied themselves to catalog them, including Leonard Mackall, William Price, and George Watson Cole. Azalea Clizbee's labors as compiler, he commented, represented an "unbelievably large amount of work . . . of which the layman has no conception." And regarding what may have seemed a steep price for the volumes that put all this labor into printed form, he noted that the hundred-dollar price did not "of course" even "cover the cost of production." [80]

Nonetheless, Heartman admitted that the catalog had imperfections. He particularly regretted that neither the manuscripts nor the small collection of Georgia and Confederate currency and Confederate music was listed.

There were also a few mistakes in collation, and the "quoting of references could have been followed up more consistently." Also, examples of Georgiana—some important, some trivial—were still missing from the collection, a fact soon to be highlighted by Douglas McMurtrie in an article for the *Georgia Historical Quarterly*. Heartman quickly added, however, that he pointed out these omissions, "not with a sense of superiority, for indeed one should be very humble in the presence of this elaborate work and the comparative perfection achieved. I am merely mentioning them to show that I did a bit more than superficially glance over the volumes. The fact is that I spent several pleasant days in the company of this catalogue." Many volumes had been added since the founder's death, he could see, but he hoped additions would continue so that "an ultimate absolute completeness will be secured."[81]

Sadly, Audrey Howland barely lived to see the catalog's publication. After several years of declining health, she died of a rare heart ailment in Asheville, North Carolina, on September 6, 1931; she was only forty-one. Her body was returned to Savannah for burial, and her funeral service was conducted in the library at Wormsloe. Its shelves held several rare volumes she had presented, along with the new three-volume catalog, created in large part through her exertions.[82]

With the catalog scheduled for publication in 1931, Wymberley W. De Renne began to pursue plans to repair his finances by selling the library. Such a step had not been rare among founders' sons. As Charles Heartman had remarked with unconscious irony in his review of the catalog, the "founders of some of the collections dispersed in recent years surely never thought that their genteel hobby would be . . . the means of saving their families from ruin." Ideally, the sale would be to the University of Georgia, in keeping with the wishes of the library's founder, who had bequeathed his books and manuscripts to the university in the event that Wymberley should "die without male issue, namely a son him surviving." Consequently, De Renne's lawyer, Charlton Theus, offered the library to the philanthropist George Foster Peabody in May 1931. It was thought that Peabody could purchase the collection and present it to the university's library as yet another of his many benefactions (which had included donation of the library building itself). In this case, Peabody felt unable to help, but he contacted the university authorities so that they could begin to search for ways to secure the collection.[83]

De Renne, however, did not feel bound to sell to the university. At about this time he received legal advice from a Savannah judge (an old family friend) that the will's restriction on the disposition of the library was not worded to make sale to some other institution impossible. By June 1931, officials from North Carolina's Duke University had visited Wormsloe and inspected the library with interest. De Renne was also advised that he could profit even more from the sale if he shipped the books to Europe, took refuge there, and sold the collection piecemeal.[84]

In any case, at some point in the 1930s, De Renne did begin to dispose of various manuscripts, some mentioned in the catalog, some not. The volume of Robert E. Lee's letters was among them, as was the collection of Nathanael Greene–Anthony Wayne letters. He also disposed of some of his father's books, which were extra copies or were for various reasons not recorded in the catalog (for not relating specifically to Georgia, for instance, like William Douglass's 1755 book relating to British settlements in America, which had no section on Georgia).[85]

By the year the catalog appeared, the library's books and manuscripts represented De Renne's principal possession on the ancestral estate, for by that time Elfrida De Renne Barrow was the owner of Wormsloe, and the De Rennes were lessees. This turn of events had for the most part occurred because the business dealings and investments relating to the De Renne Apartments had plunged Wymberley into a seemingly bottomless financial morass.[86]

As late as 1929, Wymberley had thought that he would be able to recover his fortune, at least partially. He had found a buyer for the apartments, but the sum he would realize would not satisfy a second mortgage, which covered almost all his remaining property. He needed $10,000 to cover assorted obligations, including taxes and overdue interest payments. His sisters agreed to lend him this sum, each putting up half the amount. But at this point, the Pennsylvania Company once again entered the affairs of the family, acting in its capacity as a person under the laws of the state of Georgia. To protect Wormsloe as well as the investment of Mrs. Coerr, for whom it continued to act as trustee, the company arranged to secure Wormsloe's title, assuming the first mortgage of $45,000. The company allowed the De Rennes to continue to occupy Wormsloe, to open the gardens (though the wording of the lease did not allow it), and to rent the dairy operations, all through a twenty-year lease agreement with favorable terms. The first year's rental was $10; the sums for the remaining nineteen years would be the annual total of taxes, mortgage interest, and 6 percent interest on the $10,000. But despite De Renne's hopes, his financial affairs did not improve, specifically, he wrote, because of a default by the purchaser of the apartment. This created "the possibility of a foreclosure" against De Renne.[87]

And despite all the steps taken, there seemed to be a danger that a foreclosure on De Renne's properties would still endanger Wormsloe. Consequently, Mrs. Barrow, seeking to prevent the estate from passing from the family, purchased the original Wormsloe mortgage from its holder, Julius Hirsch, in 1930. The lease agreement that the Pennsylvania Company had arranged continued in force, however. Audrey Howland next arranged to buy one-half of her sister's interest in Wormsloe, and she left her interest to De Renne in her will. Shortly after Mrs. Howland's death in 1931, De Renne sold Mrs. Barrow the half-interest left him by Mrs. Howland. Having expended, to that point, some $53,000, Mrs. Barrow received in November 1931 Wormsloe, Long Island, and the Dupon Lots, for herself and for "her heirs and assigns, in fee simple forever."[88]

The misunderstandings and misinterpretations that characterized this situation would be numerous and tangled. De Renne interpreted the arrangement with his sister as being in the nature of a loan of indefinite duration, much as he had customarily enjoyed in his dealings with Audrey— he expected that Mrs. Barrow would continue to hold Wormsloe for him, or for his heirs, until he or they could repay her and once again own the estate in fee simple. Brother and sister, however, were both bound by the original lease agreement fashioned by the Pennsylvania Company. It restricted to ten years, beginning in June 1929, the time during which Wormsloe could be bought back. This option to buy, however, was dependent on De Renne, as lessee, not defaulting on the terms of the lease, and this default had soon occurred because he had not made all of the scheduled payments. As early as March 1931, before Mrs. Howland's death, Lawton and Cunningham advised Mrs. Barrow that De Renne's option to buy was already null and void and that the Pennsylvania Company could, at her request, "declare the contract in default and then terminate it," before the amounts in default increased further. When she acquired the property several months later, she acquired with it the right and power to evict her brother at any time. She chose instead to give him more time to mend his affairs, most specifically by selling the library to the University of Georgia.[89]

Mrs. Barrow had spent considerable sums of money in redeeming Wormsloe from the original mortgage and would for several years more pay the taxes and interest payments that were the lessees' responsibility. She also continued to allow Wormsloe to be open to the public, although this in itself was not allowed by the 1929 lease and was personally disagreeable to her. But as years passed and the amount of money siphoned by Wormsloe increased, she felt that she had been put into a position that forced her to act. Not least among her worries, Wormsloe House, which under the terms of the lease was to be kept in a good state of repair, was rapidly deteriorating.[90]

Predictably, with the Depression in full swing, Mrs. Barrow was also under financial strains. Essentially, she was making expenditures to maintain three residences—the house on Chippewa Square; Yonholme, the Barrows' Blue Ridge retreat; and Wormsloe. At the same time, property values had plummeted, making it difficult to acquire money either through selling property or securing loans on it. In Savannah, real estate was routinely being lost through foreclosure and nonpayment of taxes. Given such a state of affairs, when Stanley Howland wished to sell to Mrs. Barrow his half-interest in some of the property he had inherited from Audrey, she declined; she had no ready funds for such investments.[91]

Meanwhile, De Renne's attempts to sell the library to the university were meeting with much interest but little action. As had earlier been the case with the collections of Israel Tefft, A. A. Smets, and Colonel Jones, the De Renne Georgia Library was going on the market at a time when it would be impossible to secure a price approaching its actual value. And there was also the difference of an unprecedented nationwide economic dislocation, as well as various other complications that related to the prospective purchaser being a state institution. Nonetheless, the negotiating sum mentioned by the university's officials was $100,000, an amount that could bring Wormsloe back to De Renne and provide him a small competence besides.[92]

As a longtime officer of the university alumni association, Dr. Barrow was one of De Renne's principal allies in his attempts to sell the library to the university. He was aware that De Renne was also talking with Duke University and realized that the University of Georgia's claim on the library, based on the will, would be void if De Renne predeceased his remaining son. This was so because the will provided that the library was to be left to the university if Wymberley W. De Renne died "without male heir." Theoretically, if the sale was made to some institution other than the university and Kentwyn De Renne predeceased his father, the university could assert its claim. If De Renne died before Kentwyn, however, the son would be left to dispose of the library as he pleased—unless De Renne left a stipulation in his will favoring the university and, like his father and grandfather before him, created another arrangement in which a "dead hand" continued to direct the affairs of the living.[93]

Although the university's desire throughout the negotiations was that the purchase encompass everything listed in the will as being part of the De Renne Georgia Library, including the Jones Collection and the Confederate Constitution, De Renne felt forced by his financial dilemma to attempt to raise money by selling some of the library's holdings. And at least one university official gave his blessing to De Renne's attempt to sell the Constitution. During 1935 and 1936, while still talking with Georgia and Duke, De Renne also negotiated with the noted Philadelphia book and manuscript collector-dealer A. S. W. Rosenbach to sell the Confederate Constitution separately. Charlton Theus expended considerable time and energy in attempting to convince Rosenbach that, despite the wording of the will, a way could found to sell him the document free of encumbrances. Rosenbach tabled the negotiations indefinitely, advising Theus that the time was not auspicious for a sale.[94]

The auspices were apparently not favorable for the Georgia Board of Regents either, for $100,000 was a huge sum for a state institution to gather during an economic depression, and the regents could not "contract a debt against the state." The regents' attempts to acquire the library were further complicated by expensive, ongoing construction projects, demands and stipulations from various New Deal bureaucracies, a delay created by a related Supreme Court case, and, not least, the stated reluctance of Governor Eugene Talmadge to support the library purchase.[95]

During the long years of the library negotiations, Mrs. Barrow's concern for Wormsloe continued unabated. She hoped for evidence that her brother could work himself out of the financial mire and even began to formulate ways that would allow her, with an easy conscience, to let her brother repurchase Wormsloe if he was able to get the price he wanted for the library. These included having the deed drawn in such a way that the property could not again be mortgaged or sold away from the family. Even then, however, there was the problem of how the property could be maintained in the event of another financial disaster. As time wore on with little evidence that her brother would be able to recover his fortune, she tried to bring him to a clear understanding of the realities of the situation and of their respective positions in it.[96]

Most obviously, she informed him in 1934 that she had found a prospective buyer of Wormsloe, Samuel E. Wolff of New York. De Renne would not consent to have the estate shown because he said it would not be convenient and, more important, because he thought it would be dangerous—in light of his financial state—to have a price put on the property. She next told him that the same party was willing to lease the property for ten years; during that time, Wolff promised to spend a considerable sum of money making needed repairs and renovations at Wormsloe House and would turn it over to Wymberley's heirs at the end of the period. De Renne was as unalterably opposed to the lease as to the sale and seemed impervious to the underlying point: that the property was Mrs. Barrow's to do with as she pleased and that there were ways to preserve Wormsloe—and simultaneously improve it—without draining her financially. Instead, he continued to hope for a favorable twist of fate to turn his fortunes around and particularly counted on the library selling for at least $100,000.[97]

Despite the strains of their business relationship, the personal relationship between the brother and sister remained relatively cordial throughout the late 1920s and early 1930s, with visits exchanged between Wormsloe, Chippewa Square, and Yonholme. Mrs. Barrow occasionally visited the library as her interest increased in her family's history and in historical research in general, and she also sometimes assisted as one of the hostesses at various functions held by the De Rennes at Wormsloe. But as the 1930s wore on, the subject of Wormsloe's future became more and more of a wedge between the two. Mrs. Barrow was faced with financial difficulties of her own, which would worsen if there were no change in the status quo, particularly where Wormsloe was concerned. As time passed with no improvement in her brother's financial situation, she became convinced that she would soon have to take decisive action to assume complete control of Wormsloe, however painful and embarrassing it might prove to all concerned.[98]

Few predicaments could match this one for unfortunate complications. There were miscommunications and misinterpretations, along with certain amounts of talking at cross-purposes, wishful thinking, and misunderstandings; all would lead gradually but inexorably to a bitter estrangement between the siblings. De Renne attempted to secure an ironclad concession from Mrs. Barrow, promising that Wormsloe would be returned either to him or to his heirs. Though she was willing for him to regain Wormsloe if he could salvage his fortunes, her observations told her more and more plainly that such a day would never come. Nonetheless, she still wished to come to an agreement with him that would protect both the library and Wormsloe.[99]

Consequently, De Renne assented to agreements with Mrs. Barrow, dated April 27 and May 1, 1934, under the terms of which he agreed to sell the library to the University of Georgia. From the sum he secured, she was to receive $72,000 (representing her outlay for the property, as well as annual expenses of interest and taxes), "to be paid in full and promptly within the near future." He would then be allowed a twenty-year lease, and, "if at that time, or any time previous," Mrs. Barrow was persuaded that her brother was "free from debt and financially capable as the owner of Wormsloe *to keep it*," she would give it back to him. If he died before the expiration of the lease, its terms would apply to his son. Should she die before the expiration of the lease, however, De Renne and his male heir could never regain Wormsloe but could continue to make their home there if it was "properly maintained" and met "all legal requirements." Failing this, the estate would revert to Mrs. Barrow's heirs.[100]

In December 1934, the Board of Regents seemed closer than ever before to agreeing to purchase the library, and De Renne, Charlton Theus, and Dr. Barrow traveled together to Athens to meet with the regents. De Renne was apparently confident that he would be given a check for $100,000, from which he could give his sister the sum necessary to secure the new twenty-year lease. Instead, by a vote of seven to two, the regents tabled the motion to purchase. Governor Eugene Talmadge's opposition to the sale was apparently the decisive factor in this reversal, but, since De Renne suspected his sister of bad faith in her dealings with him, it took little to convince him that his problems in bringing the regents to terms were of her making.[101]

Again, a seemingly interminable wait began, and, increasingly, the delays began to tell on the De Rennes, especially Augusta. The business reverses of the early 1920s, followed by the shock of Inigo's death in 1928, and the long years of near-penury had been difficult to bear. Now she seemed suspended between the hope that the regents would come to their rescue and the despair of fearing that they would not. Mrs. De Renne found it particularly hard to deal with the various stresses of the family's precarious financial condition. These were markedly burdensome in relation to her duties as hostess at Wormsloe and the responsibilities that she felt to uphold on a limited budget Wormsloe's fabled traditions of hospitality. Her guests, however, knew nothing of this and found her composed and serene. Gregarious, with a talent for making friends, she had long been known as a clever and generous hostess. But keeping up appearances and entertaining even moderately required ever-increasing ingenuity.[102]

Mrs. Barrow was also disappointed that the regents had not purchased the library, but she waited eighteen months more before she took further steps. Then, she decided, the time had at last come to settle the question of Wormsloe's future once and for all, though she hoped to conclude matters as amicably as possible. De Renne spoke with her at the Barrow home on June 1, 1936, on a subject that she had first raised two years earlier. She again explained her own financial situation to him: specifically, that she was having to make payments of $6,000 per annum on her Savannah residence and $7,000 a year for him to continue living at Wormsloe. Such an arrangement could no longer continue: she intended to sell the residence in town and move to Wormsloe House. Writing to request that the De Rennes meet with her and Dr. Barrow for a discussion of how best to resolve the situation, she offered to help her brother establish another home on the estate. The De Rennes declined the invitation, and no such meeting between the couples ever took place.[103]

Instead, there was an exchange of letters. De Renne wrote his sister of the progress he had made with his finances, asserting that he had reduced his indebtedness from over half a million dollars to $32,000. His tenure at Wormsloe after her acquisition of it, he wrote, he considered to have been indefinite and as a form of loan from her that he would eventually repay. He admitted that she had had to invest heavily in Wormsloe but argued that she did not have as much in it as it was worth. Moreover, his interpretation was that she had given her word that Wormsloe would go to his heirs, and he assured her that if she would have his "financial status" examined, she would "find a reasonable assurance" that he could recover his "financial independence." [104]

Mrs. Barrow responded that her "foremost desire" since their father's death had been that "Wormsloe be preserved as the home of a De Renne" and that she had made sacrifices to see that this would happen. Failing that,

Bonaventure Cemetery. From a stereograph, c. 1880, in the De Renne compilation *Photographs of Old Savannah*. (De Renne Library, Hargrett Rare Book and Manuscript Library, University of Georgia Libraries.)

Top: Wymberley W. De Renne, early 1920s. From a pen-and-ink sketch by Harry Palmer for the newspaper series "Men of Affairs in Savannah." (Courtesy of Eudora De Renne Roebling.) *Bottom:* Signature of Wymberley W. De Renne. (De Renne Collection, Hargrett Rare Book and Manuscript Library, University of Georgia Libraries.)

Wedding picture of Augusta Floyd De Renne and Wymberley W. De Renne with best man Dr. Charles Camblos Norris and maid of honor Frances Floyd, sister of the bride. (Courtesy of Eudora De Renne Roebling.)

Augusta Floyd De Renne, Germany, 1924. From a portrait by Maria Schieben.
(De Renne Collection, Hargrett Rare Book and Manuscript Library, University
of Georgia Libraries.)

Kentwyn (*left*) and Inigo De Renne, 1924. (De Renne Collection, Hargrett Rare Book and Manuscript Library, University of Georgia Libraries.)

Eudora De Renne in the formal garden at Wormsloe, 1934. From a photograph by Bayard Wootten. (De Renne Collection, Hargrett Rare Book and Manuscript Library, University of Georgia Libraries.)

Bookplate of Wymberley W. De
Renne, from Corra Harris's *A Circuit
Rider's Widow*, 1916. (De Renne
Library, Hargrett Rare Book and
Manuscript Library, University of
Georgia Libraries.)

Wymberley W. De Renne

The De Renne Apartments. Constructed 1919–20, architect Henrik Wallin
(1874–1936). (De Renne Collection, Hargrett Rare Book and Manuscript Library,
University of Georgia Libraries.)

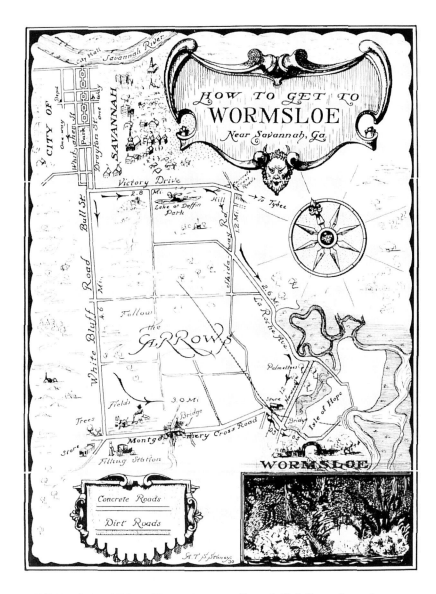

WORMSLOE GARDENS
SAVANNAH, GEORGIA
"The loveliest bit of the true South I have ever seen." Fanny Haeslip Lea

ONE ADMISSION

Good Until

N⁰ 2894

Above: A. T. S. Stoney's tourist map to Wormsloe. (De Renne Collection, Hargrett Rare Book and Manuscript Library, University of Georgia Libraries.) *Left:* Admission ticket to Wormsloe Gardens. (De Renne Collection, Hargrett Rare Book and Manuscript Library, University of Georgia Libraries.)

Wymberley W. and Augusta De Renne in the formal garden at Wormsloe, 1930.
(De Renne Collection, Hargrett Rare Book and Manuscript Library, University of
Georgia Libraries.)

Left: Wymberley W. and Augusta De Renne, Wormsloe Gardens. (De Renne Collection, Hargrett Rare Book and Manuscript Library, University of Georgia Libraries.) *Below:* Plan of Augusta De Renne's formal garden at Wormsloe. From a drawing by her brother Marmaduke H. Floyd. (De Renne Collection, Hargrett Rare Book and Manuscript Library, University of Georgia Libraries.)

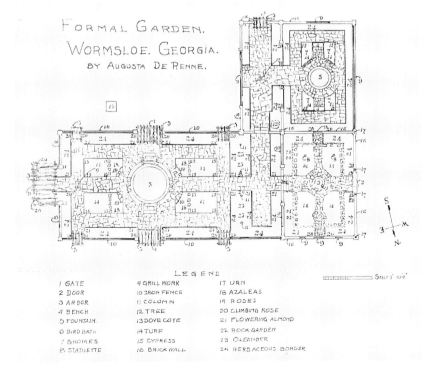

FORMAL GARDEN.
WORMSLOE. GEORGIA.
BY AUGUSTA DE RENNE.

LEGEND

1 GATE	9 GRILL WORK	17 URN
2 DOOR	10 IRON FENCE	18 AZALEAS
3 ARBOR	11 COLUMN	19 ROSES
4 BENCH	12 TREE	20 CLIMBING ROSE
5 FOUNTAIN	13 DOVE COTE	21 FLOWERING ALMOND
6 BIRD BATH	14 TURF	22 ROCK GARDEN
7 GNOMES	15 CYPRESS	23 OLEANDER
8 STATUETTE	16 BRICK WALL	24 HERBACEOUS BORDER

SCALE 1' 10'0"

Wormsloe Gardens: the fountain and pool in the original formal garden, with dovecote in the left background. (De Renne Collection, Hargrett Rare Book and Manuscript Library, University of Georgia Libraries.)

The sunken garden. Statuary (*left to right*): *Pippa Passes* by Louise Allen, *Young Girl with Ewer* by Lucy Currier Richards, and *The Dreamer* by Louise Allen. (De Renne Collection, Hargrett Rare Book and Manuscript Library, University of Georgia Libraries.)

The interior of the W. J. De Renne Georgia Library

Wormsloe *by* EDGAR L. PENNINGTON

Gardens

NOW, another of America's great hereditary estates has been opened to the public! Wormsloe, on the Savannah River, famous for its gardens and its water vistas, for its ruined forts and its library of priceless Colonial manuscripts, can today be visited by those lovers of the beautiful and historic who have longed to see this unusual place but who have had to pass it by as they traveled through the South.

Corner—Formal Garden—Sundial and fountain figures by Lucy Richards

Corner—Bowenie Garden

Page Sixteen

Left: One of the many articles on Wormsloe Gardens that appeared in the 1920s and 1930s. (De Renne Collection, Hargrett Rare Book and Manuscript Library, University of Georgia Libraries.) *Below:* Wormsloe Gardens: lawn and fountain north of the residence, 1930. (De Renne Collection, Hargrett Rare Book and Manuscript Library, University of Georgia Libraries.)

Left: Wormsloe pier and pavilion. From a Bayard Wootten postcard. (De Renne Collection, Hargrett Rare Book and Manuscript Library, University of Georgia Libraries.) *Below:* A Wormsloe slave cabin and "Aunt Liza," said to have been born there, as they appeared on the gardens tour. (De Renne Collection, Hargrett Rare Book and Manuscript Library, University of Georgia Libraries.)

Wormsloe House during the Wormsloe Gardens days. (Georgia Historical Society.)

Wormsloe House: looking toward the fireplace in the northeast parlor, 1920s. (Wormsloe Collection, Hargrett Rare Book and Manuscript Library, University of Georgia Libraries.)

Wormsloe House:
the southeast parlor,
1920s. (Wormsloe
Collection, Hargrett
Rare Book and Man-
uscript Library, Uni-
versity of Georgia
Libraries.)

A sectional view
of the library at
Wormsloe, c. 1922.
(De Renne Collec-
tion, Hargrett Rare
Book and Manuscript
Library, University of
Georgia Libraries.)

Some of the participants in the bicentennial celebration at Wormsloe. *Left to right, beginning behind cake:* Kentwyn De Renne, Augusta De Renne, Pleasant Stovall (chairman of the Georgia Bicentennial Commission), and Wymberley W. De Renne. (De Renne Collection, Hargrett Rare Book and Manuscript Library, University of Georgia Libraries.)

Catalogue
OF THE
WYMBERLEY JONES DE RENNE
GEORGIA LIBRARY
AT
Wormsloe, Isle of Hope
near Savannah, Georgia

VOLUME I
1700-1836

WORMSLOE
PRIVATELY PRINTED
1931

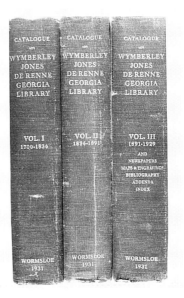

Left: Title page of the third and final catalog of the De Renne Georgia Library, 1931. (De Renne Library, Hargrett Rare Book and Manuscript Library, University of Georgia Libraries.) *Right:* A much-used copy of the 1931 catalog. (De Renne Library, Hargrett Rare Book and Manuscript Library, University of Georgia Libraries.)

Top: The De Renne Library: Purchase by the University of Georgia, April 11, 1938. *Left to right:* Wymberley W. De Renne, Charlton M. Theus, and Steadman V. Sanford, chancellor of the University System of Georgia. (Hargrett Rare Book and Manuscript Library, University of Georgia Libraries.) *Bottom:* The University of Georgia Library, where the De Renne Georgia Library was transferred in 1938. There it remained until its removal in 1953 to the university's new Ilah Dunlap Little Memorial Library. (Hargrett Rare Book and Manuscript Library, University of Georgia Libraries.)

Top: The De Renne
residence, Hill Street,
Athens. (De Renne
Collection, Hargrett
Rare Book and Man-
uscript Library, Uni-
versity of Georgia
Libraries.) *Bottom:*
Augusta De Renne
in her Athens garden.
(De Renne Collec-
tion, Hargrett Rare
Book and Manuscript
Library, University of
Georgia Libraries.)

Wymberley W. De Renne with the Permanent Confederate Constitution, May 1951. Bound for a Confederate reunion in Norfolk, Virginia, De Renne received escorts along the way, including these two North Carolina State Highway Patrol sergeants. (De Renne Collection, Hargrett Rare Book and Manuscript Library, University of Georgia Libraries.)

Dr. Craig Barrow and Elfrida De Renne Barrow, in front of the Liberty Street house (Courtesy of Malcolm Bell III.)

The Barrow residence, 17 West McDonough Street, Chippewa Square. (Cordray-Foltz Photograph Collection, Georgia Historical Society.)

Elfrida De Renne Barrow. Portrait, early 1900s, by Edward August Bell (1862–1953). (Courtesy of Elfrida Barrow Moore, Savannah.)

Elfrida De Renne Barrow and her children, Craig, Muriel, and Elfrida, 1915. (De Renne Collection, Hargrett Rare Book and Manuscript Library, University of Georgia Libraries.)

Dr. Craig Barrow as a captain of the U.S. Army Medical Corps, November 1918.
(Courtesy of Craig Barrow Bell.)

Top: Elfrida De Renne Barrow, 1920s. (Courtesy of Malcolm Bell III.) *Bottom:* Signature of Elfrida De Renne Barrow. (Hargrett Rare Book and Manuscript Library, University of Georgia Libraries.)

Elfrida (*left*) and Muriel Barrow. (Courtesy of William G. Peterkin III.)

Left: Laura Palmer Bell. (Courtesy of Elfrida Barrow Moore, Savannah.) *Right:* Harriet Monroe, champion of the New Poetry. (University of Chicago Library.)

Left: DuBose Heyward. (South Carolina Historical Society.) *Right:* John Bennett. (South Caroliniana Library, University of South Carolina.)

Wormsloe House: The north front, as altered in 1938. (Wormsloe Collection, Hargrett Rare Book and Manuscript Library, University of Georgia Libraries.)

Wormsloe House: The south front, as altered in 1938. (Wormsloe Historic Site.)

Top: Wormsloe House: First-floor hall, looking toward the formal garden. (Photograph by Taylor and Dull by courtesy of *The Magazine Antiques*.) *Bottom left:* Wormsloe House: Southeast parlor, with the portrait of George Jones by Rembrandt Peale, bronze candlesticks by Edward McCartan, and novels by Sir Walter Scott. (Photograph by Taylor and Dull by courtesy of *The Magazine Antiques*.) *Bottom right:* Wormsloe House: Northeast parlor, with the portrait of Noble Wimberly Jones by Charles Willson Peale. Tradition blames Union soldiers for defacing the marble mantels in both parlors. (Photograph by Taylor and Dull by courtesy of *The Magazine Antiques*.)

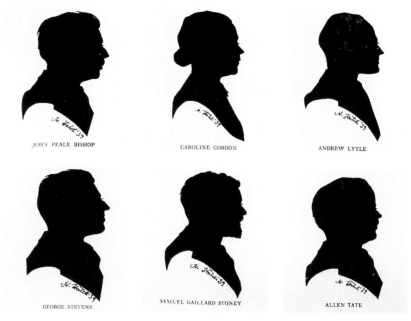

Participants in the Savannah Writers' Conference, April 1939. Silhouettes by Helen Hatch. (Courtesy of the *Georgia Review.*)

Left: Samuel Gaillard Stoney on the veranda at Wormsloe House. (Savannah Writers' Conference Papers, Georgia Historical Society.) *Right:* John Peale Bishop having his silhouette cut by Helen Hatch on the Wormsloe House veranda. (Savannah Writers' Conference Papers, Georgia Historical Society.)

Frank Allen Jenkins,
Sr., 1874–1960.
(From *Holland's:
The Magazine of the
South*, August 1950.)

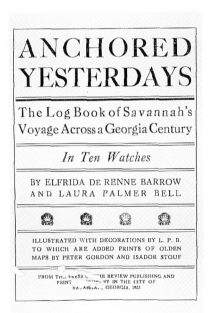

ANCHORED YESTERDAYS

The Log Book of Savannah's
Voyage Across a Georgia Century

In Ten Watches

BY ELFRIDA DE RENNE BARROW
AND LAURA PALMER BELL

ILLUSTRATED WITH DECORATIONS BY L. P. B.
TO WHICH ARE ADDED PRINTS OF OLDEN
MAPS BY PETER GORDON AND ISADOR STOUF

FROM THE PRESS OF THE REVIEW PUBLISHING AND
PRINT... NY IN THE CITY OF
SAVANNAH, GEORGIA, 1923

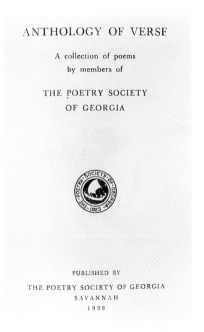

ANTHOLOGY OF VERSE

A collection of poems
by members of

THE POETRY SOCIETY
OF GEORGIA

PUBLISHED BY
THE POETRY SOCIETY OF GEORGIA
SAVANNAH
1929

Left: Title page of *Anchored Yesterdays*, 1923. (De Renne Library, Hargrett Rare
Book and Manuscript Library, University of Georgia Libraries.) *Right:* Title page
of the Georgia Poetry Society's *Anthology of Verse*, 1929, with the seal designed by
Laura Palmer Bell. (Hargrett Rare Book and Manuscript Library, University of
Georgia Libraries.)

Craig Barrow, Jr.
(Courtesy of Mrs.
Craig Barrow, Jr.)

Left: E. Merton Coulter in the De Renne Georgia Library at Wormsloe, 1937.
(Hargrett Rare Book and Manuscript Library, University of Georgia Libraries.)
Right: John Donald Wade, c. 1912. From a portrait by Kate F. Edwards. (Hargrett
Rare Book and Manuscript Library, University of Georgia Libraries.)

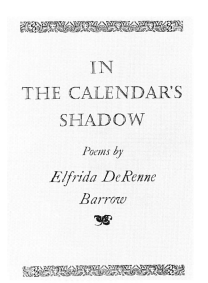

Left: Dust jacket of *In the Calendar's Shadow,* the verse of Elfrida De Renne Barrow, collected by Malcolm Bell III and printed at the Ashantilly Press in 1976. (Hargrett Rare Book and Manuscript Library, University of Georgia Libraries.) *Right: The Library at Wormsloe,* 1935, a linoleum cut by Burnley Weaver (1898–1963), based on a photograph by Bayard Wootten (1875–1959). (Wormsloe Collection, Hargrett Rare Book and Manuscript Library, University of Georgia Libraries.)

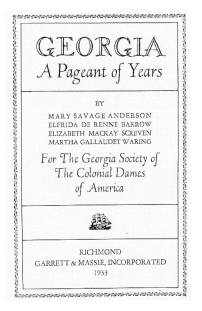

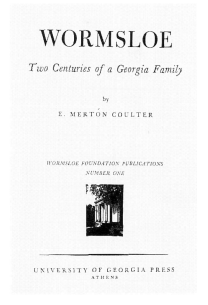

Title page of *Georgia: A Pageant of Years,* 1933. (Hargrett Rare Book and Manuscript Library, University of Georgia Libraries.) *Right:* Title page of *Wormsloe: Two Centuries of a Georgia Family,* 1955, with the Weaver cut as emblem of the series of Wormsloe Foundation Publications. (Hargrett Rare Book and Manuscript Library, University of Georgia Libraries.)

Elfrida De Renne Barrow, on the porch of Wormsloe House, 1968. (Courtesy of Malcolm Bell III.)

she wished that Wormsloe would at least "be retained in the family." And she had become persuaded that he would never again be "financially able" to resume ownership. It had already been decided between them, she reminded him, that, if she died before he could restore his fortunes, there was no question as to the disposition of Wormsloe: it would go to her children. She pointed out as well that she had done much for his "protection" and his "sustenance" and that she had provided him "not only with a home but with the home of [his] choice long after [he] had lost, through [his] independent actions, all rights of ownership." He had been given a generous amount of time to get Wormsloe back and had been offered a new lease, which he had been unable to secure. She was now ready to act.[105]

In answer to a query from Mrs. Barrow several weeks later about his intentions, De Renne wrote that "regardless of anything that may happen, I will always be grateful to you." As to what specifically he intended to do, he repeated that he needed more time but intended to repay her as soon as possible. Mrs. Barrow decided to wait no longer. On July 31, 1936, the sheriff of Chatham County presented the De Rennes with a notice of intent to repossess. Wymberley immediately acted to have the case brought before the county superior court and also made plans to bring suit to attempt to regain his title to Wormsloe. Although some predictably unpleasant exchanges followed by letter, there were some reasonably cordial communications as well. But the dispute was now public, and each sibling had partisans.[106]

The weekend before they were to appear in court, De Renne approached his sister in an attempt to forestall the trial of his suit, which his attorneys advised him he could not win. As a result of the meeting, Mrs. Barrow gave De Renne a one-year lease at a rental of $2,200 and allowed him to "extinguish" his back rent and other debts to her, totaling over $12,000, for only $6,000, if payment was made by February 20. (He raised this money by having the Knoedler Gallery of New York sell four family portraits, including Rembrandt Peale's painting of George Jones.) Finally, he was given the opportunity to secure a long-term lease of Wormsloe, "at an increased rental," if he sold the library "for $90,000.00 or more within twelve months from January 29, 1937." The sum of $90,000 was to be used to set up a trust fund to pay the rent, and it was agreed that this would probably allow him to live at Wormsloe for the rest of his life, and his son after him. But as his lawyers warned him, if he failed to sell the library, he would be "under an absolute obligation (if Mrs. Barrow so demand[ed]) to vacate Wormsloe on January

29, 1938." On the Monday following this agreement, February 1, 1937, the jury found for Mrs. Barrow in the dispossessory proceedings; consequently, securing the short-term lease and the other concessions had been very fortunate indeed for the De Rennes.[107]

The following August, De Renne and Theus attended a lengthy meeting with the regents and delivered an elaborate presentation relating to the library's treasures. The regents formally voted to investigate the possibility of buying the library at the previously mentioned price of $100,000, and De Renne gave them an option to purchase that would expire on January 29, 1938. This, of course, was the same day that he was under "an absolute obligation" to vacate Wormsloe if he could not meet the terms of the long-term lease.[108]

The sum involved was huge, but the university officials and some interested alumni set out to raise the money required. Assisting them was Professor E. Merton Coulter of the University of Georgia. He zealously promoted the sale in print and otherwise, as befitted one who, with university librarian Duncan Burnet, had worked for many years to assemble a collection of Georgiana worthy of the state's premier institution of higher learning. In articles in newspapers and in the university's alumni magazine, Coulter (himself a North Carolinian) appealed to Georgia's state pride by trumpeting the excellence of the De Renne books and the shame that would attend their being shipped to North Carolina or elsewhere. He had a reasonable fear that the library would become another tangible portion of the state's legacy lured away by tobacco dollars from Duke.

> The De Renne library is not a haphazard collection of books [Coulter wrote]. Each item was acquired because of its intrinsic importance. This library is not to be measured by quantity, though it contains thousands of books, pamphlets, and various other kinds of historical documents, but by its quality. It has a great many extremely valuable first editions and other rarities. But it is much more than an expert's or specialist's library; its greatest value for the University of Georgia (which hopes to secure it) is to be seen in the spread of its contents from the earliest colonial times down to the present.
>
> It has been Georgia's glory to make a great deal of history, but it has been her misfortune and somewhat her shame to allow the records of her honorable past to be carried beyond her borders. Others, not of Georgia, appreciating more than her citizens her past, have removed so much of what should

have been kept that it has almost come to pass that a Georgian must migrate to some other state to study the history of his forebears.

Though enlightened alumni and other shared Coulter's pride (and his fear), it proved impossible to raise more than $65,000, even tentatively.[109]

The Macon Evening News of March 8, 1938, put the predicament of the university and De Renne into perspective in an editorial: De Renne "had offered the library to the University of Georgia for a hundred thousand dollars. He needs the money. The University system may not contract a debt against the state and has no hundred thousand dollars in cash. The collection has conservatively been valued at $250,000. Despite the historic and Romantic value of the library, it might not be wise to seek tax money to buy it with. It may be only wanton wishfulness but that money could be an undying gift to Georgia culture" from some wealthy citizen.

No Croesus came forward. And so it seemed the books would go to Duke, for as the deadline approached for vacating Wormsloe, the regents had not acted. The De Rennes began to face the unthinkable—that they would have to move from Wormsloe to some place unknown, clearing the immense house of possessions accumulated during the near half-century since the family had returned from Biarritz. When January 29, 1938, arrived, the day the one-year lease agreement ended (along with the regents' option to buy the library), the De Rennes were still at Wormsloe. Two days later De Renne wrote Mrs. Barrow's attorney that he would need three months to move but would pay the rent during that period; however, he also requested that the payment then due be postponed a month. The attorney responded that De Renne would be expected to vacate Wormsloe no later than March 1, 1938, but that he did not need to take the time and trouble to move the library; Mrs. Barrow would allow him to leave it at Wormsloe, under lock and key. It was, in fact, assumed that the books would remain there until the regents could arrange to purchase them. Mrs. Barrow, however, regarded the now-overdue rent as a "fixed obligation.[110]

During the next several weeks, as the packing began, De Renne traveled to Washington, D.C., and Durham, North Carolina, to explore his remaining options. If nothing else, the trip provided a rejuvenating change of scene and a boost for his morale, luxuries after having felt beset for so long. Herbert Putnam, still Librarian of Congress, received him sympathetically and with fond memories of the elder De Renne. But he could not help Wymberley in any material way; the congressional library could not take the De Renne books on loan and employ De Renne as a librarian, as he offered.[111]

Much better fortune awaited him in Durham. The Duke University officials who met with him were concerned about the entail but, unknown to him, had been interested enough to send agents to check into the situation in Savannah. Consequently, they were fully aware of De Renne's pressing financial problems. Most important, however, they were still eager to purchase the books if a way could be found to do so without incurring legal action or a later loss of the library to the University of Georgia. As was the case with prospective buyers of the Confederate Constitution, there was the problem of the clause in the will that left the collection to Georgia if De Renne died without a son surviving him — and one son had already died an untimely death. What if, after the books came to Duke, Kentwyn predeceased his father?[112]

The Duke lawyers thought they had the answer. They offered De Renne a proposal whereby the library would be purchased, pending an inspection of it, for a minimum of $50,000 or a maximum of $72,000. The purchase price would then be put into a non-negotiable bond, payable to De Renne's son at De Renne's death. If Kentwyn died first, the bond would become void (and the books would be bound for Georgia). Under the terms of the proposed contract, De Renne would also be paid $2,500 per annum and "designated 'Curator of the Wymberley Jones De Renne Georgia Library.'" Unfortunately for Wymberley, the Duke negotiations made an uncomfortable but salient point: no one was likely to offer him the hoped-for $100,000 for the library.[113]

As the day for leaving Wormsloe forever approached, the atmosphere there became increasingly hectic. On the weekend before the move, there was a two-day sale of odds and ends that brought some money, but circumstances were so confused that some things of value were mixed with the mundane and sold for a pittance.[114]

For interested observers, there were now three major unanswered questions. Where would the De Rennes go? What of Wormsloe Gardens and the flood of tourists expected for the fast-approaching blooming season? And what of the library? Several friends had offered the De Rennes houses that they owned, as well as vacation cottages, to serve as a refuge until things could be sorted out. They chose Charles MacLean's Windsor, just west of the Isle of Hope, and moved there with a few possessions. The bulk of their furniture went to a friend's house in town, and a world of other possessions was consigned to a pickery owned by Marmaduke Floyd.[115]

As to Wormsloe Gardens, Mrs. Barrow, having decided to renovate Wormsloe House and move there, had no intention of opening Wormsloe to visitors for the full season. She informed the Chamber of Commerce that the gardens would be closed after the De Rennes departed on the first of March. But entreaties from the chamber followed, citing the number of people who had made plans to come to the gardens during the peak of the season. Mrs. Barrow consequently allowed the gardens to remain open for another month, with the provision that the chamber would run the gardens and turn over the proceeds to her brother.[116]

There was, of course, disappointment among the Savannah city fathers at the closing of a popular tourist attraction, but there was also regret throughout the state. The *Atlanta Constitution* eloquently expressed the general view, in an editorial titled "A Public Loss." While musing over the reasons that the gardens had been closed, the writer asserted that there could be "no question as to the deprivation which it imposes. Old and serene, as well as piercingly lovely, this beauty spot embodies all those intimations of life in death, of tradition molded to the uses of modern life, of security in the face of all alteration, which heartens the human spirit while delighting the human eye. It is to be hoped that only a temporary barrier has been erected to the common enjoyment of this accumulation of beauty."[117]

For various reasons, again related to misunderstandings, the De Rennes' last day at Wormsloe was even more wrenching than might have been anticipated. But finally, the house stood empty and silent. As the family prepared to leave, the young daughter was asked if she wished to take a memento with her. As a true De Renne, she selected a horse — or at least an image of one, a beautiful copper weathervane in equine form, proudly pacing, tail flying. It was placed in the automobile, and the De Rennes drove down the oak avenue together for the last time. Before leaving, however, De Renne gave himself the satisfaction of revealing to Dr. Barrow, in the course of a conversation, that the library building was empty of its books, maps, and manuscripts; little remained inside but a portrait of Audrey. As to the books' location, De Renne was uncommunicative.[118]

Unknown to all but a very few friends and relatives, De Renne had arranged several days before with Marmaduke Floyd to have the books, carefully packed in boxes according to their catalog order, hauled by truck to a bonded, fireproof warehouse in Charleston, South Carolina, where Floyd had rented a secure storage room. Likewise, the Confederate Constitution was gone from Savannah; it was then resting in a vault in New York City, through the help of one of De Renne's lawyer friends there. Among others, it was examined with a view toward a purchase by Belle da Costa Greene of the J. Pierpont Morgan Library.[119]

News of the missing library surprised the Barrows and stunned the regents, but, despite his precarious circumstances, De Renne delighted in the spectacle of the regents suddenly moving in an expeditious manner. Almost immediately, Chancellor S. V. Sanford appeared in Savannah, requesting a conference with De Renne. The disappearance of books in which the university had a residual interest, as well as fears for their safety, had brought the regents to the table in a way that nothing else ever had.[120]

Though Wormsloe was now irretrievably gone, De Renne had two institutions offering to purchase the library and two employment opportunities awaiting his decision. The regents now offered to pay him $60,000 for the library (in several annual installments), with the understanding that the Confederate Constitution and the Jones Collection and most other manuscripts would not be part of the sale (though the regents wanted an option to purchase these materials). Essentially, the regents expected the books listed in the catalog to go to the University of Georgia Library, as well as some of the listed manuscripts that had not been sold. In addition, De Renne was offered a position on the library staff, with the title of assistant librarian. Principally, he was to be curator of the De Renne Library, at a salary, to begin in September 1938, of $2,500 per annum (a sum which his brother-in-law, for one, considered "handsome").[121]

Whether stated or not, an important aspect of the negotiations, understood by all parties, was that the university, as a residuary legatee of W. J. De Renne, had an arguable claim against any other institution that might try to lease or purchase the books and that no matter what the outcome of a suit to prevent Duke from getting control of the De Renne Library, there would be considerable legal costs, as well as embarrassment. But at a very basic level, De Renne also understood, when all was said and done, that the University of Georgia was indeed the ultimate destination his father had planned for the books he had so lovingly collected. Despite his pleasure in having had "other strings to [his] bow," Wymberley soon advised Duke that he could not enter into an agreement. So the books would go to Georgia. But in consideration of Duke University's kindness to him, De Renne presented the Duke library with the volume of Robert E. Lee's telegrams from the Jones Confederate Collection.[122]

The pending sale of the library to the Board of Regents of the University System of Georgia was announced approvingly, and the signing of the contract was widely covered in the press. The *Atlanta Constitution* reported on March 21, 1938, that the negotiations had suddenly achieved such importance that, almost unprecedentedly, "a full attendance" of the regents had been secured to approve the purchase price, which would be "returned many times in the years to come." Though Georgia's history had been "long neglected except by a scattered few," the paper continued, the state had "a rich history, a saga of fortitude against apparently insurmountable odds. The story has never been fully told, yet in the De Renne Library may be found the material from which the pageant of the years will be unfolded. The library will provide rich research material heretofore available only under difficult conditions." Now easily accessible, the collection "should also greatly strengthen the graduate school at the University, for not only is the collection the most complete of Georgiana in existence, but it also contains much of importance to the South and to the nation, particularly about the War Between the States."[123]

Before the library was formally signed over to the university on April 11, 1938, E. Merton Coulter had been dispatched to Charleston to check the collection as quickly and carefully as possible. Because it was such a mass of books and other materials, however, it would be years before it could be precisely known what was there and what was not. Coulter would later have the task of preparing the collection for the shelves, and, according to an agreement, De Renne would replace or pay for any missing volumes. When the process was completed, De Renne replaced what he could and paid back almost $500. The transaction that secured the Confederate Constitution was a more quiet affair, concluded in late 1938 at a purchase price of $20,000, all but $1,000 of which went to one of De Renne's major creditors.[124]

Under the circumstances, Wymberley De Renne did very well during his years in Athens; he seems to have found academia more congenial than the business world. He would never return to the postwar prosperity he had enjoyed so briefly, but neither would he again undergo the incredible strains of the worst years at Wormsloe. With part of the income of the library sale assigned to a trust supervised by the Pennsylvania Company, his family at last had a measure of financial security. Soon after the move, they took up permanent residence on Hill Street in a two-story antebellum house with massive columns. From the quiet, wooded street where the house was located, De Renne had a three-mile walk to the university library, and he made the round-trip twice daily, always returning home for lunch. Ever the gentleman, he was never seen on the streets without his coat, regardless of summer heat; and the situation was the same in the library, where the collection that bore his surname was in the library's new second floor annex, behind a metal grille.[125]

Augusta De Renne never fully recovered from the hardships and heartbreak of the previous decades, and she endured less well than her husband what she saw as nothing less than an exile and a rustication. She still had her gardening interests, however, and garden clubs in Athens to enjoy, and she adapted her talents well to the smaller scale of the yards at Hill Street. In later years, an Atlanta magazine would profile her "Elizabethan knot garden" (based on *The Gardener's Labyrinth*, a sixteenth-century herbal), and she was much in demand for help with social occasions, famous for her inspired decorating.[126]

As the De Rennes had often noted, the sacrifices they had made during the most trying years at Wormsloe had been for their children, and both were a source of great pride to their parents. With his salary and what remained of his investments in stocks and Savannah real estate, De Renne was able, with economies, to provide well for his son and daughter, sending them to private schools in the North and to college as well. Hill Street was a good place for the children to grow up, and the house was large enough for Kentwyn to have a room for his press so that he continued his various printing projects in Athens. In 1940, he hand-printed a selection of the frontier humor of Josh Billings and saw it favorably reviewed. Later, after a time at Yale and service with the Army Signal Corps in the Pacific during World War II, he attended the University of Georgia, as had his father, and like him was drawn to journalism. A member of Chi Psi Fraternity, Blue Key, Sigma Delta Chi, and Phi Beta Kappa, Kentwyn became editor of the university newspaper as well and in 1947 received his A.B.J. degree. But ultimately, he would spend much of his adult life in New Orleans managing a commercial printing plant, Mendola Brothers, a long-established drug label and container company that he bought in the late 1950s. In 1962 he married Jean Cobb, and they had one child, a son, George Wymberley Cobb De Renne.[127]

Eudora De Renne graduated from Mount Holyoke College in Massachusetts and returned to Savannah to make her debut. In 1953 she married Wainwright Ripley Roebling, formerly of Modena Plantation of Skidaway Island, great-great-grandson of the builder of the Brooklyn Bridge. They lived in Athens for many years and had two children, Robert and Audrey.[128]

As spacious as it was, Wymberley and Augusta De Renne's Athens house almost seemed too small for the hundreds of the remaining "house books" from Wormsloe, including the extensive (and expanding) collection on gardens and horticulture. On the walls hung the Melchers portrait of W. J. De Renne and DesAnges's massive canvas of Mary De Renne, along with the smaller Brandt rendering of G. W. J. De Renne and other painted heirlooms and objets de'art.[129]

De Renne's years at the university library stretched from 1938 to 1956 and were in large part pleasant but predictably unexciting. Upon arrival he took charge not only of the De Renne Georgia Library but of the Louis S. Moore Collection, a complementary grouping of Georgiana (mainly from the late nineteenth and early twentieth centuries) and maintained registers for them both. Remarkably, the books were allowed to circulate, with some restrictions. Later other collections, such as the Egmont papers, formerly part of the library of Sir Thomas Phillipps, came into his care. De Renne's only major disappointment, eventually rectified in part, was in attempting to have his salary increased to keep pace with the times.[130]

Occasionally, he would make a discovery among the books and manuscripts that attracted the notice of newspaper reporters. And sometimes he would take some of the De Renne Library's choicest items to cultural affairs and festivals in various cities in Georgia and beyond. Most gratifying of all the excursions of those years was a trip to Norfolk, Virginia, which he made with Augusta in 1951. In that year they took the Confederate Constitution, under guard and insured for $50,000, to the final reunion of the Confederate veterans.[131]

Wymberley W. De Renne was well-liked by his co-workers and an acknowledged master of the De Renne catalog and collection. When questioned about his presence in Athens, he would sometimes reply briefly, and with wry deprecation, that he "came with the Library." But he never discussed the events that brought him to Athens (when anyone was rude enough to question him about it) and also never responded substantively to questions regarding such gems as the Jones Confederate Collection that were no longer a part of the De Renne Library.[152]

Despite attempts at reconciliation by Mrs. Barrow, the estrangement between the brother and sister was permanent and, on his side at least, very bitter. But he never rehearsed his grievances before his children and, in fact, would not entertain any talk of Wormsloe with them. Meanwhile, upstairs in the attic of the Hill Street house was most of the history of Wormsloe and the Jones–De Renne family: the entire family archive was there, boxed and removed from the library building at the same time the books had been. Throughout De Renne's lifetime these materials would remain secure but inaccessible.[153]

Ill health—circulatory problems that first appeared as vertigo—forced De Renne's early retirement from the university library in 1956. After suffering a stroke, he spent his last two years in Milledgeville at an extended care facility near the site of old Oglethorpe University; there he died in March 1966. Almost exactly three years later, Kentwyn De Renne died in New Orleans and, like his father, was buried with military honors in the De Renne crypt at Bonaventure. They were soon reunited with Augusta De Renne, who died in the Hill Street house some four months after Kentwyn's death. Her obituaries made prominent mention of her role as the designer of the gardens at Wormsloe.[154]

CHAPTER 12

The Round of Time

Failure! success!—what *was* success, but a clinging fast, unabashed by
smile or neglect, to that better part in art, in one's self, that cannot be
taken away?
—HENRY HANDEL RICHARDSON

L ike her father's father, Elfrida De Renne Barrow had begun
her days in Philadelphia. But instead of splitting her childhood between North and South, she passed her formative years
on the Continent, mostly in France, and particularly in Biarritz.
In later years this era would vividly return to her in the "delec-
tableness" of anisette—its taste of licorice evoked an "adored"
childhood syrup first enjoyed in France—and would always lead
her to savor, in remembrance, the "engaging joys" of "flavorous"
bygone days.[1]

More than either of her siblings, she was steeped in French
culture and language. And as the eldest child, Elfrida alone was
able to please her Francophile father with letters reporting the
news and social activities of the Côte Basque, while he was far
away in America. In Biarritz her artistic sensibility was kin-
dled early; she was, a local newspaper proclaimed, "*une artiste
de 12 ans!*," while in Savannah Carl L. Brandt—engaged on his

portrait of Mary Telfair—"beg[ged] to be kindly remembered" to the "little artist," hoping that she was "at work with her clever brush and pencil." Her first experiments with photography and poetry followed soon afterward.[2]

Young Elfrida's later studies in New York, guided by the once and future Charlestonian Meta Huger, gave her a firm grounding in literature, as well as the social polish that the Fifth Avenue school promised. She found living in the American metropolis exhilarating and eagerly awaited her father's visits, which often included an evening at the theatre or the opera to see such productions as *Romeo and Juliet* and *Faust*. Central Park, with its numerous attractions, was nearby for long walks in the spring and for watching the ice-skaters in winter. She and her companions "used to amble in leisure past the Reservoir . . . or walk briskly as was the case—& the demands might be—to the quick clatter of horses' hooves as busses and hansom cabs jolted to and fro—& up & down!" And there were such pleasures as making excursions to Huyler's confectionery for chocolates. But Wormsloe always waited, seldom far from her thoughts. The rejuvenated estate appeared in photographs in her room and was even more palpably present in the yellow jasmine on her window sill, sent from Wormsloe by her father.[3]

After returning to Savannah, she soon became a bride, then a young mother. But the sudden death of her own mother, whose funeral was held at the Barrows' Liberty Street house, was too soon followed by her father's death. As the new master of Wormsloe, her brother received the great abundance of condolences that came to the siblings, with occasional mentions of his sisters. For her part, Elfrida De Renne Barrow prized a sympathetic letter from Miss Huger, now an octogenarian:

> It is a great shock to me to read that your father has passed suddenly away from Earth! Who knows better than I what a loss he is to you, who were all in all to him. You were his oldest, his pride, his heart's delight. You loved and valued what he loved and valued, and in a way the headship of the family devolves upon you. True, Wymberley was a dear little boy when last I saw him & he has probably borne out the promise of his childhood and become very much a man. He will preserve his father's name and the Wormsloe house, with its hospitable traditions. But it is the women of the family who keep alive its history, its aims, its friendships, whatever has given it its stamp, and what one would most wish to preserve.[4]

The year after the death of Wymberly Jones De Renne, Dr. and Mrs. Craig Barrow moved to McDonough Street with their three young children, aged from four to ten. The recently purchased house was considered one of the finest in Savannah. It had double parlors, each with an exquisite marble mantel carved with a floral motif. From these rooms French doors led to a two-story semicircular portico; it faced Chippewa Square and, in its center, the heroic statue of General James Oglethorpe, looking defiantly toward what had been Spanish Florida. Only five years earlier, the house's former owners had expanded the antebellum structure and remodeled it extensively, adding much mahogany woodwork and ornamental plaster.[5]

The architect Henrik Wallin had taken care to preserve the Old South charm of the original house while adding a third floor and attic to the original, as well as a spacious kitchen and service area. This expansion proved helpful as the Barrows continued the traditions of hospitality that were a hallmark of Wormsloe House. Over the years, their own house, with its spacious rectangular dining room, would welcome many guests: not only Savannah friends, but also visiting professional associates of Dr. Barrow and the numerous literati who were drawn to his wife. As if in anticipation of her coming, one of the first-floor rooms had walls almost entirely covered by bookshelves, ready to be filled. Other amenities included an internal telephone system and an elevator, as well as numerous bedrooms. The second story contained a suite of rooms for the Barrows, with floor-to-ceiling windows and a balcony facing the square and several rooms for guests as well. The children's rooms were on the third floor.[6]

As was the custom, Mrs. Barrow delayed any significant involvement in local societies and organizations until all her children were in school. Thus, not until 1919 and 1921, respectively, would she make her commitment to two organizations that would claim much of her time and energy—the Georgia Society of the Colonial Dames and the Georgia Historical Society (newly open to women). But although the historical focus of these groups would increasingly appeal to Mrs. Barrow, two literary groups claimed her deepest interest: the Prosodists and the Poetry Society of Georgia.[7]

Mrs. Barrow's affinity for poetry stretched back to her childhood. In the years immediately before the Great War, she and other poetry lovers had watched with great interest the advent of the "New Poetry," championed by Chicago's Harriet Monroe; her periodical *Poetry: A Magazine of Verse* had appeared in 1912 and had helped promote a literary renaissance. In 1920 a shared love of poetry prompted Mrs. Barrow and a few other Savannah ladies, including her close friend Laura Palmer Bell, to form the Prosodists, a group devoted to studying and composing verse. At their weekly Monday afternoon meetings, they honed their poetry with readings and critiques.[8]

Savannah had a history of welcoming literary figures to its salons, theaters, and lecture halls; in the previous century the town had hosted, among others, such men of letters as William Makepeace Thackeray and Oscar Wilde. In keeping with this honorable tradition, the Prosodists invited poets to speak before local audiences. Some of them journeyed to Savannah from as nearby as Charleston—from whose renascent literary circle DuBose Heyward came—and from as far away as Chicago, for in March 1921 Harriet Monroe herself came to proselytize. Fittingly, she spoke at the Bandbox Theater of the Huntingdon Club, an organization of literary-minded ladies (including Elfrida De Renne Barrow) that took its name from the eighteenth-century patroness of learning in Georgia, Selina, Countess of Huntingdon. Dressed in a Russian tunic, Miss Monroe delighted her listeners with dramatic readings of several pieces from her seminal 1917 anthology *The New Poetry*—including excerpts from "Senlin" by Savannah native Conrad Aiken—and read some of her own verse as well.[9]

Miss Monroe spoke passionately of the growth of what would be called modern poetry; she theorized that its quickening was traceable to "the development of new ideals out of the older standards of English poetry"; its immediate origins were "a rich background of culture" and "an intimate knowledge of the elder poets, as well as those of to-day, who have bidden the old forms good-bye and who are expressing the spirit of their own age with a direct simplicity which certainly challenges thought, whether or not it touches the emotions."[10]

During her talk, Miss Monroe did not neglect to compliment her hostesses, the Prosodists: it was "out of just such groups and through just such interests," she said, "that some of the finest movements in art develop." And when she returned to Chicago from her visit to the South, she recorded her impressions of Savannah and the small group of poets that had invited her:

> If Charleston is a great lady, Savannah is a fine one. Charleston commands
> and Savannah persuades. She is tempted to sit dreaming over her past, to

linger in the two old moss-hung graveyards whose mournful beauty is a wonder-story all over the world . . . But Savannah does not forget that she is one of the great ports of the world, with all Spanish America to the south of her; and now and then she salutes the future with a sky-scraper. Or even with a poetry society—a little one, The Prosodists she calls it, to show that its five members are students of technique.[11]

Miss Monroe ended her essay with some general observations on the state of literature in the South, which spoke clearly to Mrs. Barrow:

The problem is . . . to make the local loyalties generously productive and creative instead of narrowly exclusive and prejudicial, to sweep away hindrances between the imaginative energy of elect souls and the adequate expression of that energy in the arts and in life. The energy is there . . . ; but against its vital force rise always the dead walls of conservative oppression. The people must learn that beauty is created from within—it cannot be inherited from the past or imported from overseas. . . . It is an achievement of the individual soul; and if the individual soul fails to create it, to create its own beauty in some one of the innumerable art-impulses or spiritual impulses of life, something within that soul turns to dust and ashes. And what is true of the individual is true of the group: hand-me-down art and literature, hand-me-down ethics, morals, politics—the ready-made everywhere, the self-created crowded out, speeded away—this is the dusty-ashen threat against our modern civilization.[12]

Her words were both challenging and encouraging. But a few months before, the observations of another outlander, more interested in attack than promotion, had created the atmosphere in which the poet Elfrida De Renne Barrow would make her first appearance before a national audience. Without meaning to provide any impetus to southern culture, Baltimore's resident gadfly H. L. Mencken spurred southern writers to action with his controversial 1920 essay "The Sahara of the Bozart," in which he rebuked those below the Mason-Dixon line for their cultural aridity. To Mencken, it was "amazing to contemplate so vast a vacuity" as the South. There, though poetasters were abundant, a true poet was "almost as rare as a . . . dry-point etcher or a metaphysician." With only two exceptions, there was not "a single southern poet above the rank of a neighborhood rhymester."[13]

And though all the southern states appalled Mencken to some degree, Georgia was the worst; "but little removed from savagery," it had not "in thirty years . . . produced a single idea." Joel Chandler Harris, "little more than an amanuensis for the local blacks," was "almost literally, the whole of the literature of Georgia—nay, of the entire art of Georgia." But, he argued, it had not always been thus. Antebellum southerners, among whom he would have included such Georgians as Mrs. Barrow's De Renne grandfather, had inhabited another, better world, according to Mencken's idiosyncratic, romantic view. Though Elfrida De Renne Barrow and her fellow Georgians inhabited a region even worse than an "intellectual Gobi," her grandfather had enjoyed and helped create the superior culture of the Old South, that of the slaveholding grandees, who (Mencken noted elsewhere), "with very few exceptions, were members of the American branch of the Church of England." These were "men of delicate fancy, urbane instinct and aristocratic manner—in brief, superior men—in brief, gentry." In their world, Mencken asserted, there was a "certain noble spaciousness." The "*Ur*-Confederate had leisure. He liked to toy with ideas. He was hospitable and tolerant. He had the vague thing that we call culture." William Brown Hodgson could not have agreed more, and G. W. J. De Renne would not have refused the compliment. But, Mencken lamented, they and their kind had, in one way or another, disappeared into the "red gullet of war," and "poor white trash" now held dominion.[14]

Formed in Charleston the same year that Mencken's diatribe appeared, the Poetry Society of South Carolina included members such as DuBose Heyward and Hervey Allen, who quickly returned Mencken's fire. South Carolina, after all, had been consigned by Mencken to "that vast plain of mediocrity, stupidity, lethargy, almost of dead silence" between Virginia (simply "senile") and Georgia ("crass, gross, vulgar, and obnoxious").[15]

In one of their most effective counterattacks, Heyward and Allen accepted Harriet Monroe's offer to help them showcase verse from the states of the former Confederacy: she agreed to publish a "Southern number" of *Poetry* in 1922, with the two as joint editors. A nonresident member of South Carolina's poetry society from its beginning, Mrs. Barrow had received encouragement from Heyward, and he included some of her efforts in the selection offered to *Poetry*. They were accepted, and Heyward soon wrote to her with the exciting news: "Miss Monroe is really enthusiastic over the material for the Southern issue. . . . Everyone . . . but you is more or less well-known, so you will not be in bad company. It should be a fine debut."[16]

It was. Under the simple heading "Verses," five of Elfrida De Renne Barrow's short poems were grouped, beginning with "Impressions":

I feel the sands of time
  Crunch beneath my feet—
Out on the open road
  Or in the narrow street.

And when my heart is glad
  My foot-prints are light,
Tracing faintly the sands
  That glitter cool and white.

But when my soul is sad
  Heavy sinks my tread—
Deep furrows in the dank
  Dark sands where lie the dead.[17]

Many of the characteristics of her verse were found in this poem: concise-
ness, introspection, vivid imagery, and very careful use of words, particularly seen in the choice of title, which surprises.

In the South Carolina Poetry Society, Mrs. Barrow served not only as
a member but as a generous patron as well. Her offer of the Southern Prize
of $100, "for the encouragement of Poetry in the South," helped induce
several distinguished entrants to compete, including John Crowe Ransom
and Donald Davidson, two of the Nashville poets who had begun publication of *The Fugitive* in 1922. Ransom was selected winner by a panel of
three judges in 1923 for his poem "Armageddon," a selection that set in
train an amusing series of events. To some, "Armageddon" was blithely sacrilegious, and Heyward and others feared that to publish the poem in the society's yearbook (along with the other prize poems, as was customary)
would so offend some of the organization's staunchest members and supporters that the society might be fatally weakened. On the other hand, anything that looked like censorship would displease both Mrs. Barrow and
Ransom and bring a whoop from Mencken and others, with animadver-
sions on the South's lack of sophistication, its intolerance, and its oppression
by fundamentalist minds.[18]

Under the circumstances, Heyward's way out was inspired—"Armageddon," along with those entries that had received honorable mention in

competing for the Southern Prize, would receive a separate publication, with complimentary copies for patron and poets and copies as well for those society members who wished to have one. In the yearbook, published later, there would be no need to have more than a mention of "Armageddon" because the poem would already be in print. Through such compromises, the delicate state of art in the South was shielded.[19]

The same year, 1923, the visit of another nationally known poet to Savannah was the occasion for a lecture on poetry, and for a challenge as well. In a well-attended meeting in the Colonial Dames' Room in Hodgson Hall's basement, venerable, white-haired Edwin Markham gave a "witty and poetic talk," which contained a serious charge to his listeners: it was past time that a poetry society of Georgia be formed. His listeners agreed, Mrs. Barrow one of the foremost among them. She would be "in a real sense the founder," as well as "the guiding light" of the Savannah organization. A charter member of the society that was formed, she became one of its first officers (though she would never consent to be its president) and was also chosen to describe the organization's genesis and aims in the new *Southern Literary Magazine*. As had been the case with the Charleston organization, Mrs. Barrow would be among the first to offer an annual poetry prize, an expedient that—for all the state poetry societies—proved to be one of the most successful forms of encouragement and recognition.[20]

Mrs. Barrow's own work would make her generally known in literary circles as a "poet of some reputation"; she was one of only three Georgia poets whom DuBose Heyward felt worth mentioning in his 1926 survey "Contemporary Southern Poetry." She had, he noted, "yielded to the modern influence" in her work. Her poems had their first readings before the Prosodists (which for a time continued its independent existence) or before the Poetry Society of Georgia, where deep-voiced Hortense Orcutt was a favorite reader. During the 1920s and 1930s her verse would appear in *Poetry* several more times; her last offerings were published in 1935. Her poems also made infrequent appearances in other publications, such as *Bookman*, and in what had become one of H. L. Mencken's favored southern literary periodicals, *The Reviewer* of Richmond, Virginia. Indeed, Elfrida De Renne Barrow's one appearance in the Richmond magazine preceded one of Menckenite Gerald Johnson's more trenchant pieces, "Fourteen Equestrian Statues of Colonel Simmons." Her work appeared in anthologies as well—

that of the Poetry Society of Georgia in 1929 and in *The Oglethorpe Book of Georgia Verse* the following year.[21]

Some of Mrs. Barrow's verse was also published by the Poetry Society of South Carolina, which by 1925 had all but declared victory over H. L. Mencken; he had admitted that the "revival of the South" was "among the most significant phenomena to American literature to-day." Given the Charleston organization's penchant for local color, Mrs. Barrow tended to submit to the yearbook poems drawn from her experiences in the Blue Ridge instead of her more characteristic lyrics. She was made an honorary member of the Charleston society in 1926 but ceased active membership when the society went into a decline in the 1930s, during which period the yearbooks ceased publication. Years later, however, in appreciation of her early work and support, a reborn Poetry Society of South Carolina again honored her early work and patronage.[22]

Occasionally, she made appearances in person as well as print, as in the case of the Southern Book Exposition of 1929. The exposition sought to answer the question, "Is a Renaissance of literary art dawning in the South today?" The response came in the form of displays, readings, and personal appearances. Among the authors showcased were Mrs. Barrow, Professors E. Merton Coulter and John Donald Wade, Julia Peterkin, and many others, "men and women whose living presence," the ads promised, would "bring charm in keeping with the distinction of their work."[23]

Among Mrs. Barrow's admirers was the poet and novelist Henry Bellamann, who in one of his newspaper columns furnished an account of a meeting between the two in New York City:

> A few days ago I had tea with Elfrida De Renne Barrow of Savannah. Mrs. Barrow is a poet of distinction, and a patron of arts and letters. I had the pleasure of reading some work of hers that is scheduled for future appearance in "Poetry: A Magazine of Verse."
>
> I have always had a sincere admiration for Mrs. Barrow's poetry. It is writing of an extremely distilled kind—delicate, strong, and individual. Unhurried by the urge to produce quantity—an urge that destroys so many poets at the beginning—Mrs. Barrow has been content to write a few poems and do them beautifully.
>
> A group of her poems were published in "Poetry" a year or so ago, and they have lingered in my memory as being among the loveliest things of that

year. . . . I look forward to the eventual appearance of a volume of poetry from this gifted writer.

Incidentally, I heard from Mrs. Barrow, during her brief visit here, more literary news of the South and more news of poets than I have heard all winter.[24]

Nonetheless, Mrs. Barrow prepared verse for publication only for about a dozen years, ending in 1935, perhaps in part because of the death of Harriet Monroe in 1936. As Mrs. Barrow's friend and mentor, Miss Monroe had been generous with her advice over the years, and her opinion was the touchstone Mrs. Barrow sought most eagerly; she was irreplaceable. Nonetheless, Mrs. Barrow's active enthusiasm for the Poetry Society of Georgia was unwaning and lifelong, and her patronage continued unabated, indeed increased. In 1969 she became only the fifth person to receive an honorary membership in the society; and in 1970, a longtime fellow society member, Gerald Chan Sieg (who had first won her own Poetry Society prizes as a Savannah high school girl) published a graceful and admiring tribute to Mrs. Barrow and included a representative sampling of her verse.[25]

In later years Mrs. Barrow paid a tribute of her own to the poet David McCord. In a fashion similar to that accorded Ik. Marvel by her grandfather, she complimented McCord with a special private printing by the Ashantilly Press of his poem "Take Sky," which had first appeared in the pages of the *New York Times Book Review*. Later, one of Mrs. Barrow's grandsons would gather her own poems, published and unpublished, and have the Ashantilly Press print them in a slender volume.[26]

Reflecting on her years with the Poetry Society in 1950, Mrs. Barrow remembered most vividly the many visiting poets and other men and women of letters who had visited Savannah. Among the foremost were the several Irish bards who had appeared under the society's auspices, including James Stephens and Padraic Colum and Æ (George William Russell). The last mentioned had made an indelible impression at his reading in 1931, and afterward, in the parlors at McDonough Street. There, seated on a stool, faced with numerous enthusiasts bearing copies of his books, Æ produced from his tuxedo jacket a small set of pastels and furnished his admirers' books with diminutive sketches of Irish landscapes. There were also insistently American poets like Carl Sandburg; as was his custom, he combined his poetry with folk songs self-accompanied on his guitar (and, after his appearance, prevailed on Mrs. Barrow to attend a prizefight with him). And there was Vachel Lindsay, who regaled his audience with a dramatic chanting of "General William Booth Enters Heaven."[27]

Over Mrs. Barrrow's many decades in the society, the organization would also welcome native Georgian writers, whose range was perhaps best exemplified by Daniel Whitehead Hicky, author of "Ulysses at Midnight," who came in the 1920s and—almost half a century later—James Dickey, born the same year as the Poetry Society. His reading was attended not only by the society's members but by worshipful "flower children" as well.[28]

Among the South Carolina authors who visited the Barrows at the Chippewa Square house were John Bennett and Julia Peterkin. Bennett, as author of the classic Elizabethan tale *Master Skylark* (1897), was a particular favorite of the Barrow children. Mrs. Barrow prized his literary acumen; at her request, he served many times as a judge for the annual poetry competitions of the Georgia poetry society.[29]

Bennet also took an interest in the Little House, an enterprise that had been launched by the Barrows and was in the charge of Laura Palmer Bell and Emma Huger Barrow, wife of Dr. Barrow's brother David. Located in an antebellum cottage on Gordon Street near Bull, the Little House offered books, stationery, antiques, and gifts. As Mrs. Bell explained to Bennett, "We have held exhibits from time to time, of an artistic and commercial nature, for (except in a few instances) the charming things that we have shown have all been for sale." Savannah apparently provided a discriminating clientele, for it was "easier to sell a good non-fiction book than the best of the popular novels."[30]

One of the most memorable southern writers to appear before the Poetry Society of Georgia was Julia Peterkin. "How well one remembers her tall figure," wrote Savannah journalist and society member Jane Judge, "the simple white dress she wore, her crown of red hair, and her manner as of one hearing invisible voices." It was not verse that made her famous, however, but her sympathetic novels of Negro life, including *Black April* and *Scarlet Sister Mary*, winner of the Pulitzer Prize in 1928. Distinguished as a southern author who had won H. L. Mencken's approval, Mrs. Peterkin lived a hundred miles north of Savannah, at Lang Syne Plantation; a legacy to her husband, it was one of the few old Carolina estates still "intact" and being worked as a farm.[31]

In 1931 Julia Peterkin's son William married the Barrows' daughter Elfrida in the house on Chippewa Square, and five years later the residence served as the setting for another wedding when Muriel Barrow married Malcolm Bell, Jr. This connection between the Barrows and Laura and Malcolm Bell became a double one in 1938, when Craig Barrow, Jr., married Laura Palmer Bell, her mother's namesake, at St. John's Church.[52]

After the Barrows' move to Wormsloe in 1938, friends and visiting literati frequently made the trek out Skidaway Road and down the beautiful oak avenue to the residence; there they found a Wormsloe House transformed by extensive remodeling. Gone were the elaborate Victorian trimmings, along with the entire servants' wing, though its brick foundation, screened by shrubbery, was roofed to provide an unobtrusive garage. Most of the plantation outbuildings had also disappeared, including the modern masonry dairy barn, the antebellum rice mill, and the stables. Remaining, of course, was the library building, though empty and little used for many years to come.[53]

Immediately west of Wormsloe House, the house built for Jesse Beach still stood, now occupied by Frank A. Jenkins, Sr., and his sons, Frank and George; his wife had died in 1926. Having been at Wormsloe since the 1890s, Jenkins would continue there as the sedate and indispensable head butler until his death at eighty-five in 1960. In later years, he was increasingly assisted by his son and namesake, who continued to serve at Wormsloe after his father's death. Frank, Jr., and his wife, Rosa Lee, raised three sons at the estate (all of whom earned college degrees), and the couple did not leave Wormsloe until the 1980s, after he entered the Methodist ministry.[54]

The northern facade of Wormsloe House was returned to the Greek Revival influences of its earlier days, with some contributions from the Neoclassical Revival; these were probably inspired in part by the renewed interest in columned southern plantation houses, a by-product of the popularity of such novels of the Old South as *Gone with the Wind*. There was now a slender-columned, two-story portico, beneath which double stairs climbed to the main entryway. The side veranda, newly screened to two-story height, enclosed a small sleeping porch adjacent to the second-floor master bedroom. On the other end of the house, the two bay windows—moved so that they were "one above the other on the first and second floors"—were among the few survivals from the time of Mrs. Barrow's father. As had been the case in the days of her grandfather, the piazza was made accessible only from inside the house; the middle third, now left open to the sky, was flanked by airy sunrooms. Above the piazza, the south facade was stripped of its balconies and tower (though the tower's spiral staircase was left standing). Below the piazza, the formal garden remained and, though simplified, retained the basic pattern created by Augusta De Renne. New statuary appeared, as did a wrought-iron gate ornamented with the staff of Aesculepius, in honor of Dr. Barrow's profession.[55]

Like its exterior, the interior of Wormsloe House lost most of its Victorian embellishment. The elaborate decorations and heavy furnishings that had typified the house since the early 1890s now gave way to greater simplicity. The antique furniture selected for the parlors and dining room in particular would have easily won the approbation of the family's earlier generations, including George Jones, Noble Wimberly Jones, and Letitia Van Deren Smith, whose portraits presided over various first-floor rooms.[56]

Although the home's appointments evoked the previous century, it was equipped with many modern conveniences, including a spacious kitchen and pantry, modern bathrooms on each floor, and an elevator, not so much a luxury as a necessity dictated by Dr. Barrow's declining health.[57]

By the time the Barrows began living at Wormsloe, their children were grown and married. But with them were Audrey's daughters, Virginia and Frederica Coerr, whom their aunt and uncle had cared for since their mother's death in 1931.[58]

Wormsloe House would serve many times as the site for meetings of the Poetry Society and for other literary gatherings up into the 1960s, when on a particularly memorable occasion May Sarton would read there. But the residence's first major role as host was only indirectly related to the Poetry Society. In 1939 Lowry Axley, a Savannah professor and the society's past president, staged the Savannah Writers' Conference; it brought several eminent authors to Savannah for three days in April for readings and workshops, all designed to give "lovers of literature" and "aspiring writers" a range of "stimulating contacts with writers of experience and note." Assisting Axley were the Barrows and other Poetry Society members, as well as other representatives of Savannah's literary community.[59]

Allen Tate and his wife, Caroline Gordon, were among the writers who attended. Since his days with the Fugitives, Tate had completed lives of "Stonewall" Jackson and Jefferson Davis and had contributed to the Agrarian manifesto *I'll Take My Stand;* his *Selected Poems* had appeared in 1937, the same year that his wife had published *None Shall Look Back* and *The*

Garden of Adonis. Tate's fellow Agrarian Andrew Lytle, novelist and biographer of Nathan Bedford Forrest, was also among the participants, though somewhat distracted by his continuing work on his novel of Hernando de Soto, *At the Moon's Inn.* Joining the three was their friend John Peale Bishop, who was now decades from the young intellectual who had inspired F. Scott Fitzgerald to base Thomas Parke d'Invilliers on him: he had begun to suffer health problems that would lead to his death five years later at age fifty-two. George Stevens, then editor of the *Saturday Review of Literature,* was also present, having agreed to come at Mrs. Barrow's suggestion.[40]

In furthering its literary aims the Savannah conference was a great success and would probably have been repeated had World War II not intervened. But financially, the conference only broke even. While some of the participants had hoped for a greater monetary return, there were other amenities. The Tates, for example, were the Barrows' guests at Wormsloe for the duration and were "delighted" by the estate and their hosts. One afternoon all of the writers—including Charleston's Samuel Gaillard Stoney, whose *Plantations of the Carolina Low Country* had recently appeared—visited Wormsloe for a reception; while there an artist produced silhouettes of them on the Wormsloe House veranda. Bishop, who found time to go on a "birding expedition" during his stay on the coast, must have been as impressed with Wormsloe's population of birds as had been members of the Audobon Society during a visit the previous month.[41]

Though Wormsloe House would welcome many poets and novelists over the years, historians—Charles and Mary Beard among them—were also frequent guests. As time passed, Mrs. Barrow's historical interests competed increasingly with her literary ones, and in later years most of the works she brought to print were historical in nature.[42]

As an indication of her burgeoning interest in her state's history, Elfrida De Renne Barrow had in 1921 joined the Georgia Historical Society, which had recently undergone a radical transformation from its earlier character. Despite the work of her father, U. B. Phillips, and others to convert the society into a more useful, effective organization, an insurgency arose in 1917 that created another historical organization, the Georgia Historical Association. It threatened to weaken, if not destroy, the society. The state would obviously not support two such organizations, and the association made rapid progress in recruiting new members.[43]

Ironically, one of the leaders of the rival group was none other than Robert Preston Brooks, De Renne Professor of Georgia History. And he was in good company: Governor N. E. Harris chaired the organizational meeting, and Professor Brooks, State Librarian Maud Barker Cobb, and State Compiler of Records Lucian L. Knight were among the association's first officers; Chancellor David C. Barrow of the University of Georgia was a charter member. Essentially, Brooks and his colleagues asserted that the Georgia Historical Society was little more than a Savannah entity and that, as an essentially local organization, its major focus had always been the Georgia coast during its heyday, principally the colonial and revolutionary periods; thus the society had all but ignored a large portion of the present-day state's population, along with over a dozen decades of its past. The association proposed to correct this imbalance, along with, presumably, the society's tendency toward antiquarianism, for the association's membership roll was heavy with professors from the state's colleges and universities and soon made plans for its own journal, the *Georgia Historical Review*.[44]

W. J. De Renne would probably have seen the justice of some of the insurgents' complaints and charges, and, in any event, the colleagues he left behind certainly did. A truce was called, negotiations held, and, in 1920, a fusion of the two groups was engineered. The society was helped greatly by this change: it kept its identity and its headquarters in Savannah, while at the same time increasing its membership greatly through the absorption of the association's more than five hundred members. And since it was at last no longer a strictly local organization, the society resigned its trusteeship of the Telfair Academy, which finally gained its independence.[45]

What benefit did the Georgia Historical Association receive from the merger? The society would now hold two annual meetings: one, on or around Georgia Day, would take place in Savannah; another, later in the year, would be held in another town in the state, moving the society a distance in space as well as intention from its former parochialism. Curators and officers would now also reflect the society's statewide membership (though Savannah retained a majority of curators). And there was as well a move afoot to assist those society members who were trained historians by diverting the society's publications from their former path. Most noticeably, this would lead to a lengthy moratorium on publication of the society's *Collections* and an increased emphasis on the *Georgia Historical Quarterly*, the society's journal. Though initially edited in Savannah by William Harden (who would die in 1936 at age ninety-two) and later edited in Macon, the *Quarterly* was by 1924 firmly established at the University of Georgia, creating an Athens-Savannah axis that remained intact throughout Mrs. Barrow's lifetime and beyond.[16]

Elfrida De Renne Barrow was not among those earliest female members of the society, who had joined years before the merger with the association. Chief among them was Mrs. B. H. Bullard (née Elizabeth Millar), who would be the society's grande dame and major patroness well into the 1930s and would generously pay for "the building to be thoroughly renovated and restored, both within and without, from roof to foundations." Unlike Mrs. Bullard, Mrs. Barrow intended that some of her contributions to the society be in the form of articles. In 1922 her first submission to the *Quarterly* was printed. Titled "'Memento Mori,'" it transformed the dry data of early nineteenth-century Savannah death records into a series of reflections on death and life in the early 1800s. As one reader noted, Mrs. Barrow had taken a "dour, bald topic" and made it into "something vivid" through her "humanity and imagination." [17]

In the context of local historiography, Mrs. Barrow's first article was in sharp contrast to the work of Savannah's most prolific historian of the time, her friend and fellow society member Thomas Gamble; his straightforward recitation of facts was closer in style to the antiquarian school. His *History of the City Government of Savannah, Ga., from 1790 to 1901,* was a valuable reference tool, and he would soon publish his most popular work, *Savannah Duels and Duelists.* His articles for the *Savannah Morning News* were legion and would eventually fill a substantial number of bound volumes.[18]

The unique character of Elfrida De Renne Barrow's historical work was soon displayed in a more ambitious publication, written with Laura Palmer Bell. They called this elaborate study *Anchored Yesterdays: The Log Book of Savannah's Voyage Across a Georgia Century, in Ten Watches.* A sort of overture to the Georgia bicentennial just a decade away, *Anchored Yesterdays* reviewed chronologically the major events of Savannah's history, 1733 to 1833, and used the immediacy of the present tense, as well as a generous dash of humor. Considering that the book appeared at the end of 1923—following a span of months that had seen the creation of the Poetry Society and the first publication of Mrs. Barrow's verse by Harriet Monroe (and publication of a historical piece in the *Quarterly*)—the appearance of such an accomplished piece of work was surprising. But there it was, an artistic and sophisticated treatment that brought the authors much praise, with Mrs. Bell accorded special mention for the nautical designs she contributed as decorations for the book. One reviewer also praised the book's scholarly apparatus, noting that it ended with a "bibliography giving a full list of authorities, and an excellent index." [49]

Privately printed in a limited edition of one thousand copies (with the type afterward distributed), the book was bound in "gray limp cardboard" with title labels on the front and spine. Its attractiveness, testified that a local Savannah press, the Review Printing and Publishing Company, could produce excellent work. [50]

Appearing only seven years after the death of Wymberley Jones De Renne, the book was researched in the library that he had so lovingly collected. It was easy enough for anyone to appreciate his achievement in the abstract, but there was a pronounced effect on his daughter from working at Wormsloe among her father's books (for so she continued to consider them) and using the library as he had meant it to be used.

Though both authors of *Anchored Yesterdays* deprecated any thoughts that they had pretensions to being professional historians, it was obvious to all readers that their work was well written, carefully researched, and mostly free from errors. They had sought and received assistance from learned friends such as Leonard Mackall and Anne Wallis Brumby of Athens, later the university's dean of women. As a trained historian to read the book before publication, the two had selected Professor Preston Brooks, who also reviewed the book for the *Quarterly;* the reviews at that time were often considered as important for encouragement as anything else, with the underlying thought that productive work should be promoted. With only minor reservations, Brooks pronounced *Anchored Yesterdays* "excellent"; he found that though Mrs. Barrow and Mrs. Bell had "sedulously avoided the technique of professional historiography," there was "ample evidence of a thorough examination of sources." Their judgment in the selection of sources he found "altogether admirable," adding that readers would "enjoy many a hearty laugh over the numerous whimsical and amusing extracts." A reviewer in the *Atlanta Constitution* went so far as to say that the book was "as complete in the statement of every essential fact in Georgia's evolution . . . as that of any historian who has devoted volumes to the undertaking," though it covered the same ground "in just 131 pages." [51]

Also gratifying was the opinion privately expressed by John Bennett, in his capacity as both artist and writer. He found Mrs. Bell's cover illustration of a frigate under full sail "a joy," something "to look at and to dream over." The entire book enthralled him, from the epigraph by G. K. Chesterton to the final map, and he thought the style and structure inspired. The history of Georgia, he noted, "is a fine story, and its truth more picturesque than the fallacies so long cherished by the unenquiring herd. Your poetical, or was it romantic, fancy, turning historic periods to watches, truly adds just the suggestion of romance which turns the fact to an intrigue of fantasy. I'll label it a lure." [52]

In Elfrida De Renne Barrow's increasing attraction to Georgia history (and in what would prove to be only a beginning in writing on historical subjects), it may have occurred to her that the erstwhile De Renne professor might come to act as something of a mentor to her. This was not to be. Despite his former title and numerous historical publications, the professor's grasp of the facts of Georgia's past was admittedly unthorough. And despite his love of history, he realized that teaching the subject promised little money for supporting his family. After a brief interlude in banking, he was brought back to the university (with the promise of a raise) to his life's work in its business department and, later, its administration. So Brooks passed from the scene (insofar as Georgia history was concerned), unique in having been not only the sole De Renne professor at the university, but, strangely enough, the only one ever to hold a chair of Georgia history. As he left, another player mounted the stage who could make de facto claim to Brooks's former titles and more. [53]

Though not Georgia-born like Brooks, the native North Carolinian E. Merton Coulter would make the history of his adopted state a lifelong passion; his identification with his chosen subject, and his untiring promotion of it, would lead to a statewide reputation and influence that eclipsed even that of his most illustrious predecessor, Charles C. Jones, Jr. [54]

After graduating from North Carolina's state university in 1913, Coulter did graduate work at the University of Wisconsin, where in 1915 he received his master's degree, and, two years later, his doctorate. His revised dissertation appeared in 1926 as *The Civil War and Readjustment in Kentucky*, and his earliest published work was confined to the states of the Mississippi valley, along with some work relating to his native state. [55]

After teaching in North Carolina and elsewhere (and finding professorships in his field less than abundant), Coulter arrived in Athens in 1919 to assess a job offer there. Initially, he was more than unimpressed with the university, whose campus, he thought, "resembled an over-grazed cow pasture." Nonetheless, Professor J. H. T. McPherson, who then headed the history department, was impressed by Coulter and pressured him to stay. Somewhat against his better judgment, Coulter signed a teaching contract, and he soon complained that the departure of Professor Brooks—who was embarked on his brief venture in the private sector—had resulted in what he found to be a disappointing "present condition and general outlook" at the university.[56]

Coulter soldiered on, however, soon pleased by Brooks's early return, and absorbed himself in teaching courses in American, European, and, most notably, Georgia history. His classroom style depended heavily on lectures that, though fascinating, discouraged discussion. As a researcher, scouting the stacks in the university library, he came upon U. B. Phillip's *Georgia and State Rights,* with its annotated bibliography of works on the state's history, and immediately recognized the field's interest and significance. In 1921, the *Quarterly* published the first of what would be scores of Coulter's articles on Georgia history, a study of the state's nullification movement.[57]

Mrs. Barrow and Professor Coulter undoubtedly met each other at society meetings in the early 1920s. But at such affairs he was a shy, though genial, presence—a scholar who wrote "in words of princely beauty" but whose spoken English evoked his rural North Carolina background; things were "up 'ere," not "up there," one acquaintance cited as an example. To his close friends, who called him "Merto," he was excellent, amusing company.[58]

A 1925 article on John Wesley, Coulter's first foray into Georgia's colonial history, captured Mrs. Barrow's interest and led to her getting to know him. This was the beginning of a correspondence, collaboration, and friendship between the two that would last the remainder of her life. Mrs. Barrow had long been fascinated with John Wesley's brief and rather unbecoming Georgia sojourn, and it had been treated at some length in *Anchored Yesterdays* (a book that won the professor's hearty approval, as well as a permanent place on both the reading list for his Georgia history students and in the bibliography of his long-standard history of the state).[59]

"When John Wesley Preached in Georgia" was in some ways uncharacteristic of the body of Coulter's work: it was a lengthy article chopped into sixteen numbered, titled segments. Though one of Coulter's hallmarks was his deft use of a diversity of sources, in this case he mainly tapped the two sources indispensable for his purposes: the state-published volumes of Georgia's colonial records and John Wesley's journal.[60]

The early portion of the article prepared the way for Wesley's arrival in Georgia in 1736 by describing with well-selected quotes the earlier years of the colony, its reasons for existence, and the daily life of the earliest settlers. By comparison, the section on Wesley suffered somewhat, but Coulter described the Georgia experience of the young priest—and his eventual downfall—with a humane sympathy for Wesley's youthful foibles. Nonetheless, he provided a clear-eyed (though brief) look at the young man's ill-fated romance with Sophia Hopkey and its disastrous consequences.[61]

Writing Coulter of her enjoyment of the article, Mrs. Barrow confided to him that—though worrying that she might risk Coulter's thinking that she had a fixation on the Wesley-Hopkey affair (and thus the scandalous aspects of history)—she felt the relationship should have been examined more thoroughly. To her, it was the incident that indicated most clearly Wesley's character, though she had strong views on other aspects of his life as well.[62]

Neither she nor Coulter, however, felt that he was the writer to put Wesley's Georgia experience into a full-scale biography. Both thought that task should fall to another member of the society, John Donald Wade, then a professor in the English department at the university. Like Mrs. Barrow, he had long cherished a fascination for Wesley, though his earlier study of Augustus Baldwin Longstreet and his later work suggest that his interests were more closely centered on the history and culture of the South. In any case, he went off to England to do research for his Wesley biography.[63]

Meanwhile, another of Mrs. Barrow's friends, the popular novelist Marie Conway Oemler, began work on a historical novel inspired by Wesley's days in Georgia. Titled *The Holy Lover*, it appeared in 1927 and was considered at the time to be its author's most creditable performance to that date. Its dedication page stated simply, "Elfrida De Renne Barrow: Her Book." Oemler's novel was distinguished by a decidedly unsentimental portrait of Wesley, drawn to some extent from his own journals, extracts of which were printed throughout her lightly fictionalized account.[64]

Three years later, when Wade's book was published, it contained a similar tribute to Mrs. Barrow. While stating that his interest in Wesley began "in the Methodist preoccupation of certain members of [his] family," he went on to say: "The person who set me thinking about Wesley as the subject of a biography is Mrs. Elfrida De Renne Barrow. I know that I have not developed adequately the ideas that lady had in mind and passed on, in a measure, to me. I wish that the book were better so that it might more truly represent her inferences." He also thanked an unnamed "private benefactor" (also apparently Mrs. Barrow) who, along with the Guggenheim Foundation, had enabled him "to command the time necessary for so much reading, and for so much cogitating, and for so much writing."[65]

In the tradition of the *Quarterly* (of which Coulter had begun in 1924 what would be five decades of editorship), it was Elfrida Barrow who was given Wade's *John Wesley* to review. The critique began provocatively:

> It was St. Gaudens, I believe, who set for his standard the sentiment: "You can do anything you please. It's the way it's done that makes the difference." And who better than biographers can do anything they please with their favored victims whom they resurrect from the dead and stir again into life through the pages of their cherished books where, as often as not, they jog-trot from cover to cover as they travel the commonplace highway of the average biographer's mind.
>
> Few indeed are those so fortunate as to re-act their existence . . . through an interpreter who adventures into the scenic altitudes of concept and style. . . .
>
> John Wade has achieved the difference, and has written an important and enduring book, one whose fresh vigor of thought and compelling charm of style make of its reading a true delight.[66]

After more compliments, she continued:

> This review, appearing as it does in a journal devoted to the interests of Georgia history, does not seem complete without a mention of Wesley's turbulent and aggressive sojourn in Georgia. One might wish that Mr. Wade had allowed us a longer glimpse into that formative and impressionable period of Wesley's life, scene of one of the most dramatic love episodes in history; when Wesley, with his heart a "tug of war" finally shook the dust from his feet and Sophy Hopkey from his soul and left Georgia forever after not quite two years of tempestuous living, at odds with himself and his surroundings.

She approved, however, of Wade's having titled the chapter that dealt with the Hopkey episode "Bungler" and quoted briefly from it: "She was eighteen. Always she was very lovely, always in white, obviously his adorer, obviously in need of a champion. And in Savannah it was early spring."[67]

At around the same time, the *Quarterly* published Mrs. Barrow's second and last historical article—or "near-article," as she described it. She wrote Coulter that perhaps it would at least be a diverting change from the journal's usual scholarly fare. As with "'Memento Mori,'" she had given color and interest to what seemed to be unpromising material—in this case newspaper advertisements of businesses that had flourished along Savannah's Bay Street in 1829. She chose from her source skillfully, conjuring up a feast for the senses as well as the mind, and linked the newspaper excerpts gracefully and imaginatively, with occasional touches of droll humor.[68]

The article was titled "On the Bay, One Hundred Years Ago, Being various Items compiled from the advertising columns of the *Savannah Georgian* of 1829." Noting that Bay Street at that time was "within sight and sound of a river kept busy by the coming and going of sailing brigs and trading schooners, packet sloops and steam ships," she conjured up a scene where "cargoes in profusion . . . crowded the little bluff, while the wharves literally groaned beneath their load of wholesale delicacies." She was mildly disappointed when the article did not appear in 1929, as she had planned, particularly since it made her realize that Coulter had not understood her intent of marking the centennial of 1829. Nonetheless, she had offprints prepared for presentation to friends and scholarly acquaintances. The booklets were bound in thin cardboard, with a facsimile of an 1829 *Savannah Georgian* front page on the cover.[69]

Coinciding with the beginning of her friendship with Coulter was Mrs. Barrow's entry into the publishing activities of the Colonial Dames, in which the professor would later play a part. The national society had an impressive record of issuing worthwhile publications, such as *Correspondence of William Pitt* (two volumes, 1906) and *The Letters of Richard Henry Lee* (two volumes, 1911–14). The Georgia society had made an even earlier, if more modest, beginning by issuing as a small pamphlet Walter G. Charlton's 1898 address to the society, *The Making of Georgia.*[70]

Elfrida De Renne Barrow's initial research for one of the Colonial Dames' publishing projects was carried out soon after the publication of "'Memento Mori'" and was closely related in subject. The book, published in 1924, was titled *Some Early Epitaphs in Georgia*, and she not only participated as one of the committee that researched the book but provided its epigraph as well: her poem "God's Acre," which was inspired by Savannah's Colonial Cemetery, where were located many of the tombstones that provided the book's inscriptions. These epitaphs were placed in context by biographical sketches of those they memorialized, who in many cases had been among Savannah's most eminent men of the eighteenth and early nineteenth centuries.[71]

Two former occupants of the cemetery, Noble Jones and Noble Wimberly Jones, earned prominent mention in the book, though, Mrs. Barrow later admitted, her ancestors at that time were "chronic strangers" to her. She accepted them, of course, and understood them somewhat. But they were not figures of any keen interest to her, although she had researched them in detail when she had submitted her membership application to the Society of Colonial Dames in the early 1920s.[72]

Mrs. Barrow did not become deeply interested in her Jones forebears until the early 1930s, when—during her presidency of the Georgia Society of Colonial Dames—she worked as one of four coauthors (including her cousin Mary Savage Jones Anderson, granddaughter of George Noble Jones) on the Colonial Dames' "permanent contribution" to the Georgia bicentennial of 1933. The creation of this book was less pleasant than Mrs. Barrow's earlier collaboration with Laura Palmer Bell and was certainly a more arduous task; Mrs. Barrow was particularly upset over the sectional tone of some of the passages proposed for the book and was at pains to smooth over any such controversies. But the finished product nonetheless had much in common with *Anchored Yesterdays*. This became obvious after the committee of authors, of which Mrs. Barrow was chairman, jettisoned an early plan to cast the publication as a "day book" for 1933. Although *Anchored Yesterdays* had outlined the years 1733–1833, the new book would "present a sort of calendar of most of the notable happenings in Georgia between June 5, 1539 and January 9, 1933."[73]

The research for the book occupied many months and was conducted at Hodgson Hall, at the Savannah Public Library, and, of course, at Wormsloe's Wymberley Jones De Renne Georgia Library, which provided many of the book's beautifully reproduced illustrations. When the ladies gathered to sort through what they had gleaned and to attempt to organize it and transform it into a chronicle, the task often threatened to overwhelm them. To one of the collaborators, it seemed as if they were "bailing out the ocean."[74]

They were not laboring without some scholarly assistance, however. Coulter patiently answered numerous queries from the writers, through the mails and in consultations by telephone. And he was once visited by the committee in Athens, an incident of such moment that word of it was carried in a Savannah newspaper. Finally, when the manuscript was completed, the professor consented to go over it to point out any needed corrections and to make occasional suggestions. But the ladies, Mrs. Barrow insisted, did not expect or want their work to receive any but the sternest handling from him.[75]

As the time for sending the book to the printers in Richmond neared, the much-debated working title suggested by one of Mrs. Barrow's coauthors was dropped: *Marching with Georgia* became *Georgia: A Pageant of Years*. As Mrs. Barrow explained, "Pageants have been popular this year," and the authors hoped that "pageant" would be a "lucky" word for them. In any case, Mrs. Barrow assured Coulter, the book was "guaranteed 100 percent pure and harmless . . . for infant and adult alike." Soon, however, waiting for publication, she fretted that somewhere in the manuscript sent to the press, now inaccessible and past correcting, the "supreme error" lurked.[76]

While the ladies had been working on their book, Coulter had been completing one of his own, a comprehensive history of the state commissioned by Mrs. B. F. Bullard, who would soon also bring the memoirs of William Harden to print. One of her stipulations regarding Coulter's book was that it approach the present as nearly as possible. It transpired, however, that there were exceptions to this provision, as Coulter discovered when he received a frantic telegram from Mrs. Bullard shortly after his own manuscript had been sent to be printed by the University of North Carolina Press. In effect, she told him to "stop the press" and said that an explanatory letter would follow. In it she explained that a rumor had reached her that the Colonial Dames' book, with which she knew Coulter had assisted, was going to include a mention of the Leo Frank lynching of 1915. This she thought would be disastrous to the state, and she became terrified at the thought that Coulter's book, whose manuscript she had not asked to see, might also contain a passage on the incident. If it did and was already in print, she would not allow the book to be distributed. As it happened, neither of the books contained a reference to the tragic episode, though Coulter's book (which would enjoy three printings and be the standard Georgia history for generations) would include the Frank case in a later edition, published after Mrs. Bullard's death.[77]

When it came time for the *Quarterly's* review of *Georgia: A Pageant of Years*, John Donald Wade produced a gracefully written, thoughtful essay. Though not reluctant to catalog a few errors, omissions, and stylistic lapses, he thought that, on the whole, the "ladies who put this book together did a fine thing," that they were "always direct and pointed, and that they were always aware of the many-sidedness of history." He was impressed that their book "reflect[ed] . . . the shifting *cultural* trends of the state with as great scrupulousness as those . . . purely governmental or military." Wade found a species of positive sectionalism in the book, for though it was "workman-like," such a "mechanical trick of scholarship . . . thrives as well in one soil as another. The sophistication of the writing and the mature taste involved in the selection of the thirteen delightful illustrations may well be the peculiar out-growth of Savannah." Wade wondered, consequently, if the "book's point of origin [did] not explain its distinction," since its authors were "most valid products of the coastal culture." But at the same time, Wade worried whether, after fifty years, time would "have bred up in Georgia these ladies' parallel."[78]

Coulter's masterful *Short History of Georgia* also received positive reviews, and the Barrows were among the book's greatest admirers. Dr. Barrow, his wife noted in a letter to Coulter, even described the professor as a "stylist"; he, like others, enjoyed Coulter's ability to make history read like a novel. Mrs. Barrow loved the book as well and was particularly struck by its concluding sentence: "Moored to the past by two hundred years, Georgians were enabled to face the third century with the conservatism that comes from age and with the liberalism that grows from the chastening present."[79]

The Georgia bicentennial stimulated historical interest across the state, helped along because the Georgia Historical Society had developed into a statewide organization that, like its journal, recognized as its province the entire history of the state. The very success of broadening the society's focus contributed to the formation in 1934 of a Savannah-centered organization of which Mrs. Barrow was a charter member, the Savannah Historical Research Association (SHRA). Not a rival of the Georgia Historical Society, the association was much more active, meeting monthly, with a minimum of business, to read and discuss papers that were the products of the members' research. Hodgson Hall served as the organization's meeting place, and its founder and most enthusiastic member was the society's librarian, Dolores Boisfeuillet Floyd, Augusta De Renne's sister-in-law. Indeed, the De Rennes themselves were members during the early years of the association. Among the other members were Lowry Axley and Laura Palmer Bell.[80]

Mrs. De Renne's brother Marmaduke Floyd, another member of the association, was the catalyst for a Colonial Dames book; its genesis had been a lecture he delivered to the group on his investigations of supposed Spanish ruins along the Georgia coast. Several books describing Spain's occupation of the Georgia seaboard had led coastal landowners and entrepreneurs, with "adroit salesmanship," to use the picturesque ruins as "a unique asset for exploitation to attract tourists and prospective purchasers." Consequently, many old tabby structures of the early nineteenth century had been wrongly identified as ancient Catholic missions. The Colonial Dames requested that a committee, including Floyd, Coulter, Leonard Mackall, and John Donald Wade, investigate the ruins and come to some conclusion regarding their probable origin.[81]

The final result was *Georgia's Disputed Ruins* (1937), the first of many books to be edited by Coulter, who urged readers to examine the data presented and draw their own conclusions on the nature of the ruins. Floyd provided an essay detailing his speculations and findings, and James A. Ford contributed an archaeological report on one of the ruins. Coulter also included a nineteenth-century essay by Thomas Spalding of Sapelo, which shed light on the production of tabby and on the construction of the "sugar houses" that were apparently being mistaken for ruined missions. The book was published by the University of North Carolina Press for the Colonial Dames, with a foreword by Mrs. Barrow. Such a publication, one reviewer observed, showed that her organization had "become intensely interested in the early history of [Georgia]—more interested in its history than in its traditions and myths."[82]

In 1944 examples of the work of the Savannah Historical Research Association were gathered into a special number of the *Quarterly* on the occasion of the organization's tenth anniversary. Mrs. Barrow had regretfully resigned in 1939; having moved from Savannah to "the country," she wrote, made it "practically impossible" to attend the evening meetings in town. It was she, however, who Coulter suggested should select the papers to be printed, with the assistance of association member Walter Charlton Hartridge. The association acquiesced and made her an honorary member in advance of her labors, an honor that had previously been bestowed only once, on Leonard Mackall, who had died in 1937. Also introduced by Mrs. Barrow, the SHRA number of the *Quarterly* included a brief history of the association, eight essays by members, and an annotated checklist of the papers then held by the association. Though Mrs. Barrow's papers for the association were not published, Mrs. Bell's "Vanishing Gardens of Savannah" appeared in the special issue.[83]

Two more books, both printed for the Colonial Dames, would feature forewords by Mrs. Barrow: *Letters of Don Juan McQueen* (1943) and *Letters of Robert Mackay* (1949), both of which were edited by Walter Charlton Hartridge, Jr. The Harvard-educated scion of an old Savannah family, Hartridge, like Charles C. Jones, Jr., was tall in stature, fascinated by history, and collected data, books, and manuscripts voraciously. Fortunately, unlike Colonel Jones, he had more leisure and means to pursue his interests. With only Mrs. Marmaduke Floyd as his near rival in Savannah, he had made a name for having amassed an incredible amount of material. Because of his two projects for the Colonial Dames (and others of his own) and his sharing of mutual historical interests with Mrs. Barrow, he was for many years a regular visitor at Wormsloe.[84]

From the time of their purchase of Yonholme in 1916, Mrs. Barrow and her husband had welcomed guests to their North Carolina refuge, where they always summered (though Dr. Barrow's duties at the Central Railroad's hospital kept him much in Savannah). Covered with a steeply pitched gable roof, the house boasted a spacious screened veranda and spectacular views of the surrounding mountains. Harriet Monroe loved Yonholme's setting and used it as a backdrop for some of her own poetry. She also enjoyed hikes into the mountains and, once atop the summit she had chosen, would refresh herself with her own distinctive snack: sardines and chocolate. And Yonholme had literary neighbors as well as literary guests. DuBose Heyward maintained his own retreat, Orienta, nearby, and Carl Sandburg's Connemara was only a mountain away (though he did not arrive in the Blue Ridge until the mid-1940s, when Mrs. Barrow began living year-round at Wormsloe). Historians, including Professors Coulter and Brooks, found their way to Yonholme, as did such novelists as Mary Granger and Marie Conway Oemler. The latter wrote to Mrs. Barrow after one visit, "I like to think of you in that mountain garden of yours, serene and secure."[85]

For Mrs. Barrow, the years of World War II would seem far from secure and would be sadly memorable for reasons beyond those usually to be feared—though she, like many other mothers, experienced the anxieties of seeing a son enter wartime service. Her son and other loved ones returned from the war, but unrelated deaths of the period left her bereft. In 1941, the tragically early death of her elder daughter and namesake occurred, and on the last day of August 1945, only weeks after Japan's surrender, Dr. Barrow died unexpectedly. Stricken by a cerebral hemorrhage at Wormsloe, he was taken to the Central of Georgia's hospital. It was remarked that there was "a certain appropriateness that death should come to him in the hospital to which he had dedicated his life and work, and which he had held so dear."[86]

Beneath the overarching oaks, a family burial plot was prepared, between Wormsloe House and the ancient Jones cemetery. Enclosed by a wall constructed from old bricks gathered on the plantation, it was entered through a wrought-iron gate. On the face of Dr. Barrow's slab was inscribed a line from "High Flight" by John Gillespie Magee, Jr.; it had achieved a poignant popularity during the war, particularly among those, like the Barrows' son, who had served in the U.S. Army Air Force. Craig Barrow, Jr., from this time became his mother's adviser and carefully conducted her business affairs for the rest of her life.[87]

Though not reclusive, Mrs. Barrow would spend most of her remaining days in the "fastnesses" of Wormsloe, and somber dress would become habitual to her. Wormsloe would be a source of strength, as well as delight, to her, and though she took pleasure in the blooming season, she came to prefer the variegated greens and browns that characterized her surroundings for most of the year. She was seldom alone—a friend or relative normally resided or visited with her—and she kept company with the "little creatures" of Wormsloe as well. In a Christmas card that showed numerous animals encircling a decorated tree, she noted, "All . . . are here, indeed the Crow—in numbers—eat from the bird feeder & stalk around the pool.— As for the squirrels—they frolic *en masse*—the fox, too, I have met & the deer graze about the house."[88]

Mrs. Barrow was now approaching the age at which her father, longest lived of his family, had died. Her thoughts turned to the acres that surrounded her and their probable future. For her children and grandchildren she had no fears; they would continue to protect and preserve the estate. But she could see no farther into the future and began to cast about for a way that could give her certainty in her own lifetime that Wormsloe would be perpetually preserved. She did not have to look far to see what might happen, for none of the other old Chatham County plantations were still held by families whose possession stretched back to the early eighteenth century, and many coastal estates were now given over to industrial uses or had been carved into residential subdivisions.[89]

Her initial inclination was to involve in some way the University of Georgia, alma mater of her husband and two of her children. The university's School of Forestry already had charge of several tracts, some smaller, some larger than Wormsloe—though most were near Athens. Presumably, she envisioned giving Wormsloe to the university, protected by restricting covenants and reserving a portion of the land for her family, at least for the foreseeable future. For various reasons nothing came of the talks with the administration, and it would be over a decade before she devised another expedient that seemed to have a chance of working.[90]

In the meantime, she embarked on another endeavor, very close to her heart, that also involved Wormsloe. To a historian like E. Merton Coulter, the two-century saga of Wormsloe and its masters had obvious attractions, and, beginning in the mid-1940s, he and Mrs. Barrow discussed at increasing length his writing a book on the subject. Because of her passion for privacy, she had some misgivings about such a book, particularly one that would delve into family matters in any detail—she seems to have preferred a study that would trace the evolution of the plantation itself and its role as a backdrop to history and would concentrate little on the people who had lived there.[91]

A model already existed in "Wormsloe," a monograph held by the Georgia Historical Society, prepared in the late 1930s by the Savannah Writers' Project of the Work Projects Administration. Headed by Mrs. Barrow's friend Mary Granger, the Savannah unit was best known for its published study *Savannah River Plantations* (1947), which combined articles published in the *Quarterly* beginning in 1938, and for *Drums and Shadows: Survival Studies Among the Georgia Coastal Negroes* (1940). For the latter Mrs. Barrow's daughter and son-in-law, Muriel and Malcolm Bell, Jr., had provided a series of acclaimed photographs of people, places, and artifacts. The unit's Wormsloe study, however, existed only as an unpublished typescript, less than fifty pages in length. But it was copiously annotated with references to many pertinent primary sources, and its exhaustive research—among the deeds in the Chatham County Courthouse in particular—would save Coulter much time and digging. By the late 1940s he had finally begun work on his Wormsloe manuscript. Much of his research was done at the library of the Georgia Historical Society, again revitalized, this time by an affiliation with Armstrong College; its president's wife, Lilla Mills Hawes, had become librarian and director of the society and was well on her way to becoming "the very life blood of the organization." She would be at her post for the rest of Mrs. Barrow's life.[92]

Almost a decade would pass between the proposal of the Wormsloe book and its publication. The major impediment was Coulter's lack of time. In addition to his labors as editor of the *Quarterly*, he held several visiting professorships during the period and also took over coeditorship of the Louisiana State University Press's History of the South series. For this series he wrote a history of Reconstruction, published in 1947, as well as a stout volume covering the story of the Confederacy—considered by some his masterpiece—which appeared three years later. Meanwhile, he had been forced to come to grips with the inarguable fact that the Jones–De Renne family papers in private possession in Athens would not be available for his use.[93]

Coulter continued to work on his history of Wormsloe as time allowed, and Mrs. Barrow took a step that would have a decided impact on the Wormsloe book and on the estate itself. In late 1951, she secured a charter for a nonprofit, tax-exempt corporation to be called the Wormsloe Foundation, "for the study and development of agriculture, horticulture and forestry in the state of Georgia, . . . to promote and further historical research in this State and elsewhere," and to foster the "preservation and maintenance of historical sites and documents." It was decided that, in the spirit of the various Wormsloe editions, the foundation would institute a series of publications devoted to Georgia history, to be published by the University of Georgia Press. Coulter's Wormsloe study was selected as most appropriate to inaugurate the series.[94]

The principal trustees of the foundation were members of the Barrow family, but trusteeship was not restricted to them. Elfrida De Renne Barrow was chair of the Board of Trustees, and Craig Barrow, Jr., nominally secretary and treasurer, worked energetically and effectively in a variety of roles to promote the foundation's goals. Coulter himself agreed to serve as trustee, a post he would hold for life, and he also accepted the general editorship of the series of Wormsloe Foundation Publications.[95]

Coulter's *Wormsloe: Two Centuries of a Georgia Family*, dedicated to the memory of Wymberley Jones De Renne, appeared in June 1955. As Coulter stated eloquently in the preface, "Books have floated into print down the currents of rivers; books have been launched around the shorelines of lakes; this book flows out of the blood stream of six generations of a family in

Georgia." The study traced the history of Wormsloe and its masters from the birth of the Georgia colony to the time of Coulter's writing, with particular emphasis on the first two generations; 70 percent of the book centered on the lives and times of Noble Jones and Noble Wimberly Jones. For these lives and that of George Jones, a public record was available. But the first two generations of De Rennes, having mainly devoted themselves to private pursuits, had left much less printed documentation; the lack of family papers weakened this section, as some critics observed, though within the limitations, Coulter produced accurate, serviceable accounts of the De Rennes of Wormsloe. The living generation, however, and the events that had brought Elfrida De Renne Barrow and Wymberley Wormsloe De Renne to their respective destinies were accorded a reticence that was all but impenetrable.[96]

The book was a fitting beginning for the series and set a high standard for the volumes that followed. Its simple but attractive design, suggested by Mrs. Barrow, won an award for the press and would be the pattern for the other numbers in the series—as would its scholarly format and meticulous editing. In keeping with the Wormsloe Foundation's nonprofit status, book production and related costs were paid by the foundation and totaled approximately $3,000 for the limited edition of 750 copies. Since the book sold for $5 per copy, with Coulter and the press splitting the proceeds, lack of a profit was assured. The book sold well, with only 145 copies remaining by December 1956.[97]

Appreciative reviews abounded for *Wormsloe*. Richard Harwell noted that Coulter had written "with infinite care and an honest admiration—with care for history and admiration for facts. His fine, solid book is decked with the trimmings of this historical profession: supplementary notes and bibliography; and the reader should be warned that the trimmings should not be skipped. The notes are packed with pertinent and interesting information." Preston Brooks praised the "goodly number of reproductions of Jones–De Renne family portraits and the eight photographs of the buildings, avenues and grounds of Wormsloe." Coulter's writing, according to Herbert Weaver, was "good throughout, and in many places brilliant." And Freeman H. Hart called the book "the remarkably interesting story of a very unusual family whose six generations cover the span of the more than two centuries of Georgia. A representative of each of the six generations in a unique way represented his day. Their similarities and differences form a beautiful mosaic of history, a part of the development of America as a nation." He found it of "particular interest . . . that from the deep rooting of this family in Georgia soil there came in the later generations a flowering of a choice sort that enriched the cultural development of the state." [98]

A concern harbored by some readers was raised and answered by a Savannah reviewer. "There are few harder tasks for a serious writer," wrote Fritz Simmons in the *Savannah Evening Press*, "especially if he is first and foremost an historian, than a commissioned family history. This is true because there are few, if any families who do not have in their histories lesser events and individuals and those who commission or permit family histories are usually very proud people, indeed. Mr. Coulter, though sympathetic, has included the chaff with the wheat, either directly or by implication, and the result is a credit to the integrity of both the writer and the present chatelaine of Wormsloe, Mrs. Craig Barrow." That lady herself, Coulter was soon informed, was "very pleased with the outcome" of his labors. [99]

During Mrs. Barrow's lifetime, nine other books were published in the series of Wormsloe Foundation Publications, all in limited editions of from 600 to 750 copies. All but one would represent primary documentation of the Trusteeship period of Georgia's history, typified by the second and third numbers, announced as forthcoming in *Wormsloe:* a newly found volume of William Stephens's journal, covering the years 1741 to 1745, which was published in two volumes. It was fitting that the journal was a foundation publication, since a rare earlier volume had been made available for publication by the state through the courtesy of its owner, Mrs. Barrow's father. This publication of the journal also made plain the Wormsloe Foundation's commitment to historical integrity, for in putting Stephens into print, one of Noble Jones's occasional enemies was given a forum, and Jones did not escape criticism in several of the journal's passages. [100]

There was also a satisfying continuity in the fact that two of the other Wormsloe Foundation publications were associated closely with the Earl of Egmont, since one of the quartos had been a printing of a portion of his journal. One of the books coupled the *True and Historical Narrative* of arch-Malcontent Patrick Tailfer with the Earl of Egmont's acerbic comments and corrections, which had been written in his copy of the Tailfer polemic. The other foundation publication was a long-missing volume of Egmont's journal, 1732–38, for which Wymberley Jones De Renne had long searched in vain. This journal, as published by the Wormsloe Foundation, preceded in chronology that segment published by Mary De Renne in 1886 and had been part of the Thomas Phillipps collection; it had been acquired by the Thomas Gilcrease Institute of American History and Art, Tulsa, Oklahoma, which permitted its publication.[101]

The sixth of the foundation's publications was particularly significant, for it was based on a manuscript that formed part of a rich collection bought by the Wormsloe Foundation and presented in 1957 to the University of Georgia Library. *The Journal of Peter Gordon, 1732–1735* was based on a manuscript that was found among a wide range of materials gathered by Savannah collector Keith Read (1880–1940), who had lived very near Wormsloe. This purchase by the Wormsloe Foundation was heartily approved by Coulter, particularly since university libraries beyond Georgia's borders had competed strongly for the right to buy the collection. "I myself think," Coulter wrote Mrs. Barrow, "that Georgia has been long enough a colonial dependency in a literary sense, of institutions outside the state." According to John Wyatt Bonner, head of the university library's Special Collections Department, which gratefully received the 3,625-item Read Collection, it was "unique in that almost every item [contained] new and interesting information" and that there was almost no "filler material." Though richest in materials relating to eighteenth-century Georgia, the chronological range of the manuscripts embraced the period from the 1700s through the Civil War. Among the other Read items that saw publication (though not as part of the Wormsloe series) were *Laws of the Creek Nation* (1960) and *Lachlan McIntosh Papers in the University of Georgia Libraries* (1968).[102]

Beginning in 1966, the foundation's publications centered on the Salzburgers, early Georgia's most enterprising colonists. A generous number of volumes was published, starting with *Henry Newman's Salzburger Letterbooks* and continuing with volumes of Samuel Urlsperger's *Detailed Reports on the Salzburger Emigrants*, which had been among the German-language imprints collected by Wymberley Jones De Renne. Editing (and sometimes translating) these sources was George Fenwick Jones of the University of Maryland, son of George Noble Jones II and great-grandson of the first George Noble Jones.[103]

Among the numbers in the series published before Mrs. Barrow's death, the exception to colonial-era primary sources was *Joseph Vallence Bevan,*

Georgia's First Official Historian (1964), which was written by Coulter and dedicated to Mrs. Barrow, despite her initial reluctance. She was finally persuaded that such a dedication was an appropriate tribute of respect and admiration from Coulter, though she felt uneasy in appearing in other than an official capacity in relation to the foundation's publications.[104]

An irony of the Bevan book's subtitle is that Georgia's first official historian produced no history of the state. This book belongs to a class of studies produced by Coulter that have been called "historical miniatures." He had decided that there was more challenge to him as a researcher and historian, as well as the possibility of more interest to the reader, in selecting as his subjects relatively obscure figures rather than famous ones and giving them the full "life and times" treatment. This was certainly the case with the biography of Bevan; though it had admirers, its detractors felt that such subjects coupled with such methods led to superflous detail and uneven coverage.[105]

By the time of the Bevan biography's publication, Mrs. Barrow had come to view the Wormsloe Foundation as vital to her final plans for the future of Wormsloe. In 1961 she had decided to partition the estate, reserving to her family Wormsloe House and forty-eight acres surrounding it, bordered by the river to the east and the oak avenue to the west. She also reserved two smaller parcels: ten acres at Skidaway Point, where the old bridgehead had been located, and fifteen acres south of and adjoining the Wormsloe House parcel. She then presented to the Wormsloe Foundation the two large parcels that remained, a gift of 750 acres. One parcel constituted most of the old Wimberly lands that G. W. J. De Renne had added to Wormsloe (270 acres), and the other (480 acres) included all remaining lands west and south of Wormsloe House. The larger of the foundation's parcels contained both the tabby ruins and the ancient family cemetery.[106]

Coulter saw the step as an important one; the increase of the foundation's endowment was, he stated, "a milestone in the development of historical interest in this part of the country"; it would "increase the effectiveness of the Foundation greatly in carrying out the objects set forth in its charter." The donated land would continue to be used as it had been for some time, as a benefit to such groups as the Audubon Society and to various educational institutions (the University of Georgia, Armstrong University, and Emory University being the principal beneficiaries) that wanted access to Wormsloe's forests and marshes for a variety of reasons. The gift of the parcels to the Wormsloe Foundation would also lead to the first professional archaeological excavations at the site of Noble Jones's fortified tabby residence, which were conducted in 1968 and 1969, with the results published in 1979 in a foundation publication titled *Captain Jones's Wormslow*.[107]

During the 1950s and 1960s, Elfrida De Renne Barrow continued to make contributions to the Savannah area, both as a trustee of the Wormsloe Foundation and as a private individual. In the latter capacity, she gave a portion of her Poplar Grove land for the creation in 1955 of the Youth Museum of Savannah and served as one of the museum's original trustees. She also continued in her enjoyment of the Poetry Society of Georgia and her generous patronage of it.[108]

Another signal service she performed—this one involving the foundation—was her contribution to the rejuvenation of Savannah's historic district. In the years since the Great War, the historic section of Savannah had suffered from decay and neglect, and many irreplaceable structures had been razed. In 1966, after the Scarborough House ceased to be used as a school and reverted to the heirs of G. W. J. De Renne, Mrs. Barrow and the other trustees worked successfully to have the Regency mansion transferred to the Historic Savannah Foundation. She gave up her portion of the purchase price, and the Wormsloe Foundation contributed generously toward the restoration of the structure. Two years later the foundation trustees were instrumental in supporting the publication of the landmark book *Historic Savannah*.[109]

Elfrida De Renne Barrow continued to share Wormsloe with others, including opening the grounds two days yearly for a spring tour, usually for the benefit of the Women of Christ Church. And there were especially invited guests as well. For memorable annual visits to Wormsloe House, Mrs. Barrow's friend Professor Helen I. Greene brought the most accomplished and promising young women from her history classes at the state college in Milledgeville. Professors from other schools were also allowed to bring students for tours of the gardens and the ruins. Professor Spencer B. King and his Mercer University students were astonished by the "beautiful vista" that awaited them, and they found Wormsloe's grounds both "neat and majestic." As had others, the party found an abundance of birds. King likened it to a "convention," to which "every species must have sent delegates."[110]

Journalists came as well. Hugh Russell Fraser, like many before him, was overwhelmed as he turned through the gates into what he "knew at once

[was] one of the lush, natural, tropic gardens of the world." He thought at once of Henry David Thoreau and wondered what he, "who knew far better . . . how to appraise Nature," would have thought of it. Soon after being welcomed by Mrs. Barrow into Wormsloe House, Fraser was astonished to hear her quote Thoreau and found that she had just been reading him, in fact read him often, and also thought of him frequently during her lengthy walks over the estate.[111]

Resuming their conversation about Wormsloe, Mrs. Barrow said: "Nothing bothers you here. Neither autos, nor radio nor television, if you don't want these things to. Nothing—Oh yes, nothing except the airplane. I suppose you can't keep the airplanes away. . . . Did you know . . . Thoreau predicted that, too? You know that old adage: 'Poets are prophets'? Well, I believe it. You know what he once wrote: 'They have not yet laid waste the skies!' How wonderful a prediction that was! Just think of it, even Thoreau back in those days, could see what was coming." Asking her what Thoreau would have thought of Wormsloe, Fraser found that Mrs. Barrow had a ready answer: "Oh, I don't think he would like it. It is too lush, too tropical. He was not sectional, but regional. . . . I draw a distinction between [them]. That New England landscape has a certain austerity about it. It has its own regional character. I don't think he would be happy in so lush an environment as this."[112]

When William S. Kirkpatrick of the *Atlanta Journal and Constitution Magazine* came to Wormsloe, he was also captivated and prepared a careful account of the plantation and its history that benefited from a lengthy interview (and a detailed correspondence) with Mrs. Barrow. The Wormsloe Foundation had not yet received its portion of Wormsloe, and Kirkpatrick viewed with alarm the threats that the modern world had begun to pose to the ancient estate. Kirkpatrick's appreciative essay ended with a quotation from Professor Coulter regarding Wormsloe: "It is as old as Georgia itself and is a part of more than 200 years of the history of the commonwealth. Few if any of the states of the American Union have such a heritage. To allow it to become a casualty to 'progress' would be a tragedy for which future generations would be slow to forgive us."[113]

Mrs. Barrow's Savannah friends also made more private visits to Wormsloe—the poet Conrad Aiken, for example, strolled under the oaks with his wife, both absorbed by the beauty of their surroundings. And, occasionally, there would also be a "descent" on Wormsloe from Athens by Coulter, in company with the Misses Brumby, Anne Wallis and her sister Mary Harris—"those two prime grand-ladies," as John Donald Wade described them. Far removed from these visits were incursions by Hollywood: from time to time, motion picture companies were allowed to use portions of Wormsloe as filming locations.[114]

During the last several years of her life, Elfrida De Renne Barrow took particular delight in her children and grandchildren and the interest they took in matters that were dear to her. She was gratified that one of them suggested collaborating with her in the printing of a letter from Benjamin Franklin to Noble Wimberly Jones, with a reflective essay prepared by the young man, the great-great-great-greatgrandson of the "Morning Star of Liberty." It was produced handsomely in a limited edition by the Ashantilly Press in 1966. Two years later, at Mrs. Barrow's request, the same press printed an account of this grandson's wedding at Wormsloe, solemnized six decades after her own wedding there. Written by J. Frederick Waring, it was limited in distribution to family and friends. The wedding itself was attended by one lady other than Mrs. Barrow who attended the 1906 ceremony: Ophelia Dent of Hofwyl Plantation.[115]

Such happy events were counterbalanced with sad ones. In 1961, Mrs. Barrow's half-brother Dr. Charles Camblos Norris died at Fairhill, and, though nearing eighty herself, she took the train to faraway Pennsylvania to pay her last respects. There were also the deaths of Anne Wallis Brumby in 1964 and of Laura Palmer Bell in 1968, and, the following year, that of Mrs. Barrow's niece Frederica, who had been married at Wormsloe. And though Mrs. Barrow had for a long time enjoyed the "youthful old age" that she once attributed to one of her contemporaries, chronic illness began to exact its toll. Her mind, however, remained keen, her interests broad, her love of life undiminished.[116]

Among the concerns of Mrs. Barrow's final days was a renewed threat to Wormsloe by developers of Skidaway Island. An initial plan proposed a bridge from the Bethesda vicinity across the southernmost acres of Wormsloe. This catastrophe was avoided for a lesser one when the Wormsloe Foundation granted permission for the bridge to cross its marshlands at the southern tip of the Isle of Hope. Workers began in 1969 to construct huge concrete and steel piers and spans between Jones Point and the Florida passage below, and Wormsloe's privacy, security, and integrity were forever altered. Even more portentously, Chatham County had chosen to disallow the tax exemption on the foundation's Wormsloe land, and a lawsuit was in progress.[117]

But amid these painful distractions there came, during the last several months of Mrs. Barrows life, some good news to cheer her. With the help of Coulter and others, the voluminous Jones–De Renne family archive had been purchased from the estate of her brother, to be transferred to the most fitting location: the special collections section of the University of Georgia Library. What she felt her father had wished was finally accomplished: the contents of his library—books, manuscripts, and personal papers, almost in their entirety—would at last be preserved in a secure and appropriate place.[118]

Mrs. Barrow had drafted a will that left the remaining portion of Wormsloe to her son, Craig Barrow, Jr., in fee simple. She was secure in the certainty that he and his wife, Laura Bell Barrow, and their children would preserve the estate and uphold the family's traditions into the distant future.[119]

On the first of October 1970 Elfrida De Renne Barrow died at Wormsloe, and soon its soil received her body, as it had that of Noble Jones two centuries earlier.[120] In the simple brick enclosure of the Barrow family cemetery, beneath the soaring oak canopy, a marble slab to her memory was placed. On its surface were carved the final words of one of her most memorable poems:

> *Perhaps*
> *Beyond that undeciphered bend*
> *Waits another garden's end—*
> *Another gate*
> *Swings open to another spring.*
> *This is an estimate*
> *That blinds my reckoning.*

Appendices

Information regarding the sources of material in the appendices will be found, in sequence, at the end of the Notes.

The Blood of Noble Jones

Genealogical Tables of the Jones and De Renne Families and Related Families

TABLES

Overview: The Descent of the De Renne Family from Noble Jones

1. The Jones Family, First Through Third Generation in Georgia

2. George Jones and His Descendants

3. Sarah Jones Glen and Her Descendants

4. Gibbons, Cuthbert, and Telfair

5. Fenwick, Drayton, Campbell, and Tattnall

6. Campbell and Jones

7. Gibbes, Elliott, and Butler

8. Savage, Hutchinson, Tyng, and Jones

9. George Noble Jones and His Descendants

10. Van Deren

11. Campbell-Stewart

12. Smith

13. Camblos

14. De Renne

Abbreviations and Symbols

b. = born; d. = died; m. = married; unm. = unmarried; * = issue; ± = no issue

The Descent of the De Renne Family from Noble Jones

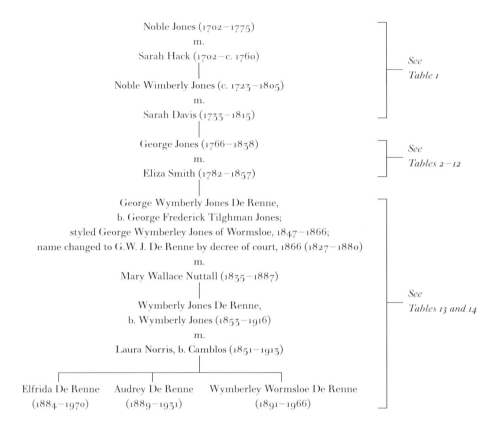

Noble Jones (1702–1775)
m.
Sarah Hack (1702–c. 1760)

See Table 1

Noble Wimberly Jones (c. 1723–1805)
m.
Sarah Davis (1733–1815)

George Jones (1766–1838)
m.
Eliza Smith (1782–1857)

See Tables 2–12

George Wymberly Jones De Renne,
b. George Frederick Tilghman Jones;
styled George Wymberley Jones of Wormsloe, 1847–1866;
name changed to G.W. J. De Renne by decree of court, 1866 (1827–1880)
m.
Mary Wallace Nuttall (1835–1887)

Wymberly Jones De Renne,
b. Wymberly Jones (1853–1916)
m.
Laura Norris, b. Camblos (1851–1913)

See Tables 13 and 14

Elfrida De Renne
(1884–1970)

Audrey De Renne
(1889–1931)

Wymberley Wormsloe De Renne
(1891–1966)

TABLE 1

The Jones Family, First Through Third Generation in Georgia

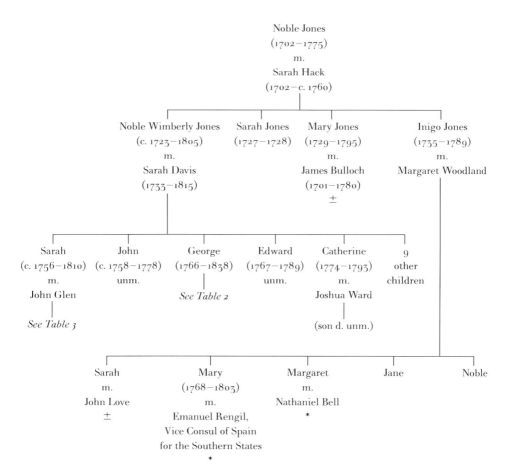

Noble Jones
(1702–1775)
m.
Sarah Hack
(1702–c. 1760)

Noble Wimberly Jones
(c. 1723–1805)
m.
Sarah Davis
(1733–1815)

Sarah Jones
(1727–1728)

Mary Jones
(1729–1795)
m.
James Bulloch
(1701–1780)
±

Inigo Jones
(1735–1789)
m.
Margaret Woodland

Sarah
(c. 1756–1810)
m.
John Glen

See Table 3

John
(c. 1758–1778)
unm.

George
(1766–1838)

See Table 2

Edward
(1767–1789)
unm.

Catherine
(1774–1793)
m.
Joshua Ward

(son d. unm.)

9
other
children

Sarah
m.
John Love
±

Mary
(1768–1803)
m.
Emanuel Rengil,
Vice Consul of Spain
for the Southern States
*

Margaret
m.
Nathaniel Bell
*

Jane

Noble

TABLE 2

George Jones and His Descendants

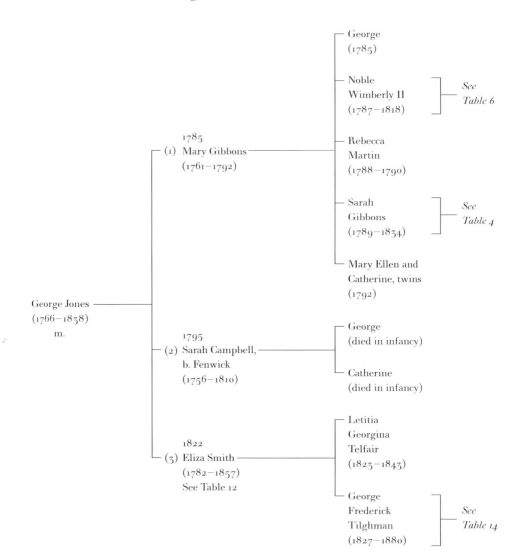

George Jones
(1766–1838)
m.

(1) 1785
Mary Gibbons
(1761–1792)

George
(1785)

Noble
Wimberly II
(1787–1818)
— *See
Table 6*

Rebecca
Martin
(1788–1790)

Sarah
Gibbons
(1789–1834)
— *See
Table 4*

Mary Ellen and
Catherine, twins
(1792)

(2) 1795
Sarah Campbell,
b. Fenwick
(1756–1810)

George
(died in infancy)

Catherine
(died in infancy)

(3) 1822
Eliza Smith
(1782–1857)
See Table 12

Letitia
Georgina
Telfair
(1823–1843)

George
Frederick
Tilghman
(1827–1880)
— *See
Table 14*

TABLE 3

Sarah Jones Glen and Her Descendants

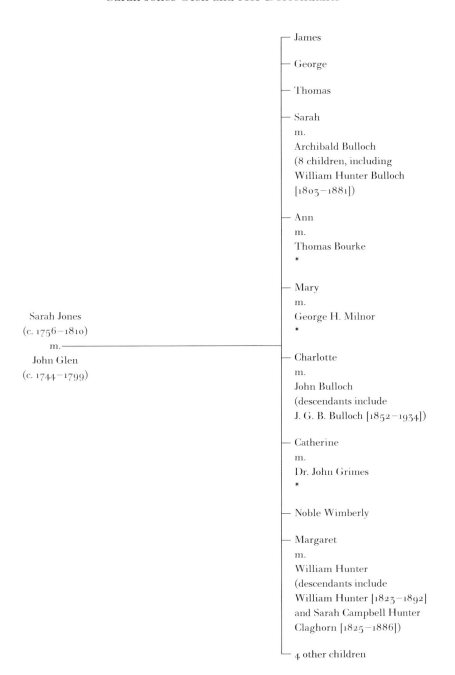

James

George

Thomas

Sarah
m.
Archibald Bulloch
(8 children, including
William Hunter Bulloch
[1803–1881])

Ann
m.
Thomas Bourke
*

Mary
m.
George H. Milnor
*

Sarah Jones
(c. 1756–1810)
m.
John Glen
(c. 1744–1799)

Charlotte
m.
John Bulloch
(descendants include
J. G. B. Bulloch [1852–1934])

Catherine
m.
Dr. John Grimes
*

Noble Wimberly

Margaret
m.
William Hunter
(descendants include
William Hunter [1823–1892]
and Sarah Campbell Hunter
Claghorn [1825–1886])

4 other children

TABLE 4

Gibbons, Cuthbert, and Telfair

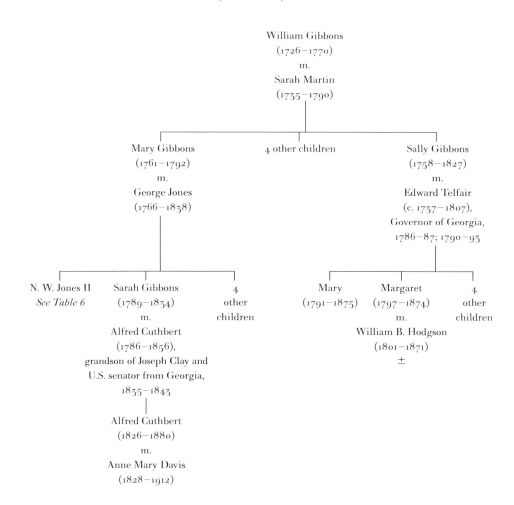

William Gibbons
(1726−1770)
m.
Sarah Martin
(1735−1790)

Mary Gibbons
(1761−1792)
m.
George Jones
(1766−1838)

4 other children

Sally Gibbons
(1758−1827)
m.
Edward Telfair
(c. 1737−1807),
Governor of Georgia,
1786−87; 1790−93

N. W. Jones II
See Table 6

Sarah Gibbons
(1789−1834)
m.
Alfred Cuthbert
(1786−1856),
grandson of Joseph Clay and
U.S. senator from Georgia,
1835−1843

Alfred Cuthbert
(1826−1880)
m.
Anne Mary Davis
(1828−1912)

4
other
children

Mary
(1791−1875)

Margaret
(1797−1874)
m.
William B. Hodgson
(1801−1871)
±

4
other
children

TABLE 5
Fenwick, Drayton, Campbell, and Tattnall

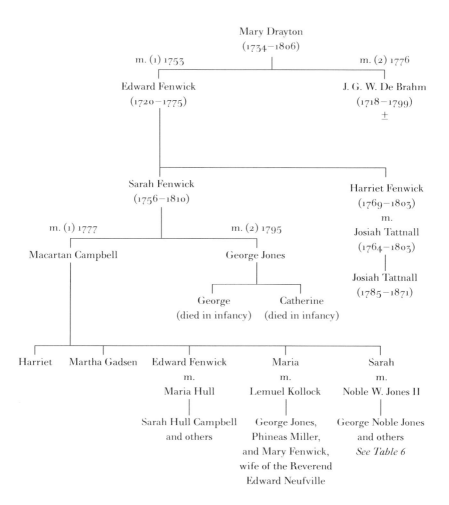

TABLE 6

Campbell and Jones

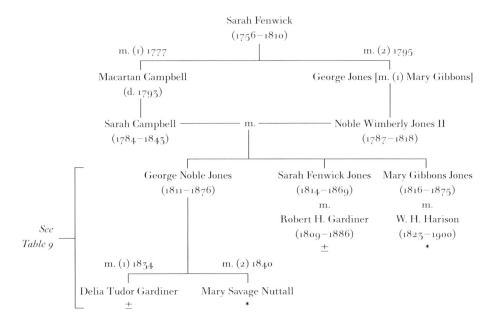

TABLE 7
Gibbes, Elliott, and Butler

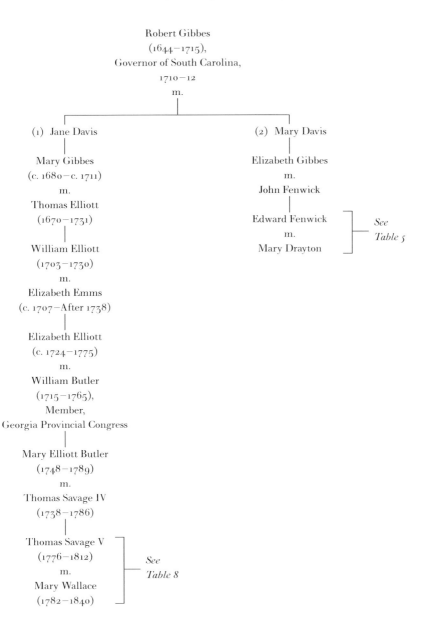

Robert Gibbes
(1644–1715),
Governor of South Carolina,
1710–12
m.

(1) Jane Davis

Mary Gibbes
(c. 1680–c. 1711)
m.
Thomas Elliott
(1670–1731)

William Elliott
(1703–1730)
m.
Elizabeth Emms
(c. 1707–After 1738)

Elizabeth Elliott
(c. 1724–1775)
m.
William Butler
(1715–1765),
Member,
Georgia Provincial Congress

Mary Elliott Butler
(1748–1789)
m.
Thomas Savage IV
(1738–1786)

Thomas Savage V
(1776–1812)
m.
Mary Wallace
(1782–1840)

*See
Table 8*

(2) Mary Davis

Elizabeth Gibbes
m.
John Fenwick

Edward Fenwick
m.
Mary Drayton

*See
Table 5*

TABLE 8

Savage, Hutchinson, Tyng, and Jones

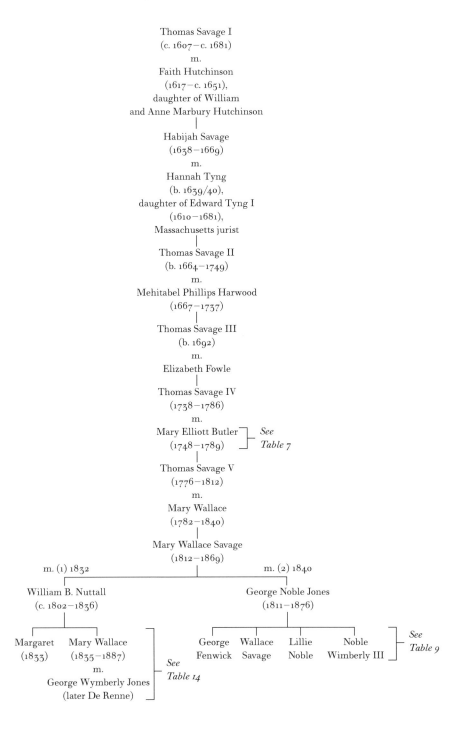

Thomas Savage I
(c. 1607–c. 1681)
m.
Faith Hutchinson
(1617–c. 1651),
daughter of William
and Anne Marbury Hutchinson

Habijah Savage
(1638–1669)
m.
Hannah Tyng
(b. 1639/40),
daughter of Edward Tyng I
(1610–1681),
Massachusetts jurist

Thomas Savage II
(b. 1664–1749)
m.
Mehitabel Phillips Harwood
(1667–1737)

Thomas Savage III
(b. 1692)
m.
Elizabeth Fowle

Thomas Savage IV
(1738–1786)
m.
Mary Elliott Butler   *See*
(1748–1789)   *Table 7*

Thomas Savage V
(1776–1812)
m.
Mary Wallace
(1782–1840)

Mary Wallace Savage
(1812–1869)

m. (1) 1832   m. (2) 1840

William B. Nuttall   George Noble Jones
(c. 1802–1836)   (1811–1876)

Margaret   Mary Wallace   George   Wallace   Lillie   Noble   *See*
(1833)   (1835–1887)   Fenwick   Savage   Noble   Wimberly III   *Table 9*
              m.   *See*
              George Wymberly Jones   *Table 14*
              (later De Renne)

TABLE 9

George Noble Jones and His Descendants

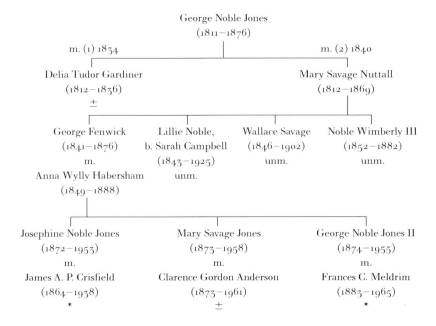

George Noble Jones
(1811–1876)

m. (1) 1834   m. (2) 1840

Delia Tudor Gardiner
(1812–1836)
±

Mary Savage Nuttall
(1812–1869)

George Fenwick
(1841–1876)
m.
Anna Wylly Habersham
(1849–1888)

Lillie Noble,
b. Sarah Campbell
(1843–1925)
unm.

Wallace Savage
(1846–1902)
unm.

Noble Wimberly III
(1852–1882)
unm.

Josephine Noble Jones
(1872–1953)
m.
James A. P. Crisfield
(1864–1938)
*

Mary Savage Jones
(1873–1958)
m.
Clarence Gordon Anderson
(1873–1961)
±

George Noble Jones II
(1874–1955)
m.
Frances C. Meldrim
(1883–1965)
*

TABLE 10

Van Deren

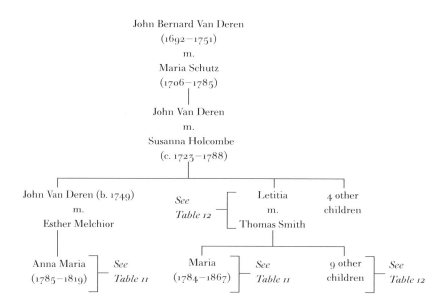

John Bernard Van Deren
(1692–1751)
m.
Maria Schutz
(1706–1785)

John Van Deren
m.
Susanna Holcombe
(c. 1723–1788)

John Van Deren (b. 1749)
m.
Esther Melchior

See Table 12

Letitia
m.
Thomas Smith

4 other children

Anna Maria
(1785–1819)

See Table 11

Maria
(1784–1867)

See Table 11

9 other children

See Table 12

TABLE 11

Campbell-Stewart

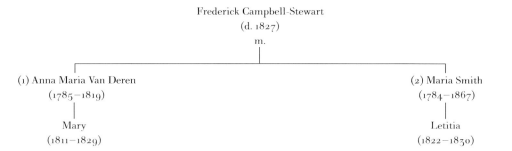

Frederick Campbell-Stewart
(d. 1827)
m.

(1) Anna Maria Van Deren
(1785–1819)

Mary
(1811–1829)

(2) Maria Smith
(1784–1867)

Letitia
(1822–1830)

TABLE 12

Smith

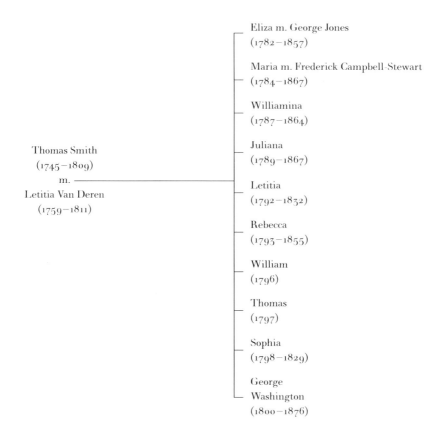

Thomas Smith
(1745–1809)
m.
Letitia Van Deren
(1759–1811)

Eliza m. George Jones
(1782–1857)

Maria m. Frederick Campbell-Stewart
(1784–1867)

Williamina
(1787–1864)

Juliana
(1789–1867)

Letitia
(1792–1832)

Rebecca
(1793–1855)

William
(1796)

Thomas
(1797)

Sophia
(1798–1829)

George
Washington
(1800–1876)

TABLE 13

Camblos

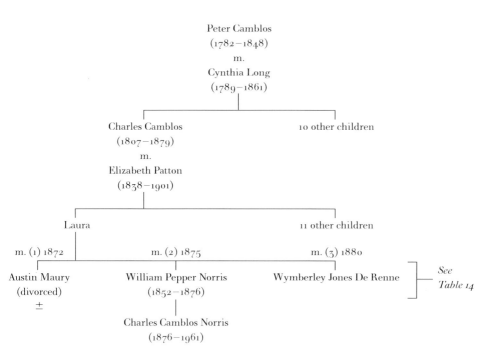

Peter Camblos
(1782–1848)
m.
Cynthia Long
(1789–1861)

Charles Camblos
(1807–1879)
m.
Elizabeth Patton
(1838–1901)

10 other children

Laura

11 other children

m. (1) 1872   m. (2) 1875   m. (3) 1880

Austin Maury   William Pepper Norris   Wymberley Jones De Renne
(divorced)   (1852–1876)
±

See
Table 14

Charles Camblos Norris
(1876–1961)

TABLE 14

De Renne

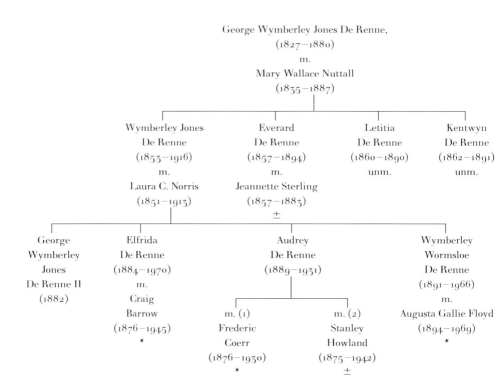

George Wymberley Jones De Renne,
(1827–1880)

m.

Mary Wallace Nuttall
(1835–1887)

| Wymberley Jones De Renne (1853–1916) m. Laura C. Norris (1851–1913) | Everard De Renne (1857–1894) m. Jeannette Sterling (1857–1883) ± | Letitia De Renne (1860–1890) unm. | Kentwyn De Renne (1862–1891) unm. |

| George Wymberley Jones De Renne II (1882) | Elfrida De Renne (1884–1970) m. Craig Barrow (1876–1945) * | Audrey De Renne (1889–1931) | Wymberley Wormsloe De Renne (1891–1966) m. Augusta Gallie Floyd (1894–1969) * |

| m. (1) Frederic Coerr (1876–1930) * | m. (2) Stanley Howland (1875–1942) ± |

Collections and Publications of the Jones–De Renne Family

A. Collections

1. The Antebellum Library of George Wymberley Jones

The manuscript catalog of Jones's antebellum library is found in a volume labeled on its spine "Miscellanea Georgiana"—an acquisition early enough to have De Renne's birth name, "George F. T. Jones," stamped above the title. In a brief prefatory note he states:

> This catalogue contains about 1250 volumes—costing about $3500. I had besides a number of other books, and engravings, not mentioned in it—in all, I believe, about 1300 volumes worth about $3700.
>
> Most of them were lost by the sack of Habersham's store at the capture of Savannah Dec. 21. 1864—and by the fire at Oaklands. Jefferson Co. Ga. April 25. 1865.

The books in the antebellum library were purchased principally in Philadelphia, Savannah, and Europe between 1844 and 1861. Most of them were apparently kept in Philadelphia until their removal to Wormsloe in 1854. Seven years later, after the Civil War began, the books were divided to be sent to safety. Instead, they met with the twin disasters mentioned by Jones above. Those that survived (joined by some replacements for several that did not, as well as other books) eventually became part of the G. W. J. De Renne Georgia Historical Collection at the Georgia State Library in Atlanta. That collection, now at the Hargrett Rare Book and Manuscript Library, will be described below.

Preparation of a subject bibliography based on the catalog showed that the antebellum library could be divided into the following sections: Ancient History, European and Asian History, British History and Biography, United States History, Books Relating to Carolina and Georgia, Description and Travel, Heraldry and Genealogy, Recreation and Leisure, Periodicals, Science and Technology, Medicine (including Medical Biography and Anthropology), Agriculture, Fine Arts, Philosophy and Psychology, Religion, Classical Greek Literature, Latin Literature and Language, British Poetry and Drama, British Literature (Novels, Essays, Literary Biography, and Miscellany), American Literature, French Literature and Language, Other Literatures, and Bibliography (Books, Libraries, Catalogs, and Bibliographies).

2. The G. W. J. De Renne Georgia Historical Collection (The De Renne Gift)

These books actually represent three separate collections. From a historical standpoint, the most important among them belong to that small group of books that G.W.J. De Renne called the "ruins" of the antebellum library that he collected as George Wymberley Jones. These volumes survived the two catastrophes that struck his collection in 1864 and 1865, and many bear one of his "George Wymberley Jones of Wormsloe" bookplates.

The other two groups were collected by Mr. and Mrs. De Renne after the war. Though De Renne made no attempt to restore all sections of his earlier collection, he took particular steps toward recreating his Georgia library by locating replacements for books that had been lost. His purchases also included books that had not been represented earlier, such as the series of sermons preached before the Trustees in the 1730s. De Renne's postbellum acquisitions came from both America and Europe and received "G.W. J. De Renne" bookplates, or none at all. This group of books is also rich in finely bound presentation copies from Colonel Charles C. Jones, Jr.

The third group of books is associated with Mary De Renne rather than her husband. It includes titles collected by her or presented to her after 1880, as well as examples of her own printing ventures, including her continuation of the Wormsloe Quartos and multiple copies of her edition of John Warwick Daniel's oration on R. E. Lee.

The diverse collection represented by these three groups of books was housed for a time in the Liberty Street residence in Savannah, along with the Mary De Renne Confederate Collection (described below), other family books, and Letitia De Renne's personal library. How all of these books and other materials were separated and assigned to their several destinations is a matter of conjecture. Indications are that Everard De Renne probably had many of the books and materials packed and shipped to New York at some time between his mother's death in 1887 and that of his sister in February 1890. These books he later left as bequests in honor of his father and mother, and they are first mentioned as separate collections in his will of July 1890.

The books remaining at the Savannah residence numbered over thirteen hundred and were inventoried as part of Letitia De Renne's estate. Nonetheless, they appear to have included volumes from each of three groups described above, that is, books from G. W. J. De Renne's antebellum and postbellum libraries and non-Confederate books that had belonged to Mary De Renne.

The unfortunate circumstance of the mixture of the collections prevents an accurate accounting of the survivors of De Renne's antebellum library, as well as a precise assessment of his postwar collecting activities. Despite the similarity of his and his daughter's intellectual interests, many titles inventoried as part of Letitia De Renne's estate seem more likely to have been her father's than hers. There is, for example, a small collection of Latin classics, with multiple copies of Horace, one of which seems to have been a survivor of the prewar collection, along with a vellum-bound 1754 edition of Pliny; it seems identical to one that De Renne had before the war. Since the numerous Greek and Roman classics of the antebellum library are represented in the De Renne Gift by only one odd volume from a broken set of Euripides, it seems unlikely that it is an accurate reflection of the classical works that De Renne owned after the war. Additionally, a seventeen-volume, calf-bound set of Horace Walpole's works and correspondence, different from and more complete than the antebellum library's set, is a notable example of what would appear to have been one of G. W. J. De Renne's postwar purchases. Numerous other volumes parallel—in title and subject—those in the prewar library.

In any case, the books listed in Letitia De Renne's property inventory, valued at $8,000, did not continue as an independent collection, and none of them are known to have resurfaced. Everard and Kentwyn divided many of these books between themselves, keeping some of them—no doubt—because they had been their father's. A Philadelphia book dealer purchased the sizable remainder.

This dispersed library of Letitia De Renne's property inventory contained no Civil War books and only one Georgia title, Colonel Charles C. Jones's *Negro Myths from the Georgia Coast* (1888), published after the deaths of both her parents. Obviously, Everard De Renne did a thorough job of removing from the Liberty Street house all books that pertained to the Georgiana and Confederate collections he would bequeath (though there would be some admixture). Of the remaining titles, many doubtless did belong to Letitia De Renne, though only a few of them—most relating to art and poetry—can be assigned to her with certainty because of their dates of publication. Only about sixty of the inventoried books were listed with publication dates; most that are listed are pre-1860.

The dispersed collection contained numerous leather-bound editions of the premier nineteenth-century English novelists, including Dickens, Eliot, and Thackeray; standard sets of the works of American and English poets; classics of French literature; and a good selection of historical works, from Gibbon and Macaulay to

Prescott and Parkman. Included as well were the popular series on British history by John Heneage Jesse and Martha Walker Freer's similar French chronicles. It is unknown whether any of these dispersed books had bookplates.

Those books preserved by Everard De Renne as two different collections went to different locations. In an 1893 codicil to his will, Everard De Renne left his mother's Confederate books (along with her manuscripts and relics) to the Ladies' Hollywood Memorial Association of Richmond, Virginia, for placement in the Confederate Museum. The other books he bequeathed to the State Library of Georgia in Atlanta as the "G. W. J. De Renne Georgia Historical Collection." Soon thereafter, the 1894 General Assembly passed a resolution stating that the "people of the State of Georgia will ever hold in grateful remembrance the State pride and the great generosity which must have animated Mr. [Everard] De Renne to make this valuable donation."

Though about half of the approximately 170 titles related to Georgia history, many of them rare and several beautifully bound, the remaining volumes formed such a disparate collection that they seem to have been brought together arbitrarily. It is difficult to understand, for example, why Everard De Renne placed under his father's name—as a collection of Georgiana—such books as Edwin W. Streeter's *Precious Stones and Gems* and John Brown's sentimental dog story *Rab and His Friends*.

Both the Atlanta and Richmond repositories received their bequests in 1894. After seeing *The De Renne Gift*, John Milledge's catalog of the books sent to the State Library, Katherine C. Stiles, vice regent for the Confederate Museum's Georgia Room, moved to retrieve some items which she knew Mrs. De Renne had considered part of her Confederate collection and to return to Georgia other De Renne volumes that she thought belonged there. Her efforts, ultimately successful, explain the presence in the collection of books that are unquestionably De Renne books but are not listed in Milledge's pamphlet or elsewhere. There are also some other books, not originally listed and without bookplates, that may indeed have belonged to the De Rennes, though some may be strays from the State Library's general collection.

Others may be replacements. Several listed De Renne books (and perhaps some unlisted) fell victim to pilferage or loss at some time between 1894 and 1911, when State Librarian Maud Barker Cobb conducted the first systematic inventory and professional cataloging of the collection. The State Library subsequently purchased some titles to take the place of those that were missing. In recent years, some of the titles purloined from the State Library have reappeared, offered for sale by dealers in rare books.

In the case of five Jones–De Renne publications of which there were multiple copies in the collection, the State Library in 1902 permanently loaned the surplus titles to other libraries across the state: Emory College Library at Oxford, Mercer College Library in Macon, the University of Georgia Library in Athens, the library of the Georgia Historical Society in Savannah, and the Wymberley Jones De Renne Georgia Library at Wormsloe.

The Museum of the Confederacy (successor to the Confederate Museum) holds several books that were part of G. W. J. De Renne's library, notably presentation copies from Colonel Charles C. Jones, Jr., such as *The Siege of Savannah in 1864*, which were presumably assigned to Mrs. De Renne's collection because of their Confederate subject matter. Among the other books in Richmond, Colonel Jones's *History of Georgia* (which stops well short of the Civil War) would more properly have been sent to the State Library's collection.

When the Georgia State Library became the Georgia State Law Library, its nonlaw books were placed elsewhere. In 1992 the Hargrett Rare Book and Manuscript Library of the University of Georgia Libraries received the De Renne books (which during their time in Atlanta had been erroneously identified as the Mary De Renne Historical Collection). The Hargrett Library maintains the G. W. J. De Renne Georgia Historical Collection under the name it was meant to bear and continues to keep it separate from other collections. Added to it in recent years from different sources have been two more survivors of G. W. J. De Renne's antebellum library.

3. THE MARY DE RENNE CONFEDERATE COLLECTION

The Ladies' Hollywood Memorial Association of Richmond, Virginia, received Everard De Renne's bequest of the Mary De Renne Confederate Collection in 1894, the same year that its sister organization, the Confederate Memorial Literary Society, received title to the "White House of the Confederacy." Until the structure could be readied for its opening as the Confederate Museum, the collection was stored in a vault in Richmond's State Bank. In early 1896 it was moved to its intended place in the museum's Georgia Room.

Though the voluminous De Renne Confederate Collection contained all manner of manuscripts, images, and relics, only its books and pamphlets are readily identified. Of the printed materials gathered by Mrs. De Renne relating to the Middle Period, the great majority dealt with the Civil War. There is no evidence that she ever prepared a catalog of her own or that Everard De Renne arranged for the books and pamphlets to be listed. If an actual shelf list was ever prepared at the museum itself, it has not been found. Consequently, a major source of information on the printed materials is the set of rudimentary, often baffling, catalogs published by the Confederate Museum in 1898 and 1905. Though they list the assorted components of the collection in all their profusion, these catalogs provide only minimal bibliographical information in their entries for books and pamphlets. Douglas Southall Freeman's elaborate 1908 *Calendar of Confederate Papers*, though very precise in its listings, includes only Confederate imprints and other wartime publications and manuscripts.

Any personal inspection of the printed materials of the De Renne Confederate Collection is hampered by the fact that its books and pamphlets were decades ago absorbed into the Museum of the Confederacy's general library (just as the relics were submerged in the general artifact collection). No notations on catalog cards assist in identifying volumes from the De Renne collection, but, as might be expected, the sumptuous bindings of the books themselves provide strong indications of the De Renne books' scattered presence on the shelves; their bookplates offer final confirmation. Identifying Confederate imprints in pamphlet form is more problematical. Nonetheless, the lineaments of Mary De Renne's achievement remain apparent.

4. THE WYMBERLEY JONES DE RENNE GEORGIA LIBRARY

Although most of the 1931 catalog's books relating to the history of Georgia from 1700 through 1929 are still present in the library, many of the other materials gathered by Wymberley Jones De Renne and Wymberley Wormsloe De Renne are elsewhere or have dropped entirely from sight. Of the printed materials, few of the newspapers—other than rarities like the *Cherokee Phoenix*—are still in the De Renne library, and neither are many of the books listed in the catalog's bibliography, though that listing includes works consulted elsewhere as well as works actually on the shelves at Wormsloe. Some that were there such as Rich's *Bibliotheca Americana Nova* (1835–46) and *The Leiter Library* (1907) are missing. Most of the maps, plans, and engravings, however, are still with the collection.

The manuscript riches of the De Renne Georgia Library received very uneven coverage in the catalog. Although there are entries for some of the major eighteenth-century acquisitions—such as the Trustees' accountant Harman Verelst's letters and reports (1741–43) and General Benjamin Lincoln's orderly book (1779–80)—a prized nineteenth-century collection like the Robert E. Lee Dispatches receives only passing mention in a footnote, and the other sections of the Jones Confederate Collection are not described. As Leonard L. Mackall noted, "letters written by prominent men, many being of great interest," were never "calendared or even listed."

Since the terms of the library sale to the regents excluded the manuscripts, some were disposed of elsewhere, while others arrived with the several installments of the De Renne Family Papers. Most were given separate manuscript numbers and entered the general manuscript collection.

The list that follows includes all identifiable manuscripts that were once in the De Renne Georgia Library at Wormsloe, including both the general historical manuscripts and the Jones–De Renne family archive (including those portions of the archive later accumulated in Athens). Related Jones–De Renne manuscripts are also listed. Unless otherwise noted, these manuscripts are in the Hargrett Rare Book and Manuscript Library, University of Georgia Libraries, Athens, Georgia. The library's collection descriptions are occasionally quoted.

FAMILY MANUSCRIPTS. (Entries whose manuscript numbers are followed by an asterisk were never in the De Renne Georgia Library.)

1. De Renne Family Papers (1732–1939), Ms. 1064: 7,420 items in 59 boxes and one volume with interleaved manuscripts.

1a. De Renne Family Papers—Oversize (1735–1916), Ms. 1064a: 61 items.

2. De Renne Family Papers (1770–1986), Ms. 2819: 47 boxes and a drawer of oversize materials.

3. Wymberley Wormsloe De Renne Family Papers (1880–1970), Ms. 1788: c. 15,000 items in 119 boxes. Portions of this collection are restricted.

4. De Renne Family Receipts and Remedies (1860s–1940s), Ms. 1120: 136 items. Recipes for cakes, sauces, vegetables, meats, desserts, fish, salads, jellies, soups, wine, breads, and drinks. The collection includes two manuscript recipe books (one Mary De Renne's). Also present are remedies for minor illnesses and various housekeeping hints, with newspaper clippings covering all of the above-mentioned topics.

5. Noble Jones—Noble Wimberly Jones—George Jones Papers (1754–1838), Ms. 1136: 80 items (mainly correspondence) "tipped into a bound volume by Wymberley Jones De Renne circa 1905."

6. Noble Wimberly Jones–Benjamin Franklin Correspondence (1768–78), Ms. 1414*: 14 items (photographic reproductions).

7. Noble Wimberly Jones (1778), Ms. 2322(M)*: 1 item. Petition for payment as member of the Continental Congress, endorsed by George Walton.

8. Thomas Smith Papers (1767–1912), Ms. 1055: 68 items. Letters and papers associated with G. W. J. De Renne's maternal grandfather and his family.

9. Thomas Smith Papers: George Washington Division (1785–1912), Ms. 1055a: 5 items. Typescripts made in 1902 of Washington-Smith correspondence (1785–86) relating to Pennsylvania land suits in which Smith represented Washington. Also correspondence relating to the originals being offered for sale to W. J. De Renne, 1911–12.

10. Thomas Smith Papers: Burton Alva Konkle Division (1902–6), Ms. 1055b: 93 items. Correspondence between W. J. De Renne and Burton Alva Konkle relating to the latter's *Life and Times of Thomas Smith, 1745–1809*, with bills, clippings, and other materials relating to the book's publication.

11. John Van Deren Land Patent (1776), Ms. 1133.

12. Frederick and Maria Campbell Stewart: Land Documents (1815–34), Ms. 1136 (oversize). Mainly printed material relating to the settlement of the estate of Frederick Campbell Stewart, uncle of G. W. J. De Renne.

13. William Bacon Stevens Letters (1847–48), Ms. 1134: 9 items. These letters were written by Stevens to G. F. T. Jones (later G. W. J. De Renne) during the time Stevens was preparing the first volume of his *History of Georgia*.

14. George Wymberley Jones De Renne Letters (1870–78), Ms. 467*: 5 items. Photostats of letters used in E. M. Coulter's research for *Wormsloe* (1955).

15. Wymberley Jones De Renne Book Lists, Ms. 2745 (M). Printed lists advertising wants of the De Renne Georgia Library.

OTHER HISTORICAL MANUSCRIPTS

1. De Renne Confederate Manuscripts (1861–1905), Ms. 1135: 54 items. "This collection of miscellaneous letters and documents pertains to a wide variety of individuals active in the cause of the Confederacy. There are a number of letters from the war years, but the majority are letters of reminiscence and anecdote from the post-war period with a few individuals represented only by signatures on documents." Since many are addressed to Colonel Charles C. Jones, Jr., they may be remnants of the Jones Confederate Collection or, in some cases, letters that had been passed along by Jones to Mary De Renne for her autograph collection.

2. De Renne Historical Manuscripts (1746–1908), Ms. 1136: 56 items. "This collection of miscellaneous letters, notes, and documents pertains almost wholly to historical figures important in the development of Georgia as colony and state. . . . Although not all items are of great historical importance (a few being retained for autographs alone), several are of pre-eminent significance, including letters of Pierce Butler (30 March 1803) to Aaron Burr, William A. Bowles (15 February 1799) to Lord Townshend, and Thomas Savage (14 December 1775)." Correspondence of W. J. De Renne is found under the subheadings "Material from 'Acts . . . 1775–1770,'" "George Gilman Smith," and "Dr. John M. Harney."

3. De Renne Historical Manuscripts (1770–1899), Ms. 2819, Box 13: 22 miscellaneous items.

4. Miscellaneous Manuscripts. The following were transferred to the general manuscript collection at various times and have all but lost their identity as part of De Renne Georgia Library. Page numbers in brackets refer to descriptions in the 1931 catalog; those entries without page citations were not included therein.

Ms. 787a.   General Benjamin Lincoln's Order Book, Volume 2 (1779–80) [217–18].

Ms. 1039.   Sir James Wright, Governor of the Province of Georgia—Answer to the Lords of Trade, 15 February 1762 [142].

Ms. 1040.   Frink, Samuel. Seven Sermons Delivered in Christ Church, Savannah, 1767–71 [183].

Ms. 1041.   *Hercules* (ship). Log Book of a Voyage from Plymouth to Savannah, 1784 [231].

Ms. 1042.   James Wilson et al.— Manuscript Memoranda relating to the Yazoo Lands, 1794–1803 [264].

Ms. 1043.   John Y. Noel—Letter of John Y. Noel, mayor of Savannah, on the burning of the city on 29 November 1796 [274].

Ms. 1044.   Georgia Commission Book "B." Typed transcripts of state military commissions, 1754–1827, with index [402].

Ms. 1045.   Young Men's Debating Club of Savannah, 1835. "The original manuscript record book of the club," including constitution by-laws and member list [447].

Ms. 1046.   Eugene LeHardy—Journal, vol. 3, 1851–53. The manuscript diary and miscellany of a civil engineer engaged in railroad construction in northwest Georgia [540].

Ms. 1047.   Wilson Lumpkin—Incidents connected with the life of Wilson Lumpkin, 1852. These two manuscript journals were the source of *The Removal of the Cherokee Indians from Georgia* (1907) [547].

Ms. 1048.   Selma, Rome and Dalton Railroad Company, Rome, Georgia. Correspondence, 1868–71 [705].

Ms. 1049.   Eugene Henry Hinton. A Historical Sketch of the Evolution of Trade and Transportation at Augusta, Georgia, c. 1912. Also, a similar sketch relating to Macon, Georgia [1113].

Ms. 1052.   Twiggs Family—Genealogy, c. 1910 [1094].

Ms. 1056.   Dr. William Duncan—Papers of a Confederate surgeon, including wartime and postwar material, 1861–73.

Ms. 1099.   Robert Milledge Charlton—Legal Briefs, 1824–31.

Ms. 1114.   Medicine—Early Georgia, 1844–94.

Ms. 1147.   Legal Commonplace Book, late eighteenth century.

Ms. 1148.   Dr. J. C. LeHardy—Medical Correspondence, 1874–79.

Ms. 1192.   Letter, John McPherson Berrien to George Jones, 9 June 1819.

Ms. 1193.   Robert Middleton—Land Warrants, 1790 (3 items).

Ms. 1194.   Jacob Waldburg Papers, 1793–1829 (3 items). Waldburg was a Chatham County merchant.

Ms. 1205.   Henry Bourguin—List of Slaves, 1799.

Ms. 1292. Friendly Fire Association, Savannah. Minutes, March–April 1809 [337].

Ms. 1420. Charles Spalding, "The Indian Difficulties of Georgia," address delivered before the Georgia Historical Society, 30 March 1844. 3 items, 1844–1918.

Ms. 1421. Bryan Family Genealogy: "The Bryan Family of South Carolina and Georgia," undated [1325–26].

Ms. 1422. Cuthbert Family Genealogy: "Remarks as to the Cuthberts," undated (c. 1900) [1326].

Ms. 1423. Index of Articles on American Indians in *The Friend: A Religious and Literary Journal*, vols. 1 to 19 [1313–14].

Ms. 1494. Berrien Family Genealogy.

Ms. 1496. Photographs of Savannah, c. 1900.
           179 photographs and views mounted on 17 plates [1281].

Ms. 1503. Christ Church, St. Simons Island, Georgia.
           Christ Church Parish History, 1904 [1009].

Ms. 1504. Bulloch, J. G. B. Address at Banquet of the Order of Washington, Hotel Cairo, Washington, D.C., 22 February 1909, and letter, Bulloch to W. J. De Renne, 3 March 1909.

Ms. 1505. Georgia Hussars, Savannah Scrapbook. Newspaper clippings, 1894–96.

Ms. 1512. Confederate States of America, Constitution. Supplementing the document are 38 items, including correspondence, photographs, and clippings [619–20].

Ms. 1516. Estaing, Charles Hector, comte D'.
           Siege de Savannah . . . (1779) [215–16].

Ms. 1650. Norwood, Thomas Manson. Letters of Nemesis. 6 items, 1871–1913, including transcripts of the Nemesis letters attacking Governor Rufus Bullock, from the *Augusta Chronicle and Sentinel* of 1871. Also correspondence relating to the making of the transcripts for W. J. De Renne.

DISPERSED MANUSCRIPTS. The following collections are now in other repositories or in non–De Renne collections in the Hargrett Library.

Charles C. Jones, Jr., Confederate Collection. Most of this collection was widely dispersed. Only its most identifiable components are listed.

Lee, Robert Edward. Official Letters, 1862–65. Virginia State Library and Archives, Richmond, Virginia. (This is the bulk of the Lee letters.) Some others are in the George H. and Katherine M. Davis Collection, Howard-Tilton Memorial

Library, Tulane University, and the Keith Read Collection, Hargrett Rare Book and Manuscript Library, University of Georgia.

Lee, Robert Edward. Official Telegrams, 1862–65. Special Collections Library, Duke University.

Jones–De Renne Family Archive, 1700s–1900s. Portions of this collection are found in various Jones and De Renne collections in Duke's Special Collections Library and in the Keith Read Collections at the Georgia Historical Society and at the Hargrett Rare Book and Manuscript Library, University of Georgia.

Harman Verelst Manuscripts, 1741–43. Special Collections Library, Duke University.

Anthony Wayne–Nathanael Greene Manuscripts, 1781–82. William L. Clements Library, University of Michigan, Ann Arbor, Michigan.

PUBLICATIONS

1. JONES–DE RENNE PUBLICATIONS, 1847–86

*Denotes Wormsloe Quartos. With the exception of *Observations on Dr. Stevens's History of Georgia*, the first seven entries below are cited verbatim from *Miscellanea Georgiana*.

*[George Walton, William Few, and Richard Howly.] *Observations upon the Effects of certain late Political Suggestions*. By the Delegates of Georgia. Printed in the year 1781. Wormsloe [printed at Philadelphia, by C. Sherman], 1847. 4.to pp. 14. 21 copies printed: 2 on plate paper, 19 on fine paper.

Theory concerning the Nature of Insanity. By George Wymberley-Jones. Wormsloe [printed at Philadelphia, by C. Sherman], 1847. 8vo. pp. 38. 48 copies printed: 4 on plate paper, 44 on fine paper.

**History of the Province of Georgia: With Maps of original Surveys*. By John Gerar William de Brahm, His Majesty's Surveyor-General for the Southern District of North America. Now first printed. Wormsloe [printed at Philadelphia, by C. Sherman], 1849. 4.to pp. 55. 6 maps, and colophon [black letter, shaped like an inverted pyramid, with the apex pointing toward the Jones arms]. 49 copies printed: 4 on plate paper, 45 on fine paper.

[*Observations on Doctor Stevens's History of Georgia*. Savannah (printed at Philadelphia, by C. Sherman?), 1849. 8vo, pp. 28. 105 copies printed: 100 on fine paper, 5 on large paper.]

**Journal and Letters of Eliza Lucas*. Now first printed. Wormsloe [printed at Philadelphia, by C. Sherman], 1850. 4.to pp. 30. & colophon [black letter, in the shape of a diamond]. 19 copies printed: 6 on the "C. H."–English paper, 13 on plate paper.

A Bachelor's Reverie: In Three Parts. I. Smoke—Signifying Doubt. II. Blaze—Signifying Cheer. III. Ashes—Signifying Desolation. By Ik: Marvel. Wormsloe [printed at Philadelphia, by C. Sherman], 1850. 8vo. pp. 40. & colophon [black letter, arranged in a rectangle]. 12 copies printed—on the C. H. Paper.

* *Diary of Col. Winthrop Sargent, Adjutant General of the United States Army, During the Campaign of MDCCXCI.* Now first Printed. Wormsloe [printed at Philadelphia, by C. Sherman], 1851. 4.to pp. 58. & colophon [black letter, in the shape of an hourglass] & two plates [engraved by G. W. Boynton, based upon drawings by Winthrop Sargent: (1) Order of Battle, March and Encampment of the Army of the United States under Major General Arthur St. Clair, during the Campaign of 1791; (2) A Plan of the Encampment and Sketch of the Action, Retreat &c., upon Nov. 4th, 1791]. 46 copies printed: 6 on the "C. H." paper, 40 on plate paper.

* Georgia (Colony). General Assembly, 1755–74. *Acts Passed by the General Assembly of the State of Georgia, 1755 to 1774.* Wormsloe [printed at Philadelphia, by T. K. Collins], 1881. Large 4to. Pp. 427 with side notes and colophon. 49 copies printed.

John Warwick Daniel. *Robert Edward Lee; An Oration Pronounced at the Unveiling of the Recumbent Figure at Lexington, Virginia, June 28th, 1883.* Savannah, Georgia [printed at Philadelphia, by T. K. Collins?], 1883. Pp. 55 with three plates. "Impression limited to one hundred copies, 25 on large paper, quarto; 75 on small paper, octavo."

Stephen Elliott. *The Rt. Rev. Stephen Elliott, D.D., Bishop of the Diocese of Georgia, at Laurel Grove, Savannah, December 31st, 1865.* [Savannah, 1885?] 8vo. 1 leaf.

* John Perceval, First Earl of Egmont. *A Journal of the Transactions of the Trustees for Establishing the Colony of Georgia in America.* Wormsloe [printed by H. O. Houghton & Co., at the Riverside Press, Cambridge, Mass.], 1886. 4to. Pp. 494 and colophon. 49 copies printed.

2. DE RENNE PUBLICATIONS, 1892–1931

Address of Colonel John Screven Delivered at the First Annual Dinner of the Sons of the Revolution on February 8, 1892 at Savannah, Georgia. [Philadelphia, 1892.] ["Forty-five copies of this book have been printed, and reserved exclusively for private distribution."] 4to. Pp. 40.

Burton Alva Konkle. *The Life and Times of Thomas Smith, 1745–1809, A Pennsylvania Member of the Continental Congress.* Philadelphia, Campion & Company, 1904. 8vo. Pp. xi, 303, with illustrations. Edition limited to 500 copies.

[Wymberley Jones De Renne.] *Books Relating to the History of Georgia in the Library of Wymberley Jones De Renne, of Wormsloe, Isle of Hope, Chatham County, Georgia.* [Savannah, Georgia: Morning News Press], 1905. Large 4to. Pp. 74, in "blue paper wrappers, with the De Renne coat-of-arms and: W. J. De Renne on the front cover." Edition limited to 250 copies.

Wilson Lumpkin. *The Removal of the Cherokee Indians from Georgia.* Wormsloe, 1907. Dodd, Mead & Company, Publishers, New York. 2 vols. Large 8vo. Pp. 369, 328, with two plates. Edition limited to 500 sets.

[Wymberley Jones De Renne.] *A Short History of the Confederate Constitutions of the Confederate States of America; 1861–1899.* [Savannah: Morning News Press, 1909.] Large 4to. Pp. [8], with plate, "facsimile of the last 4 lines of the Permanent Constitution, and of the signatures of its signers." "In gray paper wrapper, on front cover a woodcut . . . with title: The Birth of the Confederacy. . . ." Edition limited to 150 copies, "100 being on handmade paper."

Oscar Wegelin, compiler and annotator. *Books Relating to the History of Georgia in the Library of Wymberley Jones De Renne, of Wormsloe, Isle of Hope, Chatham County, Georgia.* [Savannah, Georgia: Morning News Press], 1911. Large 4to. Pp. vi, 268, xviii (index), with 35 plates: frontispiece photograph of the library at Wormsloe and 34 facsimiles. Dark paper wrapper with "The W. J. De Renne Collection, Wormsloe, 1911" on cover. Edition limited to 200 copies.

Robert Edward Lee. *Lee's Dispatches: Unpublished Letters of General Robert E. Lee, C.S.A. to Jefferson Davis and the War Department of the Confederate States of America, 1862–1865.* From the Private Collection of Wymberley Jones De Renne of Wormsloe, Georgia. Edited with an Introduction by Douglas Southall Freeman. New York and London: G. P. Putnam's Sons, 1915. 8vo. Pp. lxiii, 400. With frontispiece (from the William E. Marshall portrait of R. E. Lee) and pull-out map (Map of Eastern Virginia &c. showing Campaigns of Gen. Lee in 1862–'63–'64–'65). First impression: 506 copies; second impression: 514 copies.

Catalogue of the Wymberley Jones De Renne Georgia Library at Wormsloe, Isle of Hope near Savannah, Georgia. Compiled by Azalea Clizbee, with a Preface by Leonard L. Mackall. 3 volumes. Wormsloe, privately printed, 1931. Royal 8vo. Pp. xxxiii, 448; x, 449–895; ix, 897–1396, with photogravure frontispieces in each volume and 117 facsimiles. Edition limited to 300 numbered sets, printed by the Plandome Press, Inc., New York, in Caslon Monotype on Rives handmade paper. Bound in full buckram, gilt lettered, with gilt top. [Reprinted in smaller format in 1995 by Maurizio Martino, Storrs-Mansfield, Connecticut, in an edition limited to 150 copies.]

3. PUBLICATIONS OF ELFRIDA DE RENNE BARROW, 1922–1976

1922

Poems:

"Verses" (collection title)

"Impressions"

"Recognition"
"Twilight"
"Death"
"I Wonder"
Poetry 20 (April 1922): 19–21.
Poem:
"God's Acre"
Year Book of the Poetry Society of South Carolina 1, no. 2 (1922): 24.

1923
Poem:
"A Mountain Interlude"
Year Book of the Poetry Society of South Carolina 1, no. 3 (1923): 35.
Poems:
"Loose Leaves" (collection title)
"Futility"
"Travelling"
"Habit and Custom and I"
"Concerning the World"
"Colors"
"The Wall Between"
"Presentiment"
"Insomnia"
"Hush"
Poetry 22 (May 1923): 67–71.
Article:
" 'Memento Mori.' "
Georgia Historical Quarterly 7 (June 1923): 166–73.
Article:
"The Poetry Society of Georgia—Its Organization and Aims."
Southern Literary Magazine 1 (August 1923): 19.
Poem:
"Dawn Dream"
Reviewer 4 (October 1923): 19.
Book:
Elfrida De Renne Barrow and Laura Palmer Bell. *Anchored Yesterdays: The Log
    Book of Savannah's Voyage Across a Georgia Century, in Ten Watches.* Illustrated
    with decorations by L. P. B. to which are added prints of olden maps by Peter
    Gordon and Isador Stouf. Savannah: The Press of the Review Publishing and

Printing Company, 1923. ["One Thousand Copies printed, and the type distributed." Reprinted in new format in 1956 by the Ashantilly Press of Darien, Georgia, for the Little House of Savannah, Georgia. Handset in Caslon type and decorated with woodcuts by William Haynes.]

1924
Poem:
"Dawn Dream" [Reprinted from the *Reviewer*]
Year Book of the Poetry Society of South Carolina 2, No. 1 (1924): 20.

1925
Poem:
"Sheep"
Bookman 61 (March 1925): 28.

1926
Poems:
"Underwings" (collection title)
"Interim"
"Facing an Hour-glass"
"Twilight"
"An Old Burying-ground"
"Silence Is a Stranger Here"
"Penetralia"
Poetry 27 (February 1926): 250–53.
Poem:
"In the Homespun Hills"
Year Book of the Poetry Society of South Carolina 2, No. 3 (1926): 35–37.

1927
Poems:
"Autumnal" (collection title)
"Garden's End"
"Earth Change"
Poetry 31 (December 1927): 138–39.

1929
Poems:
"Timepieces"
"Garden's End"
"An Old Burying-ground"

"Insomnia"

"Sheep"

Anthology of Verse. Savannah: Poetry Society of Georgia, 1929.

1930

Poem:

"Ports"

Poetry 35 (January 1930): 203.

Article:

"On the Bay One Hundred Years Ago: Being Various Items Compiled from the Advertising Columns of the *Savannah Georgian* of 1829."

Georgia Historical Quarterly 14 (March 1930): 1–16.

Poem:

"Garden's End"

Thornwell Jacobs, ed. *The Oglethorpe Book of Georgia Verse.* Atlanta: Oglethorpe University Press, 1930.

1931

Review of *John Wesley* by John Donald Wade.

Georgia Historical Quarterly 15 (March 1931): 105–6.

Poem:

"Pavlova, January 23, 1931"

Year Book of the Poetry Society of Georgia 8 (1932): 46.

1933

Mary Savage Anderson, Elfrida De Renne Barrow, Elizabeth Mackay Screven, and Martha Gallaudet Waring (for the Georgia Society of the Colonial Dames of America).

Georgia: A Pageant of Years. Richmond: Garrett & Massie, 1933. Reprinted in 1974 by the Reprint Company, Spartanburg, S.C.

1935

Poems:

"In the Calendar's Shadow" (collection title)

"New Year's Eve"

"Lines of the Unknown"

Poetry 45 (January 1935): 200–201.

1937

Foreword to *Georgia's Disputed Ruins,* ed. E. Merton Coulter. Chapel Hill, 1937.

1943

Foreword to *The Letters of Don Juan McQueen to His Family*, ed. Walter Charlton Hartridge. Columbia, S.C., 1943.

1944

Foreword to the Savannah Historical Research Association Anniversary Number (1934–44).
Georgia Historical Quarterly 28 (September 1944): 111–12.

1949

Foreword to *The Letters of Robert Mackay to His Wife*, ed. Walter Charlton Hartridge. Athens, 1949.

1950

Article:
"Georgia Poetry Society's Work 'A Bright Venture.'" *Savannah Morning News*, 14 April 1950, 6.

1952

Review of *When All Is Said and Done* by Dolly Blount Lamar. *Georgia Historical Quarterly* 36 (December 1952): 397–98.

1961

Poem:
David McCord. "Take Sky."
Privately Printed for Elfrida De Renne Barrow at the Ashantilly Press, Darien, Georgia, 1961. [A poem in four stanzas originally printed in *New York Times Book Review*, 11 June 1961.]

1966

A Letter from Benjamin Franklin to Noble Wimberly Jones.
With notes by Malcolm Bell III. Privately printed for Elfrida De Renne Barrow and Malcolm Bell III, at Darien, Georgia: Ashantilly Press, 1966. [Edition limited to 375 copies.]

1968

Pamphlet:
[J. Frederick Waring.] *Wedding at Wormsloe.*
Privately printed for Elfrida De Renne Barrow at the Ashantilly Press, Darien, Georgia, 1968.

1970

Poems:

"Insomnia"

"Timepieces"

"Pavlova, January 23, 1931"

"Garden's End"

In Gerald Chan Sieg's "Elfrida De Renne Barrow . . . Poet and Writer," *Savannah News-Press Magazine,* 7 June 1970, p. 3. Reprinted in *Yearbook of the Poetry Society of Georgia, 1969–1970.*

1973

Poems:

"Garden's End"

"Pavlova, January 23, 1931"

Anthology of Verse. Savannah: Poetry Society of Georgia, 1973.

1976

Collected Verse:

In the Calendar's Shadow: Poems by Elfrida De Renne Barrow. Edited with an Afterword by Malcolm Bell III. Privately printed at the Ashantilly Press, Darien, Georgia, 1976. [This volume includes all poems previously published, as well as those that follow; though they had not seen print, many had been read at monthly meetings of the Poetry Society of Georgia:

"The Spinster"	"The Dark Entry"
"Not in the Time Table"	"The Round of Time"
"Summer Day"	"The Distant View"
"This I Ask"	"Small Words"
"Untitled Verses"	"The Confederate Monument"
"St. Helena"	"The Colonial Cemetery"
"Interval"	"Noon Mark"]

4. WORMSLOE FOUNDATION PUBLICATIONS

E. Merton Coulter. *Wormsloe: Two Centuries of a Georgia Family.* Wormsloe Foundation Publications Number One. Edition limited to 750 copies. Athens: University of Georgia Press, 1955. Pp. xv, 322.

E. Merton Coulter, ed. *The Journal of William Stephens, 1741–1743.* Wormsloe Foundation Publications Number Two. Edition limited to 500 copies. Athens: University of Georgia Press, 1958. Pp. xxxi, 263.

E. Merton Coulter, ed. *The Journal of William Stephens, 1743–1745.* Wormsloe

Foundation Publications Number Three. Edition limited to 500 copies. Athens: University of Georgia Press, 1959. Pp. xv, 288.

Pat. Tailfer, and Others. *A True and Historical Narrative of the Colony of Georgia.* With Comments by the Earl of Egmont. Edited with and introduction by Clarence L. Ver Steeg. Wormsloe Foundation Publications Number Four. Edition limited to 600 copies. Athens: University of Georgia Press, 1960. Pp. xxxiv, 169.

John Percival, First Earl of Egmont. *The Journal of the Earl of Egmont: Abstract of the Trustees Proceedings for Establishing the Colony of Georgia, 1732–1738.* Edited with an Introduction by Robert G. McPherson. Wormsloe Publications Number Five. Edition limited to 600 copies. Athens: University of Georgia Press. Pp. xxv, 414.

E. Merton Coulter, ed. *The Journal of Peter Gordon, 1732–1735.* Wormsloe Foundation Publications Number Six. Edition limited to 750 copies. Athens: University of Georgia Press, 1963. Pp. viii, 78.

E. Merton Coulter. *Joseph Vallence Bevan, Georgia's First Official Historian.* Wormsloe Foundation Publications Number Seven. Edition limited to 750 copies. Athens: University of Georgia Press, 1964. Pp. xvii, 157.

George Fenwick Jones, transcriber and ed. *Henry Newman's Salzburger Letterbooks.* Wormsloe Foundation Publications Number Eight. Edition limited to 750 copies. Athens: University of Georgia Press, 1966. Pp. xvi, 626.

Detailed Reports on the Salzburger Emigrants Who Settled in America . . . Edited by Samuel Urlsperger. Vol. 1, 1733–34. Edited with an Introduction by George Fenwick Jones. Translated by Hermann J. Lacher. Wormsloe Foundation Publications Number Nine. Edition limited to 750 copies. Athens: University of Georgia Press, 1968. Pp. xxii, 211.

Detailed Reports on the Salzburger Emigrants Who Settled in America . . . Edited by Samuel Urlsperger. Vol. 2, 1734–35. Edited with an Introduction by George Fenwick Jones. Translated by Hermann J. Lacher. Wormsloe Foundation Publications Number Ten. Edition limited to 750 copies. Athens: University of Georgia Press, 1969. Pp. xxxv, 253.

Detailed Reports on the Salzburger Emigrants Who Settled in America . . . Edited by Samuel Urlsperger. Vol. 3, 1736. Translated and edited by George Fenwick Jones and Marie Hahn. Wormsloe Foundation Publications Number Eleven. Athens: University of Georgia Press, 1972. Pp. xx, 348.

Detailed Reports on the Salzburger Emigrants Who Settled in America . . . Edited by Samuel Urlsperger. Vol. 4, 1737. Translated and edited by George Fenwick Jones and Renate Wilson. Wormsloe Foundation Publications Number Twelve. Athens: University of Georgia Press, 1976. Pp. xvi, 248.

William M. Kelso. *Captain Jones's Wormslow: A Historical, Archaeological, and Architectural Study of an Eighteenth-Century Plantation Site Near Savannah, Georgia.* Wormsloe Foundation Publications Number Thirteen. Athens: University of Georgia Press, 1979. Pp. xvi, 196.

Detailed Reports on the Salzburger Emigrants Who Settled in America . . . Edited by Samuel Urlsperger. Vol. 5, 1738. Translated and edited by George Fenwick Jones and Renate Wilson. Wormsloe Foundation Publications Number Fourteen. Athens: University of Georgia Press, 1980. Pp. xxiii, 351. [The University of Georgia Press has continued to publish the series of *Detailed Reports*, with volumes 6 through 17 published 1981–93. Volume 13 contains a cumulative index to volumes 1 through 12.]

John Linley. *The Georgia Catalog: Historic American Buildings Survey, a Guide to the Architecture of the State.* (Part I. A History of the Architecture of the State. Part II. A Catalog of Buildings Included in the Historic American Buildings Survey.) Wormsloe Foundation Publications Number Fifteen. Athens: University of Georgia Press, 1982. Pp. xiv, 402. [Published in both hardcover and paperback.]

Forty Years of Diversity: Essays on Colonial Georgia. Edited by Harvey H. Jackson and Phinizy Spalding. Wormsloe Foundation Publications Number Sixteen. Athens: University of Georgia Press, 1984. Pp. xv, 324.

Jack Leigh. *The Ogeechee: A River and Its People.* Wormsloe Foundation Publications Number Seventeen. With a map and 87 black-and-white photographs. Athens: University of Georgia Press, 1986. Unpaginated.

Wilbur H. Duncan and Marion B. Duncan. *Trees of the Southeastern United States.* Wormsloe Foundation Publications Number Eighteen. Athens: University of Georgia Press, 1988. Pp. xi, 322.

Mart A. Stewart. *"What Nature Suffers To Groe": Life, Labor, and Landscape on the Georgia Coast, 1680–1920.* Wormsloe Foundation Publications Number Nineteen. Athens: University of Georgia Press, 1996. Pp. xix, 370.

Wilbur H. Duncan and Marion B. Duncan. *Wildflowers of the Eastern United States.* Wormsloe Foundation Publications Number Twenty. Athens: University of Georgia Press, 1999. Pp. xxxvi, 380.

William Harris Bragg. *De Renne: Three Generations of a Georgia Family.* Wormsloe Foundation Publications Number Twenty-one. Athens: University of Georgia Press, 1999. Pp. xx, 632.

Wormsloe Since 1970

During the last months of Elfrida De Renne Barrow's life, depositions were being taken for a court case ultimately won by the Wormsloe Foundation in Chatham County Superior Court. The action was based on the foundation's having filed an affidavit of illegality contesting the county's revocation of its tax exemption. It was shown in the proceedings that the foundation's Wormsloe lands were accruing no profit; instead, they were being used principally by institutions of higher learning for various purposes related to study and research. And even the parcel containing the residence, though retained by the Barrow family, was open annually to the general public for the benefit of various charities, and the grounds of Wormsloe House were open to the public year-round, by appointment, although the house itself remained private. The family-owned parcels, of course, had always been on the tax books. In May 1970, the judge in the case decided that those parcels held by the Wormsloe Foundation would remain tax exempt, thus confirming the foundation's custodianship of its portion of Wormsloe.[1]

But a year later, the Georgia Court of Appeals reversed this judgment, holding that an affidavit of illegality was an "unavailable remedy." The motivation of the Chatham County authorities in revoking the tax exemption and in pursuing the case seems somewhat puzzling, but it apparently centered on a suspicion that the Barrow family intended to save money through the tax exemption for a period of time, after which Wormsloe might be sold to developers at a large profit. It would be difficult to imagine a less likely scenario. Apparently in support of this view, however, the county attorney placed much emphasis on a transaction of the 1950s, in which certain Poplar Grove property, formerly part of the foundation's endowment, had been sold. Historical perspective would have shown that the two cases were not analogous, but such perspective was sadly lacking in the story of the foundation's struggle with the Chatham County authorities.[2]

Throughout its existence, the foundation had, through its legal counsel, worked to tighten the measures that protected its Wormsloe property and to keep the holdings within the changing applications and expectations of the tax laws (particularly the Tax Reform Act of 1969), and it had amended its charter accordingly. In 1971, during the time that the case was being appealed to the Georgia Supreme Court, the foundation amended its charter once again to conform to new tax laws affecting private foundations. A previous amendment had already arranged for the University of Georgia to be given priority as recipient of the foundation's Wormsloe lands if and when the foundation was dissolved; the new amendments contained language that made it impossible for the foundation ever to "sell off" the land in the way the county authorities seemed to envision.[3]

Nonetheless, on the last day of February 1972, the Georgia Supreme Court ruled against the foundation and a month later denied a rehearing. The majority opinion construed the pertinent tax law narrowly, holding that "a charitable institution itself must be carrying on an operation on its real estate for the benefit of the public or for some other legitimate charitable purpose. Merely making the real estate available to other public or charitable institutions for their use is not sufficient to qualify for the tax exemption." Justice Benning Grice dissented. He held that the land had been "used for purely charitable purposes within the meaning of Georgia law," that it had "been used exclusively for educational, archaeological, ecological and historical research and . . . never used to produce profit for the Foundation." He was also impressed by the fact that, under the foundation's charter, "no part of this property can ever inure to the benefit of *any* individual" and that "in the event of dissolution of the Foundation, its funds and property *must* be distributed to other 'exempt organizations' under the direction of the Senior Judge of the Superior Court of Chatham County, with preference being given to the University of Georgia."[4]

Since the tax commissioner of Chatham County was charging the foundation for back taxes dating from 1965 and had valued the foundation lands at $1,000 an acre, the lien on the property had climbed steeply. Future taxes at such a high rate would have made retaining the foundation's Wormsloe lands prohibitively expensive. Circumstances had created a perfect illustration of the dictum that "the power to tax is the power to destroy."[5]

Reluctantly, the foundation decided to take the ironic step of preserving the acreage by disposing of it in a way resembling most closely the intent of its charter. A few months after the reversal by the Georgia Supreme Court in the Wormsloe Foundation case, the state of Georgia had created the Georgia Heritage Advisory Trust Commission and was preparing to acquire lands of historical and ecological importance throughout the state. The sudden availability of most of Wormsloe— 750 acres—was unexpected but welcome, and negotiations for the acquisition of the land began in the fall of 1972. The Nature Conservancy, which had become active in Georgia a few years earlier, also became involved in "extended discussions" with the state and the foundation. Ultimately, the foundation's Wormsloe lands were conveyed to the Nature Conservancy, which in late December 1972 accepted the parcels, encumbered by the lien for ad valorem taxes, to hold them for the state of Georgia. In August 1973 the state acquired the acreage from the conservancy. Valued at over $3 million, the plantation (minus the family parcels) became the property of the state of Georgia for $250,000, representing the contested accrued taxes.

The formal transfer was presided over by Governor Jimmy Carter. Attended by various local and state dignitaries, the ceremony took place in Wormsloe's library building and, observed the governor, "had the dignity and sense of dedication [befitting] an event of such importance."[6]

In the deed transferring Wormsloe to the state, the language protecting the plantation provided that the property would "forever be known as Wormsloe" and was to be "held for the general public as an historical and ecological nature preserve for scientific, historical, educational, and aesthetic purposes." The land was also to be kept "essentially in its natural state"; necessary construction was never to be allowed to impair "the essentially natural and historical character of the property." At the time the state acquired the Wormsloe lands, the Barrow family also agreed "to preserve in its present state" the family's acreage adjacent to what was now to be Wormsloe Historic Site and therefore agreed voluntarily to forgo any "development potential" of the property. In 1978 the Barrow family also conveyed a conservation easement to the state, ensuring preservation of the family properties in their natural state. And in 1997 the security of Wormsloe was greatly enhanced by the state's acquisition (with the assistance of the Wormsloe Foundation) of Pigeon Island, just below the estate's southern marshlands.[7]

After years of study and preparation and the construction of a modern visitors' center and museum near the southern end of the oak avenue, the state opened Wormsloe Historic Site to the general public in the fall of 1979. As its major interpretive site—and the focus of several of its museum displays—the park officials chose the tabby ruin, with the adjacent Jones family plot nearby, still marked by the massive stone monument placed there by G. W. J. De Renne. These sites were made accessible by a choice of trails, and in later years more paths to various other destinations were added. The Confederate earthworks were left for additional study and, possibly, opening at a later day.

As time has passed, exhibits explaining life at an eighteenth-century colonial outpost have been added, along with simulations of the wattle-and-daub huts that once housed Captain Noble Jones's marines. Occasionally, costumed reenactors present living history programs.

In 1993 the Georgia Historical Commission erected one of its markers near the museum, titled "Noble Jones' 'Wormslow,' 1736–1775." And four years later, with a grant from the Wormsloe Foundation, another of the estate's historic structures was restored: the gatehouse constructed by Wymberley W. De Renne in 1917.[8]

Finally, then, most of Wormsloe Plantation came to be held by the state and people of Georgia. But as the tercentenary of the birth of Noble Jones approached, three parcels of Wormsloe still remained with his descendants, some of whom still occupied the house built by George Jones and several times altered by the De Rennes.

Abbreviations

Full citations for all manuscript collections will be found below in Selected Sources.

BAK   Burton Alva Konkle

BRHG   *Books Relating to the History of Georgia in the Library of Wymberley Jones De Renne*

CCCH   Chatham County Courthouse, Savannah

CCJJ   Charles Colcock Jones, Jr.

CMT   Charlton M. Theus

CRG   *Colonial Records of Georgia*

CSAC   Confederate States of America, Constitution, Ms. 1512-17, UGAL

CSH   C. S. Hook

DAB   *Dictionary of American Biography*

DB   Deed Book, CCCH

DeRCM   De Renne Confederate Manuscripts, UGAL

DeRFP   De Renne Family Papers, Ms. 1064, UGAL

DeRFP+   De Renne Family Papers, Ms. 2819, UGAL

DeRGL   De Renne Georgia Library, UGAL

DeRHM   De Renne Historical Manuscripts, UGAL

DeRLC   *Catalogue of the Wymberley Jones De Renne Georgia Library* (1931)

DGB   *Dictionary of Georgia Biography*

DLB   *Dictionary of Literary Biography*

DMWP   David M. Wright Papers, GHS

DNB   *Dictionary of National Biography*

DSF   Douglas Southall Freeman

DUL   Special Collections, Duke University Library, Durham, N.C.

EDeRB   Elfrida De Renne Barrow

EMC   Ellis Merton Coulter

EMCP   Ellis Merton Coulter Papers, UGAL

GB   Grant Book (Georgia Surveyor General, Register of Grants, GDAH)

GDAH   Georgia Department of Archives and History, Atlanta

GFTJ   George F. T. Jones

GHQ   *Georgia Historical Quarterly*

GHS   Georgia Historical Society, Savannah

GJ	George Jones
GNJ	George Noble Jones
GNJP	George Noble Jones Papers, DUL
GR	*Georgia Review*
GWJ	George Wymberley Jones
GWJDeR	G. W. J. De Renne
GWJDeRP	G. W. J. De Renne Papers, DUL
GWJDeRC	G. W. J. De Renne Georgia Historical Collection, UGAL
GWS	George Washington Smith
HSP	Historical Society of Pennsylvania, Philadelphia
JFP	Jones Family Papers, GHS
JGBB	J. G. B. Bulloch
JSH	*Journal of Southern History*
KCS	Katherine C. Stiles
KDeR-A	Kentwyn De Renne, "Autobiography"
KRC	Keith Read Collection
L&C	Lawton and Cunningham
LGTJ	Letitia G. T. Jones
LLM	Leonard L. Mackall
LoC	Manuscripts Division, Library of Congress
LPCB	Letter Press Copy Book
MDeR	Mary De Renne
MNJ	Mary Nuttall Jones
MSJ	Mary Savage Jones
MoC	Eleanor S. Brockenbrough Library, Museum of the Confederacy, Richmond, Va.
MoM	*Men of Mark in Georgia*
NHS	Newport Historical Society, Newport, R.I.
NCAB	*National Cyclopaedia of American Biography*
NJ	Noble Jones
NSCDG	National Society of the Colonial Dames of America, Georgia
NWJ	Noble Wimberly Jones
ORA	*Official Records of the Union and Confederate Armies*
ORN	*Official Records of the Union and Confederate Navies*
PAAS	*Proceedings of the American Antiquarian Society*
PCR	Probate Court Records, CCCH
PMV	*Poetry: A Magazine of Verse*
PSG	Poetry Society of Georgia
PSGP	Poetry Society of Georgia Papers, GHS

PSSC	Poetry Society of South Carolina
SCHS	South Carolina Historical Society, Charleston
SCJ	Superior Court Judgments (CCCH/GHS)
SCR	Superior Court Records, CCCH
SDG	*Savannah Daily Georgian*
SEP	*Savannah Evening Press*
SHRA	Savannah Historical Research Association Papers, GHS
SMN	*Savannah Morning News*
SWC	Savannah Writers' Conference Collection, GHS
TC	Telamon Cuyler
TCC	Telamon Cuyler Collection, Ms. 1170, UGAL
TLC	T. L. Cole
TSP	Thomas Smith Papers, UGAL
	a. George Washington Division
	b. Burton Alva Konkle Division
UBP	U. B. Phillips
UBPP	U. B. Phillips Papers, Southern Historical Collection, UNC
UGAL	Hargrett Library, University of Georgia Libraries, Athens
UGAL-A	University of Georgia Archives, UGAL
UNC	University of North Carolina Library, Chapel Hill
WBS	William Bacon Stevens
WBSL	William Bacon Stevens Letters, UGAL
WC	Wormsloe Collection, UGAL
WCHC	Walter Charlton Hartridge, Jr., Collection, GHS
WHS	Wormsloe Historic Site, Savannah
WJDeR	Wymberley Jones De Renne
WPA	Works Progress Administration, Georgia Writers' Project, Savannah Unit, GHS
WTC	West Texas Collection, Porter Henderson Library, Angelo State University, San Angelo, Texas
WWDeR	Wymberley Wormsloe De Renne
WWDeRP	Wymberley Wormsloe De Renne Papers, UGAL

Notes

In most cases, the manuscript collections' abbreviations are followed by the box numbers (and sometimes the file numbers) of the material being cited.

Full bibliographic information for printed materials listed in short form in the notes is provided below in Selected Sources.

PROLOGUE. The Honor of the Past

1. Diary of GWJDeR, 1876–80, p. 40, DeRFP-13; *SMN,* 17, 18, 19 May 1880; Knight, *Georgia's Landmarks,* 2:79. The site known during the 1800s as the Old Cemetery or the "brick cemetery" (and now called Colonial Park Cemetery) is located at the intersection of Abercorn Street and Oglethorpe Avenue.

2. *Sketch of Bonaventure,* p. [5]; on-site inspections by the author. For Bonaventure, see also WPA-14 and WPA-15, GHS, and *General Index to Keepers' Record Books, Bonaventure Cemetery, Savannah, Georgia, 1850–1938* (WPA, 1939).

3. DB 3P:220, SCR; GWJDeR memorandum, 11 June 1880, DeRFP-26; John Postell, Civil Engineer, "Plan of Evergreen Cemetery at Bonaventure," [1869], with manuscript additions by GWJDeR, and "Map of Portion [of] Bonaventure Cemetery," with manuscript additions by WJDeR, Map Collection, UGAL; Knight, *Georgia's Landmarks,* 2:289.

4. *SMN,* 10 November 1877, 22 February 1878; Gamble, *History of the City Government of Savannah,* 199, 212–13, 387–88.

5. GWJDeR, "Sketch for tomb of Noble Jones in Old Cemetery, Savannah, placed there by me, 1870," DeRFP-13; NSCDG, *Some Early Epitaphs in Georgia,* 23–24.

6. Biographical sketches of NJ are found in Northern, *MoM,* 1:195–207 (by WJDeR), and in *DGB,* 1:551–53 (by Phinizy Spalding). See also Temple and Coleman, *Georgia Journeys,* 268–91. The most extended treatment of NJ's life is in Coulter's *Wormsloe,* 39–107.

7. [Stovall], *Isle of Hope,* 3; CRG, 4:619.

8. GWJDeR, Journal, 1850–75, p. 1, DeRFP-57.

9. *DGB,* 1:551–52; Coulter, *Wormsloe,* 50.

10. It has been claimed as fact that NJ held a medical degree (J. Calvin Weaver, M.D., "Early Medical History of Georgia," *Journal of the Medical Association of*

Georgia 29 [1940]: 92; Maurice Bear Gordon, *Aesculapius Comes to the Colonies* [Ventnor, N.J., 1949], 486). There is no evidence or documentation of this, however, and apparently NJ, like many other doctors of his time, practiced medicine without a degree. That he practiced is certain because contemporary accounts describe him as "Doctor Noble Jones." But in the eighteenth century that title embraced three kinds of doctors: physicians (a term then mainly applied to university-trained doctors), surgeons ("joined in one company with the barbers" when NJ left England), and apothecaries (who had their Latin from the grammar school and "learned in the school of practice rather than of theory"). Available evidence places NJ in the last-mentioned category, similar to today's general practitioner (Bernice Hamilton, "The Medical Profession in the Eighteenth Century," *Economic History Review* 4 (1951): 142, 149, 160–63).

NJ's grandson George Jones recorded that the elder Jones had begun practicing medicine before leaving England, continued in Georgia, and took his son Noble Wimberly Jones (the source of this information) "into business with him about the year 1748" ([Dr. George Jones to Dr. John Grimes], 2 June 1805, John Grimes Papers, GHS; copy in DeRFP-9). In 1758, former royal governor John Reynolds, who had come to Georgia in 1754, listed the various kinds of work NJ had done in the colony and noted that "at length he practised Physick" (Reynolds to the Earl of Hardwicke, Add. MSS. 35909, Reports and Papers Relating to America, 1710–65, British Library, London). As a practitioner of physic (the branch of medicine that treated disease by prescribing various remedies), NJ was probably self-trained, mainly through experience and reading various books on medicine, in Latin and otherwise. One of Jones's medical notebooks survives, containing material copied in his small, neat cursive from the 1749 edition of *Medulla Medicinae Universae* (DeRFP-6). According to the letter from George Jones to Dr. Grimes cited above, NJ stopped practicing medicine on a regular basis during the 1750s. A good overview of the practice of medicine in colonial Georgia, describing its dearth of trained professional physicians, is Joseph I. Waring, "Colonial Medicine in Georgia and South Carolina," *GHQ* 59 (1975): 141–53. See also Coulter, *Wormsloe*, 104–5, and Harold E. Davis, *The Fledgling Province* (Chapel Hill, 1976), 86–88.

11. Coulter, *Wormsloe*, 45–48, 91–94, 104; *CRG*, 4 (Supplement): 118. See also, for a description of the various kinds of eighteenth-century carpenters and builders, Rodney M. Baine and Louis De Vorsey Jr., "The Provenance and Historical Accuracy of 'A View of Savannah,'" *GHQ* 73 (1989): 789–90. NJ's father, Edward, was, however, a distiller—not a carpenter, as is stated ibid., 789—and the quotation regarding the "hot and passionate temper" of NJ (790) actually refers to that of the bailiff Thomas Jones. For Edward Jones's occupation and NJ's apprenticeship to the

joiner Edward Sanderson, see transcript from Joiners' Bindings, 1710–24, MS 8052/4, Guildhall Library, London, in M. H. Flower to David McCord Wright, 24 February 1966, DMWP-39, GHS.

For NJ's role in the creation of the view of Savannah attributed to Peter Gordon, see Baine and De Vorsey, "Provenance," 788–91, where the authors assert that Jones's plats of Savannah were the basis of the Englishman George Jones's Savannah sketch, which was in turn the basis for the Fourdrinier engraving long associated with Peter Gordon. George Fenwick Jones, however, argues that the source of both the George Jones sketch and the Fourdrinier engraving was a perspective view prepared by NJ from his own plats. See Jones, "Peter Gordon's (?) View of Savannah," *GHQ* 70 (1986): 97–101, and "Communications," *GHQ* 73 (1989): 363–66. That Noble Jones himself could have drafted a plat-based sketch to guide George Jones has long been suggested by NJ's similar perspective view of the Bethesda Orphan House. This image is found as a folding plate at the back of George Whitefield, *An Account of Money Received . . . for the Orphan-House* (London, 1741), and is cited by Baine and De Vorsey in "Communications," 367–68. The latter authors agree that NJ could have executed the view attributed to Gordon but hold to their original interpretation, as described above. NJ's career as public surveyor is described in detail in Farris W. Cadle, *Georgia Land Surveying History and Law* (Athens, 1991), 16–20, 24.

Pigeon (Redoubt) Island, south of Wormsloe, was apparently the site of NJ's machicolated fort. The island remained in the possession of his descendants until 1814 (Kelso, *Captain Jones's Wormslow*, 8–10; DB 2E:405).

12. Photocopy of Marriage Record, 30 July 1723, Register, Lincoln's Inn Chapel, London, England, DMWP-39, GHS; Guy Holborn, Librarian, Lincoln's Inn Library, to author, 30 March, 10 April 1995. NJ's only child to be born in Georgia was named Inigo Jones, and the Welsh arms attributed to the seventeenth-century architect were very similar to those claimed by NJ (Coulter, *Wormsloe*, 36; *DNB*, 10:999; Crozier, ed., *Crozier's General Armory*, 80; Burke and Burke, *General Armory*, 547).

13. GWJDeR, "Notes on Books, etc., relating to the Early History of Georgia," DeRFP-12 (Grace, a slave woman who remembered NJ, told GWJDeR that his great-grandfather had been a "big man"); Kelso, *Captain Jones's Wormslow*, 8–10; Ivers, *British Drums*, 146, 195; Coulter, *Wormsloe*, 74–76.

Although nineteenth-century histories of Georgia place NJ on St. Simons Island during the Spanish invasion, Ivers (164) shows that the Jones involved in defending Fort Frederica was Captain Thomas Jones. NJ's presence at St. Augustine, however, is well-documented. See Coulter, *Wormsloe*, 57, and Ivers, *British Drums*, 146.

The Spanish War began as the War of Jenkins's Ear in 1739 and by 1744 had merged into King George's War (1744–48), the American phase of the War of the Austrian Succession (1740–48).

14. Coulter, *Wormsloe*, 103–4.

15. Christening Record, 20 June 1702, Parish of St. Martin Vintry, London, England; Coulter, *Wormsloe*, 104. The parish in which NJ was born lay between St. Paul's and the Tower of London.

16. The letter from George Bancroft to George Wymberley Jones [De Renne], 7 October 1854 (enclosing transcript of Samuel Adams to NWJ, 16 July 1774) is in DeRFP-9. The Franklin-Jones correspondence, 1768–78, is held by the American Philosophical Society; other letters are in the George Jones Papers, GHS. A letter from Franklin to NWJ, 7 October 1772, in the WC, is the subject of Bell, *Some Notes and Reflections*.

17. Coulter, *Wormsloe*, 149–50; *DGB*, 1:553–54. The most comprehensive nineteenth-century account of the life of NWJ is found in Jones, *Biographical Sketches*, 124–36. With minor changes, this sketch also appears in the first volume of *MoM*, 208–18, and in Harden, *History of Savannah and South Georgia*, 2:539–44. Other sketches of Jones's life appeared in Thacher, *American Medical Biography* (1828), 340–44 (based on the 1805 eulogy by Dr. John Grimes, printed version cited below, from the original manuscript in the Grimes Papers, GHS, and having as a major source the letter from George Jones to Dr. Grimes, cited above); Lieber, ed., *Encyclopaedia Americana* (1883), 13:479 (a close synopsis of the Thacher sketch); White, *Historical Collections of Georgia*, 367 (based on the Lieber sketch); *NCAB*, 11:172; John Grimes, "Eulogy on the Life and Character of Dr. Noble Wymberley Jones," *GHQ* 4 (1920): 17–32, 141–58; *DAB*, 10:196–97 (written by E. Merton Coulter); Victor Bassett, "A Medical Biography of Dr. Noble Wymberley Jones of Georgia," *Bulletin of the Georgia Medical Society* 1 (October, December 1935, January 1936): 1–3, 29–33, 43–50 (also reprinted in pamphlet form, 1936); and *DGB*, 1:553–54 (written by Raymond C. Bailey). Lengthy obituaries appeared in the Savannah *Georgia Republican and State Intelligencer*, 14 January 1805, and the *Charleston* (S.C.) *Times*, 15 January 1805. Four chapters of Coulter's *Wormsloe* (108–81) are devoted to NWJ.

Several books published since Coulter's *Wormsloe* have devoted considerable attention to NJ and NWJ. Among them are Davis, *Fledgling Province;* Richard Beale Davis, *Intellectual Life in the Colonial South, 1585–1763*, 3 vols. (Knoxville, Tenn., 1978); and James M. Johnson, *Militiamen, Rangers, and Redcoats: The Military in Georgia, 1754–1776* (Macon, 1992).

18. *DGB*, 1:554; Grimes, "Eulogy," 17; *Charleston* (S.C.) *Times*, 15 January 1805.

19. Published sketches of the life of Dr. George Jones make use of a common source: eulogistic resolutions passed by an 1838 meeting in Savannah of Georgia's state and federal bar (*Savannah Georgian*, 20 November 1838; a copy is in DeRFP-

7). These resolutions formed the basis of sketches in *NCAB* 5: 548; *MoM* 2: 342–44 (most of the text verbatim, with additions by WJDeR); and Harden's *History of Savannah and South Georgia*, 2:544 (the resolutions "given entire"). Brief sketches of Jones's life also appear in the various volumes of biographies of members of the U.S. Congress and in *DGB*, 1:547–48 (written by H. B. Fant). Coulter's *Wormsloe* provides the most detailed treatment of the life of Dr. George Jones (182–212) and introduces the possibility that Jones, as a teenager during the Revolution, was for a time a prisoner on a British ship (279n.31). Additional sources will be found in the notes to Chapter 1.

Medical instruments of the second and third generations of the Jones family survive, though in the case of Noble Wimberly Jones only a pocket lancet is in the De Renne Family Papers; there is, however, a photograph of his medical kit and instruments, present whereabouts unknown. The more extensive set of instruments of George Jones, complete with leather case, has been on loan for many years to the Georgia Medical Society's Women's Auxiliary and has been displayed in its medical museum in the lobby of Candler General Hospital in Savannah (DeRFP-9; DeRFP+-22; Candler General Hospital, *Associates Newsletter* 4 [Spring 1977]: 4).

20. Coulter, *Wormsloe*, 206, 213–14.

21. Diary of GWJDeR, 1876–80, p. 40; GWJDeR to WJDeR, 18 June 1880, DeRFP+-1.

22. GWJ to GNJ, 2 April 1852, JFP-1, GHS.

23. The lines of verse are from Alexander Pope, "Elegy to the Memory of an Unfortunate Lady," 1.38, and Horace, *Odes*, III.xxx.1.

CHAPTER 1. The Pierian Spring

1. Everard De Renne, "Family History from Researches of G. W. J. De Renne, WC; Coulter, *Wormsloe*, 187–92, 208–9. George Jones's first marriage, to Mary Gibbons (1761–92), allied him with the Gibbons and Telfair families, and his daughter Sarah Gibbons Jones married into the Cuthbert family. His second marriage, to Sarah Fenwick Campbell, strengthened the family's ties to Charleston, which had begun when Noble Wimberly Jones practiced medicine there during the Revolution; this marriage connected the Jones family with the Fenwicks, Campbells, Draytons, Tattnalls, and Kollocks. George Jones's only son to reach manhood, Noble Wimberly Jones II, a child of his first marriage, married Sarah Campbell, daughter of George Jones's second wife from her own first marriage. Through marriages of George Jones's sisters, Catherine and Sarah, the Jones family became related to the Harts, Glens, Bullochs, Bourkes, Grimeses, and Hunters, among others. Source material on the Jones and other families is found in the Genealogy Files, David McCord Wright Papers, and Jones Family Papers, GHS; De Renne, "Family

History," and Application of Membership of EDeRB, Georgia Society of Colonial Dames, WC; DeRFP-1, DeRFP-13, and DeRFP-58; and NWJ Papers, GNJ Papers, and GWJDeR Papers, DUL. Printed sources are listed below under "Genealogical and Heraldic Studies" in Selected Sources.

2. Konkle, *Thomas Smith*, 1, 174–86; Douglas Southall Freeman, *George Washington: A Biography*, 6 vols. (New York, 1948–54), 6:32, 32n.34. The Konkle biography, commissioned by WJDeR, is the only book-length study of Thomas Smith. A brief but comprehensive sketch of his life is found in Smith, *William Smith*, 2:520–23.

3. Charles Coleman Sellers, *Charles Willson Peale* (New York, 1969), 208, 460n.18; Konkle, *Thomas Smith*, 146–47. The founder of the Van Deren family in America was John Bernard Van Deren (1692–1751), a native of the Prussian city of Konigsberg. His surname, spelled variously, appears on his will as "Van Duehren." Originally a tailor, he preached mainly in frontier settlements in the vicinity of Albany, New York, with occasional trips into New Jersey and Pennsylvania. A highly controversial figure, he engaged in a lengthy feud with another Lutheran divine, Wilhelm Christoph Berkenmeyer, who questioned Van Deren's ordination and literacy and generally denounced him as a hedge priest. A printed account of Berkenmeyer's side of one of their disputes issued from the press of John Peter Zenger in 1728. Estate records show that at his death Van Deren had a library of almost two hundred books, a considerable number for his time and place. Among the sources on Van Deren's life are Charles H. Glatfelter, *Pastors and People*, 2 vols. (Breinigsville, Pa., 1980–81), 1:30; John P. Dern, ed., *The Albany Protocol* (Ann Arbor, 1971), xxiv, xliv–xlv, 2n.10; and Arnold J. H. VanLaer, trans., *The Lutheran Church in New York* (New York, 1946), passim.

4. Konkle, *Thomas Smith*, 166, 246, 247.

5. Ibid., 263, 277, 262, 262n.3; "Miscellanea Georgiana," DeRFP-45.

6. Smith, *William Smith*, 2:523; Konkle, *Thomas Smith*, 263; Coulter, *Wormsloe*, 209–10. Born in Maryland in 1756, William Tilghman became chief justice of the Pennysylvania Supreme Court in 1806, a position he held until his death in 1827 (*DAB*, 18:545–46).

7. After her husband's death, Maria Campbell Stewart engaged in a long and ultimately unsuccessful legal fight to win back a part of her husband's estate (*Times* [London], 4 June 1839). The printed transcript of this tangled case, complete with excerpts from many of Frederick Campbell Stewart's letters, is the source of almost all of the information on Maria Campbell Stewart and her husband. A copy is found in DeRHM (oversize). Other material relating to the Campbells and Stewarts is in DeRFP-2.

8. P. M. Kollock to George J. Kollock, 24 November 1822, Johnston, ed., "Kollock

Letters," *GHQ* 30:238; Phillips and Glunt, eds., *Florida Plantation Records*, 20; "Miscellanea Georgiana," DeRFP-45. For the first five decades of his life, the only son of Noble Wimberly Jones II was known as George Jones, Jr., or as plain George Jones. Only during the Civil War years did he begin calling himself George Noble Jones (though usually signing himself G. Noble Jones). To reduce confusion, I will refer to him throughout the text as George Noble Jones.

9. GJ to Governor Charles Goldsborough, 24 July 1827, DeRFP-12.

10. Many of the Jones family's travels are recorded in Johnston, ed., "Kollock Letters," Parts II–V.

11. Coulter, *Wormsloe*, 207–8; "Wormsloe," p. 21, WPA-23, GHS; Robert Habersham to GJ, 1 December 1825, DeRFP-7; *Savannah Georgian*, 6 December 1825. John McKinnon's 1816 map of Chatham County, Georgia (GHS), shows the location of Newton, along with two other nearby Jones plantations, Lambeth (which was later absorbed by Newton) and Dean Forest. Newton was apparently named for Sir Isaac, who lived in the near vicinity of Noble Jones from 1710 to 1727 and was buried in Westminster Abbey. It is obvious why a man of Noble Jones's interests would have revered Newton but unknown whether Jones was a relation of William Jones (1675–1749), a member of Newton's circle. Lambeth was named by Noble Wimberly Jones for his birthplace. A previous owner named Dean Forest, but the Joneses' ancestors would have known the expanse of South Midlands woods, near the Welsh border, that inspired the name.

Noble Jones settled at Wormsloe in the 1730s, holding the land by a lease from the Georgia colony's Trustees. His ownership was made official after the colony became a royal province; the king's grant of Wormsloe (five hundred acres) was dated 24 December 1756. The will of Noble Jones gave his daughter Mary life tenancy of the plantation. At her death in 1795 Wormsloe became the property of her brother Noble Wimberly Jones, under the terms of Noble Jones's will. George Jones was given Wormsloe by his father, Noble Wimberly Jones, by deed of gift in 1804. Under the terms of George Jones's will, his wife was to hold Wormsloe until her death or remarriage, after which Wormsloe was to go to his son (GB "A," p. 256, GDAH; NJ's Will, 12 October 1775, File J-1, Book B, Folio 120, PCR; Deed of Gift, DB 2D:169, SCR; GJ's Will, Book G, Folio 355, PCR).

Noble Jones was granted Newton in 1756, the same year his son Noble Wimberly Jones received adjacent Lambeth. Dean Forest was a much later acquisition of George Jones; the plantation had formerly belonged to both Jonathan Bryan and James Habersham. Dean Forest was west of, and adjacent to, Newton and Lambeth. These were the Joneses' rice lands (GB "A," 251, GDAH; GB "A," 249, GDAH; "Dean Forest," WPA-15, GHS).

12. "Plan of House &c at Wormslow taken by A. J. C. Shaw 1829," DeRFP, 1064a

(Oversize); Asher Benjamin, *The American Builder's Companion*, 6th ed. (Boston, 1827), 104 and Plate 55; Kelso, *Captain Jones's Wormslow*, 13–15. In addition to Noble Jones's tabby house and the wooden structure built for George Jones in 1829, there was another dwelling house at Wormsloe, mentioned in an 1815 manuscript of George Jones. It is described as "a one story house, about 26 feet in length by 18 feet in depth, with shed rooms & a piazza." This would appear to be the dwelling house occupied by Ann Reid when she leased Wormsloe in 1819 and is perhaps also the "gentleman's house" near Bethesda described by John Bartram in 1765, "delightfully scituated on A large tide salt creek where yᵉ oisters is as thick as thay can ly within A stone cast of his house." The exact site of this house is unknown. "List of Lands. . . . (1 April 1815), DeRFP-7; Kelso, *Captain Jones's Wormsloe*, 13; John Bartram, "Diary of a Journey through the Carolinas, Georgia, and Florida from July 1, 1765, to April 10, 1766," *Transactions of the American Philsophical Society* 33, Part 1 (1942): 30.

13. Jones, *Georgia Historical Society*, 25–26; Coulter, *Wormsloe*, 236; Alexander von Humboldt, *Personal Narrative of Travels to the Equinoctial Regions of the New Continent*, 7 vols. (London, 1814–29), 5:291.

14. Coulter, *Wormsloe*, 105, 213.

15. GJ to George Jones Kollock, 2 August 1836, Kollock Collection, UGAL; Sherman Day, *Historical Collections of Pennsylvania* (Philadelphia, 1843), 543–45; Joseph Jackson, *Encyclopedia of Philadelphia*, 4 vols. (Harrisburg, Pa., 1931), 2:317–18; White, *Statistics of Georgia*, 155.

16. For examples, see "Kollock Letters," *GHQ* 30:244, 31:153, 216; GJ to George Jones Kollock, Kollock Collection, UGAL.

17. Simpson, ed., *Jones Family Papers*, 42, 45; Johnston, ed., "Kollock Letters," *GHQ* 30:328, 31:204–5; Thomas F. Gordon, *Gazetteer of the State of New Jersey* (Trenton, N.J., 1834), 106–7; John W. Barber and Henry Howe, *Historical Collections of the State of New Jersey* (New York, 1846), 99–103; Lida Newberry, ed., *New Jersey: A Guide to Its Present and Past* (New York, 1977), 144–45.

18. Gordon, *Gazetteer*, 106; Newberry, ed., *New Jersey*, 145.

19. Barber and Howe, *Historical Collections*, 101–2; Newberry, ed., *New Jersey*, 145.

20. Owen Connelly, *The Gentle Bonaparte* (New York, 1968), 249 53; Newberry, ed., *New Jersey*, 146.

21. Jones's passport description, 10 May 1850, DeRFP-12 (A "Permit of Embarkation" to London, 23 November 1810, in Ms. 1136, UGAL, gives Dr. George Jones's height as 5′8″); F. M. Kircheisen, *Napoleon* (Freeport, N.Y., 1972), 260–61. Among Jones's possessions associated with Napoleon was a large bronze copy of Vela's dying Napoleon, with the map of Europe spread on his lap.

22. Johnston, ed., "Kollock Letters," *GHQ* 31:157; Harden, *Recollections*, 53.

Dr. Jones died "at his late residence at the corner of South Broad [Oglethorpe Avenue] and Bull Street," which had apparently been rented, as was his custom with his Savannah dwelling houses. Indications are that the house is that built for George W. Anderson two years earlier; its present address is 4 West Oglethorpe Avenue (*Savannah Georgian*, 14 November 1838).

23. Simpson, ed., *Jones Family Papers*, 37, 57.

24. Coulter, *Wormsloe*, 189–92, 202–4; *MoM*, 2:344; Gamble, *Savannah Duels*, 187; Simpson, ed., *Jones Family Papers*, 37.

25. GJ's Will, Book G, Folio 355, PCR.

26. GJ's Estate Records, File Box I, Folio 74, and EJ to [GNJ], 3 January 1840, LGTJ's Estate Records, File Box I, Folio 81, PCR.

27. Johnston, ed., "Kollock Letters," *GHQ* 30:249, 251, 257, 323, 326, 341, 31:135; Lilian Handlin, *George Bancroft: The Intellectual as Democrat* (New York, 1984), 94–95; GNJ's Diploma, JFP-2, GHS.

28. Brewer, *History of Religious Education*, 258–61; John W. Barber and Henry Howe, *Historical Collections of the State of New York* (New York, 1841), 453; St. Paul's College, *Catalogue*, 1838, [2–3]; Ayres, *Muhlenberg*, 125–28, 131, 141.

29. *Appleton's Cyclopaedia of American Biography*, 4:453, 455.

30. Ayres, *Muhlenberg*, 131–32.

31. Ibid., 140.

32. Ibid., 143.

33. Newton, *Muhlenberg*, 58–60; Ayres, *Muhlenberg*, 146–48, 150, 172.

34. Ayres, *Muhlenberg*, 142. Estate records show $11 paid for a garden hose in 1840 and tuition, including flute instruction, in 1841.

35. Ayres, *Muhlenberg*, 134, 139; Newton, *Muhlenberg*, 55.

36. Protestant Episcopal Church, Diocese of Georgia, *Journal* (1842), 9; Ayres, *Muhlenberg*, 137, 334.

37. Owens, *Georgia's Planting Prelate*, 11; Protestant Episcopal Church, Diocese of Georgia, *Journal* (1842), 12; Jennings B. Sanders, "George Whitefield Two Hundred and Twenty-five Years After His First American Visit: An Interpretation," *GHQ* 48 (March 1964): 69; [Aaron Crossley Hobart Seymour], *The Life and Times of Selina, Countess of Huntingdon*, 2 vols. (London, 1844), 2:265–66; Alvin W. Skardon, *Church Leader in the Cities: William Augustus Muhlenberg* (Philadelphia, 1971), 85. Bishop Elliott tried to ameliorate the working and living conditions of Georgia's slaves and also converted many of them to the Episcopal faith.

38. Eliza Jones, Petition to the Honorable the Justices of the Inferior Court of Chatham County, [c. 1843], LGTJ's Estate Records, File Box I, Folio 81, PCR.

39. Ibid.; *Savannah Georgian*, 27 October 1843.

40. Everard De Renne, "Family History," WC (Silhouette); DeRFP+-Uninventoried Books (prayer book); DeRFP-19 (poem).

41. University of Pennsylvania, *Biographical Catalogue*, 143.

42. John Andrew Gallery, ed., *Philadelphia Architecture: A Guide to the City* (Cambridge, Mass., 1984), 37; Richard J. Webster, *Philadelphia Preserved: Catalog of the Historic American Buildings Survey* (Philadelphia, 1976), 53, 106–7, 141–42.

43. Day, *Historical Collections of Pennsylvania*, 580; Cheyney, *History of the University of Pennsylvania*, 228; University of Pennsylvania, Catalogue (1844–45), 30–31; GFTJ's B.A. diploma, University of Pennsylvania, DeRFP-1064a (Oversize).

44. Cheyney, *History of the University of Pennsylvania*, 223–24.

45. Ibid., 242; Callcott, *History in the United States*, 59–60.

46. Jones, a close student of the eighteenth century, was always partial to the works and personalities of England's Augustan Age and owned a three-volume set of Pope issued by his favorite English publisher, William Pickering. The lines of verse are from *An Essay on Criticism* (1711).

47. GJ's Estate Records, File Box I, Folio 74, PCR; Coulter, *Thomas Spalding*, 54–55; T. Reed Ferguson, *The John Couper Family at Cannon's Point* (Macon, 1994), 168; *DGB*, 1:223. Couper's library contained over five thousand volumes.

48. Expenses of GFTJ, 1844–46, in LGTJ's Estate Records, File Box I, Folio 81, PCR. A lively survey of bibliophilia and bibliomania, from ancient times to the recent past, is Nicholas A. Basbanes, *A Gentle Madness: Bibliophiles, Bibliomanes, and the Eternal Passion for Books* (New York, 1995).

49. Expenses of GFTJ, 1844–46, in LGTJ's Estate Records, File Box I, Folio 81, PCR; Korey, "Three Early Philadelphia Book Collectors," 8; Dickinson, *Dictionary of American Book Collectors*, 211; Jewett, *Notices of Public Libraries*, 120. The collections of Logan (2,600 volumes) and Mackenzie (7,000 volumes) were then—and are still—held by the Library Company of Philadelphia. Jewett's book, cited above, contains a comprehensive survey of American public libraries of the mid-1800s, while Luther Farnham's *A Glance at Private Libraries* (1855) concentrates on Boston and environs.

50. Penington obituary clipping, undated and unidentified (c. 1867), Edward Carey Gardiner Collection, Manuscript Department, HSP (hereafter cited as Penington obituary); Brotherhead, *Forty Years Among the Old Booksellers of Philadelphia*, 26.

51. Receipts from book purchases, 1840s, DeRFP-12; GWJ to Winthrop Sargent, 3 February 1855, Sargent Papers, HSP; Waring, *Cerveau's Savannah*, 68. To put the thirteen hundred volumes of Jones's library in context, the 1850 census showed that Georgia public and college libraries averaged from around two thousand to twenty-four hundred volumes (*Seventh U.S. Census, 1850*, Appendix, Vol. 1, 384–85). In a study of the antebellum libraries of eight representative southerners, Clyde Hull Cantrell found that the collectors were "by no means narrow in literary culture"

and that their libraries "had good coverage of the cultural areas known to exist prior to 1861." In comparison with those cited by Cantrell, Jones's collection was superior in most respects, with particular relative strengths in the classics, religion, the arts, and British and American history—the last mentioned including Georgiana (Cantrell, "Reading Habits of Ante-Bellum Southerners," 305–16).

52. "Miscellanea Georgiana," DeRFP-45.

53. Ibid.

54. Ruth Whelan, *The Anatomy of Superstition* (Oxford, 1989), 233, 240; Kingsley Martin, *French Liberal Thought in the Eighteenth Century* (New York, 1962), 48; Lawrence Lipking, "The Marginal Gloss," *Critical Inquiry* 3 (Summer 1977): 626. James's Bayle was the 1820 Paris edition.

55. Dibdin, *Bibliomania*, 16; Jackson, *Anatomy of Bibliomania*, 557–58. All information regarding the books in the library comes from the original manuscript catalog, found in "Miscellanea Georgiana," DeRFP-45.

56. Receipt, 4 November 1845, DeRFP-12; Keynes, *William Pickering*, 13–14, 20; Penington obituary.

57. A manuscript note by WWDeR notes that a bookplate was in NJ's copy of *The Laws of England*, whereabouts now unknown, but perhaps the source of the photographic reproductions found in the NJ Bible in the Hargrett Library and in DeRFP-6 and 58 (Oversize). Manuscript notations on envelopes in DeRFP+-37, in the hands of GWJDeR and MDeR, suggest that these photographs were produced in the 1860s or 1870s. DeRFP-6 also contains one actual bookplate, with "Noble Jones" printed in black letter, but it seems to be of later origin and is more likely associated with Dr. George Jones's son Noble.

In "Miscellanea Georgiana," George Wymberley Jones noted, "Our present coat of arms is used in the seal of a letter from Noble Jones to his son, Noble Wimberly Jones, dated Jan. 29ᵗʰ 1761." This letter apparently survives only in transcript. Also in "Miscellanea Georgiana," Jones describes the "Arms of Jones of Wormsloe" as follows: "Per bend sinister ermine and ermines, a lion rampant within a bordure engrailed, or. Crest—a demi-lion rampant or, holding between his paws a mullet pierced gules."

There are similarities between the arms and crest described and those attributed to the architect Inigo Jones. Both employ symbols associated with the semimythical tenth-century Welsh border lord Tudor Trevor. Neither, however, is found in the Garter's Ordinaries of the College of Arms, perhaps because of the tangled, idiosyncratic nature of Welsh heraldry. In any case, Noble Jones's "use of the arms followed Welsh usage and was unexceptional" (Davis, *Fledgling Province*, 177; *The New Testament* [1753], with signature and two-page manuscript prayer of NJ, Book Call Number DER 1753 J6, UGAL; Library Card Files of WWDeR, DeRFP+-11–12; "Miscellanea Georgiana," DeRFP-45; Simpson, ed., *Jones Family Papers*, 10–

12, 68n.1; Williams, ed., *Royal Tribes of Wales*, 21; Report of the College of Arms, 23 March 1993; Siddons, *Development of Welsh Heraldry*, 1:xi–xii, 194–203, 215–18, 331–33, 2:557–58; Report of the Committee on Heraldry, New England Historic Genealogical Society, 2 August 1994).

58. O'Dwyer, *Thomas Frognall Dibdin*, 7, 20. A modern admirer of Dibdin offered the best inventory of his deficiencies: "It must be admitted at once that he was the most exasperating of bibliographers—hardly a statement he makes can be accepted without checking. . . . Inaccurate, annoyingly slangy ('saucy margins,' 'creamy papyrus'), gullible . . . , and absurd ('the Beau Brummell of the bibliomaniac folly')—he was all these" ([Jackson], *Publications of Dibdin*, 10–11).

59. O'Dwyer, *Thomas Frognall Dibdin*, 21–23; Sargent, "Bibliopegia," 347.

60. Dibdin, *Introduction to Classics*, 1:265, 377, 2:554, 276, 397.

61. Hazlitt, "On Reading New Books," 17.

62. "Miscellanea Georgiana," DeRFP-45.

63. "A. A. Smets, Esq., of Georgia," 97; Smets, *Catalogue Raisonne*, 3, 20, 37–38; Smets, *Catalogue of Library*, 71, 160, 221.

64. Hubbell, *The South in American Literature*, 355–58; Updike, *Printing Types*, 2:189.

65. William Gilmore Simms to Messrs. Leavitt, Strebeigh & Co., 3 October 1866, in Tefft, *Catalogue*, 21; Jones, "Israel Keech Tefft," 62; GWJ to Israel Tefft, [undated, c. 1848], Keith Read Collection, UGAL; Mackall, "Gwinnett Autographs, Anecdotes," 27. Mackall's article traces the document that bore the autograph in question, which also contained the autograph of Noble Jones. The anecdote regarding the Gwinnett autograph was first published in 1862, with a story told by Tefft supposedly the source. It features Tefft arriving at a riverside plantation (apparently Wormsloe) to serve as a notary for the owner. The Gwinnett document blows "across his path" from a mass of papers being cleaned from a garret and discarded by servants and is given him by the owner, who is "unable to enter fully into [Tefft's] feelings" of excitement. Nothing could be more unlikely than the last quotation or the story of Jones's allowing servants to throw away eighteenth-century manuscripts, but his generosity seems an accurate detail.

66. GWJ to Peter Force, 15 August 1855, DeRFP-12; Spofford, "Washington Reminiscences," 677; Spofford, "Peter Force," 227–28; Goff, *Peter Force*, 9, 15.

67. "Miscellanea Georgiana," DeRFP-45; *DNB*, 1:878.

68. "Miscellanea Georgiana."

69. Ibid. At this time there was a struggle in the Episcopal Church between the High Church party, which supported the Oxford Movement, and the Evangelicals, who stressed preaching and missionary work; both the Smiths' Christ Church in Philadelphia and the Joneses' Christ Church in Savannah were identified with the latter. Though the charge against Bishop Onderdonk was "lasciviousness," his

High Church partisans blamed his downfall on the machinations of his Evangelical enemies. The charges were brought by Paul Trapier, rector of St. Michael's Church in Charleston, a friend of both Bishop Elliott and young Jones (S. D. McConnell, *History of the American Episcopal Church* [New York, 1904], 325; William Wilson Manross, *The Episcopal Church in the United States, 1800–1840: A Study in Church Life* [New York, 1938], 50–51, 164–65; Raymond W. Albright, *A History of the Protestant Episcopal Church* [New York, 1964], 240; Paul Trapier, *Incidents in My Life* [Charleston, S.C., 1954], 24).

70. "Miscellanea Georgiana."

71. Ibid.

72. Ibid.; Dibdin, *Introduction to Classics*, 2.111.

73. "Miscellanea Georgiana;" Dibdin, *Introduction to Classics*, 2:187.

74. Carson, *History of the Historical Society of Pennsylvania*, 1:75–77; Smith, *William Smith*, 2:523–25.

75. Smith, *William Smith*, 2:523–25. Smith's writings appeared in various journals, as well as in pamphlet form; his two lengthier works were *A Defence of the System of Solitary Confinement of Prisoners Adopted by the State of Pennsylvania . . .* (1833) and *Facts & Arguments in Favour of Adopting Railways in Preference to Canals . . .* (1825).

76. University of Pennsylvania, *Catalogue* (1843–44), 10.

77. Sargent, "Bibliopegia," 361–64.

78. *DAB*, 16:368–69.

79. Sargent, "Winthrop Sargent," 233–36; Sargent and Sargent, *Epes Sargent*, 62; Harnett T. Kane, *Natchez on the Mississippi* (New York, 1947), 119–20.

80. Commonplace Book, DeRFP-13; Sargent and Sargent, *Epes Sargent*, 64.

81. Sargent and Sargent, *Epes Sargent*, 63; Winthrop Sargent, Receipt, 8 December 1845, for copying "Appendix &c to Smith's Georgia Sermon," laid in "Miscellanea Georgiana," DeRFP-45; "Notes on Books, etc., relating to the Early History of Georgia," DeRFP-12.

82. Allibone, *Critical Dictionary*, 2:1933; GWJ to Sargent, 3 February 1855, Sargent Papers, HSP. A bibliography of most of Sargent's works is in Sargent and Sargent, *Epes Sargent*, 59–60.

83. GWJDeR to GNJ, 20 July 1871, JFP-1.

84. Norwood, *Medical Education*, 83–84; Ezell, "Southern Education," 310; Corner, *Two Centuries of Medicine*, 100.

85. Norwood, *Medical Education*, 66, 78–83; Corner, *Two Centuries of Medicine*, 94, 98.

86. University of Pennsylvania, *Catalogue* (1847–48), 20; Corner, *Two Centuries of Medicine*, 107.

87. Corner, *Two Centuries of Medicine*, 95; University of Pennsylvania, *Cata-*

logue (1847–48), 36; Jones, "Experimental Inquiry," 308–10. The master of arts degree required no additional course work. Upon application, it was conferred upon university alumni who were bachelors of arts of three years' standing.

88. Mark Bence-Jones and Hugh Montgomery-Massingberd, *The British Aristocracy* (London, 1979), 1–3 ("The Concept of the Gentleman"); Cady, *The Gentleman in America*, 5, 9, 19, 32, 100–101; Hundley, *Social Relations in Our Southern States*, xxx–xxxiii.

89. Lewis, *Rescuing Horace Walpole*, 234.

CHAPTER 2. Agricola

1. Callcott, *History in the United States*, 25. Jones's attitude toward genealogy resembled that expressed by Scott in *Waverley:* "Family tradition and genealogical history . . . is the very reverse of amber, which, itself a valuable substance, usually includes flies, straws, and other trifles; whereas these studies, being themselves very insignificant and trifling, do nevertheless serve to perpetuate a great deal of what is rare and valuable in ancient manners, and to record many curious and minute facts, which could have been preserved and conveyed through no other medium" (Scott, *Waverley*, 51).

2. "Miscellanea Georgiana," DeRFP-45.

3. Scott, *Waverley*, 50–55; Scott, *The Antiquary*, 12, 18–22, 26–29, 201–4, 303; Konkle, *Thomas Smith*, [1]; Robert Chambers, *History of the Rebellion of 1745–6* (Edinburgh, 1929), 160–61; Brown, *Scott*, 49, 63; Daiches, *Scott*, 69.

4. *DeRLC*, 3:1298. For example, Jones ordered a transcript of *De Praestantia Coloniae Georgico-Anglicanae* after seeing the Rich listing (1:88) and noting the book's location in the British Museum.

5. "Miscellanea Georgiana"; Stevens, *History of Georgia*, 1:xiiii; Mackall, "De Renne Library," 70n.10; University of Georgia, Library, *Catalogue* (1858), 5, 7, 9, 12, 17, 18. All told, the university library held fewer than four hundred titles relating to history of any kind.

6. [Hewat], *Historical Account*, 162–63; Johnson, "Hewat," 51.

7. *SDG*, 5 February 1847.

8. *SDG*, 23 January 1846; *Augusta Constitutionalist*, 21 August 1849.

9. Jack, "Preservation of Georgia History," 241; Coulter, *Bevan*, 73–75. The list of materials lent by Dr. Jones to McCall, and later used by Bevan, is found in the George Jones Papers, GHS. It includes letters of Noble Jones, receipts for repairs of boats and of "the Redoubt at Skidaway" in 1746 and 1747, and correspondence between Noble Wimberly Jones and Benjamin Franklin.

10. Coulter, *Bevan*, 78–82, 117. Despite Bevan's work, most of the state's manu-

script archives would remain scattered throughout the various departments in the state capitol until 1918 (Jack, "Preservation of Georgia History," 249–50).

11. Coulter, *Bevan*, 124–26; Martin and Spufford, *Records of the Nation*, 37, 91–92. The Senatus Academicus, "composed of the governor, the president of the Senate, the speaker of the House, the members of the Senate, and the Board of Trustees of the University," supervised "all educational institutions over which the state had any control" (Coulter, *Bevan*, 124).

12. [Harden], "Georgia Historical Society," 6–7.

13. [Stevens], "Autobiography," 527; GHS, *Dedication of Hodgson Hall*, 28; GHS, *Collections*, 3:420. In later years Tefft lived at the intersection of Bull and Jones Streets, on the corner diagonally opposite the home of his friend Alexander Smets (Harden, *Recollections*, 13).

14. [Stevens], "Autobiography," 527; GHS, *Collections*, 2:420.

15. GHS, *Collections*, 2:327; Coulter, "Stevens," 99–100. William Gilmore Simms, like Tefft, had a very considerable library. At the time it was burned in March 1865 it contained ten thousand volumes and was described as "the most valuable library, to a literary man, to be found in the Confederacy" (Oliphant et al., eds., *Letters of Simms*, 4:484n.48).

16. [Stevens], "Autobiography," 468, 524–27; Coulter, "Stevens," 92–93; Green, *Role of the Yankee in the Old South*, 5.

17. *SDG*, 13 February 1841; Coulter, "Stevens," 98–99.

18. Simms to Stevens, 30 December [1841], in Oliphant et al., eds., *Letters of Simms*, 1:296, 344n.23.

19. [Stevens], "Autobiography," 529.

20. Davis, "Elliott," 59–60, 62, 64, 68–69, 121–22; Malone, *Episcopal Church in Georgia*, 20.

21. GHS, *Dedication of Hodgson Hall*, 26–27; GHS, *Collections*, 2:326; [Stevens], "Autobiography," 530–31.

22. Coulter, "Stevens," 100–102; *DGB*, 1:290; *One Hundred Years*, 8, 10–11; Trustees' Minutes (1835–57), 169, 171, 174, UGAL-A. Stevens was not responsible for all the delays. At a meeting of the society in November 1846, it was noted that additional "transcripts from the State Paper Office, London, which have been twice shipwrecked on their journey hither, have at length been recovered, although somewhat damaged by their double submersion. As soon as they shall have been dried and rebound, they will be forwarded to Dr. Stevens at Athens, the Historiographer of the Society" (*SDG*, 18 November 1846). See also GHS, *Collections*, 18:4, 80–81.

23. "Notes on Books, etc., Relating to the Early History of Georgia," DeRFP-12; "Miscellanea Georgiana," DeRFP-45. *SDG*, 7 January 1846.

24. E. G. Withycombe, *The Oxford Dictionary of English Christian Names* (Ox-

ford, 1963), 122; Oath of Allegiance, 9 June 1865, DeRFP-12; Scott, *The Antiquary*, 27–29. The historical community of the time, in both England and America, comprised antiquaries and historians, with the former—greatly in the majority—performing such labors as those of the Georgia Historical Society: collecting, compiling, editing, and diffusing historical materials. Though some antiquaries composed monographs and books, the more creative and artistic tasks of selecting, assimilating, and shaping source material into studies or narratives were primarily considered the province of the historian.

The more pedantic and incompetent class of antiquaries had been lampooned as early as 1592, when Thomas Nashe wrote of their "very rusty wit." Robert Burton's *Anatomy of Melancholy* (1621) and John Earle's *Microcosmographie* (1628)—both of which Jones owned—had passages that ridiculed antiquaries. In the 1700s Pope derided Thomas Hearne, of "sober face, with learned dust besprent," and Scott—himself an antiquary—amused himself not only with Jonathan Oldbuck but others, like Dr. Jonas Dryasdust. Even Charles Dickens had gentle fun with Mr. Pickwick and the adventure of the curiously inscribed stone, an episode that resembles the story of Oldbuck and the Praetorium. On balance, Jones's activities would be antiquarian, but his work in these early years resembled more that of the historian (Levine, *The Amateur and the Professional*, 11–12; Piggot, *Ancient Britons and the Antiquarian Imagination*, 14–18; Piggott, "The Ancestors of Jonathan Oldbuck," 150–51, 156).

25. Joanne Shattock, *Politics and Reviewers: The "Edinburgh" and the "Quarterly" in the Early Victorian Age* (London, 1989), 6. The British reviews also provided for the "nominal icognito" of their essayists (ibid., 18).

26. *SDG*, 7 January 1846.

27. Ibid.

28. *SDG*, 23 January 1846; Harris, *Oglethorpe*, [v].

29. *SDG*, 23 January 1846.

30. *SDG*, 9 February 1846; Harris, *Oglethorpe*, 71n.2; GHS, *Collections*, 2:[38].

31. *SDG*, 9 February 1846.

32. Ibid.

33. Ibid. Harris had quoted Stevens on Oglethorpe's skills in the art of war: the general was "possessed of the most eminent military qualifications" (*Oglethorpe*, 245).

34. *SDG*, 26 February, 12 March 1846.

35. *SDG*, 12 March 1846.

36. *SDG*, 3 April 1846.

37. Ibid.; *SDG*, 7 January 1846. Bulloch, like his predecessor at the *Georgian*, Dr. Arnold, was a staunch Unionist. It has been argued that many prominent Sa-

vannah citizens, as inhabitants of Georgia's most cosmopolitan city, were less likely to subscribe to a southern sectionalism like Jones's than to a "coast-line sectionalism, based upon common colonial traditions, and the relatively intimate communication afforded by marine transportation." Consequently, many upper-class Savannahians would be less prone to be intolerant of "Yankees" and would be more at home in northern ports like New York or Philadelphia than in many Georgia towns (Shryock, *Letters of Richard D. Arnold*, 9). Savannah also served as a resort for northerners, invalid and otherwise, and as a stopping point on the way to Florida, so strident "anti-Yankee" sectionalism could be economically counterproductive.

38. McCardell, *Idea of a Southern Nation*, 3–5, 229; Cooper, *The South and the Politics of Slavery*, 59–60.

39. Weigley, ed., *Philadelphia*, 263, 319, 355, 392; Ezell, "Southern Education," 310; Franklin, *Southern Odyssey*, 63–66.

40. Hubbell, "Literary Nationalism," 182, 185, 187, 211; Kraus, *Writing of American History*, 136–37; Callcott, *History in the United States*, 35–36, 68; *SDG*, 3 April 1846; GWJDeR to Rev. Dr. J. B. Gibson, 14 April 1875, DeRFP-19; Brotherhead, *Forty Years Among the Old Booksellers of Philadelphia*, 26. Jones's attitude was akin to that of another scholarly young southerner, his close contemporary James Johnston Pettigrew of South Carolina. "As for the abominable Yankees," Pettigrew wrote in 1850, "I believe them with few exceptions to be the most despicable of the human race" (Wilson, *Carolina Cavalier*, 110).

41. Hubbell, "Literary Nationalism," 195–97, 201–3; *SDG*, 3 April 1846. For the state of literature and thought in the antebellum South, see Rubin et al., eds., *History of Southern Literature*, 81–174, and O'Brien, ed., *All Clever Men*. The latter contains fourteen discourses of the period, ably edited and superbly introduced. Eugene Genovese and Elizabeth Fox-Genovese are also insightful contributors to the subject.

42. McCardell, *Idea of a Southern Nation*, 158–59; Herbert A. Howell, *The Copyright Law* (Washington, D.C., 1942), 4–5; *SDG*, 3 April 1846.

43. *SDG*, 7 April 1846.

44. Ibid.

45. Ibid.

46. *SDG*, 22 April 1846; GHS, *Collections* 3 (Part 1): [2].

47. *SDG*, 5 February 1847.

48. Ibid. Winthrop Sargent would later launch a similar attack against French novelist Alexandre Dumas (1802–70), denouncing him as a plagiarist and whipping him with parallel columns ([Sargent], "Literary Impostures.—Alexandre Dumas," *North American Review* 78 [April 1854]:305–45).

49. *SDG*, 6 February 1847. In a reviewing milieu where John Wilson Croker's

criticism reputedly killed John Keats, censuring a deceased author appears minor. But many people in Savannah remembered McCall and Harris (both invalids) with respect and affection, and there was a particular fondness for the "indescribably bent" Harris, who had been so cheerful despite his infirmities. In Boston, however, he had his own critics, including one who satirized him as "Dr. Snivelwell" (Myron F. Brightfield, *John Wilson Croker* [Berkeley, 1940], 346–47; *SDG*, 23 January 1846; Nathaniel L. Frothingham, "Memoir of Rev. Thaddeus Mason Harris, D.D.," *Collections of the Massachusetts Historical Society* 2, ser. 4 [1854]: 146, 148; Harris, *Oglethorpe*, [xviii]; *DAB*, 8:321).

50. *SDG*, 5 February 1847; *DGB*, 2:650; *MoM*, 1:239.

51. WBS to GFTJ, 16 March 1847, WBSL.

52. Ibid.

53. WBS to GFTJ, 29 March, 25 May, 2 July 1847 (quoting GFTJ's letter of 12 June 1847), WBSL.

54. WBS to GFTJ, 25 May 1847, WBSL.

55. WBS to GFTJ, 29 March 1847 (referring to GFTJ's letter of 24 March 1847), WBS to GFTJ, 25 August 1847 (referring to GFTJ's letter of 12 August 1847), WBSL.

56. [Stevens], "Autobiography," 533; Stevens, *History of Georgia*, xiii.

57. [Stevens], "Autobiography," 532; Protestant Episcopal Church, Diocese of Georgia *Journal* (1843–48), passim; Hull, *Historical Sketch*, 60.

58. WBS to GFTJ, 25 August 1847, and WBS to GWJ, 1 December 1847, WBSL; Protestant Episcopal Church, Diocese of Pennsylvania *Journal* (1847), 95; Clark, *Reminiscences*, 77.

59. Clark, *Reminiscences*, 40–41; [Stevens], "Autobiography," 534.

60. Coulter, "Stevens," 104–5; Protestant Episcopal Church, Diocese of Georgia *Journal* (1848), 18, 27.

61. WBS to GWJ, 1 December 1847, and WBS to GFTJ, 25 August 1847, WBSL.

62. WBS to GWJ, 30 March 1848, WBSL.

63. WBS to GWJ, 19 May 1848, WBSL.

64. Ibid.

65. Ibid.

66. GWJ to Israel Tefft, 28 December 1848, GWJDeR Correspondence File, GHS; *SDG*, 21 November 1849; Morrison, *John S. Norris*, 8, 23; GHS Minute Books, 1:157; GHS, *Collections*, 18:175–76. Until monuments were erected in several other squares, Monument Square was the familiar name for Johnson Square (Waring, *Cerveau's Savannah*, 9, 56).

67. [Jones], *Observations*, [1].

68. *SDG*, 5 February 1847.

69. [Jones,] *Observations,* [3]−6.

70. Ibid., 6−7.

71. Ibid., 7, 12.

72. Ibid., 8, 12; Washington Irving, *Diedrich Knickerbocker's A History of New York* (New York, 1927), 15, 23.

73. [Jones], *Observations,* 17n., 22, 19.

74. Ibid., 23.

75. Ibid., 27−28.

76. As in the case of Agricola on Harris, Jones's *Observations* quotes one of Horace's odes against Dr. Stevens: *Parturiunt montes, nascetur ridiculus mus* (The mountains heave, and give birth to a laughable mouse) (*SDG,* 23 June 1846; [Jones], *Observations,* 8; *Augusta Constitutionalist,* 21 August 1849).

77. *Augusta Constitutionalist,* 21 August 1849.

78. GHS Minute Books, 1:157; *SDG,* 21 November 1849. The allusion is to two Greek critics. Longinus was credited with the masterpiece of literary criticism titled *On the Sublime.* Zoilus was noted for the bitterness and severity of his criticism, particularly that he directed at Homer, for which he was said to have been thrown from a precipice (*Lempriere's Classical Dictionary,* 334−35, 674).

79. Hull, *Historical Sketch,* 60; [Jones], *Observations,* 4n.

80. *SDG,* 3 December 1847; *North American Review* 67 (1848): 316; *Southern Quarterly Review* 13 (1848):471−72, 499, 501; Oliphant et al., eds., *Letters of Simms,* 1:296n.135.

81. Oliphant et al., eds., *Letters of Simms,* 6:200−201. Over half a century later, the librarian of the Georgia Historical Society would comment dryly that the society, having "contributed liberally" toward printing the two volumes of Stevens's history, had acquired "a large number of copies, many of which are still in its possession." The book was still being offered, at $2 per volume, as late as 1920 ([Harden], "Georgia Historical Society," 6; *GHQ,* 4:127).

82. Sabin, *Bibliotheca Americana,* 9:320; Jones, *Georgia Historical Society,* 15, 28.

CHAPTER 3. Book-Madness

1. A receipt from the Philadelphia printing and engraving firm of Mason and Mason, dated 27 October 1847, shows, beside entries for 12 and 25 August 1847, that Jones had "G. F. T. Jones" erased from the "arms plate" and "Geo. Wymberley Jones" engraved thereon; he also had the motto altered at this time. In the Stevens-Jones correspondence, Stevens first addresses Jones as "George W. Jones" in the letter of 2 November 1847, in which he notes that he has changed Jones's name in the

preface of his *History of Georgia*. The previous extant letter (to "Geo. F. T. Jones, Esq.") was dated 25 August 1847, responding to Jones's of 12 August 1847 (Receipt, DeRFP-12; WBS to GWJ, 25 August, 2 November 1847, WBSL).

2. The derivation of the name is unknown. It was for a time assumed that Wimberly was the surname of the family of Noble Jones's wife, just as another theory had her maiden name as Wormsloe; it was actually Hack. There might, of course, have been some collateral relationship to the Wimberlys in either the Jones or Hack family. Also, at St. Margaret's Westminster, the church the Joneses attended in the years before they left England, there is a monument to Gilbert Wimberley (died 1653), who is buried in the church. A former rector of the church and prebendary of Westminster, Wimberley was a royalist who was "deprived by the Commonwealth." During the reign of Charles II, he returned to St. Margaret's (LLM to S. N. Rhoads, 29 April 1918, DeRGL Accession File, UGAL; Arthur Roland Maddison, *Lincolnshire Pedigrees*, 4 vols. (London, 1902–6), 3:1093; Douglas Wimberley to J. G. B. Bulloch, 22 September 1909, DeRFP-40; David McCord Wright, "The English Roots of Noble Jones," DMWP-39).

3. "Miscellanea Georgiana," DeRFP-45; *DNB*, 3:164.

4. Ivor H. Evans, *Brewer's Dictionary of Phrase and Fable*, 14th ed. (New York, 1991), 769; Scott, *Redgauntlet*, 401. The original motto, *Vigilias ago* (I keep watch) was retained by George Noble Jones's branch of the family. For a soldier long in charge of a frontier outpost, this motto was very fitting. Since accepted usage was that such mottoes could be altered at will (unlike the arms and crest), Noble Jones himself may have created the motto.

5. DB 3P:220; George Jones's monument; Bonaventure Cemetery, Savannah, Ga.

6. Gamble, *History of the City Government of Savannah*, 199; Sears, *Sacred Places*, 100. The Evergreen Cemetery Company of Bonaventure was incorporated in December 1847, the same year the property was purchased (*Sketch of Bonaventure*, 6, 13).

7. DB 3P:220; George Jones's monument, Bonaventure Cemetery, Savannah, Ga. "Map of Portion [of] Bonaventure Cemetery," Map Collection, UGAL; *DAB*, 3:523.

8. See for example, GWJ to GNJ, 2 April 1852 (JFP:1), in which GWJ reports receiving a letter asking whether he will sell Dean Forest Plantation, a property of GNJ. The hyphenated surname "Wymberley-Jones" almost never appears as part of a signature of George Wymberley Jones and is not employed where GWJ's name appears on Dr. George Jones's Bonaventure monument (or on the monument of GWJDeR), but it is used in all of the Wormsloe editions and associated works except the Walton quarto (1847) and Mary De Renne's *Lee* (1883). It appears as a sur-

name in Wormeley, "Reminiscences of Newport in the Fifties," 11. For compound (or double) surnames and changed names in general, see Baring-Gould, *Family Names,* 390–407.

9. Lower, *Patronymica Britannica,* 173–74; Burke and Burke, *General Armory* (1842), unpaginated (under "Jones, or Johnes"); Burke, *General Armory* (1884), 547.

10. Lower, *English Surnames* (1849), 1:vii; Lower, *English Surnames* (1842), 152; Lower, *Patronymica Britannica,* xxviii; *Lettres de Madame de Sévigné de sa Famille et de ses Amis,* 14 vols. (Paris, 1862–68), 7:9. De Renne was—and is—pronounced (də ren′).

11. GJ's Estate Records, File Box I, Folio 74; LGTJ's Estate Records, File Box I, Folio 81, PCR.

12. LGTJ's Estate Records, File Box I, Folio 81, PCR. DB 3F:375, 386; Plantation Journal, 1, DeRFP-57; DB 3F:382; Conveyance . . . to George Wymberley Jones, Negro Slaves, 20 February 1849, DeRFP-12; Record Book, DeRFP-13.

13. Plantation Journal, 3, 5, 6, DeRFP-57.

14. Hodgson Journal, 34–35, CCJJ Papers, UGAL.

15. Lewis, *Horace Walpole,* 141–42; Coulter, *Wormsloe,* 216. Several sources make the mistake of assuming that the imprint signified that Jones actually had a printing press at Wormsloe, like those of Walpole at Strawberry Hill and Sir Egerton Brydges at Lee Priory (Jones owned books printed at both places). All of Jones's Wormsloe editions were printed in Philadelphia, however, as is noted (based on documentary evidence) in the description of each of his titles in the *DeRLC* (1931).

16. Wymberley-Jones, *Theory Concerning the Nature of Insanity,* [3], [5]; Receipt, C. Sherman to GWJ, 7 December 1847, laid in the DeRGL copy of *Theory,* UGAL. The cost of forty-eight copies (including paper, composition, presswork, and folding) was $30.

17. "Miscellanea Georgiana," DeRFP-45.

18. *Theory,* [4], [7]–8.

19. Ibid., 8–10, 20.

20. Ibid., 27–29; Albert Deutsch, *The Mentally Ill in America: A History of Their Care and Treatment from Colonial Times* (Garden City, N.Y.), 64–66.

21. *Theory,* 19.

22. Ibid., 32–35.

23. *Report of the Episcopal Female Prayer Book Society 1847,* [2]–3.

24. [Jones], *Observations,* [27].

25. Callcott, *History in the United States,* 112.

26. Dibdin, *Bibliomania,* 77; Sargent, "Bibliomania," 277.

27. GHS, *Collections,* 3 (Part 1): [3]–4.

28. Spofford, "Washington Reminiscences," 675–76; *DLB,* 30:89.

29. Weigley, ed., *Philadelphia*, 174–75; Wolf, *Brief History of the Library Company of Philadelphia*, 31.

30. Walton et al., *Observations upon the Effects of Certain Late Political Suggestions*, [5], [7]–8; Paul H. Smith, ed., *Letters of Delegates to Congress, 1774–1789*, 24 vols. (Washington, D.C., 1976–96), 16:350n.1 (the *Observations* are at 16:561–66). Jones included the pamphlet's text in full but omitted the table and included only those statistics "possessing interest at present." His reprint (leaf size approximately 13″ × 10″) was much larger than the original, whose leaves were approximately 8″ × 6″ (*Observations*, [3]–[4]; *DeRLC*, 1:223 and 2:509). The delegates' original manuscript survives in the New York Public Library.

31. Ms. note on front flyleaf of [Jones], *Observations*, GWJDeRC, UGAL. For Madison's complicated views and sometimes contradictory actions in this matter, based in large part on Virginia's aim of securing navigation rights to the Mississippi River, see Edmund C. Burnett, ed., *Letters of the Members of the Continental Congress*, 8 vols. (Washington, D.C., 1921–38), 5:456–59, and Irving Brant, *James Madison: The Nationalist, 1780–1787* (New York, 1948), 70–88.

32. Jones intended the "official" number of copies of this first of the series to be twenty-one, but C. Sherman actually produced twenty-two copies (for $16.25). The Library Company of Philadelphia still holds the pamphlet that Jones reprinted. An additional copy of the original pamphlet was later discovered by Charles C. Jones, Jr.; finely bound, with the authors' autographs added, it ultimately became a part of the DeRGL. A third copy is in the Cornell University Library (Receipt, C. Sherman to GWJ, 2 October 1847, laid in the DeRGL copy of *Observations;* "Miscellanea Georgiana," DeRFP-45; Mackall, "De Renne Georgia Library," 68n.9).

33. "Miscellanea Georgiana," DeRFP-45; Reports of the Bodleian Library, 23 March and 2 September 1992. Austin, an associate of the London publisher John Bell (1745–1831), based his faces on "the new Didot types of 1783–84," the precursors of "modern" typefaces (*DNB*, 4:168–69; Morison, *Four Centuries of Fine Printing*, 40–41). Bell was the first to discard the "long s," which was used during Jones's time in printing such eighteenth-century materials as his friend Winthrop Sargent's *The Loyal Verses of Joseph Stansbury and Doctor Jonathan Odell* (Albany, N.Y., 1860) and Plowden J. C. Weston's *Documents Connected with the History of South Carolina* (London, 1856).

Another characteristic of the quartos was that Jones, in keeping with his previous statements on the matter, had none of them copyrighted. Using the copy presented to the Georgia Historical Society, the historian George White reprinted the *Observations*, with minor omissions, in his *Historical Collections of Georgia* (1855). White described Jones as "a young gentleman whose praiseworthy efforts to rescue from oblivion many important facts connected with the early history of Georgia, entitle him to the gratitude of her citizens" (106–10).

34. De Brahm, *History*, [3]; *DGB*, 1:246–47. Understandably confused by the esoterica of nineteenth-century book formats, several bibliographers have labeled the antebellum Wormsloe Quartos folios, apparently because they often have signature marks every two leaves, a common characterestic of folios. This is also, however, characteristic of a "quarto in twos," in which the printed sheet was cut in half, and each half (each with its own signature mark) was folded once. More commonly with quartos, the sheet (bearing only one signature mark) was folded twice, yielding a signature mark every four leaves. Had the Wormsloe Quartos been printed on laid paper, as were many such books, there would have been no confusion; the watermark would have appeared within the spine fold and the chain lines would have been horizontal (as is the case with the postbellum Egmont quarto) rather than vertical, as with folios. But the quartos were printed on machine-made paper, devoid of any marks. The sizes of nineteenth-century folios and quartos could be so similar that size is often not a decisive indicator of format. See particularly William Savage, *Dictionary of the Art of Printing* (London, 1841), 560, and Philip Gaskell, *A New Introduction to Bibliography* (Oxford, 1972), 84–85, 106n.B, and Figures 47 and 48.

35. De Vorsey, *De Brahm's Report*, 273n.210; GHS, *Collections*, 18:176; De Brahm, *History*, 4. For differences between the two copies of De Brahm, see De Vorsey, 46–47, 273n.210.

36. Carpenter, *Harvard University Library*, 74–75; [Potter], *Library of Harvard University*, 21, 49; Jewett, *Notices of Public Libraries*, 31, 34–35. At the midpoint of the nineteenth century, the Harvard library—consisting of the Gore Hall library, the law library, and various "society libraries connected with the college"—held 84,200 volumes, making it the largest in the United States, more than ten times the size of the library at the University of Georgia. Ironically, Harvard's librarian was Thaddeus William Harris, son of the Oglethorpe biographer savaged by "Agricola" (Jewett, 31, 156).

37. De Brahm, *History*, [3], passim. In 1856, perhaps as a sincere form of flattery, the South Carolina scholar-planter Plowden J. C. Weston (1819–64) privately printed most of the text (but none of the maps) of the Harvard De Brahm manuscript devoted to his state. He mentioned Jones's De Brahm quarto (though mistaking it for a folio), remarking on its "great typographical excellence" and its limited number of copies. His own book, a small quarto, was restricted to 121 copies, beautifully printed on various papers at the Chiswick Press in London (Weston, *Documents*, [3]–4, [157]; *DeRLC*, 2:583; Anthony Q. Devereux, *The Rice Princes: A Rice Epoch Revisited* [Columbia, S.C., 1973], 75, 89, 120). Louis De Vorsey's 1971 edition of De Brahm made available the British Library's De Brahm volumes in handsome form, with an excellent introduction and copious notes.

38. De Brahm, *History*, 24. When the Smithsonian Institution librarian Charles

C. Jewett published his survey of public libraries in 1851, he included the referenced quotation in the Savannah section, noting that the book had been "privately printed by G. W. Jones, of Georgia, in 1849, from an old MS. in the Harvard University Library" (Jewett, *Notices of Public Libraries*, 158).

The location of the library mentioned by De Brahm as being on the Savannah River, 96¼ miles from the sea, is often assumed to have been (and indeed may have been) in Augusta, but De Brahm elsewhere (p. 4) gives the distance from Augusta to the sea as 150 miles.

39. David McNeely Stauffer, *American Engravers upon Copper and Steel*, 3 vols. (New York, 1907), 1:28; *DeRLC*, 2:522; GHS, *Collections*, 18:175; De Brahm, *History*, 4. Plates based on photographs of the British Library manuscript renderings of the omitted drawings are in De Vorsey, *De Brahm's Report*, following page 142.

40. De Brahm, *History*, [3].

41. Bassett, *Middle Group American Historians*, 100–107; Callcott, *History in the United States*, 128–36; Jameson, *History of Historical Writing*, 111.

42. Ravenel, *Charleston*, 476, 478.

43. Ibid.; *DAB*, 9:130; Bremer, *The Homes of the New World*, 1:378–79, 390.

44. Pinckney, ed., *Letterbook*, ix, xxiv; Bell, *Major Butler's Legacy*, 76–77, 539–40.

45. The letterbook, with its "dry parchment covers and faded brown ink on fragile pages," is now in the library of the South Carolina Historical Society in Charleston. Some of the related papers are in the Duke University Library (Pinckney, ed., *Letterbook*, xxvii). Jones's Lucas journal—reproduced from a copy in the Rare Book Collection of the University of North Carolina at Chapel Hill—was reissued in 1967 by the Reprint Company of Spartanburg, South Carolina, in the same volume with Harriott Horry Ravenel's *Eliza Pinckney* (New York, 1896). The original letterbook was published by the University of North Carolina Press in 1972 in a scholarly edition containing excellent introductory material and extensive annotation. In 1997 a paperback edition, with a new introduction, was published by the University of South Carolina Press.

46. [Pinckney], *Journal and Letters of Eliza Lucas*, [33], passim; "Miscellanea Georgiana," DeRFP-45.

47. Pinckney, ed., *Letterbook*, xv–xvi; *Journal*, 24, 25–30.

48. *Journal*, [5], 20, 30.

49. Pinckney, ed., *Letterbook*, xxvii; *Journal*, 7, 16, 28–29.

50. "Miscellanea Georgiana," DeRFP-45.

51. John M. Clayton, Letter of Introduction of GWJ, 4 May 1850, DeRFP-12.

52. Passport of GWJ, 10 May 1850, with Endorsements, DeRFP-12.

53. *DAB*, 15:549; Stevens, *Recollections*, 13.

54. Stern, "Henry Stevens," 4–5.

55. Stevens, *Recollections*, 13; Keynes, *William Pickering*, 30, 39–41.

56. Sargent, *Diary*, [3]. Most of Sargent's manuscripts were given to the Ohio Historical Society in 1926 by Winthrop Sargent VII, but "the original of Winthrop Sargent's diary of the St. Clair expedition cannot be found" and is represented by the Wormsloe quarto. In this case, the printing of a rare manuscript did save it from oblivion, and the most recent studies of St. Clair's defeat draw heavily on the diary. The *Ohio Archaeological and Historical Quarterly* reprinted the quarto, minus the illustrations, in its number of July 1924 (33:237–73) (Frederick S. Allis, Jr., *Guide to the Microfilm Edition of the Winthrop Sargent Papers* [Boston: 1965], 31; Prucha, *Sword of the Republic*, 25n.16).

Though there was no direct connection between the events chronicled in this quarto and Georgia history, Sargent in 1798 became governor of the Mississippi Territory, originally part of Georgia. There was also a link with Jones's Smith grandfather: Arthur St. Clair (1734–1818), also born in Scotland, was one of Thomas Smith's "most intimate friends in their struggles in a new land" (Konkle, *Thomas Smith*, 5).

57. Prucha, *Sword of the Republic*, 22–27.

58. Sargent, *Diary*, 34, 48.

59. Ibid., 36, 38–39; Wiley Sword, *President Washington's Indian War: The Struggle for the Old Northwest, 1790–1795* (Norman, Okla., 1985), 186. One authority has noted of St. Clair's defeat that in "proportion to numbers involved, this was the severest disaster to American arms up to the Battle of the Little Big Horn in 1876" (John K. Mahon, *History of the Militia and the National Guard* [New York, 1983], 51).

60. "Miscellanea Georgiana," DeRFP-45; Sargent, *Diary*, [59].

61. Mott, *Golden Multitudes*, 129; Marvel, "A Bachelor's Reverie," *Southern Literary Messenger* 15 (September 1849): 601–9. The "Reverie" was reprinted in *Harper's New Monthly Magazine* 1 (October 1850): 620–27, with the notation on 620, "From a new work soon to be issued by Baker and Scribner."

62. Marvel, *A Bachelor's Reverie*, [3]–4, 6–7, 11, 14, 17 (all citations to the *Reverie* are to the Wormsloe edition). The publications of the Elzevir family, produced in Holland in the sixteenth and seventeenth centuries, were much prized by bibliophiles.

63. Ibid., 18–19.

64. Ibid., 22.

65. Ibid., 22–25.

66. Ibid., 25, 30, 34, 38–39.

67. Ibid., 40.

68. Mott, *Golden Multitudes*, 307 (other books of 1850 that met the required sale of 225,000 volumes were *David Copperfield* and *The Scarlet Letter*).

69. Winthrop Sargent to "Ik. Marvel," 8 November 1850 [copy], laid in the DeRGL copy of *A Bachelor's Reverie*, UGAL.

Ik (pronounced "Ike") Marvel" was the pseudonym of Donald G. Mitchell, who preferred the pen name spelled as shown ("without the period") and apparently formed it from the names of two of his favorite authors, Izaak Walton and Andrew Marvel. The Wormsloe edition uses a variation—"Ik: Marvel" (Kime, *Donald G. Mitchell*, 9).

In his preface to the 1883 edition of *Reveries of a Bachelor*, Mitchell wrote that, soon after the publication of the original reverie, it had received the "honor of a private printing, in elegant quarto [*sic*] form, and an edition of twelve copies, by a curious bibliophile and (I trust) worthy gentleman, then living at Savannah, Ga." (Marvel, *Reveries of a Bachelor* [1883], xvi).

Jones found Mitchell's subsequent works unappealing and felt that the author had "written himself out"; he wrote Winthrop Sargent that even if Mitchell lived to be eighty, his "best epitaph" would still be "Author of a Bachelor's Reverie." Though the author lived to eighty-six, his biographer notes that from the 1850s until his death (a peaceful one, in his library), Mitchell "was chiefly known as the author of *Reveries of a Bachelor*" (GWJ to Winthrop Sargent, 3 February 1855, Sargent Papers, HSP; Kime, *Donald G. Mitchell*, 31).

70. Marvel, *A Bachelor's Reverie*, [41]. Three of the original leather-bound copies are in the GWJDeRC, UGAL.

71. "Miscellanea Georgiana," DeRFP-45.

CHAPTER 4. Ancestral Fields

1. Mary Oakley McRory and Edith Clarke Barrows, *History of Jefferson County, Florida* (n.p., 1958), 97–98; Martin, *Florida*, 75; Phillips and Glunt, eds., *Florida Plantation Records*, 16.

2. Phillips and Glunt, eds., *Florida Plantation Records*, 16–17; Doherty, *Richard Keith Call*, 49–51, 70–71, 80; Martin, *Florida*, 33n.3. The *Catalogue of the Litchfield Law School* shows that William B. Nuttall graduated with the class of 1823.

3. "Miscellanea Georgiana," DeRFP-45; Park, *Major Thomas Savage*, 41; Phillips and Glunt, eds., *Florida Plantation Records*, 16.

4. Hoffmann and Hoffmann, *North by South*, 217.

5. Phillips and Glunt, eds., *Florida Plantation Records*, 16, 46; Long, *Florida Breezes*, 166, 168; Jerrell H. Shofner, *History of Jefferson County* (Tallahassee, 1976), 59. Murat's plantation, Lipona, was just east of El Destino. Though the friendship of William Nuttall and Achille Murat ended bitterly, correspondence

and clippings in the Jones Family Papers, GHS, suggest that Mrs. Nuttall (by then Mrs. George Noble Jones) renewed her acquaintance with members of the family of the then-deceased Murat in the 1860s and through them "had the entre at the Court of St. Cloud" (A. J. Hanna, *A Prince in Their Midst: The Adventurous Life of Achille Murat on the American Frontier* [Norman, Okla., 1946], 153, 196; Clipping, 29 December 1902, JFP-3).

6. Long, *Florida Breezes*, 169–70.

7. "Miscellanea Georgiana," DeRFP-45; Abbey, ed., "Documents Relating to El Destino," 183–86; Mary Savage Nuttall to Mary Wallace, 8 March [1837], and Undated Memorandum of WJDeR, DeRFP-24.

8. Mary Savage Nuttall Jones to Mary Wallace Nuttall Jones, October 1863, in private possession; "Miscellanea Georgiana," DeRFP-45, Abbey, ed., "Documents Relating to El Destino," 211–13; Hoffmann and Hoffmann, *North by South*, 217.

9. Phillips and Glunt, eds., *Florida Plantation Records*, 17–19; Abbey, ed., "Documents Relating to El Destino," 186n.18; Shofner, *History of Jefferson County*, 41; Mary Wallace Savage to Mary Wallace, 9 July [1840], DeRFP-24; Ferguson, *Kingscote*, 5.

10. [Gardiner and Gardiner, eds.], *Early Recollections*, [1], 142–43, 186–87, 216–17.

11. Ibid., 188–89.

12. Ibid.

13. Ferguson, *Kingscote*, 1–2, 5–7; [Gardiner and Gardiner, eds.], *Recollections*, 215; Hester, "Kingscote," 1.

14. Phillips and Glunt, eds., *Florida Plantation Records*, 18–20, 37n.53, 541–43; Abbey, ed., "Documents Relating to El Destino," 186, 212n.24. George Noble Jones also owned a third Florida plantation, Oscilla Eldorado, unmentioned in the Phillips and Glunt book (JFP-Folder 94).

15. Phillips and Glunt, eds., *Florida Plantation Records*, 21–22.

16. Elliott, *This Was My Newport*, xv.

17. Ferguson, *Kingscote*, 3, 4; Anthony Trollope, *North America* (New York, 1951), 27; Wormeley, "Reminiscences," 9; Van Rensselaer, *Newport*, 18; *Hand-Book of Newport*, 18; James, *The American Scene*, 152.

18. Ferguson, *Kingscote*, 3, 11; Mason, *Newport*, 51; Curtis, *Lotus-Eating*, 195.

19. Hoffmann and Hoffmann, *North by South*, 215–16; *Hand-Book of Newport*, 119.

20. Maria Campbell to Mrs. Thomas Gardner, [18 May 1840], DeRFP-24.

21. "Miscellanea Georgiana," DeRFP-45; Mary Wallace Savage to Mary Wallace, 9 July [1840], DeRFP-24; Johnston, ed., "Kollock Letters," *GHQ* 31:296.

22. Leonard J. Panaggio, "America's Oldest Summer Cottage," *Atlanta Journal*

and *Constitution Magazine*, 5 August 1973, 10, 38; Wayne Andrews, *American Gothic: Its Origins, Its Trials, Its Triumphs* (New York, 1975), 6, 63, 65; Ferguson, *Kingscote*, 39; S. Fenwicke Campbell to Mary Wallace Nuttall, 7 May 1841, JFP-1; Paul F. Miller, Preservation Society of Newport County to the author, 5 November 1992; Antoinette F. Downing and Vincent J. Scully, Jr., *Architectural Heritage of Newport, Rhode Island, 1640–1915* (New York, 1952), Plates 155, 157; *Hand-Book of Newport*, 63.

23. Susan M. Kollock, ed., "Letters of the Kollock and Allied Families, 1826–1884," *GHQ* 33 (December 1949): 350; *DGB*, 1:464–65. The square opposite the Telfair mansion was later renamed Telfair Square.

At the mansion (in the early 1860s at least) "good-looking little negro boys and men dressed in liveries" waited at table, a practice that one guest, the British journalist William Howard Russell, wrote "smacks of [Hodgson's] Orientalism" (Russell, *My Diary North and South* [Boston, 1863], 157).

24. Mary Savage Nuttall Jones to "My dear Aunt," 24 July 1850, in private possession; Unidentified clipping, c. 9 November 1877, DeRFP-4; Carson, *History of the Historical Society of Pennsylvania*, 1:77.

25. Park, *Major Thomas Savage*, 41; Ferguson, *Kingscote*, 9–10.

26. Johnston, ed., "Kollock Letters," *GHQ* 32:132, 135; GWJ to Mary Savage Nuttall Jones, 24 January 1852, EDeRBC.

27. DB 3L:178. A suit arising from this marriage settlement and that of Mrs. George Noble Jones was brought at some point in early 1880, though the court record has apparently disappeared. The only evidence of the suit is a draft of the answer to the bill of complaint found in JFP-2.

28. "Miscellanea Georgiana," DeRFP-45; Marriage Certificate, GWJ and Mary Wallace Nuttall, 21 October 1852, DeRFP-12; Marriage Notice, *Newport Mercury*, 23 October 1852; Trinity Parish Records, 1786–1861, Marriage #35, NHS; Van Rensselaer, *Newport*, 253, 255–56; Elliott, *This Was My Newport*, xxiii.

29. Passport of GWJ, 7 October 1852 (in brown leather passport case stamped in gold "G. Wymberley Jones"), and "Account Book of Samuel Street, My Travelling Courier—A Swiss—from Nov. 1852 London to May 1853 Liverpool," DeRFP-12. Street's phonetic spelling (and accent) are most obvious in his numerous notations of having paid the "hotel beel."

30. "Account Book of Samuel Street," DeRFP-12; William Dana Orcutt, *The Kingdom of Books* (Boston, 1927), opposite 8.

31. "Account Book of Samuel Street," DeRFP-12; "Miscellanea Georgiana," DeRFP-45; crystal Jordan water flask, with notes of GWJDeR and WJDeR, DeRFP+-47. Lieutenant W. F. Lynch, U.S.N., conducted "the first scientific survey of the Dead Sea" in 1848 and published his *Narrative of the United States' Expedition to the River Jordan and the Dead Sea* the following year. Like Washington

Smith, he was an "earnest Christian" who visited the Holy Land "to widen and to deepen the foundations of [his] religious faith" (*DAB*, 6:524–25; Smith, *William Smith*, 525). The Jordan water was used at family christenings for generations; in 1906 GWJ's great-grandson Craig Barrow, Jr., was christened with what remained of it.

The Joneses' 1853 stay in Newport is documented in detail in "Expenses in Newport from June 20th to Oct. 29th 1853" (DeRFP+-7).

32. Wormeley, "Reminiscences," 8, 11–12. Mary is listed as "M. Wymberley-Jones" in her leather-bound Queen of Clubs journal, containing rules and regulations, transcripts of literary selections, and lists of meetings (DeRFP-23).

33. [Tuckerman], *Newport Reading Room*, ix, 1–3, 21.

34. Ferguson, *Kingscote*, 10–11; *New York Daily Tribune*, 5 October 1854; George Bancroft to GWJ, 7 October 1854, DeRFP-9; Mary Savage Nuttall Jones to "My dear Aunt," 24 July 1850, in private possession; [Fuller], *Belle Brittan*, 172.

35. Record Book, DeRFP-13.

36. Plantation Account Book, DeRFP-57; Plantation Journal, DeRFP-12.

37. Plantation Account Book, 6, 122–23, DeRFP-57; Record Book, DeRFP-13.

38. "Miscellanea Georgiana," DeRFP-45; Plantation Journal, DeRFP-12; Williamina Smith to GWJ, 1 February 1857, DeRFP-7.

39. Williamina Smith to GWJ, 1 February 1857, DeRFP-7; Juliana Smith to GWJ, 11 February 1857, ibid.; Plantation Account Book, p. 6, DeRFP-57.

40. Plantation Journal, DeRFP-12; For Deziray (spelled variously, of Santo Domingan descent) and Golding, see Registers of Free Persons of Color, vol. 3:13, 32, GHS.

41. Plantation Journal, DeRFP-12; Record Book, DeRFP-13; GNJ to GWJ, 1 January 1856, and GWJ to GNJ, 15 January 1856, JFP-1.

42. GWJ to GNJ, 11 March 1856, JFP-1; Plantation Journal, DeRFP-12.

43. GWJ to Peter Force, 15 August 1855, DeRFP-12.

44. William B. Hodgson to James H. Hammond, 7 October 1849, James H. Hammond Papers, LoC.

45. "Miscellanea Georgiana," DeRFP-45; Plantation Account Book, DeRFP-57; Ledger, DeRFP-12.

46. GWJ to GNJ, 15 January 1856, JFP-1.

47. Plantation Journal, DeRFP-12. Stained cotton was often the result of yellowing from "untimely rains" or seepage of seed oil after careless ginning. GWJ's proportion of white to stained was within the "fair average" for Sea Island cotton (Rosengarten, *Tombee*, 75–76).

48. Plantation Journal, DeRFP-12; Eaton, *History of the Old South*, 209; Rosengarten, *Tombee*, 75.

49. Plantation Account Book, DeRFP-57; Bill of Sale, 5 April 1859, DeRFP-13;

Plantation Journal, DeRFP-12. William B. Hodgson had purchased a steam engine the previous year and noted that it had enabled him to "emancipate from slavery 18 mules & 4 little nigger drivers" (William B. Hodgson to James H. Hammond, 19 June 1859, James H. Hammond Papers, LoC).

50. GWJ's manuscript notes in his copy of Whitemarsh B. Seabrook's *Memoir of the Origin, Cultivation and Uses of Cotton*, GWJDeRC; Plantation Journal, DeRFP-12.

51. Plantation Journal, DeRFP-12. Among the "eatables" imported from the West Indies were the tanyah (also called tania and tannier) and arrowroot—both of which have starchy, edible rootstocks—as well as benne, the herb also known as sesame, whose seeds are used as flavorings.

52. Plantation Journal, DeRFP-12; Diary, DeRFP-13; De Renne Family Receipts and Remedies, UGAL.

53. Plan of Wormsloe House, DeRFP-Oversize; Plantation Journal, DeRFP-12.

54. *CRG* 6:340–41; Betty Wood, *Slavery in Colonial Georgia* (Athens, 1984), 90–91. The slaves that came to GWJ are listed by him by name and monetary value in the Record Book, DeRFP-13.

55. Plantation Journal, DeRFP-12.

56. Ibid. For "plantation slavery from the point of view of masters," with recommendations regarding housing and other necessities, see James O. Breeden, ed., *Advice Among Masters: The Ideal in Slave Management in the Old South* (Westport, Conn., 1980).

57. Plantation Journal, DeRFP-12; Plantation Account Book, DeRFP-57.

58. GWJ to Andrew Johnson, 28 August 1865, "Amnesty Papers," National Archives Microfilm M1003, Roll 20; Bryson, *An American Consular Officer*, 150–52.

59. "Miscellanea Georgiana," DeRFP-45; Malcolm Cowley, ed., *Adventures of an African Slaver* (Garden City, N.Y., 1928), xvii–xxi; William Stanton, *The Leopard's Spots: Scientific Attitudes Toward Race in America* (Chicago, 1970), 52–53; Samuel Wilberforce, *History of the Protestant Episcopal Church in America* (New York, 1849), 419, 423.

60. Plantation Account Book, DeRFP-57; "Miscellanea Georgiana," DeRFP-45; GWJ to GNJ, 2 April 1852, JFP-1; Savannah Tax Digests, 1850, 1860, GHS; Haunton, "Savannah," 35, 36, 40.

Wharf lots 4 and 5, east of Bull Street, had belonged to Noble Jones; wharf lot 4 had been left to GWJ by his father, and his 1849 purchase brought the two properties back together. Of his $3,724 net income for 1851, GWJ spent $3,590 to rebuild the wharf and repair the stores on lot 5 (Plantation Account Book, DeRFP-57).

Of Savannah's 997 real property owners in 1860, GWJ and twenty-one others were among the top 2 percent, owning at least $80,000 worth of property apiece, while GNJ was among the top sixteen property owners with holdings valued at

$100,000 or more. In 1860 Savannah, a "mere eighty-six individuals possessed over half the real property, measured by value" (Savannah Tax Digest, 1860, GHS; Haunton, "Savannah," 36).

61. Kelly, *Short History of Skidaway Island*, 23–24, 26, 36; "Modena Plantation," WPA-16, GHS.

62. Johnson et al., *Ecological Survey of the Coastal Region of Georgia*, 11–13; Coulter, *Wormsloe*, 106.

63. Transcript by GWJ of the notice in the *Georgia Gazette*, 8 June 1780, DeRFP-30.

64. DB 3F:373, DB 3K:354, DB 3K:355, DB 3P:514; "Note on Stouf's Survey of Wimberly," DeRFP-58; "Extract of Title of Wimberly" and "Extract of Title of Long Island," DeRFP+-10.

65. "Memorandum for counsel—Wormsloe right of way, 1857," DeRFP-30.

66. Ibid.; *SMN*, 10 July 1857. The subscribers to the bridge were J. R. Pritchard, J. F. Waring, Alvin M. Miller, William H. Wade, Charles Van Horn, William R. Symons, Serenus Meyers, and a Mr. Martin ("List of the association of Subscribers to the Skidaway Ferry bridge," DeRFP-29).

67. MDeR, "Record of War Times," WC.

68. Ibid.

69. Ibid.

70. Durham, "Savannah," 11; Babits, "Battery Wimberly," 6.

71. Jones, *Siege of Savannah*, 98, 102, 152; Elma S. Kurtz, ed., "War Diary of Cornelius R. Hanleiter, Georgia Light Artillery, Army of Tennessee, C.S.A., Thompson Artillery," *Atlanta Historical Bulletin* 14, Part 3 (September 1969): 68, 70, 72; Babits, "Battery Wimberly," 6; Georgia Historical Society, *The U.S.S. Water Witch* (Savannah, 1974), 32; Jones, *Historical Sketch of the Chatham Artillery*, 38, 43, 46; Myers, ed., *Children of Pride*, 777–78; Coulter, *Wormsloe*, 233–34; *ORA*, Series I, vol. 6:305 (1861), vol. 14:649 (1862), 853–59 (1863), and vol. 35, part 2:611 (1864).

The actual name of the Wormsloe works is a vexed question. Colonel Charles C. Jones's detailed plan of the locations of the artillery in the Savannah vicinity and their distances from Oglethorpe Barracks on Liberty Street, dated October 1864, shows seven guns on the Isle of Hope but does not name the fortifications at Wormsloe. The *tête du pont* in the plantation's northeastern corner "12,866 yds." from the barracks (and located on a portion of Wimberly Plantation by then absorbed into Wormsloe) is called "Skidaway Bridge," and the earthwork at the southern tip of Wormsloe, "14,666 yds." from the barracks, is called simply "Jones Point." WJDeR called the position "Lawton Battery" in Knight's *Georgia's Landmarks* (1:88). (A copy of Jones's plan is found in his extra-illustrated copy of *Siege of Savannah*, UGAL.) The 1881 engraving of Union Brigadier General Orlando M. Poe's "Map of Savannah and Vicinity," from two manuscript maps dated 25 September 1866, based in part on Confederate maps, calls the Jones Point earthwork "Fort Wimberly" (*OR A Atlas*, Plate LXX, 2). The same name, curiously, is given to the tabby ruins at Wormsloe on Charles G. Platen's 1875 map of Chatham County (GHS), citing a map by John R. Tebeau.

Another minor but confusing problem arises from the various spellings of Wimberly. From 1860 a tract of old Wimberly Plantation north of and adjacent to the northeasternmost portion of Wormsloe—including a smaller parcel that contained the Wimberly plantation house—was in possession of Captain Joseph S. Claghorn and his wife; they called the house and plantation of approximately sixty-eight acres "Wymberly." Much later, when a residential subdivision was created on the site in the 1940s, it was named "Wymberley" (Wymberley Tract, Ms. 1060, GHS; Ruth Saffold DeTreville, *Captain Claghorn of the Chatham Artillery of Savannah* [N.p., 1978], 23, 38–39).

GWJ helped to create this confusion of spellings with the engraving of Charles Willson Peale's portrait of NWJ that he commissioned in the 1840s. Up until that point, his grandfather's middle name and the plantation name had both appeared with the original spelling, "Wimberly." The engraving identified its subject as "N. W. Jones," so GWJ was not attempting to give his grandfather's name a new spelling. But since his own name, with its different spelling, appeared immediately below, the assumption was widely and mistakenly made that the proper spelling was of N. W. Jones's middle name, and, consequently, his plantation, was "Wymberley." Adaptations, like the Claghorns,' apparently followed this error.

72. Certificates of Disability: 3, 5 March 1862, 2 April 1862, 19 November 1862, and "Surgeon's Certificate of Exemption," 29 September 1863, DeRFP-12.

73. GWJ to Andrew Johnson, 28 August 1865, "Amnesty Papers," National Archives Microfilm M1003, Roll 20; Plantation Account Book, DeRFP-57. Henry Berner Jones, M.D., kindly reviewed the certificates of exemption and disability, a description of other characteristics of GWJ's continuing illness and invalidism, the circumstances of his death, and the death certificate; he found the evidence suggestive of and consistent with a diagnosis of chronic nephritis.

74. MDeR, "Record of War Times," WC; Archie Vernon Huff Jr., *Greenville: The History of the City and County in the South Carolina Piedmont* (Columbia, S.C., 1995), 139; Durham, "Savannah," 11.

75. MDeR, "Record of War Times," WC.

76. Undated, unidentified newspaper clipping, with GWJ's annotation: "Miss Telfair's letter to Mrs. Thompson, Litchfield, 1863. intercepted and published in a Northern paper—about Kentwyn," DeRFP-20.

77. Ibid.; GWJ to William B. Hodgson, 1 September 1861, in Copy 2 of De Brahm's *History*, DeRGL.

78. Various receipts for rooms, board, tuition, and stabling in Greenville, S.C., 1861–63, DeRFP-13; James M. Richardson, *History of Greenville County, South Carolina* (Atlanta, 1930), 76; Archie Vernon Huff, Jr., *Greenville: The History of the City and County in the South Carolina Piedmont* (Columbia, S.C., 1995), 91; Linda Friddle, ed., *Famous Greenville Firsts* (Greenville, S.C., 1986), 39–40.

79. Plantation Account Book, 1, DeRFP-57; Quartermaster's receipt for sixty-four bales of hay, 3 February 1862, DeRFP-13. GWJ's intermittent supervision of Wormsloe apparently ended in 1864, when his deteriorating health led him to take refuge at Oaklands. Edward Nelson, who became his overseer, agreed in the contract drawn up by Jones not "to use any severity to the negroes . . . nor to suffer them to be ill-treated by other persons" (Contract, GWJ and Edward M. Nelson, 10 January 1864, DeRFP-58; Receipt, 1 January 1866, DeRFP-29).

80. Durham, "Savannah," 12; "Miscellanea Georgiana," DeRFP-45.

81. WJDeR, "History of My Life," DeRFP-14.

82. Mary Savage Nuttall Jones to Mary Wallace Nuttall Jones, October 1863, in private possession; MDeR, "Record of War Times," WC; *ORA*, Series I, vol. 44: 164, 185, 188–89.

83. William B. Hodgson to GWS, 29 March 1865, DeRFP-12. Union troops began arriving in Louisville on 28 November, and the Fourteenth and Twentieth Corps were encamped there, along with Judson Kilpatrick's cavalry division, from 29 November to 1 December (though elements of the Union cavalry preceded the main body of troops). Oaklands Plantation was located within four miles of Louisville (*ORA*, Series I, vol. 44:37, 44, 55, 185, 188, 197).

84. Durham, "Savannah," 46–48; William B. Hodgson to GWS, 29 March 1865, DeRFP-12; "Miscellanea Georgiana," DeRFP-45.

85. Coulter, *Wormsloe*, 234; *ORA*, Series I, vol. 44:794, 807. Though one hundred Federal soldiers were sent to garrison "Wimberly," it is uncertain whether the reference is to the Jones Point works or to the fortifications at the Skidaway bridgehead near Claghorn's Wymberly; the latter were more important to Sherman's establishing connection with the Union naval forces.

86. *ORA.*, Series I, vol. 47, Part 2:60–62; Oubre, *Forty Acres and a Mule*, 46–51; Hodgson, "Journal," 30, CCJJ Papers, Ms. 215, Box 8, Folder 4, UGAL.

87. Linnius Howell, Land Title, 13 July 1865, DeRFP-26; Bristol Drayton, Land Title, 15 July 1865, Unbound Miscellaneous Papers, 1862–69, and Register of Land Titles Issued to Freedmen, April–September 1865, Roll 36, Records of the Assistant Commissioner for the State of Georgia, Bureau of Refugees, Freedmen, and Abandoned Lands, 1865–69, National Archives. Long Island was later rented out to sharecroppers.

88. Hodgson, "Journal," 35; William B. Hodgson to GWS, 29 March 1865, DeRFP-12.

89. William B. Hodgson to GWS, 29 March 1865, DeRFP-12.

90. GWJ, Oath of Allegiance, 9 June 1865, DeRFP-12; Jonathan Truman Dorris, *Pardon and Amnesty Under Lincoln and Johnson* (Chapel Hill, 1953), 221–23.

91. *ORA*, Series I, vol. 47, Part 3:595–96; William B. Hodgson to GWS, 29 March 1865, DeRFP-12; Petition of GWJ to rent property and collect rents, [16 June 1865], DeRFP-26; Unidentified and undated clipping regarding lease of Wormsloe, 19 June 1865, DeRFP-31; *Savannah Daily Herald*, 24 June, 1 July 1865, 15 June 1866.

92. Middleton, ed., *Life in Carolina and New England*, 179; "Miscellanea Georgiana," DeRFP-45.

93. GWJ to Andrew Johnson, 19 July, 28 August 1865, with endorsements, "Amnesty Papers," National Archives Microfilm M1003, Roll 20; Official Pardon of GWJ, 29 August 1865, DeRFP-12.

94. Petition for Change of Name, 11 January 1866, approved 12 January 1866, DeRFP-13; Steamer trunk of GWJDeR, in private possession.

As E. Merton Coulter noted, GWJDeR "changed the family name to De Renne, separating it as here written, but the subsequent generations have not done so uniformly" (Coulter, *Wormsloe*, x). As did Coulter in *Wormsloe*, in this book I consistently employ the spelling of De Renne that was devised by the name's creator.

CHAPTER 5. The Noblest Road

1. Richard Ollard, *Clarendon and His Friends* (New York, 1988), 311; Dalmasso, *Montpellier*, 12–16, 95–99; James, *Art of Travel*, 283–84.

2. "Mirabel," DeRFP-2; Georgiana King Diaries, NHS; Wymberley De Renne, "History of My Life," DeRFP-14.

3. King Diaries, NHS; James, *Art of Travel*, 288.

4. Dalmasso, *Montpellier*, 15–16; *The Hachette Guide to France* (New York, 1988), 498–99; James, *Art of Travel*, 288.

5. Joseph I. Waring, *A History of Medicine in South Carolina, 1825–1900*, 3 vols. (Columbia, S.C., 1967), 2:245; *DAB*, 9:130; Ravenel, *Charleston*, 479; Brotherhead, *Forty Years Among the Old Booksellers*, 27.

6. Goff, *Peter Force*, 13–14; Spofford, "Washington Reminiscences," 679.

7. Sargent and Sargent, *Epes Sargent*, 61–64; *Appleton's Cyclopaedia of American Biography*, 5:398.

8. Death Notices of Maria Campbell Stewart and Juliana Smith, DER 1867/C3 and DER 1867/S52, DeRGL; James, *Art of Travel*, 282; Auditor's Report, Estate of Maria Campbell Stewart, DeRFP-2; GNJ to George Washington Smith, 22 July 1867, DeRFP-2; Plan of Tomb, DeRFP-1064a (Oversize), Folder 29.

9. "Miscellanea Georgiana," DeRFP-45; Milledge, *De Renne Gift*, passim; Estate of Letitia De Renne, File D-363, PCR.

10. *DGB*, 2:964; Tefft, *Catalogue*; Smets, *Catalogue of the Private Collection of Autographs*; Smets, *Catalogue of the Private Library*. Tefft's collection of signers of the Declaration of Independence, including the Button Gwinnett autograph presented by GWJ, is in the New York State Library, Albany, along with a copy of the 1867 sale catalog, in which most prices paid are entered in the margins in manuscript. The copy of the Smets library catalog in the DeRGL has penciled annotations of the incredibly low prices fetched by Smets's books.

11. "British Museum," DeRFP-42; Stern, *Antiquarian Bookselling*, 195.

12. "List of Georgia Papers in the Public Record Office, London," DeRFP-47; Ben Weinreb and Christopher Hibbert, *The London Encyclopaedia* (New York, 1993), 625; Baedeker, *London and Its Environs*, 150−51; Martin and Spufford, eds., *Records of the Nation*, 39−40, 92; Public Record Office, *Guide to the Public Records*, 33−34, 48−50.

13. *DNB*, 17:606; Green, "William Noel Sainsbury," 28−31. See also Sainsbury, "The British Public Record Office and the Materials in It for Early American History," *PAAS* 8 (1893):376−89.

14. William Starr Basinger to Thomas G. Basinger, 25 July 1905, CSAC-17; William Starr Basinger to GWJDeR, 2 May 1867, GWJDeR Papers, DUL.

15. Shryock, ed., *Letters of Richard D. Arnold*, 135, 143; *SMN*, 11 January 1869; William Starr Basinger to GWJDeR, 12 August 1867, GWJDeR Papers, DUL; Plantation Account Book, DeRFP-57. Most of this was commercial property, to which GWJDeR added throughout the 1870s, including his purchase of a wharf lot and offices west of and adjoining his other riverfront property.

16. Plantation Account Book, 19, DeRFP-57; WJDeR, "Wormsloe," Accession File, DeRGL; *SMN*, 18 December 1868; Duncan, *Freedom's Shore*, 28, 30; Coulter, *The South During Reconstruction*, 73; GWJDeR to George Fenwick Jones, 25 May 1871, DeRFP-30.

17. *SMN*, 1 April 1897; *Acts of the General Assembly, 1870*, 453.

18. Report of the Commissioners of Public Roads, Chatham County, Georgia, 9 December 1871, DeRFP-30; Georgia (State), General Assembly, *Acts (1870)*, 453.

19. *SMN*, 7 October 1871; Georgia (State), General Assembly, *Acts (1871)*, 242; GWJDeR to George Fenwick Jones, 25 May 1871, DeRFP-30.

20. GWJDeR to George Fenwick Jones, 25 May 1871, DeRFP-30; John Thomson to GWJDeR, 24 April 1878, DeRFP+-5; Diary, 1876−80, DeRFP-13.

21. GWJDeR to George Fenwick Jones, 21, 25 May 1871, DeRFP-30; Report of the Commissioners of Public Roads, Chatham County, Georgia, 9 December 1871, DeRFP-30.

22. Report of the Commissioners of Public Roads, Chatham County, Georgia, 9 December 1871, DeRFP-30; Chatham County Superior Court, Presentments of the Grand Jury, January Term Superior Court, 1872, undated, unidentified newspaper clipping, DeRFP-30.

23. DB 4K:342, SCR; "Notes on Books, etc., Relating to the Early History of Georgia," DeRFP-12; Morrison, *John S. Norris*, 41, 43; "The City of Savannah, Georgia," *Hunt's Merchants' Magazine* 29 (1853): 57.

24. "Notes on Books, etc., Relating to the Early History of Georgia," DeRFP-12; Diary, 1876–80, DeRFP-13; Undated, unidentified clipping, DeRFP+-36.

25. Diary, 1876–80, DeRFP-13; *SMN*, 30 January 1876, 3 February, 19 March 1878; Stereographs of Wormsloe, WWDeRP-119. The antebellum well house, constructed by Bruno Deziray and Prince Golding, now stands on the grounds of the Beach Institute in Savannah, a gift in honor of the Reverend Frank A. Jenkins, Jr.

26. Undated, unidentified clipping, DeRFP+-36; Morrison, *John S. Norris*, 41; Diary, 1876–80, DeRFP-13.

27. Inventory, Estate of Letitia De Renne, File D-363, PCR.

28. Diary, 1876–80, DeRFP-13.

29. Jones, *Georgia Historical Society*, 29; Diary, 1876–80, DeRFP-13.

30. Bell, "Romantic Wines of Madeira," 335; Diary, 1876–80, DeRFP-13. The diary contains a list of GWJDeR's wines and their locations in the various cellars and attics in the Liberty Street residence.

31. Diary, 1876–80, DeRFP-13.

32. Ibid.; Billie Burn, *An Island Named Daufuskie* (Spartanburg, S.C., 1991), 144–54.

33. Mayor Edward C. Anderson to GWJDeR, 7 October 1875, and GWJDeR to Anderson (copy), 12 October 1875, DeRFP-12; *SMN*, 7 October 1875; GWJDeR to W. W. Lincoln, 20 February 1873, Christ Church of Savannah, Vestry Minutes (1864–1901), GHS.

34. Christ Church of Savannah, Chatham County, Vestry Minutes (1864–1901), 153–54 (pew), 180 (stone plaque), GHS; GWJDeR, "Correspondence about my gift of a pew in Christ Church to the Bishop of Georgia & his successors forever, 1873," DeRFP+-3.

35. Diary, 1876–1880, DeRFP-13; Protestant Episcopal Church, Diocese of Georgia, *Journal* (1876), 31, (1877), 24–25. Among other benefactions, GWJDeR sent a generous contribution to the congregation of Temple Mickve Israel the year the new Jewish synagogue was consecrated. His contribution, he wrote, was "a testimony of respect for the people who worship God after the ancient fashion of their fathers—who care for their own poor,—as they have learned from Him to do—and who always lend a willing, helping hand to every public project of benevo-

lence." A transcript of this letter was sent to GWJDeR's grandson almost fifty years later, with a cover letter that noted that the "letter was so highly esteemed by the congregation of Mickve Israel that it was made part of their minutes" (Lee Roy Myers to WWDeR, 7 April 1926, containing copy of GWJDeR to S. Yates Levy, 25 February 1878, WWDeRP-9).

36. *SMN*, 20 September, 1 October 1878.

37. Whitehill, *Independent Historical Societies*, 177–78; [Mackall], "William Harden," 77–78. Dr. Arnold expressed his esteem for GWJDeR and his forebears in an 1868 address that mentioned the family's distinction "in the annals of Georgia, both in a political and a literary point of view." Dr. George Jones, he said, "has left lineal descendants among us . . . who have always proved the truth of the French proverb, the 'Noblesse oblige'—which I translate freely—a gentleman cannot forget himself " (Arnold, *Address*, 12, 14).

38. GNJ to Wallace Savage Jones and George Fenwick Jones, 7 July 1871, and GWJDeR to GNJ, 20 July 1871, JFP-1; *SMN*, 27 June 1871; Certificate of Death of William Brown Hodgson, Municipal Archives, New York City.

39. GWJDeR to GNJ, 20 July 1871, JFP-1.

40. Ibid.

41. Hodgson, *Science of Language,* [iii].

42. DB 4.V:172, SCR; *SMN*, 18 September 1885; Haygood S. Bowden, *Two Hundred Years of Education: Bicentennial, 1733–1933, Savannah, Chatham County, Georgia* (Richmond, 1932), 278; *SMN/SEP*, 14 November 1976. MDeR arranged for the second building to be deeded to the city in May 1882 for use as a school.

On 19 May 1952, in recognition of GWJDeR's contributions to education in Chatham County, the Board of Education named a new Savannah school the George W. J. De Renne Elementary School. Located at Mills B. Lane Avenue and Hopkins Street, the institution opened in 1953 and is now known as De Renne Middle School (*SMN*, 20 May 1952; "School History," De Renne Middle School, Savannah, Georgia).

43. Minute Book, 2:61, 106–7, GHS.

44. GWJDeR to William Harden, 4 June 1871, GWJDeR Correspondence File, GHS; GWJDeR to Edward Harden, 31 January 1872, Minute Book, 2:106–7, GHS. The volumes of letters are found as Mss. 595 (Oglethorpe) and 884 (Wright), GHS. The Oglethorpe volume remains in its original red leather binding, with "General Oglethorpe's Letters. 1735–1744" stamped in gold on the front.

Another contribution—certified copies from the Georgia secretary of state's office of the commissions of John Reynolds, the first royal governor—went unpublished until 1920, at which time De Renne's letter of 6 December 1875 was published with them. One of the commissions, including detailed instructions "drawn up in the office of the Board of Trade," was published in 1946, from the copies of the colonial records secured by the state of Georgia in the early 1900s ("The Two Royal Commissions Issued to John Reynolds as Governor of Provincial Georgia," *GHQ* 4 [1920]: 159–78; Albert B. Saye, ed., "Commission and Instructions of Governor John Reynolds, August 6, 1754," *GHQ* 30 [1946]: 125–162; *CRG*, 20:vii).

45. GWJDeR to Edward Harden, 31 January 1872, Minute Book, 2:107, GHS.

46. Ibid.

47. Minute Book, 2:118–19, GHS; GHS, *Collections*, 3:vi. There has never been a satisfactory explanation of this volume's being numbered 3, when Hodgson's previous volume of the *Collections* was numbered 3, Part 1.

48. GHS, *Collections*, 3:[v]–vi; W. Grayson Mann to GWJDeR, 3 June 1873, GWJDeR Correspondence File, GHS; William Hunter to GWJDeR, 3 June 1873, DeRFP-12; GWJDeR to W. Grayson Mann, 7 June 1873 (copy), DeRFP-12; William Neyle Habersham to GWJDeR, 10 June 1873, DeRFP-12.

49. GWJDeR to W. Grayson Mann, 19 June 1873, GWJDeR Correspondence File, GHS; Minute Book, 2:151, GHS; *SMN*, 13 February 1874; *DGB*, 1:513. The original hall of the society later became a "bar room" ([Mackall], "William Harden," 81).

50. Minute Book, 2:194–95, GHS; Easton Yonge to GWJDeR, 8 December 1875, DeRFP-16; *SMN*, 6 March 1877.

51. Minute Book, 2:197, GHS.

52. GWJDeR to Gov. James M. Smith, January 1876, DeRFP-16.

53. Minute Book, 2:197, 204, 209, GHS; Niles, *Principles and Acts of the Revolution*, 390–94; *SMN*, 2 May 1876.

54. Coulter, *Georgia*, 359.

55. Myers, ed., *Children of Pride*, [7]–8.

56. Ibid., 14–17, 20.

57. Bonner, "Charles Colcock Jones," 325–26, 330.

58. Ibid., 324–25; Penn, "Charles Colcock Jones," 72.

59. Minute Book, 2:117, GHS.

60. *DeRLC*, 2:696, 704, 721, 746–47, 760; David S. Edelstein, *Joel Munsell: Printer and Antiquarian* (New York, 1950), 17, 20, 275, 321.

61. GWJDeR to CCJJ, 4 December 1870, GWJDeR Letters, Ms. 467, UGAL.

62. Stevens returned to Savannah in 1873 to preach at the sesquicentennial of Christ Church (*DGB*, 2:933; Coulter, "William Bacon Stevens," 108).

63. CCJJ to GWJDeR, 1 March 1875, Keith Read Collection-15, UGAL.

64. GWJDeR to CCJJ, 19 February, 12 March 1875, 19 July 1874, GWJDeR Letters, Ms. 467, UGAL.

65. GWJDeR to CCJJ, 9 March 1878, Ms. 467, UGAL.

66. Ibid.; *DGB*, 1:550.

67. Jones, *Georgia Historical Society*, 21–22; Lawton, "Telfair Academy of Arts," 15–16.

68. *SMN*, 15 February 1876; Henry R. Jackson to GWJDeR, 25 February 1875, DeRFP-13.

69. GHS, *Dedication of Hodgson Hall*, [5]–8, [9]; *SMN*, 15 February 1876.

70. GHS, *Dedication of Hodgson Hall*, 15–23; *SMN*, 15 February 1876. In the absence from Savannah of General A. R. Lawton, the conveyance had to be effected through a letter. For the GHS publication on the dedication, a more elaborate version was desired, with which GWJDeR assisted Lawton, providing the last five paragraphs. "I shall not hesitate to 'strut in borrowed plumes,'" wrote Lawton, "without any acknowledgment except to the lender!" (A. R. Lawton to the President and Members of the GHS, 12 February 1876, in *SMN*, 15 February 1876, and in GHS, *Dedication of Hodgson Hall*, 10–12; A. R. Lawton to GWJDeR, 31 March 1876 [endorsed in GWJDeR's hand: "Gen. Lawton's thanks for draft of last paragraphs of his letter to Ga. Hist. Soc. conveying Hodgson Hall. 1876."], DeRFP-13).

The trust deed prohibited eating, drinking, and "entertainment or amusements of any kind" in Hodgson Hall. Consequently, when a newspaper reported that a legal opinion would be sought, making it possible to allow chess playing in the hall, GWJDeR suggested that he would take legal action to prevent it. Although he himself had advised Mrs. Hodgson that chess playing might be excepted from her strictures, she was adamantly against it. "Professional ingenuity can no doubt show how to evade any obligation however sacred," he wrote General Henry R. Jackson, "and the demoralization consequent upon (I do not say resulting from) the war may induce even so respectable a body as the Georgia Historical Society to try a trip on that road;—I know not. But I do not intend to allow my dead friend's wishes to be disregarded and her purposes come to naught, if I can stay it." The society decided not to pursue the matter, and as late as the 1970s, amusements of all kinds continued to be forbidden in the hall. "When once the membership infringed upon these Victorian rules," noted a historian of the society, "the wind rose, windows rattled, a glass fell and broke, and mysterious voices were heard!" For a time "proscribed amusements" were "confined to the new annex," but in recent years, the hall has safely seen a certain amount of "Feasting" and "drinking" (GWJDeR to Henry R. Jackson [copy], 9 June 1876, and Henry R. Jackson to GWJDeR, 15 June 1876, DeRFP-13; Britt, *Overture to the Future*, 6).

71. *SMN*, 15 February 1876; GHS, *Dedication of Hodgson Hall*, 29; MDeR to WJDeR, 15 February 1876, DeRFP-14.

72. Gamble, *History of the City Government of Savannah*, 331–32; Will of Mary Telfair, DeRFP-48. Hodgson Park had been renamed Forsyth Park when Forsyth

Ward was laid out in 1851. A unanimous resolution and petition of the GHS (framed by GWJDeR in February 1875) called unsuccessfully for the city council to return the park to the name it had been "commonly called" (Minute Book, 2:175–77, GHS).

73. Diary, 1876–80, DeRFP-13. An obituary noted that GWS "was never in public life, and was a frequent traveller and resident abroad and was a man of great learning and varied attainments. . . . He was quite wealthy and made many munificent charitable gifts. . . . He has gone to his reward, and taken the sweet savor of good deeds with him" (*Philadelphia Public Ledger*, 25 April 1876).

74. "Telegraphic despatches [relating to the death of GWS]," DeRFP-4; GWS to GWJDeR, 16 April 1876, DeRFP-4; "A Fortunate Heir," unidentified clipping, c. 1876, DeRFP-4; Will of GWS, City Archives, Philadelphia.

75. CCJJ to GWJDeR, 2 August 1876, DeRFP-Autograph Book; GWJDeR to CCJJ, 6 August 1876, in vol. 1 of Jones's extra-illustrated copy of *Dead Towns of Georgia*, UGAL; Jones, *Dead Towns of Georgia*, [5].

76. Jones, *Dead Towns of Georgia*, 251–53.

77. Diary, 1876–80, DeRFP-13; Receipt, Moran & Reilly, dated 1 June 1875, for moving monument to Wormsloe and placing it at the burial ground, 13–15 May 1875, DeRFP+-7; Plantation Journal, DeRFP-12; "Notes on Books, etc., relating to the Early History of Georgia," DeRFP-12; GWJDeR, "Sketch for tomb of Noble Jones in Old Cemetery, Savannah, placed there by me 1870," DeRFP-13; Coulter, *Wormsloe*, 236.

78. GWJDeR to CCJJ, 25 December 1876, in vol. 2 of Jones's extra-illustrated copy of *Dead Towns of Georgia*, UGAL.

79. GWJDeR to CCJJ, 6 August 1876, ibid., vol. 1.

80. Penn, "Charles Colcock Jones," 39–40, 66; CCJJ to GWJDeR, 11 January 1878, DeRFP-Autograph Book.

81. CCJJ to GWJDeR, 4 February 1878, DeRFP-Autograph Book; GWJDeR to CCJJ, 17 February 1878, Ms. 467, UGAL.

82. CCJJ to GWJDeR, 11 February 1878, DeRFP-Autograph Book; Minute Book, 4:252–53, GHS; GWJDeR to CCJJ, 17 February 1878, GWJDeR Papers, Ms. 467, UGAL.

83. CCJJ to GWJDeR, 27 April 1878, DeRFP-Autograph Book; Jones, *Dead Towns of Georgia*, [3].

84. *SMN*, 7 May 1878.

85. Jones, "Colonel Charles C. Jones," 306; Penn, "Charles C. Jones," 48; J. R. Saussy to GWJDeR, 10 June 1878, DeRFP-13.

86. *Times* (London), 12 June 1878; Mrs. Stephens to D. E. R., 13 June 1878, and W. J. Noble to D. E. R., 14 June 1878, DeRFP-29; "Answers to Advertisement in

London Times about 'Wormslow,' " ibid.; Record Book, DeRFP-13. Unsurprisingly, the area referred to by Mrs. Stephens is heavily populated with Joneses, situated as it is on the Welsh border. Coincidentally or not, another Herefordshire parish is called Wormilow Hundred, and, oddly, the "West Riding place-name Womersley" survives in surnames as both "*Womersley* and *Wimberley*" (M. A. Faraday, ed., *Hereford Militia Assessments of 1663* [London, 1972], 169, 209; Royal Commission on Historical Monuments, England, *Inventory of the Historical Monuments in Herefordshire*, 3 vols. [London, 1931–34], 3:214–15; Reaney, *Origin of English Surnames*, 39).

87. Diary, 1876–80, DeRFP-13; Christ Church of Savannah, Chatham County, Vestry Minutes (1864–1901), 151, GHS; Joseph E. Johnston to GWJDeR, 8 March 1878, DeRFP+-1.

88. *Savannah Daily Advertiser,* 28 May 1875; Emerson, *Historic Southern Monuments*, 119–21; *SMN,* 8 October 1931.

89. Foster, *Ghosts of the Confederacy,* 41; Hamilton Branch to GWJDeR, 19 April 1878, in private possession, as are the Branch and other letters that follow through note 87, unless cited otherwise. For Hamilton Branch's Civil War career, see Mauriel Phillips Joslyn, *Charlotte's Boys: Civil War Letters of the Branch Family of Savannah* (Berryville, Va., 1996). The Margaret Branch Sexton Collection, UGAL, contains newspaper correspondence of the 1920s and 1950s in which Branch's daughter argues that her father was the sole model for the statue, though her father's letters to GWJDeR (apparently unknown to her) support the account in the text.

90. Hamilton Branch to GWJDeR, 5 June 1878.

91. *NCAB,* 40:559; Hamilton Branch to GWJDeR, 8 October 1878.

92. Maurice J. Power to GWJDeR, 29 March 1879, William Harden to GWJDeR, 24 July 1879, and W. Grayson Mann to GWJDeR, 16 February 1880, DeRFP-33; "The Confederate Soldier," Fine Arts Accession Record Sheet, Telfair Academy of Arts and Sciences, Savannah, Georgia.

According to A. R. Lawton, "The first work of art which the [Telfair] Academy acquired was through gift on February 12th, 1880, . . . of a bronze statuette, a replica of the bronze Confederate Soldier which tops the Confederate Monument. . . . The statue and the replica in little were both gifts of Georgia's generous citizen, George Wymberley Jones De Renne (Lawton, "Telfair Academy of Arts," 17).

Since the Telfair Academy was not formally opened until 1883, the Confederate soldier was apparently on exhibit for a time at Hodgson Hall. It returned there for an exhibition in 1997 but had been in storage for years. The other "replica in little" is in private possession.

93. *SMN,* 25 April, 12 May 1879; *SMN,* 8 October 1931; Diary, 1876–80,

DeRFP-13. The cost of the statue alone was $2,500 (Receipt, Maurice J. Power to GWJDeR, 8 April 1879, with endorsement).

94. GWJDeR to the President of the Ladies' Memorial Association, 21 May 1879, printed in *SMN*, 4 June 1879.

95. GWJDeR to the President of the Ladies' Memorial Association, 28 April 1880, Ladies' Memorial Association Papers, Ms. 473, GHS.

96. Bartlett, "Early Settler Memorials," 108. *The Confederate Soldier* appeared in gilt on the cover of Frances Butler Leigh's *Ten Years on a Georgia Plantation Since the War* (London, 1883).

97. Diary, 1876–80, DeRFP-13. These remaining monuments would be moved to Bonaventure after GWJDeR's death. NJ's cenotaph was placed at the end of the lane immediately east of that leading to Dr. George Jones's monument. Behind that monument, the NWJ slab was placed over the sealed opening to the crypt containing the remains moved from the Old Cemetery in 1880.

98. Diary, 1876–80, DeRFP-13; Louis DesAnges to MDeR, 21 July 1873, DeRFP+-1.

99. GWJDeR to WJDeR, 18 June 1880, DeRFP+-1; Diary, 1876–80, De RFP-13.

100. Coulter, *Wormsloe*, 241–42.

101. Everard De Renne, Biographical File, Alumni Records, Princeton University; J. Thomas Scharf, *History of Westchester County, New York*, 2 vols. (Philadelphia, 1886), 2:351; Everard De Renne to GWJDeR, 5 August, 3 July 1879, DeRFP+-1.

102. *SMN*, 12 June 1879; Kentwyn De Renne, Medal, 1er Prix de Gymnastique, in private possession; C. W. Everest to GWJDeR, 4 December 1871, DeRFP-19; Rensselaer Polytechnic Institute, *Register of All Students, 1824–1929* (Troy, N.Y., 1930), 59, 299, 402; Kentwyn De Renne Alumni File, Archives and Special Collections, Folsom Library, Rensselaer Polytechnic Institute. In an incident at St. John's School, where fighting was prohibited, Kentwyn's roommate used "infamous language to him about himself, his country [the South], and his family." Kentwyn asked "that he might be allowed to avoid him, or to try to whip him into decency — though a boy larger and stronger than himself," a request his father supported. Though the headmaster moved Kentwyn into Everard's room, he assured GWJDeR that, under the circumstances, his son would not have been punished for "an attempt at personal chastisement" (GWJDeR to Rev. J. B. Gibson, 14 April 1875 [copy], and Gibson to GWJDeR, 17 April 1875, DeRFP-19).

103. Diary of Letitia De Renne, 1876, DeRFP+-9; Bridget Phillips to GWJDeR, 31 May 1872, DeRFP-13; CCJJ to MDeR, 25 August 1882, DeRFP-Autograph Book.

104. *Acts of the General Assembly, 1875,* [309]–10; Will of GWJDeR, File D-305, PCR. The will was also printed as a seven-page pamphlet by J. B. Lippincott & Company, Philadelphia (copy in DeRFP-12).

105. WJDeR to GWJDeR (copy), 7 May 1880, DeRFP-14; GWJDeR to WJDeR, 18 June 1880, DeRFP+-1.

106. The Savannah City Council, for example, would not approve GWJDeR's petition to be allowed to provide a large park for the use of the patients of the City Hospital of Savannah. Citizens in the area had opposed this use of the four lots involved. In a letter to the editor commenting on the action of the council and the citizens, "A Friend to Progress" wrote, "Richly do we deserve that the munificent citizen who, like his Master, is 'always going about doing good,' should shake the dust of this city from his feet and never again take any interest in her welfare" (*SMN,* 29, 31 May, 1 June 1878).

107. *SMN,* 5 August 1880; GWJDeR to WJDeR, 30 July 1880, DeRFP-12; [Kentwyn De Renne to WJDeR, August 1880], DeRFP-12. Kentwyn De Renne, in the letter previously cited, noted that his father had died of "exhaustion"; the death certificate lists "debility." Both are consistent with the last stages of nephritis (Death Certificate of GWJDeR, City Archives, Philadelphia).

108. Telegrams of T. A. Biddle and Company to WJDeR, 4, 5, 6 August 1880, DeRFP-12.

109. James J. Farrell, *Inventing the American Way of Death, 1830–1920* (Philadelphia, 1980), 157–59; [Kentwyn De Renne to WJDeR, August 1880], DeRFP-12.

110. Everard De Renne to WJDeR, 31 August 1880, DeRFP-12; Protestant Episcopal Church, Diocese of Georgia, *Journal* (1881), 16; *SMN,* 30 August 1880.

111. *SMN,* 5, 30 August, 8 September 1880.

112. *SMN,* 5 August 1880.

113. Minute Book, 2:313–15, GHS.

114. MDeR to Moxley Sorrel, 8 October 1880, Minute Book, 2:318–20, GHS; Moxley Sorrel to MDeR, 13 October 1880, "Extracts from the Minutes of the GHS," DeRFP-16.

115. Jones, *Georgia Historical Society,* [3], 21. One of Jones's few errors in his sketch of GWJDeR was in stating that his "graduating thesis" was his *Theory Concerning the Nature of Insanity* (ibid., 24).

116. Ibid., 27.

117. Ibid., 30.

118. CCJJ to MDeR, 11 January 1881, DeRFP-Autograph Book; Jones, "Sketch of Dr. G. W. De Renne." The introductory note to the sketch said, "We have alluded in previous numbers to the splendid gift by Dr. De Renne, of the bronze statue of a

Confederate soldier to the Memorial Association of Savannah, and to the presentation to our Society of his beautiful 'Wormsloe Quartos,' by Mrs. De Renne. We are sure our readers will thank us for allowing them to see the following tribute of Colonel Jones" (ibid., 193).

In 1913 "portions" of Jones's sketch of GWJDeR, "with occasional paraphrase," appeared in the second volume of Harden's *History of Savannah* (544–49). Seventy years later an entry on GWJDeR by Morton R. McInvale appeared in *DGB*, 1:251–52.

CHAPTER 6. The Altar of Memory

1. KCS to MDeR, 15 July 1882, DeRFP-13; John W. Beckwith to MDeR, 9 December 1880, DeRFP-23.

2. A. R. Lawton to MDeR, 12 June 1883, DeRFP-12; MDeR to Mrs. Jeremy F. Gilmer, 4 September 1883, Gilmer Memorial Volume, MoC.

3. "Diet List," DeRFP-23; MDeR to WJDeR, 12 May 1881, DeRFP-14; Georgiana King Diaries, NHS. As early as the fall of 1863, MDeR—who was 5′9″—weighed 242 pounds (Memorandum of GWJ in Everard De Renne, "Family History," EDeRBC).

4. CCJJ to MDeR, 17 January 1881, DeRFP-Autograph Book.

5. Ibid.; CCJJ to MDeR, 17 February 1881, and CCJJ to GWJDeR, 15 April 1879, DeRFP-Autograph Book.

6. *Acts*-Ms. Volume, GWJDeRC; Lamar, "Georgia Law Books," 122.

7. CCJJ to MDeR, 17 January, 17 February 1881, 4 March 1881, DeRFP-Autograph Book; *DeRLC* 2:797–98; Ms. copy of dedication, DeRHM.

8. Georgia (Colony), General Assembly, *Acts Passed by the General Assembly* (*1881*), Ms. volume and printed volume, GWJDeRC; MDeR to CCJJ, 21 July 1881, Jones Papers, DUL.

9. CCJJ to MDeR, 25 July, 22 August 1881, DeRFP-Autograph Book; Receipt, T. K. Collins, Book and Job Printer, DeRHM.

10. Georgia (Colony), General Assembly, *Acts Passed by the General Assembly* (*1881*), 6–7; [Jones,] "A Notable Work," *Augusta Chronicle and Constitutionalist*, 12 November 1881.

11. Georgia (Colony), General Assembly, *Acts Passed by the General Assembly* (*1881*), 6–7.

12. Ibid.; [Jones,] "A Notable Work."

13. CCJJ to MDeR, 11 January 1881, DeRFP-Autograph Book; MDeR's List of Presentation Copies of *Acts*, DeRFP-41.

14. [Jones,] "A Notable Work"; Stevens, *Stevens's Historical Collections* [1881

catalog], 34; CCJJ to MDeR, 11 January 1882, 30 September 1885, DeRFP-Autograph Book.

15. Penn, "Charles Colcock Jones, 116–22; *SMN,* 15 June 1884.

16. Penn, "Charles Colcock Jones, 119–21, Jones, *Memorial . . . with Regard to a Subscription on the Part of the State to His History of Georgia;* Winsor, *Narrative and Critical History of America,* 5:406; Joel Chandler Harris, *Stories from Georgia* (New York, 1896), 4.

17. CCJJ to MDeR, 25 April 1882, 9 June, 1 September, 28 November 1883, DeRFP-Autograph Book; Bonner, "Charles Colcock Jones," 334.

18. CCJJ to MDeR, 24 October, 30 September, 11 November 1885, DeRFP-Autograph Book.

19. CCJJ to MDeR, 22 October 1885, DeRFP-Autograph Book; Stevens, *Stevens's Historical Collections,* 34.

20. MDeR to CCJJ, 1 January 1886, DeRFP-Autograph Book.

21. CCJJ to MDeR, 4, 25 January 1886, DeRFP-Autograph Book.

22. Houghton, Mifflin & Co. to CCJJ, 25 January 1886, Jones Papers, DUL; MDeR to CCJJ, 29 January 1886, mounted in Jones's copy of *Acts,* Rare Book Room, Duke University Library; MDeR to CCJJ, 6 January 1886, Jones Papers, DUL.

23. MDeR to CCJJ, mounted in Jones's copy of *Acts,* Rare Book Room, DUL.

24. Houghton, Mifflin & Co. to CCJJ, 25 January, 3 February 1886, Jones Papers, DUL; CCJJ to MDeR, 25 January 1886, DeRFP-Autograph Book.

25. CCJJ to MDeR, 4 January 1886, DeRFP-Autograph Book; Egmont, *Journal,* x; Stevens, *Stevens's Historical Collections,* 34; Houghton, Mifflin & Co. to CCJJ, 3 February 1886, Jones Papers, DUL.

26. CCJJ to MDeR, 4 January 1886, DeRFP-Autograph Book; MDeR to CCJJ, 8 January 1886, Jones Papers, DUL.

27. Egmont, *Journal,* [v], ix.

28. *DeRLC,* 2:844–46.

29. MDeR's List of Presentation Copies of Egmont's *Journal,* DeRFP-41; CCJJ to MDeR, 18 August 1886, DeRFP-Autograph Book; *SMN,* 5–8 May 1886; CCJJ to MDeR, [May 1886], Keith Read Collection-26, GHS; Jefferson Davis to MDeR, 7 November 1886, DeRFP-42.

30. CCJJ to MDeR, 9 January 1882, DeRFP-Autograph Book; Stephen W. Sylvia and Michael J. O'Donnell, *The Illustrated History of Civil War Relics* (Orange, Va., 1978), [127].

31. Harwell, *Cornerstones of Confederate Collecting,* 5; Harwell, *In Tall Cotton,* [ii]; CCJJ to MDeR, 9 January 1882, DeRFP-Autograph Book. In the catalog of his library, Colonel Nicholson noted that a major influence on his Civil War collecting was "Le Cercle autour du Pôele," which met at Penington's bookstore for discus-

sions of the war and whose members included Winthrop Sargent and Charles Sumner (Nicholson, *Catalogue*, [v]).

32. E. P. Alexander to MDeR, 13 April 1884, DeRCM; CCJJ to MDeR, 9 January 1882, DeRFP-Autograph Book. Several of the letters of Confederate officers are addressed to the Reverend Jones, making it probable that he presented them to Mrs. De Renne; the same holds true for letters addressed to Colonel Jones.

33. CCJJ to MDeR, 9 January 1882, DeRFP-Autograph Book.

34. Ibid.

35. R. A. Brock to MDeR, 4 February, 5 June 1882, DeRFP-Autograph Book; Harwell, *Confederate Hundred*, xvi–xviii.

36. R. A. Brock to MDeR, 4 February, 5 June, 11 July, 21 September 1882, DeRFP-Autograph Book. Richard Harwell notes that "Southerners were not soon collectors of Confederate books themselves (with the notable exceptions of [R. A.] Brock and Charles C. Jones, Jr." (Harwell, *Confederate Hundred*, xviii). While most of Jones's collection is today located at Duke University and the University of Georgia, the troves of Brock and Nicholson are part of the excellent Civil War collection at the Henry E. Huntington Library in San Marino, California.

37. Myers, ed., *Children of Pride*, 1689, 1691; Confederate Memorial Society, *Year Book* (1917), [140]; KCS to MDeR, 20 May, 29 May, 15 July, 1882, DeRFP-13. In explaining her devotion to the Cause, Miss Stiles wrote, "Our Heroes in their graves escaped much, but oh! it hurts me so when anyone says, 'They died for nothing.' They did not gain freedom, but they kept their honor & principles & have certainly made a name for themselves as a distinct people, which I hope will last as long as time does" (KCS to MDeR, 15 July 1882, DeRFP-13).

38. William Starr Basinger to Thomas G. Basinger, 25 July 1905, Confederate Constitution, Ms. 1512–17, UGAL.

39. Freeman, *Calendar*, [501]; "Confederate Museum," undated (c. 1896) and unidentified, DeRFP-20; *Catalogue of the Confederate Museum* (1898), 82–105.

40. *Catalogue of the Confederate Museum* (1898), passim; R. A. Brock to MDeR, 27 April 1882, DeRFP-Autograph Book.

41. Freeman, *Calendar*, 164; *Catalogue of the Confederate Museum* (1898), passim; Susan B. Harrison to Leonard L. Mackall, 26 May 1919, laid in copy 1 of Milledge, *De Renne Gift*, UGAL.

42. [De Renne,] *Short History of the Confederate Constitutions*, [2]; *DeRLC*, 2:620.

43. "Two Relics of the War," *New York Sun*, 26 March 1883.

44. Ibid.; Irvine, "The Fate of Confederate Archives," 840–41; *DAB*, 5:196. Irvine's masterful account of the disposition of the archives of the Confederacy, published in 1939, has never been surpassed.

45. E. S. Parker to MDeR, 9 April 1883, Correspondence: Purchase of the Confederate Constitution, MoC; F. G. de Fontaine to MDeR, with enclosures, 15 [April] 1883, ibid.

46. F. G. de Fontaine to MDeR, with enclosures, 15 [April] 1883, ibid.

47. MDeR to Mrs. J. F. Gilmer, 4 September 1883, Gilmer Memorial Volume, MoC; Mrs. F. G. de Fontaine to MDeR, 24 June 1883, Correspondence: Purchase of the Confederate Constitution, MoC.

48. George T. Hanning to MDeR, 25, 27 June, 2 July 1883, Correspondence: Purchase of the Confederate Constitution, MoC.

49. Lieber Cottage, Historic Building Data Sheet, NHS; Mrs. F. G. de Fontaine to MDeR, 1 July 1883, Correspondence: Purchase of the Confederate Constitution, MoC.

50. Authorization of F. G. de Fontaine, 30 June 1883; Certification of George T. Hanning, 4 July 1883; Receipt, 4 July 1883; George T. Hanning to MDeR, 6 July 1883, Correspondence: Purchase of the Confederate Constitution, MoC.

51. William Starr Basinger to Thomas G. Basinger, 25 July 1905, Ms. 1512–17, UGAL; Irvine, "Fate of Confederate Archives," 826–27.

52. CCJJ to MDeR, 1 September 1883, R. A. Brock to MDeR, 9 August 1883, DeRFP-Autograph Book.

53. E. J. Hale and Son to MDeR, 19, 28 May, 2 June 1883, ibid.

54. Corcoran purchased the Provisional Constitution for $800 in early February 1884 and presented it to the Southern Historical Society (Beers, *The Confederacy*, 3; W. W. Corcoran to J. William Jones, 6 February 1884, *SHSP* 12 [1884]: 140).

55. *SMN*, 30 May, 3, 14 June, 1884; F. G. de Fontaine to MDeR, 24 June 1884, with circular of the Georgia Historical Society, Confederate Constitution, Ms. 1512-17, UGAL; Beers, *The Confederacy*, 400.

56. Foster, *Ghosts of the Confederacy*, 88.

57. CCJJ to MDeR, 28 November 1883, DeRFP-Autograph Book; *DeRLC*, 2:815–16; MDeR to KCS, 26 November 1883, laid in Daniel's *Lee*, UGAL.

In addition, MDeR had prepared for presentation as gifts twenty-five large paper impressions of the book's frontispiece photograph of General Lee (*DeRLC*, 3:1265).

Also in 1883, the Lee Memorial Association published *Ceremonies Connected with the Inauguration of the Mausoleum and the Unveiling of the Recumbent Figure of General Robert Edward Lee*, which is sometimes confused with the De Renne *Lee* because of its inclusion of the Daniel oration.

Not long after her *Lee* appeared (around 1884 or 1885), MDeR brought to the press a minor but satisfying prize, Bishop Stephen Elliott's remarks at the interment at Laurel Grove Cemetery of the dead—known and unknown—of the Savannah Volunteer Guards (Eighteenth Georgia Battalion). Those present at the occasion (31 December 1865) recalled the few words as very fitting and memorable, and a newspaper account reported that Elliott "prefaced the closing burial service with a brief but touching allusion to the solemn occasion, which thrilled the hearts of all present." No copy appeared to have survived. MDeR, however, was able to locate a transcript—"pencil notes taken by one of the hearers"—and had it printed for distribution as "At Laurel Grove, Savannah, December 31st, 1865." This leaflet is so obscure that it is identified in the 1931 De Renne catalog as probably printed in 1866; its connection to Mrs. De Renne was obviously unknown to the catalog's preparers (MDeR to Hamilton Branch, 20 May 1885, Margaret Branch Sexton Papers, UGAL; *Savannah Daily Herald*, 1 January 1866; *DeRLC*, 2:682).

58. Application for Power to Appoint an Agent in Savannah, approved 11 December 1880, Estate Records of GWJDeR, File D-305, PCR; Notes of Conversation with Alexander Robert Lawton Jr., 30 January 1955, WCHC-95, GHS. Alexander Robert Lawton, Jr. (1884–1963), was the grandson of GWJDeR's contemporary General Alexander Robert Lawton (1818–96) and the son of WJDeR's contemporary Colonel Alexander Rudolph Lawton (1858–1936), also sometimes called A. R. Lawton, Jr.

59. MDeR to WJDeR, 12 November 1880, DeRFP-14; Letters of Guardianship of Kentwyn De Renne: Harry Peale (30 November 1880) and MDeR (18 January 1881), DeRFP-19; Application for Maintenance and Support, approved 7 July 1881, Estate Records of GWJDeR, File D-305, PCR.

60. Application for Maintenance and Support, approved 7 July 1881, Estate Records of GWJDeR, File D-305, PCR; Biographical Notes, DeRFP-19; *SMN*, 23 April 1884, 12 April 1885; Notes of Conversation with Alexander Robert Lawton, Jr., 30 January 1955, WCHC-95, GHS.

61. Samuel Peter Orth, *History of Cleveland, Ohio*, 3 vols. (Chicago and Cleveland, 1910), 2:939–40; Emma Betts Sterling Diaries, Western Reserve Historical Society, Cleveland, Ohio.

62. Everard De Renne, Alumni File, Princeton University; Certificates of Medical Instruction, DeRFP-19; Everard De Renne, M.D. Diploma, University of the City of New York, 9 March 1882, DeRFP-1064a; MDeR to Wallace Savage Jones, 27 April [1882], JFP-1; MDeR to WJDeR, 17 February [1880], DeRFP-14.

Savannah-born Ward McAllister (1827–95) had by the 1860s made himself the "social boss" of New York City. Even in his heyday, however, his "many vanities and affectations laid him open . . . to extravagant ridicule," which probably explains Everard De Renne's unwillingness to be associated with him. McAllister's publication in 1890 of his memoirs, *Society as I Have Found It*, led to his undoing, for the book "was deemed fatuous even in an era not notably hostile to that quality."

Among McAllister's antebellum reminiscences was a canard directed at "Mr. Jones, who [went] to Newport every summer." Details in the Jones anecdote seemed to point irrefutably to George Noble Jones; in the DeRGL's autographed copy of one of the four hundred copies of the deluxe edition, there is an indignant notation by Leonard L. Mackall, describing the insinuations as "very unfair." Oddly enough, McAllister's marginal addenda to his copy of the book, deposited with the New-York Historical Society, show that "Mr. Jones" was actually Savannahian William H. Miller; under the circumstances, the use of such a pseudonym was fatuous indeed (*DAB*, 11 : 547 – 48; Auchincloss, *Vanderbilt Era*, 187; McAllister, *Society as I Have Found It*, 95 – 99; Copies of *Society as I Have Found It*, DeRGL [Mackall notes at p. 95], and New-York Historical Society [Call #Y-Q 1890.M; addenda at pp. 95 and 98]).

63. Sterling Diaries; *Cleveland Plain Dealer*, 18 April 1883.

64. Transcript of Diary of Leillian Macauley, in Sterling Diaries. Macauley was the friend and traveling companion of Jeannette De Renne.

65. Ibid.; Everard De Renne, Alumni File, Princeton University; New York City Directories, 1886 – 91; CCJJ to Dr. Everard De Renne, 22 December 1891, LPCB, 1890 – 91 (F-2060), Jones Papers, DUL.

66. Transcript of Diary of Leillian Macauley, in Sterling Diaries.

67. A. R. Lawton to MDeR, 12 June 1883, DeRFP-12.

68. MDeR et al., Complainants, vs. Pennsylvania Company, Defendant, in Equity, Decided 7 June 1881, SCJ-117, GHS.

69. A. R. Lawton to MDeR, 12 June 1883, DeRFP-12; MDeR et al., Complainants, vs. Pennsylvania Company, Defendant, in Equity, Decided 13 July 1883, SCJ-127, GHS; DB 51 : 319, SCR.

70. MDeR to WJDeR, 12 May 1881, DeRFP-14.

71. Ibid.; MDeR to CCJJ, 21 July 1881, Jones Papers, DUL; MDeR to Mrs. J. F. Gilmer, 4 September 1883, Gilmer Memorial Volume, MoC. Giving up visits to Europe was made somewhat more bearable by Mrs. De Renne's increasing dissatisfaction with democratization of foreign travel after the Civil War. Her comments regarding unwelcome changes at the Alpine town of Oberammergau are a case in point: "The detestable Tourists . . . are doing their best to vulgarize the whole thing. There is a great staring new building with 'Gaye's Hotel' on one side and 'Hotel Gaye' on the other where droves of human creatures are lodged and fed, and Omnibuses bring and carry away loads of Cookies and Caygills. Fancy their attempting applause [at the Passion Play], and getting up and stamping out as at a Theatre, to be on time for Omnibuses!" (MDeR to WJDeR, 14 July 1880, DeRFP-14).

The English firm of Thos. Cook & Son was most heavily involved in taking tourists ("Cookies") throughout western Europe, but the obscure Mr. Caygill, a former

Cook employee, provided some competition between 1879 and 1884 (Piers Brendon, *Thomas Cook: 150 Years of Popular Tourism* [London, 1991], 156–57, 338n.68).

72. MDeR to Mrs. J. F. Gilmer, 4 September 1883, Gilmer Memorial Volume, MoC.

73. MDeR, Death Certificate, Town Clerk's Office, Litchfield, Conn.; *SMN*, 1 September 1887.

74. "Impressions de Voyage," DeRFP-14; *SMN*, 3 September 1887.

75. *SMN*, 1 September 1887.

76. CCJJ to Letitia De Renne, 27 September 1887, LPCB, 1887–88 (F-2054), Jones Papers, DUL.

77. *SMN*, 15 October 1887, 30 May 1888; Will of MDeR, File D-343, PCR.

78. Philadelphia City Directory, 1889–90; Estate Records of Letitia De Renne, File D-363, PCR; Georgia Writers' Project, *Drums and Shadows* (Athens, 1940, new ed. 1986), 99.

79. Estate Records of Letitia De Renne, File D-363, PCR; DB 6W:25, SCR.

80. Will of MDeR, File D-343, PCR; Estate Records of Letitia De Renne, File D-363, PCR; Will of Everard De Renne, Liber 514:216, Surrogate's Court, City and County of New York.

81. Will and Codicil of Everard De Renne, Liber 514:216, Surrogate's Court, City and County of New York. The Georgia State Library, then located in the capitol building in Atlanta, served as the respository of such printed records as the acts and journals of the legislature, as well as of publications and other materials, including for a time some manuscripts, bearing on the history of the state (Phillips, "Public Archives of Georgia," 447–48).

82. Will and Codicil of Everard DeRenne, Liber 514:216, Surrogate's Court, City and County of New York; Account Book, entry for 11 May 1895, DeRFP+-8.

83. *SMN*, 21, 22 March 1894; Milledge, *DeRenne Gift*, [3], 16; State of Georgia, *Annual Report of the State Librarian* (1918), 6, 9; Bonner, *Milledgeville*, 187–88.

84. *Memoirs of Georgia*, 1:864–65; *Atlanta Constitution*, 3 February 1899; Milledge, *De Renne Gift*, passim.

85. Milledgeville, *De Renne Gift*, [3].

86. Ibid., passim.

87. Correspondence and Reports of the State Librarian, Georgia State Library, Atlanta; Ella May Thornton to EDeRB, 8 April 1930, WC.

88. Collier et al., *White House of the Confederacy*, 23–25; Confederate Memorial Literary Society, *Year Book* (1917), [140]; Confederate Memorial Literary Society, *In Memoriam Sempiternam*, 72; "The South's Museum," *SHSP* 23 (1895): 354–58, 373–74.

89. *Catalogue of the Confederate Museum* (1898), [82]–105; "A National Repos-

itory," *SHSP* 22 (1894): 389. Some of the materials meant to be in the Confederate Museum wound up at the Georgia State Library, and vice versa. Rebuffed in an attempt to have State Librarian John Milledge hand over to her "the Last Order of the Confederate Government," mistakenly included with the "De Renne Gift," the indomitable Miss Stiles had the Georgia General Assembly's House of Representatives pass a resolution delivering the document to her (*Acts of the General Assembly* [*1897*], 602).

90. *Catalogue of the Confederate Museum* (1898), [82]; Clifford Dowdey, *Experiment in Rebellion* (Garden City, N.Y., 1950), 110; Beveridge, "Where Southern Memories Cluster," 34.

91. Beveridge, "Where Southern Memories Cluster," 34; Hill, *Victory in Defeat*, 15; "Manuscript of Confederate Constitution on Exhibition for Historians," *SHSP* 36 (1908): 371–72.

92. Hill, *Victory in Defeat*, 6; Collier, *White House of the Confederacy*, 25.

93. James, *American Scene*, 276; Kammen, *Mystic Chords of Memory*, 381.

94. James, *American Scene*, 275, 277.

95. Ella May Thornton to EDeRB, 8 April 1930, WC ("Many of the [De Renne] volumes are beautifully bound," Thornton wrote, "and the whole has served as a nucleus around which has been built an interesting and valuable Georgia library of considerable size"); Report of the Vice Regent of the Georgia Room [Katherine C. Stiles] from 6 December 1900 to 6 December 1901, MoC ("Mrs. De Renne . . . collected the nucleus around which gathered the invaluable contents of this building"); Hill, *Victory in Defeat*, 15; [Jones], "A Notable Work," *Augusta Chronicle and Constitutionalist*, 12 November 1881. The De Renne Gift's books (along with the other Georgia books of the State Library) are cataloged in Ella May Thornton, comp., *Finding-List of Books and Pamphlets Relating to Georgia and Georgians*, which also listed books relating to Georgia history held by Atlanta's Carnegie Library, the Library of Congress, the University of Georgia Library, and the De Renne Library at Wormsloe (with the 1911 De Renne catalog as its source). The most complete listings of the Mary De Renne Collection are found in the two Confederate Museum catalogs (1898, 1905) and Freeman's *Calendar*.

CHAPTER 7. Wandering Scion

1. Stephen R. Wise, *Lifeline of the Confederacy: Blockade Running During the Civil War* (Columbia, S.C., 1988), 114–17, 164, 275, 299; *ORN*, Series 2, vol. 1:192; "History of My Life" and George Fenwick Jones's Account Book, DeRFP-14.

2. Mary Savage Jones to Mary Nuttall Jones, 1 October 1863, in private possession; "History of My Life," DeRFP-14; "Tribute of Regard [for George Fenwick

Jones]," JFP-3; James, *Autobiography*, 110; Mayor, *La Tour de Peilz*, 79; Student Registry, Bellerive, in *Bellerive, Souvenir du Jubilé*; Ron Chernow, *The House of Morgan* (New York, 1990), 20.

3. "History of My Life," DeRFP-14.

4. Ibid.; George Fenwick Jones's Account Book, DeRFP-14.

5. "History of My Life" and George Fenwick Jones's Account Book, DeRFP-14; Mary Savage Jones to Mary Nuttall Jones, 11 January, 21 July 1864, in private possession.

6. Mary Savage Jones to Mary Nuttall Jones, 11 January 1864, in private possession. It would be over a year, of course, before the name change became legal.

7. Mary Savage Jones to Mary Nuttall Jones, 9 February 1864, in private possession; George Fenwick Jones's Account Book, DeRFP-14; Lillie Noble Jones to General J. Franklin Bell, 12 May 1908, JFP-3; Wallace Savage Jones, "Journal of a Tour in Switzerland and Italy," 1856, in private possession.

8. Prior, *Vevey*, [5]−7; James, *Tales*, 3.

9. Muller, *Vevey*, 14; Prior, *Vevey*, 10−12, 16, 19−20.

10. Muller, *Vevey*, 14−15; Prior, *Vevey*, [5], 14−15; "Panoramas du Lac et des Montagnes des Environs de Vevey," folding plate in Prior, *Vevey*.

11. Michielin, *La Tour-de-Peilz*, unpaginated; Mayor, *La Tour de Peilz*, 79; WJDeR to "Meine lieben Aeltern [My dear Parents]," 27 January 1870, DeRFP-14; MSJ to MNJ, 9 February, 20 June 1864, in private possession.

12. MSJ to MNJ, 20 June 1864, in private possession; WJDeR, Résumés de l'Application et de la Conduite, Bellerive, DeRFP-14; James, *Autobiography*, 110.

13. MSJ to MNJ, 9 February, 21 July 1864, in private possession; WJDeR, Résumés de l'Application et de la Conduite, Bellerive, DeRFP-14; Boudin, "Notice sur le Château de Mirabel," 358−63, 368; "Description de Mirabel," DeRFP-2.

14. MSJ to MNJ, 21 July 1864, in private possession; Résumés, WJDeR, Lycée Imperial de Montpellier, DeRFP-14.

15. Secondy, *Histoire du Lycée de Montpellier*, 160; Georgiana King Diaries, NHS; Letitia De Renne, 1ᵉʳ Prix de Couture, Pension Hammer, Montpellier, DeRFP+-Miscellaneous Books; Various résumés of the De Renne brothers, Lycée Imperial, DeRFP-14.

16. Student Registry, Bellerive, in *Bellerive, Souvenir du Jubilé*; Phillips and Glunt, eds., *Florida Plantation Records*, 23, 177−81; Copy of the Burial Register of the British Chaplain, Dieppe, France, 16 August 1869, JFP-2.

17. WJDeR, Résumés de l'Application et de la Conduite, Bellerive, DeRFP-14; Mayor, *La Tour de Peilz*, 79; Notarized Certificate of Edwin Sillig, June 1871, DeRFP-14.

18. Hart, *German Universities*, 290−91.

19. Ibid., 360–61; Callcott, *History in the United States*, 216.

20. "Leipzig," *Encyclopaedia Britannica* (11th ed.), 16:400–401; Schauffler, *Romantic Germany*, 237, 249, 251.

21. Howitt, *Student-Life of Germany*, 146.

22. Hart, *German Universities*, 309; Howitt, *Student-Life of Germany*, 248–49, 285.

23. Hawthorne, "Feast of Blood," [405]; Jerome K. Jerome, *Three Men on Wheels* (Cambridge, Mass., 1900), 258–59; Reighard, "German Students and Their Absurd Duels," 228; Hart, *German Universities*, 70; Perry, *German University Education*, 82.

24. Hawthorne, "Feast of Blood," 406; *Geschichte des Corps Saxonia zu Leipzig*, 425; WJDeR's marginalia to his copy of "Duelling in German Universities. By an English Student," *Strand* 13 (February 1897): 148–53 (cited hereafter as WJDeR's Marginalia), DeRFP-20.

25. Perry, *German University Education*, 81; WJDeR's Marginalia.

26. Hawthorne, "Feast of Blood," 406; Reighard, "German Students and Their Absurd Duels," 230–31; Baldick, *The Duel*, 148; Hart, *German Universities*, 72–74.

27. Truman, *Field of Honor*, 57–58; Hart, *German Universities*, 72–73; WJDeR's Marginalia.

28. Howitt, *Student-Life of Germany*, 138; "Duelling in German Universities," 152–53.

29. Truman, *Field of Honor*, 65–66; Morris, "The Art of Duelling Among German Students," 17; Hawthorne, "Feast of Blood," 408. Inscriptions on WJDeR's duelling ribbons indicate that he fought the customary three duels (DeRFP-20).

30. Memorandum of EDeRB, c. 1955, WC; Truman, *Field of Honor*, 56.

31. Jerome, *Three Men on Wheels*, 261; Baldick, *The Duel*, 149; Hart, *German Universities*, 77–78, 80.

32. Certifications and other documentation from the Universities of Leipzig and Strassburg, relating to the studies of "Herr Wymberley De Renne aus Newport," 1871–74, DeRFP-17.

33. WJDeR's Oriental travels are documented by seven letters (12 May–30 June 1875, principally to MDeR) and an unbound journal, 15 May–6 July 1875 (cited hereinafter as Journal). In notes 33 to 53 all manuscript citations relating exclusively to WJDeR's time in the Far East are to DeRFP-14.

34. WJDeR to MDeR, 12 May 1875.

35. Ibid.

36. Journal.

37. Ibid.; WJDeR to MDeR, 7 June 1875.

38. Ibid.

39. Ibid.

40. Ibid.

41. Ibid.

42. Ibid.; Cortazzi, *Victorians in Japan*, xi.

43. Journal; Mementos and souvenirs of the tour, including a wooden helmet, are in DeRFP+-29, 46.

44. Journal; Cortazzi, *Victorians in Japan*, 223.

45. Journal; MDeR to GNJ, 18 February 1871, JFP-1; John Lowe, *Into Japan* (London, 1985), 78.

46. Journal.

47. Ibid.; WJDeR to Everard De Renne, 27 June 1875.

48. Journal.

49. Journal; WJDeR to MDeR, 30 June 1875.

50. Journal.

51. Journal; G. B. Endacott, *A History of Hong Kong* (London, 1958), [1], Map 3; Elfed Vaughan Roberts et al., *Historical Dictionary of Hong Kong and Macau* (Metuchen, N.J., 1992), 121.

52. Journal.

53. Ibid.; WJDeR to MDeR, 30 June 1875.

54. Journal; WJDeR to GWJDeR, 30 June 1875.

55. WJDeR, Diploma, Bachelor of Laws, Columbia University, 17 May 1876, and Notice of Admittance to the New York Bar, 24 May 1876, DeRFP-14.

56. Diary of Letitia De Renne, 1876, DeRFP+-9; Address Book of WJDeR, c. 1876 (containing addresses and list of calls made, "Uptown" and "Downtown"), DeRFP+-7; W. H. Drayton to GWJDeR, 26 April 1876, DeRFP-4.

57. MDeR to WJDeR, 28 May 1880, DeRFP-14.

58. WJDeR, Receipt for Initiation Fee and Annual Dues, Union Club, 7 October 1876, DeRFP-14; Joseph Tweedy to Elizabeth A. Mellick, 27 October [1878], Tweedy Letters, WTC.

59. WJDeR to GWJDeR, 8 May 1880, DeRFP-14.

60. WJDeR to MDeR, 8 May 1880, ibid.

61. Copy of Indenture between WJDeR and GWJDeR, 31 December 1877, DeRFP-13. This was a considerable amount of money at the time. During the same period, for example, Harvard University president Charles Eliot's annual salary was $5,000, with which he "kept a comfortable home, entertained, owned a summer house, a boat, and put his own two sons through Harvard." Theodore Roosevelt's annual income at the time from his father's estate was $8,000, "a princely sum" (McCullough, *Mornings on Horseback*, 205). For most of the money amounts in this book, 1827–1916, a very rough approximation of present-day purchasing

power may be calculated by multiplying by ten. A valuable discussion of purchasing power and inflation, 1750–1970, is found in Gerald Reitlinger's *The Economics of Taste*, 3 vols. (London, 1961–70), 3:9–17.

62. WJDeR to GWJDeR, 8 May 1880, DeRFP-14; Jordan, ed., *Colonial Families of Phildelphia*, 1:93. Death Certificate of William Pepper Norris, City Archives, Philadelphia, Pa.

63. Billington, *Land of Savagery, Land of Promise*, 64, 69, 345–50; Smith, *Virgin Land*, 174, 181.

64. WJDeR to GWJDeR, 8 May 1880, DeRFP-14.

65. Joseph Tweedy to Elizabeth A. Mellick, 27 October [1878], Tweedy Letters, WTC.

66. Ibid.; Clemens, *Concho Country*, 110.

67. Clemens, *Concho Country*, 52–53, 83–84, 88; "Knickerbocker Ranch," 32, WTC; Tom Green County Historical Society, *Historical Montage of Tom Green County*, 22–23.

68. Green, "Land Settlement in West Texas," 3, 270; O. Henry (William Sidney Porter), "A Departmental Case," in McClintock and Simms, eds., *O. Henry's Texas Stories*, 3.

69. Smith, *Virgin Land*, 174; Walter Prescott Webb et al., *The Handbook of Texas*, 2 vols. (Austin, Tex., 1952), 2:69–70; Clemens, *Concho Country*, 73–78.

70. Green, "Land Settlement in West Texas," 255; "Knickerbocker Ranch," 32, WTC; Stephens and Holmes, *Historical Atlas of Texas*, 43. The railroad would not reach the population center of the region until 1888 (Green, "Land Settlement in West Texas," 260).

71. Clemens, *Concho Country*, 69, 72, 79.

72. Ibid., 88–89. When WJDeR arrived in the town in 1878, it was known as San Angela, apparently a corruption of Santa Angela; by the time he left five years later, it had become known as San Angelo. To reduce confusion, the town is always referred to in the text as San Angelo, its present name.

73. Clemens, *Concho Country*, 110–11; "A Sheep Ranch in Tom Green County," undated, unidentified newspaper clipping, WTC.

74. Joseph Tweedy to Mrs. O. B. Tweedy, 29 April 1879, Tweedy Letters, WTC; Joseph Tweedy to WJDeR, 6 April 1891, DeRFP-17; "Knickerbocker Ranch," 32, WTC.

75. MDeR to WJDeR, 16 October 1879, 12 January, 17 March, 6 July 1880, and WJDeR to MDeR, 7 May 1880, DeRFP-14.

76. MDeR to WJDeR, 17 March 1880, ibid.

77. WJDeR to GWJDeR, 7 May 1880, ibid.

78. Ibid.

79. Ogden Tanner, *The Ranchers* (Alexandria, Va., 1977), 98, 107; Viola and Wilson, eds., *Texas Ranchman*, 16–17.

80. Clemens, *Concho Country*, 126–27; Viola and Wilson, eds., *Texas Ranchman*, 16.

81. WJDeR to GWJDeR, 7 May 1880, DeRFP-14.

82. Ibid.

83. GWJDeR to Thomas A. Biddle & Co., 24 May, 18 June, 1 August, 1880, DeRFP-14; Memorandum of Agreement between WJDeR and George A. Bremer, 29 May 1880, DeRFP-17; "Knickerbocker Ranch," 37, WTC.

84. WJDeR to MDeR, 7 May 1880, and WJDeR to GWJDeR, 7 May 1880, DeRFP-14.

85. WJDeR to GWJDeR, 7 May 1880, ibid.

86. WJDeR to MDeR, 7 May 1880, ibid.

87. Ibid.

88. GWJDeR to WJDeR, 18 June 1880, DeRFP+-1. WJDeR made use of the telegraph station and post office at Fort Concho during his early days in the region.

89. George Williams to "Niece Helen," 27 July 1880, David Williams Letters, WTC.

90. MDeR to WJDeR, 6, 14 July 1880, DeRFP-14.

91. GWJDeR to WJDeR, 30 July 1880, DeRFP-12; Thomas A. Biddle & Co. to WJDeR (Telegram), 4 August 1880, DeRFP-12.

92. Thomas A. Biddle & Co. to WJDeR (Telegram), 6 August 1880, DeRFP-12; Everard De Renne to WJDeR, 31 August 1880, DeRFP-12.

93. David Welsh to WJDeR (Receipt), 2 October 1880, DeRFP-17; Joseph Tweedy to Mrs. O. B. Tweedy, 3 December 1880, Tweedy Letters, WTC.

94. "Knickerbocker Ranch," 37–38, WTC.

95. WJDeR to MDeR, 27 October 1880, DeRFP-14.

96. Burt, *Perennial Philadelphians*, 110; Baltzell, *Philadelphia Gentlemen*, 71–80; *Philadelphia Public Ledger*, 27 February 1879.

97. Marriage Certificate, Austin C. Maury and Laura Camblos, City Archives, Philadelphia; Copy of Proceedings, Laura Maury, by her next friend W. Rhodes Murphy, versus Austin C. Maury, in Divorce, Court of Common Pleas, June Term 1874, Philadelphia, DeRFP-25; Interview with Ophelia Dent, September 1955, WCHC.

98. MDeR to WJDeR, 12 May 1881, DeRFP-14; WJDeR to A. R. Lawton, 15 May 1881, in Mary De Renne et al., Complainants, and the Pennsylvania Company, Defendant, in Equity, June Term, 1881, SCJ-117, GHS; A. R. Lawton to MDeR, 12 June 1883, DeRFP-12; J. Franklin Jameson to Richard A. Roberts, 29 January 1929,

in Donnan and Stock, eds., *An Historian's World*, 297. Although Jameson knew WJDeR, he was incorrect in some of the details of the story, writing that De Renne was "cut . . . off with a small allowance because he married a person, excellent in every way, whom the father did not wish him to marry."

99. Will of GWJDeR, File D-305, PCR; Biddle Account Documents, DeRFP-14; "De Renne Will Case," undated, unidentified newspaper clipping, DeRFP+-36. Papers relating to the court proceedings involving Everard De Renne's heirs are in DeRFP-14 and in SCJ-186, GHS. On the envelope containing the Biddle material, cited above, is a notation by WJDeR: "Biddle's Account, Showing I never received but 8400 out of the $30,000. Although I paid the $2100 a year until my brother Everard's death, after his death his heirs tried to have the will so construed as to get it."

100. "The Buena Ventura Ranch," Broadside [1891], in private possession; License to Practice Law, 26 April 1881, and Authorization to Practice Law in Tom Green County, 28 May 1881, DeRFP-14; Terry Clyde Maxwell, "Avifauna of the Concho Valley of West-Central Texas with Special Reference to Historical Change" (Ph.D. dissertation, Texas A&M University, 1979), 21, 34–38, Phelan, *Texas Wild*, 37, 40, 46, 62; "Knickerbocker Ranch," 40, WTC. Copies of deeds, maps, and other materials relating to WJDeR's Texas land acquisitions are in DeRFP-17.

101. Plan of the Buena Ventura Ranch House, DeRFP-17; Katherine Tweedy, "Buena Ventura," *Southwestern Sheep and Goat Raiser*, March 1941, 54; *San Angelo Standard-Times*, 27 March 1977.

102. *San Angelo Standard Times*, 27 March 1977.

103. Among the eastern women who did remain in Texas was Mrs. Joseph Tweedy.

104. Memorandum of the birth and death of GWJDeR II, DeRFP-14; Letter of Elizabeth Smith, 28 August 1882, Fort Concho Archives, San Angelo, Texas.

105. Charles C. Norris to Susan Miles, 19 August 1955, Susan Miles Collection, WTC; Interview with Ophelia Dent, September 1955, WCHC.

106. Sketch of gravestone, Susan Miles Collection, WTC; Photograph of grave site, c. 1882, DeRFP+-22.

107. Letter of Elizabeth Smith, 28 August 1882, Fort Concho Archives, San Angelo, Texas; Clemens, *Concho Country*, 93–94; Viola and Wilson, eds., *Texas Ranchman*, 17–18; Susan Miles, "Wymberley De Renne," Susan Miles Collection, WTC.

108. Susan Miles, "Wymberley De Renne," Susan Miles Collection, WTC.

109. Business Papers, Buena Ventura Ranch, DeRFP-17.

110. Ibid.; WJDeR to Col. John A. Turner, 23 August 1883, in *Texas Stockman*, 19 February 1884.

111. Business Papers, Buena Ventura Ranch, DeRFP-17. WJDeR's accumulation of Texas property is recorded in detail in the Tax Assessment Rolls for Tom Green and Concho Counties, WTC.

112. Woods, *British Gentlemen in the Wild West*, 44–45; Susan Miles, "The Vernons," Susan Miles Collection, WTC; *DNB*, 20:276, 21:148; [Cokayne], *Complete Peerage*, 12:264–65; *Times* (London), 3 May 1883.

113. Business Papers, Buena Ventura Ranch, DeRFP-17. After her marriage, Laura De Renne was engaged in court proceedings relating to the estate of her deceased husband, William Pepper Norris, and there was also a dispute over her brother Pierre's management of her financial affairs in Philadelphia. In any event, it seems that her fortune was not as considerable as WJDeR had supposed (DeRFP-25).

Oddly, WJDeR was also long mistaken regarding his wife's age. In a memorandum of c. 1891 (DeRFP-58), recording the birth dates of his wife and four children, he gives her birthday as 10 December 1848, which would have made her several years his senior. The 1891 birth certificate of WWDeR, however, gives her age as "triente six ans," which would have made her younger than he. Her certificate of marriage to Austin Maury (Philadelphia City Archives), gives her age as twenty-nine in June 1872 (and Maury's as twenty-five). The reason for these discrepancies is unknown. The Camblos Family Bible (in private possession) shows, however, that she was born on 10 December 1851, and this date appeared on her plaque in the De Renne crypt.

114. WJDeR to William Vernon, 1 December 1883, DeRFP-17.

115. WJDeR to William Vernon, 4, 13 December 1883, and WJDeR to W. J. Skinner, 15 December 1883, ibid.

116. WJDeR to W. J. Skinner, 22 December 1883, ibid.

117. W. J. Skinner to WJDeR, 1, 9, 24 January 1884, ibid.; *San Angelo Weekly Standard*, 28 January 1888, 3 January 1891; *San Angelo Standard-Times*, 27 March 1977.

118. W. J. Skinner to WJDeR, 10 November 1894, DeRFP-17.

119. WJDeR, Family Record, DeRFP-58; "In Memoriam . . . Wymberley Jones De Renne," GHS, *Proceedings* (1917), 14.

120. Russell, *Biarritz*, 4, 5, 12; Horace G. Hutchinson, *Portraits of the Eighties* (New York, 1920), 14; Joanne, *Biarritz*, 24.

121. Russell, *Biarritz*, 10, 12; "Biarritz," *Harper's New Monthly Magazine* 69 (1884): 11, 12; De Joantho, *Biarritz Illustré*, 102; "Biarritz," *Littell's Living Age* 16

(1857): 172; Sturrock, *French Pyrenees*, 19; Harold Kurtz, *The Empress Eugénie, 1826–1920* (Boston, 1964), 65–66.

122. "Biarritz," *Harper's New Monthly Magazine* 69 (1884): 6; Russell, *Biarritz*, 6; Joanne, *Biarritz*, 25–29; De Joantho, *Biarritz Illustré*, 153; Biarritz Golf Club, *Constitution and Regulations* (Biarritz, 1892) and British Club, Biarritz, *Rules and Regulations* (Biarritz, 1891), DeRFP+-Miscellaneous Books (WJDeR's membership is listed in both books).

123. Armand Praviel, *Biarritz, Pau and the Basque Country* (Boston, 1926), 49; Russell, *Biarritz*, 1; Charles Graves, *The Rich Man's Guide to Europe* (Englewood Cliffs, N.J., 1966), 249; Joanne, *Biarritz*, 27.

124. Praviel, *Biarritz*, 165; Fenhagen, "Descendants of Judge Robert Pringle," 224; Report of Jean R. Casenave, Biarritz, 16 September 1993; Duncan Pringle to Wymberley De Renne, 9 October [1907], laid in *A Bachelor's Reverie*, DeRGL.

125. Will and Codicil of MDeR, PCR; MDeR to WJDeR, 12 November 1880, DeRFP-14.

126. WJDeR, Family Record, DeRFP-58.

127. "List of Boxes & trunks containing articles having been in use in my household, during eight years' residence in Biarritz, France," DeRPP+-9.

128. L&C to WJDeR, 7 May 1891, DeRFP-19; "Impressions de Voyage," DeRFP-14; Ludlow Ogden to WJDeR, 9 March 1894, and Agreement, Ludlow Ogden et al. and WJDeR, 26 May 1894, DeRFP-19. Kentwyn died at age twenty-nine, two years after being diagnosed with cirrhosis of the liver and interstitial nephritis; heart failure was a contributing cause of death. Everard's death, at thirty-six, was caused by chronic interstitial hepatitis, complicated by edema of the lungs and ascites (Death certificates of KDeR and EDeR, Municipal Archives, New York City).

129. Gregory, *Savannah and Its Surroundings*, 19; Avery, "The City of Savannah, Georgia," 256–71; Lindsey and Britt, *Isle of Hope*, unpaginated.

On WJDeR's return the recently published *Historic and Picturesque Savannah* awaited him. It described his late father as one "to whom both the State and the city are indebted for public-spirited service and liberality in preserving and publishing early records of the colony. . . . Mr. De Renne at all times cherished a remarkable affection for the traditions and memories of his family and the State. The Georgia Historical Society reaped the benefit of his researches in valuable documents and publications. To his liberality, also, will the Confederate monument remain a lasting witness" (Wilson, *Historic and Picturesque Savannah*, 193–94).

130. Acte de Naissance de De Renne, Wymberley Wormsloe, Extrait des Registres de l'Etat-Civil de la Ville de Biarritz, DeRFP+-9; "Impressions de Voyage," DeRFP-14.

1. February 1891 apparently marked the beginning of the first phase of WJDeR's move back to Savannah. In any case, he was in Savannah before 20 February, when he purchased the first of his Bonaventure lots (Indenture, Evergreen Cemetery Company of Bonaventure and WJDeR, 20 February 1891, DeRFP-26).

2. Papers relating to farming operations at Wormsloe during WJDeR's time are in DeRFP-29, and oyster leases and information regarding "oyster pirates" are in DeRFP-29 and 30. Such products of WJDeR's dairying operations as "Wormsloe Curd" and "Wormsloe Cream" were offered for sale by the Savannah grocer M. S. Gardner (*SMN*, 8 September 1912).

3. Interview with the Reverend Frank A. Jenkins, Jr., 28 April 1991.

4. WJDeR to L&C, 23 May [1904], and 1904 memorandum for L&C, headed "Wormsloe. 1904," DeRFP-29; Diary of GWJDeR, 1876−80, p. 41; Account Book (1895), DeRFP+-8; Correspondence of Jesse Beach, DeRFP-29; Interview with the Reverend Frank A. Jenkins, Jr., 28 April 1991. The granite monument in Sandfly Cemetery, apparently placed there by WJDeR, reads "IN MEMORY OF / JESSE BEACH / AN HONEST MAN, A GOOD MAN, / A FAITHFUL SERVANT / DIED AT / WORMSLOE / NOVEMBER 11, 1911 / MAY HE REST IN PEACE.

5. Brown Cash Book, 1899−1916, DeRFP-15; Correspondence of Jesse Beach, DeRFP-29.

6. The Reverend Frank Allen Jenkins, Jr., "Wormsloe Plantation," 1−2. From a later perspective, the Reverend Jenkins (1920−94) recalled the interrelationships of those who worked at Wormsloe as "a beautiful part of the history of the planta-tion." In reminiscing, he wrote: "I remember the Collins, the Householders and the Hersheys, who were all dairymen.

I can recall the Scotts, who were farmers; the Coreys, who were plumbers; and the Nelsons, who were rivermen.

Now these men all had long-term relationships with the owners of Wormsloe. Of course, they were bound together for economic reasons, but in addition, had a deep interest in their craft and in each other. Everyone trying to get nowhere too fast, as it appears to be today, was not their life-style, but rather a pace that gave them a sort of inner peace."

Of his own experiences at Wormsloe, he wrote: "I feel that Wormsloe had that peculiar social awareness that allows for growth—that allows for security. Person-ally, it has been a way of life to me, not completely unabrasive, but yet balanced by a genuine concern of one human being for another" (ibid., 10−11).

7. WWDeR to Augusta De Renne, 24 November 1918, WWDeRP-8; Interview with Ophelia Dent, September 1955, WCHC-95.

8. WJDeR to GNJ II, 21 July 1897, JFP-1; Elfrida De Renne to WJDeR, [18 July 1899], WWDeRP-1; S. Duncan Pringle to WWDeR, 25 June 1916, DeRFP-14.

9. Journal and Cash Book, 1894, with notes on Wines, DeRFP+-8; Tourilli Fish and Game Club of the Province of Quebec, *Annual Reports* (Assorted), DeRFP-51 and DeRFP+-36; Address Book, DeRFP+-8; Audrey De Renne to WJDeR, 12 August 1901, WWDeRP-3.

10. Mayer, *Once upon a City*, 27; Clark, *View of Westport*, unpaginated. Near Westport was the burial place of the abolitionist John Brown, though it is doubtful the De Rennes visited it. To the contrary, Audrey, as a young schoolgirl in New Jersey, would not attend assemblies if she knew "John Brown's Body" was to be sung, as it was on Lincoln's birthday and other patriotic occasions; it made her "furious." Even more than her siblings she was self-consciously southern: in her gray riding habit she considered that she "looked like a *Georgian* indeed," and to a New York doctor's teasing question of whether she liked New York or Savannah best, "said very proudly SAVANNAH" (Audrey De Renne to WJDeR, 23 February 1903, 7 April 1901, c. October 1899, WWDeRP-5,3,1).

11. Correspondence of Jesse Beach, DeRFP-29.

12. Percy Buchanan to Mrs. John Bentley, 20 February 1979, Wormsloe Plantation Folder, Vertical Files, GHS; WJDeR to Dr. Craig Barrow, 22 November 1911, EDeRBC; WJDeR to Dr. Francis Murray, 25 February 1903, WWDeRP-5; Elfrida De Renne to WJDeR, [12 April 1901], WWDeRP-3.

For a time during the early 1900s, New York City held a special attraction for WWDeR. He was an ardent fan of cartoonist Charles "Bunny" Schultze, creator of the popular "Foxy Grandpa" comic strip, which at the time rivaled the more long-lived Buster Brown and Katzenjammer Kids strips. Schultze not only corresponded with Wymberley (signing with his characteristic bunny sketch) but occasionally came to visit at the De Rennes' New York hotel (WWDeRP-3, passim). For a biographical sketch of Schultze, see Judith O'Sullivan, *The Great American Comic Strip: One Hundred Years of Cartoon Art* (New York, 1990), 184–85.

13. *SMN*, 22 July 1894, 22 June 1900; Petition and Judgment, 24 July 1894, SCJ-180, and 21 June 1900, SCJ-209, GHS. The court allowed the expenditure of $7,600 from the corpus of the estate for the 1894 alterations and additions to Wormsloe House (on which expenditures WJDeR paid 8 percent per annum in addition to his rental payment) and $4,000 for the additions of 1900. The architects for the 1894 and 1900 additions were, respectively, Henry Urban and H. W. Witcover.

14. *SMN*, 22 July 1894; Blueprints and Photographs, 1894–97, DeRFP+-10 and 24, DeRFP-29, DeRFP-Oversize: Folder 29, and WC. The service stairs at the western end of the house and the eastern end's spiral staircase were apparently also designed to serve as fire escapes.

15. *SMN*, 22 July 1894; Blueprints and Photographs, 1894–97, DeRFP+-10 and 24, DeRFP-29, DeRFP-Oversize: Folder 29, and EDeRBC.

16. Specifications of Two Mantel Pieces and Eight Bronze Sphinxes, with Plan of Mantel, DeRFP+-10; Photograph of Mantel and Mural, WHS; Photograph, WC.

17. *SMN*, 22 June 1900; Blueprints and Photographs, 1900–1914, DeRFP+-10 and 24; DeRFP-Oversize: Folder 29; and EDeRBC. The first of WJDeR's piers, built in 1899, was wooden; six feet above high water, it was eight feet wide and almost two hundred feet long (Memorandum, 9 February 1899, DeRFP+-3). It apparently replaced the pier of GWJDeR's time and some years later was itself replaced by the concrete pier and pavilion still extant. An undated clipping, c. 1914, notes that the pavilion, "entirely of reinforced concrete, now rests on six immense reinforced concrete piles sunk in the water. . . . Because they were made of concrete the regular pile driver could not be used, and instead they were sunk with suction pumps" (DeRFP+-36).

18. "Wormsloe," 29, WPA-23, Item 4218; Edward Lovell's Sons to WJDeR, 18 June 1906, DeRFP-29.

19. *SEP*, 2 November 1915; *SMN*, 13 February 1914; Audrey De Renne to WJDeR, 20 April 1904, WWDeRP-7; Letter [signature undecipherable] to "Lieber corpsbruder!" [WJDeR], 28 February 1914, DeRFP-15, mentioning "the merry hours we had in your house." Duncan is constantly mentioned in the children's letters from the 1890s and early 1900s, in WWDeRP, Boxes 1 through 7.

20. Account Book (1895), DeRFP+-8; Jenkins, "Wormsloe Plantation," 5. Of the employees who had come from France, the most devoted was Mathilde Garderes, "Nana" to the children.

21. Wine Orders and Receipts, DeRFP+-5. WJDeR's 1895 inventory of wine and other spirits at Wormsloe lists over one hundred bottles of Madeira, over three hundred bottles of sherry (plus one and a half demijohns of Molyneux sherry), nineteen bottles and one and a half demijohns of brandy, and some sixty bottles of whiskey and liqueurs—all his father's (and some his grandfather's), purchased from Everard De Renne's heirs. Listed as his "own importation" are over eighty boxes and over 450 bottles of various spirits (Ledger, DeRFP-15). Various notes by WJDeR on Madeira and related subjects are in his 1894 Journal (DeRFP+-8), and DeRFP+-5 contains lists, orders, correspondence, and miscellaneous items relating to the Jones–De Renne cellars, c. 1790–1911.

22. Luther Anderson to WJDeR, 30 January 1915, DeRFP-40; Interview with Ophelia Dent, September 1955, WCHC; Letter of Ophelia Dent, 3 February 1972, in private possession. Dent, of Hofwyl Plantation, was a close friend of Audrey

De Renne; she often visited the De Rennes at Wormsloe and frequently traveled with them.

23. Photographs, 1895–1905, DeRFP+-24; "An Index Map of Wormsloe, Showing the improvements being made, Spring of 1897," "Wormsloe, Detail Plat. Section A," "Wormsloe, Detail Plat. Sections B & C," DeRFP+-(Oversize Drawer); W. J. Stevenson, Gardener, to WJDeR, 16 June, 4 August, 15 September 1904, DeRFP-29.

24. Photographs, 1895–1905, DeRFP+-24; Receipt, F. H. Morse to WJDeR, 15 March 1897, DeRFP+-7; Plan of Water Supply System at Wormsloe, DeRFP-Oversize, Folder 29; "Wormsloe, Detail Plat. Sections B & C," DeRFP+-(Oversize Drawer).

25. "Wormsloe, Detail Plat. Sections B & C," DeRFP+-(Oversize Drawer); Audrey De Renne to WJDeR, 4 November 1901, WWDeRP-3; Marmaduke Floyd, "A New Map of Wormsloe" [showing bridle paths], DeRFP+-24; "Race Track, Wormsloe" [ms. plan], DeRFP+-10. With the plan is an unidentified clipping showing and describing William C. Whitney's track at his farm at Westbury, Long Island, New York—apparently the model for the Wormsloe track.

26. Elfrida De Renne to WJDeR, [c. 25 February 1899], WWDeRP-1, and [c. 14 March 1900], WWDeRP-2. Two books published during WJDeR's time included photographs of Wormsloe. There were five views in *Art Work of Savannah* (1893) and six in Jones, *Art Work of Savannah and Augusta, Georgia* (1902).

27. *Lakewood, New Jersey* (Lakewood, N.J., 1894), unpaginated; *Waumbek's Penny Daily* (Jefferson, N.H.), 20 July, 31 July, 7, 21 August 1901; Letter of Ophelia Dent, 3 February 1972, in private possession.

28. Audrey De Renne to WJDeR, 20 November 1899, WWDeRP-1; Audrey De Renne to WJDeR, WWDeRP-3; Photographs, 1895–1905, DeRFP+-24.

29. Photographs, 1895–1905, DeRFP+-24; Jenkins, "Wormsloe Plantation," 2; "Wormsloe," 38, WPA-23, Item 4218; Irving, *Sketch Book*, 218. On a map of Wormsloe and its fields, (DeRFP+-10), WJDeR labeled this avenue "Wymberley Avenue," though it is usually called simply the Oak Avenue and the one farther east the Old Avenue. A persistent oral tradition regarding the Oak Avenue and its dedication is recorded in the WPA file on Wormsloe.

30. *SMN*, 20 June, 3 August 1894, 1 April 1897.
Wormsloe's impressive entrance gateway was constructed in the winter of 1912–13 and was apparently meant to have been dedicated in 1912, the year that WWDeR reached his majority; the original drawings by Wallin and Young show "1912" rather than "1913" on the face of the arch. But for unknown reasons the contract with the Savannah Engineering and Construction Company was not signed until

27 November 1912. It called for the concrete work to be completed by January 1913 and the iron work to be finished by the next month, all at a cost of $3,100. Various problems delayed until April or May 1913 the delivery and installation of the gates and locks, which were the work of the International Steel and Iron Construction Company of Evansville, Indiana.

Wrought-iron fencing flanked the gateway, which was itself sixty-two feet across, with the central arched opening fifteen feet across and almost twenty feet in height. In addition to the double gates under the arch, smaller gates were constructed on either side (Specifications for Concrete and Iron Gateway, with related correspondence, DeRFP+-3; Photographs and Drawings, DeRFP+-24; Blueprints, DeRFP+-Oversize).

31. *Georgia Reports,* 105:259; *Southeastern Reporter,* 31:167; L&C to WJDeR, 9 October 1908, DeRFP-30; *SMN,* 23 April 1908, 10 May 1912; Correspondence, WJDeR and George W. Owens, August–September 1909, and Clippings, DeRFP-30.

32. W. O'D. Rockwell, "Map of Wormsloe and Vicinity, Compiled from Authentic Maps, April 20th 1908," DeRFP+-(Oversize Drawer).

33. "Plan of Lots . . . of the Dupon Subdivision, 1913," DeRFP-30; DB 11J:62, SCR.

34. *SMN,* 15 November 1889, 10 April 1887; Maps of Poplar Grove, DeRFP-1064a (Oversize); "Map Showing Proposed De Renne Avenue . . . July 12th 1906," ibid.; DB 9M:179, SCR; Frederick Law Olmsted to E. R. Conant ("For the Information of Mr. De Renne"), 20 March 1916, DeRFP-26; Receipt, Olmsted Brothers to WJDeR, 17 April 1916, ibid.

35. Beirne Gordon to WJDeR, 24 March 1898, DeRFP+-1; [Duncan], *Roll of the Georgia Hussars,* 18, 520–23, 560; Secretary, Georgia Hussars, to WJDeR, 11 April 1895, DeRFP+-1. Of course, guests unassociated with military organizations were also taken to view the ruins of the fortified residence. Joseph F. Sabin, New York book dealer and son of the famed bibliographer, wrote of his visit: "The remains of that old Fort take one a long time back—the *then* and the *now* bridged by history to you who know—by imagination to one who has been your delighted visitor" (Joseph F. Sabin to WJDeR, 20 February 1911, DeRFP-40).

36. William W. Gordon to WJDeR, 11 March 1895, DeRFP+-1, [Duncan], *Roll of the Georgia Hussars,* 523; Olive Kuser to Augusta De Renne, [9 May 1932], DeRFP+-1. Kuser's letter relayed her memories of her father-in-law's vivid description of his day at Wormsloe in 1895. He was with the New Jersey team.

37. Photograph of the De Renne Cup, WHS; Copy of Resolutions passed by the Oglethorpe Light Infantry, 3 February 1896, DeRFP+-1; DB 7P:374, SCR;

Secretary, Savannah Military Rifle Range Association, to WJDeR, 4 May 1896, DeRFP-16.

38. *SMN*, 15 December 1908; Photographs of Captain Duncan's Anniversary Celebration, DeRFP-15; William Law Wakelee to WJDeR, 10 December 1908, DeRFP-16 (Wakelee died 3 June 1909). The luncheon, catered by A. M. Barbee & Son of Isle of Hope, featured diamondback terrapin, partridges a la Barbee, various cold meats and vegetables, cheese, fruits, wine and whiskey, and coffee, both mocha and Java.

39. Davies, *Patriotism on Parade*, 50; WJDeR's Application for Membership in the SR, 4 January 1892, Sons of the Revolution Collection, GHS; WJDeR's Certificate of Membership, 7 January 1892, DeRFP+-9; Society of the Sons of the Revolution in the State of Georgia, *Constitution and List of Members* (1892), 12–14, 33–42. De Renne's organization (SR) should not be confused with the Sons of the American Revolution (SAR), founded in 1889.

40. Society of the Sons of the Revolution in the State of Georgia, *Constitution and List of Members* (1892), [4], 35, 37, 38.

41. *Address of Colonel John Screven*, 15.

42. Ibid., 5, [30–31]. WJDeR's manuscript library catalog, c. 1898 (DeRFP-41), notes that the book was printed in Philadelphia. Its title page bears no place of publication, and the book appears in none of the other De Renne library catalogs.

43. Davies, *Patriotism on Parade*, 47. The SR membership lists, previously cited, list members by place of residence.

44. Bulloch, *History and Genealogy*, [119]–27; Manuscript Genealogical Charts, DeRFP+-32. WJDeR's personal, annotated copy of Bulloch's *History* is in the WC.

45. Bulloch, *History of the Glen Family*, 98; JGBB to WJDeR, 17 December 1896, DeRFP-16. One of De Renne's copies of Bulloch's *History* contains a manuscript chart by Bulloch titled "Descent of Colonel [Noble] Jones from the Royal House of Wales" (WC).

46. WJDeR to JGBB, undated draft on Bulloch's of 11 March 1899, DeRFP-16; W. P. W. Phillimore (London genealogist) to JGBB, 21 October 1899, ibid.; W. A. Lindsay, College of Arms, to JGBB, 24 November 1899, ibid.; WJDeR to JGBB, 10 January 1901, ibid.

47. Account book (1895), DeRFP+-8.

48. BAK to WJDeR, 9 January, 12 February 1902, TSP-b; Introduction by BAK, 7 June 1902, to "The Correspondence between George Washington and His Attorney, Thomas Smith, Esq. of Carlisle and Bedford, Pa., in the Years 1785–86," TSP-a. Unless otherwise noted, citations in notes 46–55 are to TSP-b.

In 1902 WJDeR provided a framed photographic enlargement of his miniature of Judge Smith and briefly loaned the original so that a copy could be painted and placed in the collection at Independence Hall by early 1903. In late 1904 WJDeR presented an oil portrait of Thomas Smith by Edward A. Bell, also based on the miniature, to replace the first copy, which WJDeR found too "rubicund" in relation to the original miniature. The Bell portrait is now in storage (Specimen Folder, SN.13.266, Thomas Smith by Edward A. Bell, Independence National Historic Park, Philadelphia).

De Renne was offered the Washington-Smith letters in 1911 for $3,000 but declined to buy them (Charles F. Humrich to WJDeR, 28 September 1911, TSP-a).

49. BAK to WJDeR, 8 July, 11 August 1902.

50. BAK to WJDeR, 3, 8 September, 1902; WJDeR to BAK, 12 September 1902 (draft).

51. BAK to WJDeR, 12 November 1902; BAK to WJDeR, 30 May 1903; W. H. Campion to WJDeR, 20 June 1903. Campion undertook to publish the book for WJDeR for $600, plus "10% commission on the manufacture and sale of the work."

52. BAK to WJDeR, 18 August, 26 October 1903; WJDeR to BAK, 28 August 1903.

53. BAK to WJDeR, 25 December 1903, 2 March 1904.

54. WJDeR to BAK, 1 March 1904 (Copy); Konkle, *Thomas Smith*, [xv – xvi].

55. WJDeR to BAK, 1 March 1904 (Copy). Two of the many positive reviews appeared in the *American Historical Review* 10 (1904): 182 – 83, and the *Nation* 79 (18 August 1904): 146 – 47.

56. BAK to WJDeR, 2, 16 March 1904.

57. WJDeR to BAK, 20 March 1904 (Draft).

58. Campion and Company to WJDeR, 5 April 1904; "Report on the Langworthy MSS. Search," in BAK to WJDeR, 27 June 1905, DeRFP-13; WJDeR to BAK, 5 January 1906 (Draft), DeRFP+-3; BAK to WJDeR, 1, 13, 24, February 1913, DeRFP-40; Leonard L. Mackall, "Edward Langworthy and the First Attempt to Write a Separate History of Georgia, with Selections from the Long-Lost Langworthy Papers," *GHQ* 7 (1923): [1]–17; Konkle, "Edward Langworthy," *GHQ* 11 (1927): 166 – 70.

Campion's original estimate of $600 for producing five hundred copies of *Thomas Smith* eventually more than doubled, and the company relinquished its 10 percent commission ($123.05). By April 1904, ninety-four copies had been sold (at $3.50), twenty-three were still in stores, fifty-one had been distributed as "editorial copies," and six had been sent to WJDeR. More than two years later, there were still 279 copies on hand, and most of them seem to have been disposed of in 1909 at twenty-five cents apiece. WJDeR's payments to Campion and Company finally exceeded $900 (Campion and Company to WJDeR, 20 June 1903, 5 April 1905, with bill; Receipt, Campion and Company to WJDeR, 12 May 1904; Campion and Company to WJDeR, 24 October 1906, DeRFP-42, and 31 August 1909, DeRFP-16).

59. *New York Times, Philadelphia Inquirer,* 25 October 1944.

60. A. B. Caldwell to WJDeR, 7 September 1905, DeRFP-42. The De Renne–Smith correspondence is in the De Renne Historical Manuscripts, Ms. 1136, UGAL.

61. A. B. Caldwell to WJDeR, 13 September 1905, DeRFP-42; WJDeR to A. B. Caldwell, 21 January 1906, DeRFP-6. The portraits that have been published as likenesses of Noble Jones are actually either Noble Wimberly Jones (for example, Coulter, *Georgia,* opposite 84) or Noble Wimberly Jones II (for examples, Lockwood, ed., *Gardens of Colony and State,* 285, and James M. Johnson, *Militiamen, Rangers, and Redcoats* [(Macon, Ga., 1992], 14).

62. Rough and final manuscript drafts are in DeRFP-6, and a typescript draft, with corrections in WJDeR's hand, is in the WC.

63. *MoM,* 1:204–5.

64. Ibid., 205–6.

65. GHS, *Collections,* 6:7, 179. Another reason that WJDeR probably felt compelled to refute the charge definitively related to the essay on NWJ taken from Colonel Jones's *Biographical Sketches of the Delegates from Georgia to the Continental Congress,* which he had suggested be printed in *Men of Mark in Georgia.* Colonel Jones had been given access to GWJDeR's papers during Mrs. De Renne's widowhood and had apparently noted the charge then. But when Jones mentioned Habersham's letter in the sketch, he omitted its accusatory conclusion so that the behavior of the younger Jones merely appeared ungrateful in light of the Crown's generosity, without its being suggested that his father had been malfeasant. Jones's solution to the dilemma was diplomatic since it allowed him to praise both Habersham and Jones, but it was more eulogy than history.

66. WJDeR to A. B. Caldwell, undated draft on A. B. Caldwell to WJDeR, 9 December 1907, DeRFP-42.

67. *MoM,* 2:[342]–44; Harden, *History of Savannah,* 2:533–49.

68. L. L. Knight to WJDeR, 24 November 1910 and 25 November 1911 (with WJDeR's note of 28 November 1911), DeRFP-40; WJDeR's Manuscript, "Wormsloe," 27 November 1911, DeRGL Accession File, UGAL; Knight, *Georgia's Landmarks, Memorials and Legends,* 1:87–89. WJDeR also provided a copy of his Wormsloe sketch to the Georgia Society of the Colonial Dames of America, which had it printed in the *Savannah Press,* 30 December 1916.

69. UBP to Waldo Leland, 16 January 1905, J. Franklin Jameson Papers, LoC; CHS to WJDeR, 15 November 1905, DeRFP-38.

70. Marshall, *Historic Houses of Athens,* 21; Wilson Lumpkin, "House Build-

ing," Lumpkin Folder, Vertical Files, UGAL; *Hearst's Sunday American,* 14 September 1913.

71. *DGB,* 2:644–45; Anita Butts Sams, "Memories of Monroe-Born Martha Lumpkin," *North Georgia Life,* October 1963, 17.

72. Sams, "Memories," 17; Lumpkin Folder, Vertical Files, UGAL. The Lumpkin Family Bible is in the possession of Mrs. William Tate, Athens, Ga.

73. Donnan and Stock, eds., *An Historian's World,* 325; UBP to Waldo Leland, 16 January 1905, J. Franklin Jameson Papers, LoC.

74. CSH to WJDeR, 20 October, 15 November 1905, DeRFP-38.

75. CSH to WJDeR, 18 November 1905, ibid.

76. CSH to WJDeR, 26 November 1905, ibid.

77. Ibid.

78. CSH to WJDeR, 26, 27 November 1905, DeRFP-38; Receipt for $600, Mrs. M. L. Compton to CSH, 27 November 1905, DeRFP+-7.

79. CSH to WJDeR, 27 November 1905, DeRFP-38. In 1907 Compton reportedly sold the Lumpkin House and remaining land to the university for $10,000, a figure she had mentioned to Hook. She did, however, stipulate in the deed that "if the house symbolic of her father's character were ever removed from the premises or destroyed manually, the penalty would be reversion of the property to the heirs." Soon after she sold the house she moved to Decatur, Georgia, where she died in 1917, a few months short of her ninetieth birthday. Happily for her, she was afforded a good deal of attention in the Atlanta press during her final decade (Marshall, *Historic Houses of Athens,* 21; *Hearst's Sunday American,* 14 September 1913; Lumpkin Folder, Vertical Files, UGAL).

80. Coulter, *Wormsloe,* 247.

81. WJDeR's manuscript introduction to *Removal of the Cherokee Indians,* DeRFP+-13; WJDeR to [David C. Barrow], undated draft, DeRFP+-1. The two Lumpkin manuscript volumes are found as Ms. 1047, UGAL.

82. WJDeR to [David C. Barrow], undated draft, DeRFP+-1.

83. David C. Barrow to WJDeR, 18 August 1906, DeRFP-40; David C. Barrow to WJDeR, 9 November 1906, DeRFP+-1; WJDeR to David C. Barrow, 14 March 1907, Barrow Papers-2, UGAL-A.

84. W. S. Pottinger to WJDeR, 6 February 1907, DeRFP 38; Robert H. Dodd to WJDeR, 8 April 1908, DeRFP-42; "Memorandum of Agreement for selling Lumpkin's 'Cherokee Indians,'" 13 April 1908, ibid.

85. WJDeR to William Harden, 6 June 1907, William Harden to WJDeR, 24 July 1907, W. S. Pottinger to WJDeR, 5 July 1907, DeRFP-38. Harden's penciled editing annotations remain in the manuscript volumes.

86. WJDeR to W. S. Pottinger, 10 April 1907 (Draft), on W. S. Pottinger to WJDeR, 9 April 1907, DeRFP-38.

87. *DeRLC*, 3:1055–56; "Finis Cherokees," WJDeR's note on envelope containing Dodd & Livingston to WJDeR, 24 June 1911, DeRFP-42; Memorandum, Morning News Press, 26 June 1916, laid in Vol. 1 of *Removal of the Cherokees*, DeRGL. A 1911 plan to have the Americus Book Company take over distribution from Dodd & Livingston (successors to Dodd, Mead) apparently did not succeed, although there is a specimen title page in the DeRGL. The memorandum cited above shows that 225 bound sets of the book remained in 1916, along with 160 unbound sets. Since passing into the public domain, however, the book has been reprinted twice (two volumes in one) by the Arno Press and the New York Times (New York, 1969) and by Augustus M. Kelley (New York, 1971).

88. Mott, *Golden Multitudes*, 312; Mackall, "The Wymberley Jones De Renne Georgia Library," 73n.16.

WJDeR considered reprinting at least two other works. The first was the *Report of the Committee Appointed to Examine into the Proceedings of the People of Georgia*, originally published in Charleston in 1736. A. S. W. Rosenbach, who sold the small quarto pamphlet to WJDeR in 1909 for $375, identified it as, "with one exception, the first book printed south of Virginia." At that time only one other copy was known to exist, and it was not complete, as was the one purchased by WJDeR. The second work under consideration was of more recent vintage: the "Nemesis" letters, anti-Reconstruction philippics written in 1871 by WJDeR's friend Senator Thomas M. Norwood and published in the *Augusta Chronicle and Sentinel* (A. S. W. Rosenbach to WJDeR, 16, 24 March 1909, DeRFP-54; *DeRLC*, 1:69; WJDeR to T. K. Oglesby, 29 October 1913, DeRFP-40; Letters of Nemesis, Ms. 1650, UGAL; Bragg, "The Junius of Georgia Redemption," 86–122).

CHAPTER 9. Maecenas

1. Penn, "Charles Colcock Jones," 39–40, 66.

2. Ibid., 54–55, 72; Grady, *New South*, 3–13; Jones and Gordon, *Old South*, 15–18; *Augusta Chronicle*, 20 July 1893.

3. CCJJ to Everard De Renne, 8 March 1890, 22 December 1891, LPCB 1890 and LPCB 1890–91, DUL; CCJJ to Eliot Danforth, 1 May 1891, LPCB, 1891–92, ibid.; CCJJ to Joseph F. Sabin, 15 December 1892, LPCB, 1892–93, ibid.; WJDeR to DSF, 15 May 1914 (Draft), DeRFP-38; Telamon Cuyler to WJDeR, 25 November 1909, DeRFP-42; Haywood Pearce Jr., *Benjamin H. Hill: Secession and Reconstruction* (Chicago, 1928), 310.

In addition to the bound manuscripts, WJDeR also apparently purchased from Colonel Jones a good number of miscellaneous Confederate imprints. This seems likely since during later years, when he was gathering his Georgia books in earnest, WJDeR never actively sought Confederate items and warned dealers that he was not in the market for such things. Yet his Georgia library held a fairly comprehensive group of more than two hundred specimens of Confederate printing, many not relating specifically to Georgia, and an accession from Colonel Jones seems the most likely source—particularly since the early manuscript catalog of De Renne's library contains the entry "Confederate States—Many pamphlets relating to—." Unless an inventory eventually surfaces, there can never be a full accounting of the exact contents of what WJDeR described as the "Jones Collection of Confederate Manuscripts, Portraits, etc." The collection was sold and otherwise disposed of after his death, and it has been impossible to trace the present-day location of many of the items. The three printed De Renne catalogs (and the two early manuscript library catalogs and the catalog of autographs) give scant mention to these Confederate materials.

4. W. M. Davant to Leonard L. Mackall, 9 May 1918, CSAC.

5. *DeRLC*, 2:619–20; Confederate Memorial Literary Society, *In Memoriam Sempiternam*, 72.

6. *BRHG* (1905), 63 and folding plate opposite. Unless otherwise noted, all material cited in notes 7 though 17 is from CSAC.

7. William Starr Basinger to Thomas G. Basinger, 25 July 1905; William Starr Basinger to WJDeR, 10 August 1905.

8. A. McC. Duncan to WJDeR, 15 May, 17 June 1907; Wade Hampton de Fontaine to WJDeR, 26 August 1907.

9. Unidentified clipping, 31 December 1908, quoting the *Richmond Journal.*

10. *Richmond News Leader*, 30 December 1908.

11. Ibid.; Confederate Memorial Literary Society, *Yearbook* (1908–09), 12–13, 27–29; Freeman, *Calendar*, 11; Gignilliat, "The Thought of Douglas Southall Freeman," 184.

12. G. W. Owens to WJDeR, 15 February 1909.

13. DSF to KCS, 9 March 1909. MDeR's Constitution was no doubt meant to be in the museum as well; probably only inadvertence (or Everard De Renne's lack of familiarity with his mother's holdings) kept it from joining the other materials. Under the circumstances, however, no one in Richmond attempted to claim it.

14. Ibid. When W. W. Corcoran's presentation of the Provisional Constitution to the Southern Historical Society had been reported in the society's *Papers* in 1884, Colonel Jones—also confused by the use of the word "original"—had immediately written to MDeR. "How can this be," he asked, "when you have the original engrossed document, duly signed and authenticated in your possession? There must certainly be some mistake about the Richmond document. I cannot understand how or why a paper of this sort should have been executed in duplicate." When MDeR wrote to explain the difference in the two documents, he responded, "Be-

yond doubt, the Constitution which you have is by far the most valuable document." The confusion of such an authority as Jones regarding these documents makes the later controversy somewhat more understandable (CCJJ to MDeR, 10, 13 March 1884, DeRFP-Autograph Book).

15. G. W. Owens to KCS, 16 March 1909.

16. KCS to G. W. Owens, 24 March 1909; Freeman's and Eckenrode's Certificate of Authenticity, 27 March [1909].

17. "Rare Document of Confederacy," *SMN*, 23 May 1909. This article reprints "Two Relics of the Confederacy" and contains its own share of errors, including a suggestion that it was Miss Stiles who first contacted WJDeR regarding the mystery of the Constitutions.

18. *DeRLC*, 3:1079–81; A. McC. Duncan to WJDeR, 8 June 1909. Duncan's letter shows that the mischievous word "original" continued in use.

The Constitution that William Starr Basinger mentioned to WJDeR, sometimes known as the "Cobb Constitution," was the manuscript draft of the Permanent (De Renne) Constitution. Delivered to the printer in parts beginning on 22 February 1861, it bears a certification of authenticity signed by the secretary of the Confederate Congress on 27 February 1861. Almost entirely in the hand of T. R. R. Cobb, the draft covers some forty manuscript pages (and one printed page) and was printed in thirteen copies, numbering twenty-seven pages each, for the Committee on the Constitution's Corrections. The committee's corrected draft for use during the debate by the Congress as a whole received a larger printing and was dated 9 March 1861.

In final form, the Permanent Constitution was approved by Congress on 11 March 1861 (the date it bears), and the vellum document, "transcribed in the traditional Spencerian style," was "laid on the table for signing" on 16 March 1861. Unlike the parchment Provisional Constitution of 8 February 1861, sold by de Fontaine to W. W. Corcoran in 1883, the Permanent (De Renne) Constitution has never been fully reproduced in facsimile; WJDeR declined a request to have such a reproduction included in the 1910 edition of *The Harvard Classics*. Many printed versions of the Provisional and Permanent Constitutions were issued during the war, and WJDeR eventually acquired several specimens, as well as the lithographed version of the Provisional Constitution created by de Fontaine in 1883.

In 1912 WJDeR declined to accept A. L. Hull's offer to sell him the Cobb Constitution. After having been on loan to the University of Georgia library from 1908, it was reclaimed by Hull's descendants in 1982 and offered for sale at $200,000. It was purchased for an undisclosed price by the Karpeles Manuscript Library, which has museums in Montecito, California, and several other cities (Harwell, Annotations to *Confederate Imprints* [Catalog 114, Broadfoot's Bookmark], Wendell, N.C.,

1982, 2–4; Parrish and Willingham, *Confederate Imprints*, 43; Beers, *The Confederacy*, 3–4; Hull, "The Making of the Confederate Constitution," 281; Lee, *Confederate Constitutions*, 81n.72, 87–88, 124n.5; William Patten, *Harvard Classics*, to WJDeR, 7 January 1910, with WJDeR's endorsement ["NO"], 9 January 1910, DeRFP-41; A. L. Hull to WJDeR, 5 December 1912, DeRFP-40; Letter of Suzanne E. Barrett, Karpeles Manuscript Library, 13 September 1991).

19. Worthington C. Ford to WJDeR, 26 June 1905, LoC Archives (letters cited in notes 19–21 are from this source); Herbert Putnam to WJDeR, 5 April 1909; WJDeR to Herbert Putnam, 26 May 1909; WJDeR to Gaillard Hunt, 17 June 1909.

20. WJDeR to Herbert Putnam, 17 June 1909; WJDeR to Gaillard Hunt, 17 June 1909.

21. Gaillard Hunt to WJDeR, 15 June 1909, 8 March 1910; WJDeR to Herbert Putnam, 27 December 1914.

22. Henry Alexander White, *Robert E. Lee and the Southern Confederacy, 1807–1870* (New York, 1897), v; Connelly, *Marble Man*, 42, 115, 119; Norwood, *An Appeal to the Men and Women of the South to Build a Christian Pantheon in Honor of Our Confederate Heroes*, 14–15. Other of WJDeR's friends had more than a passing interest in Robert E. Lee. J. Florance Minis, for example, had been a student at Washington College during Lee's tenure as president. Minis's wife, Louisa, a major donor to the Confederate Museum's Georgia Room, was the daughter of Confederate general Jeremy F. Gilmer, and her mother was a friend of Mary De Renne (Kole, *Minis Family*, 125; Confederate Memorial Literary Society, *Catalogue of the Confederate Museum* [1905], 126).

23. Harold E. Mahan, "The Arsenal of History: The Official Records of the War of the Rebellion," *Civil War History* 29 (March 1983): [5], 16n.51.

24. UBP to WJDeR, 26 February 1910, DeRFP-38; Freeman, *Calendar*, 13, 164, 501; DSF to WJDeR, 14 June 1910, DeRFP-38. Unless noted otherwise, materials cited in notes 25 through 60 are from DeRFP-38.

25. DSF to WJDeR, 8 October 1910, 2 July 1915; DSF to Louis V. Naisawald, Box 71, Freeman Papers, LoC.

26. DSF to WJDeR, 6 February 1911, 5 December 1910, 5 August 1915; WJDeR to Robert E. Lee Jr., 28 October 1910.

27. DSF to WJDeR, 6 February 1911. With this letter, Freeman sent WJDeR an inscribed copy of a book he had recently edited, *Memoirs of Service with John Yates Beall, C.S.N.* (DeRFP+- Miscellaneous Books).

28. Dodd, Mead to WJDeR, 1 November 1910, 11 February 1911; Dodd, Mead to DSF, 16 March 1911.

29. DSF to WJDeR, 2 June 1911.

30. Ibid.; DSF to WJDeR, 7, 26 June 1911, 29 April 1912.

31. DSF to WJDeR, 29 April 1912, 24 October 1913.

32. WJDeR to DSF, 26 September 1913. WJDeR underwent surgery in September 1913, perhaps related to an otherwise unexplained "accident in Canada," since a detailed 1914 letter by his doctor makes no mention of the operation or the need for it. A diabetic condition, diagnosed in 1912, was treated with initial success through diet. His health continued to deteriorate, however. In 1914 he began taking Digipuratum for a heart complaint. The same year he was found to have a cirrhotic liver, as well as ascites and "oedema of both lower extremities from the knee downwards" (DSF to WJDeR, 23 September 1913; Lillie Noble Jones to WWDeR, 25 June [1916], DeRFP-14; Dr. Francis W. Murray to Dr. Craig Barrow, 21 November 1914, WC).

33. Bragg, "'Our Joint Labor,'" 4, 8n.16, 14–15. See this article for a more detailed account of the preparation and publication of Lee's Dispatches.

34. Cheek, "Douglas Southall Freeman," 37; DSF to WJDeR, 8, 23 September 1913; WJDeR to DSF, 26 September 1913.

35. Note on draft of WJDeR to DSF, 30 April 1914; WJDeR to DSF, 15 May 1914; DSF to WJDeR, 26 June 1911, 1 May 1914; Bragg, "'Our Joint Labor,'" 25.

36. DSF to WJDeR, 7, 15 September 1914.

37. DSF to WJDeR, 15 September 1914.

38. DSF to WJDeR, 1 May 1914; WJDeR to DSF, 15 May 1914; Irvine, "Fate of Confederate Archives," 823–26; Freeman, The South to Posterity, 96–101. See also Bragg, "Charles C. Jones, Jr., and the Mystery of Lee's Lost Dispatches." In brief, Colonel Jones had been lent a mass of official correspondence by Davis's wartime secretary; Jones kept the majority of the letters and telegrams through subterfuge and had the correspondence bound into several volumes.

39. WJDeR to DSF, [21 September 1914]; DSF to WJDeR, 15, 22 September 1914.

40. Freeman, ed., Lee's Dispatches, xxxv, xxxvii–xviii; Enclosure to DSF to WJDeR, 15 September 1914.

41. WJDeR to DSF, [21 September 1914].

42. DLB, 17:160; DSF to WJDeR, 22 September 1914; WJDeR to DSF, [21 September 1914].

43. DSF to WJDeR, 15, 22 September 1914.

44. DSF to WJDeR, 16 February 1911, 17 October 1914, Edward Dodd to WJDeR, 13 October 1914.

45. DSF to WJDeR, 17 October 1914; G. P. Putnam's Sons to WJDeR, 21, 29 (with estimate of 28 October), 30 October 1914. Putnam's was not disposed to publish the book except at WJDeR's expense. "Our judgment," they wrote, "is adverse to the probability of securing for the proposed volume a sufficiently extended sale

to render the publication remunerative" (G. P. Putnam's Sons to WJDeR, 21 October 1914).

46. WJDeR to DSF, 30 October 1914.

47. Ibid.

48. DSF to WJDeR, 4 November 1914.

49. Bragg, "'Our Joint Labor,'" 21, 24; "Lee Letters: Newspaper Clippings," DeRFP-42.

50. DSF to G. P. Putnam's Sons, 22 December 1914; WJDeR to G. H. Putnam, undated draft of Putnam to WJDeR, 11 May 1915.

51. G. H. Putnam to WJDeR, 11 May 1915. Major Putnam was, incidentally, a brother of Librarian of Congress Herbert Putnam.

52. WJDeR to G. H. Putnam, undated draft on Putnam to WJDeR, 11 May 1915.

53. WJDeR to G. P. Putnam's Sons, 4 June 1915.

54. "Lee Letters: Newspaper Clippings," DeRFP-42; "Unpublished Dispatches from Gen. Lee," *New York Times Review of Books*, 27 June 1915, 1. Posterity has also valued *Lee's Dispatches*. In 1978, Richard Harwell included the book in his *In Tall Cotton: The 200 Most Important Confederate Books for the Reader, Researcher and Collector* (39–41), and in 1995 historian Gary W. Gallagher, surveying the military histories of the Civil War, selected *Lee's Dispatches* as one of the one hundred classics "essential to any comprehensive Civil War library" (*Civil War* 49 [February 1995]: 42, 46). In *Lee the Soldier* (Lincoln, Neb., 1996), edited by Gallagher, he and the historians Robert K. Krick and T. Michael Parrish placed Freeman's classic in "The R. E. Lee 200: An Annotated Bibliography of Essential Books on Lee's Military Career," calling it a "crucial edition of primary sources necessary for an appreciation of Lee's military decision making and his influence on President Davis" (580).

55. *Philadelphia Press*, 28 August 1915; *Worcester Gazette*, 12 July 1915; *Richmond Times-Dispatch*, 5 August 1915; *Atlanta Constitution*, 4 November 1915; Charles Edgeworth Jones to WJDeR, 28 August 1915, "Personal Comments on Lee Letters [Scrapbook]," DeRFP-42.

56. DSF to WJDeR, 5 August 1915.

57. Bill, First Impression, *Lee's Dispatches*, 31 May 1915; Bill, Second Impression, *Lee's Dispatches*, 26 August 1915; Statements of Account, 31 July 1915, 31 January 1916, 31 January 1918.

58. "Personal Comments on Lee Letters [Scrapbook]," DeRFP-42.

59. Lillie Noble Jones to WJDeR, 6 August [1915], ibid. Lillie Noble Jones (1843–1925) remained in Italy after the death there in 1902 of her brother, the diplomat Wallace Savage Jones. (Her brother Noble W. Jones III had died of malaria in Savannah twenty years earlier.) Miss Noble Jones, as she was known, served as hostess for Wallace during his consulships in Messina, Sicily (1885–91), and

Rome, Italy (1893–97). Both are buried in Rome's Protestant cemetery (*SMN*, 9 May 1882, 29 December 1902; W. S. Jones obituary clipping [unidentified], 3 January 1903, Lillie Noble Jones to Major General J. Franklin Bell, 12 May 1908, JFP-3).

60. DSF to WJDeR, 2 July 1915.

61. E. L. Burlingame to DSF, 24 November 1915, Scribner Author Files, Princeton University Library; Cheek, "Reflections," 29. As was the case with *Removal of the Cherokee Indians*, publishers became more enthusiastic about *Lee's Dispatches* after it passed into the public domain. In 1957, four years after Freeman's death, Putnam's published a "New Edition" of the dispatches, in smaller format, with the map reduced and bound in—though the "Signed First Printing" contained the map as a folding plate. It included a foreword by Grady McWhiney and eleven additional dispatches found by him, principally at the Duke University library. No information is available on the size of the edition or the number of copies sold, though its critical reception was largely respectful. The major criticism was that it had reprinted the errors of the original edition "with canine fidelity." In 1994 the Louisiana State University Press reprinted in paperback, in slightly smaller format, the 1957 edition of *Lee's Dispatches*. This latest edition contained no additions or changes except to delete the map (Freeman, ed., *Lee's Dispatches*, New ed., with Additional Dispatches and a Foreword by Grady McWhiney, New York, 1957 [reprint, Baton Rouge, 1994], new material: v–x, 361–75; Joseph H. Harrison Jr., Review of *Lee's Dispatches* [1957 ed.], *Virginia Magazine of History and Biography* 66 [1958]: 375; Letter of Irene O'Neill, The Putnam Publishing Group, 23 November 1985).

CHAPTER 10. A Befitting Temple

1. Account Book (1895–96), DeRFP+-8. Only rarely did any of WJDeR's father's plundered books return to Wormsloe. In the first such instance in 1911, after his library had become widely known, WJDeR received in the mail William Douglass's *Summary, Historical and Political . . . of the British Settlements in North America* (1755). The sender, the Massachusetts Historical Society's Samuel A. Green (1830–1918), had been given the book in Richmond in April 1865 and had always assumed—presumably because of the bookplate—"that it was 'looted'—taken from a private library during the War." He also shared a happy reminiscence of traveling in 1851 in the area of Niagara Falls with "a Mr. Jones of Savannah . . . accompanied by two or three ladies" (apparently George Noble Jones). "The party was very civil to me," Green wrote, "a young man just out of college; and made an impression on my youthful mind." Mr. Jones, he recalled, "carried a shawl—then much in style."

WJDeR responded, "I do not know how to thank you for the delicacy of feeling which prompted" the return of books, "most valuable . . . as the only ones I have of my father's antebellum library." Though admitting he had never heard of "the Niagara excursion," WJDeR wrote, "I am very glad that you entertain such pleasant recollections of my people" (Samuel Green to WJDeR, 27 May 1911; WJDeR to Samuel Green, [Draft, c. 30 May 1911], both laid in Douglass's *Summary*, DeRGL).

2. Manuscript Library Catalogue (c. 1898), DeRFP-41; "List of Boxes & trunks containing articles having been in use in my household, during eight years residence in Biarritz, France," Inventory of Personal Property at Wormsloe, 1896–99, DeRFP+-9; WJDeR to GNJ II, 21 July 1897, JFP-1.

3. Manuscript Library Catalogue (c. 1898), DeRFP-41; *DeRLC*, 1:345.

4. Book Receipts, DeRFP-53; Manuscript Library Catalogue (c. 1902), DeRFP+-10.

5. MDeR to WJDeR, 12 November [1880], DeRFP-14.

6. GWJDeR to CCJJ, 31 March [1875], laid in De Brahm's *History*, DeRGL; Lyman C. Draper, *Essay on the Autographic Collections of the Signers of the Declaration of Independence and of the Constitution* (New York, 1889), 4, 11; Callcott, *History in the United States*, 97–98.

7. "W. J. De Renne—Index of Autographs—and Letters. 1896," DeRFP-16; WJDeR to Telamon Smith [Cuyler], 25 October 1903, TCC-169.

8. "W. J. De Renne—Index of Autographs—and Letters. 1896," DeRFP-16; *DeRLC*, 1:215–18.

9. "W. J. De Renne—Index of Autographs—and Letters. 1896," DeRFP-16.

10. WJDeR to Telamon Smith [Cuyler], 25 October 1903, TCC-169; Receipt, Joseph Sabin to WJDeR, 11 November 1910, DeRFP-54; Receipt, Joseph Sabin to WJDeR, 12 November 1912, DeRFP-40; Joseph Sabin to WJDeR, 24 March 1911, DeRFP-40; WJDeR to Joseph Sabin, 31 March 1911, Henry B. Dawson Papers, William L. Clements Library, University of Michigan. Clements (1861–1934), a noted collector of Americana, later acquired the Wayne-Greene correspondence from WJDeR's heir. The letters were published as "After Yorktown: The Wayne-Green Correspondence, 1782," in Howard H. Peckham, ed., *Sources of American Independence*, 2 vols. (Chicago, 1978), 2:361–427.

11. Manuscript Library Catalogue (c. 1898), DeRFP-41; Winsor, *Narrative and Critical History of America*, 5:392–406.

12. Bernard Quaritch to WJDeR, 10 July 1905, DeRFP-40; "The House of Henry Stevens," *Publishers' Weekly*, 29 June 1907, 1912–13; Henry Stevens, Son & Stiles to LLM, 8 April, 31 July 1916, DeRFP-43; Receipt, Henry Stevens, Son & Stiles, 25 June 1902, DeRFP-53.

The catalogs themselves offered special delights. "No ephemeral literature," wrote one bibliophile, "approaches in fascination a bookseller's catalogue. To receive one at breakfast, skim through it with one's bacon and eggs, send off a post-card by the first mail for some long-sought rarity—or even a telegram if circumstances demand it—these are among the highest pleasures of life" (A. N. L. Munby, *The Alabaster Hand* [London, 1949], 140–41). Munby also wrote on that most omnivorous of all bibliomaniacs, Sir Thomas Phillipps (1792–1872), who wanted a copy of every book ever printed.

WJDeR's "black book," in which he listed dealers, publishers, and librarians, is in DeRFP-44. Among his listings are fifteen New York dealers, ten from London, and nine in Germany and Austria. The favorite Savannah bookstore of both WJDeR and WWDeR was that of "old Mr. Jacob Gardner" on East Broughton Street (WWDeR to Augusta De Renne, 24 November 1918, WWDeRP-8).

13. CSH to LLM, 31 July 1916, 24 June 1918, DeRFP-43. Hook also occasionally went on research trips for WJDeR, on some of which he visited the South Carolina Historical Society in Charleston. There he was assisted in securing information on WJDeR's family in the eighteenth century by the redoubtable Mabel Webber (1869–1941). A society mainstay and longtime editor of its journal, Webber watched with interest the continuing expansion of the DeRGL (CSH to WJDeR, 15 November 1905, DeRFP-38; "Mabel Louise Webber," *South Carolina Historical and Genealogical Magazine* 42 (October 1941): 203–4.

14. CSH to LLM, 31 July 1916, 24 June 1918, DeRFP-43.

15. CSH to LLM, 7 June 1918, ibid.

16. CSH to WJDeR, 22 November 1905, DeRFP-38; Burrille Atkinson to WJDeR, 17 April 1907, Harry F. Dunwody to WJDeR, 23 April 1907, WJDeR to Burrille Atkinson, 29 April 1907, Burrille Atkinson to WJDeR, 1 October 1907, DeRFP-40.

17. CSH to WJDeR, 30 June 1905, DeRFP-34.

18. Mackall, "De Renne Georgia Library," 82.

19. TLC to WJDeR, 25 October 1905, DeRFP-40; *DeRLC*, 3:1025–26.

20. TLC to WJDeR, 25 October 1905, DeRFP-40.

21. WJDeR to TLC, 27 October 1905 (Draft, on letter previously cited), DeRFP-40.

22. TLC to WJDeR, 30 October 1905, DeRFP-40; *SMN*, 7 November 1905; TLC to WJDeR, 10 April 1908, DeRFP-38.

23. Draft of instructions to the Launder Bindery, undated, Ms. 1136, UGAL; *DeRLC*, 1:145–48; Agreement with Statute Law Book Company, 1 June 1907, DeRFP-53; *Georgia Colonial Laws* (reprinted 1932), [v]. Another disagreement between WJDeR and Cole seems to have delayed Cole's acquisition of the copies of the three acts found only in the Ewen copy. In any case, they were not supplied during De Renne's lifetime, and Cole died in 1932, the same year that photographs were

secured from De Renne's heir and the compendium was finally printed (on "best all-rag paper") and bound together "in green fabrikoid," in an edition of thirty copies. See *DeRLC* (1:146) for a listing of the "collections of the original Acts and Session Laws up to 1770." Theoretically, the *Acts* quarto of 1881 and the 1932 State Law Book Company collection would contain all legislation passed in Georgia from 1755 to 1774, printed and unprinted, but it was later discovered that the quarto "omits 9 Acts not previously printed by Johnston &c & not in full in Watkins & Marbury & Crawford." *CRG*, 18 (1910) and 19, Parts 1 and 2 (1911), also published much Georgia colonial legislation. There has still been no complete printing of Georgia's colonial legislation. Since the state of Georgia by this time had copied all of the PRO legislation, *CRG*, 18, contains the bulk of the laws first printed in the 1881 quarto ("The Wormsloe Ga. Acts . . ." [ms. of LLM], Ms. 1136, UGAL, and "Concordance showing correspondence of pages in known copies of Georgia Laws 1755–1770, printed by James Johnston," [typescript by LLM], DeRFP-43).

24. Manuscript Catalogue (c. 1902), DeRFP+-10; *BRHG* (1905).

25. *DeRLC*, 1:xx; WJDeR to Duncan Burnet, 22 March 1906, DeRGL Accession File, UGAL. WJDeR received many complimentary acknowledgments from those to whom he presented catalogs. Among the most prized was from Nina Flandé, a family friend who resided in the French town of Pau. She pronounced his gathering of Georgia books *"un vrai trésor d'érudition"* (Nina Flandé to WJDeR, 10 June 1905, DeRFP-40).

26. *BRHG* (1905), 7–26.

27. Ibid., 33–38; Charles Edgeworth Jones to WJDeR, 10 May 1909, DeRFP-38.

28. *BRHG* (1905), 63–64.

29. Ibid., [3].

30. Wymberley Jones De Renne Book Lists, Ms. 2745 (M), UGAL; *BRHG* (1911): 260–68; Receipt from Jay A. Farnsworth, Job Printer, Westport, New York, DeRFP-40.

31. WJDeR to Walter G. Charlton, 16 May 1910, DeRFP-47; Herbert Putnam to WJDeR, 24 April 1916, DeRFP-40; A. S. W. Rosenbach, *An American Jewish Bibliography* (Philadelphia, 1926), 60.

32. Wymberley Jones De Renne Book Lists, Ms. 2745 (M), UGAL; *BRHG* (1911), 30, 196, 205.

33. Blueprints of Library in the Residence at Wormsloe, Folder 29 DeRFP (Oversize); Photograph of Library (1899), DeRFP+-24.

34. WJDeR to C. Lucian Jones, undated draft on Jones's of 27 March 1916, DeRFP-40.

35. Wallin and Young, Statement of Cost of Library for Mr. W. J. De Renne, 15

May 1908, DeRFP+-3; Library Blueprints, DeRFP+-Oversize. Labor and materials for the library totaled over $12,000. One of De Renne's books, A. Rivela and H. v. Pernull's *The Dead Cities of Sicily* (Palermo, Sicily, 1905) shows, as Figure 61, a structure similar to the library building, particularly in the distinctive design of the four-columned portico; considering that the library was dedicated to Dr. Noble Jones, it is intriguing that the similar Roman structure is a temple to Aesculapius, the god of medicine (DeRFP+-. Miscellaneous Books).

36. Library Blueprints, DeRFP+-Oversize; Rita DeLorme, "Tile Tracing," *Savannah Magazine* 5 (March–April 1994): 11.

37. Library Photographs and Blueprints, DeRFP+-24 and DeRFP+-Oversize.

38. Ibid., LLM to George Stikeman, 18 April 1918, DeRFP-43.

39. Library Photographs, DeRFP+-24; Carl L. Brandt to WJDeR, 8 August 1895, DeRFP-14.

40. A. McC. Duncan to WJDeR, 13 August 1907, DeRFP-53; Wallin and Young, Statement of Cost of Library for Mr. W. J. De Renne, 15 May 1908, DeRFP+-3; Library Blueprints, DeRFP+-Oversize; WJDeR to Preston Brooks, undated draft on Brooks's of 23 April 1908, DeRFP-40; Blank invitation to a "private view," WC; Mackall, "De Renne Georgia Library," 73; Receipt, Launder Bindery to WJDeR, 15 August 1905, DeRFP-53; Receipt, Launder Bindery to WJDeR, 18 July 1910, DeRFP-54; Joseph F. Sabin to WJDeR, 20 February 1911, DeRFP-40. (The date *1907* appears beneath the De Renne arms in the mosaic floor of the portico, but actual construction was done in 1907–8.)

41. Mackall, "De Renne Georgia Library," 84. The growth of the library eventually led to the installation of additional shelves on the walls adjacent to the windows.

42. Ron Chernow, *The House of Morgan* (New York, 1990), 116–20; WJDeR to Claud Estes, 2 January 1912 (Draft), DeRFP-40.

43. Correspondence, WWDeRC-1,2; Elfrida De Renne, Diary, 1904–5, WC; Knight, *Standard History*, 6:2819. Dr. Barrow won the 1909 Reliability Contest, in which drivers followed a course from Savannah to Atlanta (Savannah Automobile Club to Dr. Craig Barrow, 27 November 1909, WC).

44. *SEP*, 3 January 1906; *SMN*, 4 January 1906.

45. *SEP*, 3 January 1906; *SMN*, 4 January 1906.

46. Knight, *Standard History*, 6:2819. One of WJDeR's few real estate investments, the Liberty Street house had been purchased, renovated, and expanded by him in 1896 (DB 7Q:83, SCR; Memorandum of Agreement between G. H. Gruver & Company and WJDeR, 24 July 1896, DeRFP+-9).

47. Knight, *Standard History*, 6:2819; Correspondence and Clippings, WC; *SMN*, 1 September 1945.

48. Correspondence, WWDeRC-1,2; *SMN*, 29 November 1907; "Dr. Coerr to Wed," undated, unidentified clipping in DeRFP+-36; *New York Times*, 21 November 1912; Datebook 1916, DeRFP-14; WJDeR to Dr. Craig Barrow, 8 October 1914, WC. Wymberley De Renne Coerr (1913–96) later achieved distinction in the U.S. diplomatic service (*New York Times*, 23 October 1996).

49. Duncan Pringle to WJDeR, 9 October [1903], laid in *A Bachelor's Reverie*, DeRGL; WJDeR to Worthington Ford, 12 December 1907, Ford to WJDeR, 27 December 1907, J. Franklin Jameson Papers, LoC.

50. Henry James, *The Ivory Tower*, 23; St. George's School, Newport, R.I., *Lance* (1908), 40, 46, 50, 97, 106, 121. To family and friends, WWDeR was often known as "W. W." during his boyhood, "Wymberley" thereafter. A copy of "The International Races at Savannah" is in DeRFP+-39. For a detailed account of Savannah's racing days, see Julian K. Quattlebaum, *The Great Savannah Races* (Athens, 1983).

51. Transcripts, University of Georgia, Columbia University, DeRFP+-10; Preston Brooks to WJDeR, 20 November 1909, DeRFP-40; *Pandora*, 1911–12; W. W. De Renne, "College Periodicals," *Georgian*, May 1911, 275–77.

52. Transcripts, Columbia University, DeRFP+-10; Audrey Coerr to WWDeR, 9 February [1924?], DeRFP-18; W. W. De Renne and Geo. S. Kaufman, "That Infernal Machine. A Play in One Act," [Copyright 1915 by Geo. S. Kaufman], Kaufman Papers, LoC. In this comic three-character trifle, a bashful businessman argues with his friend over whether to use the titular machine—a dictatograph—to propose to his stenographer. One authority on Kaufman sees the play as "a glimpse into the style that would eventually bring acclaim . . . as a playwright. The seeds of his comedic style are discernible in the dialogue, which is fast-paced and filled with repartee" (Rhoda-Gale Pollack, *George S. Kaufman* [Boston, 1988], 7).

53. De Renne Library Correspondence, DeRFP-40, 41, 42, 44, passim.

54. A. R. Lawton to William W. Wright, 10 April 1909, DeRFP-40; A. O. Bacon to WJDeR, 11 May 1911, J. R. Lamar to WJDeR, 12 May 1911, DeRFP+-1; GHS, *Annals* (1915), 10.

55. *NCAB*, 1:509; *Memoirs of Georgia*, 1:724–26; *Atlanta Journal*, 5 September 1910; *New York Times*, 6 September 1910.

56. U. B. Phillips to Waldo Leland, 16 January 1905, J. Franklin Jameson Papers, LoC; *Atlanta Constitution*, 6 September 1910. The Moore manuscript was "presented to a northern library" shortly before Brown's death (*Atlanta Journal*, 5 September 1910). Some two thousand of Brown's books went as a bequest to the Georgia Insitute of Technology in 1910. "Because the collection is especially strong in the humanities, and because of a desire that its resources be put to the best use, it has now been transferred to the Georgia State University Library, where it will remain on permanent loan" ("Bibles, Boccaccio, and Julius Brown," *Information In-*

terchange: A Newsletter of Policies and Services, Georgia State University Library 1 [April 1974]: 1).

57. *Memoirs of Georgia*, 1:724−25; Julius Brown to WJDeR, 10 October 1907, 30 January, 12 March 1908, DeRFP-40.

58. *DeRLC*, 2:673, 700, 786, 796, 3:897−98; *BRHG* (1911), 244−45.

59. *DGB*, 1:121−22; Joseph Mackey Brown to WJDeR, 9 November 1910, DeRFP-16.

60. Julius Brown to WJDeR, 10 October 1907, DeRFP-40.

61. *DGB*, 1:237−38; Coulter, *Wormsloe*, 288n.15; Telamon Smith [Cuyler] to WJDeR, 26 March 1903, DeRFP-42. Cuyler later claimed that he and WJDeR had agreed to split Georgia collecting between them, with De Renne concentrating on books and Cuyler on manuscripts. But by the time the two met, WJDeR had lost most of his interest in manuscripts and would in any case have outmatched Cuyler in competing for Georgia items of any kind. Cuyler always appears to have invested more money, time, and energy into being a boulevardier than a collector.

62. Scoggins, "Telamon Cuyler and Korea," 7, 8, 15. Cuyler also applied the name "Beverwyck" to his middle Georgia plantation in Jones County, near the hamlet of Wayside, but later settled on "Wychehil" as its name.

Regarding Cuyler's name change, WJDeR wrote, "I congratulate you on changing the order of your name—You will be much safer from prying eyes in your correspondence & delivered from the nuisance of opening other peoples' letters" (WJDeR to TC, 4 December 1904, TCC-169).

Besides Cuyler, two other midstate acquaintances of WJDeR's were the Macon historians and collectors George Gilman Smith (1836−1913) and Claud Estes (1857−1917). Smith, chronicler of Georgia Methodism, also wrote a 555-page history of Georgia; he felt so beholden to Colonel Jones for his material that his index listed pages 1−555 after the colonel's name, but he had also made use of the De Renne Collection at the State Library. He regretted that he was "too lame" to visit Wormsloe; crippled by a wound during the Civil War, he had been in a rolling chair ever since. Estes, a lawyer believed to own "one of the prize libraries of the State," offered to sell his Georgia books to De Renne. He was also considered an authority on Georgia's Confederate troops (Harold Lawrence, ed., *Methodist Preachers in Georgia, 1783−1900* [Tignall, Ga., 1984], 505; Smith, *The Story of Georgia and the Georgia People*, 658; George Gilman Smith to WJDeR, 10 May, 10 August 1905, DeRHM; *Macon Telegraph*, 31 July 1917; Claud Estes to WJDeR, 16 December 1911, DeRFP-40).

63. TC to A. B. Caldwell, 9 May 1907, TCC-114.

64. WJDeR to TC, 13 March, 4, 30 December 1904, TCC-169; TC to WJDeR, 14 November 1907, DeRFP-42; WJDeR to TC, 27 February 1906, WC.

65. TC to WJDeR, 31 January 1910, DeRFP-40; A. M. Broadley, *Chats on Auto-graphs* (London, 1910), 13, 321–24. The Broadley-Cuyler correspondence is in TCC-154. In his book, Broadley mentioned that his "enthusiastic friend" was the "proud possessor of a holograph document containing seven times the name of Button Gwinnett." After the deaths of WJDeR and Charles Edgeworth Jones (1867–1931), Cuyler claimed, dubiously, that he had gotten "quite a batch of documents" from them, including some in the hand of Button Gwinnett. One of these was purchased for $3,000 in 1936 by the firm of Thomas F. Madigan. Mrs. Madigan wrote Cuyler in 1939 that several authorities had "questioned its authenticity" and that she had compared it with other documents that had recently come on the market, purport-edly written by Gwinnett. Though none matched Gwinnett's holograph will (for-merly owned by Colonel Jones and by that time in the J. Pierpont Morgan Library), all matched the handwriting in the body of a document (purchased from Cuyler) supposedly signed by Sir James Wright (Mrs. Thomas F. Madigan to TC, 4 De-cember 1939, TCC-155).

66. TC to WJDeR, 8 November 1909, DeRFP-42; Telamon Smith Cuyler, *A Roster of the Surviving General Officers of the Confederate States Army, 1861–1865* (Mamaroneck, N,Y., 1905). A copy of the roster is in the Charles Edgeworth Jones Papers at Duke. The Cuyler collection at the University of Georgia contains little information on the Beverwyck Quartos (TCC-154 contains most of what there is) and lacks copies of most of the quartos. The *National Union Catalogue* lists only three Cuyler titles, two of them quartos, the second of which is a brief genealogical work on his family, of which there is a copy in DeRFP-42.

67. TC to WJDeR, 12 February 1905, DeRFP-42; TC to A. B. Caldwell, 9 May 1907, TCC-114; Works Progress Administration, *Georgia Land Grants*, collected by Telamon Cuyler (N.p., n.d.); Works Progress Administration, *Georgia Colonial Wills*, collected by Telamon Cuyler [Savannah, 1938]; *DGB*, 1:238. In his *Telamon Cuyler* (p. [5]), Cuyler remarks of himself that he "looks the cultured aristocrat and would be noted in any company."

68. A. McC. Duncan to WJDeR, 8 June 1909, DeRFP-16. U. B. Phillips, who was present when Cuyler was given his first glimpse of the Jones Confederate Col-lection, wrote WJDeR: "I shall doubtless develop a strong sense of being tantalized by my distance from your library; but even if worst comes to the worst, I shall never be so dejected as our entertaining friend Cuyler after his view of the revelation. Luckily, you see, I haven't the collector's jealous instinct" (UBP to WJDeR, 18 April 1909, DeRFP-38).

69. TC to Governor Joseph M. Terrell, 26 March 1905, TCC-169; TC to WJDeR, 27 October 1910 (Telegram), DeRFP-40. Between 1902 and 1918 (when the De-partment of Archives and History was finally established) the successive compilers

of records did much work in gathering and publishing Georgia's colonial, revolutionary, and Confederate records. Almost all of the records gathered in England in the 1830s by the Reverend Charles Wallace Howard had been destroyed by fire in 1891 while on loan to an Emory College professor, Henry A. Scomp. The copying process had to be done and paid for anew by the state, though WJDeR, in one of his early forays into the publication of manuscripts, considered financing the project himself (Bryan, "Recent Archival Developments in Georgia," 57; Henry N. Stevens to WJDeR, 14 August 1902, DeRFP-40).

70. "Telamon S. Cuyler Is Back in Atlanta Dazed, Demented," *Atlanta Journal*, 2 February 1911; *New York Times*, 5 April 1915. Several clippings lampooning Cuyler's change of name are found in TCC-113; many of WJDeR's Cuyler clippings are in DeRFP+-36.

71. Scoggins, "Telamon Cuyler and Korea," 4, 6–7; Phillips, "Public Archives of Georgia," 454; Cobb, "Condition of Georgia's Archives," 34–35; Jack, "Preservation of Georgia History," 248–51.

72. According to data from the accession folder of the Collection of Georgia Books and Manuscripts of Telamon Cuyler (1873–1951), the university paid Cuyler $3,000 in 1937 and an additional $1,500 to his estate in 1956 for materials that had not been transferred earlier. The papers, dated 1659–1951, contain around sixty-two thousand items. Many of Cuyler's books are shelved in the general library.

After having been located for several years in the capitol building, the Department of Archives and History was in 1930 moved to the picturesque Rhodes Castle, a former residence of some twenty rooms on Peachtree Street, where problems with the security and safety of the holdings eventually arose again. The move back to the capitol's environs, to the Archives and Records Building (constructed at a cost of over $6 million) came in 1965 (Bryan, "Recent Archival Developments in Georgia," 58; Sparks, "Magnificent Home for Georgia's Past," 11). Even in the new building, pilferage was not unknown, but stringent regulations regarding original records finally seem to have made them safe.

73. Ford, "Manuscripts and Historical Archives," 77–78.

74. UBP to WJDeR, 6 February 1905, DeRFP-38; Dillon, *Ulrich Bonnell Phillips*, 12; Phillips, "Public Archives of Georgia," 439–74; UBP to WJDeR, 23 February 1905, DeRFP-38; Van Tassel, "The American Historical Association and the South," 482. Among the best sources on UBP are the biographies by Merton L. Dillon (1985) and John Herbert Roper (1984) and *Ulrich Bonnell Phillips: A Southern Historian and His Critics* (Westport, Conn., 1990), edited by John David Smith and John C. Inscoe.

75. GHS Minute Book, 3:105; WJDeR to Otis Ashmore, 28 February 1896, WJDeR Correspondence File, GHS.

76. WJDeR to William Harden, 5 May 1896, WJDeR Correspondence File, GHS; Georgia Historical Society, *Descriptive Circular,* (1903) [1−2].

77. *SMN,* 9 January 1900; WJDeR's Eulogy on Colonel John Screven, 5 February 1900, KRC-7, UGAL; GHS, *Collections,* 5, Part 2, [3].

78. *SMN,* 13 February 1903.

79. Ibid.; Georgia Historical Society, *Descriptive Circular* (1903), [3].

80. UBP to Lucien H. Boggs, 23 February 1903, UBPP.

81. Ibid.

82. UBP to George J. Baldwin, 17 April 1903, UBPP. Phillips felt that the society's most important policy should be "to keep the old fossils out of office, and prevent the Society from becoming antiquarian rather than historical. The antiquarian tendency is always the most dangerous foe to the usefulness and life of historical societies. Of course, the genealogists and the collectors of arrow-heads, who think they are historical students, must be coddled sometimes; for practical work men of true historical interest and training must be had." He identified William Harden himself as "sort of a fossil—though well meaning." Another suggestion, that the society should "apply for State aid," would much later be acted on (and seen as the society's salvation) when in 1966 the society's library became a branch depository of the Georgia Department of Archives and History, staffed by state archivists, bringing "the blessing of having the State assist in paying some of the bills that had become so burdensome." This relationship ended in 1997, when the state privatized the GHS Library, while continuing its status as a branch depository. Since "the Society's library and archives will be administered by the Society," there was a "phasing out" of three of the state archivists (UBP to George J. Baldwin, 17 April 1903, UBPP; UBP to Waldo Leland, 16 January 1905, J. Franklin Jameson Papers, LoC; UBP to George J. Baldwin, 4 May 1903, UBPP; Britt, *Overture to the Future,* 13; *GHS Footnotes* 23 (Spring−Summer 1997): [1])

83. UBP to George J. Baldwin, 2, 5, 9 May 1903, 11 July 1908, George J. Baldwin to UBP, 4 May 1903 (Telegram), 19 June 1903, UBPP; GHS, *Collections,* 6:4. The Montiano letters were published in 1909, in the first part of volume 7 of the *Collections.*

In regard to the society's publications in general, UBP advised that enough be printed—both for sale and distribution (to university libraries more than to other historical societies)—to be "within easy access of workers." Strictly limited editions, he felt, defeated the purpose. As an example, he wrote, "The Wormsloe Quartos are comparatively useless, because a copy can never be had when a student wants to use it" (UBP to Lucien Boggs, 3 March 1903, UBPP).

84. George Parker Winship to WJDeR, 19 October 1905, DeRFP-40.

85. A. R. Lawton to UBP, 20 February 1909, UBP Correspondence File, GHS.

86. Ibid.

87. A. R. Lawton to UBP, 9, 22 March 1909, UBP to A. R. Lawton, 29 March 1909, UBP Correspondence File, GHS; WJDeR to A. R. Lawton, 1 April 1909, WJDeR Correspondence File, GHS. The previous year Phillips had expressed his "very great pleasure" that WJDeR had published the Lumpkin manuscripts and "rendered a large service to Georgia and to American historical scholarship." Phillips had considered the Lumpkin manuscripts the "most valuable . . . in private hands in Georgia" and had hoped the society would secure them for him to edit (UBP to WJDeR, 10 May 1908, DeRFP-38; UBP to Lucien Boggs, 26 March 1903, UBP to George J. Baldwin, 17 April 1903, UBPP).

88. *SMN*, 5 April 1909; UBP to the Telfair Academy, 16 August 1909, Telfair Family Papers-4, GHS.

89. "A Visit to 'Wormsloe' in April, A D 1909, with Original Photographs, Taken and Arranged by Telamon Cuyler. Paris 1909," DeRFP+-24; Ulrich B. Phillips, Review of *DeRLC*, *American Historical Review* 38 (October 1932): 174.

90. "Memoranda by U. B. Phillips for a conference with the committee of the Georgia Historical Society, at Wormsloe, April 9, 1909," UBP Correspondence File, GHS.

91. Ibid.; A. R. Lawton to UBP, 10 January 1913, DeRFP-33; List of Members, Georgia Historical Society, January 15, 1914, DeRFP-33. The Hawkins manuscripts were finally published in 1916 as volume 9 of the *Collections;* there would not be another volume until 1952.

92. UBP to George J. Baldwin, 2 May 1903, UBPP; *BRHG* (1911), 141−43.

93. *DeRLC*, 3:1082−83, 1119−20. The correspondence regarding the Spanish transcripts is in DeRFP-33.

94. GHS, *Collections,* 7, Part. 2, 40.

95. Charles Edgeworth Jones to WJDeR, 16 July 1910, WJDeR to Charles Edgeworth Jones, [27 July 1910 (Draft)], DeRFP-16; WJDeR to Walter G. Charlton, 16 May 1910, DeRFP-47; *DeRLC*, 3:961.

96. WJDeR to Walter G. Charlton, 16 May, 14 May 1910 (Telegram), DeRFP-47.

97. *BRHG* (1905); *BRHG* (1911). WJDeR to C. DeW. Willcox, 21 May 1912, DeRFP-33, notes that six hundred items were added to the library between April 1911 and May 1912.

98. *NCAB*, 55:355−56. The firm of Henry Stevens, Son & Stiles applauded WJDeR's decision to employ a cataloger: "Cataloguing is easy enough to those who are used to doing it, but worrying, tiresome work to the amateur. We think you were quite wise in securing professional assistance" (Henry Stevens, etc., to WJDeR, 26 January 1911, DeRFP-54). Correspondence between WJDeR and Oscar Wegelin (1876−1970) regarding the 1911 catalog is in DeRFP-16; the original glass

negatives for the facsimiles that illustrated the catalog are in DeRFP-42A. Wegelin undertook to advertise the catalog, which he described as "A Bibliography of Georgia," and took orders for it, as is shown by a leaflet in the American Antiquarian Society's copy of the catalog. The printing of the 1911 catalog cost WJDeR just over $1,000 (Bill, dated 1 April 1911, DeRFP-38).

99. *BRHG* (1911), 142. Reviews of the 1911 catalog appeared in the *Atlanta Constitution*, 12 May 1911, the *Boston Evening Transcript*, 21 July 1911, and the *Nation* 93 (17 August 1911): 141.

100. WJDeR to Worthington Ford, 1 November 1910 (Draft), DeRFP-41; C. Mildred Thompson to WJDeR, 20 July 1910, DeRFP-42; C. Mildred Thompson to WJDeR, 5 May 1911, DeRFP+-1.

101. David C. Barrow to WJDeR, 22 February 1907, WJDeR to David C. Barrow, 7 March 1907, David C. Barrow Papers-2, UGAL-A; WJDeR to Preston Brooks, 28 May 1914 (Draft), DeRFP-40; Resolution of the Trustees, 16 June 1914, Minutes of the Board of Trustees, Vol. 6, 1887–1914, UGAL-A. The resolution calls for the "W. J. De Renne Chair of Southern History," but other correspondence, the *Pandora* (1915–19), and the University *Bulletin* (1915–20) call it the "De Renne Chair of Georgia History." Brooks resigned from the university in 1919 and went into banking. When he returned at Chancellor Barrow's request the next year, it was to become dean of the School of Commerce (commonly called the business school), where he stayed until retirement. Perhaps for this reason, his memoir, *Under Seven Flags*, gives very little information about his years as a history professor (*DGB*, 1:116–17).

102. Preston Brooks to WJDeR, 9 October 1907, 2 January 1908, 28 September 1914, DeRFP-40. WJDeR normally answered any queries sent to his library, but he could be stern with researchers who displayed a weak grasp of certain facets of Georgia history. As one transgressor wrote apologetically: "I regret my careless mention of 'criminals' in conjunction with 'debtors.' It is one of those unfortunate phrases which one finds in print and consequently takes for granted" (Lawrence Shaw Mayo to WJDeR, 7 March 1914, DeRFP-40).

Also during 1914 James Ross McCain (1881–1965) wrote WJDeR that he was "so well known as the best student of Georgia colonial history" that he hoped he would read and make suggestions on his Ph.D dissertation, "The Executive in Proprietary Georgia, 1732–1752." WJDeR did so and also invited McCain to come to Wormsloe to do research in the library. McCain's dissertation was later expanded into *Georgia as a Proprietary Province: The Execution of a Trust* (Boston, 1917), "a seminal work in the history of the Georgia colony" (J. R. McCain to WJDeR, 5 March, 13 April 1914, DeRFP-40; *DGB*, 2:648).

103. Preston Brooks to WJDeR, 2 January 1909, DeRFP-40.

104. *DeRLC*, 3:1372–73. For a chronological bibliography of Brooks's works see his selected writings, *Georgia Studies;* his historical works, listed on pages 295–98, include such race-related entries as "A Local Study of the Race Problem" (1911) and a letter to the *Nation*, "A Southern Professor on Lynching" (1916).

105. Brooks, *History of Georgia* (1913; 2d ed., rev. and abridged, 1918); Illustrations from the De Renne Library used in the *History;* Robert Preston Brooks Collection-1, UGAL; Brooks, comp., *Preliminary Bibliography of Georgia History*. The three-hundred-book bibliography was "a basis for a more extended bibliography, as well as a guide for University students pursuing courses in Georgia history." Since copies were also to be sent to university alumni, it was hoped that it would prompt contributions, for the alumni would be "impressed by the lack of material in the University bearing on our local history."

In 1914, university librarian Duncan Burnet asked WJDeR for a contribution of $250–$500 to buy Georgiana for the library. De Renne sent a $500 check by return mail, which Burnet invested, using the income from the "De Renne fund" to purchase books as late as 1939. Those volumes, many of which remain in the general collection of the library, are identified by a special bookplate that Burnet prepared (Duncan Burnet to WJDeR, 11 April 1914, DeRFP-40; WJDeR to Duncan Burnet, 15 April 1914, Accession File, DeRGL; Burnet, "The Libraries of the University System of Georgia," *Lavonia* (Ga.) *Times*, 27 October 1939).

106. A. R. Lawton to WJDeR, 29 December 1913, DeRFP-33. WJDeR himself had become a member of the AHA in 1905. From its inception in 1884 ("the year that trained historians took over the job of recording America's past"), the AHA had maintained a tenuous presence in the South, which, "though never heavily represented," was always "*well* represented" in the organization. The region was, for a time, considered to present "the greatest obstacles to the spread of scientific history" in the United States. Helping to nudge the South into the mainstream, the AHA stirred historical interest through reports on southern archives and publications of southern state bibliographies. Perhaps most helpfully, many historians, both northern and southern, began during the late nineteenth and early twentieth centuries to write more consciously as Americans and admitted that the traditional sectional histories of both regions had been "biased and bad." The Charleston convention, visited by Lawton and the other Savannahians, heard William A. Dunning, "a professional historian who had made his reputation in Southern history, deliver his presidential address"—"a fitting climax to the pioneer period of scientific history in the South." There was a similar resonance to the Boston-raised Jameson being asked to serve as the main speaker at the Georgia Historical Soci-

ety's seventy-fifth anniversary (BAK to WJDeR, 4 March 1905, DeRFP-13; Van Tassel, *Recording America's Past,* vii; Van Tassel, "The American Historical Association and the South," 467, 470, 476–77, 479–81).

107. *SEP,* 12 February 1914; *SMN,* 13 February 1914.

108. "Georgia's Foremost Citizen," undated, unidentified clipping, DeRFP+-36; J. Franklin Jameson to WJDeR, 23 February 1914, J. Franklin Jameson Papers, LoC; Donnan and Stock, eds., *An Historian's World,* 297.

Brooks recalled that Jameson's address, "The History of Historical Societies," was delivered "at great length to a somewhat restless group" (Brooks, "Wormsloe House," 150).

Governor Slaton had earlier visited Wormsloe in 1911 and had written WJDeR: "The pleasure of my visit to Savannah was immeasurably enhanced by the privilege of a visit to Wormsloe, and the opportunity of observing the invaluable service you had rendered Georgia. The basis of patriotism is attachment to locality. I believe the love of every Georgian for his native State would be stimulated by a knowledge of your home and the work in which you are engaged" (John M. Slaton to WJDeR, 14 December 1911, DeRFP-40). WJDeR took Slaton's side in the controversy over Leo Frank; he followed the Frank trial and aftermath closely (collecting numerous clippings) and sent monetary contributions to Frank (DeRFP-36).

109. Herbert Putnam to WJDeR, 18 June 1909, LLM to Herbert Putnam, 8 May 1916, Library of Congress Archives, LoC.

110. Worthington Ford to WJDeR, 26 June 1905, ibid.; Worthington Ford to WJDeR, 15 June 1915, in "Personal Comments on Lee Letters," DeRFP-42; Dillon, *Ulrich Bonnell Phillips,* 77; *NCAB,* 4:225–26.

111. Worthington Ford to WJDeR, 6, 10 October, 1 November 1910, DeRFP-41; "Earliest Georgia Papers," DeRFP-33. As his father had been, WJDeR was generous with his gifts to the GHS, including copies of the quartos and rare maps (GHS Acknowledgments, DeRFP-40, passim; *DeRLC,* 3:1209, 1217).

112. Herbert Putnam to WJDeR, 24 April 1916, Library of Congress Archives, LoC. The map WJDeR offered was "Carolinas, Upper Florida, & Louisiana," c. 1720; it is reproduced opposite page 38 of GHS *Collections,* 7, Pt. 1.

Though unmentioned by him, security and preservation may have also concerned Putnam. The environment of the books and manuscripts in the Wormsloe library was not comparable to that of the Library of Congress, which, for example, had no fireplaces. Also, given the effect of temperature and humidity on library materials, the Georgia coast was not the best location for a collection of rarities. WJDeR, however, took various steps to protect his materials, not least of which was having the great doors securely locked when the library was not in use. Standard procedure was for the building to be "opened on all fine days (windows). On dark & wet days to be left closed with fans turned on from 10 to 12 AM." At least in part because of the need of fans for ventilation, the caretaker at Wormsloe was directed "to keep electricity up for the library only" when the De Rennes were not in residence. Whatever the case, the books of the De Renne Georgia Library today seem to have suffered no obvious damage from their decades on the Isle of Hope (*Guide to the Library of Congress* [Washington, D.C., 1988], 10; Entry for 26 April–19 May 1913, Brown Cash Book, 1899–1916, DeRFP-15; Entry for 9 January 1916, 1916 Date Book, DeRFP-14).

113. LLM to Herbert Putnam, 8 May 1916, DeRFP-14; Birrell, *Obiter Dicta,* 291; WJDeR to Herbert Putnam, 26 May 1916 (Draft), DeRFP-43.

114. Dickinson, *Dictionary of American Book Collectors,* 215–16. The best sources on Mackall's life are *GHQ* 22 (March 1938)—a number issued "In Memoriam Leonard Leopold Mackall," and William W. Mackall, *Character Sketch of the Late Leonard Leopold Mackall.* Sketches of both Mackall and WJDeR appear in Dickinson's *Dictionary of American Book Collectors.*

115. GHS Minute Book, 6:437–38; GHS Minute Book, 7:53, 85–90.

116. WJDeR to Charles Edgeworth Jones, 10 April 1916, DeRFP+-1.

117. Most of the voluminous Mackall correspondence is in DeRFP-43.

118. WJDeR to David C. Barrow, 12 August 1914, DeRFP-40; Laura De Renne to Dr. Craig Barrow, [11 February 1912], WC; Specifications of the Labor and Materials Required in the Erection of a Family Burial Vault, Bonaventure Cemetery, DeRFP+-10; Blueprints of Family Burial Vault, DeRFP+-33; Death Certificates of Laura De Renne and WJDeR, Municipal Archives, New York City.

119. Dr. Francis W. Murray to Dr. Craig Barrow, 21 November 1914, WC. Dr. Murray (1855–1929) was a member of the Union Club like the De Renne brothers and had followed much the same course of medical study as Everard had (*NCAB,* 27:227–28).

120. Record of Check ($2,000), WJDeR to Gari Melchers, 20 February 1915, DeRFP-15. The Gari Melchers portrait of WJDeR was exhibited at the Telfair Academy, along with three other portraits and thirteen paintings by Melchers, 7–27 February 1916. This marked the first event at the Telfair for which electric lighting was used for evening exhibitions. A total of 5,805 visitors were recorded during the period, 1,877 of them coming on the last day alone. During the Gari Melchers Retrospective Exhibition of 1990–91, the portrait was again exhibited at the Telfair, 5 June–5 August 1990 (Telfair Academy of Arts and Sciences, Special Exhibition Catalogue [1916]), DeRFP+-Miscellaneous Books; GHS Minute Book, 7:160; Diane Lesko and Esther Persson, eds., *Gari Melchers: A Retrospective Exhibition* [St. Petersburg, Fla., 1990]).

121. *SEP,* 2 November 1915. Captain Duncan, who died of ptomaine poisoning, bequeathed to WJDeR his "ollapodrida" of clippings, scrapbooks, and manuscript notes on Georgia's (particularly Savannah's) military history. This collection is submerged, unidentified, within the DeRFP, principally in Boxes 45, 46, 47, 48, and 57.

122. WJDeR to LLM, 16 April 1916 (Draft), DeRFP-43; LLM, Manuscript notes opposite the title pages of *History of Georgia* and *Charters* . . . , both dated August 1916, DeRGL; *SMN,* 24 June 1916; Audrey Coerr to WWDeR, [11 March 1923], DeRFP-18; Marcel Proust, *À La Recherche du Temps Perdu,* 3 vols. (Paris: Gallimard, 1954), 3: 188; *SMN,* 27 June 1916.

123. R. P. Brooks, "Notable Contribution to State by Late Wymberley De Renne," *Atlanta Constitution,* 7 July 1916.

124. GHS, *Proceedings* (1917): 14–15.

125. DSF to WWDeR, 23 June 1916 (Telegram), DeRFP-14. Six years after his death a comprehensive sketch of WJDeR appeared in *The National Cyclopaedia of American Biography,* illustrated by the Melchers portrait and a facsimile signature (*NCAB,* 18 : 390–91).

CHAPTER 11. Mortmain

1. For examples of the Pennsylvania Company's buying, selling, building, and lending see Superior Court Judgments: Boxes 180:14717, 196:15420, 206:15816, and 224:16568, GHS. The extensive 1903 renovation of the De Renne Block on Bay Street included electrification of the buildings (for lights and fans) and replacement with interior staircases of the narrow exterior stairs, shown in George N. Barnard's wartime photograph of the Savannah waterfront. This property would remain with GWJDeR's descendants, at least in part, until the mid-1980s, after which it became a riverfront hotel (Photograph 50, Barnard, *Photographic Views;* Clipping, c. May 1903, DeRFP+-36; DB 123P: 308–18, DB 127R: 301–15, SCR). WJDeR's income is shown in Ledgers, DeRFP-12.

2. The status of the De Renne estate in 1916 is shown in the Schedules of Distribution, Estate of GWJDeR, DeRFP-13.

3. Schedules of Distribution, Georgia and Pennsylvania Accounts of the Estate of GWJDeR, EDeRBC; WWDeR to L&C, 3 January 1917, WC; DB 13D:189, SCR; "List of De Renne Property and Tenants," DeRFP-13, L&C, Estate of De Renne, Schedule of Receipts, 1 February 1917 to 31 January 1918, WC.

4. Will and Estate Records of WJDeR, PCR.

5. Ibid.; *SMN,* 25 June 1916; *SEP,* 2 July 1916. There was a further proviso in the will to WWDeR's benefit: if one of his sisters predeceased WJDeR, her share would go to him.

In present-day dollars the legacies of the heirs of GWJDeR and WJDeR were much greater. The estate of J. Pierpont Morgan, for example, was valued at around $68 million at his death in 1913 but was calculated to be worth over $800 million "in 1989 dollars" (Ron Chernow, *The House of Morgan* [New York, 1990], 158).

6. DB 13D:196, SCR; DB 13D:195, SCR; Financial Records, 1917, WWDeRP-79; WWDeR to Mrs. Fontaine Barden, 31 March 1938, DeRFP+-2. The sums paid to the sisters in February are the only such payments in the financial records for 1917; if there was some informal quid pro quo, no record of it has been found.

7. Audrey Coerr to WWDeR, 8 November 1923, and other of her letters of the 1920s, DeRFP-18; George Bird Evans, "A Man of Principle," [2], in Charles C. Norris, *Eastern Upland Shooting* (Traverse City, Mich., 1990), a reprint of the 1946 edition.

8. WJDeR to Dr. Craig Barrow, 22 November 1911, WC; WWDeR, Diploma, Bachelor of Arts Degree, 7 June 1916, DeRFP+-10.

9. WWDeR, Military Records, DeRFP+-8, and WWDeR File, National Archives and Records Administration; WWDeR to Augusta Floyd, 3 February 1918, WWDeRP-8.

10. *DGB*, 1:316; *SEP*, 16 December 1949.

11. *SMN*, 10 March 1918.

12. "At Home" Announcement, Dempsey Hotel, DeRFP-58; WWDeR to Augusta De Renne, 21, 24 November 1918, WWDeRP-8.

13. WWDeR to Augusta De Renne, 29 October 1918, WWDeRP-8; WWDeR, Military Records, DeRFP+-8. The Thirty-first ("Dixie") Division was composed of National Guardsmen from Georgia, Florida, and Alabama (Shipley Thomas, *History of the A.E.F.* [New York, 1920], 482).

14. WWDeR to T. P. Ravenel, 19 February 1912, WWDeR Correspondence File, GHS; Minute Book, 6:377, GHS; WWDeR to William Harden, 28 April 1920, WWDeR Correspondence File, GHS; *GHQ* 16 (1932): 56. Though it was announced in 1921 that manuscripts from the De Renne library were to be published in the *Georgia Historical Quarterly*, based on selections of the *Quarterly*'s editorial board, nothing seems to have come of the plan (*GHQ* 5 [March 1921]: 71).

15. Financial Records, 1915–35, WWDeRP-79; Georges Bignault, Landscape Architect, to WWDeR, 16, 22 February 1917, WWDeRP-8; Legal Agreement relating to Construction of Gate House, 8 August 1917, DeRFP-30. During the same period, another structure, used in part as a smithy for working wrought iron, apparently was built near the water to the west of the gatehouse.

16. Library Announcement, 10 July 1916, DeRFP+-36.

17. Financial Material, 1916–18, WWDeRP-79; Minutes, Board of Regents, University System of Georgia, Fiscal Year 1 July 1937, through 30 June, 1938, 22, UGAL-A; Mackall, "Preface," *DeRLC*, 1:xxi. Individual biographical summaries

and lists of associated materials from Setz's voluminous "Partial List of Letters, Papers and Documents Relating to Noble Jones, His Descendants and Connections" are found in the DeRFP with some of the manuscripts they helped to identify and organize.

The eccentric William Price (1860–1936), a lifelong bachelor like Mackall, later wrote that "the stars themselves directed [his] humble destiny within Wormsloe's noble horizons." He was described in Yale's 1910 record of the Class of 1883 (p. 207), as his class's "most multiplex linguist and doubtless he excels us all in his store of uncommon, interesting, but unremunerative knowledge." Long after he left Wormsloe for Texas, he kept up with the De Rennes and occasionally received much-needed money gifts from WWDeR (William Price to WWDeR, 10 April 1923, 17 February 1925, DeRFP-58).

18. LLM to Oscar Wegelin, 18 July 1916, DeRFP-43.

19. WJDeR to Charles Edgeworth Jones, 10 April 1916, Charles Edgeworth Jones Papers, DUL; Cole, comp., *Catalogue of the Library of E. D. Church*, 1:v; Grolier Club, *Grolier 75*, 14.

20. Mackall, "Preface," *DeRLC*, 1:xxi; Financial Material, 1916–18, WWDeRP-79. Most of LLM's correspondence relating to the library and the catalog is in DeRFP-43 and in the De Renne Georgia Library Accession File, UGAL.

21. Grolier Club, *Grolier 75*, 54–55; Mackall, "Preface," *DeRLC*, 1:xxi; *Library Journal* 42 (July 1917): 579.

22. LLM to T. L. Cole, 1 January 1918, DeRFP-43; Mackall, "Preface," *DeRLC*, 1:xxi.

23. Mackall, "De Renne Georgia Library," 63; Mackall, "Preface," *DeRLC*, 1:xxiii; Dickinson, *Dictionary of American Book Collectors*, 215–16. As a harbinger of his speech to the Georgia Historical Society, Mackall had in April 1918 addressed the Georgia Senate on the subject of the De Renne Georgia Library (LLM to WWDeR, 15 April 1918, DeRFP-43).

24. WWDeR to Audrey Coerr, 5 July 1924, DeRFP-44 (describing the work done on the catalog from 1916 to 1924); McKay, comp., *American Book Auction Catalogues*, 19–21; Mackall, "Preface," *DeRLC*, 1:xxiii.

Azalea Hallett Clizbee (1877–1935) also produced a few brief genealogical reference works, mainly tombstone inscriptions and baptismal records, all in the New York Public Library. Her "Curtis Walters, American Binder; An Appreciation" appeared in the *American Book Collector* 2 (August–September 1932): 124–34.

25. *Savannah City Directory* (1920).

26. *SEP*, 1 July, 13 August 1919; *SMN*, 21 June, 11 July 1906; L&C, Estate of De Renne, Schedule of Receipts, 1 February 1917 to 31 January 1918, WC; *SEP*, 26 June 1920; DB 15M:59, SCR.

27. *SEP*, 1 July, 13 August 1919; DB 14H:176–79, DB 14D:446, DB 15D:400, SCR (Copies of pertinent indentures are also in DeRFP-27); Notes of Conversation with A. R. Lawton, 30 January 1955, WCHC; *SMN*, 1 January, 16 March 1920; DB 14M:5, SCR.

28. *SMN*, 26 September 1920; *Savannah City Directory* (1920). The heirs of GWJDeR apparently sold the Clinton Street residence in 1919 (Trust Officer, Pennsylvania Company, to EDeRB, 29 July 1919, WC). Among the properties purchased for the construction of the De Renne Apartments was the house and lot that WJDeR had purchased in the 1890s, where the Barrows had lived. Additional information regarding the apartments was provided from the files of the De Renne Plaza Condominiums, successor to the De Renne Apartments. The sixty-fifth anniversary of the building was celebrated with a restoration of "the lobby's original appearance and grandeur."

29. *SEP*, 4 September 1919, 17 September 1920; *SMN*, 1 January 1920; Tindall, *Emergence of the New South*, 111; Coulter, *Georgia*, 431.

30. *SEP*, 17 March 1920.

31. *SMN*, 11 January 1920; DB 15T:198, SCR; Audrey Coerr to WWDeR, 11 March 1923, DeRFP-18.

Audrey and Wymberley were allies from childhood. Only two years separated them, while Elfrida was five years older than Audrey and entered young adulthood when the other two—whose personalities were more compatible—were still at play. Ophelia Dent's frequent presence with the De Rennes was to accommodate Audrey, who wished to have a young girl her age with them. From the time Audrey learned of Wymberley's financial disaster, she went to extraordinary lengths to assist him. Ironically, his reverses came when he was almost the age his father had been when his Buena Ventura dream had evaporated, but he had no safety net of generous annuities (DeRFP-18 and WWDeRP-1,2,3, passim).

32. DB 25C:258, SCR; L&C to WWDeR, EDeRB, and Audrey Howland, 16 August 1929, WC.

33. Augusta De Renne to Mrs. J. F. Minis, 14 August 1919, DeRFP+-1; KDeR-A:4; Mrs. Gamble Latrobe to Eudora De Renne Roebling, 9 October 1969, DeRFP+-2; William Garrard to WWDeR, 13 November 1924, DeRFP+-1; *SMN*, 28 October 1929.

34. *GHQ* 6 (1922): 128; *GHQ* 12 (1928): 72, 95; Meldrim, *An Historic Pilgrimage*, [1]; Gamble, comp., *Georgia Miscellany*, 2:158–59, Savannah Public Library (1921 meeting of the Colonial Dames in the Wormsloe Library); *SMN*, 5 April 1925, 29 March 1926, 31 March 1927, 16 February 1929; Lockwood, comp., *Gardens of Colony and State*, 223; *Atlanta Constitution*, 12 December 1926.

35. *SEP*, 1 April, 24 September 1927, 12 February 1936; *Atlanta Constitution*,

17 March 1929; Savannah Board of Trade to Louis S. Moore, 7 March 1929, Wormsloe Vertical File, UGAL.

Though she came to prefer such organizations as the Colonial Dames and the Married Woman's Card Club, Augusta De Renne was also among the early leaders of Savannah's League of Women Voters, and—unlike others in the League who wanted to delay women's initial participation—she advocated that women should vote in the election of November 1920 (*SEP*, 17 September 1920).

36. Coulter, *Wormsloe*, 26–27; WWDeR to Augusta De Renne, 21 November 1918, WWDeRP-8; De Renne, "The Formal Garden at Wormsloe," 24. During a trip to England in 1922, Mrs. De Renne examined several gardens, including those at Stratford-on-Avon (Augusta De Renne to WWDeR, 30 July 1922, DeRFP-18).

37. De Renne, "The Formal Garden at Wormsloe," 24–25; Cooney, comp., *Garden History of Georgia*, 372. In 1923, the former De Renne mansion was acquired from the Georgia Hussars by the Knights of Columbus of Savannah, who still own it. The wrought iron in question, however, was described as having been from the Padelford house, since former owner Edward Padelford's name was more associated with the house than the De Renne's had been (DB 18T:164, SCR).

38. De Renne, "The Formal Garden at Wormsloe," 24–25; Cooney, comp., *Garden History of Georgia*, 372; Lockwood, comp., *Gardens of Colony and State*, 292.

39. De Renne, "The Formal Garden at Wormsloe," 24–25; Cooney, comp., *Garden History of Georgia*, 372. WWDeR had purchased the statuary in August 1916 from the Fine Arts Academy in Buffalo, New York. "Pippa Passes" and "The Dreamer" were the work of Louise Allen. "Sundial: Lilies" and "Young Girl with Ewer" were done by Lucy Currier Richards (Receipt, 19 August 1916, DeRFP+-7). The addition of the formal garden apparently led to the removal of the porte cochere, which had disappeared by 1929.

40. De Renne, "The Formal Garden at Wormsloe," 24–25. Since most of the slave cabins had been razed, the bricks that survived were used for the garden's walls; the flagstones, hauled from Savannah, had served as ship ballast (Cooney, comp., *Garden History of Georgia*, 370).

41. *The Garden Club of Georgia Yearbook* (1932), 6.

42. Susan Myrick, "Wormsloe Rich in Georgia History," *Macon Telegraph*, 24 March 1929; "The Intangible Lure of Wormsloe Gardens," *Resorts Life*, 19 March 1931, 6; *Hearst's Sunday American*, 17 March 1929. The expedient of turning an estate into a "money-making venture, by opening it to a mass public" would soon become commonplace. Biltmore House, in Asheville, North Carolina, was opened to the public in 1930, only thirty-five years after its formal opening as a residence. The trend would not begin in England until 1949, when the sixth Marquess of Bath opened Longleat to paying visitors (*Biltmore House and Gardens* [Asheville, N.C.,

1976], 3; David Cannadine, *The Decline and Fall of the British Aristocracy* [New Haven, 1990], 645–46).

43. *SEP*, 26 February, 24 September 1927; *SMN*, 31 March 1927, 30 March 1929.

44. *Hearst's Sunday American*, 17 March 1929; *SEP*, 24 September 1927, 8 February 1930; Interview with the Reverend Frank A. Jenkins, Jr., 28 April 1991; Steed, *Georgia*, 54–57. Open over several springs, daily from 11 to 6, the tearoom quickly became popular with tourists and also served as a "social rendezvous" for Savannahians, particularly the "horsey" set, who made it a destination when riding to "the salts." During the period that the gardens were open to the public, admission fees ranged from fifty cents to a dollar. Hours ranged from 9 or 10 in the morning until 5:30 P.M. or sundown (*SMN*, 15 March 1930; "Elizabeth's Letter," *SEP*, undated clipping, c. March 1930, DeRFP-31; Various Wormsloe Gardens brochures, DeRFP-31; *SMN*, 14 April 1929).

45. Interview with the Reverend Frank A. Jenkins, Jr., 28 April 1991; *Atlanta Journal*, 16 March 1929.

46. *SEP*, 24 September 1927, 17, 24 March 1928.

47. *Atlanta Journal*, 1 May 1932; Savannah Unit, Federal Writers' Project, *Savannah*, 169; *SMN*, 5 April 1929; *SEP*, 30 March 1926, 26 April 1933; *Hearst's Sunday American*, 17 March 1929; Interview with the Reverend Frank A. Jenkins, Jr., 28 April 1991; Announcement of Opening of Library to Researchers, 1935, WWDeRP-70; Amos Aschbach Ettinger, *James Edward Oglethorpe: Imperial Idealist* (Oxford, 1936), viii; Inscription in Wade's *Longstreet*, DeRGL; Heywood Pearce, Jr., *Benjamin H. Hill: Secession and Reconstruction* (Chicago, 1928), viii. The announcement noted that a "charge of one dollar is made for one afternoon's work" and that "meals and acccommodations" were available "at the residence" for "out-of-town students." Work could be done only on Monday and Thursday afternoons, from two until six; daily use was available through "special arrangements."

48. *SEP*, 28 January 1933. In 1933, Governor Eugene Talmadge traveled to New York City to speak at Flag Day and to place a stone excavated from Fort Wymberley at the "Liberty Pole" that was the focus of the annual exercises. Stones from all thirteen colonies were eventually dedicated (*SEP*, 23 May 1933; *SMN*, 17 June 1933).

49. *Macon Evening News*, 16 February 1929; *SEP*, 28 May 1929.

50. *SMN*, 13 March, 14 April 1929, 15 March 1930. Clippings of many of the 1929 articles on Wormsloe Gardens are in DeRFP-31.

51. *SEP*, 24 March 1928. WWDeR's list of contacts and much of his correspondence relating to his promotion of Wormsloe Gardens are in DeRFP-58. A 1929 Wormsloe Gardens brochure featured four color views by Savannah photographer George Foltz. As the work of two Savannah firms—the Dixie Engraving Company

and Braid and Hutton, Printers—the brochure was praised as a "very fine example" of what local craftsmen could do. WWDeR later commissioned A. T. S. Stoney (soon to provide plans and drawings for *Plantations of the Carolina Low Country*) to create a tourist map to Wormsloe. For several seasons, beginning in 1929, WWDeR also published pamphlet guides to several southern cities, particularly Savannah and Charleston. Of the kind distributed free to tourists by various advertisers, the pamphlets contained historical information and attractive maps and were enthusiastically supported by coastal businesses and tourist attractions (Undated clippings and map, DeRFP-31; Requests for Savannah and Charleston Pamphlets, 1929–34, DeRFP-58 and DeRFP+-4). Some of the brochures are in DeRFP+-38.

52. KDeR-A: 11, Kammen, *Mystic Chords of Memory,* 305, 338–39.

53. R. Jervis Cooke, "Sand and Grit: The Story of Fort McAllister" (Typescript, UGAL, n.p., n.d.), 70–71; Kammen, *Mystic Chords of Memory,* 304.

54. Herschel Brickell, "Literary Landscape," 380. Brickell also mentioned favorably *The Savannah Cook Book* by Harriet Ross Colquitt. Published in 1933, it featured an introduction by Ogden Nash and included, from the Wormsloe library, GWJDeR's accounts of the culinary attractions of his 1878 outing to Daufuskie Island and of Leta's party at Wormsloe (Harriet Ross Colquitt, comp. and ed., *The Savannah Cook Book* [New York, 1933], 174–75).

55. *SMN,* 27 March 1929; Ben Ames Williams, *Great Oaks* (New York: E. P. Dutton, 1930); "Author, Who Saw Wormsloe, Describes It in Her Novel," unidentified clipping, DeRFP-31; Fanny Heaslip Lea, *Good-bye Summer* (New York: Dodd, Mead, 1931).

In Lea's novel, it is the Cary family that has owned its plantation since 1735. "And the Carys are still there," notes one of the twentieth-century characters. Another responds: "That's romance! Gentlemen and ladies, and Spanish moss on all the trees, and hundreds of camellia bushes, and azaleas blooming thick along a river, and a crumbled fort, and deep in the forest a spot that was once the slaves' cemetery . . . when I was your age, darling, there was still a little wooden headboard standing, carved by hand, primitive as an African idol . . . the wood was rotting away and full of worm-holes." Wormsloe's oaks are also described: "There are trees all round the house that have been there two hundred years or more, so hung with gray moss that when you stand under them and look up at the sky, you might be standing in a very old, very ghostly, very frail cathedral, not made with hands" (Lea, *Good-bye Summer,* 16–17).

56. Julien Green, *Each Man in His Darkness* (London: Quartet Books, 1990), 5; Green, *Diary,* 47–48. In Green's *Each Man in His Darkness,* the residence at the fictional Wormsloe is described in a way that suggests its relation to the actual

structure: "Tall and broad, the old wooden house stood out in a dark mass against the sky. It looked like a great chest." It is also described as "sumptuously melancholy." Inside there is a statue closely resembling one owned by the De Rennes: "The first thing to meet his eye was a large and well-nigh naked woman of polished bronze who carried a torch in her fist. She stood at the foot of the stairs smiling at the visitor and he, suitcase in hand, looked at her attentively" (Green, *Each Man in His Darkness*, 5, 9, 21). In 1962, two New York producers came to Savannah to "take certain pictures of the avenue at Wormsloe" that were to be used in a proposed — but apparently unproduced — production of another of Julien Green's works, his play *South* (WC).

57. *Atlanta Constitution*, 17 March 1929.

58. *SEP*, 24 September 1927; "An Exhibition of Etchings and Drawings by Christopher Murphy, Jr. Plainfield, New Jersey" (six views of Wormsloe, lent by WWDeR, were part of the 1928 exhibit), DeRFP+-36; "Seven Pencil Sketches of Historic Wormsloe To Be at High Museum," *Atlanta Journal*, 12 February 1933; Cornelia Cunningham Sketches, DeRFP-58; Wormsloe Postcards, DeRFP+-24; *SEP*, 2 February 1934; Bayard Wootten to Augusta De Renne, 17 April 1935, WWDeRP-11; *Wormsloe* (1937), DeRFP-30.

59. Albert R. Rogers to WWDeR, 28 January 1933, DeRFP-34; *SMN*, 13 February, 21 April 1933; *Mid-Week Pictorial*, 25 February 1933; Mrs. Eugene Talmadge to Mr. and Mrs. WWDeR, 27 April 1933, DeRFP-58.

60. "An Historical Map of Georgia, drawn by Cornelia Cunningham, edited by W. W. De Renne," DeRFP+-(Oversize Drawer); "Georgia Bi-centennial Souvenir Stamps," DeRFP-34; "Georgia Bi-centennial Calendar," DeRFP+-36; "Three Georgia Bi-centennial Publications of Importance" [leaflet], DeRFP+-36; *SMN*, 19 October 1932.

61. Cooney, comp., *Garden History of Georgia*, 18–20, 370–73; Lockwood, comp., *Gardens of Colony and State*, [262], 285–92. The Mary Jones anecdote, found on page 290 of Lockwood, apparently first appeared in 1913 in WJDeR's description of Wormsloe for Knight's *Georgia's Landmarks, Memorials and Legends*, 1:88. It appears in some form or other in almost all of the Wormsloe Gardens literature. It was also the subject of one of Ray Robert's radio features on Atlanta's WGST, "The Story Behind the Picture," and was also printed in his Sunday newspaper column of the same name (*Atlanta Constitution*, 10 September 1933). Though surviving widows and daughters of the masters of Wormsloe did receive a life tenancy at the plantation, there is no evidence that the Mary Jones legend had anything to do with it. Professor E. Merton Coulter's extensive digging into the primary sources of the Jones family history unearthed no mention of Mary Jones's heroics.

62. KDeR-A:5, 7; Interview with the Reverend Frank A. Jenkins, Jr., 28 April 1991; Matthew Baird III to WWDeR, 10 December 1928, WWDeRP-10; Mrs. Gamble Latrobe to Eudora De Renne Roebling, 9 October 1969, DeRFP+-2.

63. KDeR-A:5, 8−9, 11, 15; Interview with the Reverend Frank A. Jenkins, Jr., 28 April 1991.

64. Steed, *Georgia*, 54.

65. Ibid., 55−57.

66. WWDeR, "In Re: Wormsloe, Summary of Facts" and untitled memorandum, c. 1929, DeRFP+-10; *SMN*, 7 June 1929; KDeR-A:8.

67. WWDeR to Audrey Coerr, 5 July 1924, DeRFP-44. Correspondence relating to Azalea Clizbee's work on the 1931 catalog is in Boxes 18, 44, and 52 of the DeRFP. This, however, is one of the few conspicuously incomplete correspondence files in the DeRFP; there is no correspondence for 1928−31.

68. Azalea Clizbee to WWDeR, 31 May 1923; Audrey Coerr to WWDeR, 2 July [1924], DeRFP-44.

69. EDeRB to G. W. Owens, 20 April 1917, Memorandum, H. W. Johnson to EDeRB, WWDeR to EDeRB, [9 November 1917], WC.

70. WWDeR to Audrey Coerr, 5 July, 10 October, 3 November 1924, DeRFP-44.

71. WWDeR to Audrey Coerr and EDeRB, 27 June 1925, DeRFP-44; Azalea Clizbee to Audrey Coerr, 12 February 1924, DeRFP-52; Azalea Clizbee to WWDeR, 28 June, 25 July 1924, WWDeR to Azalea Clizbee, 5 July 1924, Conde Nast to WWDeR, 14 September 1924, WWDeR to Audrey Coerr, 10 October 1924, DeRFP-44. The original understanding (later altered) was for the 350 copies of the proposed 600-page catalog to be produced, per page, as follows: composition, $6; presswork, $4; paper, $5; and binding, $1, with an estimated total of $9,600 for printing.

72. Statement, C&S Bank, Trustee, De Renne Catalogue Fund, 17 November 1924, Bill, Walker Engraving Company, September 1924, DeRFP-44; Audrey Coerr to WWDeR, 10 November 1924, DeRFP-18; Azalea Clizbee to WWDeR, 15 May 1925, DeRFP-44.

73. Azalea Clizbee to WWDeR, 25 July 1924, 15 May, 9 September 1925, DeRFP-44.

74. Azalea Clizbee to WWDeR, 25 July 1924, 15 May 1925; Audrey Coerr to WWDeR, 2, 21 July 1924, Azalea Clizbee to WWDeR, 28 June 1924, 6 May 1927, DeRFP-44.

75. Marriage Record, Audrey Coerr and Stanley Howland, 26 February 1929, Register of Deeds, Buncombe County Courthouse, Asheville, N.C.; Receipt, Plandome Press, 15 July 1927, Azalea Clizbee to WWDeR, 6 May 1927, DeRFP-44; Mackall, *Leonard Leopold Mackall*, 30. Information regarding Stanley Howland was kindly supplied by his daughter Mrs. William J. Cocke.

76. Library of Congress to Stanley Howland, 27 August 1931, Putnam File, LoC; Heartman, "Catalogue of the De Renne Library," 19; *DeRLC*, 1:[xvii].

77. "Announcement of Publication" (1930), laid in *DeRLC*, Special Collections, Ina Dillard Russell Library, Georgia College, Milledgeville, Ga.

78. Phillips, Review of *DeRLC*, 174−75.

79. Heartman, "Catalogue of the De Renne Library," 19.

80. Ibid., 21. Given Heartman's and others' comments, it is plain that the cost of the catalog was ultimately in excess of $30,000, though the accounts for the last years of the project are missing. WWDeR reported to the regents that the catalog "was prepared . . . at a cost of approximately $30,000." Duncan Burnet, librarian of the University of Georgia, was told that "the De Renne catalogue cost, preparation and printing, $150,000" (Minutes, Board of Regents, 20 August 1937, 22, GDAH; Burnet to S. V. Sanford, 19 August 1936, Louis S. Moore Collection Accession File, UGAL).

81. Minutes, Board of Regents, 20 August 1937, 23, GDAH; Douglas McMurtrie, "Located Imprints of the Eighteenth Century Not in the De Renne Catalogue," *GHQ* 18 (March 1934): 27−65. McMurtrie's list contains seventy-one items, located in eighteen repositories. It has much of minor interest but also includes titles long sought after by WJDeR, such as the Reverend John J. Zubly's *The Stamp-Act Repealed* (1766) and the elusive 1777 "Lancaster Constitution." And as one commentator noted, "the builder of the library could never have passed a night entirely unperturbed as long as he knew that Yale had the unique 1795 Yazoo Act which when first passed created such a scandal the case was carried to the Supreme Court" (Cannon, *American Book Collectors*, 251).

In 1995 the *DeRLC* was reprinted in three volumes, much reduced in size, by Maurizio Martino, Storrs-Mansfield, Conn., in an edition "strictly limited" to 150 copies.

82. *SMN*, 8, 9 September 1931; Certificate of Death, Audrey Howland, Register of Deeds, Buncombe County Courthouse, Asheville, N.C.

83. Will of WJDeR, PCR; CMT to George Foster Peabody, 28 May 1931, Peabody to CMT, 2 June 1931, Peabody to Harry Hodgson, 2 June 1931, Accession File, DeRGL; Dyer, *University of Georgia*, 157. Peabody wrote Hodgson, "As you know, I have no cash," but added that he would subscribe $1,000 worth of stock if there was a move to purchase the collection for the university library and suggested that Dr. Barrow "might be able to handle a negotiation."

84. Dr. Craig Barrow to Chancellor Charles M. Snelling, 10 June 1931, Accession File, DeRGL; Marmaduke Floyd to Anderson Bouchelle, 11 March 1938, Floyd Papers, GHS. "Under my view," asserted WWDeR's adviser, "Wymberley De Renne has the power to will his qualified fee subject to the contingency of his

dying without male issue surviving him. In the event male issue should survive, I think the provision of his will would be valid whether he left the property to the University of Georgia or not" (Samuel B. Adams to Dr. Craig Barrow, 24 June 1931, WC).

85. Cannon, *American Book Collectors*, 250. There is generally no documentary evidence of these dispersals, other than a few to be mentioned below.

86. "In Re: Wormsloe."

87. Ibid.; "Sale of De Renne Apartments Closed," *SEP*, 6 June 1929. Despite the initial complications, the 1929 purchaser retained ownership, and the apartments did not pass from his family until 1975. Thereafter the De Renne Apartments became the De Renne Plaza Condominiums.

88. *SEP*, 6 June 1929; Dr. Craig Barrow to the Pennsylvania Company, 1 July 1930, G. L. Groover to Dr. Craig Barrow, 16 November 1931, WC; DB 27V : 371, SCR; Junius G. Adams to Dr. Craig Barrow, 29 October 1931, WC; DB 22X : 286; DB 23U : 339; DB 31A : 353. Copies of documents relating to this matter that involved the Grace Securities Corporation of Richmond, Virginia, are in DeRFP-27.

89. L&C to Mrs. Craig Barrow, 16, 17 March 1931, WC. Audrey Howland's trustee, Philadelphia lawyer Roland Morris, also agreed that "it would be far better from a legal point of view to not only declare null and void, but to formally terminate, the lease," so that there would be "no question as to Mr. De Renne's rights to ever re-purchase [Wormsloe]." It was feared that WWDeR's sale of the library would put him in a position to secure title to Wormsloe again. To protect Wormsloe from passing to outsiders, the sisters wished "the terms of the sale [to] forever prevent a resale to anyone outside the family" (Dr. Craig Barrow to Roland S. Morris, 14 July 1931, Morris Duane to Dr. Craig Barrow, 25 August 1931, WC). First Pennsylvania Banking and Trust Company, the successor to the Pennsylvania Company, merged in 1990 with CoreStates Bank N.A. "Unfortunately, all records with respect to the administration of the De Renne Estate and Trust have long since been destroyed" (Daniel Brainard Slack, CoreStates Bank N.A., to the author, 8 April 1992).

90. EDeRB to WWDeR, 4 June 1936, EDeRB to WWDeR and Augusta Floyd De Renne, 31 July 1936, DeRFP+-1.

91. Dr. Craig Barrow to Junius G. Adams, 20 November 1933, ibid. As another example of the financial pressures on Mrs. Barrow, the $30,000 loan she had obtained to get clear title to Wormsloe in 1931 was "secured by certain stocks and bonds, and on account of the fall in the market value of such securities, the Bank desire[d] her to take up the loan" at a time when it was difficult to borrow money on Savannah real estate (T. M. Cunningham to Roland S. Morris, 14 July 1932, WC).

92. S. V. Sanford to CMT, 21 June 1934, S. V. Sanford to CMT, 20 October 1934, Harmon Caldwell to CMT, 26 June 1936, Caldwell Papers, UGAL-A.

Although Charles Edgeworth Jones succeeded in selling for $2,000 his father's four-volume set of autographs of members of the Continental Congress, the bulk of the massive Jones autograph collection netted only $2,639.51 at an auction in Philadelphia in 1894 (Penn, "Charles Colcock Jones," 90, 92).

93. Dr. Craig Barrow to Chancellor Charles M. Snelling, 10 June 1931, Accession File, DeRGL.

94. WWDeR to A. S. W. Rosenbach, 14 June 1935, CMT to A. S. W. Rosenbach, 28 April 1936, CMT, "Memorandum of Authorities: Construction of the Will of W. J. De Renne," A. S. W. Rosenbach to WWDeR, 24 June 1935, Correspondence File I:48:37, Rosenbach Museum and Library, Philadelphia, Pa. WWDeR also met with Rosenbach in Philadelphia for further discussions in April 1936 (CMT to A. S. W. Rosenbach, 28 April 1936, ibid.).

95. *SMN*, 9 March 1938; S. V. Sanford to Harold Hirsch, 19 April 1934 (copy), WC; CMT to S. V. Sanford, 30 July 1934, 29 January 1935, S. V. Sanford to CMT, 20 October 1934, Caldwell Papers, UGAL-A.

96. Dr. Craig Barrow to Roland S. Morris, 14 July 1931, EDeRB to H. W. Johnson, 28 April 1934, WC.

97. "In Re: Wormsloe."

98. *SMN*, 5 April 1929, 12 February 1933; EDeRB to WWDeR, 4 June 1936, DeRFP+-1.

99. CMT to H. W. Johnson, 27 April 1934, EDeRB to H. W. Johnson, 28 April 1934, H. W. Johnson to EDeRB, 1 May 1934, WWDeR to H. W. Johnson, 1 May 1934, WC.

100. EDeRB to H. W. Johnson, 28 April 1934, ibid.

101. "In Re: Wormsloe"; Board of Regents Minutes, 21 December 1934, 96, GDAH; CMT to S. V. Sanford, 29 January 1935, Caldwell Papers, UGAL-A.

102. Joseph Robinson to Augusta De Renne, 9 June 1936, WWDeRP-11; Mrs. Gamble Latrobe to Augusta De Renne, [3 May 1938], Mrs. Gamble Latrobe to Eudora De Renne Roebling, 9 October 1969, DeRFP+-2.

103. WWDeR to EDeRB, 3 June 1936, EDeRB to WWDeR, 4 June 1936, DeRFP+-1.

104. WWDeR to EDeRB, 3 June 1936, ibid.

105. EDeRB to WWDeR, 4 June 1936, ibid.

106. WWDeR to EDeRB, 1 July 1936, WC; EDeRB to Mr. and Mrs. WWDeR, 31 July 1936, WWDeR to Mrs. Fontaine Barden, 12 August 1936, EDeRB to WWDeR, 28 September 1936, DeRFP+-1; WWDeR, "Statement of Transactions in Connection with the Lease and Purchase of Wormsloe," DeRFP+-6.

107. A. B. Lovett and CMT to WWDeR, 2 February 1937, DeRFP+-3; *SEP*, 1 February 1937; *SMN*, 2 February 1937; Barrow v. De Renne, Dispossessory Proceedings, Affidavits and Counter-Affidavits, Superior Court, Chatham County, June Term 1936, SCR. WWDeR wrote in his "Statement of Transactions," "After several conferences Craig Barrow, Jr., suggested the plan [for the one-year lease, the reduction of back rent, etc.] which was finally adopted."

At its New York gallery in November 1936, M. Knoedler and Company opened "an exhibition of American portraiture of the late eighteenth and early nineteenth centuries" that created much interest in the work of the artists of that period. The Jones—De Renne family portraits offered for sale by Knoedler were two by Charles Willson Peale (Noble Wimberly Jones and Letitia Van Deren Smith), one by Rembrandt Peale (Dr. George Jones), and one by Jeremiah Theus (*A Child of the Smith Family*). The portraits were purchased in early 1937 for EDeRB by her friend Mrs. Joseph Bickerton (*New York Times*, 5, 8 November 1936; Knoedler & Co. Catalogue [typescript, c. 1937] and Fine Arts Accession Record Sheets, Telfair Academy of Arts and Sciences, Savannah, Georgia).

Charlton M. Theus (1894–1955), WWDeR's lawyer, was a descendant of the artist Jeremiah Theus (*SMN-SEP Magazine*, 9 April 1967, 4).

108. Minutes, Board of Regents, 20 August 1937, 21–23, GDAH.

109. Geneva H. Emily, "Duncan Burnet: An Optimistic Philosophy," *Athens* (Ga.) *Advertiser*, 22 July 1964, 8; E. M. Coulter, "De Renne Library History Thrills All Georgians," *Atlanta Constitution*, 5 September 1937; E. M. Coulter, "The Wymberley Jones De Renne Georgia Library," *Georgia Alumni Record* 17 (October 1937): 38; C. S. Sanford to S. V. Sanford, 8 December 1937 (Copy), EDeRBC. James H. Cobb, representing the Savannah newspapers, noted that the story of the library sale had "unusual reader appeal for Savannah, both because of the location of the library here and the number of university alumni" who lived in the area; as early as 1934 he had received President Sanford's promise that he would notify Cobb immediately when a deal for the library was closed (James H. Cobb, Jr., to S. V. Sanford, 14 June 1934, and Sanford to Cobb, 22 June 1934, Caldwell Papers, UGAL-A).

110. WWDeR to H. W. Johnson, 31 January 1938 (Copy), H. W. Johnson to WWDeR, 2 February 1938 (Copy), EDeRBC.

111. "Statement of Transactions"; WWDeR to Herbert Putnam, 7 February 1938, Putnam Papers, LoC.

112. A. S. Brower to Dr. R. L. Flowers, 8 March 1938, enclosing proposed agreements, R. L. Flowers Correspondence File, University Archives, DUL.

113. Ibid.

114. *SEP*, 25 February 1938; Marmaduke Floyd to Anderson Bouchelle, 11 March 1938, Floyd Papers, GHS.

115. "Statement of Transactions"; Marmaduke Floyd to Anderson Bouchelle, 11 March 1938, Floyd Papers, GHS.

116. H. W. Johnson to Dr. Craig Barrow, 10 February 1938, WC; *SMN*, 1 March 1938; WWDeR to Charles G. Day, 8 April 1938, DeRFP+-3.

117. *Atlanta Constitution*, 23 February 1938.

118. "Statement of Transactions."

119. Ibid.; Carroll J. Dickson to WWDeR, 17 February 1938, DeRFP+-4.

120. "Statement of Transactions"; *SMN*, 12 March 1938.

121. Minutes, Board of Regents, 18 March 1938, 201–2, GDAH; Marmaduke Floyd to Henry and Frances Floyd Caldwell, 14 March 1938, Floyd Papers, GHS.

Apparently because of a budget cutback, WWDeR's salary was actually $2,400 from 1938 through 1945. Average annual salaries at the University of Georgia at the beginning of this period were $3,300 (professors), $2,580 (associate professors), $2,092 (assistant professors), and $1,491 (instructors). Because of WWDeR's lack of a degree in library science, his original official title was archivist, History Department; at the time of his retirement, he was listed as assistant professor in libraries (Salary Statistics, J. D. Bolton Papers, Box 57, UGAL-A; WWDeR's Personnel File and Employment Records [1938–55], UGAL-A).

122. WWDeR to A. S. Brower, [14 March 1938 (Draft)], A. S. Brower to WWDeR, 22 March 1938, DeRFP+-4; WWDeR to Mrs. Fontaine Barden, 31 March 1938, DeRFP+-2; WWDeR to W. G. Land, Duke University Library, 25 April 1938, W. G. Land to WWDeR, 16 May 1938, DeRFP+-4.

Indications are that it was at about this time that most of the the the R. E. Lee letters were sold to financier Bernard Baruch, though at least one of them went to Savannah collector Keith Read, along with other De Renne library manuscripts. Most of Read's books and manuscripts relating to the Confederacy were acquired by Emory University in 1938. Called the Keith M. Read Confederate Collection, it consisted of approximately "9,000 manuscripts, 3,000 books and pamphlets, 1,000 magazines and newspapers, 200 broadsides, many maps, pieces of sheet music, and miscellaneous ana." Unfortunately, the collection was scattered throughout the special collections department and the general library, making it practically impossible to determine which of these Read items were originally part of the De Renne collection.

Like the volume of Lee letters, the other volumes of the Jones Confederate Collection were broken up and seem to have been dispersed by the Pennsylvania rare book dealer James Lewis Hook. He also disposed of some of the 1931 catalogs and some of the "house books" (the term for those general De Renne volumes not assigned to the library). There is evidence that some of the De Renne library manuscripts, from the family archive and otherwise, were acquired by Duke from

WWDeR in 1938 and that others, acquired by Mr. and Mrs. Marmaduke Floyd, also later went there. Some of the celebrated eighteenth-century Verelst manuscripts, for example, which are mentioned in the introduction to the 1931 catalog, were acquired from Mrs. Floyd in 1951. In a related matter, most of the furnishings of the library building were acquired for sale by Joseph D. Green, a Charleston office equipment dealer (Catesby L. Jones to WWDeR, 18 February 1938, DeRFP+-4; English, *Roads to Research*, 73; WWDeR to James Lewis Hook, 14 July 1938 (Copy), James Lewis Hook to WWDeR, 21 May, 16 July 1938, DeRFP+-4; Accession Files, Special Collections Library, DUL; Joseph D. Green to WWDeR, 24 September 1938, DeRFP+-4).

123. *Atlanta Constitution*, 21 March, 12 April 1938; *Atlanta Journal*, 3 April 1938; *SEP*, 11 April 1938; "The University Acquires Premier Library of Georgia History," *Georgia Alumni Record* 18 (September 1938): 11.

124. *Charleston News and Courier*, 19 March 1938; *SEP*, 19 March 1938; Minutes of the Board of Regents (Box 2: July 1937–December 1939), 1 August 1939, 5–6, UGAL-A; Documents Relating to the Sale of the Confederate Constitution, 11 September 1939, DeRFP+-6; Record Book 59, Folios 176–77, Clerk's Office, Superior Court, Clarke County, Georgia; *Annual Report from the Regents of the University System of Georgia* (1939), 10–11; L. W. McRae to Marion Smith, 13 December 1939 (Copy), Caldwell Papers, UGAL-A; CMT to WWDeR, 21 November 1942, DeRFP+-6. See also Dolly Blount Lamar, *When All Is Said and Done* (Athens, 1952), 129–30.

The Permanent Constitution of the Confederate States of America is not available for examination by researchers and is displayed to the general public only once a year, on Confederate Memorial Day. The document is, however, accessible on CD-ROM in the university library and also through the World Wide Web.

125. WWDeR to Marmaduke Floyd, c. December 1938, Floyd Papers, GHS; Dorothy Darsey to WWDeR, 15 February 1952, DeRFP-58; R. V. Watterson to WWDeR, 10 May 1939, DeRFP+-6; CMT to WWDeR, 3 November 1939, ibid.; Interview with Mrs. William Tate, 6 July 1994.

126. Marmaduke Floyd to Henry and Frances Floyd Caldwell, 14 March 1938, Floyd Papers, GHS; Margaret Beauchamp Armistead, "Medieval Herb Garden in Georgia," *Atlanta Journal and Constitution Magazine*, 21 September 1952, 42–43.

127. KDeR-A:16, 23, 27, 33; Kentwyn De Renne, ed., *Selections from the Writings of Josh Billings, or, Proverbial Philosophy of Wit and Humor* (Athens: Kentwyn De Renne, 1940); *SMN*, 9 December 1962, 14 March 1969.

Josh Billings (size/format 16mo) was issued in a "limited edition of three hundred and twenty-four numbered copies," with "seventy-six pages of text." The book was drawn from the humorous works of Billings (pseudonym of Henry Wheeler Shaw [1818–85]). It featured period illustrations by Thomas Nast (1840–1902) and an introduction by Carl Purington Rollins, the typographer of the Yale University Press (Prospectus, *Josh Billings*, DeRFP-20; Copy of *Josh Billings*, Georgia Room, UGAL).

128. *Athens Banner-Herald*, 23 August 1953, 4 August 1969.

129. The De Renne Garden Collection includes over five hundred titles, dating from the sixteenth century through the 1960s. It was acquired in 1970 by Callaway Gardens, Pine Mountain, Georgia, to "be the nucleus of a library for the Gardens." The De Renne books and the others that accumulated around them were for years "housed in the library/conference room in the office of the Director of Gardens and the President of the Resort." In 1994 the De Renne Garden Collection, along with some of the other older books, was placed on permanent loan with the Cherokee Garden Club Library at the Atlanta History Center (Fred C. Galle to Eudora De Renne Roebling, 8 February 1971; Letters of Patricia L. Collins, Director of Education, Callaway Gardens, to the author, 23 April 1991 [including "Evaluation of the De Renne Garden Books in the Callaway Gardens Library"] and 30 July 1994; and Blanche Farley, Librarian, Cherokee Garden Library, to the author 21 May 1997, all in private possession).

130. Registers, De Renne Collection, 1938–42, Special Collections Division, Box 117, UGAL-A; Correspondence, Box 105, ibid.; Personnel File of WWDeR, UGAL-A; WWDeR Clipping File, Biographical Files, UGAL.

Louis Stone Moore (1885–1934) of Thomasville, Georgia, was an attorney and collector and a 1906 graduate of the University of Georgia law school. At his home, Tockwotton, he assembled a collection of Georgiana considered second only to the De Renne Georgia Library: "approximately 4,000 bound volumes and several thousand unbound pamphlets and maps." Though it had "none of the unique rarities" of the De Renne library, there were "somewhere between 450 and 650 quite scarce things," purchased from many of the same dealers that WJDeR had patronized. In October 1936, E. Merton Coulter and University of Georgia president Harmon W. Caldwell went to Thomasville to bid for the library at an executor's sale and purchased it for $5,000. This was the university library's first major accession of printed Georgiana (and would be followed the next year by many of Telamon Cuyler's Georgia manuscripts). Librarian Duncan Burnet and Coulter together packed the Moore collection in Thomasville and had it transported to Athens "in a large College of Agriculture truck," which they protectively "trailed" in Coulter's car all the way to Athens. Most of the Moore books were eventually transferred to the university's general library, where they are identified by an elaborate bookplate prepared after their purchase (*Macon Telegraph*, 16 March 1930; *Thomasville Press*, 1 June 1934; English, *Roads to Research*, 58; Duncan Burnet to S. V. Sanford, 19 August 1936, Moore Collection Accession File, UGAL; Burnet, Memorandum re: Moore Collection, 2 August 1946, ibid.).

131. *Atlanta Journal*, 24 May 1951; *Norfolk Virginian-Pilot*, 30 May 1951.

132. Interview, John Wyatt Bonner, 15 July 1991; Interview, Mrs. William Tate, 6 July 1994.

133. Sarah B. Temple to WWDeR, 15 February 1954, DeRFP+-4; Inventory of WWDeR's Hill Street House, DeRFP+-9.

Both the estranged siblings continued to maintain affectionate relations with their half-brother, Dr. Charles Camblos Norris. An eminent Philadelphia physician, he was head of obstetrics and gynecology at the University of Pennsylvania Medical School from 1927 until 1941. He was also distinguished as a sportsman and an author, famous for his "hunting bible," *Eastern Upland Shooting*. Though Dr. Norris never shot during his visits to Wormsloe, WWDeR was occasionally one of his hunting companions in North Carolina and elsewhere (*Philadelphia Inquirer*, 27 February 1961; Evans, *Recollections of a Shooting Guest*, 178; George Bird Evans to the author, 12 January 1991).

134. WWDeR to W. P. Kellam, 23 April 1955, Personnel File of WWDeR, UGAL-A; *Athens Banner-Herald*, 3 April 1966; *SMN*, 14 March 1969; *SEP*, 4 August 1969. Mrs. Kentwyn De Renne died in New Orleans on 23 July 1991.

CHAPTER 12. The Round of Time

1. EDeRB to J. L. Weller, [1 January 1960, 14 April 1961], in private possession.

2. Correspondence, WWDeRP-1, e.g., from the Pavillon Henry IV in Biarritz: "The Empress of Austria is here. She is always dressed in black with a white umbrella and always has a young man with her" (Elfrida De Renne to WJDeR, 21 December 1895); "L'Exposition Artistique de Biarritz-Association," 14 March 1897, DeRFP-20; Carl L. Brandt to WJDeR, 8 August 1897, DeRFP-14; Elfrida De Renne to WJDeR, c. June 1899, WWDeRP-1.

3. Elfrida De Renne to WJDeR, [c. 29 May 1899], WWDeRP-1; Elfrida De Renne to WJDeR, 2 May 1901, WWDeRP-3; EDeRB to J. L. Weller, undated, c. 1956, in private possession; *SMN*, 1 March 1913.

4. Meta D. Huger to EDeRB, 27 June 1916, WC.

5. DB 13H:342; *SMN*, 28 June 1912.

6. Savannah Ward Books (Lots 37 and 38, Brown Ward), GHS; *SMN*, 28 June 1912; DB 42H:65. The house is now owned and occupied by a law firm.

7. National Society of the Colonial Dames (Georgia), *Register of the Georgia So-*

ciety Colonial Dames of America (Baltimore, 1937), 5, 25, 84; GHS Membership List, 1921, Archives, GHS.

8. Cahill, *Harriet Monroe*, 58−59; *SMN*, 10 March 1921; Strong, "Poetry Society of Georgia," 29. The newspaper article cited above identifies the Prosodists as Mrs. Craig Barrow, Mrs. Frank McIntire, Mrs. W. F. McCauley, Mrs. Malcolm Bell, and Miss Jane Meldrim (later Mrs. Erastus Hewitt). Later accounts of the group's membership differ. Jane Judge's "Personal Impressions," 13, identifies only Barrow, Bell, and McIntire as still members, as does Strong's article cited above. Mrs. Strong makes no claim to membership in her article but is listed among the Prosodists in the 1959−60 Poetry Society of Georgia Yearbook, along with the three cited earlier, and with the addition of Mrs. Stewart Huston (Harriet Lawrence). Jane Meldrim Hewitt, omitted from some listings, is described in the 1988−89 yearbook as the "last living member of the group."

9. Judge, "Personal Impressions," 1, 12, 13; Wilson, *Savannah*, 194; Huntingdon Club Materials, Vertical Files, GHS; Dubose Heyward to EDeRB, 10 January 1922, WC; *SMN*, 10 March 1921. The GHS also holds a collection of papers of the Huntingdon Club, but access to them is restricted.

10. *SMN*, 10 March 1921.

11. Ibid.; *PMV* 18 (May 1921):94.

12. *PMV* 18 (May 1921):96.

13. Hobson, *Serpent in Eden*, 14; Mencken, *Prejudices*, 69−70, 71. Mencken's exceptions were Robert Loveman and John McClure, both now obscure.

14. Mencken, *Prejudices*, 70−73; Mencken, "Editorial," 151.

15. *Year Book PSSC* (1921): 5−7, 14−16; Mencken, *Prejudices*, 73.

16. Durham, "Rise of DuBose Heyward," 69; Durham, *DuBose Heyward*, 29; Dubose Heyward to EDeRB, 10 January 1922, WC. Though there is no indication that they knew it, Heyward and Mrs. Barrow were distantly related. He was the great-great-grandson of Elizabeth Savage Heyward, sister of EDeRB's great-great-grandfather, Thomas Savage V (Genealogy Chart, DuBose Heyward Papers, SCHS).

17. *PMV* 20 (April 1922): 19.

18. *Year Book PSSC* (1923): 14; Cowan, *Fugitive Group*, xv−xvi; Ransom, *Armageddon*, 16; DuBose Heyward to Hervey Allen, two letters, undated [1923], Heyward Papers, SCHS; Durham, *DuBose Heyward*, 27−28. The Fugitives were "indignant" over Monroe's suggestion (in the Southern Number of Poetry and in her later review of Heyward and Allen's *Carolina Chansons*) that southern poets should devote themselves to specifically southern subjects; by and large, Mrs. Barrow seems to have agreed with their view (Rubin, *Wary Fugitives*, 144).

19. DuBose Heyward to Hervey Allen, undated [1923], Heyward Papers, SCHS;

Durham, *DuBose Heyward*, 28. The Southern Prize was awarded annually, 1923–32, with the exception of 1929 and 1931, when "no poems submitted were considered of suitable quality by the judge." Among the winners other than Ransom were Donald Davidson, for "Fire on Belmont Street," 1926, and Josephine Pinckney, for "An Island Boy," 1927 (Coxe, "Charleston Poetic Renaissance," 205).

20. Judge, "Personal Impressions," 14–15; Coxe, "Charleston Poetic Renaissance," 60; *SMN*, 21 February 1923; Minutes of Meeting, 20 February 1923, PSGP-8; Barrow, "Poetry Society of Georgia," 19; Pinckney, "Charleston's Poetry Society," 55–56; Strong, "Poetry Society of Georgia," 39. Laura Palmer Bell was another of the Prosodists who earned recognition in the society for her poems. She also was responsible for the society's seal, "a frail little craft on a perilous sea sailing under the benison of a new moon" (Strong, "Poetry Society of Georgia," 30).

21. Coxe, "Charleston Poetic Renaissance," 36; Sader, ed., *Comprehensive Index to English-Language Little Magazines*, 1:236–37; Heyward, "Contemporary Southern Poetry," 54; Barrow, "Dawn Dream," *Reviewer* 4 (October 1923); 19; Poetry Society of Georgia, *Anthology of Verse*, 5–10; Jacobs, ed., *Oglethorpe Book of Georgia Verse*, 497–98.

22. *Year Book PSSC* (1925): 9, (1926); 10, (1969): 24; Barrow, *In the Calendar's Shadow*, 58.

23. *Atlanta Constitution*, 16, 19–21 March 1929. Mrs. Barrow was also among the "state's oustanding writers" recognized at an Athens banquet by the Georgia Press Association in 1934 (*Athens Banner-Herald*, 24 February 1934).

24. *SEP*, 13 June 1923.

25. Monroe, *Poet's Life*, 468; *SMN*, 16 November 1969; Sieg, "Elfrida De Renne Barrow," *Savannah News-Press Magazine*, 7 June 1970, 3.

26. *New York Times Book Review*, 11 June 1961, 1; David McCord, *Take Sky* (Darien, Ga., 1961). David McCord (1897–1997) found the Ashantilly Press's folded single-sheet presentation of his poem "really an enchanting piece of printing" (David McCord to EDeRB, 12 December 1961, WC). For an overview of the work of the Ashantilly Press and other twentieth-century Georgia private presses, see Zachert, *Fine Printing in Georgia*.

27. *SMN*, 14 April 1950; Judge, "Personal Impressions," 15–17.

28. Barrow, "Poets, Writers and Men of Letters," SHRA; *The Poetry Society of Georgia Yearbook*, 1969–70. Readings by visiting writers were held most often at the Telfair Academy, the Lawton Memorial Hall, and the Savannah Public Library.

After Mrs. Barrow's death, a new Poetry Society of Georgia prize was offered: the Conrad Aiken Prize in Memory of Elfrida De Renne Barrow. The 1969–70 yearbook "was a month late, in order to carry a tribute to Mrs. Barrow, whose real memorial is the Poetry Society itself" (PSG *Yearbook*, 1970–71, unpaginated; PSG *Yearbook*, 1971–72, 27).

29. EDeRB to John Bennett, 9 October 1928, Bennett Papers, SCHS; *DLB* 42:83.

30. John Bennett to Laura Palmer Bell, 17 April 1925, Bell to Bennett, 25 April 1925, Bennett Papers, SCHS.

31. Judge, "Personal Impressions," 16; *DLB*, 9:281, 283; Landess, *Julia Peterkin*, 17; Hobson, *Mencken*, 211.

32. *SMN*, 1 November 1931, 26 July 1936, 20 April 1938.

33. *SMN*, 15 July 1938. Wormsloe's transformation from tourist attraction to private estate was noted in a detailed entry in *Georgia*, 267–68.

34. Interview with the Reverend Frank Jenkins, Jr., 28 April 1991; *Savannah Tribune*, 16 January 1960; Lillian Bragg [no relation to the present writer], "Frank Jenkins, Sr.," WC; *SEP*, 7 June 1984. Several of these structures were documented by the Historic American Buildings Survey in 1934 and are found in HABS File GA-2126, LoC. They include an interior and exterior view of one of the slave cabins and views of the rice mill and well house. A photograph was also taken of the "old fort" at the time. See also Linley, *Georgia Catalog*, 297.

35. *SMN*, 15 July 1938; Clason Kyle, "Wormsloe on the Skidaway," Columbus, Ga., *Sunday Ledger-Enquirer Magazine*, 15 December 1968, 23.

36. "Three Gracious Savannah Homes," *House and Garden*, March 1940, 24–25; Lee Giffen, "Wormsloe, the Home of Mrs. Craig Barrow," *Antiques*, March 1967, 372–73. Other appearances in print of the remodeled Wormsloe House included Margaret Godley, "Wormsloe," *Holland's*, August 1950, 9–12; Hamilton Basso, "Savannah and the Golden Isles," *Holiday*, December 1951, 48; Medora Field Perkerson, *White Columns in Georgia* (New York, 1952), 112–14; Calder Willingham, "Georgia," *Holiday*, June 1956, 42–44; Frederick Doveton Nichols, *The Early Architecture of Georgia* (Chapel Hill, 1957), 93–95; W. S. Kirkpatrick, "Historic Wormsloe in One Family 223 Years," *Atlanta Journal and Constitution Magazine*, 19 April 1959, 24–26, 29; Gladys Freeman, "Houses and Gardens of Georgia's Historic Savannah," *Town and Country*, March 1962, 72–75, 124–25; and Ledlie William Conger, *Sketching and Etching Georgia* (Atlanta, 1971), Plate III and text. Recent photographs of Wormsloe House interiors, the library, and the formal garden are found in James A. D. Cox (text) and N. Jane Iseley (photography), *Savannah Tour of Homes and Gardens* (Savannah, 1996), [64]–[67].

Among the sources specifically including photographs of the grounds and formal garden, post-1938, are Coulter, *Wormsloe*, following 256; "Wormsloe Plantation," *SMN Magazine*, 21 March 1965, 1, 6, 7; Kyle, "Wormsloe on the Skidaway," 22–23;

and William Mitchell (text) and Richard Moore (photography), *Gardens of Georgia* (Atlanta, 1989), 34–35.

37. Blueprints, Alterations to Residence, Wormsloe, August 1938, WC.

38. Roland S. Morris to EDeRB, 28 December 1931, WC.

39. *Savannah Writers' Conference* (brochure), SWC; Toledano, "Savannah Writers' Conference—1939," 145, 147.

40. Toledano, "Savannah Writers' Conference," 149; Lowry Axley, "Savannah Writers' Conference," *SMN*, 12 March 1939.

41. Lowry Axley to EDeRB, 12 April 1939, Lowry Axley to John Peale Bishop, 15 April 1939, Allen Tate to Lowry Axley, 18 April 1939, Lowry Axley to Allen Tate, 20 April 1939, SWC; Caroline Gordon to Edna Lytle, 23 May 1939, Edna Lytle Papers, Special Collections, Heard Library, Vanderbilt University; *SMN*, 5 March 1939.

42. Charles Beard to EDeRB, 22 April 1930, Mary R. Beard to EDeRB, 15 May 1938, 14 July 1942, J. G. De Roulhac Hamilton to EDeRB, 31 January 1954, WC; Thomas Gamble to EDeRB, 2 May 1933, DeRFP-18. In her letter of 14 July 1942, Mrs. Beard wrote: "Day dreams include visions of you both on the Isle of Hope with all its charms of human and vegetable life. Eliza Lucas Pinckney in the old planting days wrote in her Diary about her 'love of the vegetable kingdom'—a love I share in these days. But even now I love the human kingdom which has for its flowering such personalities as you both."

43. Membership List, 1921, Archives, GHS; King, "Georgia Historical Society," 300.

44. Brooks, "Need for a New Historical Organization in Georgia," 12, 19, 24, 29–31; *Proceedings of the First Annual Session of the Georgia Historical Association* (1917), [4], 75; *Proceedings of the Third Annual Session of the Georgia Historical Association* (1919), 49. Another major aim of the association—the creation of a state department of archives—was accomplished before the organization ended its brief existence (Bryan, "Recent Archival Developments in Georgia," 57–58).

45. *GHQ* 4 (June–September 1920): 75–79, 93–105.

46. Ibid., 103–5; King, "Georgia Historical Society," 301; *GHQ* 7 (March 1923): 70; *GHQ* 9 (March 1925): 89; Spalding, *Book of Accessions*, 3.

47. GHS, *Annals* (1915): 67; *GHQ* 7 (June 1923): 177; *GHQ* 24 (June 1940): 178–80; *SMN*, 14 November 1941; Barrow, "'Memento Mori'"; *Year Book PSSC* (1923): 84. Periodically, the society has made other efforts to become more inclusive and less Savannah-centered. The most wide-ranging is the latest, known as Initiative 2000, which divided the state into six districts, with their own regional vice presidents, and offered local historical organizations across the state

affiliate memberships and various services (*GHS Footnotes* 21 [Fall 1995]: 2, 4, 6).

48. *SEP,* 31 July 1945. Gamble (1868–1945), a journalist and twice mayor of Savannah, was also known as the "Father of Armstrong Junior College" (*DGB* 1: 337–38).

The premier Savannah historian of Mrs. Barrow's later life was Alexander A. Lawrence (1906–79), whose first book, *James Moore Wayne, Southern Unionist* (Chapel Hill, 1943), appeared during Gamble's final years and was followed by several excellent books, including *Storm over Savannah* (Athens, Ga., 1951) and *A Present for Mr. Lincoln* (Macon, Ga., 1961) (*DGB* 2 : 606–7).

49. *SMN,* 16 December 1923; *SEP,* 22 December 1923; *GHQ* 8 (March 1924): 73.

50. *DeRLC,* 3 : 1162.

51. Barrow and Bell, *Anchored Yesterdays,* [9]; *GHQ* 8 (March 1924): 71–73; *Atlanta Constitution,* 30 December 1923. In 1956, the book was issued in a new edition, "handset in the Caslon types," by the Ashantilly Press of Darien, Georgia, as its first publication (*SMN,* 9 September 1956).

52. John Bennett to EDeRB, 8 March 1924, Bennett Papers, SCHS.

53. *GHQ* 8 (March 1924): 72; Brooks, *Under Seven Flags,* 22–23; Brooks, *Georgia Studies,* 17.

54. Montgomery, "A Few Words About E. Merton Coulter," 10–11.

55. Ibid., 7–9.

56. Ibid., 10; Woodward, "Ellis Merton Coulter" (article), 59–60.

57. Woodward, "Ellis Merton Coulter" (dissertation), 53, 223.

58. *Atlanta Journal,* 9 December 1956.

59. EDeRB to EMC, [February 1926], EMCP-8, folder 14; Coulter, *Georgia,* 483, 485, 486.

60. E. Merton Coulter, "When John Wesley Preached in Georgia," *GHQ* 9 (December 1925): 317–51.

61. Ibid.

62. EDeRB to EMC, [February 1926], EMCP-8, Folder 14.

63. EDeRB to EMC, [1927], EMCP-9, Folder 2.

64. Oemler, *Holy Lover,* [vii]. Oemler, one of Georgia's two major novelists of the period, also knew Margaret Mitchell, who made significant borrowings from two of Oemler's novels for *Gone with the Wind* (Darden Asbury Pyron, *Southern Daughter: The Life of Margaret Mitchell* [New York, 1991], 315–17).

65. *SEP,* 7 May 1927; *New York Times,* 15 May 1927; Wade, *John Wesley,* viii, xiii.

66. *GHQ* 15 (March 1931): 105.

67. Ibid., 106.

68. EDeRB to EMC, [1929] and 1 July [1929], EMCP-10, Folder 2; Elfrida De Renne Barrow, "On the Bay," *GHQ* 14 (March 1930): 1–16.

69. Barrow, "On the Bay," 1; EDeRB to EMC, 10 January [1930], EMCP-10, Folder 12; "On the Bay," bound offprint, WC.

70. Lamar, *History of the National Society of the Colonial Dames*, 81; Walter G. Charlton, *The Making of Georgia: An Address Delivered at the Request of the Georgia Society of the Colonial Dames* [Savannah, 1898].

71. National Society of the Colonial Dames of America (Georgia), *Some Early Epitaphs in Georgia*, 23–26.

72. EDeRB to EMC, [1929], EMCP-10, Folder 2. EDeRB was president of the Georgia Society Colonial Dames, 1929–33, and by 1937 had been made a life member. During EDeRB's presidency, the historian of the society noted, "Many men of letters were invited to address the members on historical and educational subjects, a reference library was started at Colonial Dames House, and a Committee formed on 'Historical collections and exhibits'" (Anderson, comp., *History of the Georgia Society of the Colonial Dames*, 32).

73. EDeRB to EMC, [1932], EMCP-11, Folder 12; EDeRB to EMC, [January 1931], EMCP-11, Folder 2; *GHQ* 17 (December 1933): 318.

74. EDeRB to EMC, [1932], EMCP-11, Folder 12; Anderson et al., *Georgia*, ii, 17, 20, 81, 113.

75. *SEP*, 11 January 1933; EDeRB to EMC, [1933], EMCP-12, Folder 2. Mrs. Barrow eventually came to call Coulter "the Patron Saint of Lady Historians," a title he accepted with good humor (EDeRB to EMC, 3 January 1938, EMCP-27).

76. EDeRB to EMC, three letters, [1933], EMCP-12, Folder 2.

77. Elizabeth M. Bullard to EMC, 9 October, 5 December, 1931, EMCP-11; Elizabeth M. Bullard to EMC (telegram and letter), 23 January 1933, Elizabeth M. Bullard to EMC, 9 July 1934, EMCP-12. *A Short History of Georgia* was revised and enlarged for a second edition, titled *Georgia: A Short History*, in 1947; its coverage was expanded for a third edition, published under the same title in 1960.

78. *GHQ* 17 (December 1933): 318–19.

79. EDeRB to EMC, 2 November [1933], EMCP-12; Coulter, *Short History of Georgia*, 415.

80. *GHQ* 28 (September 1944): 111, 209, 225–26. Charles F. Groves to Raiford J. Wood, 18 April 1934, SHRA. According to the collection description of the association's papers, the SHRA functioned until the 1970s.

81. Coulter, ed., *Georgia's Disputed Ruins*, v, vii–ix, 3–4.

82. Ibid., vi–xi; *JSH* 4 (1938): 101.

83. EDeRB to Elizabeth Groover, 8 May [1939], EMC to Alexander A. Lawrence, 31 August 1944, Minutes, 27 September 1944, SHRA Minute Book, 1944–51,

SHRA; *GHQ* 28 (September 1944): 111–12, 196–208, 216–17. Mrs. Barrow's unpublished papers were "Holly Leaves: Savannah's Christmas Diary, 1870–1895,"
read 28 December 1934; "Poets, Writers and Men of Letters Who Have Appeared
Under the Auspices of the Poetry Society of Georgia from February 1923 to December 1936," read 27 January 1937; and "Some Facts Concerning the Squares of
Old Savannah," read 27 February 1935. On the last-mentioned date, Bell also read
her similar paper, "Some Curious Information About the Squares of Savannah."
Since the 1928 South Carolina Poetry Society's yearbook had announced a Barrow-
Bell collaboration on a historical work to be titled *The Old Squares of Savannah*
(p. 55), these papers were apparently drawn from the research for that book, which
was never completed or published.

The SHRA special number of the *Quarterly* marked the second time that Savannah had suggested such an issue to Athens. Mrs. Barrow had earlier proposed the
memorial number to Leonard L. Mackall (*GHQ* 22 [March 1938]; EDeRB to EMC,
[1938], EMCP-26).

84. *SMN*, 20 August 1974; O'Hara, "Mrs. Marmaduke Floyd," 293, 298–99;
Hartridge-Barrow correspondence, WC. Hartridge's voluminous papers are in the
Georgia Historical Society, as are some of Mrs. Floyd's; other Floyd manuscripts are
at Duke University.

85. EDeRB to Harriet Monroe, [June 1924], Poetry Magazine Papers, Univer-
sity of Chicago Library (several poems in Harriet Monroe's *The Difference and
Other Poems* [1925] were drawn from her time in the Blue Ridge); DuBose Hey-
ward to Hervey Allen, 22 August 1933, DuBose Heyward Papers, SCHS; EDeRB to
EMC, [1930], EMCP-10, Folder 12; Brooks, "Wormsloe House and Its Masters," 151;
Marie Conway Oemler to EDeRB, 20 September 1929, WC.

86. *SEP*, 10 September 1941, 31 August 1945; *Central of Georgia Magazine* 35
(September 1945): 1. In 1952 a plaque in Dr. Barrow's memory was unveiled at the
Central of Georgia Hospital during its Silver Jubilee (*SEP*, 2 August 1952).

87. Interview with the Reverend Frank A. Jenkins, Jr., 28 April 1991; Peggy
Noonan, *What I Saw at the Revolution* (New York, 1990), 259.

88. Interview with the Reverend Frank A. Jenkins, Jr., 28 April 1991; EDeRB to
J. L. Waller, undated Christmas card (c. 1950s), in private possession.

89. Edith Inglesby, "From the Ashes of the Old, a New and Different Empire,"
SMN Magazine, 4 March 1962, 6–7. Among others, the article listed these plantations and their current uses or owners: Causton's Bluff (housing), Deptford (housing), Mulberry Grove (industries), Coleraine (sugar refinery), Brampton (Dixie As-
phalt Company), and Hermitage (Union Bag–Camp Paper Corporation).

90. EMC to EDeRB, 24 November 1947, EMCP-46; *Bulletin, the University
of Georgia* 44 (June 1944): 4. The 1948 correspondence relating to the proposed

uses of Wormsloe by the university included plans for the cutting and sale of some of the timber, as well as the creation of a "Southeastern Arts Center," similar to the MacDowell Colony at Peterborough, New Hampshire, and to Yaddo in Saratoga Springs, New York (Jonathan Clark Rogers Papers, UGAL-A). Mrs. Barrow would not have looked favorably upon harvesting Wormsloe's timber; she made few changes in the natural environment of the estate because she enjoyed so much "the peacefulness of its age." She was a firm believer in what she called the "advantages of neglect." Nonetheless, in 1974 a pine-beetle infestation made cutting down many of the old trees a necessity (Interview with the Reverend Frank A. Jenkins, Jr., 28 April 1991; *SMN*, 22 February 1974).

91. EMC to EDeRB, 24 November, 4 December 1947, EMCP-46; EDeRB to EMC, [28 November 1947], EMCP-23, Folder 14; EDeRB to EMC, [c. 24 May 1948], EMCP-24, Folder 9; EMC to EDeRB, 18 June 1948, EMCP-46; EDeRB to EMC, 13 August [1949], EMCP-25, Folder 6.

92. WPA—Savannah Writers' Project, Collection Description, GHS; "Wormsloe," WPA-23; Lilla M. Hawes to EMC, 18 July 1949, EMCP-159; Britt, *Overture to the Future*, 12; Spalding, "Treasure House for Georgia's Past," 58. An unpublished WPA map of Wormsloe, like those in *Savannah River Plantations*, is in the EDeRBC.

Savannah native Mary Granger (1897–1970) was a graduate of Barnard College and Columbia University. Before her days with the Savannah Writers' Project she published three books: two contemporary novels—*Widow of Ephesus* (1926) and *Lucy and Three* (1930)—and a work of historical fiction, *Wife to Pilate* (1929). In 1932 she was awarded the last of the Poetry Society of South Carolina's Southern Prizes for "A Sonnet Sequence." She taught for a time at Armstrong Junior College in Savannah and the Women's College of the City of New York. Becoming interested in "river engineering and navigation" during World War II, she ultimately joined the U.S. Corps of Engineers, from which she retired in 1967 (*SEP*, 18 November 1970).

Lilla Mills Hawes (1908–94) was the society's director from 1948 until 1976, when she began a very active retirement, mainly centered at Hodgson Hall (*SMN*, 19 August 1994).

93. Montgomery, "A Few Words About E. Merton Coulter," 12–13; EMC to EDeRB, 24 May, 18 June 1948, EMCP-46.

94. Charters, Book 22, 456–58, SCR; *SMN*, 19 December 1951; Minute Book, Wormsloe Foundation, Inc., 27 December 1951, 22 November 1952, 9 January 1954; Agreement, the University of Georgia Press and the Wormsloe Foundation, Inc., 22 September 1954, Files, Wormsloe Foundation, Inc.

95. Minute Book, Wormsloe Foundation, Inc., passim. Other nonfamily trustees included Henry L. Ashmore of Armstrong State College and J. Frederick Waring, author of *Cerveau's Savannah* (Savannah, 1973).

96. Coulter, *Wormsloe*, [v], ix, 255–57; *SMN*, 26 June 1955.

97. *Atlanta Journal*, 11 January 1956; EDeRB to EMC, [1955], EMCP-99-1; Receipt, Manufacturing Costs of *Wormsloe*, 21 June 1955, Ralph Stevens to Craig Barrow Jr., 20 December 1956, Files, Wormsloe Foundation, Inc. Mrs. Barrow had *Wormsloe* bound in black cloth, in keeping with the customarily dark bindings of the quartos (EDeRB to EMC, [1955], EMCP-99-1).

98. *GHQ* 40 (March 1956): 92–93; *GHQ* 40 (June 1956): 151; *Mississippi Valley Historical Review* 42 (December 1955): 560; *Virginia Magazine of History and Biography* 64 (January 1956): 115.

99. *SEP*, 27 June 1955; Craig Barrow, Jr., to EMC, 17 June 1955 (Copy), Files, Wormsloe Foundation, Inc.

100. Coulter, ed., *Journal of William Stephens*, 1:xvii–xviii; *CRG*, Supplement to vol. 4, iii.

101. Ver Steeg, ed., *True and Historical Narrative*, x–xi; McPherson, ed., *Journal of the Earl of Egmont*, x.

102. Coulter, ed., *Journal of Peter Gordon*, 21–22; EMC to EDeRB, 24 October 1956, EMCP-104; *SMN*, 14 July 1957; English, *Roads to Research*, 57–58. *Laws of the Creek Nation* (edited by Antonio J. Waring) and *Lachlan McIntosh Papers in the University of Georgia Libraries* (edited by Lilla Mills Hawes) were, respectively, Miscellanea Publications 1 and 7 of the University of Georgia Libraries. At the suggestion of Richard Harwell, the foundation published for the University of Georgia Libraries a pamphlet by Harwell titled *The Confederate Constitution* (1979).

103. *JSH* 57 (November 1991): 721–24.

104. Coulter, *Joseph Vallence Bevan*, [v]; EDeRB to EMC, [c. 4 March 1964], Craig Barrow Jr., to EMC, 10 March 1964, EMCP-105.

105. Woodward, "Ellis Merton Coulter" (dissertation), 40, 48–50. After Mrs. Barrow's death Wormsloe Foundation Publications Number Eleven (1972) was dedicated "In Memory of Elfrida De Renne Barrow, Author, Scholar, Patron of the Arts."

106. *SMN*, 16 February 1961; "Map of Wormsloe and Vicinity Compiled from Authentic Maps and Aerial Photographs," [27 December 1960], WC; DB 77D: 267, SCR.

107. *SMN*, 16 February 1961; Affidavit of Craig Barrow Jr., 12 March 1970, File 7593, SCR.

108. *The Youth Museum Story* (N.p., 1965), 2–3 (the name of the museum was later changed to the Savannah Science Museum); *SMN*, 2 October 1970.

109. DB 89X:451, 553, 555, 557, 561, 563, SCR; *SMN*, 8 February 1968; *SMN/SEP*, 14 November 1976.

In 1979 the East Broad Street School reverted to the heirs of GWJDeR; it was purchased the next year by the St. John's Housing and Development Corporation (*SMN*, 13 December 1984).

110. *Atlanta Journal*, 15 March 1954; Interview with Helen I. Greene, 9 March 1994; Spencer B. King, Jr., *Sound of Drums* (Macon, Ga.), 539.

111. *SEP*, 31 August 1957.

112. *SEP*, 31 August, 2 September 1957.

113. W. S. Kirkpatrick, "Historic Wormsloe in One Family 223 Years," *Atlanta Journal and Constitution Magazine*, 19 April 1959, 24–26, 29; Kirkpatrick-Barrow Correspondence, WC.

114. Interview with the Reverend Frank A. Jenkins, Jr., 28 April 1991; EMC to EDeRB, 2 August 1948, EMCP-46.

Though he retired from teaching as professor emeritus in 1958, Coulter continued to serve as editor of the *Georgia Historical Quarterly* until 1974 and was a fixture at the university until his death at age ninety in 1981. In his latter years he found a burrow that suited him on the ground floor of Phi Kappa Hall, a columned antebellum structure just east of the Arch. There he continued to work, surrounding himself with a massive collection of eighteen thousand books and one hundred thousand manuscripts. When it was willed by Coulter to the university library, the collection was appraised at $410,000 (*Atlanta Journal*, 16 October 1967; F. N. Boney, *A Walking Tour of the University of Georgia* [Athens, 1989], 22–23; *Columns: The University of Georgia Faculty Staff News*, 19 October 1981, 2).

Two Twentieth-Century Fox films, *The View from Pompey's Head* and *The Three Faces of Eve*, used Wormsloe briefly for filming in 1955 and 1957 respectively; the latter used the oak avenue for its final scene (Correspondence, WC).

115. Bell, *Some Notes and Reflections upon a Letter from Benjamin Franklin to Noble Wimberly Jones*; [Waring], *Wedding at Wormsloe*, 2. As had been her grandmother, Laura Bell Barrow, younger daughter of Craig Barrow, Jr., was also married in Wormsloe House.

116. *Philadelphia Inquirer*, 27 February 1961; *Athens Banner-Herald*, 23 February 1964; *SMN*, 4 January 1968; *GHQ* 36 (December 1952): 397.

117. *SMN*, 4 August 1967; Kelly, *Short History of Skidaway Island*, 83; Affidavit of Illegality, 22 January 1970, File 7593, SCR.

118. EMC to EDeRB, 31 January 1970, EMCP-105; Spalding, *Book of Accessions*, 77–78.

119. Last Will and Testament of EDeRB, PCR.

120. *SMN*, 2 October 1970; Monument of EDeRB, Wormsloe.

APPENDIX 1. The Blood of Noble Jones

The bulk of the information for these charts and tables came from the Genealogy Files, DMWP, and JFP, GHS; Everard De Renne's "Family History" and
EDeRB's Application of Membership to the Georgia Society of Colonial Dames,
WC; materials in DeRFP-1, DeRFP-13, DeRFP-45 ("Miscellanea Georgiana"),
and DeRFP-58, UGAL; and NWJ Papers, GNJ Papers, and GWJDeR Papers, DUL.
Other information was secured through correspondence with descendants of the
various families. Pertinent publications are listed under "Genealogical and Heraldic Studies" in Selected Sources.

APPENDIX 2. Collections and Publications of the Jones–De Renne Family

A. COLLECTIONS

1. The Antebellum Library of George Wymberley Jones. "Miscellanea Georgiana," containing the manuscript catalog of this library, is found in DeRFP-45.

2. The G. W. J. De Renne Georgia Historical Collection (The De Renne Gift).
Major sources for this section are John Milledge's pamphlet *The De Renne Gift*
(1894), the manuscript on which the pamphlet is based (found in the Hargrett Library's accession file for this collection), and in the card catalogs for the collection
prepared by the Georgia State Library and the Hargrett Library. The General Assembly's resolution of gratitude for the De Renne Gift and the resolution regarding
"the Last Order of the Confederate Government" are found, respectively, in *Georgia Laws* (1894), 291, and *Georgia Laws* (1897), 602.

3. The Mary De Renne Confederate Collection. The two catalogs of the Confederate Museum (1898 and 1905) and Douglas Southall Freeman's *Calendar of
Confederate Papers* (1908) are the most important printed sources of information
for this collection. Some supplementary printed studies are listed under "Works
Relating to Civil War Manuscripts, Literature, and Collecting" in the Selected
Sources. The collection's books were also personally inspected by the author. During the research for this book, emended subject bibliographies were prepared for
the three collections listed above. Copies have been deposited with the De Renne
Family Papers at the Hargrett Library.

4. The Wymberley Jones De Renne Georgia Library. The several manuscript
and three printed catalogs of the library are the major sources for printed materi-

als. Information regarding the manuscript collections is found in the Hargrett Library's card catalog for manuscripts, the numerical notebooks listing the manuscripts, and the collection description notebooks and files.

B. PUBLICATIONS

1. Jones–De Renne Publications, 1847–86. The most valuable information regarding the earliest printed works of the Jones–De Renne family is found in DeRFP-41, DeRFP-43, and DeRFP-45 ("Miscellanea Georgiana"). Multiple copies of each title were also inspected by the author. Full bibliographical information is found in the *DeRLC*.

2. De Renne Publications, 1892–1931. Information was secured from the *DeRLC* and from examination of the books listed.

3. Publications of Elfrida De Renne Barrow, 1922–76. The afterword of *In the Calendar's Shadow* contains the best listing of her verse, supplemented by Sader, ed., *Comprehensive Index to English-Language Little Magazines*. The Poetry Society of Georgia Collection, GHS, was also useful. The periodicals and books in which her poetry and prose appeared were also examined.

4. Wormsloe Foundation Publications. The bibliographical information relating to these books was obtained from an examination of the books themselves.

APPENDIX 3. WORMSLOE SINCE 1970

1. Documents relating to the court case are found in File 7593, SCR. Elfrida De Renne Barrow was succeeded as chair of the Wormsloe Foundation by the historian J. Frederick Waring (1902–72). After his death, Laura Bell Barrow (Mrs. Craig Barrow, Jr.) was elected chairman, a post she still held in 1999. From the foundation's creation until his death in 1978, Craig Barrow, Jr., served variously as secretary and treasurer of the foundation. His son, Craig Barrow III, was elected to succeed him as treasurer.

2. *SEP*, 14 May 1971; *Reports . . . Court of Appeals* 123 (1972), 765–66; File 7593, SCR. The case had been transferred to the Court of Appeals from the Georgia Supreme Court (*Georgia Cases* [1971], 481).

3. Charters, Books 29 (424–29) and 50 (278–79), SCR; Minute Book, Wormsloe Foundation, Inc., passim.

4. *Georgia Reports* 228 (1973): 722–33.

5. *SMN*, 2 March 1972; Memorandum, Joe D. Tanner to Governor Jimmy Carter, 15 December 1972, RG 86-SG1-Ser.1, Department of Natural Resources, GDAH (hereinafter cited as Memorandum).

6. *SMN*, 25 October 1972; *Addresses of Jimmy Carter* (Budget Message, 11 Jan-

uary 1973), 176; Memorandum; DB 101"O":987, SCR; Press Release, Office of the Governor, 30 December 1972, RG 86-SG1-Ser.1, Department of Natural Resources, GDAH; *Atlanta Journal,* 31 December 1972, 11 January 1973; *SEP,* 31 December 1972, 18 August 1973; DB 102 S:349, SCR; Joe D. Tanner to Lilla Mills Hawes, 14 August 1973, Wormsloe Plantation Vertical File, GHS; Jimmy Carter to Mr. and Mrs. Craig Barrow, Jr., 21 August 1973, Minute Book, Wormsloe Foundation, Inc.

7. DB 102 S:349, SCR; Joe D. Tanner to Craig Barrow, Jr., 27 July 1977, David E. Morine to Craig Barrow, Jr., 29 July 1977, RG 86-SG1-Ser. 1, Department of Natural Resources, GDAH; Copy of Indenture, 11 September 1978, WHS. In 1982 the Wormsloe Foundation donated to the Telfair Academy the four family portraits that had been sold by the Knoedler Gallery in 1937 (*Georgia Gazette,* 6 January 1982).

The series of Wormsloe Foundation publications continued after Elfrida De Renne Barrow's death and the state's acquisition of Wormsloe. Professor Coulter edited four more publications before his death, three of them additional volumes of the Salzburger Reports (1972, 1976, 1980); the fourth was William Kelso's account of his excavations at Wormsloe, *Captain Jones's Wormslow* (1979), which finally placed the eighteenth-century ruins in appropriate context.

There have been seven widely varied publications since Coulter's death: John Linley's architectural guide, *The Georgia Catalog* (1982); *Forty Years of Diversity* (edited by Harvey H. Jackson and Phinizy Spalding), a collection of essays on colonial Georgia based on papers prepared for a symposium marking the 250th anniversary of Georgia's founding (and dedicated to the memory of E. Merton Coulter); *The Ogeechee: A River and Its People* (1986), a popular photographic survey by Jack Leigh; *Trees of the Southeastern United States* (1988), a profusely illustrated field guide by Wilbur H. Duncan and Marion B. Duncan; and Mart A. Stewart's *"What Nature Suffers to Groe"* (1996), an environmental history of the Georgia coast, 1680–1920; and, in 1999, the Duncans' *Wildflowers of the Eastern United States* and the present volume.

The foundation also continued to contribute toward the preparation and publication of other historical works, including the *Georgia Historical Quarterly Index, Volumes I–LX, 1917–1976* (1991).

8. Interpretive Prospectus for Wormsloe, Savannah, Georgia, August 1978, WHS; *SMN/SEP,* 24 August 1980; *SMN,* 6 February 1984, 7 July 1991; *SEP,* 9 July 1990, 12 November 1991; *Islands Closeup,* 29 April 1993; Victoria and Frank Logue, *Georgia Outdoors* (Winston-Salem, N.C., 1993), 129–31; Roulhac Toledano, *The National Trust Guide to Savannah* (New York, 1997), 47. In 1981, during the governorship of George Busbee, Wormsloe was dedicated as a Heritage Preserve (Record Book 160 U-658, SCR).

Selected Sources

Primary Sources

Manuscripts and Other Unpublished Sources

American Antiquarian Society, Worcester, Massachusetts
    Inscriptions and Laid-in Materials, De Renne Publications
British Library, London, England
    Reports and Papers Relating to America, 1710–65
Buncombe County Courthouse, Asheville, N.C.
    Register of Deeds
Chatham County Courthouse, Savannah, Georgia
    Probate Court Records
    Superior Court Records
City Archives, Philadelphia, Pennsylvania
    Certificates of Death
    Wills
Clarke County Courthouse, Athens, Ga.
    Probate Court Records
    Superior Court Records
William L. Clements Library, University of Michigan, Ann Arbor, Michigan
    Henry B. Dawson Papers
Duke University, Durham, N.C.
    Special Collections, William R. Perkins Library
        Accession Files
        George Wymberley Jones De Renne Papers, 1782–1916
        Marmaduke Floyd Collection
        Charles Colcock Jones Jr. Papers, 1763–1926
        Charles Edgeworth Jones Papers, 1815–1929
        George Noble Jones Papers, 1786–1872
        Noble Wimberly Jones Papers, 1766–1811
    University Archives, William R. Perkins Library, Robert Lee Flowers Correspondence File

Emory University Library, Atlanta, Georgia
  Keith M. Read Confederate Collection
Fort Concho Archives, Fort Concho National Historic Landmark, San Angelo,
  Texas
  Letter of Elizabeth Smith, 28 August 1882
Georgia Department of Archives and History, Atlanta, Georgia
  Department of Natural Resources, Correspondence Files
  Georgia, Surveyor General, Register of Grants
  Minutes, Board of Regents of the University System of Georgia (Microfilm)
Georgia Historical Society, Savannah, Georgia
  Chatham County, Georgia, Tax Digests, Ms. 5125
  Chatham County, Superior Court, Judgments, Ms. 5125-SP
  Christ Church of Savannah, Georgia, Vestry Minutes, Ms. 978
  Map Collection
  Marmaduke Hamilton and Dolores Boisfeuillet Floyd Papers, Ms. 1308
  Genealogy Files
  Georgia Historical Society Archives, Ms. 1361 AD
    George Wymberley Jones De Renne Correspondence File
    Wymberley Jones De Renne Correspondence File
    Wymberley Wormsloe De Renne Correspondence File
    Georgia Historical Society Membership Lists
    Georgia Historical Society Minute Books
    U. B. Phillips Correspondence File
  John Grimes Papers, Ms. 332
  Walter Charlton Hartridge, Jr., Collection, Ms. 1349
  Stewart Huston Collection, Ms. 1267
  Jones Family Papers, Ms. 440
  George Jones Papers, Ms. 439
  Ladies' Memorial Association Papers, Ms. 473
  James Edward Oglethorpe Papers, Ms. 595
  Poetry Society of Georgia, Ms. 1215
  Keith Read Collection, Ms. 648
  Savannah, Georgia, Registers of Free Persons of Color, Ms. 5600CL-130
  Savannah, Georgia, Tax Digests, Ms. 5600CT
  Savannah, Georgia, Ward Books
  Savannah Historical Research Association Papers, Ms. 994
  Savannah Writers' Conference Papers, Ms. 711
  Sons of the Revolution in the State of Georgia Collection, Ms. 1454
  Telfair Family Papers, Ms. 793

Vertical Files
   Huntingdon Club
   Plantations: Wormsloe
Work Projects Administration, Georgia Writers' Project, Savannah Unit,
   Ms. 1355
David McCord Wright Papers, Ms. 1277
James Wright Papers, Ms. 884
Wymberley Tract Collection, Ms. 1060
Georgia State Library, Atlanta, Georgia
Correspondence and Reports of the State Librarian
Historical Society of Pennsylvania, Philadelphia, Pennsylvania
   Boles Penrose Pictorial Philadelphia Collection
   Edward Carey Gardiner Collection
   Winthrop Sargent Papers
Independence National Historic Park, Philadelphia, Pennsylvania
   Specimen Folder: Portrait of Thomas Smith
Library of Congress, Washington, D.C.
   Douglas Southall Freeman Papers
   James H. Hammond Papers
   Historic American Buildings Survey Records
   J. Franklin Jameson Papers
   George Simon Kaufman Papers
   Library of Congress Archives
Municipal Archives, New York, New York
   Certificates of Death
Museum of the Confederacy, Richmond, Virginia
   Correspondence: Purchase of the Confederate Constitution
   Gilmer Memorial Volume
   Report of the Vice Regent of the Georgia Room, 6 December 1901
National Archives, Washington, D.C.
   Amnesty Papers (Microcopy M1003, Roll 20)
   Military Records: W. W. De Renne
   Records of the Assistant Commissioner for the State of Georgia, Bureau of
      Refugees, Freedmen, and Abandoned Lands, 1865–69. Record Group 105
      (Microcopy 798)
Newport Historical Society, Newport, Rhode Island
   Historic Building Data Files
   Georgiana King Diaries
   Trinity Parish Records, 1786–1861

Ohio Historical Society, Columbus, Ohio
    Winthrop Sargent Papers
Princeton University, Princeton, New Jersey
    Princeton University Archives, Seeley G. Mudd Manuscript Library
        Alumni Records
        Scribner Author Files
Rensselaer Polytechnic Institute, Troy, New York
    Archives and Special Collections, Folsom Library
        Alumni Records
Rosenbach Museum and Library, Philadelphia, Pennsylvania
    Correspondence File I:48:37
South Carolina Historical Society, Charleston, South Carolina
    John Bennett Papers
    DuBose Heyward Papers
Surrogate's Court, City and County of New York, New York
    Probate Records
Telfair Academy of Arts and Sciences, Savannah, Georgia
    Catalogue (Typescript), M. Knoedler & Company, c. 1937
    Fine Arts Accession Records
University of Chicago Library, Chicago, Illinois
    Poetry Magazine Papers, 1912–36
University of Georgia, Athens, Georgia
    Hargrett Rare Book and Manuscript Library
        Accession Files: De Renne Georgia Library, Telamon Cuyler, and Louis S.
            Moore Collections
        Robert Preston Brooks Papers, Ms. 1300
        Confederate States of America, Constitution: Correspondence and Miscel-
            lany, Mss. 1512–17
        Ellis Merton Coulter Personal Papers, Ms. 1710
        Telamon Cuyler Collection, Ms. 1170
        De Renne Confederate Manuscripts, Ms. 1135
        De Renne Family Papers, Ms. 1064
        De Renne Family Papers, Ms. 1064 (Oversize)
        De Renne Family Papers, Ms. 2819
        De Renne Family Receipts and Remedies, Ms. 1120
        De Renne Historical Manuscripts, Ms. 1136
        De Renne Historical Manuscripts, Ms. 1136 (Oversize)
        George Wymberley Jones De Renne Letters, Ms. 467
        Wymberley Wormsloe De Renne Papers, Ms. 1788
        Charles C. Jones, Jr., Papers, Ms. 215

Kollock Collection, Ms. 8

Map Collection (Printed and Manuscript)

Keith Read Collection, 1732–1905, Ms. 921

Margaret Branch Sexton Collection, Ms. 25

Thomas Smith Papers:

    Burton Alva Konkle Division, 1902–1906, Ms. 1055b

    George Washington Division, 1785–1912, Ms. 1055a

William Bacon Stevens Letters, Ms. 1134

John Donald Wade Papers, Mss. 837, 2945

Wormsloe Collection

University Archives

David C. Barrow Papers

J. D. Bolton Papers

Harmon W. Caldwell Papers

Minutes of the Board of Regents of the University System of Georgia

Minutes of the Board of Trustees of the University of Georgia

Jonathan Clark Rogers Papers

University of Georgia Library Directors' Papers

University of North Carolina, Chapel Hill, North Carolina

Southern Historical Collection, Wilson Library

Ulrich B. Phillips Papers, Ms. 2832

Vanderbilt University, Nashville, Tennessee

Special Collections, Heard Library

Edna Lytle Papers

West Texas Collection, Porter Henderson Library, Angelo State University, San Angelo, Texas

Assessment Rolls of Property and Rolls of Unrendered Property in Tom Green and Concho Counties (Microfilm)

Knickerbocker Ranch Papers

Susan Miles Collection

Tweedy Family Letters

David Williams Letters

Western Reserve Historical Society, Cleveland, Ohio

Emma Betts Sterling Diaries, Ms. 3323

Wormsloe, Isle of Hope, Savannah, Georgia

Files and Minute Book, Wormsloe Foundation, Inc.

Wormsloe Historic Site, Savannah, Georgia

Interpretive Prospectus for Wormsloe, Savannah, Georgia

Miscellaneous Files, Publications, and Photographs

General Sources: Books, Pamphlets, and
Articles from Periodicals

Abbey, Kathryn T., ed. "Documents Relating to El Destino and Chemonie Plantations, Middle Florida. . . ." *Florida Historical Quarterly* 7 (January, April 1929): 179–213, 291–329, and 8 (July, October 1929): 3–46, 79–111.

Avery, I. W. "The City of Savannah, Georgia." *Harper's New Monthly Magazine* 76 (January 1888): 256–71.

Baedeker, Karl. *London and Its Environs*. New York, 1908.

Barnard, George N. *Photographic Views of Sherman's Campaign*. Republication of the 1866 edition. New York, 1977.

Bell, Malcolm, III. *Some Notes and Reflections upon a Letter from Benjamin Franklin to Noble Wimberly Jones*. Darien, Ga., 1966.

Bellerive, Vevey, Switzerland. *Souvenir du Jubilé 50ᵐᵉ de la Fondation de l'Etablissement*. Vevey, 1886.

Bragg, William Harris, ed. "The Junius of Georgia Redemption: Thomas M. Norwood and the 'Nemesis' Letters." *Georgia Historical Quarterly* 77 (Spring 1993): 86–122.

Bremer, Fredrika. *The Homes of the New World*. New York, 1854.

Brickell, Herschel. "The Literary Landscape." *North American Review* 235 (April 1933): 376–84.

"The Buena Ventura Ranch." Broadside [1891]. In private possession.

Coulter, E. Merton, ed. *The Journal of Peter Gordon*. Athens, 1963.

———. *The Journal of William Stephens*. 2 vols. Athens, 1958–59.

Curtis, George William. *Lotus-Eating: A Summer Book*. New York, 1877.

De Brahm, John Gerar William. *History of the Province of Georgia*. Wormsloe, 1849.

De Joantho, Louis. *Biarritz Illustré*. Biarritz, France, 1885.

De Vorsey, Louis Jr., ed. *De Brahm's Report of the General Survey in the Southern District of North America*. Columbia, S.C., 1971.

Donnan, Elizabeth, and Leo F. Stock, eds. *An Historian's World: Selections from the Correspondence of John Franklin Jameson*. Philadelphia, 1956.

"Duelling in German Universities. By an English Student." *Strand* 13 (February 1897): 148–53.

Egmont, John Perceval, First Earl of. *A Journal of the Transactions of the Trustees for the Establishing the Colony of Georgia in America*. Wormsloe, 1886.

Freeman, Douglas Southall, ed. *Lee's Dispatches . . . 1862−65*. New York, 1915.

[Fuller, Hiram.] *Belle Brittan on a Tour, at Newport, and Here and There.* New York, 1858.

Gamble, Thomas, comp. *Georgia Miscellany*, 11 vols. and index. Savannah Public Library, Savannah, Georgia.

Georgia (Colony). General Assembly. *Acts Passed by the General Assembly of Georgia, 1755−1774.* Wormsloe, 1881.

————. *Georgia Colonial Laws, 17th. February 1755—10th. May 1770.* Washington, D.C., 1932.

Georgia Historical Society. *Collections of the Georgia Historical Society.* Vols. 1−18. Savannah, 1840−1976.

————. Descriptive Circular. [Savannah, 1903].

————. *Proceedings of the Dedication of Hodgson Hall by the Georgia Historical Society. . . .* Savannah, 1876.

Green, Julien. *Diary, 1928−1957.* New York, 1964.

Hand-Book of Newport. Newport, R.I., 1852.

Hart, James Morgan. *German Universities: A Narrative of Personal Experience.* New York, 1874.

Hawthorne, Julian. "A Feast of Blood." *Galaxy* 16 (September 1873): 405−9.

Howitt, William. *The Student-Life of Germany.* Philadelphia, 1842.

Hundley, Daniel R. *Social Relations in Our Southern States.* Edited, with an Introduction, by William J. Cooper Jr. Baton Rouge, 1979.

James, Henry. *The American Scene.* New York, 1987.

————. *The Art of Travel.* Edited by Morton Dauwen Zabel. Garden City, N.Y., 1958.

Johnston, Edith Duncan, ed. "The Kollock Letters, 1799−1850." *Georgia Historical Quarterly* 30 (September, December 1946): 218−58, 312−56; 31 (March, June, September, December 1947): 34−80, 121−63, 195−232, 289−322; and 32 (March, June 1948): 32−67, 119−43.

Jones, Charles C. Jr. "Memorial . . . with Regard to a Subscription on the Part of the State to His History of Georgia." N.p., [1882].

Lakewood, New Jersey. Lakewood, N.J., 1894.

Lumpkin, Wilson. *The Removal of the Cherokee Indians from Georgia.* 2 vols. Wormsloe, 1907.

McPherson, Robert G., ed. *The Journal of the Earl of Egmont.* Athens, 1962.

Mason, George C. *Newport Illustrated, in a Series of Pen and Pencil Sketches.* Newport, R.I., 1854.

Morris, Fritz. "The Art of Duelling Among German Students." *Illustrated Sporting News* 2 (9 January 1904): 16−17.

Myers, Robert Manson, ed. *The Children of Pride: A True Story of Georgia and the Civil War.* New Haven, 1972.

National Society of the Colonial Dames of America. Georgia. *Chatham County Map Portfolio. . . .* Athens, 1942.

————. *Some Early Epitaphs in Georgia.* Durham, N.C., 1924.

Niles, Hezekiah, ed. *Principles and Acts of the Revolution in America.* Samuel V. Niles's republication, revised and expanded, of the 1822 edition. New York, 1876.

Oliphant, Mary C. Simms, et al., eds. *The Letters of William Gilmore Simms.* 6 vols. Columbia, S.C., 1952–82.

Perry, Walter C. *German University Education, or The Professors and Students of Germany.* 2d ed. London, 1846.

Phillips, Ulrich Bonnell, and James David Glunt, eds. *Florida Plantation Records from the Papers of George Noble Jones.* St. Louis, 1927.

Pinckney, Elise, ed. *The Letterbook of Eliza Lucas Pinckney, 1739–1762.* Chapel Hill, N.C., 1972; paperback ed., with a new introduction. Columbia, S.C., 1997.

[Pinckney, Eliza Lucas.] *Journal and Letters of Eliza Lucas.* Wormsloe, 1850.

Prior, William P. *Vevey and Its Environs.* Vevey, 1855.

Reighard, K. Farrand. "German Students and Their Absurd Duels." *Cosmopolitan* 22 (January 1897): 227–34.

[Sargent, Winthrop]. *Diary During the Campaign of 1791.* Wormsloe, 1851.

Shryock, Richard H. *Letters of Richard D. Arnold, M.D., 1808–1876.* Durham, N.C., 1929.

Simpson, John Eddins, ed. *Jones Family Papers, 1760–1810.* Savannah, 1976.

Steed, Hal. *Georgia: Unfinished State.* New York, 1942.

Ver Steeg, Clarence L., ed. *A True and Historical Narrative of the Colony of Georgia.* Athens, 1960.

Walton, George, et al. *Observations upon the Effects of Certain Late Political Suggestions.* Wormsloe, 1847.

[Waring, J. Frederick.] *Wedding at Wormsloe.* Darien, Ga., 1968.

Weston, Plowden Charles Jennett, ed., *Documents Connected with the History of South Carolina.* London, 1856.

White, George. *Historical Collections of Georgia.* New York, 1854.

————. *Statistics of the State of Georgia.* Savannah, 1849.

GOVERNMENT AND OFFICIAL DOCUMENTS

Addresses of Jimmy Carter. Atlanta, 1975.

Candler, Allen D., and Lucian L. Knight, eds. *The Colonial Records of the State of Georgia.* 26 vols. Atlanta, 1904–16.

GEORGIA (STATE). GENERAL ASSEMBLY

Acts of the General Assembly of the State of Georgia (Georgia Laws). Atlanta, 1870,
   1871, 1875, 1894, 1897.

State of Georgia. *Annual Reports of the State Librarian.* Atlanta, 1907–18.

U.S. Naval War Records Office. *Official Records of the Union and Confederate
   Navies in the War of the Rebellion.* 30 vols. and index. Washington, D.C., 1894–
   1927.

U.S. War Department. *The War of the Rebellion: A Compilation of the Official
   Records of the Union and Confederate Armies.* 70 vols. in 128. Washington,
   D.C., 1880–1901.

MEMOIRS AND AUTOBIOGRAPHIES

Brooks, Robert Preston. *Under Seven Flags: An Autobiographical Sketch.* Athens,
   1957.

Cheek, Mary Tyler Freeman. "Douglas Southall Freeman: My Father as a
   Writer." *Richmond Literary and Historical Quarterly* 1 (1979): 33–41.

———. "Reflections." *Virginia Magazine of History and Biography* 94 (1986):
   25–39.

Clark, Thomas M. *Reminiscences.* 2d ed. New York, 1895.

[Cuyler, Telamon.] *Telamon Cuyler: Sportsman, Historian and Man of Letters.*
   N.p., c. 1943.

De Renne, Kentwyn. "Autobiography." Typescript. 3 April 1946. In private possession.

Elliott, Maud Howe. *This Was My Newport.* Cambridge, Mass., 1944.

Evans, George Bird. *Recollections of a Shooting Guest, Including the Unfinished
   Manuscript of Charles C. Norris.* Clinton, N.J., 1978.

[Gardiner, Robert Hallowell IV, and William Tudor Gardiner, eds.] *Early Recollections of Robert Hallowell Gardiner, 1782–1864.* Hallowell, Maine, 1936.

Harden, William. *Recollections of a Long and Satisfactory Life.* Savannah, 1934.

James, Henry. *Autobiography.* New York, 1956.

Jenkins, Frank Allen, Jr. "Wormsloe Plantation: Impressions of a Servant During
   Fifty Years of Service." Typescript. 16 February 1991. In private possession.

Long, Ellen Call. *Florida Breezes; or, Florida, New and Old.* Facsimile reprint of
   the 1883 ed. Gainesville, Fla., 1962.

McAllister, Ward. *Society as I Have Found It.* New York, 1890.

Middleton, Alicia Hopton, ed. *Life in Carolina and New England During the
   Nineteenth Century.* Bristol, R.I., 1929.

Monroe, Harriet. *A Poet's Life: Seventy Years in a Changing World.* New York,
   1938.

[Stevens, William Bacon.] "Autobiography of Bishop Stevens." *Church Magazine* 4 (November, December 1887): 462–75, 519–36.

[Stovall, Pleasant A.] *The Isle of Hope: Impressions of a Summer Visitor.* [Savannah, 1907].

Viola, Herman J., and Sarah Loomis Wilson, eds. *Texas Ranchman: The Memoirs of John A. Loomis.* Chadron, Neb., 1982.

Wormeley, Katharine Prescott. "Reminiscences of Newport in the Fifties." Edited with an Introduction by Richard L. Champlin. *Newport History* 41 (Winter 1968): 1–17.

MISCELLANEOUS SOURCES

City Directories: New York, Philadelphia, Savannah. Various dates.

Georgia Historical Association. *Proceedings.* 1917–19.

Georgia Historical Society. *Annals.* 1915–16.

———. *GHS Footnotes* 21 (Fall 1995), 23 (Spring–Summer 1997).

———. *Proceedings.* 1914, 1917.

Litchfield Law School, Litchfield, Conn. *Catalogue of the Litchfield Law School, from 1798 to 1827 Inclusive.* Published by the Students. Litchfield, Conn., 1828.

Protestant Episcopal Church. Diocese of Georgia. *Journal . . . Diocese of Georgia.* Various places of publication, 1842–48, 1876–77, 1881.

Protestant Episcopal Church, Diocese of Pennsylvania. *Journal . . . Diocese of Pennsylvania.* Philadelphia, 1846–48.

Report of the Episcopal Female Prayer Book Society, 1847. [Philadelphia, 1848.]

St. Paul's College, Flushing, N.Y. *Catalogue.* 1838.

Sketch of Bonaventure, Charter, By-Laws and Regulations of the Evergreen Cemetery Company of Bonaventure. Savannah, 1880.

Society of the Sons of the Revolution in the State of Georgia. *The Constitution . . . and List of Members. . . . Savannah.* 1892, 1894, 1905.

Telfair Academy of Arts and Sciences. *Special Exhibition Catalogue.* Savannah, 1916.

University of Georgia, Athens. *Bulletin* (1915–20, 1944).

———. *Pandora* (1911–12).

University of Pennsylvania, Philadelphia. *Biographical Catalogue of the Matriculates of the College. . . .* Philadelphia, 1894.

———. *Catalogue of the Trustees, Officers, and Students of the University of Pennsylvania.* Philadelphia, 1843–44, 1844–45, 1845–46, 1846–47, 1847–48.

University System of Georgia. *Annual Report for 1938 by the Regents. . . .* Atlanta, 1939.

Secondary Sources

GENERAL HISTORICAL AND BIOGRAPHICAL WORKS:
BOOKS, DISSERTATIONS, AND ARTICLES

Anderson, Mary Savage, comp. *A History of the Georgia Society of the Colonial Dames of America.* Richmond, Va., 1950.

Anderson, Mary Savage, Elfrida De Renne Barrow, Elizabeth Mackay Screven, and Martha Gallaudet Waring. *Georgia: A Pageant of Years.* Richmond, Va., 1933.

Arnold, Richard Dennis. *An Address Before the Georgia Medical Society.* Savannah, 1868.

Art Work of Savannah. Chicago, 1893.

Auchincloss, Louis. *The Vanderbilt Era: Profiles of a Gilded Age.* New York, 1989.

Ayres, Anne. *The Life and Work of William Augustus Muhlenberg.* New York, 1880.

Babits, L. E. "Battery Wimberly: A Preliminary Topographical and Documentary Survey." Typescript. 1992.

Baldick, Robert. *The Duel: A History of Duelling.* New York, 1965.

Baltzell, E. Digby. *Philadelphia Gentlemen: The Making of a National Upper Class.* Glencoe, Ill., 1958.

Barrow, Elfrida De Renne. " 'Memento Mori.' " *Georgia Historical Quarterly* 7 (1923): 166–73.

———. "On the Bay One Hundred Years Ago: Being Various Items Compiled from the Advertising Columns of the Savannah Georgian of 1829." *Georgia Historical Quarterly* 14 (1930): 1–16.

Barrow, Elfrida De Renne, and Laura Palmer Bell. *Anchored Yesterdays: The Log Book of Savannah's Voyage Across a Georgia Century, in Ten Watches.* Savannah, 1923.

Bartlett, T. H. "Early Settler Memorials." *American Architect and Building News* 22 (3 September 1887): 107–9.

Bassett, John Spencer. *The Middle Group of American Historians.* New York, 1917.

Bell, Malcolm, Jr. *Major Butler's Legacy: Five Generations of a Slaveholding Family.* Athens, 1987.

———. "The Romantic Wines of Madeira." *Georgia Historical Quarterly* 38 (December 1954): 322–36.

Beveridge, Edyth Carter. "Where Southern Memories Cluster." *Ladies' Home Journal,* September 1906, 34–45.

Billington, Ray Allen. *Land of Savagery, Land of Promise: The European Image of the American Frontier in the Nineteenth Century.* New York, 1981.

Bonner, James C. "Charles Colcock Jones: The Macaulay of the South." *Georgia Historical Quarterly* 27 (December 1943): 324–38.

———. *Milledgeville: Georgia's Antebellum Capital.* Athens, 1978.

Boudin, J. L. "Notice sur le Château de Mirabel." *Revue du Midi* 26 (1897): 355–71.

Bragg, William Harris. "Charles C. Jones, Jr., and the Mystery of Lee's Lost Dispatches." *Georgia Historical Quarterly* 72 (Fall 1988): 429–62.

———. " 'Our Joint Labor': W. J. De Renne, Douglas Southall Freeman, and Lee's Dispatches, 1910–1915." *Virginia Magazine of History and Biography* 97 (January 1989): 3–32.

Brewer, Clifton Hartwell. *A History of Religious Education in the Episcopal Church to 1835.* New Haven, 1924.

Britt, Albert S., Jr. *Overture to the Future at the Georgia Historical Society.* Savannah, 1974.

Brooks, Robert Preston. *Georgia Studies: Selected Writings of Robert Preston Brooks.* Edited with an Introduction by Gregor Sabba. Athens, 1952.

———. *History of Georgia.* Atlanta, 1913.

———. "The Need for a New Historical Organization in Georgia." *Proceedings of the First Annual Session of the Georgia Historical Association.* Atlanta, 1917.

———. "Wormsloe House and Its Masters." *Georgia Historical Quarterly* 40 (1956): 144–51.

Bryan, Mary Givens. "Recent Archival Developments in Georgia." *American Archivist* 16 (January 1953): 55–61.

Bryson, Thomas A. *An American Consular Officer in the Middle East in the Jacksonian Era: A Biography of William Brown Hodgson, 1801–1871.* Atlanta, 1979.

Burt, Nathaniel. *The Perennial Philadelphians: The Anatomy of an American Aristocracy.* Boston, 1963.

Cady, Edwin Harrison. *The Gentleman in America.* Syracuse, N.Y., 1949.

Cahill, Daniel J. *Harriet Monroe.* New York, 1973.

Callcott, George H. *History in the United States, 1800–1860: Its Practice and Purpose.* Baltimore, 1970.

Carson, Hampton L. *A History of the Historical Society of Pennsylvania.* 2 vols. Philadelphia, 1940.

Cheyney, Edward Potts. *History of the University of Pennsylvania, 1740–1940.* Philadelphia, 1940.

Clark, Raymond C. *A View of Westport, N.Y., on Lake Champlain, Gateway to the Adirondacks.* Elizabethtown, N.Y., 1972.

Clemens, Gus. *The Concho Country.* San Antonio, Tex., 1980.

Cobb, Maud Barker. "The Condition of Georgia's Archives." *Proceedings of the Georgia Historical Association* 1 (1917): 32–35.

Collier, Malinda W., et al. *White House of the Confederacy: An Illustrated History.* Richmond, Va., 1993.

Connelly, Thomas L. *The Marble Man: Robert E. Lee and His Image in American Society.* New York, 1977.

Cooney, Loraine M., comp. *Garden History of Georgia, 1733–1933.* Atlanta, 1933.

Cooper, William J., Jr. *The South and the Politics of Slavery, 1828–1856.* Baton Rouge, 1978.

Corner, George W. *Two Centuries of Medicine: A History of the School of Medicine, University of Pennsylvania.* Philadelphia, 1965.

Cortazzi, Hugh. *Victorians in Japan.* London, 1987.

Coulter, E. Merton. *Georgia: A Short History.* Chapel Hill, 1960.

———. *Joseph Vallence Bevan: Georgia's First Official Historian.* Athens, 1964.

———. *A Short History of Georgia.* Chapel Hill, 1933.

———. *The South During Reconstruction.* Baton Rouge, 1947.

———. *Thomas Spalding of Sapelo.* University, La., 1940.

———. "When John Wesley Preached in Georgia." *Georgia Historical Quarterly* 9 (December 1925): 317–51.

———. "William Bacon Stevens: Physician, Historian, Teacher, Preacher." *Georgia Historical Quarterly* 33 (June 1949): 91–109.

———. *Wormsloe: Two Centuries of a Georgia Family.* Athens, 1955.

———, ed. *Georgia's Disputed Ruins.* Chapel Hill, 1937.

Dalmasso, Alain. *Montpellier et sa région.* N.p., 1975.

Daniel, John Warwick. *Robert Edward Lee: An Oration.* Savannah, 1883.

Davies, Wallace Evan. *Patriotism on Parade: The Story of Veterans' and Hereditary Organizations in America, 1783–1900.* Cambridge, Mass., 1955.

Davis, Virgil Sim. "Stephen Elliott: A Southern Bishop in Peace and War." Ph.D. dissertation, University of Georgia, 1964.

De Renne, Augusta Floyd. "The Formal Garden at Wormsloe." *Junior League Magazine* 16 (June 1930): 24–25.

[De Renne, Wymberley Jones.] *A Short History of the Confederate Constitutions of the Confederate States of America, 1861–1899.* Savannah, 1909.

Dillon, Merton L. *Ulrich Bonnell Phillips: Historian of the Old South.* Baton Rouge, 1985.

Doherty, Herbert J., Jr. *Richard Keith Call: Southern Unionist.* Gainesville, Fla., 1961.

[Duncan, Alexander McC.] *Roll of Officers and Members of the Georgia Hussars.* Savannah, 1907.

Duncan, Russell. *Freedom's Shore: Tunis Campbell and the Georgia Freedmen.* Athens, 1986.

Durham, Roger S. "Savannah: Mr. Lincoln's Christmas Present." *Blue and Gray Magazine* 8 (February 1991): 8–18, 42–53.

Dyer, Thomas G. *The University of Georgia: A Bicentennial History, 1785–1985.* Athens, 1985.

Eaton, Clement. *A History of the Old South.* 2d ed. New York, 1966.

Emerson, Mrs. B. A. C. *Historic Southern Monuments: Representative Memorials of the Heroic Dead of the Southern Confederacy.* New York, 1911.

Ezell, John S. "A Southern Education for Southrons." *Journal of Southern History* 17 (August 1951): 303–27.

Ferguson, J. Walton. *Kingscote: Newport Cottage Orné.* Newport, R.I., 1977.

Ford, Worthington C. "Manuscripts and Historical Archives." *Annual Report, American Historical Association* (1915): 77–84.

Foster, Gaines M. *Ghosts of the Confederacy: Defeat, the Lost Cause, and the Emergence of the New South.* New York, 1987.

Franklin, John Hope. *A Southern Odyssey: Travelers in the Antebellum North.* Baton Rouge, 1976.

Freeman, Douglas Southall. *R. E. Lee.* 4 vols. New York, 1947.

———. *The South to Posterity: An Introduction to the Writing of Confederate History.* New York, 1939.

Gamble, Thomas. *A History of the City Government of Savannah, Ga., from 1790 to 1901.* [Savannah, 1901.]

———. *Savannah Duels and Duellists, 1733–1877.* Savannah, 1923.

Genovese, Eugene D. *Roll, Jordan, Roll: The World the Slaves Made.* New York, 1975.

Georgia: A Guide to Its Towns and Countryside. American Guide Series. Athens, 1940.

Georgia Writers' Project. *Drums and Shadows: Survival Studies Among the Georgia Coastal Negroes.* Athens, 1940, 1986 (Brown Thrasher ed., introduction by Charles Joyner).

Geschichte des Corps Saxonia zu Leipzig, 1812 bis 1912. Leipzig, 1912.

Gignilliat, John L. "The Thought of Douglas Southall Freeman." Ph.D. dissertation, University of Wisconsin, 1968.

Grady, Henry W. *The New South.* Savannah, 1971.

Green, Fletcher M. *The Role of the Yankee in the Old South.* Athens, 1972.

Green, Samuel S. "William Noel Sainsbury." *Proceedings of the American Antiquarian Society* 10 (April 1895): 28–31.

Green, William Elton. "Land Settlement in West Texas: Tom Green County, A Case Study, 1874–1903." Ph.D. dissertation, Texas Tech University, 1981.

Gregory, G. A. *Savannah and Its Surroundings.* Savannah, 1890.

[Harden, William.] "The Georgia Historical Society." *Georgia Historical Quarterly* 1 (March 1917): 6–13.

Harden, William. *A History of Savannah and South Georgia.* 2 vols. Chicago, 1913.

Harris, Thaddeus Mason. *Biographical Memorials of James Oglethorpe, Founder of the Colony of Georgia, in North America.* Boston, 1841.

Harwell, Richard. *The Confederate Constitution.* Athens, 1979.

Haunton, Richard H. "Savannah in the 1850's." Ph.D. Dissertation, Emory University, 1968.

Hester, Anne Jones. "Kingscote—First of the Newport Summer 'Cottages.'" Typescript. In private possession.

[Hewat, Alexander.] *Historical Account of the Colonies of South Carolina and Georgia.* London, 1779.

Hill, Tucker. *Victory in Defeat: Jefferson Davis and the Lost Cause.* Richmond, Va., 1986.

Hobson, Fred. *Mencken: A Life.* New York, 1994.

————. *Serpent in Eden: H. L. Mencken and the South.* Chapel Hill, 1974.

Hodgson, William Brown. *The Science of Language.* Newport, R.I., 1868.

Hoffmann, Charles, and Tess Hoffmann. *North by South: The Two Lives of Richard James Arnold.* Athens, 1988.

Hull, A. L. *A Historical Sketch of the University of Georgia.* Atlanta, 1894.

————. "The Making of the Confederate Constitution." *Publications of the Southern History Association* 9 (September 1905): [272]–92.

"In Memoriam. Report of Committee on the Death of the Late Wymberley Jones De Renne." *Proceedings of the Seventy-Eighth Annual Meeting of the Georgia Historical Society.* Savannah, 1917.

Irvine, Dallas D. "The Fate of Confederate Archives." *American Historical Review* 44 (June 1939): 823–41.

Irving, Washington. *Diedrich Knickerbocker's History of New York.* New York, 1927.

Ivers, Larry E. *British Drums on the Southern Frontier.* Chapel Hill, 1974.

Jack, Theodore H. "The Preservation of Georgia History." *North Carolina Historical Review* 4 (July 1927): 239–51.

Jameson, J. Franklin. *The History of Historical Writing in America.* Boston, 1891.

Joanne, Paul Benigne. *Biarritz and the Basque Country.* London, 1912.

Johnson, A. Sydney, et al. *An Ecological Survey of the Coastal Region of Georgia.* Washington, D.C., 1974.

Johnson, Elmer D. "Alexander Hewat: South Carolina's First Historian." *Journal of Southern History* 20 (February 1954): 50–62.

Jones, Charles C., Jr. *Biographical Sketches of the Delegates from Georgia to the Continental Congress.* Boston, 1891.

————. *The Dead Towns of Georgia.* Savannah, 1878.

————. *The Georgia Historical Society: Its Founders, Patrons, and Friends.* Savannah, 1881.

————. *Historical Sketch of the Chatham Artillery.* Albany, N.Y., 1867.

————. *The Siege of Savannah in December, 1864.* Albany, N.Y., 1874.

————. "Sketch of Dr. G. W. De Renne." *Southern Historical Society Papers* 11 (1883): 193–201.

Jones, Charles C., Jr., and John Brown Gordon. *The Old South.* Augusta, Ga., 1887.

[Jones, Charles Edgeworth.] *Art Work of Savannah and Augusta, Georgia.* Chicago, 1902.

Jones, Charles Edgeworth. "Col. Charles C. Jones, Jr., LL.D, Late of Augusta, Ga." *Gulf States Historical Magazine* 1 (March 1903): [301]–10.

Jones, George Wymberley. "Experimental Inquiry into the Correctness of M. Poiseuille's Explanation of the Purgative Action of Certain Substances." *American Journal of the Medical Sciences* 16 (1848): 308–10.

————. *Observations on Doctor Stevens's History of Georgia.* Savannah, 1849.

Jordan, John W., ed. *Colonial Families of Philadelphia.* 2 vols. New York, 1911.

Kammen, Michael. *Mystic Chords of Memory: The Transformation of Tradition in American Culture.* New York, 1991.

Kelly, V. E. *A Short History of Skidaway Island.* N.p., 1980.

Kelso, William M. *Captain Jones's Wormslow.* Athens, 1979.

Kime, Wayne R. *Donald G. Mitchell.* Boston, 1985.

King, Spencer B., Jr. "The Georgia Historical Society: Achievements and Aspirations." *Georgia Historical Quarterly* 47 (1963): 293–304.

Knight, Lucian Lamar. *Georgia's Landmarks, Memorials and Legends.* 2 vols. Atlanta, 1913–14.

————. *A Standard History of Georgia and Georgians.* 6 vols. Chicago, 1917.

Konkle, Burton Alva. *The Life and Times of Thomas Smith, 1745–1809.* Philadelphia, 1904.

Kraus, Michael. *The Writing of American History.* Norman, Okla., 1953.

Lamar, Joseph R. "Georgia Law Books." *Report of the Fifteenth Annual Session of the Georgia Bar Association* (1898): 118–46.

Lamar, Mrs. Joseph Rucker. *A History of the National Society of the Colonial Dames of America from 1891 to 1933.* Atlanta, 1934.

Lawton, Alexander R. "The Telfair Academy of Arts (Georgia Historical Society, Trustee)." *Georgia Historical Quarterly* 1 (March 1917): 13–24.

Lee, Charles Robert, Jr. *The Confederate Constitutions.* Chapel Hill, 1963.

Levine, Philippa. *The Amateur and the Professional: Antiquarians, Historians and Archaeologists in Victorian England.* Cambridge, Eng., 1986.

Lewis, Wilmarth S. *Horace Walpole.* New York, 1961.

———. *Rescuing Horace Walpole.* New Haven, 1978.

Lindsey, Elizabeth Chaplin, and Albert Sidney Britt Jr. *Isle of Hope, 1736–1986.* Savannah, 1986.

Linley, John. *The Georgia Catalog: Historic American Buildings Survey, a Guide to the Architecture of the State.* Athens, 1982.

Lockwood, Alice G. B., comp. *Gardens of Colony and State.* New York, 1934.

McCardell, John. *The Idea of a Southern Nation: Southern Nationalists and Southern Nationalism, 1830–1860.* New York, 1979.

McCullough, David. *Mornings on Horseback.* New York, 1981.

[Mackall, Leonard.] "William Harden." *Georgia Historical Quarterly* 20 (March 1936): 77–83.

Mackall, William W. *A Character Sketch of the Late Leonard Leopold Mackall.* Savannah, 1938.

Malone, Henry Thompson. *The Episcopal Church in Georgia, 1733–1957.* Athens, 1960.

Mandeville, G. Henry. *Flushing, Past and Present: A Historical Sketch.* Flushing, N.Y., 1860.

Marshall, Charlotte Thomas. *Historic Houses of Athens.* Athens, 1987.

Martin, G. H., and Peter Spufford, eds. *The Records of the Nation: The Public Record Office, 1838–1988, the British Record Society, 1888–1988.* Woodbridge, Eng., 1990.

Martin, Sidney Walter. *Florida During the Territorial Days.* Athens, 1944.

Mayer, Grace M. *Once upon a City: New York from 1890 to 1910.* New York, 1958.

Mayor, Jean-Claude. *La Tour de Peilz.* N.p., 1957.

Meldrim, Mrs. Peter W. *An Historic Pilgrimage Through Savannah and Some of Its Environs.* [Savannah, 1921.]

Memoirs of Georgia. 2 vols. Atlanta, 1895.

Meyerson, Martin, and Dilys Pegler Winegrad. *Gladly Learn and Gladly Teach: Franklin and His Heirs at the University of Pennsylvania, 1740–1976.* Philadelphia, 1978.

Michielin, S. *La Tour-de-Peilz.* Montreux, Switzerland, 1986.

Montgomery, Horace. "A Few Words About E. Merton Coulter." *Georgia Historical Quarterly* 58 (1974): 6–14.

Morrison, Mary Lane. *John S. Norris, Architect in Savannah, 1846–1860.* Savannah, 1980.

Muller, Fédia. *Vevey.* Neuchatel, Switzerland, 1964.

"A National Repository." *Southern Historical Society Papers* 22 (1894): 387–89.

Newton, William Wilberforce. *Dr. Muhlenberg.* Boston, 1890.

Norwood, Thomas M. *An Appeal to the Men and Women of the South to Build a Christian Pantheon in Honor of Our Confederate Heroes.* Savannah, Ga., [1906?].

Norwood, William Frederick. *Medical Education in the United States Before the Civil War.* Philadelphia, 1944.

O'Hara, Constance. "Mrs. Marmaduke Floyd: A Triumphant Life." *Georgia Historical Quarterly* 52 (September 1968): 293–304.

One Hundred Years of Life: Emmanuel Episcopal Church, Athens, Georgia, 1843–1943. Athens, 1943.

Oubre, Claude F. *Forty Acres and a Mule: The Freedmen's Bureau and Black Land Ownership.* Baton Rouge, 1978.

Owens, Hubert B. *Georgia's Planting Prelate.* Athens, 1945.

Peabody, William Bourn Oliver. *Life of James Oglethorpe, the Founder of Georgia.* Boston, 1844.

Penn, Neil S. "Charles Colcock Jones, Jr., Georgia Archaeologist, Collector, and Historian." Master's thesis, Duke University, 1958.

Phelan, Richard. *Texas Wild: The Land, Plants, and Animals of the Lone Star State.* N.p., 1976.

Phillips, Ulrich Bonnell. *American Negro Slavery: A Survey of the Supply, Employment and Control of Negro Labor as Determined by the Plantation Regime.* New York, 1918.

———. *Georgia and State Rights.* Washington, D.C., 1902.

———. *Life and Labor in the Old South.* Boston, 1929.

———. "The Public Archives of Georgia." *Annual Report, American Historical Association* (1903): 439–74.

Piggott, Stuart. "The Ancestors of Jonathan Oldbuck." *Antiquity* 29 (1955): 150–56.

———. *Ancient Britons and the Antiquarian Imagination.* New York, 1989.

Prucha, Francis Paul. *The Sword of the Republic: The United States Army on the Frontier, 1783–1846.* New York, 1969.

Public Record Office. *Guide to the Public Records.* London, 1949.

Ravenel, Mrs. St. Julien. *Charleston: The Place and the People.* New York, 1906.

Rosengarten, Theodore. *Tombee: Portrait of a Cotton Planter, with the Journal of Thomas B. Chaplin (1822–1890).* New York, 1986.

Russell, Count Henry. *Biarritz and Basque Countries.* London, 1873.

Sargent, Charles Sprague. "Winthrop Sargent." *Ohio Archeological and Historical Quarterly* 33 (July 1924): 229–36.

Sargent, Emma Worcester, and Charles Sprague Sargent. *Epes Sargent of Gloucester and His Descendants.* Boston, 1923.

Savannah Unit, Federal Writers' Project. *Savannah.* American Guide Series. Savannah, 1937.

Schauffler, Robert Haven. *Romantic Germany.* London, [1909].

Scoggins, Helen Virginia. "Telamon Cuyler and Korea." Master of Arts thesis, University of Georgia, 1960.

[Screven, John.] *Address of Colonel John Screven Delivered at the First Annual Dinner of the Sons of the Revolution on February 8, 1892, at Savannah, Georgia.* [Philadelphia, 1892.]

Sears, John F. *Sacred Places: American Tourist Attractions in the Nineteenth Century.* New York, 1989.

Secondy, Louis. *Histoire du Lycée de Montpellier, de l'ancien college des Jesuites a la Citadelle (1630–1988).* Montpellier, France, 1988.

Smith, George Gilman. *The Story of Georgia and the Georgia People.* 2d ed. Macon, 1904.

Smith, Henry Nash. *Virgin Land: The American West as Symbol and Myth.* Cambridge, Mass., 1970.

Smith, Horace Wemyss. *Life and Correspondence of the Rev. William Smith, D.D.* 2 vols. Philadelphia, 1880.

"The South's Museum." *Southern Historical Society Papers* 23 (1895): 354–81.

Spalding, Phinizy. *The Book of Accessions, Georgia Depositories, 1973–1980.* Savannah, 1981.

———. "Treasure House for Georgia's Past." *Atlanta Journal and Constitution Magazine* 6 May 1973, 54–58, 61.

Sparks, Andrew. "Magnificent Home for Georgia's Past." *Atlanta Journal and Constitution Magazine,* 2 October 1966, 11–12, 14.

Stephens, A. Ray, and William M. Holmes. *Historical Atlas of Texas.* Norman, Okla., 1989.

Stevens, William Bacon. *A History of Georgia.* 2 vols. Vol. 1, New York and Savannah, 1847; Vol. 2, Philadelphia, 1859.

Strong, Katharine H. "The Poetry Society of Georgia." *Georgia Review* 8 (Spring 1954): 29–40.

Sturrock, John. *The French Pyrenees.* London, 1988.

Tanner, Ogden. *The Ranchers*. Alexandria, Va., 1977.

Temple, Sarah B. Gober, and Kenneth Coleman. *Georgia Journeys*. Athens, 1961.

Tindall, George Brown. *The Emergence of the New South, 1913–1945*. Baton Rouge, 1967.

Tom Green County Historical Society. *Historical Montage of Tom Green County*. San Angelo, Tex., 1986.

Truman, Ben C. *The Field of Honor*. New York, 1884.

[Tuckerman, Arthur.] *The Newport Reading Room, 1853–1953: An Informal History*. Newport, R.I., 1954.

Van Rensselaer, Mrs. John King. *Newport, Our Social Capital*. Philadelphia, 1905.

Van Tassel, David D. "The American Historical Association and the South, 1884–1913." *Journal of Southern History* 23 (1957): 465–82.

————. *Recording America's Past: An Interpretation of the Development of Historical Studies in America, 1607–1884*. Chicago, 1960.

Wade, John Donald. *John Wesley*. New York, 1927.

Waring, Joseph Frederick. *Cerveau's Savannah*. Savannah, 1973.

Webb, Walter Prescott, ed. *The Handbook of Texas*. 2 vols. Austin, 1952.

Weigley, Russell F., ed. *Philadelphia: A 300-Year History*. New York, 1982.

White, George. *Historical Collections of Georgia*. 3d ed. New York, 1855.

Whitehill, Walter Muir. *Independent Historical Societies*. Boston, 1962.

Wilson, Adelaide. *Historic and Picturesque Savannah*. Boston, 1889.

Wilson, Clyde N. *Carolina Cavalier: The Life and Mind of James Johnston Pettigrew*. Athens, 1990.

Winsor, Justin, ed. *Narrative and Critical History of America*. 8 vols. Boston, 1886–89.

Woods, Lawrence M. *British Gentlemen in the Wild West*. New York, 1989.

Woodward, Michael Vaughan. "Ellis Merton Coulter and the Southern Historiographic Tradition." Ph.D. dissertation, University of Georgia, 1982.

————. "Ellis Merton Coulter: The Late Dean of Georgia Historians." *Atlanta Historical Journal* 27 (Summer 1983): 55–70.

Wormsloe: An Historical Plantation Dating from 1733. Wormsloe, 1937.

SOURCES RELATING TO BOOKS, PRINTING, AND COLLECTING: BOOKS, DISSERTATIONS, AND ARTICLES

GENERAL BIBLIOGRAPHICAL WORKS

Bowers, Fredson. *Principles of Bibliographical Description*. New York, 1962.

Brown, James Duff. *A Manual of Practical Bibliography*. London, [1906].

Esdaile, Arundell. *A Student's Manual of Bibliography*. London, 1932.

Gaskell, Philip. *A New Introduction to Bibliography*. New York, 1972.

Glaister, Geoffrey Ashall. *Glaister's Glossary of the Book*. 2d ed. Berkeley and Los Angeles, 1979.

Harrod, Leonard Montague. *Harrod's Librarians' Glossary*. 7th ed. Aldershot, Eng., 1990.

McKerrow, Ronald B. *An Introduction to Bibliography for Literary Students*. 2d impression with corrections. Oxford, 1928.

National Union Catalog, Pre-1956 Imprints: A Cumulative Author List Representing Library of Congress Printed Cards and Titles Reported by Other American Libraries. 685 vols. [London], 1968–80.

WORKS RELATING TO THE HISTORY OF PRINTING, PUBLISHING, AND BOOKSELLING

Brotherhead, William. *Forty Years Among the Old Booksellers of Philadelphia, with Bibliographical Remarks*. Reprint of the 1891 ed. Freeport, N.Y., 1972.

Derby, J. C. *Fifty Years Among Authors, Books and Publishers*. New York, 1884.

"The House of Henry Stevens, 1839–1907." *Publishers' Weekly* 71 (29 June 1907): 1912–13.

Keynes, Geoffrey. *William Pickering, Publisher: A Memoir and a Check-List of His Publications*. Rev. ed. London, 1969.

Meynell, Francis. *English Printed Books*. London, 1946.

Morison, Stanley. *Four Centuries of Fine Printing*. New ed. New York, 1960.

Stern, Madeleine B. *Antiquarian Bookselling in the United States*. Westport, Conn., 1985.

———. "Henry Stevens: 'G. M. B.'" *American Book Collector* 6 (May–June 1985): 3–9.

Stevens, Henry. *Stevens's Historical Collections*. London, 1881.

Updike, Daniel Berkeley. *Printing Types: Their History, Forms, and Use*. 2 vols. Cambridge, Mass., 1966.

Zachert, Martha Jane K. *Fine Printing in Georgia, 1950s–1990: Six Prize-Winning Private Presses*. Athens, 1994.

WORKS RELATING TO BOOK COLLECTORS, BOOK COLLECTING, AND LIBRARIES

"A. A. Smets, Esq., of Georgia." *De Bow's Review* 13 (July 1852): 97–98.

Brooks, Robert Preston, comp. *A Preliminary Bibliography of Georgia History*. Athens, 1910.

Burnet, Duncan. "The Libraries of the University System of Georgia." *Lavonia* (Ga.) *Times*, 27 October 1939.

Cannon, Carl L. *American Book Collectors and Collecting from Colonial Times to the Present*. New York, 1941.

Cantrell, Clyde Hull. "The Reading Habits of Ante-Bellum Southerners." Ph.D. dissertation, University of Illinois, 1960.

Carpenter, Kenneth E. *The First 350 Years of the Harvard University Library*. Cambridge, Mass., 1986.

Carter, John. *Taste and Technique in Book-Collecting*. New York, 1948.

Clizbee, Azalea, comp. *Catalogue of the Wymberley Jones De Renne Georgia Library*. 3 vols. Wormsloe, 1931.

Cole, George Watson, comp. *A Catalogue of Books Relating to the Discovery and Early History of North and South America Forming a Part of the Library of E. D. Church*. 5 vols. New York, 1907.

Coulter, E. M. "The Wymberley Jones De Renne Georgia Library." *Georgia Alumni Record* 17 (October 1937): 38.

[De Renne, Wymberley Jones.] *Books Relating to the History of Georgia in the Library of Wymberley Jones De Renne, of Wormsloe, Isle of Hope, Chatham County, Georgia*. [Savannah], 1905.

Dibdin, Thomas Frognall. *The Bibliomania; or, Book-Madness*. London, 1809.
———. *An Introduction to the Knowledge of Rare and Valuable Editions of the Greek and Latin Classics*. 4th ed. 2 vols. London, 1827.

Dickinson, Donald C. *Dictionary of American Book Collectors*. New York, 1986.

English, Thomas H. *Roads to Research: Distinguished Library Collections of the Southeast*. Athens, 1968.

Farnham, Luther. *A Glance at Private Libraries*. Boston, 1855.

Goff, Frederick. *Peter Force*. N.p., 1950.

Grolier Club. *Grolier 75: A Biographical Retrospective to Celebrate the Seventy-Fifth Anniversary of the Grolier Club, in New York*. New York, 1959.

Hazlitt, William. "On Reading New Books." *Monthly Magazine*, N.S. 4 (July 1827): 17–25.

Heartman, Charles. "Catalogue of the Wymberley Jones De Renne Georgia Library." *American Book Collector* 1 (January 1932): 19–23.

Jackson, Holbrook. *The Anatomy of Bibliomania*. Reprint of 1930 ed. Savannah, 1989.

[Jackson, William A.] *An Annotated List of the Publications of the Reverend Thomas Frognall Dibdin, D.D.* Cambridge, Mass., 1965.

Jewett, Charles C. *Notices of Public Libraries in the United States of America*. Washington, D.C., 1851.

Jones, Charles C., Jr. "Alexander A. Smets." In *Memorial Biographies of the New England Historic Genealogical Society,* Vol. 5. Boston, 1894.

———. "Israel Keech Tefft." In *Memorial Biographies of the New England Historic Genealogical Society,* Vol. 5. Boston, 1894.

Korey, Marie Elena. "Three Early Philadelphia Book Collectors." *American Book Collector* 2 (November–December 1981): 2–13.

Lehmann-Haupt, Hellmut, et al. *The Book in America: A History of the Making, the Selling, and the Collecting of Books in the United States.* New York, 1939.

Mackall, Leonard L. "Gwinnett Autographs, Anecdotes." *New York Herald Tribune Books,* 17 April 1927.

———. "The Wymberley Jones De Renne Georgia Library." *Georgia Historical Quarterly* 2 (June 1918): 63–86.

McKay, George L., comp. *American Book Auction Catalogues, 1713–1934, a Union List.* Introduction by Clarence S. Brigham. New York, 1937.

McMurtrie, Douglas. "Located Imprints of the Eighteenth Century Not in the De Renne Catalogue." *Georgia Historical Quarterly* 18 (March 1934): 27–65.

Milledge, John. *The De Renne Gift.* Atlanta, 1894.

O'Dwyer, E. J. *Thomas Frognall Dibdin: Bibliographer and Bibliomaniac Extraordinary, 1776–1847.* Pinner, Eng., 1967.

Phillips, Ulrich Bonnell. Review of *Catalogue of the Wymberley Jones De Renne Georgia Library at Wormsloe, Isle of Hope, near Savannah, Georgia. American Historical Review* 38 (October 1932): 174–75.

[Potter, Alfred Claghorn.] *The Library of Harvard University: Descriptive and Historical Notes.* Cambridge, Mass., 1934.

Rich, Obadiah. *Bibliotheca Americana Nova.* 2 vols. London, 1835–46.

Sabin, Joseph. *Bibliotheca Americana: A Dictionary of Books Relating to America, from Its Discovery to the Present Time.* 29 vols. New York, 1868–92 [Joseph Sabin], 1928–1936 [Wilberforce Eames].

[Sargent, Winthrop, VI.] "Bibliomania: M. Libri's Case." *North American Review* 76 (1853): 273–98.

———. "Bibliopegia." *North American Review* 79 (1854): 344–71.

Smets, Alexander A. *Catalogue of the Private Collection of Autographs of the Late Mr. A. A. Smets, of Savannah, Ga.* New York, 1868.

———. *Catalogue of the Private Library of the Late Mr. A. A. Smets, Savannah, Ga.* New York, 1868.

———. *Catalogue Raisonne of the Curious Manuscripts, Early Printed and Other Rare Books, Composing Part of the Library of Mr. A. A. Smets.* Savannah, 1860.

Spofford, Ainsworth R. "The Life and Labors of Peter Force, Mayor of Washington." *Records of the Columbia Historical Society, Washington, D.C.* 2 (1899): 219–35.

————. "Washington Reminiscences." *Atlantic Monthly* 81 (May 1898): 668–79.

Stevens, Henry. *Recollections of James Lenox and the Formation of His Library.* New York, 1951.

Tefft, Israel Keech. *Catalogue of the Entire Collection of Autographs of the Late Mr. I. K. Tefft, of Savannah, Ga.* New York, 1867.

Thornton, Ella May, comp. *Finding-List of Books and Pamphlets Relating to Georgia and Georgians.* Atlanta, 1928.

"The University Acquires Premier Library of Georgia History." *Georgia Alumni Record* 18 (September 1938): 11, 15.

University of Georgia, Library. *Catalogue of Books in the Library of the University of Georgia.* Athens, 1858.

[Wegelin, Oscar, comp.] *Books Relating to the History of Georgia in the Library of Wymberley Jones De Renne, of Wormsloe, Isle of Hope, Chatham County, Georgia.* [Savannah], 1911.

Wolf, Edwin, 2d. *"At the Instance of Benjamin Franklin": A Brief History of the Library Company of Philadelphia, 1731–1976.* Philadelphia, 1976.

WORKS RELATING TO CIVIL WAR LITERATURE, MANUSCRIPTS, AND COLLECTING

Bartlett, John Russell. *A Catalogue of Books and Pamphlets Relating to the Civil War in the United States, and on Subjects Growing out of That Event, Together with Works on American Slavery, and Essays from Reviews and Magazines on the Same Subject.* Boston, 1866.

Beers, Henry Putney. *The Confederacy.* Reprint of *Guide to the Archives of the Government of the Confederate States of America* (1968). Washington, D.C., 1986.

Confederate Memorial Literary Society, Richmond, Confederate Museum. *Catalogue of the Confederate Museum, of the Confederate Memorial Literary Society, Corner Twelfth and Clay Street, Richmond, Virginia.* Richmond, Va., 1905.

————. *Catalogue of the Confederate Museum, Twelfth and Clay Streets, Richmond, Va.* Richmond, Va., 1898.

————. *In Memoriam Sempiternam.* Richmond, Va., 1896.

————. *Year Book.* Richmond, Va., 1907, 1908–9, 1913–14, 1917.

Freeman, Douglas Southall. *A Calendar of Confederate Papers with a Bibliography of Some Confederate Publications.* Richmond, Va., 1908.

Harwell, Richard Barksdale. *The Confederate Hundred: A Bibliophilic Selection of Confederate Books.* 2d ed. Wendell, N.C., 1982.

————. *Confederate Imprints* (Catalog 114, Broadfoot's Bookmark). Wendell, N.C., 1982.

————. *Cornerstones of Confederate Collecting.* 3d ed. Wendell, N.C., 1982.

————. *In Tall Cotton: The 200 Most Important Confederate Books for the Reader, Researcher and Collector.* Austin, 1978.

Nicholson, John Page. *Catalogue of Library of Brevet Lieutenant-Colonel John Page Nicholson . . . Relating to the War of the Rebellion, 1861–1866.* Philadelphia, 1914.

Parrish, T. Michael, and Robert M. Willingham, Jr. *Confederate Imprints: A Bibliography of Southern Publications from Secession to Surrender.* Austin, 1987.

COLLECTED AND REFERENCE WORKS

Allibone, S. Austin. *A Critical Dictionary of English Literature and British and American Authors.* 3 vols. Philadelphia, 1858–71.

Appleton's Cyclopaedia of American Biography. 9 vols. New York, 1894–1922.

Dictionary of American Biography. 20 vols. Edited by Allen Johnson and Dumas Malone. New York, 1928–36.

Dictionary of Georgia Biography. 2 vols. Edited by Kenneth Coleman and Charles Stephen Gur. Athens, 1983.

Dictionary of Literary Biography. Vols. 1–97. Detroit, 1978–.

Dictionary of National Biography. 21 vols. with supplement. Edited by Leslie Stephen. London, 1885–90.

Evans, Ivor H. *Brewer's Dictionary of Phrase and Fable.* 14th ed. New York, 1991.

Lempriere's Classical Dictionary. 3d ed. London, 1984.

Lieber, Francis, ed. *Encyclopaedia Americana.* 13 vols. Philadelphia, 1829–33.

National Cyclopaedia of American Biography. Vols. 1–63. Clifton, N.J., 1891–1984.

Northen, William J., ed. *Men of Mark in Georgia.* 7 vols. Atlanta, 1907–12.

Thacher, James. *American Medical Biography.* 2 vols in one. Boston, 1828.

GENEALOGICAL AND HERALDIC STUDIES

Baring-Gould, S. *Family Names and Their Story.* London, 1910.

Bulloch, Joseph Gaston Baillie. *The Cuthberts, Barons of Castle Hill, and Their Descendants in South Carolina and Georgia.* N.p., 1908.

————. *A History and Genealogy of the Families of Bulloch, Stobo, De Veaux, Irvine, Douglass, Baillie, Lewis, Adams, Glen, Jones, Davis, Hunter, with a Genealogy of Branches of the Habersham, King, Stiles, Footman, Newell, Turner, Stewart, Dunwody, Elliott, with Mention of Bryan, Bourke, Williams, Wylly, Woodbridge, and Many Other Families.* Savannah, 1892.

————. *A History of the Glen Family of South Carolina and Georgia.* [Washington, D.C.], 1923.

Burke, John, and John Bernard Burke. *A General Armory of England, Scotland, and Ireland.* London, 1842.

Burke, Sir Bernard. *The General Armory of England, Scotland, Ireland, and Wales.* London, 1884.

[Cokayne, George Edward.] *The Complete Peerage, or A History of the House of Lords and All Its Members from the Earliest Times.* Rev. and enlarged ed. 13 vols. London, 1959.

Crozier, William Armstrong, ed. *Crozier's General Armory: A Registry of American Families Entitled to Coat Armor.* New York, 1904.

Ewen, C. L'Estrange. *A History of Surnames of the British Isles.* New York, 1931.

Fenhagen, Mary Pringle. "Descendants of Judge Robert Pringle." *South Carolina Historical Magazine* 62 (1961): 151–64, 221–36.

Kole, Kaye. *The Minis Family of Georgia, 1733–1992.* Savannah, 1992.

Leach, M. Atherton, ed. *Some Account of the Draytons of South Carolina and Philadelphia.* Lancaster, Pa., 1921.

Lower, Mark Antony. *English Surnames: An Essay on Family Nomenclature. . . .* 2 vols. London, 1849.

————. *English Surnames: Essays on Family Nomenclature. . . .* London, 1842.

————. *Patronymica Britannica: A Dictionary of the Family Names of the United Kingdom.* London, 1860.

Morgan, T. J., and Prys Morgan. *Welsh Surnames.* Cardiff, 1985.

Newton, William. *A Display of Heraldry.* London, 1846.

Park, Lawrence. *Major Thomas Savage of Boston and His Descendants.* Boston, 1914.

Pringle, Alexander. *Records of the Pringles or Hoppringills of the Scottish Border.* London, 1933.

Quinn, Alice Hawkins. *Descendants of Robert Gibbes (1644–1715), Colonial Governor of South Carolina.* 3 vols. N.p., 1991.

Reaney, P. H. *The Origin of English Surnames.* London, 1967.

Siddons, Michael Powell. *The Development of Welsh Heraldry.* 3 vols. Aberystwyth, Wales, 1991–93.

Smith, D. E. Huger. "An Account of the Tattnall and Fenwick Families in South

Carolina." *South Carolina Historical and Genealogical Magazine* 14 (January 1913): 3–19.

Williams, Richard, ed. *The Royal Tribes of Wales.* Liverpool, 1887.

Wimberley, Douglas. *Memorials of the Family of Wimberley. . . .* Inverness, Scotland, 1893.

Literary Works, Studies, and Miscellany

Axley, Lowry. "Savannah Writers' Conference." *Savannah Morning News,* 12 March 1939.

Barrow, Elfrida De Renne. "Georgia Poetry Society's Work 'A Bright Venture.'" *Savannah Morning News,* 14 April 1950, 6.

———. *In the Calendar's Shadow: Poems by Elfrida De Renne Barrow.* Edited and with an Afterword by Malcolm Bell III. Darien, Ga., 1976.

———. "The Poetry Society of Georgia—Its Organization and Aims." *Southern Literary Magazine* 1 (August 1923): 19.

Bernbaum, Ernest. *Guide Through the Romantic Movement.* 2d ed. New York, 1949.

Birrell, Augustine. *Obiter Dicta.* 2d ser. New York, 1887.

Brooks, Van Wyck. *The Flowering of New England, 1815–1865.* New York, 1940.

Brown, David. *Walter Scott and the Historical Imagination.* London, 1979.

Cowan, Louise. *The Fugitive Group: A Literary Study.* Baton Rouge, 1959.

Coxe, Maurice. "The Charleston Poetic Renaissance." Ph.D. dissertation, University of Pennsylvania, 1958.

Daiches, David. *Sir Walter Scott and His World.* New York, 1971.

De Renne, Kentwyn, ed. *Selections from the Writings of Josh Billings, or Proverbial Philosophy of Wit and Humor.* Athens, 1940.

Durham, Frank. *DuBose Heyward: The Man Who Wrote Porgy.* Columbia, S.C., 1954.

———. "The Rise of DuBose Heyward and the Rise and Fall of the Poetry Society of South Carolina." *Mississippi Quarterly* 19 (Spring 1966): 66–78.

Heyward, DuBose. "Contemporary Southern Poetry, II: The Poets." *Bookman* 63 (March–August 1926): 52–55.

Hubbell, Jay B. "Literary Nationalism in the Old South." In *American Studies in Honor of William Kenneth Boyd.* Edited by David Kelly Jackson. Durham, 1940.

———. *The South in American Literature, 1607–1900.* Durham, N.C., 1954.

Irving, Washington. *The Sketch Book of Geoffrey Crayon, Gent.* Edited by Haskell Springer. New York, 1988.

Jacobs, Thornwell, ed. *The Oglethorpe Book of Georgia Verse.* Atlanta, 1930.

James, Henry. *The Ivory Tower.* New York, 1945.

———. *Tales of Henry James.* Selected and Edited by Christof Wegelin. New York, 1984.

Judge, Jane. "Personal Impressions of Literary Persons Who Have Visited Savannah from 1882 until the Present Day." Typescript. C. 1931. In Savannah Historical Research Association Papers, Georgia Historical Society.

Landess, Thomas. *Julia Peterkin.* New York, 1976.

McClintock, Marian, and Michael Simms, eds. *O. Henry's Texas Stories.* Dallas, 1986.

Marvel, Ik. *A Bachelor's Reverie.* Wormsloe, 1850.

———. *Reveries of a Bachelor, or A Book of the Heart.* New York, 1883.

Mencken, H. L. "Editorial." *American Mercury* 17 (June 1929): 150–52.

———. *Prejudices: A Selection.* New York, 1959.

Monroe, Harriet. *The Difference and Other Poems.* New York, 1925.

Mott, Frank Luther. *Golden Multitudes: The Story of Best Sellers in the United States.* New York, 1947.

O'Brien, Michael, ed. *All Clever Men, Who Make Their Way: Critical Discourse in the Old South.* Athens, 1992.

Oemler, Marie Conway. *The Holy Lover.* New York, 1927.

Parrington, Vernon Louis. *The Romantic Revolution in America, 1800–1860.* New York, 1927.

Pinckney, Josephine. "Charleston's Poetry Society." *Sewanee Review* 38 (January–March 1930): 50–56.

Poetry Society of Georgia. *Anthology of Verse: A Collection of Poems by Members of the Poetry Society of Georgia.* Savannah, 1929.

———. *Year Book.* 1924–25, 1969–70, 1970–71.

Poetry Society of South Carolina. *Year Book.* 1921, 1923, 1925.

Ransom, John Crowe. *Armageddon.* Charleston, S.C., 1923.

Riley, Sam G. *Magazines of the American South.* New York, 1986.

Rubin, Louis D., Jr. *The Wary Fugitives: Four Poets and the South.* Baton Rouge, 1978.

Rubin, Louis D., Jr., et al., eds. *The History of Southern Literature.* Baton Rouge, 1985.

Sader, Marion, ed. *Comprehensive Index to English-Language Little Magazines, 1890–1970.* 8 vols. Millwood, N.Y., 1976.

Scott, Sir Walter. *The Antiquary.* New York, 1885.

———. *Redgauntlet.* Oxford, 1985.

———. *Waverley*. Harmondsworth, Eng., 1972.

Sieg, Gerald Chan. "Elfrida De Renne Barrow." *Savannah News-Press Magazine*, 7 June 1970, 3; reprinted in Poetry Society of Georgia *Yearbook*, 1969–70, [vi–ix].

Toledano, Ben C. "Savannah Writers' Conference—1939." *Georgia Review* 22 (Summer 1968): 145–59.

Afterword and Acknowledgments

When I first visited Wormsloe in the summer of 1985, I knew little about the De Renne family or their Jones ancestors. In fact, another, unrelated Jones had brought me to Wormsloe: Colonel Charles C. Jones, Jr. I was conducting research on a biographical sketch of the colonel (never to be written), and my main interest in the Isle of Hope was that Jones had been stationed there during the early months of the Civil War. For background data, I wanted information about the area's Confederate fortifications, and I rightly assumed that the museum at the Wormsloe Historic Site would be a logical place to start.

Auspiciously, Colonel Jones's own words—an evocative quote from *The Dead Towns of Georgia*—greeted me from a wall in the museum's lobby. But as I rode back toward Savannah up the oak avenue with the information I had sought, I found that I was not thinking about Colonel Jones but about the remarkable individuals whose images had appeared in the museum's displays and of their protean house, whose present incarnation loomed indistinctly to my right, through a thick screen of foliage. As fascinating as was Colonel Jones, the story of the De Rennes struck me as much more compelling.

After several twists and turns, two related journal articles came from my research. Both touched on the De Rennes (as well as Colonel Jones) and led to the discovery that numerous manuscripts were available in the Hargrett Rare Book and Manuscript Library that had been inaccessible when E. Merton Coulter had written his classic *Wormsloe*, with its abbreviated study of the De Renne family. Though there was no finding guide to these papers, which were still in process, it seemed that they might support a small book: basically a revision and expansion of the two journal articles, augmented with appendices surveying the various Jones—De Renne collections, as well as some photographs, mainly of books from the De Renne Georgia Library. In late 1989 the Wormsloe Foundation approved my proposal that the book (now imagined as a full-scale biography of Wymberley Jones De Renne) appear as one of its publications. I began research in earnest in the spring of 1990. By that Christmas, the amount of new material that had come to light merited an expansion of the book to its present form.

Vital to this evolving process was Eudora De Renne Roebling, to whom I had written requesting an interview. We met on Easter Sunday 1990, when she and her husband, Rip, visited me and my wife during a trip to Athens. Mrs. Roebling answered numerous questions and shared reminiscences, and I sketched out for her the book as it then stood—with the Bonaventure prologue then marking G. W. J. De Renne's principal appearance in the book. We were invited to visit the Roeblings later in the year; she thought that she might have some things that would be helpful to my research.

She was more than correct. There were hundreds of De Renne photographs (which until that time had been thin on the ground indeed) and masses of manuscripts, along with a stunning array of furniture, family portraits, and heirlooms that had left Wormsloe House over half a century earlier. It was as if the protagonist of Henry James's *The Aspern Papers* had immediately been handed the manuscripts he dreamed of. In his case, that would have left no story. In my case, it made it possible for me to tell the story thoroughly, and I will always be grateful for Mrs. Roebling's kindness and generosity and for the extraordinary hospitality of her and her husband during the several trips it took to explore such a voluminous trove of papers and other materials.

In 1990 I also made research trips west to Texas and north through most of the seaboard states east of the Mississippi, as far as Westport, New York. The expenses of travel and related research, then and later, were considerable, but the Wormsloe Foundation kept them from being prohibitively so, and attached no conditions to this support. As important—while the book was being researched and written during summers, on weekends, and in the corners of days spent teaching eighth graders—the foundation's trustees maintained an imperturbable patience regarding a book that originally was scheduled for publication in the early 1990s. For all these reasons, and more, I am deeply grateful to the trustees, individually and as a group.

At Wormsloe the family could not have been more hospitable or accommodating. Visits to the estate were always pleasant and productive. Research done there and conversations held there were essential to this book.

As might be expected, my obligations to institutions and individuals in Savannah are numerous. At the Georgia Historical Society's Hodgson Hall, Anne P. Smith, with the able assistance of Eileen Ielmini and others, helped make all my visits both fruitful and very pleasant. On several occasions Joe Thompson, superintendent of Wormsloe Historic Site, unselfishly shared his knowledge of Wormsloe's history and terrain. Gerald Chan Sieg graciously gave me the benefit of her memories of the Poetry Society of Georgia. I am also obliged for assistance from Elizabeth Scott Shatto and Pamela D. King at the Telfair Academy of Arts and Sciences, Erick Erickson at the CEL Regional Library, Katherine Keena at the Juliet Gordon Low Center, Helen Peterson at the De Renne Plaza Condominiums, Michael Powers at the Knights of Columbus hall on Liberty Street (the former De Renne house),

Benjamin B. Jones of the Sons of the Revolution in the State of Georgia, and the staff at Bonaventure Cemetery.

At the Chatham County Courthouse, Glenda F. Ricks cordially assisted with records of the probate court. In the vast deed room of the Office of the Clerk of the Superior Court, the staff was uniformly helpful, and the merry band of title searchers and courthouse functionaries always made research a very diverting and entertaining experience.

Muriel Barrow Bell and Malcolm Bell, Jr., had given valuable assistance during the preparation of the two journal articles that preceded the study of the De Rennes, and their generous interest continued during the research and writing of the book, furthering my labors in countless ways. Mrs. Bell's confidence in my work was essential to my completing it, and I only wish that the finished product approached Mr. Bell's *Major Butler's Legacy,* a model of multigenerational family histories. When the Bells moved from Savannah several years ago, I easily understood a comment by one of their friends, that it was as if the fountain had disappeared from Forsyth Park.

Through the Bells we had the pleasure of meeting Robert Manson Myers, among others. He shared insights into southern history in general, and the history of the Joneses of Liberty County in particular, and his kind expressions of interest in my work were very gratifying.

The Reverend Frank A. Jenkins, Jr., gave me the benefit of his many memories of twentieth-century Wormsloe and its masters, and his sharp recall of his father's reminiscences carried me back into the previous century as well. He also walked over a good part of the estate with me on a very pleasant day and, as usual, accompanied his facts with penetrating insights. He was a remarkable man, and I am indebted to his wife, Rosa Lee, for joining him in welcoming me to their home and for providing me with several particulars of his life.

Before I met Caroline Jones Wright, I had already profited from the extensive research on the Jones family by her husband, David McCord Wright, and from her own inspired work on the complexities of the Jones family tree. My debt to her and her family only increased after meeting her and enjoying the hospitality of her house on Chatham Square. I find it impossible to think of her valuable contributions to my research without remembering a circle of helpful people, including her brother George Fenwick Jones (who had already helped me on several fronts but whom I met through her), her daughter Anna Habersham Wright Smith, her son Peter Wright, and her friends Emory Jarrott and the Reverend John Reynolds, the latter of Oxford, England, and a descendant of Georgia's first royal governor. I am indebted to her and to them all.

Josephine Jones Connerat and her daughter Laura Lawton were also very helpful with information and antebellum correspondence, dispensed under the benign gaze of a portrait of William Neyle Habersham. I am very grateful to them and also to many others in Savannah who obligingly assisted me in several ways, including Clermont Lee, Spencer Connerat, Alfred S. Britt, Lilla Mills Hawes, and Glenn Carey Godbee. And along with everyone else interested in the history and literature of Savannah and Georgia, I owe a great debt to Mills Lane of the Beehive Press for his superlative series of books.

Beyond Savannah, but connected to it in my mind because of the De Renne connection, Jean Cobb De Renne was good enough to supply me with a copy of the autobiographical sketch written by her husband, Kentwyn Floyd De Renne. And Wymberley De Renne Coerr and his daughter Susan De Renne Coerr furnished needed information regarding the Coerr family.

It was my good fortune that the greatest bulk of manuscripts that support this book were located at the Hargrett Rare Book and Manuscript Library, University of Georgia Libraries. Under the direction of Mary Ellen Brooks, it offers the perfect balance between ensuring the security of its holdings and providing efficiently for the needs of researchers. I am very grateful to Mary Ellen, and to all the others at the Hargrett Library, for many years of courteous assistance.

Though my constant visits must have ultimately seemed more like visitations, all the staff members were uniformly helpful and accommodating. I am particularly indebted to Nelson Morgan, who went the extra mile numerous times; Larry Gulley, who had a knowledge of the collections (and the often unexpected correspondences between them) that can never be duplicated by a computer; and to Linda Aaron, Melissa Bush, Joe Cote, and Nancy Stamper, as well as to Amy Romesburg and Krista Harris. Many thanks to them all.

Sarah Lockmiller photographed what must have seemed an endless stream of items from the Hargrett Library and never produced a print that was less than excellent. Katie Brower has proved a worthy successor to her. Wilson Page and Gilbert Head provided much-needed help in navigating the acres of papers in the University Archives. My gratitude is due them, and also to the staffs of the General and Science Libraries at the University, and to William Gray Potter, Director of Libraries.

Susan Frances Barrow Tate and John W. Bonner, long mainstays of the university library's Special Collections section (as it was then known) shared their memories of Wymberley W. De Renne and other figures of the time; both provided valuable leads to other sources. My visits with Mrs. Tate were among the most richly memorable of my research experiences, and I will never forget her wit, her candor, and her compendious memory.

I also owe thanks to several of the university's professors, who expressed interest in the book or rendered aid to it: Kenneth Coleman, Phinizy Spalding, F. N. Boney, Thomas G. Dyer, John C. Inscoe, R. A. LaFleur, Robert Harris, and Ludwig O. Uhlig. My thanks also to Stanley W. Lindberg of the *Georgia Review*, who helped me with material relating to the Savannah Writers' Conference of 1938.

In addition to the staffs of all those institutions mentioned in the Selected Sources, I am also grateful to Sally MacEwen of the Classics Department at Agnes Scott College and to Sarah Hawk, her student back in 1991, who assisted me with some challenging lines of Latin; to Carroll Parker, the state librarian, for allowing access to the De Renne books then at the Georgia State Library, and to Martha Lappe of the library staff; to Debbie Curtis, architectural historian at the Georgia Department of Natural Resources; to Kenneth H. Thomas, historian and genealogist; and to the amazing Franklin Garrett, historian at the Atlanta History Center.

Thanks are also owed to the staffs of the Stetson Library, Mercer University, and Washington Memorial Library, particularly to Willard Rocker, master of the myriad treasures of the Genealogical Room, and to the Reference and Interlibrary Loan Staff (particularly Judy Atwater, now departed).

I also wish to express my appreciation to individuals and institutions elsewhere. In Charleston, South Carolina: Elise Pinckney, Mrs. S. Henry Edmunds, the South Carolina Historical Society, and Elizabeth Young Newsom of Waring Historical Library of the Medical University of South Carolina. In Columbia, South Carolina: Eleanor M. Richardson of the South Caroliniana Library. In Durham, North Carolina: William R. Erwin, Jr., of Special Collections, Duke University Library; Thomas F. Harkins of the Duke University Archives; and Kay Robin Alexander of Duke University Press. In Chapel Hill, North Carolina: Richard A. Schader, Manuscripts Department, and Libby Chenault, Rare Book Department, University of North Carolina Library. In Asheville, North Carolina: Dr. and Mrs. Joshua Camblos, and, in Wilmington, North Carolina, Tom Broadfoot.

Other individuals and institutions to which I am obligated include Suzanne Barrett, of the Karpeles Manuscript Library, located in several cities; Mary L. Robertson, Huntington Library; Donald C. Dickinson, Graduate Library School, University of Arizona; Donald O. Dewey, California State University; Diane Guerine, the Greater Cleveland Genealogical Society; Ingrid Abram, Bay Village, Ohio; Joan L. Clark, Cleveland Public Library; and Marcella Van Deren, Bloomington, Illinois.

Among Richmonders I wish to thank Mary Tyler McClenahan, daughter of Douglas Southall Freeman, to whom I am deeply indebted; the infinitely patient and helpful Guy R. Swanson and his colleague Corrine P. Hudgins of the Museum of the Confederacy; the staffs of the Virginia Historical Society and the Virginia Department of Archives and History; and Nelson D. Lankford and Sara B. Bearrs of the *Virginia Magazine of History and Biography* (wherein appeared an earlier version of "Maecenas," superbly edited); in Charlottesville, Robert A. Rutland and Richard H. F. Lindemann of the University of Virginia Library; and, in West Virginia, Wayne R. Kime and Robert Heffner, Jr., Fairmont State College, and Mr. and Mrs. George Bird Evans of Bruceton Mills.

At the Library of Congress I benefited from the help of John D. Knowlton (Manuscript Division), who generously allowed me access to a pivotal collection he was processing; Peter Van Wingen and Robert R. Shields (Rare Books and Special Collections Division); and Susan E. Watkins (Law Library). Nearby I was assisted by Michael P. Musick of the National Archives and Anne K. Toohey at the National Library of Medicine.

Among numerous helpful Philadelphians, I am indebted to Kevin Crawford, the College of Physicians of Philadelphia; Leslie A. Morris, Rosenbach Museum and Library; independent researcher Susan Gray Detweiler; Gail M. Pietrzyk of the University Archives and Records Center, University of Pennsylvania; Roy E. Goodman and Marie E. Lamoureux, American Philosophical Society; and Karen Nipps, Library Company of Philadelphia.

Also in Pennsylvania, thanks are owed to William C. Fischer of Media and Elsa R. Lichtenberg, Swarthmore Public Library.

Among those in New England who assisted me were Craig Barrow Bell; Paul F. Miller, the Preservation Society of Newport County; Jean Rainwater, Brown University Library; Daniel J. Slive, the John Carter Brown Library; Henry L. P. Beckwith, Jr., New England Historic Genealogical Society (for very generous assistance); Robert L. Volz, Chapin Library, Williams College; Jennie Rathbun, Houghton Library, Harvard University; Nancy S. Beveridge, Litchfield Historical Society; Joan H. Sussler, Lewis Walpole Library; William R. Massa, Jr., Yale University Library; Thomas Nixon, Sterling Memorial Library, Yale; Paul C. Allen and Patricia Middleton, Beinecke Rare Book and Manuscript Library, Yale.

In New York City, particular thanks to Julian Leslie Weller (who shared a wonderful series of letters from Elfrida De Renne Barrow); Jessica A. Sloop and Elisa Urbanelli, Landmark Preservation Commission; Abigail Lavine, Debra Randorf, and Mariam Touba, New York Historical Society; Christopher Gray, Office for Metropolitan History; and Claudia Funke, Rare Books Librarian of the New York Public Library and the nonpareil of helpful librarians.

Elsewhere in New York I am obliged to Lynne Farrington, Olin Library, Cornell University; Ralph Ketchum, Syracuse University; and Mrs. Raymond C. Clark, Jessica R. Smith, and Rita Warren of Westport.

For help with information relating to the Protestant Episcopal Church I am grateful to the Very Reverend Theodore Bean, St. Paul's Episcopal Church, College Point, New York; T. Matthew DeWaelsche, Archives of the Episcopal Church,

Austin, Texas; the Reverend James A. Trimble, Rector, Christ Church, Philadelphia; and Newland F. Smith III, United Library, Evanston, Illinois.

In Texas, which I found to be as wonderful a state as the Texans have always claimed, my obligations are great. I owe special thanks to Ginnie and A. H. Denis for their remarkable hospitality at the old Buena Ventura ranch house (including a delicious meal—and talk of sheep—in the dining room where W. J. De Renne had entertained the Knickerbocker ranchers) and to Mrs. Denis for a guided tour of the Kickapoo country by truck and for letters filled with invaluable information. In San Angelo, I became particularly indebted to Betty Jane Smith, Katharine Tweedy Waring, Betty Varner, Marie Russell (Tom Green county clerk), and John Neilson and Evelyn G. Flynn, Museum Research Library and Archives, Fort Concho National Historic Landmark. Thanks also to Margaret T. Taylor of Paint Rock, the Concho county clerk, who saw me off to a good start on my Texas researches.

For expert assistance with some French translations and for correspondence with (and telephone calls to) France and Switzerland, I was very lucky to have the help of Sunny McClendon (a student at Agnes Scott College when she first came to my aid), who proved herself a resourceful and tenacious researcher. Much appreciation is owed to Jean R. Cazenave, Biarritz historian; Archives d'Architecture de la Côte Basque, Biarritz; A. Irigoyen, Bibliotheque Municipale, Biarritz; Alain Paul, Archives du Gard, Nimes; Jean Le Pottier, Archives départementales de l'Hérault, Montpellier; Jeanine Sillig, Tour-de-Peilz (who provided invaluable records of her distinguished ancestors); Albert Curchod, archivist, Greffe Municipal, Tour-de-Peilz; Marjolaine Guisan, Archives Communales, Vevey; and Françoise Lambert, Musée Historique du Vieux-Vevey.

I was fortunate enough to meet the Austrian scholar Gabriele Eder in Athens when she was conducting research for her edition of the correspondence of the musicologist Guido Adler and the philosopher Alexius Meinong. She kindly assisted me with some translations and also conducted some correspondence for me in Austria and in the Czech Republic; I am much indebted to her for her exceptional generosity. Thanks also are owed to the Roudnice Lobkowicz Collection, with which her help was crucial.

In the course of preparing this book, many dealers in used and rare books helped me in numerous ways and are owed my thanks. Among them are Lilly Brannon of Golden Bough Vintage Books, Macon, Georgia, who supplied several hard-to-find titles; Chan and Miegan Gordon of the Captain's Bookshelf, Asheville, North Carolina, who helped me locate Mrs. Burnley Weaver (who in turn gave me information on her husband's career as an artist, for which I am grateful), and Frank O. Walsh III, of the Yesteryear Book Shop, Atlanta, Georgia, who furnished me with several useful descriptions of those Wormsloe Quartos that have come on the market during the past several years (the *Acts* quarto, for example, has been offered for $1,500).

Researching and writing this book brought home to me my heavy obligations to those historians of the old school under whom I studied at Georgia College, among them James C. Bonner, Martin Abbott, Helen I. Greene (who talked with me about her friend Elfrida De Renne Barrow), and exemplary mentors William I. Hair and Frank B. Vinson.

Sarah Gordon of Georgia College's Department of English had earlier introduced me to many of the figures in the book's last chapter and more recently read *In the Calendar's Shadow* and discussed it with me, for which I am very grateful.

I am greatly indebted to many individuals at the University of Georgia Press, particularly Karen Orchard, Malcolm Call, and Kristine Blakeslee. The press's selection of Trudie Calvert as copyeditor and Sandy Hudson as designer was a wonderful gift, and I am most grateful that this book had the benefit of their artistry and expertise.

Closer to home, I must mention my parents, Fran and Harris Bragg, who raised me in a home where books, reading, and learning were highly valued—a wonderful gift—and to their parents, Nell and William Hardin and Eunice and Noel Bragg, for giving them (and consequently me) the same gift.

Mary Frances Smith, my wife's mother, cheerfully accompanied us on several book-related adventures, and my wife's aunt and uncle Grace and John L. Tatum long ago gave me two of the major necessities of a writer: a large desk and a roomy bookcase. I am indebted to them for these and many other reasons.

Linda and Albert Bloodworth, Danny and Kathie Greene, Bill Moffat, and Neel Stallings listened patiently to various effusions regarding this book, and I thank them kindly.

For many reasons I owe many thanks to Alice Golson, Berta Morton, Sally Wicker, Sue Greene, Ruth Moughon, Helen Pearson, Suellen Boyette, Mary Ann Hamrick, Carolyn White Williams, Elizabeth Knox, Joyce Lawrence, Martha Odom, Anne Greene Stewart, Louise Morton, Dot and Emmett Bragg, Duffie and Don Lawler, Florence Greene Childs, Dauphin Vesro Childs, Jr., Coxie and Mac Davis, Mary Ellison, Dotty and Jerry Walker, Ethel and Jimmy Rearden, Anne Winters, Mildred Wooten, Mariellyn Lunceford, and Ruth Waller Hill.

My wife, Wanda, was indispensable to the creation of this book. Words can never thank her sufficiently for all she has done and all she has tolerated over the past several years.

Index

Candler, Allen, 298

Canot, Theodore, 96

Cantrell, Clyde Hull, 452–53 (n. 51)

Captain Canot (Canot), 96

Captain Jones's Wormslow (Kelso), 393, 561 (n. 7)

Caractères (Bruyere), 274

Carlyle, Thomas: quoted, 252

Carpenter, Rev. Charles Colcock Jones, 334

Carpenter, Ruth Jones, 281

Carroll, Charles, 58

Carson, Hampton L., 238, 239

Carter, Jimmy, 437

Cattle ranching, 200, 203, 204–5

Caxton, William, 20

Central of Georgia Railroad, 171, 211, 301, 331

Chambers, Sarah E., 218

Chappell, George S., 333

Charles I, King of England, 184

Charles II, King of England, 462 (n. 2)

Charles Scribner's Sons, 272

Charlton, Walter G., 380

Charters, etc., of the Provinces of North America, The, 310

Chats on Autographs (Broadley), 293

Chemonie Plantation, 82

Cherokees, 71; removed from Georgia, 245, 249, 251

Chesterton, G. K., 376

Chew, Benjamin, 241

China, 195–96

Chiswick Press, 216, 465 (n. 37)

Christ Church, Savannah, xvii, 10, 48, 120, 318, 454–55 (n. 69)

Church, E. D., 321, 338, 339

City of Peking, 192–93

Civil War and Readjustment in Kentucky (Coulter), 376

Claghorn, Captain Joseph, 100, 473–74 (n. 71)

Claghorn family, 232

Clarendon, Earl of, 18, 109

Claudel, S., 333

Clayton, John M., 71

Cleveland, President Grover, 230, 290

Clinton Street residence, Philadelphia, 107, 145, 171, 535 (n. 28)

Clizbee, Azalea Hallett, 323, 336, 337–39, 340, 534 (n. 24)

Cobb, James H., 544 (n. 109)

Cobb, Jean. *See* De Renne, Mrs. Kentwyn

Cobb, Maud Barker, 373

Cobb, T. R. R. (Tom), 255, 259, 513–14 (n. 18)

Coerr, Frederic, 288

Coerr, Mrs. Frederic (Audrey De Renne; *see also* Howland, Mrs. Stanley), 220, 288, 339, 503 (n. 10), 504–5 (n. 22); and the catalog of the De Renne library, 337, 338; childhood of, 230, 288; in Europe, 317, 337; financial assistance offered to W. W. De Renne by, 325, 535 (n. 31); inheritance of, 316, 532–33 (n. 5); marriages of, 287–88, 318, 339; in Philadelphia, 317–18, 337; and Wormsloe Plantation, 230, 231, 317, 325

Coerr, Frederica, 371, 395

Coerr, Virginia, 371

Coerr, Wymberley Jones De Renne ("Pym"), 288, 522 (n. 48)

Cogswell, Joseph Green, 10–11

Cohen, Solomon, 125

Cole, George Watson, 321–22, 340

Cole, T. L., 279–81, 322, 519–20 (n. 23)

Collections of the Georgia Historical Society, 298, 373, 480 (n. 47), 526 (n. 83), 527 (n. 91); criticized by George F. T. Jones, 39, 40, 46, 53; and G. W. J. De Renne, 65, 121, 123, 124, 126, 136, 147; "Toma Chi Chi" on, 43–44; volumes one and

Cuyler, Telamon Cruger Smith, 291–94, 300, 523 (n. 62), 524 (nn. 65, 67, 68); collection of, 294–95, 523 (n. 61), 524 (n. 66), 525 (n. 72), 547–48 (n. 130)

da Costa, Jacob, 171
Damrosch, Walter, 333
d'Angers, David, 142
Daniel, John Warwick, 167, 489–90 (n. 57)
Dartmouth, Lord, 124
Davant, W. M., 254
Davidson, Donald, 365, 550 (n. 19)
Davis, Jefferson, 157–58, 161, 167, 176, 259, 371; correspondence with Lee, 253, 260, 516 (n. 54)
Davis, Sarah, 5
Dead Cities of Sicily, The (Rivela and Pernull), 520–21 (n. 35)
Dead Towns of Georgia, The (Jones), 133–37, 175
Dean Forest Plantation, 10, 60, 449 (n. 11), 462–63 (n. 8)
De Brahm, John Gerar William, 60, 129, 465–66 (n. 38); work of, printed by G. W. Jones, 50, 67–68, 69, 135, 150, 465 (n. 37)
de Bury, Richard, 18
Declaration of Independence, 100, 256, 259, 276, 477 (n. 10)
Defence of the System of Solitary Confinement of Prisoners, A (Smith), 455 (n. 75)
de Fontaine, Felix, 166, 167; and the Confederate Constitution, 162–64, 255, 257, 259, 513–14 (n. 18)
de Fontaine, Mrs., 164, 165
de Fontaine, Wade Hampton, 255
Deletions (Phillips), 304
Dent, James T., 225
Dent, Ophelia, 225, 395, 504–5 (n. 22), 535 (n. 31)
De Renne, Audrey (daughter of

Wymberley Jones De Renne). *See* Coerr, Mrs. Frederic; Howland, Mrs. Stanley
De Renne, Elfrida (daughter of Wymberley Jones De Renne). *See* Barrow, Mrs. Craig
De Renne, Eudora (daughter of Wymberley Wormsloe De Renne). *See* Roebling, Mrs. Wainwright R.
De Renne, Everard (son of George Wymberley Jones De Renne): and Colonel Jones, 253; death of, 174, 212, 221, 226, 499 (n. 99), 501 (n. 128); death of wife of, 169–70; and G. W. J. De Renne's funeral, 146; education of, xvi, 102, 143, 169, 186, 531 (n. 119); estate left by, 174, 221, 226–27, 229, 504 (n. 21); and the family heritage, 143, 173, 273; marriage of, 169; and the Mary De Renne Confederate Collection, 176, 512 (n. 13); mentioned, 57, 92, 142, 195, 211, 484 (n. 102); and Ward McAllister, 169, 490–91 (n. 62); wines collected by, 143, 229, 504 (n. 21); and Wormsloe Plantation, 221; and Wymberley's marriage, 209
De Renne, Mrs. Everard (Jeannette Sterling), 169, 170
De Renne, George Wymberley Cobb (son of Kentwyn Floyd De Renne), 357
De Renne, George Wymberley Jones (*see also* Jones, George Frederick Tilghman): agricultural pursuits of, 90–94, 471 (n. 47); books collected by, 71–72, 173–74, 178, 273, 275, 517–18 (n. 1); books printed by (*see also under* Wormsloe Quartos), 61–64, 65–69, 92, 279, 463 (nn. 15, 16), 464 (n. 33); character and appearance of, xiv, 146; children of, xix, 142–43, 187; during the Civil War, 99, 100–101, 103–4, 105, 106, 108, 474 (n. 73); death of, 145–46, 168, 172, 209, 210, 211, 222, 485 (n. 107); education of,

De Renne, George Wymberley Jones
(*continued*)
xvi, 89; estate inherited by, 60, 133, 199;
estate left by, 144, 315–16, 323; Europe
toured by, 71–72, 87–88; and the family
arms and motto, 57, 237, 453–54
(n. 57), 462 (n. 4); family heritage
preserved by, 134–35, 138, 242, 243, 437,
482–83 (n. 86), 501 (n. 129); family
remains relocated by, xii, xix, 57–58, 60,
142; and the Georgia Historical Society
(*see under* Georgia Historical Society);
Georgiana collected by, 112, 113–14, 130,
175, 501 (n. 129); hospitality of, 118–20;
ill health of, 100–101, 103, 105, 110, 111,
114, 126, 145, 474 (n. 73), 475 (n. 79);
interest in Confederacy of, 138–42, 148,
158, 284, 483 (nn. 89, 92), 483–84
(n. 93), 485–86 (n. 118), 501 (n. 129);
at Liberty Street, Savannah, 116–19;
magnum opus of, 137, 150–51, 154, 156,
157; marriage of, 82, 85–87; mentioned,
xviii, 80, 85, 163, 165, 194, 238, 250,
454–55 (n. 69); in Montpellier, France,
109–10, 112; name change of, to De
Renne from Jones, 7, 59–60, 107–8,
463 (n. 10), 476 (n. 94); philanthropic
activities of, 120–21, 123, 145, 146, 478–
79 (n. 35), 485 (n. 106), 501 (n. 129);
portrait of, 285, 357; post Civil War, xvi,
106–7, 109–10, 112; publicity disliked
by, 146, 147; real estate investments of,
97, 114, 472–73 (n. 60), 477 (n. 15);
relationship with son Wymberley, 198,
203, 207; and slavery, 60, 61, 92, 95–97,
122; will of, 144, 167–68, 170–71, 211,
315, 393, 485 (n. 104), 558 (n. 109);
wines collected by, 118, 119, 143, 229, 478
(n. 30); and Wormsloe Plantation, xix,
57, 58, 60–61, 89–92, 94, 103, 115–16,
133, 224, 317, 327, 392, 475 (n. 79);
writings of, 61–64, 74, 463 (nn. 15, 16);

and Wymberley's marriage, 207–8,
209, 498–99 (n. 98); and Wymberley's
ranching interests, 203–4, 205, 206, 207,
209, 212, 499 (n. 99)
De Renne, George Wymberley Jones (son
of Wymberley Jones De Renne), 214
De Renne, Mrs. George Wymberley Jones
(Mary Wallace Nuttall): books published
by, 150, 151, 152–53, 154, 155–57, 158,
391; childhood of, 80, 84–85; children
of, 143; Civil War memoirs of, 99–100,
101–2, 103–4, 110, 158; Confederate
collection of, 152–53, 158–62, 163–67,
174, 273, 489–90 (n. 57), 517–18 (n. 1);
death of, 172, 220, 253, 264; and death
of husband, 145, 146, 147, 149; estate left
by, 211; and Europe, 87–88, 114, 171,
490–91 (n. 71); and her mother's
wedding, 84–85; husband's name
preserved by, 148, 485–86 (n. 118);
ill health of, 150; marriage of, 82, 87;
mentioned, 77, 78, 84, 132, 142, 169,
509 (n. 65), 514 (n. 22); in Newport, RI,
88, 89, 90; philanthropic activities
of, 172; portrait of, 142, 227, 357; and
relationship with eldest son, 149, 198,
203–4, 207, 208–9, 211, 220; and
Wormsloe Plantation, 91, 327; and
Wymberley's marriage, 207, 208–9,
210, 211
De Renne, Inigo Jones (son of Wymberley
Wormsloe De Renne), 102, 142, 168, 169,
211, 326; death of, 335, 347
De Renne, Kentwyn (son of George
Wymberley Jones De Renne): death of,
173, 221, 501 (n. 128); and the death of
his father, 145–46; education of, 143, 484
(n. 102)
De Renne, Mrs. Kentwyn (Jean Cobb), 357,
548 (n. 134)
De Renne, Kentwyn Floyd (son of
Wymberley Wormsloe De Renne), 326,

336, 356, 357, 358; and the De Renne
Library, 345, 352; printing by, 335, 356,
546–47 (n. 127)

De Renne, Letitia "Leta" (daughter of
George Wymberley Jones De Renne),
92, 142, 169, 170, 172; death of, 173, 221;
and her father's funeral, 146; education
of, 186, 198; and her father's estate,
168; ill health of, 143, 149–50, 171–72,
173; reading enjoyed by, 118, 143–44;
relationship with Wymberley, 209, 220;
and Wormsloe Plantation, 119, 173

De Renne, Mary. See De Renne,
Mrs. George Wymberley Jones

De Renne, Wymberley Jones (son of
George Wymberley Jones De Renne),
330, 364, 388, 390; and the American
West, 143, 192, 199, 200; autograph
collection of, 275–77; and a
bibliography of Georgia, 298–99,
301, 303; biography of Thomas Smith
published by, 237–41, 244, 250, 508–9
(n. 58); birth of, 88; births of children
of, 213–14, 219, 220, 222; Bonaventure
lots purchased by, 222, 502 (n. 1); book
dealers frequented by, 277–78, 279,
518–19 (n. 12); books collected by, 221,
244–45, 251, 273–74, 320, 390–91, 541
(n. 81); books printed and published by,
235–36, 258, 260, 267–68, 270–71,
296, 507 (n. 42), 511 (n. 88); catalogs
published by, 254, 259, 274, 276, 281–
83, 293, 296, 303, 309, 311, 340, 511–12
(n. 3), 520 (n. 25), 527–28 (n. 98);
character of, 185, 199, 311–12, 532
(n. 125); Confederate collection of, 252,
253, 260, 266, 275, 276, 293; and the
Confederate Constitution, 254–56, 258–
60, 513 (n. 17), 513–14 (n. 18); death of,
250, 274–75, 310, 315, 318, 319, 360,
361, 375, 511–12 (n. 3); death of father
of, 145, 146, 211, 485 (n. 107); and the

De Renne book collections, 273, 517–18
(n. 1); disinheritance of, 211–12, 220,
499 (n. 99); and duelling, 188, 189, 190,
190–91, 495 (n. 25); education of, 102,
103, 110, 143, 182, 184–85, 186, 187–88,
190, 191, 197, 279; estate left by, 308, 316,
318; eulogy for, 311–12; in Europe, 181,
182–83, 219–20, 221, 223, 225; and
the family arms and motto, 237; family
heritage preserved by, 222, 236–44, 273,
507–8 (n. 48); Far East toured by, 191,
192–97; fellow collectors of, 290–94,
523 (n. 62); and the Georgia Historical
Society (see under Georgia Historical
Society); Georgiana collected by, 244–
45, 246, 273, 274, 275–76, 277, 278–81,
289–90, 291, 303, 511–12 (n. 3), 523
(n. 61), 527 (n. 97); health of, 264, 269,
309, 310, 515 (n. 32); horses and riding
loved by, 200, 203, 230; hospitality
of, 208, 209–10, 228, 229; hunting
and fishing enjoyed by, 203–4, 220,
225; inheritance of, 144–45, 199, 209,
273, 496–97 (n. 61); and the Lee
manuscripts, 260, 261–62, 263–64, 293;
and legal practice, 197, 198–99, 212;
library constructed by, 283–86, 308,
520–21 (nn. 35, 40), 530–31 (n. 112);
and the Lumpkin papers, 244–51, 262,
277–78, 527 (n. 87); marriage of, 142,
144, 169, 199–200, 206–7, 208, 210,
211, 498–99 (n. 98); and military
organizations, 233–35, 236, 506 (n. 36),
507 (n. 38); in New York State, 225–26,
503 (nn. 10, 12); Oglethorpe researched
by, 302–3; portrait of, 310, 339, 357,
531 (n. 120), 532 (n. 125); relationship
with parents, 149, 198, 199, 203–4, 207,
208–9, 211, 220; in Savannah, 223, 502
(n. 1); and sheep ranching, 144–45, 204–
6, 207, 208, 209, 212, 215–16, 216–18,
535 (n. 31); sketches of Jones family

De Renne, Wymberley Jones (*continued*)
written by, 241–44, 251, 509 (n. 65); in
Texas, 144–45, 200–201, 202, 203–4;
visitors to library of, 304–5, 306–7, 528
(n. 102); wines collected by, 229, 504
(n. 21); workforce enlisted at Wormsloe
by, 223, 224–25, 229, 502 (n. 6), 504
(n. 20); and Wormsloe Plantation, 178,
221, 223, 244, 273, 310, 509 (n. 68);
Wormsloe rejuvenated by, 226–28,
229–30, 231–33, 503 (nn. 13, 14), 504
(n. 17), 505 (nn. 25, 29, 30)

De Renne, Mrs. Wymberley Jones (Laura
Camblos Norris), 209–11, 212–13, 219,
220, 221, 287; antecedents of, 207;
background of, 211, 500 (n. 113); courted
by Wymberley De Renne, 199, 206–7;
death of, 310, 318, 360; estate of, 217, 500
(n. 113); ill health of, 214, 226, 229, 310;
marriages of, 199, 208, 211; in the North,
230–31; at Wormsloe, 229

De Renne, Wymberley Wormsloe (son
of Wymberley Jones De Renne), 389,
505–6 (n. 30), 522 (n. 50), 548 (n. 133);
birth of, 222; childhood of, 228, 230,
231, 288, 320; death of, 358; and the
De Renne Library, 288, 319, 336–38,
353–55; education of, 289, 318; financial
difficulties of, 323, 325–26, 336–37,
342–43, 345, 346, 347, 348, 351–52;
financially assisted by Audrey, 325, 535
(n. 31); and the Georgia Historical
Society, 319, 326, 372, 533 (n. 14);
"house books" owned by, 357, 547
(n. 129); ill health of, 226, 288–89, 318,
358; inheritance of, 316, 317, 532–33
(n. 5); and the Jones–De Renne papers,
388, 396; and journalism, 289; marriage
of, 318–19, 322; publishing by, 537–38
(n. 51); real estate investments of, 323–
24, 325, 326, 535 (n. 28); relationship
with sister Elfrida, 346, 347, 358; at the
University of Georgia, 354, 355–56,

357–58, 545 (n. 121); in World War I,
318, 319, 322; and Wormsloe Gardens,
330, 331, 537–38 (n. 51); Wormsloe left
by, 351–53; and Wormsloe Plantation,
317, 320, 326, 336, 343–44, 345–46,
347, 348–50, 351, 352, 360, 437, 533
(n. 15), 542 (n. 89)

De Renne, Mrs. Wymberley Wormsloe
(Augusta Gallie Floyd), 334, 335, 347,
383, 535–36 (n. 35); death of, 358;
gardening loved by, 327–28, 356, 357,
358; and the gardens at Wormsloe,
327–28, 358, 371, 536 (n. 36); marriage
of, 318–19

De Renne Apartments, 323–24, 325, 342,
343, 535 (n. 28), 542 (n. 87)

De Renne Garden Collection, 547 (n. 129)

De Renne Georgia Library. *See* Wymberley
Jones De Renne Georgia Library

De Renne Gift, The (Milledge), 175, 277

De Renne Hospital for Incurables,
Philadelphia, PA, 144

Derry, Joseph T., 242

DesAnges, Louis, 142, 227, 357

Descartes, René, 63

de Sévigné, Madame, 59

de Sismondi, J. C. L. S., 18

de Soto, Hernando, 372

*Detailed Reports on the Salzburger
Emigrants* (Urlsperger), 391

de Thou, Jacques-Auguste, 28

Deziray, Bruno, 91, 478 (n. 25)

Diary of Col. Winthrop Sargent, 72

Dibdin, Thomas Frognall, 18, 19, 20, 64,
112, 454 (n. 58)

Dickens, Charles, 24, 457–58 (n. 24)

Dickey, James, 369

Dictionary of National Biography, 302

Dictionnaire historique et critique (Bayle),
18, 22

*Diedrich Knickerbocker's A History of New
York* (Irving), 52

Documents Connected with the History of

Ford, Henry, 332

Ford, James A., 384

Ford, Worthington, 259, 271, 288, 295, 307

Forrest, Nathan Bedford, 372

Forsyth, John, 37

Forsyth Park, Savannah, 131, 132, 141, 481–82 (n. 72)

Fort Concho, TX, 202, 207

Fort Duquesne, 26

Fort Frederica, xvii, 70, 445 (n. 13)

Fort Sumter, 100, 101

Fort Wymberley, 331, 334–35, 537 (n. 48)

Forty Years of Diversity (Jackson and Spalding), 561 (n. 7)

Franco-Prussian War, 186, 191

Frank, Leo, 382, 530 (n. 108)

Franklin, Benjamin, xviii, 4, 65, 395

Fraser, Hugh Russell, 393–94

Freedmen, 114–15

Freeman, Douglas Southall, 177, 264, 312, 514 (n. 27), 517 (n. 61); and the Confederate Constitution, 256, 257–58; and the Lee dispatches, 261–67, 268–69, 270, 271–72

French, Daniel Chester, 302

Fugitive, The, 365

Fugitives, 371, 549 (n. 18)

G. P. Putnam's Sons, 267, 269, 515–16 (n. 45), 517 (n. 61)

Gallagher, Gary W., 516 (n. 54)

Gamble, Thomas, 374, 553 (n. 48)

Garden, Alexander, 29

Garden Club of America, 328, 334

Garden Club of Georgia Yearbook, The, 328

Gardener's Labyrinth, The, 356

Garden History of Georgia, 1733–1933, 334

Gardens of Colony and State, 334

Garderes, Mathilde, 504 (n. 20)

Gardiner, Delia Tudor (wife of George Noble Jones), 81

Gardiner, Robert Hallowell, II, 81, 82

Gardner, Jacob, 518–19 (n. 12)

Genealogy, 29, 456 (n. 1)

General History of the British Empire in America (Wynne), 29

George III, King of England, 67

Georgia, 66; bicentennial of, 333–34, 381, 383; and the Civil War, 100, 104, 106; colony, xvi, xix, 37–38, 40; gathering of historical records of, 32–33, 46, 113–14, 123–24, 294, 524–25 (n. 69); viewed by H. L. Mencken, 363–64

Georgia: A Pageant of Years (Barrow et al.), 382–83

Georgia: A Short History (Coulter), 382, 554 (n. 77)

Georgia's Disputed Ruins (Coulter), 384

Georgia's Landmarks, Memorials and Legends (Knight), 244, 539 (n. 61)

Georgia: Unfinished State (Steed), 334–35

Georgia and State Rights (Phillips), 297, 377

Georgia as a Proprietary Province (McCain), 528 (n. 102)

Georgia Catalog, The (Linley), 561 (n. 7)

Georgia Department of Archives and History, 295, 524–25 (n. 69), 525 (n. 72), 526 (n. 82), 552 (n. 44)

Georgia Gazette (Johnston), 307

Georgia Heritage Advisory Trust Commission, 436

Georgia Historical Association, 372–73, 552 (n. 44)

Georgia Historical Commission, 437

Georgia Historical Quarterly, 341, 377, 379, 533 (n. 14), 561 (n. 7); Elfrida Barrow published by, 375, 379–80; *Georgia: A Pageant of Years* reviewed in, 382–83; Mackall published by, 322, 339; and the Savannah Writers' Project, 387; and the SHRA, 384

Georgia Historical Review, 373–74

Georgia Historical Society: affiliated

society at Athens, 301; and Agricola, 36, 37, 38, 40, 43–44, 46–47; and the attorneys general's opinions volume, 166–67; and Col. Charles C. Jones, Jr., 128–29, 136–37, 297; creation of, 33; and G. W. J. De Renne, 36, 40, 43, 50, 121, 126–27, 131–32, 136, 146, 157, 464 (n. 33), 485 (n. 106), 501 (n. 129); and G. W. J. De Renne's death, 146–47; G. W. J. De Renne as president of, 24, 125–26; and Elfrida De Renne Barrow, 361, 372, 374; and Hodgson Hall, 131–32, 481 (n. 70); Mackall's paper presented to, 322, 534 (n. 23); membership in, 297, 299, 300, 301; mentioned, 35, 37, 67, 113, 243, 250, 279–80, 457–58 (n. 24), 480 (n. 49); merger with Georgia Historical Association, 372–73; and Oglethorpe, 38, 123–25, 479–80 (n. 44), 480 (n. 47); and Phillips, 296, 297–98, 299, 300–301, 372, 526 (nn. 82, 83); and the Provisional Confederate Constitution, 163; 75th anniversary of, 305–6, 529–30 (n. 106); statewide focus of, 383, 552–53 (n. 47); and W. B. Stevens, 34, 53–54, 55, 461 (n. 81); and W. J. De Renne, 228, 296–97, 298–99, 301–2, 305, 307, 311, 372, 373, 530 (n. 111); and "Wormsloe," 387; and W. W. De Renne, 319, 326, 372, 533 (n. 14)

Georgia Hussars, 168, 233–34; and the Liberty Street house, 173, 221, 315, 536 (n. 37)

Georgia Institute of Technology, 522–23 (n. 56)

Georgia Medical Society, xix, 446–47 (n. 19)

Georgian. See Savannah Daily Georgian

Georgia Society of Colonial Dames: and Augusta De Renne, 326, 535–36 (n. 35); and Elfrida De Renne Barrow, 361, 380–82, 554 (n. 72); publishing actitivities of, 380–81, 382, 384, 385, 509 (n. 68)

Georgia State Library, 124, 174–75, 415, 418–19, 492 (n. 81), 492–93 (n. 89), 493 (n. 95), 523 (n. 62)

Georgia State University Library, 522–23 (n. 56)

Gibbons, Mary, 447 (n. 1)

Gilmer, General Jeremy F., 514 (n. 22)

Glen, Sarah Jones (daughter of Noble Wimberly Jones), 236, 447 (n. 1)

Glen family, 10, 447 (n. 1)

"God's Acre" (Barrow), 380–81

Goethe, Johann Wolfgang von, 187, 309

Golden Book: Story of Fine Books and Bookmaking, The (McMurtrie), 335

Golding, Prince, 91, 478 (n. 25)

Gone with the Wind, 370, 553 (n. 64)

Good-bye Summer (Lea), 332, 538 (n. 55)

Gordon, Caroline, 371

Gordon, William W., 234

Gould, Jay, 140

Gounod, Charles-François, 184

Grace (slave), 445 (n. 13)

Grady, Henry W., 253

Grahame, James, 29

Grandville, 23

Granger, Mary, 385, 387, 556 (n. 92)

Grant, Ulysses S., 163, 202, 241, 269

Greatbach, William, 47

Great Oaks (Williams), 332

Green, Joseph D., 545–46 (n. 122)

Green, Julien, 332–33, 538–39 (n. 56)

Greene, Belle da Costa, 354

Greene, General Nathanael, 275, 276, 342

Greene, Professor Helen I., 393

Greenville, SC, 101, 102–3

Grice, Justice Benning, 436

Grierson, Colonel Benjamin, 202

Grimes, Dr. John, 443–44 (n. 10)

Grimes family, 447 (n. 1)

Grinnell, E. Morgan, 203

Grinnell, Lawrence L., 203

Grotius, Hugo, 22

Guizot, François, 18

Gulf States Historical Magazine, 298

Gutenberg, Johannes, 20

Gwinnett, Button, 21, 454 (n. 65), 477 (n. 10), 524 (n. 65)

Habersham, James, 242–43, 298, 299, 449 (n. 11), 509 (n. 65)

Habersham, William Neyle, 26, 119–20

Habersham family, 10

Hack, Sarah (wife of Noble Jones). *See* Jones, Mrs. Noble

Hale, E. J., 166

Hallowell, Robert. *See* Gardiner, Robert Hallowell

Hammond, James Henry, 96, 97

Hanning, George T., 164, 165, 167

Hardee, General W. J., 104

Hardee, Mr. and Mrs. J. L., 119–20

Harden, Edward J., 121, 125, 126

Harden, William, 242, 244, 250, 264, 374, 382; and the Georgia Historical Society, 121, 124, 296; viewed by Phillips, 526 (n. 82)

Harper's New Monthly Magazine, 76

Harris, Charles, 67

Harris, Joel Chandler, 154, 364

Harris, N. E., 373

Harris, Thaddeus Mason, 459–60 (n. 49); criticized by Agricola, 38–39, 40, 45, 46, 461 (n. 76), 465 (n. 36); and the Georgia Historical Society, 40

Harris, Thaddeus William, 465 (n. 36)

Hart, Freeman H., 389

Hart, James Morgan, 187, 188

Hart family, 447 (n. 1)

Hartridge, Walter Charlton, Jr., 384, 385

Harvard College Library, 67, 152, 465 (nn. 36, 37)

Harvard University, 11, 496–97 (n. 61)

Harwell, Richard, 389, 488 (n. 36), 516 (n. 54), 557 (n. 102)

Hawes, Lilla Mills, 387–88, 556 (n. 92)

Hawkins, Benjamin, 65, 301, 527 (n. 91)

Hawthorne, Nathaniel, 17

Hayday, James, 19, 22, 24

Hazlitt, William, 20

Hearne, Thomas, 457–58 (n. 24)

Heartman, Charles F., 340–41

Henderson, Amos, 91

Henry, O., 201

Henry E. Huntington Library, 488 (n. 36)

Henry Newman's Salzburger Letterbooks, 391

Henry Stevens, Son & Stiles, 277, 278, 527–28 (n. 98)

heraldry, 30, 57, 237, 453–54 (n. 57), 462 (n. 4)

Hewat, Alexander, 31, 45

Hewitt, Jane Meldrim (Mrs. Erastus), 549 (n. 8)

Hexapla (Bagster), 22

Heyward, Dorothy, 333

Heyward, DuBose, 333, 362, 365, 385; and Elfrida Barrow, 364, 366, 549 (n. 16)

Heyward, Elizabeth Savage, 549 (n. 16)

Hicky, Daniel Whitehead, 369

Hill, Benjamin H., 253–54, 330

Hillsborough, Earl of, 243

Hirsch, Julius, 343

Historia sui temporis (de Thou), 28

Historical Account of the Rise and Progress of the Colonies of South Carolina and Georgia (Hewat), 31, 45

Historical Collections of Georgia (White), 464 (n. 33)

Historical Sketch of the Chatham Artillery (Jones), 129

Historical Sketch of Tomo-Chi-Chi (Jones), 129

Historical Society of Pennsylvania, 24, 241, 309

Punch, 108

Putnam, G. H., 269, 277, 288, 530–31 (n. 112)

Putnam, Herbert, 259, 260, 306–8, 351

Quaritch, Bernard, 277

quarto: defined, 465 (n. 34)

Queen of Clubs, 88, 89

R. E. Lee (Freeman), 272

"R. E. Lee 200, The" (Krick and Parrish), 516 (n. 54)

R. Habersham and Sons, 103

Rabelais, François, 22

Ranke, Leopold von, 187

Ransom, John Crowe, 365, 550 (n. 19)

Ravenel, Harriott Horry, 466 (n. 45)

Read, Keith, 391, 545–46 (n. 122)

Reck, Baron Georg Philip Friederich von, 31

Recollections and Letters of General Robert E. Lee (Lee), 261

Reconstruction of Georgia, The (Thompson), 304

Redoubt Island. *See* Pigeon Island

Redwood Library, Newport, 83, 152

Reed, Henry Hope, 15–16, 62

Reed, William Bradford, 16

Reid, Ann, 449–50 (n. 12)

Reid, Robert, 139

Religious Instruction of the Negro (Jones), 283

Remains Concerning Britain (Camden), 18

Reminiscences of the Last Days, Death and Burial of General Henry Lee (Jones), 129

Removal of the Cherokee Indians from Georgia, 249, 251, 262, 511 (n. 87), 517 (n. 61)

Report of the Committee Appointed..., 511 (n. 88)

Reprint Company, 466 (n. 45)

Resolutions of the Trustees..., 283

Reveries of a Bachelor (Marvel), 76, 468 (n. 69)

Review Printing and Publishing Company, 375

Revolutionary War, 4, 8, 24, 124, 446–47 (n. 19); forgotten controversy of, 65; Massachusetts during, 42; mentioned, 47, 69, 72, 447 (n. 1); and N. W. Jones, xvii, xviii

Reynolds, J. Barlow, 203

Reynolds, John, 443–44 (n. 10), 479–80 (n. 44)

Rich, Obadiah, 22, 30, 39, 65, 456 (n. 4); death of, 71; and the Harvard College Library, 67

Richards, David, 140, 141

Richardson, Henry Handel: quoted, 359

Richardson, Samuel, 71

Richmond, VA, 159–60, 255, 256, 261, 262, 272

Richmond Journal, 256

Richmond News Leader, 256

Ritchie, Margaret E., 174

Ritchie family, 172

Rivela, A., 520–21 (n. 35)

River Jordan, 88, 470–71 (n. 31)

Riverside Press, 155, 156, 157

Robert, Ray, 539 (n. 61)

Robert E. Lee, the Southerner (Page), 261

Roebling, Audrey, 357

Roebling, Robert, 357

Roebling, Wainwright Ripley, 357

Roebling, Mrs. Wainwright R. (Eudora De Renne), 335, 357

Rollins, Carl Purington, 546–47 (n. 127)

Roosevelt, Theodore, 198, 496–97 (n. 61)

Roosevelt, Mr. and Mrs. Theodore, Sr., 198

Rosenbach, A. S. W., 283, 345, 511 (n. 88)

Round Hill School, Northampton, MA, 10–11, 13, 81

Rousseau, Jean Jacques, 184

Roxburghe, Duke of, 19

Shanghai, 195–96

Shaw, Henry Wheeler. *See* Billings, Josh

Sheep ranching, 200, 203, 204–5

Sherman, C., 62, 464 (n. 32)

Sherman, William T.: equestrian statue of, 226; mentioned, 104, 105, 158, 174, 475 (n. 85)

Short History of Georgia, A (Coulter), 382, 554 (n. 77)

Short History of the Confederate Constitutions, A (De Renne), 258–59

SHRA. *See* Savannah Historical Research Association

Sibley, John Langdon, 67

Sieg, Gerald Chan, 368

Silk Hope Plantation, 79

Sillig, Edouard-Frederic, 182, 185, 186

Sillig, Edwin, 184

Simmons, Fritz, 390

Simms, William Gilmore, 17, 33, 34, 55, 130, 457 (n. 15)

Skidaway Island, xv, 97, 100, 114–15, 174; bridge to, 98–99 115–16, 232, 395; development of, 395–96

Skinner, W. J., 215, 217, 218

Slaton, John M., 306, 530 (n. 108)

Smets, Alexander A., 20, 21, 22, 24, 457 (n. 13); death of, 112; sale of collection of, 112–13, 344, 477 (n. 10)

Smillie, Robert T., 106, 114

Smith, Al, 333

Smith, Eliza. *See* Jones, Mrs. George

Smith, George Gilman, 242, 523 (n. 62)

Smith, George Washington. *See* Smith, Washington

Smith, Gustavus Woodson, 140

Smith, James M., 126

Smith, Juliana, 72; death of, 112

Smith, Letitia Van Deren, 4, 5, 59, 544 (n. 107); portrait of, 59, 371

Smith, Rebecca, 199

Smith, S. L. S., 214

Smith, Thomas, 3–4, 111, 448 (n. 2), 467 (n. 56); biography of, 237–41, 244, 250; portrait of, 507–8 (n. 48)

Smith, Washington: death of, 133, 198; estate left by, 199, 316; and G. W. J. De Renne, 10, 23–24, 107; leisure enjoyed by, 60; mentioned, 6, 16, 71, 104, 105, 470–71 (n. 31); and North Africa, 85; obituary of, 482 (n. 73); and the Smith estate, 112; writings of, 24, 344 (n. 24), 455 (n. 75)

Smith, William, 3–5, 15, 118

Smith, Williamina, 107

Smith, Winthrop, 218

Smith & English, 17

Smith family, 7, 57, 111–12, 144

Smithsonian Institution, 465–66 (n. 38)

Society as I Have Found It (McAllister), 490–91 (n. 62)

Society for the Prevention of Cruelty to Animals, 121

Society of the Cincinnati, 25

Some Early Epitaphs in Georgia, 380–81

Sons of the Revolution (SR), 228, 235–36, 250

Sorrel, Moxley, 131, 138, 147, 159

Southampton slave insurrection, 41

South Carolina Historical Society, 466 (n. 45), 519 (n. 13)

South Carolina Poetry Society. *See* Poetry Society of South Carolina

Southern Book Exposition, 367

Southern Historical Society, 130, 152, 163, 489 (n. 54); and the Confederate Constitution, 256, 257, 512–13 (n. 14)

Southern Historical Society Papers, 148, 159, 257

Southern Literary Magazine, 366

Southern Literary Messenger, 74

Southern Quarterly Review, 55

University of Leipzig, 187–88, 191
University of North Carolina, 466 (n. 45)
University of North Carolina Press, 382, 384, 466 (n. 45)
University of Pennsylvania, 4, 15, 16, 24; School of Medicine at, 26–27, 455–56 (n. 87)
Upjohn, Richard, 82–83
Upton Letters, The (Benson), 305
Urban, Henry, 283, 503 (n. 13)
Urlsperger, Samuel, 391
USS *Rhode Island*, 181

Valentine, Edward, 167
Vanderbilt, Cornelius, 140
Vanderbilt estate, 225
Van Deren, John, 4
Van Deren, John Bernard, 448 (n. 3)
Van Deren, Letitia. *See* Smith, Letitia Van Deren
Van Deren family, 5
Vannerson, Julian, 264
Veck, W. S., 202
Venables-Vernon, William Frederick Cuthbert. *See* Vernon, Will
Verelst manuscripts, 545–46 (n. 122)
Vernon, Lord, 217, 218
Vernon, Will, 216, 217–18
View from Pompey's Head, The, 558 (n. 114)
Virgil, 20
Virginia Historical Society, 160

Wade, John Donald, 330–31, 367, 395; Barrow's *Georgia: A Pageant of Years* reviewed by, 382–83; biography of Wesley by, 378–79; and *Georgia's Disputed Ruins*, 384
Wallace, John and Mary, 79
Wallin, Henrik, 283, 310, 324, 361
Wallin and Young, 505–6 (n. 30)

Walpole, Horace, 23, 28, 39, 61, 84, 463 (n. 15); and Smets's collection, 113
Walpole, Sir Robert, 28
Walton, George, 66, 276
Walton, Izaak, 468 (n. 69)
Wappoo Creek Plantation, 70, 71
Ward, John Elliott, 253
Waring, J. Frederick, 395, 560 (n. 1)
War of Jenkins's Ear, 71, 445 (n. 13)
War of the Austrian Succession (1740–48), 450 (n. 13)
War of the Rebellion, 261
Washington, George: and Eliza Lucas Pinckney, 70; letter of, 275; mentioned, 4, 25, 238; and the Northwest Territory, 73; papers of, edited, 69
Watkins, George, 152
Watkins, Robert, 152
Waugh, Evelyn: quoted, 315
Waverley (Scott), 30, 57, 456 (n. 1)
Wayne, Anthony, 72, 276, 342
Wayne, James Moore, 50, 107
Weaver, Herbert, 389
Webber, Mabel, 519 (n. 13)
Webster, Daniel, 83
Weekly Register, 126
Wegelin, Oscar, 303, 321, 527–28 (n. 98)
Wesley, John, 281, 377–79
Weston, Plowden J. C., 464 (n. 33), 465 (n. 37)
Westport, NY, 226, 503 (n. 10)
Wharton, Edith: quoted, 336
"What Nature Suffers to Groe" (Stewart), 561 (n. 7)
"When John Wesley Preached in Georgia" (Coulter), 377–78
Whigs, xviii, 24, 126, 127
White, George, 464 (n. 33)
White, Henry A., 260–61, 269
Whitefield, George, xvii, 13, 31, 281
Whitney, William C., 505 (n. 25)

Wormsloe Plantation (*continued*)
published of, 505 (n. 26); post Civil War, 106–7, 114, 119, 478 (n. 25); produce grown at, 94, 95, 103, 223–24, 472 (n. 51); as property of the state of Georgia, 436–37, 561 (n. 7); rejuvenation of, 178, 221, 226–28, 231–33, 503 (nn. 13, 14), 504 (n. 17), 505 (n. 29), 505–6 (n. 30); in *The Savannah Cook Book*, 538 (n. 54); slaves at, 60, 61, 89, 91, 95–96, 103, 117, 475 (n. 79); timber of, 555–56 (n. 91); track constructed at, 230, 505 (n. 25); visitors to, 394; and W. J. De Renne, 221–22, 223, 224–25, 229, 502 (n. 6), 504 (n. 20); and W. W. De Renne, 316, 317, 320, 325, 533 (n. 15)

Wormsloe Quartos, 153, 154, 335, 465 (n. 34); accessibility of, 526 (n. 83); and G. W. J. De Renne, 65–74, 92, 125–26, 138, 464 (n. 33), 468 (n. 69); and the Georgia Historical Society, 296, 485–86 (n. 118); and Mary De Renne, 150–53, 155–58, 160; and W. J. De Renne, 281, 309

Wright, Sir James, xviii, 243, 524 (n. 65); correspondence of, printed by G. W. J. De Renne, 124, 126, 127, 129, 154

Wycliffe, John, 22

Wymberley-Jones, G. (*see also* De Renne, George Wymberley Jones), 56, 462–63 (n. 8)

Wymberley Jones De Renne Georgia Library: available to scholars, 330–31, 537 (n. 47); catalog of, 320–21, 322, 336–42, 342, 540 (n. 71), 541 (n. 80); and Elfrida De Renne Barrow, 381; and the Georgia Historical Society, 298–99, 533 (n. 14); library designed for, 273, 283, 530–31 (n. 112); mentioned, 547–48 (n. 130); selling of, 341–42, 344–45, 346, 347, 349–51, 542 (n. 89); and W. W. De Renne, 319, 320–21, 322–23, 330, 357

Wymberly Plantation, 100

Wymberly House, 232

Wynne, John Huddlestone, 29

Yale College, 11

Yamasee Indians, xv

Yankees, 41, 458–59 (n. 37), 459 (n. 40)

Yazoo Act, 292, 541 (n. 81)

Yazooists, xix

Yokohama, 193–94, 195

Yonholme, 344, 346, 385

Young, Edward Warren, 283, 310, 505–6 (n. 30)

Youth's Historical Society, 121

Zenger, John Peter, 448 (n. 3)

Zoilus, 54, 461 (n. 78)

Zubly, Rev. John J., 541 (n. 81)

De Renne: Three Generations of a Georgia Family is set
in 11 on 14 Monotype Walbaum with Walbaum display.
This handsome neoclassical face was originally cut by the German
type designer Justus Walbaum between the years 1805 and 1828.
The book was designed by Sandra Strother Hudson.
The illustrations were arranged by Louise OFarrell.
The maps were prepared by Heidi Perov Perry.
De Renne: Three Generations of a Georgia Family
was composed by G&S Typesetters, Inc., Austin, Texas;
printed by McNaughton & Gunn, Inc., Saline, Michigan;
and bound by John H. Dekker & Sons, Inc., Grand Rapids, Michigan.
The papers in this book are acid-free and have an effective
shelf-life of at least three hundred years.